# People and Stories in World History:
# A HISTORICAL ANTHOLOGY

**BALLARD & TIGHE**
PUBLISHERS

Brea, California

## AUTHORS

**Gregory Blanch, Ph.D.**, received a bachelor of arts degree in history from The Ohio State University and a master's degree in education from California State Polytechnic University. He earned his doctorate from the Claremont Graduate University. He is the co-author of *Explore World History*, 2nd ed.

**Roberta Stathis, Ph.D.**, received a bachelor of arts degree in anthropology and social sciences and a master's degree in education from California State University, San Bernardino. She earned her doctorate from the Claremont Graduate University. She is the co-author of *Explore World History*, 2nd ed.

## GENERAL HISTORICAL EDITOR

**Cheryl A. Riggs, Ph.D.**, is professor and chair of the history department at California State University, San Bernardino.

## REVIEWERS

**Diane L. Brooks, Ed.D.**, is the past director of the Curriculum Frameworks and Instructional Resources Office, California Department of Education.

**David Vigilante, M.A.**, is the associate director of the National Center for History in the Schools, UCLA.

*People and Stories in World History:*
# A HISTORICAL ANTHOLOGY

An IDEA® Content Resource from Ballard & Tighe

EDITOR: Heera Kang
ART DIRECTOR: Liliana Cartelli
CONSULTING EDITORS: Patrice Gotsch, Nicole Rask
EDITORIAL STAFF: Kristin Belsher, Allison Mangrum
PROOFREADERS: Antoinette Kennedy, Laurie Regan
DESKTOP PUBLISHING SPECIALIST: Kathleen Styffe
PRINTING COORDINATOR: Cathy Sanchez

2003 Printing
ISBN 1-55501-544-1    Catalog #2-813

# Table of Contents

# About the Book

*People and Stories in World History: A Historical Anthology* chronicles events and people involved in world history from Roman times to the French Revolution. You will read about real people—artists, writers, scientists, merchants, slaves, rulers, engineers, explorers, scholars, religious leaders, and farmers—who shaped the world we live in today. You will learn about these people by reading excerpts from letters, ship's logs, sacred books, literature, speeches, and even recipes.

Here are some of the people you will meet:

 Cleopatra, the Egyptian queen who dreamed of ruling the world

Mansa Musa, the king whose pilgrimage to Mecca put West Africa on the map

 Malinche, the woman who was a key to the Spanish conquest of the New World

Zheng Ho, a Chinese explorer and commander of the Treasure Fleet

 Cardinal Richelieu, the power behind the French throne

Benjamin Franklin, a man of the Enlightenment

You also will read about compelling events in world history, including:
- How beans, peppers, tomatoes, and chocolate changed the world
- A slave army that was the pride of the Ottoman Empire
- Christmas Day A.D. 800 when Charlemagne was crowned emperor of the Romans
- A speech that started the Crusades
- The night in 1453 when Constantinople fell

All these stories and more are in the pages that follow. Like the people who lived before us, we continue in the struggle to understand our place in the world. As you read this anthology, consider how our history comprises all human history and includes ties to people from all over the world.

## Most readings will have the following features:

Key dates you will learn about in the reading

A map that shows you where the events you are reading about took place

A picture of the person, place, or event you are reading about

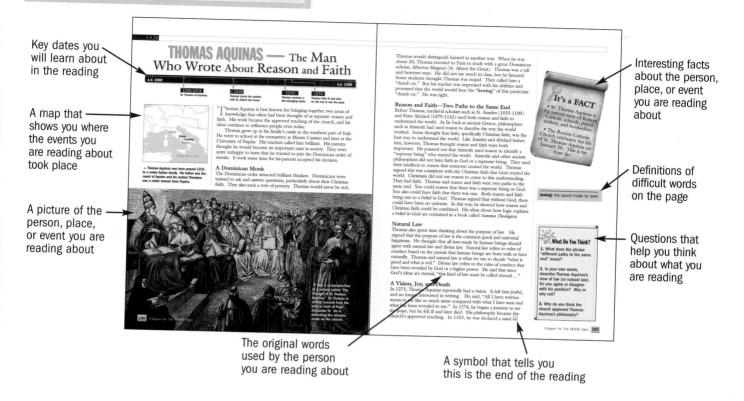

Interesting facts about the person, place, or event you are reading about

Definitions of difficult words on the page

Questions that help you think about what you are reading

The original words used by the person you are reading about

A symbol that tells you this is the end of the reading

---

Some readings are designed to help you analyze excerpts of historical writings. Here is an example of one primary source reading:

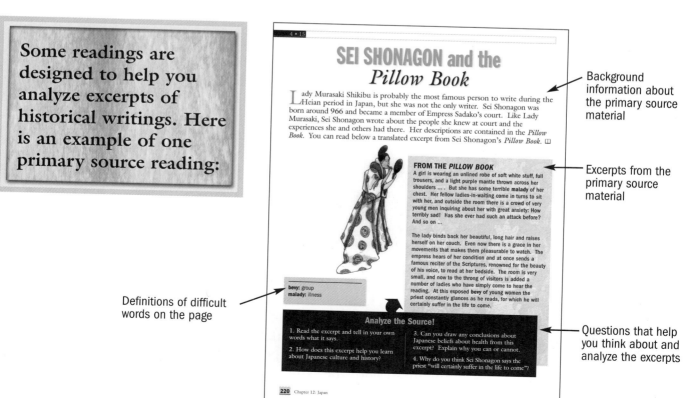

Background information about the primary source material

Excerpts from the primary source material

Definitions of difficult words on the page

Questions that help you think about and analyze the excerpts

# A BATTLE OVER BONES:
# The Story of Kennewick Man

This is the story of Kennewick Man. No one knows what his real name was. No one knows what language he spoke or what his beliefs were. We do know that he was a real man who lived and died a long time ago in the Pacific Northwest, in the state we now call Washington. We also know that many people have fought over his bones.

▲ This photograph shows an area along the Columbia River where the skull of the Kennewick Man was found. Today, this area has been covered up.

## The Find

The date was July 28, 1996. It was a lovely summer day. Thousands of people stood alongside the Columbia River near Kennewick, Washington. They were eager to see a boat race on the river that day. Some people, including two college students, went into the water to cool off. The bank of the river was lined with small, smooth river rocks. The college students walked in the water near a part of the riverbank that had eroded away. All of a sudden, they saw something that was very out of place. They saw a human skull. Whose skull was it? Was the person killed? Did anyone report a missing person? The college students had lots of questions, but not many answers.

## The Search for Answers

The students picked up the skull and placed it under some bushes. When they got back to town, they called the sheriff. The sheriff called the local police. It's not every day that people find skulls in Kennewick, Washington! The police went to the spot where the students had placed the skull. As they looked around, they saw other bones in the shallow water. They decided not to touch any of the bones. They thought it was time to call Floyd Johnson, the coroner for Kennewick. As coroner, it was Floyd Johnson's job to investigate deaths that might be from unnatural causes.

After seeing the bones, Floyd Johnson called Dr. James C. Chatters, an anthropologist who knew a lot about human skeletons. He was an expert on human bones. He said, "Bones are my thing." He also loved puzzles. Dr. Chatters was the perfect person to solve the mystery of the skull and bones.

### What Do You Think?

What's the difference between a natural and unnatural cause of death? Why do you think Coroner Floyd Johnson called an anthropologist? What do you think the anthropologist will find?

▲ Kennewick is located in a region of the United States called the Pacific Northwest.

## The Experts

The search was on for a solution to this mystery. Dr. Chatters, Coroner Johnson, and the police went back to the site where the bones were found. They found more bones. Eventually, they found almost all the bones of the skeleton, including all the teeth. The bones were discolored. Soil was stuck to them. Dr. Chatters concluded that the bones were very old. At first, he thought they might be the bones of a European, a white pioneer who died in the late 1800s. He didn't think they looked like the bones of an American Indian.

After further examination and scientific tests, Dr. Chatters began to have second thoughts. The main reason he doubted himself is because he found a projectile point—something like an arrowhead—in one of the hip bones. The shape of the projectile point told him that it was probably at least 4,500 years old. If these were the bones of a European settler from the 1800s, what was a 4,500-year-old arrowhead doing in the man's hip bone?

▲ Can you see where Coroner Johnson found the projectile point in the hip bone?

## Testing, Testing

James Chatters and the other experts had a problem that many anthropologists face—conflicting evidence. They agreed that the bones were old, and they thought the skeleton looked like it belonged to a European, not an American Indian. On the other hand, the arrowhead in the hip bone was probably at least 4,500 years old. Since there weren't any Europeans in Washington 4,500 years ago, this added to the mystery. Dr. Chatters told a newspaper reporter, "I've got a white guy with a stone point in him. … That's pretty exciting."

▲ Scientists can use DNA and radiocarbon tests to discover how old something is.

He decided to name the bones "Kennewick Man." Dr. Chatters did not have enough evidence to make strong conclusions. He needed more information. He decided to conduct DNA and radiocarbon tests.

## A Battle over Bones

On August 26, 1996, the DNA results were in and they rocked the scientific community. The bones of Kennewick Man were between 9,200 and 9,500 years old. No one had ever found a skeleton that old in the Americas. What a discovery for science!

### What Do You Think?

What did Dr. Chatters know as a fact? What was his opinion? Who else do you think might be interested in the bones?

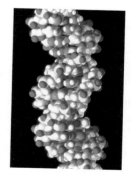

▲ DNA is the basic make-up of all living things.

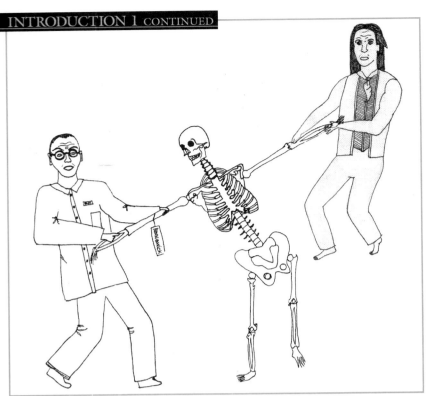

▲ A high school student named Anny Franzoy drew this cartoon to express her ideas about the Kennewick Man controversy. This kind of cartoon is called a "political" (or "editorial") cartoon. Political cartoons express in pictures an opinion about a current event. Americans have used cartoons to make statements about political events since the late 1700s. It wasn't until the late 1800s, however, that technology made it possible for cartoons to be reproduced easily. As you look at a political cartoon, think about the artist's message and consider how the message is relayed. How effectively does the cartoon tell the artist's opinion?

## What Do You Think?

Do you think scientists want to study things for the sake of science or personal gain? Who do you think had a right to name the bones—the scientists or the Indians? Who do you think will win the battle?

However, four days later, on August 30, the Army Corps of Engineers said all scientific testing on the bones must stop. The Corps also took possession of the skeleton. Why did the Army Corps of Engineers get involved? The answer is that the bones were found on land owned by the federal government. The Corps was responsible for enforcing the laws about how to handle American Indian remains and artifacts found on government land. One of the laws said that the age of the Kennewick skeleton meant it was "of Native American ancestry." The law also required the Army Corps of Engineers to inform Indian tribes "reasonably known to have a cultural relationship" to the bones.

Five Indian tribes—the Umatilla, Yakama, Nez Perce, Wanapum, and Colville—claimed Kennewick Man. A leader of the Umatilla tribe, Armand Minthorn, said: "From our oral histories, we know that our people have been part of this land since the beginning of time." The Umatilla renamed the bones, "Oyt.pa.ma.na.tit.tite," which means "The Ancient One." The Indian tribes did not think the scientists should do tests and study one of their ancestors. They thought that was disrespectful. Minthorn said that their ancestor should not be studied "for the sake of science and for [the scientists'] own personal gain."

A group of anthropologists strongly disagreed. They sued the government for the right to study the skeleton further. Dr. Chatters said that if Kennewick Man were reburied, "experts will lose the chance to directly examine this rare phenomenon." An editorial in a newspaper agreed: "The information from ancient Kennewick Man is simply too important to all peoples to be buried by one people."

The battle lines were clear. The Indian tribes thought Kennewick Man was their ancestor. They wanted to bury him. The scientists wanted to study Kennewick Man. They wanted to learn more about the earliest people in the Americas. Who would win this battle?

## The Decision

Two anthropologists, Douglas W. Owsley of the Smithsonian Institution and Richard J. Jantz of the University of Tennessee, Knoxville, wrote a letter to the Army Corps of Engineers. They said, "If a pattern of returning remains without study develops, the loss to science will be incalculable and we will never have the data required to understand the earliest populations in America."

The president of the Society of American Archaeology wrote a letter to the *New York Times* that asked Indians to "permit additional studies" on Kennewick Man. In September 2000, however, the federal government said that Kennewick Man belonged to the Umatilla Indians. The Indians thought this was the right decision. They said, "Let him come home to his people." They did not want scientists to dig up and study American Indians. Armand Minthorn said, "Today thousands of native human remains sit on the shelves of museums and institutions, waiting for the day when they can return to the earth, and waiting for the day that scientists and others pay them the respect they are due."

The scientists continued to disagree with the Indian tribes. Because they felt so strongly about the scientific value of Kennewick Man, a group of scientists took their case to court. They wanted the right to study the skeleton of Kennewick Man. A judge agreed with them and said testing could continue. But the battle for the bones of Kennewick Man is not over. Who will eventually win the battle over the bones? Who should win? 📖

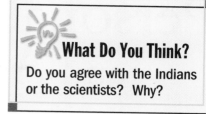

**What Do You Think?**
Do you agree with the Indians or the scientists? Why?

# Find Out More ...

Has the case been settled? Get the latest information about the Kennewick Man and the battle over his bones by doing further research, especially on the Internet. Use the keywords "Kennewick Man" to read what the scientists, Indians, and government officials have to say about the case. You also can read about the Native American Graves Protection and Repatriation Act (NAGPRA), the law that governs how the discovery of Native American remains and artifacts must be handled, protected, and preserved.

**Also see** David Hurst Thomas's book, *Skull Wars: Kennewick Man, Archaeology, and the Battle for Native American Identity.* New York: Basic Books, 2000.

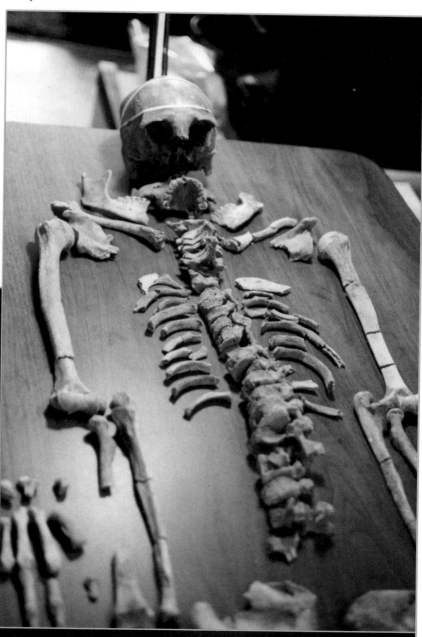

▲ These are the bones of the skeleton called Kennewick Man. Scientists and American Indians still disagree about what should be done with the bones.

# Personalities of History and Archaeology

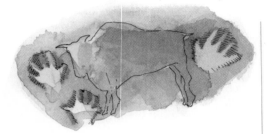

## Q. How did Mary Leakey decide to become an archaeologist?

A. While traveling with her family in France, she saw cave paintings and decided then and there to become an archaeologist. She was only 11 years old at the time! Mary Leakey had no trouble making up her mind.

## Q. How do you become a historian or an archaeologist?

A. Today, almost all historians and archaeologists are college graduates. After they earn a bachelor of arts degree, most continue studying for advanced degrees. They study history, anthropology, languages, geography, and other social sciences. Most like to read and are curious about the past.

▲ Barbara Tuchman won a Pulitzer Prize for her book about World War I.

## Q. Which archaeologist made the most important discovery in Egypt?

A. Many different archaeologists have made important discoveries in Egypt. However, one of the most famous archaeologists who worked in Egypt was Howard Carter. Carter discovered the tomb of a young boy named Tutankhamen ("King Tut") who ruled Egypt more than 3,000 years ago. Howard Carter was curious, hard working, and very lucky!

▲ Howard Carter discovered King Tut's tomb. It had not been disturbed by grave robbers. Lucky Howard!

▲ Figuring out what the Rosetta Stone said was quite a homework assignment for Jean Champollion.

## Q. How long did it take Jean Champollion to decipher the writing on the Rosetta Stone?

A. It was a long process that began in 1808. He didn't publish any of his findings until 1822. In a book published in 1824, he shared more of his ideas. This book was the basis for all later discoveries that gave us the ability to read Egyptian hieroglyphs. Jean Champollion had determination!

## Q. Who is known as the "father of history"?

A. Herodotus. He was born about 2,500 years ago in what is present-day Turkey. He wrote about things he saw in his travels throughout the Middle East. The Greek word for history means, "I have seen."

## Q. What do historians study?

A. Historians study the past. Some historians are interested in ancient Greece or Rome. Others are interested in Latin America or United States history. Barbara Tuchman, an important American historian, was interested in both American and world history. She won prizes for her work. People love to read her history books because they contain such good stories. 📖

# HERODOTUS —
# Father of History

◀ Herodotus wrote about his travels.

550 B.C.

509
Roman Republic is founded

c. 484- c. 425
Herodotus

c. 450- c. 443
Herodotus travels throughout the ancient world

400 B.C.

Herodotus was a Greek storyteller and the world's first historian. What we know about his life comes partly from his writing, but mostly from the writings of others. He was born about 484 B.C. in Halicarnassus (now Bodrum, Turkey), a Greek city in southwest Asia Minor. At the time, the Persians ruled this part of the world.

## A Traveling Man
Herodotus traveled to many places during his lifetime. He gained valuable, firsthand knowledge of Southwestern Asia. His travels took him through most of the Persian Empire, Libya, Syria, and Egypt. When he was in Egypt around 450 B.C., he saw how Egyptians made mummies. He wrote, "As much of the brain as possible is extracted through the nostrils with an iron hook." He described the entire process in great detail. Modern scientists say his description was very accurate.

▲ Herodotus had to walk or ride horses or in carts to get from place to place. He traveled throughout the ancient world, including to Athens. Athens was the center of Greek culture.

## The Beginning of Modern History
In 443 B.C., Herodotus went to live in the colony of Thurii on the island known today as Sicily. He devoted the rest of his life to the writing of his great work, entitled *History*. The word "history" comes from a Greek word meaning, "I have seen." *History* tells about the wars between Persia and Greece (499-479 B.C.). It is the first known attempt to write history. The book talks about customs, legends, and traditions in the ancient world. It also describes the actual fighting between Greece and Persia. Herodotus's attempt to create moral lessons from the study of great events forms the basis of Greek and Roman historical traditions. Herodotus is thought of as the founder of these traditions.

## The Father of History
We think Herodotus died between 430 and 420 B.C. His work provides important details about the time in which he lived and the places he visited. Herodotus wrote the first historical account, which is why we think of him today as the "father of history." 📖

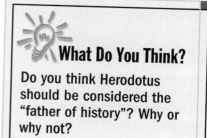

## What Do You Think?
Do you think Herodotus should be considered the "father of history"? Why or why not?

# JEAN CHAMPOLLION — The Man Who Solved the Mystery of Egyptian Hieroglyphs

A.D. **1700**                                                                                    A.D. **1900**

**1790-1832**
Jean Champollion

**1808**
Champollion
begins work on the
Rosetta Stone

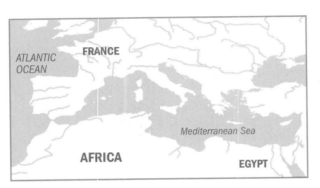

▲ Jean Champollion was born in France, but often is called the "father of Egyptology."

How did a French boy end up solving the mystery of Egyptian hieroglyphs? Jean Champollion was born in France in 1790. He began studying at home. He taught himself several languages and had many academic interests, including ancient Egypt. Before he was 20 years old, he was teaching history and politics. He spent most of his time studying ancient Egyptian language and architecture. Champollion traveled to museums in Europe examining Egyptian objects. He became an expert on ancient Egypt.

## The Big Discovery—Clues in Stone

At the time, no one could read the ancient Egyptian language. Champollion spent years trying to figure it out. The Rosetta Stone, a large block of volcanic rock, was the key that would help him unlock the mystery of Egyptian hieroglyphs. French soldiers discovered the Rosetta Stone near the town of Rosetta, Egypt in 1799. It was special because it was inscribed with the same message in three languages.

## Cracking the Code

Champollion began to examine the Rosetta Stone in 1808. One of the languages on the stone was ancient Egyptian. Using his knowledge of languages, he figured out that one of the other languages on the stone was similar to the late forms of the Egyptian language. This bit of information was the clue he needed. After more years of work, Champollion identified about 12 of the hieroglyphs. In 1822, he wrote a letter to the French Academy, an important scientific organization, to share his findings.

▲ Jean Champollion examined the writing on the Rosetta Stone. You can see the Rosetta Stone today in the British Museum in London.

## The Father of Egyptology

Champollion continued to write about his work with hieroglyphs until he died in 1832. He helped unlock the mystery of Egyptian hieroglyphs. He was not Egyptian, but he is often referred to as the "father of Egyptology." 📖

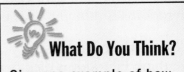

**What Do You Think?**

Give one example of how Champollion used critical thinking.

# HOWARD CARTER — The Man Who Discovered King Tut's Tomb

A.D. **1850**

A.D. **1950**

**1874-1939**
Howard Carter

**1891**
Howard Carter's
first trip to Egypt

**1922**
Howard Carter
discovers tomb
of Tutankhamen

The man who discovered King Tutankhamen's tomb described it as "the most beautiful monument I have ever seen—so lovely that it made one gasp with wonder and admiration."

▲ Howard Carter was born in England, but spent much of his life in Egypt.

Howard Carter was born in London in 1874. His father was a painter. He hoped Howard would continue the business, but Howard had other plans. When he was 17 years old, he set sail for Egypt to work as a "tracer," a person who copies drawings and inscriptions on paper for further study. Working at dig sites was hard, but he loved it. He later became the Inspector General of Monuments in Egypt.

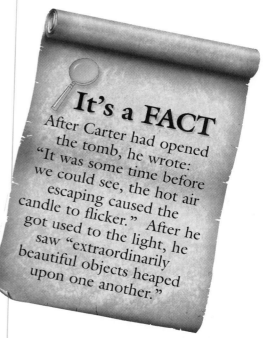

**It's a FACT**
After Carter had opened the tomb, he wrote: "It was some time before we could see, the hot air escaping caused the candle to flicker." After he got used to the light, he saw "extraordinarily beautiful objects heaped upon one another."

## Searching For History

Howard Carter made exciting discoveries in Egypt. Because of his hard work, he discovered the tombs of Thutmose IV and Queen Hatshepsut, the first woman to call herself "pharaoh." In 1908, he met George Herbert, a wealthy Englishman who collected Egyptian artifacts. Herbert agreed to support Carter's search for an unopened pharaoh's tomb. Many people did not believe one existed.

## An Amazing Find

Over the next several years, Carter made many discoveries. Then, in 1922, Carter began digging in the Valley of the Kings. Carter found the tomb of a young king named Tutankhamen. "King Tut" ruled Egypt in 1333 B.C. The discovery of King Tut's tomb was one of the most amazing finds in archaeology. The treasures inside had not been stolen, damaged, or destroyed. It took experts over a decade to make a list of all of the artifacts. These are now in the Egyptian Museum in Cairo, Egypt. Carter later retired from archaeology and eventually returned to England where he died in 1939. □

**What Do You Think?**

Why do archaeologists think it is important to list every item found in a tomb?

# BARBARA TUCHMAN —
# Making History Come Alive

A.D. **1900**                                                                                                A.D. **2000**

**1912-1989**
Barbara Tuchman

**1937**
Tuchman begins reporting on the Spanish Civil War

**1939-1945**
World War II

**1960**
Pulitzer Prize for *Guns of August*

▲ Barbara Tuchman was born in the United States, but traveled to Europe to see events there for herself.

Barbara Tuchman never called herself a historian. "I did not write to instruct but to tell a story," she said. Her stories made history come alive.

Barbara Wertheim was born in New York City in 1912. She had a lifelong interest in history. In 1933, she graduated from Radcliffe College. She started her career as a writer for her father's magazine, *The Nation*. She traveled to Europe in 1937 to write about the civil war in Spain. During World War II, she became an editor for the U.S. Office of War Information. In 1940, she married Dr. Lester R. Tuchman.

▲ Barbara Tuchman won a Pulitzer Prize for her book about World War I.

## Writing about History

At the end of the war, Barbara Tuchman began her career writing about history. Tuchman prepared to write several of her books by traveling to the places where the events happened. In one of her most important books, *The Guns of August*, Tuchman visited the places in Europe where soldiers fought the first land battles of World War I. Her descriptions helped people feel as if they were seeing things for themselves. It made history come to life. Barbara Tuchman also said that history "must be written in terms of what was known and believed at the time, not from the perspective of hindsight."

## Achieving Recognition

Barbara Tuchman wrote many articles and books about different topics. Two of her books, including *The Guns of August*, won Pulitzer Prizes. The Pulitzer Prize is one of the most important awards a writer can win. Barbara Tuchman had a rare talent for writing history. She died on February 6, 1989 at her home in Connecticut.

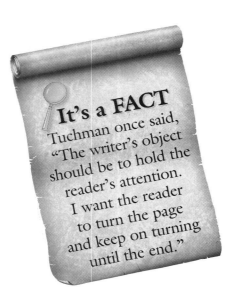

## It's a FACT

Tuchman once said, "The writer's object should be to hold the reader's attention. I want the reader to turn the page and keep on turning until the end."

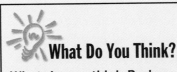

## What Do You Think?

What do you think Barbara Tuchman meant when she said that history must be written in terms of what was known and believed at the time?

# MARY LEAKEY —
# Bone Collector

◄ Mary Leakey found fossil bones in Olduvai Gorge in Africa.

A.D. **1900**                                                                    A.D. **2000**

**1913-1996**
Mary Leakey

**1959**
Leakey discovers
a skull more than
two million years old

**1978**
Leakey discovers
oldest fossil
footprints known

"Given the choice, I'd rather be in a tent than in a house," said Mary Leakey. She loved to be in the field hunting for fossils. Mary Leakey made a name for herself in archaeology at a time when most archaeologists were men.

Mary Nicol was born in 1913. Her father was a painter, but he also had a great interest in archaeology. He took his family on many trips around Europe. During a trip to France, Mary saw cave paintings drawn by people who lived thousands of years ago. She also got to go along on excavations. She described the experience as "powerfully and magically exciting." From that time on, she wanted to be an archaeologist.

## Preparing for Her Life's Work

As a young woman, she enrolled at a college in London and began to take anthropology classes. She became an expert on ancient stone tools and developed a talent for drawing these items. Her ability to draw was the reason she met her future husband, Louis Leakey. Louis Leakey was already a famous archaeologist. He needed someone to illustrate his new book.

## Digging in Africa

In 1936, Mary Nicol went on Louis Leakey's dig in Africa. Later that year, they were married. After many years of work in Africa, Mary Leakey made three very important discoveries, including a fossilized skull of an ape dated at about 20 million years old.

In 1978, Mary Leakey found the earliest fossilized footprints known. This was the first record of human beings walking upright. She called this discovery "immensely exciting—something so extraordinary that I could hardly take it in or comprehend its implications for some while."

## An Exciting Life

In 1994, Mary Leakey wrote the story of her exciting life in a book called *Disclosing the Past*. She remained interested in archaeology all her life. Mary Leakey died at her home in Africa in 1996. 📖

ENGLAND
EUROPE
ASIA
AFRICA
ATLANTIC OCEAN
Olduvai Gorge

▲ Mary Leakey was born in England, but she spent most of her life in Africa.

### What Do You Think?

**1.** Archaeologists today do not keep the artifacts they find. Why do you think this is so?

**2.** Which of Mary Leakey's discoveries do you think is most important? Why?

# DIGGING History

**A MAGAZINE ABOUT HISTORY & ARCHAEOLOGY**

**DNA TESTING SOLVES MYSTERY**

## Prince or Imposter?

European scientists used DNA tests to discover that a 200-year-old, dried-out heart belonged to Prince Louis, the son of King Louis XVI and Marie Antoinette. The prince was put in prison in 1795 during the French Revolution. He was only 10 years old. Some people had believed the young prince was rescued and that an imposter died in his place. Other people thought Louis died in prison. They say that after Louis died, the heart was secretly taken out of the prison and preserved in vinegar before it dried out. It ended up in a church in Paris, France.

Scientists compared DNA from the heart with strands of Marie Antoinette's hair that were found in a locket. Even though the tests showed the heart belonged to Prince Louis, many questions remain. Who took the heart out of prison? Why did he or she preserve it?

▶ Scientists used DNA tests to find out that Prince Louis died in prison during the French Revolution.

# The Case of Piltdown Man

Many people prefer a simple explanation of what is going on in the world around them. Sometimes, simple explanations seem so believable that we are willing to ignore other possible answers—even if the truth is right in front of our noses. There are many examples of smart, educated people being tricked into believing something that turned out to be a hoax. The case of Piltdown man is a very good example of this happening.

Scientists who search for fossils like to be first with a new idea and an important discovery. When the bones of Neanderthal man were discovered in 1856, scientists raced to find an older set of fossil remains. One of those people was Charles Dawson. Dawson liked fossils. He spent much of his spare time collecting them for the British Museum. In 1912, he brought some old skull bones to the museum. He said he found the bones near the small town of Piltdown, England.

This was exciting news. Scientists had been looking for a so-called "missing link." Were these bones evidence of human evolution between modern humans and apes?

Continued on page 18

# Underwater Treasure

Treasure hunters were looking for gold and other riches in old shipwrecks in the Mediterranean Sea in 1998 when they found something they didn't expect—a 2,500-year-old sunken ship.

Archaeologists were called in to examine the cargo and the style of the ship. They confirmed that the ship belonged to the ancient Phoenicians, a seafaring people who were excellent traders. The Phoenicians also were the people who gave us our alphabet.

One archaeologist said, "This is an exciting ship because it is from ... a culture that is known to us only from land excavations and the accounts of their enemies."

New technology has made underwater finds like this possible. A few years ago, it was not possible for people to dive deeper than 100 feet (which is a little more than the length of a basketball court). The pressure of the water at lower depths could crush a person's body. Today, advanced equipment allows people to dive much deeper, but it is very expensive. Most archaeologists don't have the money to buy this new technology. That's where treasure hunters come in.

Treasure hunters get money from investors to pay for the expensive technology. Their primary goal is to make money. In the past, they have sold the cargo from shipwrecks. The problem is that making money by selling the cargo is not what archaeologists want to do with ancient ships.

In the case of the Phoenician shipwreck, treasure hunters agreed to pay for the technology and archaeologists studied the ship and its cargo. The treasure hunters made money by filming the excavation and by organizing museum exhibits of some of the cargo. William Murray, chairman of the underwater archaeology committee of the Archaeological Institute of America, said: "If academic archaeologists are going to deal with deep-water shipwrecks, it's going to have to be through cooperative efforts like this."

Dawson and Arthur Woodward, an official from the museum, went back to the Piltdown site. They dug around and discovered more bones. At the end of 1912, they presented their discovery, called "Piltdown man," to other scientists in England. Most scientists doubted that the fossils were real. However, a year later a tooth was discovered. Five years after that another skull was found. Many people thought these discoveries proved that the Piltdown man fossils were real. But were they? How old were they really?

These were difficult questions for scientists in the early 1900s. For one thing, they had very few fossils to compare to Piltdown man. Not many fossils had been discovered yet. For another thing, they didn't have the technology to conduct advanced scientific tests.

As the decades passed, however, more fossil discoveries were made and comparisons could take place. From about 1930 to 1950 each new fossil discovery seemed to cast more doubt on the Piltdown discovery and the men who made it. The fossil evidence scientists were finding in other parts of the world didn't fit with the Piltdown bones.

Continued on page 19

**There are many examples of smart, educated people being tricked into believing something that turned out to be a hoax.**

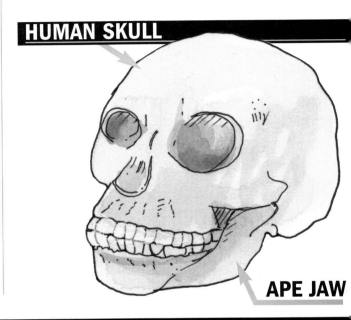

HUMAN SKULL

APE JAW

## HOAXES OF HISTORY: A GIANT FRAUD

# The Cardiff Giant— Stone Man?

In some cases, we never find out who was behind a hoax or why they tried to fool everyone. But, sometimes we do. Take the case of the Cardiff Giant. In 1866, a New York cigar maker named George Hull visited his sister in Iowa.

A minister in the area insisted that since the Bible says, "There were giants in the earth in those days," there must have been real giants. Hull disagreed. He didn't think this interpretation of the Bible was correct. In fact, he decided to fool all of the people who believed the idea that giants lived on the earth at one time.

In 1868, Hull went to Chicago and bought a huge block of stone. He hired a stonemason to carve a 10-foot statue of a giant from the stone block. The statue weighed about 3,000 pounds—almost as much as a car! To make the statue appear old, Hull poured acid and other chemicals over different parts of it. It cost him about $2,200 to create this giant fake.

Hull secretly shipped the statue to a relative's farm near Cardiff, New York. And that's where he had it buried.

In 1869, Hull's New York relative hired some workers to dig a new well. They discovered the giant on Saturday, October 16, 1869. At the time, people were very excited about this new "discovery" of a fossilized man. Lots of people came to the site to see the discovery. Hull went to the farm and charged the people 50 cents to take a peek!

A lot of people were fooled by the giant fake. One estimate is that Hull made almost $100,000 in two months. A famous scientist of the time said the giant was "the most remarkable object yet brought

Continued from page 18

The experts were confronted with confusing and conflicting information. How did scientists finally determine that Piltdown man was a hoax? Well, there is an old saying, "Science never sleeps." This means that scientists are always conducting new experiments and looking for new discoveries. They also are always trying to find new and better ways to understand and evaluate information. In the early 1950s, scientists developed new tests to find out the age of objects.

When they tested the bone fragments of Piltdown man, they found that the bones were not very old at all. The bones had been soaked in a mixture of chemicals to make them seem very hard and very old. The tests showed that the skull was from a modern human. The jaw was from an orangutan, a type of ape.

In 1953, scientists in England formally announced that Piltdown man was a hoax. Since that time, many, many people have been trying to discover who planted the fake bones and why they did it. Any guesses?

◀ An archaeologist and chef teamed up to recreate a 2,700-year-old feast. The archaeologist called this effort "experimental archaeology."

## DISCOVERING WHAT PEOPLE ATE LONG AGO

# Dining in Style

Patrick E. McGovern, an archaeology professor at the University of Pennsylvania, used new scientific methods to find out what foods and drinks were in bowls and pitchers in an ancient site (c. 700 B.C.) in central Turkey.

By analyzing the molecules in these containers, he found that people ate lamb with lentils and drank a beverage that was like wine or beer.

McGovern teamed up with a chef, Pam Horowitz, who came up with recipes based on his findings. Then they held a big dinner featuring foods that people might have eaten 2,700 years ago.

One person who attended the dinner said the lamb stew was "fantastic." Another said, "It was cooked so the lentils were crunchy, with a nutty flavor." 📖

to light in this country." Others thought it was either a fossil or a prehistoric statue. Some people offered to buy it. Eventually, a scientist proved that it was a hoax. Hull was forced to admit that the giant was a fake.

However, even after he admitted the hoax, some people continued to insist that the statue was the fossilized remains of an ancient man. One person said, "It probably would not be true that you fool all the people some of the time if they didn't want it that way. There's a craving for marvels, the tall tale, the haunted house, the whodunit, the two-headed calf."

The Cardiff Giant was exhibited all over the U.S. for many years. It was later placed in the New York State Historical Association's Farmers' Museum in Cooperstown, New York.

▶ Workers discovered the Cardiff Giant near Cardiff, New York in 1869. It turned out to be a giant hoax!

# ROMULUS & REMUS —
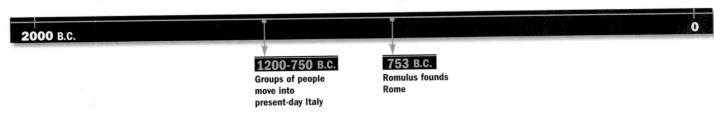
# The Founding of Rome

| 2000 B.C. | | | 0 |
|---|---|---|---|

**1200-750 B.C.**
Groups of people
move into
present-day Italy

**753 B.C.**
Romulus founds
Rome

▲ The mythical story of the founding of Rome begins with two brothers—Romulus and Remus.

It's a FACT
Romans believed
dignity and
discipline were
very important
qualities.

The story of Romulus and Remus is a tale about the mythical founders of Rome. It is an example of how people create myths to explain their origins or other past events.

## A Threat to the New King

The story begins when an ancient king died leaving two sons. By tradition, the older son should have become the new king. But the younger son pushed his brother aside and made himself the new king. When the new king heard that his older brother's wife had given birth to twin sons, he began to worry. What if the twin boys grew up and pushed him aside? The new king came up with what he thought was the perfect solution—throw them into the Tiber River! Surely, the babies would drown and never bother him again.

## A Clever Mother

To save her babies, the mother placed the twins in a basket that floated on the river. Then the story says a female wolf heard the babies crying. She felt sorry for them and began feeding and caring for them. Later, a shepherd found the boys and named them Romulus and Remus. According to the myth, when the boys grew up, they found out about the father and mother who had given birth to them. They decided to build a town of their own in the central region of Italy. This region had seven important hills. The problem was they couldn't agree on which one of the hills to build their town.

## Building a City Is Serious Business

Romulus decided to build the town on Palatine Hill, but Remus wanted it on Aventine Hill. Romulus attracted supporters to help him build the town. These supporters made Romulus their king. They began by building walls around the town. Romulus demanded that everyone respect the town walls. If they wanted to enter or leave the town, they had to use the gates. Remus wasn't very happy about this.

Remus was jealous of his brother and decided to show him what he thought of the silly town walls. He jumped right over the wall and laughed, "Ha! You think these walls are going to protect your town?" He thought he really showed Romulus a thing or two.

Romulus became angry with his brother. Remus did not show respect to the town walls. Romulus became so angry that he killed Remus. Romulus is supposed to have said, "So will die whoever else shall leap over my walls." According to this myth, Romulus founded the town in 753 B.C. and named it after himself. This is the legend of the founding of Rome. 📖

▲ According to legend, the mother of Romulus and Remus set the twins afloat on the Tiber River. The basket kept the water out.

## What Do You Think?

1. Which parts of this story might be someone's imagination?

2. What does this legend tell you about what ancient Romans thought was important?

◀ Legend says a female wolf found Romulus and Remus. She fed and cared for them.

# The Law of the Twelve Tables

1300 B.C.                                                                    0

**1200-750 B.C.**
Earliest Romans
move into
present-day Italy

**494 B.C.**
Roman Republic
gives plebeians
the right to elect
tribunes

**450 B.C.**
Senate writes
laws on bronze
tablets

EUROPE

ITALY
• Rome

Mediterranean Sea

AFRICA

▲ Patricians made up only 10% of Rome's population. The rest of the people were plebeians.

**tablet:** a thin sheet used as a writing surface

Patricians were rich landowners and army leaders in ancient Rome. They came from old, wealthy families. Only about 10% of Rome's population were patricians, but they were the most powerful group. Patrician men elected consuls and senators to govern Rome.

Most Romans were artisans, small farmers, traders, and laborers. These people were called plebeians. Like the patricians, they were Roman citizens and paid taxes. Plebeian men served in the army. However, plebeians didn't have many important rights.

## The Plebeians Gain Political Rights

As some plebeians became richer and more powerful, they began to demand more rights. In 494 B.C., they gained the right to elect people to represent them and protect their rights. These elected officials were called "tribunes." Tribunes had the power to stop discussions in the Senate about laws they didn't like. All they had to do was shout "Veto," which means "I forbid."

## Written Laws

During the early part of the Roman Republic, laws were not written down. Only consuls and senators—the patricians—knew what the laws were. Plebeians did not think this was fair. They wanted the laws written down so everyone would know what they were. Around 450 B.C., they gained this right. The Senate wrote the laws on twelve bronze **tablets**. This was a great victory for the plebeians. These written laws are known as the Law of the Twelve Tables. The Law of the Twelve Tables stated the basic rights of all free citizens. The laws covered private, criminal, religious, and public matters. Why was the Law of the Twelve Tables important? It meant the laws were written down and available to everyone to read. Also, it established the principle of equal justice before the law.

# The Law of the Twelve Tables

## From Table I

If anyone summons a man before the judge, he must go. If the man summoned does not go, let the one summoning him call the bystanders to witness and then take him by force. If he runs away, let the summoner lay hands on him. When parties make a settlement of the case, the judge shall announce it. If they do not reach a settlement, let them each state his own side of the case in the meeting place or Forum before noon ...

## From Table III

When a debt has been **acknowledged**, or judgment about the matter has been pronounced in court, thirty days must be the legitimate time of grace. After that, the debtor may be arrested by laying on of hands. Bring him into court. If he does not satisfy the judgment, or no one in court offers himself as surety in his behalf, the **creditor** may take the **defaulter** with him ...

## From Table VI

Females shall remain in **guardianship** even when they have attained their majority ...

## From Table VII

Let them keep the road in order. If they have not paved it, a man may drive his team where he likes. Should a tree on a neighbor's farm be bent crooked by the wind and lean over your farm, you may take legal action for removal of that tree. A man might gather up fruit that was falling down onto another man's farm.

## From Table X

None is to bury or burn a corpse in the city.

## From Table XI

Intermarriage shall not take place between plebeians and patricians.

## Analyze the Source!

1. Choose one of the laws above and tell in your own words what the law means. Then give reasons why you agree or disagree with the law.

2. Compare one of these laws with our laws today. How does the Law of the Twelve Tables reflect democratic principles?

# HANNIBAL OF CARTHAGE —
# The Man Who Crossed the Alps with Elephants

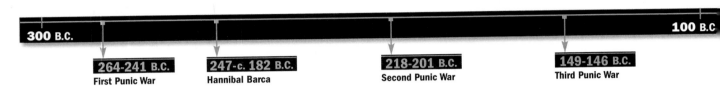

| 300 B.C. | | | | 100 B.C |
|---|---|---|---|---|

**264-241 B.C.**
First Punic War

**247-c. 182 B.C.**
Hannibal Barca

**218-201 B.C.**
Second Punic War

**149-146 B.C.**
Third Punic War

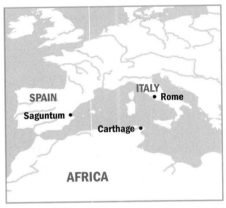

▲ Hannibal was born in Carthage. He lived in Spain, Italy, and North Africa.

**It's a FACT**
Hannibal's elephants were not much use in battle. They became frightened easily and ran in many directions, including back through Hannibal's soldiers!

Hannibal is considered one of Carthage's most famous sons. To keep a promise to his father, it is said, Hannibal waged battles against the powers of Rome.

## Carthage and Rome

The Phoenicians, a seafaring people from the eastern Mediterranean region, established Carthage as an important trading center. It was located in northern Africa in what today is Tunisia. Over time, Carthage became a powerful city-state, more powerful than Rome at the time. Carthage and Rome were often allies against the Greek cities of Italy. Eventually, Rome and Carthage went to war against one another. They fought three wars, called the Punic Wars.

The first Punic War lasted from 264 to 241 B.C., when the Romans forced the Carthaginian General Hamilcar Barca to surrender. Rome and Carthage signed a treaty—an agreement that described the conditions for peace. The second Punic War (218-201 B.C.) was fought because Carthage captured Saguntum, a city in Spain that had an alliance with Rome. Historians argue that the last Punic War (149-146 B.C.) was fought because Rome wanted to destroy the city of Carthage once and for all.

## A Promise to be Rome's Enemy Forever

According to a legend, Hamilcar Barca made his 9-year-old son Hannibal Barca promise to be Rome's enemy forever. Hannibal was born in 247 B.C. during the first Punic War. His father taught him how to be a soldier. Hannibal dedicated his life to battling Rome. This was Hannibal's way to do his duty as a citizen of Carthage and to honor his father

Hannibal was only 26 years old when he was chosen to lead the Carthaginian army. His first task was to gain more territory in Spain. He moved his troops into Saguntum, an independent city that had a treaty with Rome. Rome protested loudly. When Saguntum finally surrendered to Hannibal, Rome said Carthage had violated the treaty it had signed to end the first Punic War. Rome demanded that Hannibal surrender. When he refused, the second Punic War began in 218 B.C.

## Crossing the Alps on Elephants

Hannibal spent a winter getting ready to bring his army to Italy for battle. To get to Italy he had to cross two mountain ranges. First there were the Pyrenees, and then the Alps. Hannibal and approximately 35,000 soldiers crossed these mountain ranges with the help of horses and 37 elephants. After a long and difficult journey over the Alps, Hannibal arrived in northern Italy. His first battles against Rome were successful. As the months went by, he conquered several Roman cities. Hannibal could have marched on to Rome, but he chose to let his troops rest. This gave Rome a chance to plan a way to defeat him. The Roman armies did not go into one great battle against Hannibal's army. Instead, they fought small battles against his soldiers on the edge of the territory he controlled.

## Defeated by Rome

Hannibal was running out of food and other supplies for his soldiers. This situation dragged on for several years. Meanwhile, Rome started an attack on the city of Carthage. Hannibal decided to leave Italy and return home to protect Carthage. He arrived in Carthage in time to fight a battle against the Romans. At the decisive battle of Zama, Hannibal lost 20,000 of his soldiers, but he escaped with his life. Rome and Carthage signed another treaty, but this was not what Hannibal had been fighting for all his life. He had one last opportunity to lead an army against Rome. This time most of the war was fought on water. Hannibal was defeated by the Romans, who demanded his surrender. Rather than surrendering, he poisoned himself. The year was probably 182 or 183 B.C.

Today, Hannibal is remembered as a brave general who led thousands of soldiers and a pack of elephants across the Alps. He fought against Rome to avenge his father's loss in the first Punic War and to protect and uphold the honor of his country. □

### What Do You Think?

1. Why do people remember Hannibal? What significant things did he do with his life?

2. Are the qualities of a leader today different than the qualities of a leader from 1,000 or 2,000 years ago? Why or why not?

▲ Hannibal and 35,000 Carthaginian soldiers crossed the Alps with 37 elephants. Imagine what you would have felt like if you were a Roman soldier and you saw them coming.

# POLYBIUS on Roman Government

250 B.C. | 0

**218-201 B.C.**
Hannibal leads an attack on Rome during the second Punic War

**200-118 B.C.**
Polybius

**48 B.C.**
Julius Caesar becomes the sole ruler of Rome

More than 2,000 years ago, the Greek historian Polybius asked this question: "Who is so thoughtless and lazy that he does not want to know in what way and with what kind of government the Romans in less than 53 years conquered nearly the entire inhabited world and brought it under their rule—an achievement previously unheard of?"

## What a Government Those Romans Have!

Polybius saw firsthand Rome's rise to power. He came to Rome from his native Greece. Romans admired the ideas and culture of Greece and many Romans wanted his friendship. Polybius went with one of Rome's greatest generals on military campaigns in Spain and Africa. He was a strong supporter of Rome's expansion. He wrote admiringly about Rome's government.

▼ Polybius described these three kinds of government. He also explained how each one of these governments could turn out badly.

## THREE KINDS OF GOVERNMENT

| MONARCHY | ARISTOCRACY | DEMOCRACY |
|---|---|---|
| Ruled by one person | Ruled by a few people | Ruled by many people |

## A Mixed Government

Polybius described three kinds of governments: monarchy (rule by one person), aristocracy (rule by a few people), and democracy (rule by many people). He thought that each of these kinds of governments may start out all right, but over time each ends up badly. For example, he thought a monarchy eventually turns into a dictatorship, an aristocracy becomes dominated by a few ruling families, and a democracy declines into mob rule.

Polybius believed that the Roman Republic avoided these problems by having a "mixed" government. Rome took parts of all three kinds of governments. The consuls (elected by the Senate) were a kind of monarchy. The Senate was drawn from the aristocracy. The assemblies allowed a voice for the people. He believed these three parts of government provided a good system of checks and balances. He thought that Rome's government avoided many mistakes other empires had made. You can read here part of Polybius's observations about Rome's three kinds of government. 📖

# Polybius on the Government of the Roman Republic

The elements by which the Roman constitution was controlled were three in number. ...

All the aspects of the administration were, taken separately, so fairly and so suitably ordered and regulated through the agency of these three elements that it was impossible even for the Romans themselves to declare with certainty whether the whole system was an aristocracy, a democracy or a monarchy. ...

When one part having grown out of proportion to the others aims at supremacy and tends to become too predominant, it ... can be counterworked and thwarted by the others. ...

All in fact remains in status quo [condition as it was before a change]... because any aggressive impulse is sure to be checked and from the outset each estate stands in dread of being interfered with by the others.

### In other words ...

The Roman constitution was controlled by three different groups. The management of Rome's government ran so smoothly that even Romans couldn't say for sure whether their government was an aristocracy, a democracy, or a monarchy. When one part of the government begins to become larger and more powerful, the other two parts of government work to stop that from taking place. In the end, everything stays the same because any attempt by one part to gain more power is stopped by the others very quickly.

**Analyze the Source!**

1. Explain how the Roman Republic had a mixed government.

2. What ideas about government do you think America's founders might have gotten from the Roman Republic?

# JULIUS CAESAR — Roman General and Statesman

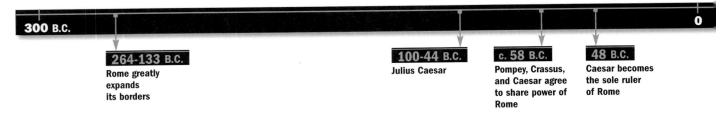

| 300 B.C. | | | | 0 |
|---|---|---|---|---|

**264-133 B.C.**
Rome greatly expands its borders

**100-44 B.C.**
Julius Caesar

**c. 58 B.C.**
Pompey, Crassus, and Caesar agree to share power of Rome

**48 B.C.**
Caesar becomes the sole ruler of Rome

▲ Caesar is remembered as a determined leader of Rome.

▼ Caesar was the first Roman leader to cross the English Channel. He set up a permanent Roman settlement in England.

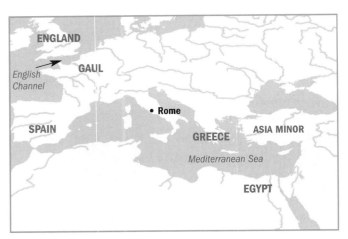

Between 264 B.C. and 133 B.C., Rome fought to expand its power over lands throughout the Mediterranean. When Julius Caesar was born in 100 B.C., however, Romans were battling one another. Civil wars were fought between groups of Romans who wanted to rule. It was during this troubled time that Julius Caesar lived. He came from a patrician family, but it was not a rich or important family. When he was 15, his father died. Shortly after, Caesar married the daughter of an important Roman senator. His new father-in-law was not happy about the marriage. He sentenced Caesar to die. To avoid this, Caesar left Rome to become a soldier. When his father-in-law died in 78 B.C., Caesar returned to Rome.

## A Proud and Determined Man

One story about Julius Caesar shows how very proud and determined he was. While he was sailing to Greece in 75 B.C., Caesar was captured by pirates. The pirates agreed to trade Caesar for 20 pieces of gold. But Caesar told the pirates that he was worth at least 50. Throughout his capture, he was friendly with the pirates, but he also promised himself that he would track them down and kill them after the money was paid. And that's just what he did.

## A Roman Leader on the Rise

Beginning in 72 B.C., Caesar was elected to one important political office after another. By about 58 B.C., Caesar had gathered together a group of friends who had a great deal of political influence. One of the men was Pompey, a Roman general, and the other man was Crassus, a rich patrician. Together these men ruled Rome. Caesar continued to be an important military leader. He conquered Gaul (present-day France) and was the first Roman leader to cross the English Channel. He set up a permanent Roman base in what is now England.

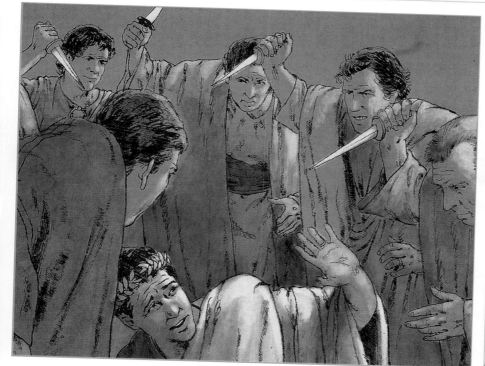

◄ According to one account, on the day Julius Caesar was killed, a fortune teller stopped him and said, "Beware the Ides of March."

**scandal:** a situation that brings disgrace or is considered shameful by the community

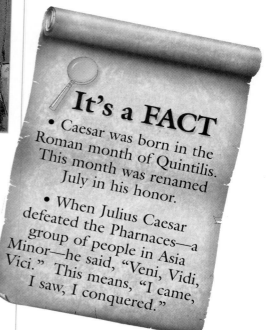

## It's a FACT

• Caesar was born in the Roman month of Quintilis. This month was renamed July in his honor.

• When Julius Caesar defeated the Pharnaces—a group of people in Asia Minor—he said, "Veni, Vidi, Vici." This means, "I came, I saw, I conquered."

Over time, Caesar, Pompey, and Crassus began to distrust one another. They were all very ambitious and willing to betray one another for personal gain. When Crassus was killed in battle, the tension between Caesar and Pompey increased. Eventually, Caesar went to war against Pompey. Caesar crushed Pompey's army and won the war in 48 B.C. Pompey fled to Egypt. Caesar followed him, but found that Pompey had been killed by order of the young Egyptian king, Ptolemy XIII. While in Egypt, Caesar began a relationship with Cleopatra, who soon was named queen of Egypt. Caesar and his army fought various groups of Egyptians who did not want Cleopatra to become queen of Egypt.

### Rome Will Have No King!

When Caesar returned to Rome, Cleopatra soon followed him there with their son, Caesarean. Cleopatra's visit caused a **scandal**. Caesar was already married, and Romans were suspicious of this exotic queen from the East. Would she encourage Caesar to declare himself "king" of Rome? Some were concerned about the power he already had. Rome had been a republic for many years. The citizens wanted nothing to do with kings. The senators were afraid that Caesar was going to do away with the Republic. To "save" the Roman Republic from becoming a dictatorship, a group of senators stabbed Caesar to death as he entered the Senate on the Ides of March (March 15) in 44 B.C. In his will, Caesar named his nephew Octavian as his heir. He also left large amounts of money to the city and to individuals. 📖

### What Do You Think?

1. Julius Caesar was a determined man. However, his actions resulted in his death. When does too much determination get in the way of sound judgment?

2. After Caesar's death, the people of Rome honored him. Why do you think the average Roman thought so highly of him?

# CLEOPATRA —
# Queen of the Nile

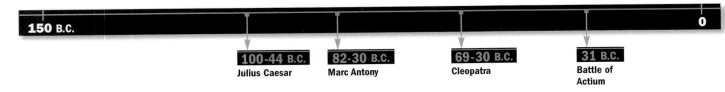

150 B.C.                                                                                                    0

100-44 B.C.          82-30 B.C.          69-30 B.C.          31 B.C.
Julius Caesar        Marc Antony         Cleopatra           Battle of
                                                             Actium

Cleopatra, the woman we call the "Queen of the Nile," was born in 69 B.C. Alexandria was the capital of Egypt, a kingdom ruled by her father, Ptolemy XII. Egypt was a wealthy, independent province in the Roman Empire. But Cleopatra's family wasn't really Egyptian. They were from an area north of Greece called Macedonia. One of Cleopatra's ancestors was a general in the army of Alexander the Great.

It's a FACT
- Cleopatra was the only member of her family who learned to speak Egyptian.
- Cleopatra's father, Ptolemy XII, was nicknamed "the flute player."

## An Ambitious Queen

Cleopatra became queen of Egypt when she was only 18 years old. In keeping with Egyptian traditions, Cleopatra married her 10-year-old brother, Ptolemy XIII. They were co-rulers of Egypt. However, since Cleopatra was a woman, her brother was the primary ruler of Egypt. Ptolemy had several advisors who wanted to rule Egypt on behalf of the young king. Cleopatra was a determined young woman. She was not content for Egypt to be simply another kingdom in the Roman Empire. She dreamed of returning Egypt to a position of power in the world.

## Cleopatra and Julius Caesar

Cleopatra and her brother's advisors disagreed about how Egypt should be ruled. Within two years, the advisors drove her out of Egypt. She went to nearby Syria and recruited an army to help her gain control of Egypt. While she was in Syria, Julius Caesar, a great Roman general, arrived in Egypt. He found Egypt close to civil war. He tried to persuade Cleopatra and her brother to rule together peacefully, but that seemed impossible. The 20-year-old Cleopatra charmed the 52-year-old Julius Caesar into joining forces with her. After six months of terrible warfare, Ptolemy's army was defeated. He died while fleeing from Julius Caesar's army. Cleopatra became sole ruler of Egypt.

EUROPE

Rome
MACEDONIA
• Actium

Mediterranean Sea

ASIA
SYRIA

Alexandria •

EGYPT

AFRICA

▲ Cleopatra was not an Egyptian. She was Macedonian Greek.

Cleopatra is a powerful historical figure. Here you can see actress Lillie Langtry as Cleopatra in an 1890 play.

## Not Welcome in Rome

With the problem of who would be Egypt's ruler settled, Julius Caesar and Cleopatra began a love affair. Cleopatra followed Caesar back to Rome with their son, Caesarean. Her visit created a scandal in Rome. Caesar was already married, and Romans were suspicious of this exotic queen from the East. To make matters worse, some Romans feared that Julius Caesar was going to declare himself king. This fear was so great that several senators decided Caesar must die. On March 15, 44 B.C., a group of senators stabbed him to death as he entered the Senate. Cleopatra had no friends in Rome and feared for her life. She returned to Egypt immediately.

## Cleopatra and Marc Antony

Three men—Octavian, Marc Antony, and Lepidus—decided to find and kill the men who murdered Julius Caesar. They also decided to share rule of the Roman Empire. While Antony was leading his army in the East, he met Cleopatra. Cleopatra still wanted Egypt to become a world power. She thought Antony could help her accomplish this goal. Antony thought Cleopatra's Egyptian armies could help him become the most powerful man in the Roman Empire. They joined political and military forces and also began a romantic relationship. Eventually, Cleopatra and Antony fought Octavian to decide who would rule Rome and Egypt. In the decisive battle of Actium in 31 B.C., Cleopatra and Antony were defeated. They went back to Egypt, but within a year they both killed themselves. Octavian became Augustus, emperor of the Roman Empire.

Cleopatra was an intelligent and powerful woman. She came very close to making her dream come true and returning Egypt to a position of power in the world.

### What Do You Think?

**1.** Most of what we know about Cleopatra is from the Romans' perspective. Why do you think their image of Cleopatra was negative?

**2.** Why do you think the Romans were suspicious of Cleopatra when she came to Rome?

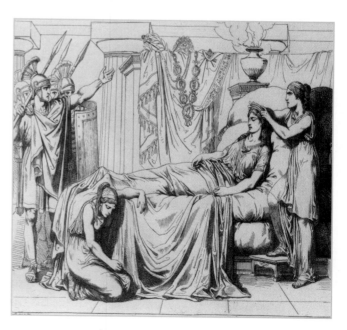

Cleopatra killed herself in 30 B.C. Some believe she ordered a servant to bring her a poisonous snake hidden in a basket of figs.

# CICERO —
# Rome's Greatest Orator

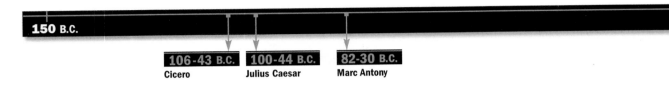

150 B.C.                                                                0

106-43 B.C.    100-44 B.C.    82-30 B.C.
Cicero         Julius Caesar  Marc Antony

In the Rome that existed in 50 B.C., there were two ways to gain fame and power. One way was to be born into a well-known senatorial family. Another way was to become a hero in battle. However, Cicero found a third way to gain fame and power. He sometimes is called Rome's greatest orator. He was the first person to gain powerful positions in Rome based upon his ability to speak in public. How did this man achieve so much and make a place for himself in history?

▲ Cicero was born in Italy about 60 miles southeast of Rome. He lived in Rome, but traveled to Greece and Sicily.

## An Excellent Education

Marcus Tullius Cicero was born in 106 B.C. His family was not wealthy but not poor. As a young boy, Cicero and his brother were given an excellent education. Cicero's father insisted that he study with many of the well-known scholars of the day. Cicero studied poetry, law, philosophy, and most importantly, public speaking or oratory. He also learned a great deal about the teachings of the Greeks. Cicero's father understood that by getting a good education, Cicero would be able to work in Rome's government. Later in his life, Cicero said, "What greater and better gift can we offer the republic than to teach and to instruct our young?" Because of his skill in public speaking, Cicero was asked to defend people charged with crimes.

## The Cost of Success

Cicero was usually successful in defending people charged with crimes. However, a Roman leader became very angry with Cicero when he successfully defended a man accused of murdering one of the leader's family members. As a result, Cicero left Rome for about two years. He traveled to Greece and other eastern provinces. He became very impressed with Greek philosophy. When he was about 30 years old, Cicero returned to Rome. By this time, his public speaking ability was far greater than anyone else's in the empire. He decided to begin a political career. Over the next 20 years, Cicero argued many important law cases. Cicero also wrote several essays on philosophy and public speaking. He served as a Roman senator, a leader in one of Rome's provinces, and as Roman consul.

## Roman Politics

During this time, Romans were fighting among themselves for control of Rome and all its land. In these conflicts, Cicero sided with Pompey, one of Rome's great generals, and against Julius Caesar. Eventually, Caesar defeated Pompey. This left Cicero no choice but to leave Rome again. Later, however, he returned when Caesar offered his friendship. For the next few years, Cicero lived as a private citizen.

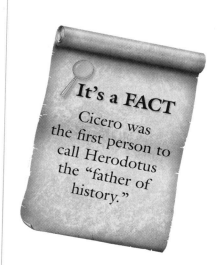

◄ **Cicero used his public speaking ability to gain positions of power in Rome.**

## The Dangers of Public Speaking

After Julius Caesar was killed in 44 B.C., Cicero decided to return to political life. He spoke harshly about Marc Antony, one of Rome's new leaders. This decision cost Cicero his life. He was captured and killed by Antony's soldiers in 43 B.C. Cicero is credited with preserving much of the original Greek philosophy. However, he is best remembered because of his wonderful writing and speaking skills. Today, when people hear the name Cicero, they think of Rome's greatest orator. 📖

**It's a FACT**
Cicero was the first person to call Herodotus the "father of history."

### THE SIX GREATEST MISTAKES

# Cicero recorded what he considered to be the six greatest mistakes human beings make:

**1.** The idea that a person advances by crushing others.

**2.** The tendency to worry about things that cannot be changed.

**3.** Insisting that something is impossible because we cannot do it ourselves.

**4.** Refusing to set aside unimportant preferences.

**5.** Neglecting learning and neglecting to develop the habit of reading and study.

**6.** Attempting to make others believe and live as we do.

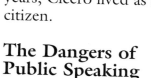

## What Do You Think?

**1.** Cicero said, "the more laws, the less justice." What do you think he meant by this statement? Is this true today? Why or why not?

**2.** Do you agree or disagree with Cicero's "six greatest mistakes" of human beings? Why?

**3.** Cicero asked, "What is so beneficial to the people as liberty, which we see not only to be greedily sought after by men, but also by beasts, and to be preferred to all things?" What do you think he meant by this?

# AUGUSTUS —
# First Roman Emperor

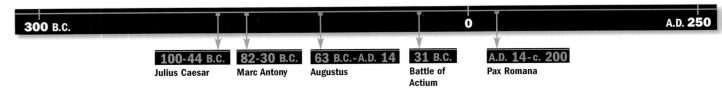

300 B.C.       0       A.D. 250

**100-44 B.C.**
Julius Caesar

**82-30 B.C.**
Marc Antony

**63 B.C.-A.D. 14**
Augustus

**31 B.C.**
Battle of
Actium

**A.D. 14-c. 200**
Pax Romana

As a young boy, Octavian had no idea that his life would be different from other boys. But Octavian's great uncle, Julius Caesar, took a liking to him. As a result, his life and the story of ancient Rome were changed forever. Octavian was born on September 23, 63 B.C. He was named Gaius Octavius. He learned military skills as well as how to think and debate. When Julius Caesar was murdered, Octavian discovered that Caesar had named him his heir. He then took the name Gaius Julius Caesar Octavius. In English, the name is shortened to Octavian.

## After Julius Caesar's Death

Naturally, Octavian was very upset about Caesar's murder. He persuaded Caesar's army to help him **avenge** his great uncle's death. He joined forces with Marc Antony, a respected Roman leader, and Lepidus, a Roman general. They made sure that Caesar's murderers were killed. Then they divided the Roman Empire into thirds. Octavian would rule the western provinces, Antony would rule the eastern provinces, and Lepidus would rule the provinces in Africa. This arrangement, however, did not satisfy either Octavian or Marc Antony for long. Both men wanted to control the entire empire. Lepidus was soon forced out. Antony joined forces with Cleopatra, the Egyptian queen. Eventually, Octavian defeated Antony and Cleopatra at the battle of Actium (in present-day Greece) in 31 B.C.

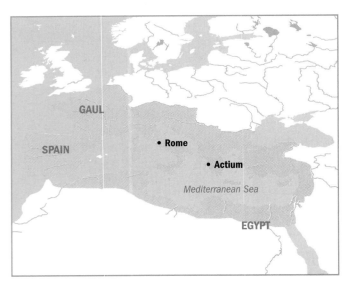

▲ **Augustus was born near Rome. He traveled throughout the Roman Empire (shaded).**

**avenge:** to take revenge; to get back at someone for wrong or injury

## From Octavian to "Augustus"

After the battle of Actium, Octavian returned to Rome in triumph at the age of 34. The Senate gave him many titles and honors. One of the titles was "Augustus," which means "revered one." He is most often referred to as "Augustus." Augustus ruled the Roman Empire for about 40 years.

During Augustus's reign, the Roman Empire expanded to include Spain, Gaul (present-day France), and Egypt. Augustus provided many services for the people of Rome. As part of his plan to improve the life of average Romans, Augustus had many bridges, **aqueducts**, and libraries built. He tried to strengthen Roman families by passing laws that required marriage and emphasized traditional Roman values such as loyalty between husbands and wives. He developed a civil service—an organization of government workers—to help govern the Roman Empire.

Augustus also encouraged artists and writers. His reign is sometimes referred to as a golden age of Latin literature because he was a friend to poets and historians. He supported the work of Virgil who wrote the **epic** poem *The Aeneid* during this period.

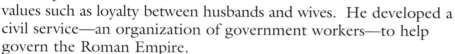

Augustus brought peace to the Roman Empire. The people considered him a fair and wise ruler.

## The Pax Romana

During the rule of Augustus, the Roman Empire became more united. Civil wars that had raged for years ended. The Roman people considered Augustus a fair and wise ruler. After he died in A.D. 14, they worshiped him as a god. Augustus is reported to have said, "I found Rome brick and left it marble." He brought peace, prosperity, and order to the empire. This continued for almost 200 years. This period of time is called the *Pax Romana*, which means "Roman peace."

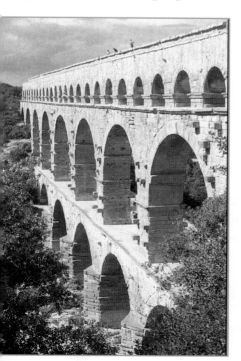

Augustus tried to improve the lives of Roman citizens. He built aqueducts to provide fresh water.

### What Do You Think?

1. Toward the end of his life, Augustus said, "Young men, hear an old man to whom old men harkened when he was young." What do you think he meant?

2. Augustus encouraged trade and the exchange of ideas throughout the Roman Empire. How might this have contributed to Rome's peace and prosperity?

3. Augustus was a great military general and political leader. In your opinion, what are the personal qualities that a great general should possess? Which of these qualities did he possess?

### It's a FACT

Augustus was a patron of the arts and a friend to some of the greatest writers the world has ever known, such as Virgil, Ovid, and Horace.

# Rome's Greatest Poets

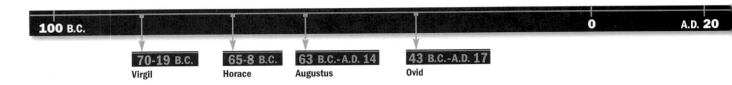

| 100 B.C. | | | | 0 | A.D. 20 |

**70-19 B.C.**
Virgil

**65-8 B.C.**
Horace

**63 B.C.-A.D. 14**
Augustus

**43 B.C.-A.D. 17**
Ovid

Romans honored men who wrote beautiful poems. Rome's greatest poets—Horace, Virgil, and Ovid—lived during the golden age of Latin literature. Wealthy Roman leaders such as Augustus encouraged writers and supported their work. Roman poets wrote about many different topics. They praised the dignity of human beings and celebrated the pleasures of a peaceful and happy life. They also wrote about Roman gods and goddesses, but humans were always the central theme. You can read here about Rome's greatest poets and the poetry they created.

## Horace

Horace's family was not rich, but they had enough money to make sure that Horace had an excellent education. Augustus greatly admired Horace's poetry. One reason might be that Augustus is a hero in the poems. Horace's poems are filled with the glories of the age of Augustus.

## Virgil

Like Horace, Virgil came from a family of modest means. Virgil also had an excellent education. He wrote poems in praise of the new age of Augustus. Virgil's most famous poem is *The Aeneid*. Virgil thought *The Aeneid* would be to the Romans what Homer's *Iliad* and *Odyssey* were to the Greeks. *The Aeneid* tells the story of a Trojan hero, Aeneas, who travels throughout the Mediterranean. Aeneas escapes the city of Troy after the Greeks destroyed it. After a long journey around the Mediterranean world, Aeneas sails to an area near the Tiber River (in present-day Italy). According to Roman legend, Aeneas chose this area to start the town of Lavinium. Legend says that Romulus and Remus, the mythical founders of Rome, were descendants of Aeneas.

### Ovid

Ovid's most famous work is *Metamorphoses*, which means "changes." At first, Augustus liked Ovid. However, his work made fun of Roman marriage, Roman warfare, and Roman life. This irritated Augustus, who sent Ovid away from Rome. Ovid spent the last nine years of his life in the harsh, cold climate of a Roman province far away from the city he loved. 📖

## Horace's Thoughts on Augustus

With Caesar [Augustus] the guardian of the state
Not civil rage nor violence shall drive out peace,
Nor wrath which forges swords
And turns unhappy cities against each other.

## From Virgil's *The Aeneid*

Your task, Roman, and do not forget it, will be to govern the peoples
of the world in your empire. These will be your arts—
and to impose a settled pattern upon peace, to pardon the
defeated and war down the proud.

## From Ovid's *Metamorphoses*

Wherever Rome's influence extends, over the lands it has civilized,
I will be spoken, on people's lips: and, famous through all the ages,
if there is truth in poet's prophecies,—vivam—I shall live.

**Analyze the Source!** Read these excerpts and tell in your own words what each means.

# JESUS of Nazareth

| 100 B.C. | 0 | A.D. 50 |

**63 B.C.-A.D. 14**
Augustus

**c. A.D. 30**
Jesus is put to
death

▲ **Jesus lived in the Roman Empire (shaded). His followers spread his message throughout Judea and the rest of the empire.**

▲ **The Christian Bible contains the Old and New Testaments. It includes writings from the disciples of Jesus.**

**Judaism:** the religion of the Jewish people
**rebellious:** refusing to obey; revolting against someone in authority or power
**superstitious:** believing in magic or having an irrational fear of something

Jesus is a complex historical and religious figure. His life is easy to understand for Christians who believe the Bible—both Old and New Testaments—is the word of God. For those who do not see the Bible as a completely factual source, the life of Jesus is more complicated. Most of what we know about Jesus comes from what others wrote about him. One way to understand his life is to look at these writings. Some of the people who wrote about Jesus held traditional Roman beliefs in many gods. Some of the people who wrote about him were Jews. They believed in one God, but they didn't believe that Jesus was his son. Others who wrote about Jesus were Christians who believed Jesus was the son of God. Examining the writings of these different groups provide information about the life of Jesus.

## What Romans Wrote about Jesus

Romans controlled most of the Mediterranean world when Jesus lived. Most Romans thought Christianity was a small group within **Judaism**. Romans saw Christians as **rebellious**, **superstitious** troublemakers. Several Romans shared this view in their writings. The Roman historian Tacitus (A.D. 54-119) wrote about the death of Jesus by order of Pontius Pilate, the governor in the area. Tacitus described how Christianity developed in Judea and how it later became popular in Judea and in Rome. Other Roman writers such as Suetonius and Pliny the Younger also wrote about Jesus and the early Christians. From their perspective, Christianity should have been done away with. However, Pliny commented on how Christians were strong in their beliefs. We can conclude from the writings of these Romans that Jesus lived and that many people worshiped him as the Jewish Messiah (or "savior") described in the Old Testament of the Bible.

## What Jews Wrote about Jesus

Flavius Josephus, a Jewish historian, wrote about Jesus. Josephus lived during the time that Jesus was alive. His writings included information about John the Baptist, a follower of Jesus. Josephus also wrote about the religious teachings of Jesus. Historians disagree as to whether or not the accounts of Josephus are true. He did not convert to Christianity. His writings about Jesus's life are still the subject of argument.

## What Christians Wrote about Jesus

Paul of Tarsus (also called St. Paul) wrote four letters that contain information about the life of Jesus. These letters were written to the people of Rome, Galatia, and Corinth. According to Paul's writing, Jesus was born to a poor Jewish family during the time when the Roman emperor Augustus ruled.

Jesus's words and actions are recorded in the New Testament of the Christian Bible. The Bible tells many stories about the life of Jesus. Some stories tell about Jesus as a young man who began to preach in the area around his home. Jesus used stories to teach people what he believed was important. One story was about the "Golden Rule"—treating others as you would have them treat you. Another story was about the importance of loving others as you love yourself.

According to Christians, as more people came to listen to him, Jesus asked several men to help spread his message. These men were his disciples or followers. As the message of Jesus became more popular, some Romans became concerned that the people of the Roman Empire would not worship Roman gods. Romans believed that worshiping their gods kept Rome safe and strong. When Jesus was about 33 years old, he led a group of his followers into Jerusalem to celebrate the Jewish feast of Passover. Shortly after he arrived in Jerusalem, the Romans arrested him and sentenced him to death. He was nailed to a cross on which he died. According to the New Testament in the Bible, Jesus rose from the dead. Christians celebrate this event on Easter.

The ideas Jesus taught have influenced people throughout the world. Today, Christianity is one of the world's largest and most influential religions. ▢

## It's a FACT

- Christians celebrate the birth of Jesus on December 25, but no one knows the date on which he was actually born.

- Jesus had 12 disciples—Peter (or Simon), Andrew, James, John, Philip, Bartholomew, Thomas, Matthew, James (the younger), Thaddeus, Simon, and Judas.

## What Do You Think?

1. Why do you think historians would want to know what different groups of people said about Jesus?

2. Other figures in history such as Confucius believed in the "Golden Rule." Why do you think people in other parts of the world share some beliefs?

◄ This picture shows the birth of Jesus according to Paul.

# PETER'S "Good News"

| 100 B.C. | 0 | A.D. 100 |
|---|---|---|

**63 B.C.-A.D. 14**
Augustus

**c. A.D. 30**
Jesus is put to death

**c. A.D. 64**
Peter is put to death

Jesus preached a message of peace and love of God in the Roman province of Judea. He taught that people should treat one another as they wished to be treated. He also taught that there was only one God and that it was important to love God and your neighbor. Peter and the other disciples of Jesus helped spread this message throughout the Roman Empire.

## The Beginnings of Christianity

Many people became interested and excited about Jesus's ideas. In the Jewish religion, some people (called prophets) were thought to be interpreters of messages from God. The Jewish prophets, including Abraham and Moses, said that God would send a Messiah (or savior) to save them. Some Jews believed that Jesus was the Messiah that had been promised to them.

Not everyone believed Jesus was the Messiah. Some Jews did not think he was the true Messiah. Some thought his teachings were in conflict with their beliefs. Others thought his ideas threatened the authority of the Roman Empire. Pontius Pilate, the Roman governor of the province, put him on trial and sentenced him to death. The Romans thought this would be the end of his teaching.

## Spreading Christianity

However, many people continued to believe Jesus was the Messiah the prophets said would come. They believed that after death, there was a kingdom in heaven for people who believed in him. Peter, one of Jesus's followers, began to lead these people who became known as Christians. Peter and others, especially Paul of Tarsus, traveled all over the Roman Empire telling people about Jesus and his teachings. Christians were eager to share their beliefs with others.

You can read on the next page an excerpt from the Christian Bible. Historians believe this represents Peter's teaching about Jesus. In this passage, Peter is saying that the people who put Jesus to death did not know any better. ☐

**It's a FACT**

Peter was put to death in Rome during Emperor Nero's rule.

▲ In the end, sharing his beliefs cost Peter his life. Christians believe he was put to death in the exact spot where the Basilica of St. Peter in Rome is located today.

# Peter's "Good News"

... I know that you [Pontius Pilate] acted in ignorance, as did also your rulers.

But what God foretold by the mouth of all the prophets, that his Christ should suffer, he thus fulfilled.

Repent therefore, and turn again, that your sins may be blotted out, that times of refreshing may come from the presence of the Lord, and that he may send the Christ appointed for you, Jesus, whom heaven must receive until the time for establishing all that God spoke by the mouth of his holy prophets from of old.

## Analyze the Source!

1. Read the passage and tell in your own words what Peter was saying.

2. From this passage, how would you describe Peter's attitude toward Pontius Pilate and the Romans?

3. How do the ideas in this passage reflect the ideas Jesus taught?

# PAUL OF TARSUS— On the Road to Damascus

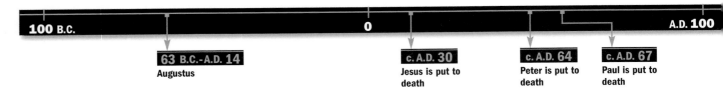

| 100 B.C. | | 0 | | | A.D. 100 |

**63 B.C.-A.D. 14**
Augustus

**c. A.D. 30**
Jesus is put to death

**c. A.D. 64**
Peter is put to death

**c. A.D. 67**
Paul is put to death

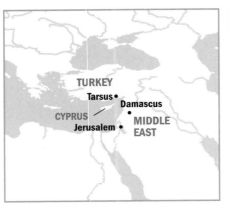

▲ On his journey to Damascus, Paul had a vision of Jesus that changed his life.

Most of what we know about Paul of Tarsus is from his own letters. They tell the story of his life and about his decision to become a Christian. Paul was born a Roman citizen in the seaport city of Tarsus (in present-day Turkey) around A.D. 5. In his early life, he became a member of a Jewish sect or group called the Pharisees. Pharisees thought it was important to be true to the laws that the prophet Moses had delivered to the Jews. Paul became a rabbi or teacher in this sect, but he earned his living as a tentmaker. Paul became aware of Christianity when people were just beginning to learn about it. He saw it as a threat to his strongly held religious beliefs.

▲ Paul was born in Tarsus. He traveled throughout the region that is now known as the Middle East. We know about Paul's life through his own writings. He also wrote about the teachings of Jesus.

## Paul Becomes a Christian

In one of his letters, Paul remembers exactly when he decided to become a Christian. While he was on the road to Damascus, he saw a vision of Jesus and temporarily lost his sight. This event made him believe that Jesus was the son of God. It was the most important moment in his life. At first, Paul spent time completely alone in the desert. Then he began traveling throughout the Roman world telling people about Christianity. He started Christian communities everywhere he went. As a **missionary**, he made three journeys around the Aegean coast and to Cyprus. First, he went to the area that is now southeastern Turkey. Eventually, hundreds of Christian churches were built in this area. His second and third journeys were longer. During these journeys, he is thought to have written his famous letters to the Romans and Corinthians.

## Christian Persecutions

Paul wanted to make a fourth journey, this time to Spain. However, in A.D. 56, he was arrested in Jerusalem. Many Christians were being persecuted at that time. To the Romans, Christianity was a superstitious, troublesome sect. Eventually, Paul was taken to Rome for trial. It is not clear whether Paul was found innocent and released by the Romans. He may have been released, traveled again to the east, and arrested again. He was executed in Rome sometime around A.D. 67.

## A Christian Hero

Paul left a lasting mark on history. More than any other early Christian, he spread the news of Christianity across the Roman world. He believed it was his duty to tell all people, not just Jews, about the ideas of Christianity. Some people believe Paul deserves credit for turning a small Jewish sect into a worldwide religion—Christianity. Today, he is called Paul of Tarsus or St. Paul. The letters he wrote are included in the New Testament of the Christian Bible. 📖

**It's a FACT**

Roman Catholics celebrate the feast day of St. Paul on June 29th.

---

**conversion:** a change where one adopts a new religion

**missionary:** a person who goes to a foreign country to do religious work

### 💡 What Do You Think?

**1.** After Paul decided to become a Christian on the road to Damascus, he had a hard time persuading others that his **conversion** was real. Have you ever changed your mind about something important and had a hard time getting other people to believe you? Why do you think it is so difficult for people to believe that others can change?

**2.** Should Paul be given credit for spreading Christianity throughout the Roman world? Why or why not?

# THE ROMAN WEEKLY
## A Newspaper for Roman Citizens
**A.D. 99**

## Bringing Rome to New Romans

## TWO KILLED NEAR FORUM

Two Romans were killed last night on their way home from a party at the imperial palace. They were the victims of a street robbery. Their valuables, including an expensive ring, other jewelry, and a bag of coins, were missing. Citizens are warned to be careful if they have to be on the streets of Rome after dark.

Romans take pride in bringing culture to other parts of the empire. Recently, Roman engineers took their building skills to the city of York in Britain. They built Roman baths, an arena for games, a theater for plays, and a racetrack.

In Gaul, Romans built an aqueduct to bring fresh water to the Roman city of Nimes. This gives people fresh water for cooking and washing. Soon homes in the provinces will have all the comforts of a Roman home, including central heating, plumbing, and toilets. People no longer have to live in the city of Rome to enjoy Roman culture.

◀ Romans were the first people to build aqueducts. By A.D. 97, aqueducts brought 85 million gallons of water into Rome every day. That's enough water to fill 850 large swimming pools!

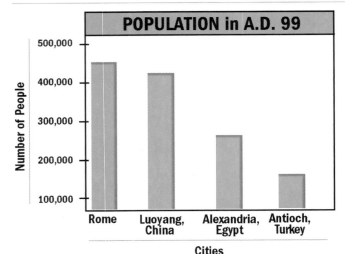

**POPULATION in A.D. 99**

Number of People

500,000
400,000
300,000
200,000
100,000

Rome | Luoyang, China | Alexandria, Egypt | Antioch, Turkey

Cities

## WE'RE #1
### ROME TOPS IN POPULATION

Romans who were at last week's games in the Colosseum won't be surprised to learn that Rome has lots of people. According to recent population figures, Rome is the biggest city in the world with an estimated population of 450,000. Close behind Rome is the city of Luoyang in China with an estimated population of 420,000. Other big cities on the list include Alexandria, Egypt (250,000) and Antioch, Turkey (150,000).

# Around the Empire

**N**ews from the Western Provinces ... Soldiers guarding the Rhine-Danube frontier from barbarians report that they suffered a very cold and harsh winter. However, the troops are disciplined and ready for combat. Workers have begun building a new stretch of road in Gaul to allow soldiers to travel more quickly to that area.

▲ Roads were first built for soldiers, but many others use them to travel through the empire.

**A**nd from the Eastern Provinces ... A religious shrine in Jerusalem was dedicated to the god Jupiter. There have been reports of violent clashes between different religious groups in the region. Roman soldiers are trying to keep the peace.

## LOCAL NEWS

## Post Office Reminder

Do you have a letter that needs to arrive in the provinces at a certain time? Keep in mind that carriers for the postal system can cover about 170 miles a day. A letter from Rome to London will take a minimum of six days. Bad weather, sickness, slow horses, and other factors can cause delays and the loss of letters and packages.

## Baths Reopened

The public baths near the Forum have been repaired and reopened. The cold and hot pools are in good working order. The exercise area has been remodeled. Come bathe, exercise, enjoy a snack, and visit with friends! Don't miss the new mosaics—they are beautiful!

## FASHION

# "MILKY" SMOOTH SKIN

Almost 40 years ago, Roman women learned that Nero's wife Poppaea bathed in milk. She kept donkeys to provide milk for her baths! Today, many still use donkey's milk in face creams. However, Roman women are finding new ingredients from other parts of the empire. Some women crush Libyan barley and then add honey and ground deer antlers to make a special cream.

Crushed snails continue to be popular in beauty creams. The most elegant Roman women scent their creams with exotic fragrances from India and China. Women keep their special creams in glass jars or elegant gold and silver containers. Today's Roman woman starts with a clean, smooth face before applying make-up and dressing in silks.

## This Week in History . . .

**19 years ago,** in A.D. 80, Emperor Titus opened the Colosseum. He declared an official holiday and invited Romans to come to the arena to see gladiators fight. The Colosseum seats 45,000 to 55,000 people.

**20 years ago,** in A.D. 79, Mt. Vesuvius erupted. First, there were earthquakes and then the top of the mountain blew off. Pompeii and Herculaneum, towns at the foot of Vesuvius, were covered with dust, ash, and poisonous gases. At least 2,000 people were killed.

**35 years ago,** in A.D. 64, a great fire destroyed much of the city of Rome. Christians were blamed for the fire, but some suspect Emperor Nero might have been responsible.

**130 years ago,** in 31 B.C., Octavian (later to be called "Augustus") defeated Marc Antony and Cleopatra at the battle of Actium.

**172 years ago,** in 73 B.C., the slave Spartacus led a slave revolt in Rome. It lasted two years, but was eventually crushed.

**363 years ago,** in 264 B.C., the first gladiators fought in Rome. They performed as part of a religious ceremony for a man who had died.

## DEAR CALPURNIA

*Dear Calpurnia,*
*My husband and I were invited to dinner at another couple's house last week. They served only vegetables sprinkled with olive oil! When we invited them to dinner, we served cheese, herbs, bacon, walnuts, figs, boiled eggs, olives, chicken, oysters, snails, sweets, and wine. They can afford to serve more than vegetables. Do you think we should remain friends with them?*

*Rattled in Rome*

Dear Rattled,
If your friends can afford to serve more than vegetables, maybe they are telling you something. Face the fact—Romans prepare more important feasts for more important people. Maybe your "friends" don't think you are very important. Drop them!

*Dear Calpurnia,*
*My family is very rich, and we live a life of luxury. I am 15 years old and have everything I want—except one thing. I am in love with a Christian girl named Lygia. My father has forbidden me to see her, but I love her. She loves me, too. What should I do?*

*Lovesick*

Dear Lovesick,
It's always more difficult for couples who have different religions. And being a Christian these days is dangerous. Follow your heart, but be careful and think about the life of luxury you will be giving up.

*Dear Calpurnia,*
*I am tired of seeing what is happening in Rome today. The city is filthy. People dump garbage, dead animals, and every awful thing you can think of in the streets. It smells terrible! Most of the poor people don't do any work. The government ought to do something!*

*Sensitive Roman Nose*

Dear Sensitive,
Lighten up. If you have been reading the news, you should know that Rome is the largest city in the world. Yes, it has problems, but it's still a great city. Don't blame the poor people. They live in cheap, poorly made apartments that are likely to fall down or burn down. They don't have much to eat.

## THE SPANIARD
# A Crowd Pleaser

Last week, crowds celebrating the festival of the god Jupiter attended games at the Colosseum. The games lasted 12 days. The most popular games were on Friday, and attendance topped 50,000 people. In the morning, there were battles between wild animals. Elephants fought buffalo. Tigers fought lions. There also were crocodiles, bulls, hippopotamuses, and other frightening beasts.

In the afternoon, gladiators fought one another with spears, nets, swords, and chains. Most of the gladiators were men, but two women fought in a contest to the death. The favorite gladiator of the day was the Spaniard. The audience cheered him on in his contest against a gladiator from the eastern provinces. The games ended at dusk.

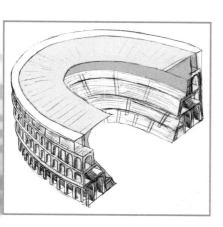

# A Look Inside the Colosseum

You enjoy the spectacles of the Colosseum, but do you appreciate the Roman skill that went into building this magnificent arena? This sketch gives you an insider's look at the construction of the arena you love so much. There's not a bad seat in the arena!

## Gaius Appuleius Docles Wins Exciting Chariot Race

Once again, Gaius Appuleius Docles rode the winning chariot at the recent race at the Circus Maximus. His team of four Arabian horses easily beat all competitors. In the third lap of the seven-lap race, the red team was a strong challenger, but then a wheel broke. Keep an eye on the young man from North Africa. He rode an excellent race and came in second. It looks as if he will have a promising future.

▶ The chariot race next week will have 12 teams of horses. Attendance last week at the Circus Maximus was over 200,000 each day.

## Christians Underground?

A rumor is being spread that Christians are meeting secretly underground in a place called the Catacombs. Apparently, they are trying to avoid persecution. Christians reject Rome's official religion, which honors the gods Jupiter, Juno, Mars, Venus, Apollo, and many others. Christians believe in only one god and refuse to worship the Roman gods. The penalty for being a Christian is death.

## Roman Holiday

Romans are preparing for the three-day feast of Jupiter. As part of the festivities, Romans will be crossing the Tiber to the old Etruscan countryside. There will be much celebration!

## Meeting of Stoics

There will be a meeting of citizens interested in Stoicism. The Stoic philosophy promises to help you realize your full human potential. Stoic philosophers will discuss ways to detach yourself from worrying about the opinions of others.

# Editorial

Emperor Trajan just became leader of the Roman Empire last year (A.D. 98), and he already is doing an excellent job. The soldiers respect him for his honorable military service. All Romans look up to him for his leadership. It appears that Trajan will become one of Rome's great emperors. Trajan's goals for the future include the following: **1)** conquer more territory, **2)** defeat Rome's enemies, and **3)** improve Rome's transportation and water systems.

Trajan plans to add four new provinces to the Roman Empire by conquering territory in the Middle East. He also wants to defeat Parthia, Rome's traditional enemy in the East.

Trajan has ambitious plans to improve Rome's transportation and water systems. He wants to repair and build new roads, bridges, and aqueducts. These projects will help make travel faster and bring water to more towns. We applaud Emperor Trajan for his work and his plans for the future. His efforts will benefit the people of the Roman Empire.

# ENTERTAINMENT NEWS

## What's Happening...

Everyone is excited about the Greek play at the Roman theater. An actor wearing a mask performs while a chorus describes the meaning. Buy your ticket soon. The play is selling out fast!

A musician playing a stringed instrument called the lyre is creating a sensation among Roman music lovers. Avoid the crush of crowds at the Colosseum. Enjoy the pleasures of music at the Roman concert hall.

# Classified Ads

**FOR SALE**
- ☞ Chariot, two years old, in great condition. Must see to believe.
- ☞ Ten acres of good farm land five miles north of Rome. Great value!
- ☞ Elegant villa and five acres along the Tiber River. Beautiful views.

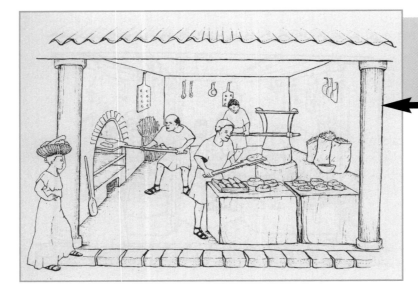

Bakery Equipment
## GREAT BUSINESS OPPORTUNITY

## MISCELLANEOUS/PERSONALS
- ☞ Need help learning Greek? Call Marcus.
- ☞ Roman general interested in finding strong men for new gladiator school. Call Galba.
- ☞ Come to a reading of Virgil's poems at the emperor's palace. Refreshments will be served.

# MARCUS AURELIUS —
## Stoic Emperor

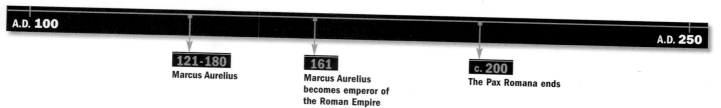

A.D. **100**                                                                    A.D. **250**

**121-180**
Marcus Aurelius

**161**
Marcus Aurelius
becomes emperor of
the Roman Empire

**c. 200**
The Pax Romana ends

Of all the Roman emperors, a few stand out—some for the good they did, and some for the harm. Of those who stand out for the good they did, there is Marcus Aurelius. Why is Marcus Aurelius a heroic figure in Roman history? Some say it is because he carried out his duties with honesty and integrity.

## Early Life and Education

Marcus Aurelius was born in Rome on April 26, A.D. 121. His family was wealthy and politically important. When his parents died, the Emperor Hadrian became interested in his welfare. He made sure Marcus received an excellent education. Marcus loved learning, especially philosophy. Philosophy is concerned with questions about the world. How did it begin? What is the purpose of life? Do people decide their actions or are they controlled by fate or gods? How should people live their lives? Philosophers think about and discuss such questions. Different groups or "schools" of philosophy have different answers.

## A Victorious Emperor

Marcus Aurelius became emperor in 161, at a time when the Roman Empire faced major problems. First, Rome was at war with the Parthians in the East. Marcus Aurelius and his army were victorious in battle against the Parthians. Another major problem was that the Roman soldiers returned from battle with a disease that spread throughout the empire. People became sick and died. Groups of Germanic peoples—the Romans called them barbarians—attacking the northern border of the empire was also a problem. Eventually, Marcus Aurelius ended these attacks. Later emperors would not be so successful.

▲ Marcus Aurelius was born in Rome, but he spent most of his life away from Rome on government business.

▲ Marcus Aurelius was the fifth of the "Five Good Emperors" as described by the famous British historian Edward Gibbon.

## It's a FACT

The movie *Gladiator* takes place at the end of the reign of Marcus Aurelius. However, much of the story is fiction.

**luxury:** something extra that makes life more comfortable and enjoyable
**reign:** the time during which a ruler is in power

### *Meditations* and the Stoic Philosophy

Marcus Aurelius wrote a book that today we call *Meditations*. The title he gave it was a Greek phrase meaning, "to himself." This book tells us about his views of the Roman Empire. It also gives an idea of his values and beliefs. It includes his thoughts about events, things he read, and ideas that occurred to him.

### PRINCIPLES OF STOICISM

- Live life in harmony with nature.
- Do not be concerned with material things.
- Control things that are within your power.
- Do not worry about things that are not within your power.
- Be self-sufficient and just.

### Stoicism

In *Meditations*, Marcus Aurelius explained his beliefs in the Stoic philosophy or "Stoicism." Stoicism is a system of moral principles, similar to a moral code, that started in Greece. It is a way of thinking about how human beings should live their lives. The Stoics believed that people should live as one with nature. People should be just, self-disciplined, and courageous. Stoics were not concerned with material things. Marcus Aurelius tried to live his life by these principles. He avoided personal **luxuries**. He put the needs of the Roman Empire above his own. He wrote, "avoid all actions that are haphazard or purposeless; and secondly let every action aim solely at the common good." Marcus Aurelius's belief in Stoicism helped him deal with the problems he faced. His beliefs helped him make decisions and take actions.

### The End of the Pax Romana

Late in his **reign**, Marcus Aurelius toured the eastern part of the Roman Empire. During this trip, his wife died. He wrote with great love and admiration about her in *Meditations*. In 177, he announced his son, Commodus, would help him rule and become sole emperor when he died. Together, they planned to continue expanding the Roman Empire. When Marcus Aurelius died in 180, the period known as the Pax Romana continued for only several more decades. □

### What Do You Think?

1. How does having a moral code help a person deal with problems?

2. Do you think it is important for leaders to have a moral code?

3. What advantages and obstacles did Marcus Aurelius have in life?

# "BARBARIANS" in the Empire

A.D. **100**                                                                                                    A.D. **400**

**121-180**
Marcus Aurelius

**161**
"Barbarians" enter
the Roman Empire

**c. 200**
The Pax Romana ends

**late 300s**
"Barbarian invasions" create
chaos in the Roman Empire

▶ This map shows some of the groups of "barbarians" that invaded the Roman Empire. The Visigoths, a Germanic people, attacked the city of Rome in 410. Then another Germanic group, the Vandals, attacked the city, destroying much of its art and beauty. The word we use to describe people who destroy property—vandals—comes from this group of people.

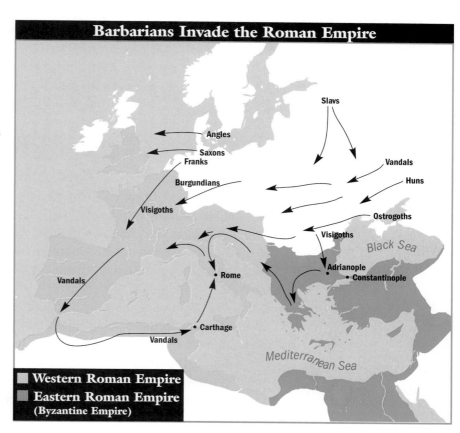

**Barbarians Invade the Roman Empire**

Slavs

Angles

Saxons
Franks

Vandals

Burgundians

Huns

Visigoths

Ostrogoths

Visigoths

Black Sea

Adrianople

Vandals

Constantinople

Rome

Vandals

Carthage

Vandals

Mediterranean Sea

☐ Western Roman Empire
☐ Eastern Roman Empire
(Byzantine Empire)

Beginning in A.D. 161, groups of people the Romans called "barbarians" began to enter the Roman Empire. Some were peaceful. Many joined the Roman army and helped to defend the empire. By the late 300s, however, the large number of barbarians coming into the Roman Empire had become a serious problem. Some groups, such as the Huns, Vandals, and Visigoths, wanted to conquer territories. These so-called "barbarian invasions" created chaos for the Roman Empire. Romans no longer could count on the government to keep the law and order.

You can read on the next page how several Romans described the barbarian invasions. The first excerpt was written by the leader of the Christian community in Carthage around A.D. 250. Procopius, a historian, wrote the second excerpt in the early 400s telling about the Vandal invasions in North Africa. Lastly, in the late 300s, Ammianus Marcellinus, a retired soldier, described the invasion of the feared Huns.

# Letter from the Bishop of Carthage

The world has grown old and lost its former vigor. ... the mountains are gutted and give less marble ... the fields lack farmers, the seas sailors, the encampments soldiers ... there is no justice in judgments, competence in trades, discipline in daily life.

# Procopius on the Vandals

[The king of the Vandals] robbed [the Romans] of their estates, which were both very numerous and excellent, and distributed them among the nation of the Vandals. ... And it fell to the lot of those who had formerly possessed these lands to dwell in extreme poverty. ... [T]he land that he did not deem worthy he allowed to remain in the hands of former owners, but assessed so large a sum to be paid in government taxes that nothing whatsoever remained to those who were able to retain their farms.

# Ammianus Marcellinus on the Huns

The people called Huns ... are a race savage beyond all parallel. At the very moment of birth the cheeks of their infant children are deeply marked by an iron, in order that the hair, instead of growing at the proper season on their faces, may be hindered by the scars. ... The Huns grow up without beards, and without any beauty.

... They never shelter themselves under roofed houses ... they wander about, roaming over the mountains and the woods. ... There is not a person in the whole nation who cannot remain on his horse day and night. On horseback they buy and sell, they take their meat and drink, and there they recline. ... None of them plow, or even touch a plow handle, ... but are homeless and lawless, perpetually wandering with their wagons, which they make their homes.

... being excited by an unrestrained desire of plundering the possessions of others, [they] went on ravaging and slaughtering all the nations in their neighborhood. ... As soon as they obtained permission of the emperor [of Rome] to cross the Danube, ... they poured across the stream day and night, without ceasing. ... In this way, through the turbulent zeal of violent people, the ruin of the Roman Empire was brought about. ... The defenses of our provinces were much exposed, and the armies of barbarians spread over ...

## Analyze the Source!

1. Tell in your own words what each excerpt says.

2. What problems did the "barbarian invasions" create for Romans?

3. How do you think the invasions affected the way Romans thought about Roman government?

# THE BYZANTINE EMPIRE —
## The New Rome

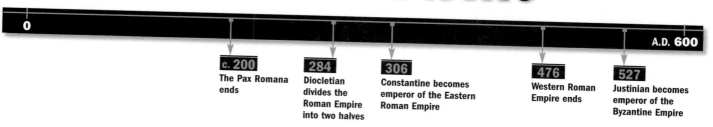

| 0 | | | | | | | A.D. **600** |

**c. 200**
The Pax Romana ends

**284**
Diocletian divides the Roman Empire into two halves

**306**
Constantine becomes emperor of the Eastern Roman Empire

**476**
Western Roman Empire ends

**527**
Justinian becomes emperor of the Byzantine Empire

By the late 200s, problems in the Roman Empire had become too great for one man to handle. In 284, Emperor Diocletian divided the Roman Empire in half, making himself ruler of the eastern half and another man ruler of the western part. The two halves were supposed to be equal, but the power had shifted to the east.

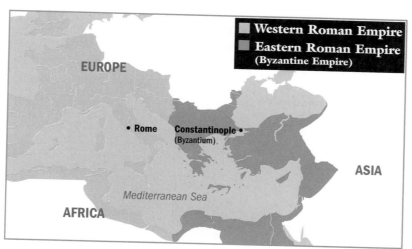

◄ Constantine made Constantinople the new capital of the Eastern Roman Empire. He called it "new Rome."

## The Fall of the Western Roman Empire

After Diocletian, Constantine became emperor of the Eastern Roman Empire in 306. Constantine built a new capital city—Constantinople—on the site of the old Greek city Byzantium. He called Constantinople the "new Rome." He reunited the eastern and western parts of the Roman Empire and decided to stay in the eastern half. Emperors after Constantine tried to keep the Roman Empire united. However, it slowly began to separate.

As the Eastern Roman Empire flourished, Rome and the Western Roman Empire faced problems. There wasn't enough money to pay for the army and government services. People were forced to pay high taxes. The government could not solve the problems people were facing. To make matters worse, Germanic groups from the north and east began invading.

Some of the Germanic groups wanted to find a place to live. Others, such as the Huns, came to conquer an empire. Historians generally agree that the Western Roman Empire officially ended in 476. In that year, Odoacer, a leader of a Germanic group, took control of Rome and forced out the last Roman emperor, Romulus Augustulus. By 500, Rome was in ruins and the Western Roman Empire was in chaos.

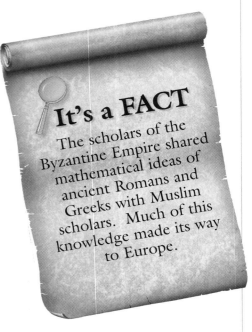

## Constantine and the Byzantine Empire

The Eastern Roman Empire escaped many of the problems that confronted Rome. They defended themselves from invaders. The Eastern Roman Empire became known as the Byzantine Empire. It lasted for another 1,000 years after the Western Roman Empire lost power.

Constantine and the early rulers of the Byzantine Empire were Romans. Their Roman ideas and culture greatly influenced them as they ruled. They had a Senate in their government and organized their armies the way Romans did. They built arenas similar to the Colosseum, a stadium like the Circus Maximus, and buildings that were exactly like buildings in Rome. They even spoke Latin.

Over time, however, Rome's influence was not as great. Perhaps the most significant reason for this is that Constantinople was located on an important trade route between Europe and Asia. Most people there were not Roman; they were Greek or from other areas. The city was a crossroad for people from the East and the West.

One area of disagreement between Rome and the Byzantine Empire had to do with religion and government. The Byzantine Empire was a Christian empire. Constantine was a Christian, and Constantinople was filled with Christian churches. Christians in the Byzantine Empire did not all agree on the same teachings. However, they did agree the emperor should have power over the church. Religion was almost a branch of the government. Over time, Christians in the Byzantine Empire disagreed strongly with Christians of the old Western Roman Empire. One of the most important disagreements was about whose power was greater—the state or the church.

▶ **Constantinople (present-day Istanbul) is located on two continents— Asia and Europe. A narrow passage of water called the Bosporus separates the Asian and European sides of the city.**

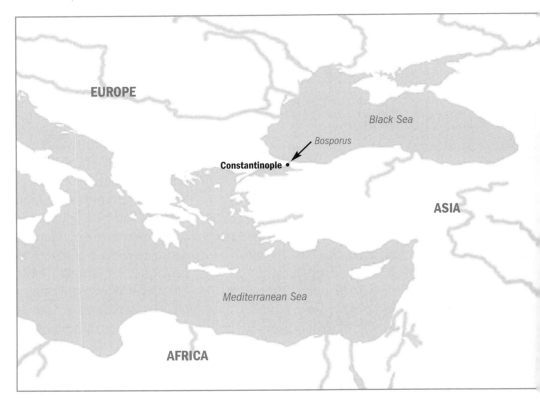

# Justinian and the Byzantine Empire

Justinian became emperor in 527 and ruled the Byzantine Empire for almost 40 years. He was known as "the emperor who never slept" because he was ambitious and worked hard to restore the power and glory of the Roman Empire. His wife, Theodora, and generals, scholars, and administrators helped him to do this.

Justinian's armies won back much of the Roman territory lost in the west—including land in Italy and North Africa. He also forced the Germanic groups out of Rome, but the city was left in ruins.

One of Justinian's most important accomplishments was the Justinian Code. He asked a group of scholars to organize all the Roman laws into one law code.

▲ Justinian is remembered as the greatest emperor of the Byzantine Empire. He is shown here with his wife, Empress Theodora.

## THE JUSTINIAN CODE

Justinian knew to have good government, you needed to have good laws. He was responsible for making sure that the people followed the law. But what were the laws? The Byzantines had lots of good Roman laws—too many. Some were not useful, others confusing.

Justinian had an idea! He organized a group of people to look at the laws. The group included Latin and Greek scholars. They made sure the laws were clear. After all, people need to understand the laws if they are going to follow them. He asked the scholars to organize all the Roman laws into one law code. It was a lot of work, but they finished in 533. This law code is called the Law Code of Justinian or the Justinian Code. It stated people's rights and described Roman legal customs.

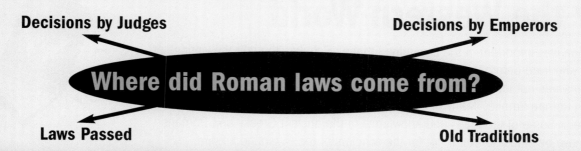

**Decisions by Judges**   **Decisions by Emperors**

**Where did Roman laws come from?**

**Laws Passed**   **Old Traditions**

▲ During Justinian's rule, the Hagia Sophia was a Christian church. However, when the Turks captured Constantinople in 1453, they converted it into a mosque. Today, people from all over the world visit the Hagia Sophia to admire its beauty.

# Preserving Learning for the Western World

Education was important in the Byzantine Empire. Scholars thought the writings of people who lived before them—the ancient Greeks and Romans—should be kept safe. This was not important to the Germanic peoples who took power in the Western Roman Empire. Many of the writings in that part of the empire were destroyed. Some of the ideas and knowledge of the ancient Greeks and Romans would have been lost forever if not for the scholars of the Byzantine Empire.

## Constantinople— Capital of the Byzantine Empire

Constantinople was the capital of the Byzantine Empire. The city developed on both sides of a narrow waterway called the Bosporus. One part of the city was on the continent of Asia and the other was on the European continent. During Justinian's rule, Constantinople was a bustling city of as many as 350,000 people.

Scholars in the Byzantine Empire used their knowledge of mathematics, geometry, and physics to build wonderful buildings and roads. Constantinople was filled with markets, theaters, palaces, government buildings, an arena, baths, warehouses, bakeries, and inns. There were also many churches, including the Hagia Sophia, a stunningly beautiful Christian church built during Justinian's rule. More importantly, Byzantine scholars worked hard to preserve the knowledge of ancient Romans and Greeks.

Constantinople wasn't the only city in the empire. Many other cities—perhaps as many as 1,500—also were part of the Byzantine Empire. Talented Byzantine artists created beautiful pictures, including thousands of mosaics, that show the riches of the empire and the lives of the people who lived in it.

## It's a FACT

- The Justinian Code is the foundation of most European legal systems.

- During a riot in Constantinople in 532, Justinian's wife Theodora organized an army of 35,000 in just one day!

## The End of the Byzantine Empire

Emperor Justinian's accomplishments were great but very costly. When he died in 565, his successors did not have many resources left to rule the empire. However, the Byzantine Empire continued long after Justinian died. It didn't end until the year 1453, when the Turks captured the capital city of Constantinople. They renamed Justinian's magnificent city "Istanbul" and made it the capital of their Ottoman Empire.

## Gifts to the Western World

The Western world owes a great debt to the Byzantine Empire. When most of present-day Europe was in chaos (from the 500s through the 900s), the Byzantine Empire had an orderly government, central rule, and effective laws.

When some Europeans in the 1300s wanted to learn more about ancient Greek and Roman ideas, they looked to Constantinople for some of the works of Greek writers such as Plato and Homer. The Byzantine Empire preserved the Roman way of life and much Greek and Roman knowledge for the world. 📖

### What Do You Think?

1. What were the similarities and differences of the Byzantine Empire and the Western Roman Empire?

2. Why is Justinian called the Byzantine Empire's greatest emperor?

3. What "gifts" did the Byzantine Empire give to the Western world? Which is most important? Why?

# MUHAMMAD — The Prophet

**A.D. 500**

**570-632**
Muhammad

**622**
Muhammad flees
to Medina

**630**
Muhammad returns to
conquer Mecca and makes
it the center of Islam

**A.D. 700**

On the Arabian Peninsula in the 500s, your life depended on your family and tribe. They fed you, protected you, and gave you work. Muhammad was born in 570 in the city of Mecca. His parents died when he was young. He had a difficult childhood. However, he later became a businessman and one of the most important religious leaders of all time.

## Early Life

Muhammad was part of the Quraysh tribe. His grandfather and uncle raised him. For work, he tended his family's flock of sheep. His uncle, Abu Talib, took him on long trading journeys. By the time Muhammad was 25, he was a successful trader with a reputation for being trustworthy. At about this time, Muhammad met and married Khadija. He enjoyed his happy and prosperous life.

## The First Revelation and the Hijra

As Muhammad grew older, he began to have questions about his life and his place in the world. He would go to caves in the mountains outside of Mecca to think in peace. One writer suggested that Muhammad asked questions such as the following: "How is it that I was an orphan but am now a rich man? I have a good wife and children, yet I am not entirely happy." He was troubled by the greedy **merchants** he saw in Mecca. No one cared about the poor or sick.

During one of the times he was away in the mountains, Muhammad reported that he received his first revelation from the archangel Gabriel. Muhammad was very upset. He didn't know what it meant. He told his wife, Khadija, and his uncle what happened. Khadija believed that Muhammad was a prophet from God. She was the first person to accept Islam, which is the religion that developed from Muhammad's teachings. Muhammad reported that he received more revelations directing him to start preaching Islam, so he did. He began to gather followers, later called Muslims. However, not all people in Mecca liked his ideas. Some thought he was their enemy and tried to kill him.

▲ This is Muhammad's name written in Arabic. His name means "highly praised."

**merchant:** a shopkeeper; a person who buys and sells things

Black Sea

Mediterranean Sea

SYRIA    ASIA

PERSIA

Persian Gulf

• Medina

Red Sea

• Mecca

AFRICA

▲ Muhammad was born in Mecca. He traveled by camel caravan around the Arabian Peninsula and as far as Syria.

In 622, Muhammad and his followers fled Mecca and went to the town of Medina. This journey from Mecca to Medina is called the Hijra. This marks one of the holiest days in the Islamic religion.

## Revelations and the Qur'an

Over the next several decades, Muslims believe that Muhammad received other revelations from the archangel Gabriel and was told the direct words of God. Muhammad shared these words or verses with his followers. Some of them memorized the messages. Each day they recited the verses. Once a year Muhammad recited all of the verses revealed to him to be certain the words were correct and in the right order. Muhammad's followers wrote the verses down. In this way, the book we know as the Qur'an came to be.

## The Spread of Islam

Muhammad's flight to Medina was a turning point in his life. In Medina he attracted many more followers. He became extremely influential. In 630, he returned in triumph to Mecca. The people of Mecca thought he would take revenge on them, but he treated them as brothers and sisters. He destroyed all of the idols in the holy site of the Kaaba. By doing this, he was destroying the old tribal system in which people were only loyal to family and tribe. Muhammad preached that there was only one God. By believing in one God, the tribes of the Arabian Peninsula would be bound together by faith. Tribes throughout the Arabian Peninsula converted to Islam. When Muhammad died in 632, he had united Arabs through Islam. During the next 100 years, Arab armies, united by one religion, conquered an empire that was larger than Rome's. 📖

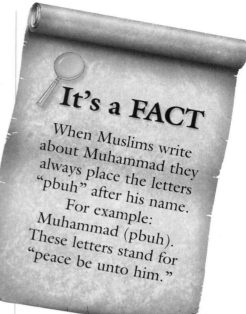

## It's a FACT

When Muslims write about Muhammad they always place the letters "pbuh" after his name. For example: Muhammad (pbuh). These letters stand for "peace be unto him."

### MUHAMMAD THE PEACEMAKER

The Kaaba is a one-room building that contains a black stone Muslims believe fell from heaven. The Kaaba is one of the holiest sites in Islam. During Muhammad's time, workers removed the black stone so that they could make some repairs to the building. When it was time to replace the stone, there was a great conflict. Four important leaders of Muslim tribes each thought that they should have the honor of replacing the black stone. The four leaders threatened war with the others. Muhammad thought of a way to solve this conflict peacefully. He placed the black stone in the middle of a square carpet. Each of the four leaders lifted a corner and together they carried the black stone into the Kaaba.

### What Do You Think?

1. What disadvantages did Muhammad overcome?

2. What was Muhammad concerned about in life?

3. How did religion unite the tribes of the Arabian Peninsula?

# ABU BAKR — First Man to Convert to Islam

A.D. 500                                  A.D. 700

**570-632**
Muhammad

**573-634**
Abu Bakr

**622**
Muhammad flees
to Medina

**630**
Muhammad returns to
conquer Mecca and makes
it the center of Islam

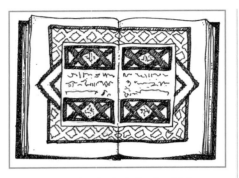

▲ The Qur'an is the holy book of Islam.

In 573, Abu Bakr was born on the Arabian Peninsula into the Quraysh tribe. This also was Muhammad's tribe. As children, Muhammad and Abu Bakr became friends. As young boys, they were both known for their honesty. Later, Abu Bakr became a rich merchant. Historians say Abu Bakr used his wealth to help those less fortunate than himself. He became known as a man who would always do the right thing.

## First Among Men

After Muhammad's first revelation, Abu Bakr was among the first people he told about his experience. Abu Bakr immediately accepted Islam and Muhammad as a prophet. Later, Muhammad was reported to have said, "I called people to Islam. Everybody thought it over, at least for a while. But this was not the case with Abu Bakr. The moment I put Islam in front of him he accepted it without hesitation." Abu Bakr also started to preach about Islam to others. Because of his reputation and the respect people had for him, many people converted to Islam.

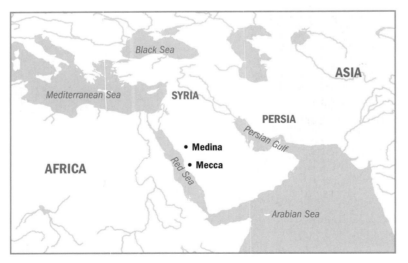

▲ Abu Bakr was born in Mecca. He and Muhammad were childhood friends.

## Abu Bakr Risks His Life

Not everyone accepted Islam. In fact, many people in Mecca were unhappy about Muhammad's teachings. Some people even threatened to kill Muhammad and Abu Bakr. Despite these threats, Abu Bakr continued to preach about Islam. He also continued to keep a watchful eye on his boyhood friend, Muhammad. As time went by, some of the followers of Islam—called Muslims—were mistreated by Muhammad's enemies. Muslims who were slaves or who did not have strong family protection were easy targets. Many times, Abu Bakr used his wealth to rescue Muslims from persecution.

## The Hijra

Eventually, some citizens of Mecca wanted to put an end to Islam. Muhammad decided to leave Mecca and go to Medina. When Abu Bakr heard this, he got ready to make the journey with Muhammad. Together, they and other Muslims made the trip to Medina. This journey is called the Hijra. It is one of the most important events in the history of Islam.

## A Representative for the Prophet

During the next few years, Abu Bakr helped Muhammad convert tribes to Islam across the Arabian Peninsula. They became more and more successful, winning battles and converts to their faith. In 630, they returned to conquer the city of Mecca. Muhammad destroyed the idols that tribes had placed in the holy site of the Kaaba. This signified the end of the old tribal system in which people were only loyal to family and tribe. Muhammad taught that by believing in one God, the tribes of the Arabian Peninsula would be bound together by their faith.

**It's a FACT**

Abu Bakr's original name was Abdul Kabah, which means "servant of the Kaaba." Muhammad called Abu Bakr "Siddiq," which means "a person whose love of God is never spoiled by doubts."

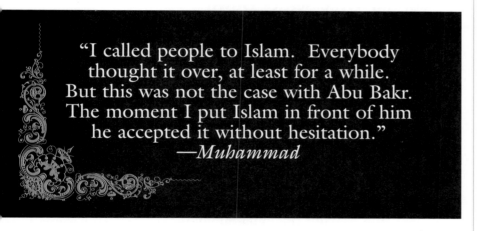

"I called people to Islam. Everybody thought it over, at least for a while. But this was not the case with Abu Bakr. The moment I put Islam in front of him he accepted it without hesitation."
—*Muhammad*

Within two years after capturing Mecca, Muhammad became ill and died. Abu Bakr took on many of Muhammad's important duties. But, there was not a formal plan for succession when Muhammad died. Muslims discussed what they should do. Many were worried about what would happen. However, they were reminded that Muhammad had died, not Islam. Finally, it was decided that Abu Bakr would be Muhammad's successor. He took the title of caliph, which means "successor." Abu Bakr died two years later. Before his death, another Muslim, Umar, was selected to be the next caliph. 📖

**What Do You Think?**

1. What did Abu Bakr have in common with Muhammad?

2. How did Abu Bakr's experiences influence his attitude and actions?

# The Quraysh Tribe

A.D. 200                                                           A.D. 700

**early 400s**
The Quraysh tribe settles in Mecca

**570-632**
Muhammad

▲ The Quraysh tribe settled in Mecca and became one of the most powerful tribes on the Arabian Peninsula.

**graze:** to feed on growing grasses or other plant materials

▲ Bedouins, including the Quraysh tribe, traveled in camel caravans such as this.

Long before Muhammad, and continuing to this day, Bedouin tribes have lived on the Arabian Peninsula. Bedouins are nomadic people. They keep herds of goats, sheep, and camels. They do not have permanent homes. They travel the desert and make camps at regular stops across the peninsula. They stop at desert oases for water and for shade from blistering heat. Oases also are places where they can trade goods and meet other groups and where their animals can **graze**.

## A Bedouin Tribe Settles Down

One tribe of Bedouins regularly stopped at a camp near Mecca. They were the Quraysh tribe. Originally, they were camel drivers and caravan guides. In the early 400s, the Quraysh settled in Mecca. Trade made them very rich. They sent out their own trade caravans. They made agreements with other tribes to make sure that caravans traveled safely through the desert to their trading center. In addition, they had control of the holy site of the Kaaba. This meant they could make other tribes pay to worship and trade in Mecca.

## A Powerful Tribe

The Quraysh became one of the most powerful tribes on the Arabian Peninsula and the chief family in Mecca. Muhammad was a member of the Quraysh tribe, but his family was not rich. When Muhammad first began preaching about Islam, most members of the Quraysh tribe opposed his ideas. However, the tribe later became devoted followers of Islam. The founders of the great Umayyad and Abbasid dynasties of Islam were members of the Quraysh tribe. Muhammad taught that social distinctions should not be based on a person's family background. However, the Quraysh tribe and other wealthy, powerful tribes enjoyed a higher status in the Muslim community. ▢

 **What Do You Think?**

1. Bedouins did not have permanent homes. They camped at stops across the Arabian Peninsula. What are the advantages and disadvantages of this lifestyle?

2. Why do people make social distinctions?

# KHADIJA — The First Woman of Islam

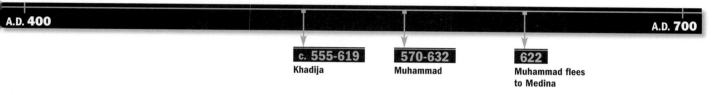

A.D. **400**                                                                                     A.D. **700**

**c. 555-619**
Khadija

**570-632**
Muhammad

**622**
Muhammad flees
to Medina

To understand Islam it is important to understand Khadija and the role she played in the life of Muhammad. An Islamic proverb says, "Islam did not rise except through Ali's sword and Khadija's wealth."

## Mixing Business and Pleasure

Khadija was a wealthy **widow** who owned a large trade caravan. The trade caravan had business throughout the Arabian Peninsula. Like other wealthy traders, Khadija needed someone to help sell her goods in cities faraway. She found one man in particular, Muhammad, who would be the perfect person for the job. As they worked together, Khadija came to know Muhammad. She was impressed with his honesty and business skill. After a short time, she proposed that they marry. Muhammad was 25 and Khadija was 40. She soon became pregnant with the first of their six children. In between births, she continued to help with the business.

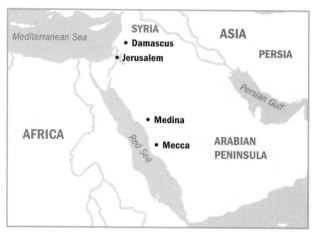

▲ Khadija lived in Mecca. She owned trade caravans that had business throughout the Arabian Peninsula.

**widow:** a woman whose husband has died

"She believed in me when all others disbelieved; she held me truthful when all others called me a liar; she sheltered me when others abandoned me; she comforted me when others shunned me ..."
—*Muhammad*

## Embracing Islam

When Muhammad was about 40 years old, he experienced his first revelation. It upset him greatly. He hurried home to tell Khadija. He told her that God had given him a mission to bring people the Qur'an, the holy book of Islam. One of the most important messages from God was, "There is no God but Allah, and Muhammad is his Prophet." Khadija immediately believed that Muhammad was God's prophet. She became the first woman to convert to Islam.

When Muhammad began to preach to Arab tribes that there was only one God, many doubted him. Khadija, however, strongly supported her husband and the early Islamic community.

▲ Khadija is remembered for her kindness and good character.

## An Inspiration for Muslim Women

As the first woman of Islam, Khadija has a significance for all Muslim women. She was an independent woman who was a successful businesswoman and a devoted wife. She was known for her kindness and her good character. She always helped the less fortunate.

After six children and 24 years of marriage to Muhammad, Khadija died at the age of 65. After her death, Muhammad talked about her in the most loving way: "She believed in me when all others disbelieved; she held me truthful when all others called me a liar; she sheltered me when others abandoned me; she comforted me when others shunned me; and Allah granted me children by her while depriving me of children by other women."

Although there have been many other great Islamic women, Khadija remains the most highly regarded woman among Muslims. 📖

### It's a FACT

Khadija had two titles: "Al-Tahira," which means "the pure one" and "Ameerat Quraysh," which means "Princess of Quraysh."

### What Do You Think?

**1.** Khadija was a successful businesswoman before she met Muhammad. What were some obstacles she had to overcome to be successful? What obstacles do women today face in achieving success?

**2.** How was Khadija's life like the lives of many women today?

**3.** Khadija was Muhammad's wife, friend, business partner, and the mother of his children. How do you think she influenced his ideas about women?

# Passages from the QUR'AN

The Qur'an contains messages Muhammad shared with his early followers. They memorized the messages and wrote them down. Muhammad's followers, called Muslims, believe the Qur'an is from God and that he gave these messages in their language, Arabic. For this reason, Muslims always read the Qur'an in Arabic. They believe translations might be wrong or that the message might be misunderstood. The passages below are ideas in the Qur'an. 📖

## Ideas in the Qur'an

**The Opening Prayer**
In the name of Allah, the Beneficent, the Merciful. ...
Keep us on the right path.
The path of those upon whom Thou hast bestowed favors.
Not (the path) of those upon whom Thy wrath is brought down ...

**Description of the Future of People Who Have Lived Good Lives**
And the companions of the right hand; how happy are the companions of the right hand!
Amid ... water flowing constantly,
And abundant fruit,
Neither **intercepted** nor forbidden ...

**Description of the Future of People Who Have Lived Evil Lives**
And those of the left hand, how wretched are those of the left hand!
In hot wind and boiling water,
And the shade of black smoke,
Neither cool nor honorable ...

### Analyze the Source!

1. Tell what the passages say in your own words.

2. Why might the words be especially powerful for people on the Arabian Peninsula?

3. How do the passages establish a standard of behavior for Muslims?

4. How are the ideas similar to other religious ideas you have learned about?

**intercept:** to stop or cut off

# The Sunni and Shiite Muslims

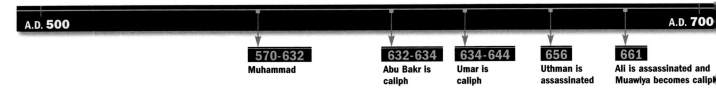

| A.D. 500 | | | | A.D. 700 |
|---|---|---|---|---|

**570-632**
Muhammad

**632-634**
Abu Bakr is caliph

**634-644**
Umar is caliph

**656**
Uthman is assassinated

**661**
Ali is assassinated and Muawiya becomes caliph

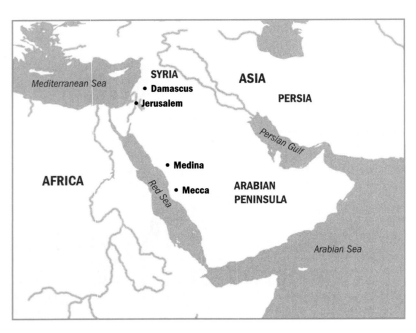

▲ Muhammad was born in Mecca in 570. He died in Medina in 632. After he died, Muslims struggled over who would take his place as the leader of Islam.

More than 1,300 years ago, Muslims began to disagree about the rightful successor to the Prophet Muhammad. The argument continues to this day.

When Muhammad died in 632, there was no plan for someone to take his place as the leader of Islam. Some Muslims thought it should be Ali, Muhammad's cousin and son-in-law. Others thought that Muhammad's most faithful friend, Abu Bakr, would be the best choice. It was decided that Abu Bakr would become the first caliph. He held that position for only two years (632-634) before he died. Muhammad's longtime friend and close advisor, Umar, became the next caliph. He was caliph for 10 years.

## Uthman's Troubled Times

While Umar was caliph, Ali helped him govern the growing Muslim community. When Umar died, Ali wanted to become caliph. Instead, a council chose a man named Uthman to be the third caliph. He came from a tribe that had fought against Muhammad. Uthman continued Umar's policy of expanding into new territories. However, there were many problems while he was caliph. He was accused of filling important governing positions with his family members and friends. He was assassinated in 656.

### MUHAMMAD'S SUCCESSORS

1st Caliph—Abu Bakr

2nd Caliph—Umar

3rd Caliph—Uthman

4th Caliph—Ali

## Ali Becomes the Fourth Caliph

After Uthman's death, Ali finally became caliph. Historians describe this as a "watershed" event—an event that changes history. Until this time, all Muslims regarded the caliph as legitimate heir to Muhammad. When Ali became caliph, however, some questioned whether he was the rightful successor. Uthman's supporters rose up in rebellion against Ali. Some of them thought Ali had helped murder Uthman.

## The Struggle for Power

Now two groups struggled over who was the rightful caliph. One group supported Ali. The other group supported a man named Muawiya. Muawiya was the powerful governor of Syria and one of Uthman's relatives. He refused to recognize Ali as caliph. Eventually, Ali and Muawiya agreed to allow a neutral third party to decide who was the rightful caliph. Before the decision was made, however, Ali was assassinated. So, in 661, Muawiya became caliph. He moved the capital of Islam from Mecca to Damascus, Syria.

## The Division between Shiites and Sunnis

Ali's followers remained faithful to him and to what they believed was the correct line of succession. Muslims who follow their faith through the line of Muhammad and Ali have come to be known as Shiite Muslims. Shiites believe that only those who are blood **descendants** of Muhammad are the legitimate heirs to his authority. In contrast to the Shiite Muslims, the Sunni Muslims do not believe that only blood descendants of Muhammad are his rightful successors. From the time of Ali and Uthman, Islam split into these two distinct groups. 📖

### It's a FACT

- Ali was Muhammad's cousin. When he married Muhammad's daughter, he also became Muhammad's son-in-law.

- Ali's followers are called "Shi'at Ali," or "the Party of Ali."

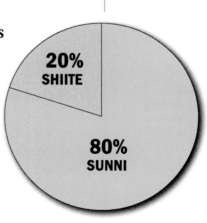

20% SHIITE

80% SUNNI

◄ Today, the Sunni represent more than 80% of all Muslims in the world.

### What Do You Think?

**1.** Muhammad did not have a clear plan for succession. How might things have been different if he had chosen a successor?

**2.** Why do people sometimes disagree about who should be leader?

**descendant:** a person related to someone who lived in the past

# The Splendors of Islamic Art

Art is more than paintings and sculptures. Since Muhammad began teaching his ideas to the people of the Arabian Peninsula in the early 600s, Muslims have created stunning pottery, metalwork, glassware, **textiles**, and calligraphy. Today, many examples of early Islamic art can be seen in museums, galleries, and private art collections.

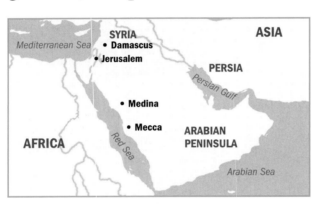

▲ Muslims living on the Arabian Peninsula created amazing pottery, metalwork, glassware, textiles, and calligraphy. They continue to create this art today.

► These Islamic coins are decorated with sayings from the Qur'an.

textile: a woven fabric; cloth

## Ceramics

Southwestern Asia—the area sometimes referred to today as the Middle East—gets very little rainfall. This also was true in the past. As a result, the people did not have a lot of water to grow reeds and straw. This meant they could not make baskets to use as containers. Instead, they created objects made of clay to store food and other goods. Over time, they created beautiful plates, bowls, vases, and pitchers. They decorated these ceramic pieces with colors and designs, and baked them in hot ovens.

## Metalwork

Islamic artists created coins, plates, pitchers, jewelry, and other objects out of metals such as gold, silver, and copper. They also used iron and steel to make swords, knives, and other weapons. The metal pieces were decorated with beautiful designs and sayings from the Qur'an.

## Glassware

The people of southwestern Asia became famous for their beautiful glassware. They created glass dishes, pitchers, bottles for perfume, and other glass containers. Because glass breaks so easily, we do not have many examples of the glassware created by early Islamic artists.

## Textiles

People in southwestern Asia had been making beautiful textiles and carpets long before Muhammad's time. However, because Muslims pray five times each day, small carpets to pray on became much more important with the rise of Islam. Cloth was needed for clothing, but textiles also were created to be hung on walls. These textiles had beautiful designs, which often included sayings from the Qur'an.

## Calligraphy

Islamic artists excelled in calligraphy, the art of fine writing. Why did they become such skillful calligraphers? One reason is that Muslim artists do not show Muhammad or any sacred figures. Therefore, writing about religious ideas became very important. Muslims thought the Qur'an contained beautiful ideas. They wanted to make these ideas beautiful to look at as well. Islamic artists decorated the walls of mosques and other buildings with sayings from the Qur'an. They also used calligraphy on pottery, metalwork, glassware, and textiles. The Qur'an and other writings, especially scientific writings, sometimes were illustrated with pictures. Calligraphy was used as part of the illustrations.

Calligraphy gave Muslims a way to write the words of God as beautifully as possible. Muslim scholars spent hours practicing calligraphy. They wrote the "letters" with a brush. Sometimes, scholars wrote the words so that the words themselves made a design. For example, the beliefs of Islam—the pillars of faith—can be written so that they look like a ship. 📖

▲ This is an early-1900s textile shop in what is today Uzbekistan. You can see silk, cotton, and wool fabrics and a few carpets.

# Where Can I See Examples of Islamic Art?

You can find a wonderful collection of Islamic art at New York's Metropolitan Museum of Art (the Met). Also, look in your local paper to find out about Islamic art exhibitions that are touring a city near you. Or, you can take a virtual tour of the Met's Islamic collection by visiting their web site, **www.metmuseum.org.** Look for "Islamic Art" on their "Collection" page.

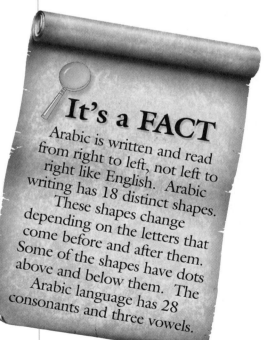

## It's a FACT

Arabic is written and read from right to left, not left to right like English. Arabic writing has 18 distinct shapes. These shapes change depending on the letters that come before and after them. Some of the shapes have dots above and below them. The Arabic language has 28 consonants and three vowels.

# MECCA — Trading Center and Holiest Muslim City

Five times each day, Muslims everywhere stop what they are doing and turn in the direction of the city of Mecca to pray. Every Muslim who is able must make a pilgrimage, or hajj, to this city. The holiest place in this holiest Muslim city is the Kaaba in the courtyard of the Great Mosque. This is the shrine that Muslims pray toward and visit during their hajj. Mecca also is the birthplace of Muhammad.

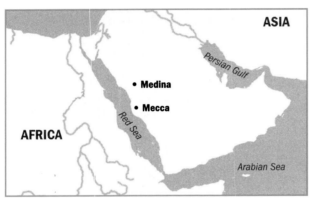

▲ Muslims consider Mecca to be their holiest city.

## The Geography and Climate

Mecca is located in the present-day Kingdom of Saudi Arabia. It is about 50 miles east of the Red Sea in a dry, sandy valley. It is hot and dry and gets very little rainfall. When the rains do come, there can be floods. Sandstorms are a fact of life and can last for days. The city's elevation is approximately 900 feet above sea level. It is surrounded by the Sirat Mountains. Muhammad went to caves in these mountains to study and think. It was there that Muslims believe he had revelations.

## The Holiest Place in Mecca

The Great Mosque can hold almost 300,000 people. The outer part of the mosque surrounds a courtyard 600-feet wide and 800-feet long. It is larger than two football fields! The Kaaba, a cube-shaped building, is in the center of this courtyard. It is about 50-feet high and about 45-feet wide. It is covered by black silk that shows excerpts from the Qur'an. There is only one door into the Kaaba. Inside is an empty room, and there are religious writings on the wall. When Muhammad and his followers fled Mecca in 622, they went to Medina. There, Muhammad called upon them to pray in the direction of the Kaaba.

**It's a FACT**

Within 100 years after Muhammad's teachings, the Islamic Empire was larger than the ancient Roman Empire.

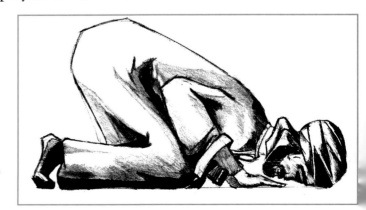

▶ Muslims stop five times each day to pray toward the city of Mecca.

## Mecca of the Past

Before Muhammad, the people of the Arabian Peninsula were not united. Their loyalty was to their families and their tribes. Tribes constantly fought one another. Most of the battles were over control of water, grazing lands, and trade routes. The Arabian Peninsula was a natural land bridge that connected the Mediterranean world or "West" with China and India in the "East." Mecca was the one place where all the tribes agreed to as a place of peace. People knew that fighting was not tolerated, so they brought their goods to trade in Mecca. It developed into an important trading center around 400. Mecca was a place where caravans stopped on the trade routes through the region. It linked the Mediterranean world with China, India, and eastern Africa. In Mecca, you could find Indian spices and perfumes, Chinese silk, and Egyptian cloth. You also could find a lively exchange of ideas.

▲ The holiest place in the holiest Muslim city of Mecca is the Kaaba. The Kaaba is a cube-shaped building in the center of the courtyard of the Great Mosque.

**It's a FACT**
The first mosque was Muhammad's home in Medina.

Muhammad was born in Mecca around 570. At first, Muhammad's teachings were not accepted. He fled to the city of Medina in 622. This event is called the Hijra. In Mecca, the people of the Arabian Peninsula worshiped many gods. They placed images or "idols" of those gods in the Kaaba for safekeeping. Muhammad returned in 630 and ordered all pagan idols in the Kaaba to be destroyed. Mecca became the capital of the Islamic empire. Over time, it did not remain an important political capital, but it has continued to be the religious capital of Islam.

In Islam, the fifth pillar of faith says it is the responsibility for Muslims who are financially and physically able to make the hajj to Mecca. Since the time of Muhammad, Muslims have taken the responsibility of the hajj very seriously. In fact, historians say that before the European age of exploration in the late 1400s and early 1500s, the pilgrimage to Mecca was the largest movement of people. Muslims from as far away as West Africa, Spain, China, and Indonesia made the long, difficult, and dangerous journey to Mecca. Some came by sea. Others made the journey over land.

### Mecca Now

Today, approximately two million Muslims make the pilgrimage to Mecca each year. Most of them come from countries other than Saudi Arabia. Islamic law is strictly enforced in Mecca and throughout Saudi Arabia. For example, alcoholic drinks are forbidden. Women are expected to dress very modestly. As Muslims travel to Mecca, they ask God to forgive their sins. They return home committed to living better lives.

Only Muslims are allowed in Mecca. The government in Saudi Arabia has built modern hotels, better roads, and other services for these visitors. Mecca's economy depends on the money visitors spend in the city. Farmers grow dates and rice on nearby oases, but most of the food Meccans eat is imported from other areas. The economy of Saudi Arabia depends on its greatest natural resource—oil. 📖

Today, approximately two million Muslims make the pilgrimage to Mecca each year. Most of them come from countries other than Saudi Arabia.

# Mosques

It is said that the first mosque—or Muslim place of worship—was the place where Muhammad lived when he went to Medina in 622. It was there that a freed African slave called Muhammad's followers to prayer. They prayed to God facing Mecca, the city where the Kaaba was located. As Muhammad's ideas attracted more followers, Muslims needed a place to pray and worship God.

## Form Follows Function

Architects have a saying: "Form follows function." This means that the purpose of a building (its function) will influence its shape and design (its form). If you look at mosques in different parts of the world, you will see that they share many similarities. This is because they fulfill the same function. For example, all mosques have a prayer hall, usually in a rectangular shape, that faces Mecca. Muslim men and women pray separately. Therefore, the prayer hall may be separated into two parts or else there is a separate room for women. There also is a space in front of the prayer hall where Muslims symbolically cleanse themselves before entering the prayer hall.

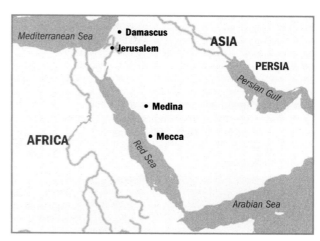

▲ Muslims pray to God facing Mecca, the city where the Kaaba is located.

◄ This photograph shows the courtyard of the Great Mosque of Mecca. Muslims are called to prayer from a tall slender tower called a minaret.

## The Architecture of Mosques

Many mosques have domes as part of their architecture. Historians think Muslims got the idea of the dome from the Byzantine Empire. Most mosques also have at least one tall tower called a minaret. Traditionally, a person (the muezzin) called all the Muslims to prayer from this tower. Today, minarets often are just for decoration. Sometimes, there is a loud speaker in the minaret that calls Muslims to prayer. Mosques do not have chairs. People kneel on rugs and pray. A mosque's religious leader, the imam, speaks to his fellow Muslims from a raised platform, or pulpit, called a minbar.

Large mosques often have courtyards. Many have schools attached to them. In the past, some mosques also had hospitals. The mosque is primarily a place for worship, but it also is a center of the Muslim community.

## Decorations

From earliest times, Muslim artists decorated the walls of mosques with sayings from the Qur'an. Muslims thought the Qur'an contained beautiful ideas. They wanted to make these ideas as beautiful to look at as they were to read. 📖

▼ The Hagia Sophia was created as a church during the Byzantine Empire, but was converted into a mosque. Historians think Muslims got the idea of the dome from the Byzantines.

# MUAWIYA — Founder of the Umayyad Dynasty

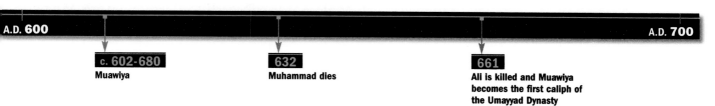

**c. 602-680**
Muawiya

**632**
Muhammad dies

**661**
Ali is killed and Muawiya
becomes the first caliph of
the Umayyad Dynasty

Muawiya founded one of the greatest dynasties in the history of Islam. He overcame many problems to accomplish this. As caliph, his most important achievement was the new system he introduced to select future caliphs.

## The Last of the "Four Rightly Guided Caliphs"

After Muhammad died in 632, four men succeeded him, in turn. As you have read, these men were Abu Bakr, Umar, Uthman, and Ali. At times, there were disagreements about who should become caliph, but these men are called the "Four Rightly Guided Caliphs." They are called "Rightly Guided Caliphs" because they were among Muhammad's closest and earliest followers. Each of them is said to have lived a simple and good life. It also is said that they treated others kindly and with mercy.

## Problems in the Islamic Empire

Uthman, the third caliph and a member of the Umayyad tribe, was assassinated in 656. Several days later, Ali became caliph. His supporters convinced him that he should be caliph. Ali knew that the Islamic Empire faced critical problems. He thought many of these problems were the result of poor management by the men Uthman had appointed to govern. One of these men was Muawiya, the governor of Syria and a member of the Umayyad tribe.

## Conflict between Ali and Muawiya

Ali decided to solve the problem of poor management by appointing new governors. All of the governors, except Muawiya, accepted Ali's orders. Muawiya said he would not obey Ali until Uthman's murder was avenged.

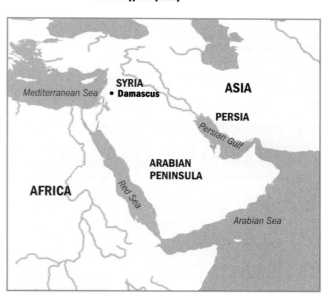

▲ After he became caliph, Muawiya moved the capital of the Islamic Empire to Damascus, Syria.

council: a group of people called together for discussion
raid: a sudden or surprise attack

Some thought Ali had been involved in Uthman's murder. Muawiya also wanted to become caliph himself. As the conflict between Ali and Muawiya increased, Ali moved the capital out of Arabia. Eventually, war broke out between Muawiya's army and Ali's forces. When the two armies met on the battlefield, Muawiya asked for a **council** to decide who should be caliph. Ali agreed to this idea, but this action angered some Muslims who wanted to kill both Ali and Muawiya. They were not successful in assassinating Muawiya, but they killed Ali in 661.

### Muawiya Becomes Caliph

With Ali dead, Muawiya had the power to become caliph. As the governor of Syria, he already controlled a large part of the Islamic Empire. He soon took control of Egypt and the area that is present-day Iraq. Muawiya moved the capital to Damascus, Syria. He then began a series of **raids** against the Byzantines. Over time, Muawiya was successful in expanding the size of his Islamic Empire.

▼ Muawiya established a system of hereditary succession. In this system, the ruler's child or other relative becomes the next ruler.

HEREDITARY SUCCESSION

RULER | RULER DIES | NEW RULER

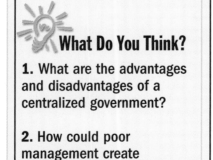

### What Do You Think?

1. What are the advantages and disadvantages of a centralized government?

2. How could poor management create problems in an empire?

### Muawiya's Legacy

The most lasting change that Muawiya introduced was the way caliphs were chosen. Before Muawiya, a council selected the caliph. Muawiya convinced people that the next caliph should be his son. In doing this, he changed the system of selecting a caliph to a system of hereditary succession. This was the beginning of the Umayyad Dynasty, which lasted for 90 years. 📖

# ABDUL MALIK —
# Umayyad Dynasty Lives

**A.D. 600** _____ **A.D. 800**

**c. 646-705**
**Abdul Malik**

**661-750**
**Umayyad Dynasty**

As a boy, Abdul Malik spent much of his time in Medina. He went to a religious school and made friends with people who would help him later in his life. At the age of 16, Abdul Malik was assigned to a government job in Medina. However, there was fighting in the city and he and his father had to flee. Eventually, his father became caliph, but died shortly thereafter. According to the line of succession, this meant Abdul Malik would become the new caliph— the fifth caliph of the Umayyad Dynasty. As caliph, he became both a political and religious leader.

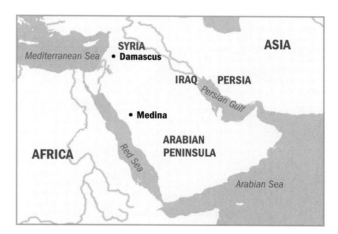

## Bringing Order and Change

When Abdul Malik became caliph, many people opposed the Umayyads and their rule. One group was located in northern Syria and Iraq. Another group was in Persia. After many battles and several years, Abdul Malik stopped the fighting and ended this Muslim civil war.

Abdul Malik ruled as caliph for 21 years. During that time, he made many changes to the Islamic Empire. For example, he established Arabic as the official language of the government. Previously, people had spoken Greek, Persian, and Arabic. Abdul Malik also produced the first Islamic-style coins. He got the idea of making coins for the Islamic Empire from the Persians and Byzantines. Coins would give people a common currency. They also would be a powerful symbol because the coins were **inscribed** with sayings from the Qur'an.

## The Umayyad Dynasty Continues

The last years of Abdul Malik's life were generally peaceful. Of course, there was the question of who would become the caliph after he died. Would it be his brother or one of his sons? Abdul Malik felt that the next caliph should be one of his sons. When he died, his son Walid became the next caliph. The line of succession for the Umayyads was assured—at least for the time being. ▢

▲ **Groups from northern Syria, Iraq, and Persia opposed Abdul Malik.**

**inscribe:** to mark or carve into stone or other material

### What Do You Think?

**1.** Abdul Malik was responsible for making the first Islamic-style coins. What do coins tell about a society?

**2.** What are the advantages and disadvantages of having one language for the government?

# AL-KHWARIZMI — A Math Wiz!

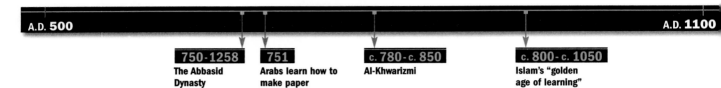

A.D. **500**

| 750-1258 | 751 | c. 780-c. 850 | c. 800-c. 1050 |

**The Abbasid Dynasty**

**Arabs learn how to make paper**

**Al-Khwarizmi**

**Islam's "golden age of learning"**

A.D. **1100**

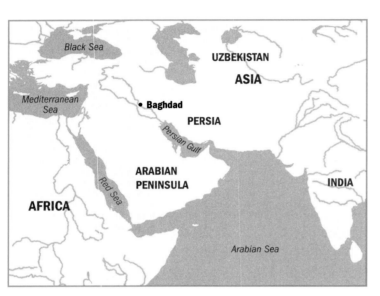

Historians disagree on many things having to do with the life of Abu Ja'far Muhammad Ibn Musa al-Khwarizmi. For example, we are not sure of the exact date of his birth and death. We think he was born around 780 in the town of Khwarizmi in present-day Uzbekistan. When he was a child, his parents moved to an area south of Baghdad. As you will find out, these details of al-Khwarizmi's life are less important than the contributions he made to the development of mathematics, **astronomy**, and **geography**. On these issues, historians strongly agree.

▲ The Abbasid Dynasty stretched from India to western Africa. The Abbasids built the city of Baghdad and made it their capital. Al-Khwarizmi moved to Baghdad as a child.

**astronomy:** the study of the universe, including the stars and planets
**geography:** the study of the earth's surface and features

## Al-Khwarizmi Joins the House of Wisdom

Al-Khwarizmi lived during the reign of the Abbasid Dynasty. Their empire stretched from India to the western shores of Africa to Baghdad. Many important events occurred during their reign. One of the most significant events happened in 751. Arabs learned how to make paper! The ability to record ideas on paper started a chain reaction in the world of learning.

In 813, Ma'mun became caliph. He strongly supported learning. One of his greatest achievements was to establish a place of learning called the House of Wisdom. The House of Wisdom was a place where scholars translated Greek scientific works and where they studied and taught other sciences. Al-Khwarizmi became a member of the House of Wisdom and is linked to what has been called the golden age of Islamic science. The House of Wisdom was active for over 200 years.

## A Zero and a Hero

Who is responsible for the subject we know today as modern mathematics? The answer is many people throughout history, including al-Khwarizmi. He introduced the concept of algebra. Algebra is advanced mathematics that allows scholars to solve difficult mathematical problems. Al-Khwarizmi was the first person to use the expression "al jabr," from which came the English word *algebra*. Al-Khwarizmi also is known as the person who introduced the use of Arabic numerals to the West. This led to our present-day use of nine Arabic numerals together with the zero sign as a placeholder.

Al-Khwarizmi's work was not limited to mathematics. While he was at the House of Wisdom, he wrote books on astronomy. In addition, he and a group of geographers produced the first globe of the known world at that time.

## Al-Khwarizmi's Legacy

Al-Khwarizmi's work greatly affected Western ideas about science and mathematics. His work in astronomy and geography was translated into European languages as well as Chinese. His work also formed the basis for a great deal of scientific and mathematical learning in medieval Europe (A.D. 500-1500). We think he died around 850. ⬚

### What Do You Think?

1. What evidence supports the statement that Muslims valued knowledge and learning?

2. Which is more important—developing new knowledge or passing knowledge to other people? Why?

# NUMBER SYSTEMS

| Arabic | Roman |
| --- | --- |
| 1 | I |
| 2 | II |
| 3 | III |
| 4 | IV |
| 5 | V |
| 6 | VI |
| 7 | VII |
| 8 | VIII |
| 9 | IX |
| 10 | X |

◄ Al-Khwarizmi introduced the use of Arabic numerals to the West. You can see the difference between Arabic and Roman numerals.

# IBN SINA and a Golden Age

**c. 800-c. 1050**
Islam's "golden age of learning"

**c. 980**
Ibn Sina is born in central Asia (modern-day Uzbekistan)

**1037**
Ibn Sina dies in Persia (present-day Iran)

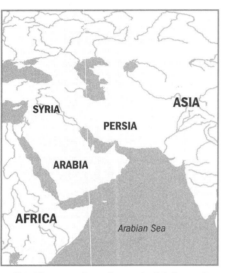

▲ Ibn Sina was born in central Asia and died in Persia.

Between 800 and 1050, the Islamic Empire enjoyed what historians call a "golden age of learning." Muslim scholars and others in the Muslim tradition studied science, mathematics, philosophy, music, and poetry. Ibn Sina was a leading scholar. In the Western world, he was known as "Avicenna." Together with other scholars, he preserved past learning and created new knowledge through experiments and discoveries.

Historians estimate that Ibn Sina wrote more than 450 books! Of these, only about 240 have survived. He wrote on many topics, including astronomy, logic, and mathematics. His greatest contributions were in the area of medicine. He had already gained great knowledge of medicine by the time he was 16 years old. He wrote two important medical books. *The Canon of Medicine* was the source of medical education for several hundred years. In *The Book of Healing*, Ibn Sina brought together ancient Greek philosophy with Muslim religious thinking. One historian commented that this book had "enough information to fill more than 5,000 pages of a modern book." Ibn Sina is remembered as an extremely gifted scholar and writer. 📖

## Analyze the Source!

1. Tell in your own words what the passage says.

2. Ibn Sina suggests that the best way to learn is from practice. Do you agree or disagree? Why?

## Ibn Sina on Medicine

Medicine is not one of the difficult sciences, and therefore I excelled in it in a very short time, to the point that distinguished physicians began to read medicine with me. I cared for the sick, and there opened up to me indescribable possibilities of therapy which can only be learnt from practice.

# OMAR KHAYYAM — Math Wiz, Astronomer, and Poet

A.D. **500**                      A.D. **2000**

**750-1258**
The Abbasid Dynasty

**c. 800-c. 1050**
Islam's "golden age"

**1048-1131**
Omar Khayyam

**1859**
Omar Khayyam's poetry is translated into English

Omar Khayyam lived during a difficult time in history. He was born in 1048 in Persia (present-day Iran). In 1055, when he was seven years old, the Turks invaded the capital city of Baghdad. Abbasid caliphs remained as figureheads, but the Turks had the real power. Islam's golden age was over.

Omar Khayyam wanted to learn, but it was not easy to be a scholar during this time. However, he overcame obstacles and became an outstanding mathematician and astronomer. Before he was 25 years old, he had written several books. He studied the stars and planets. He calculated the length of a year as 365.242198 days. Scientists today say it is 365.242190 days.

In 1092, the man who supported Omar Khayyam's work was killed. And some Muslims opposed Khayyam's ideas. During these hard times, Khayyam wrote a collection of poems called *The Rubaiyat*. Western readers learned about these poems when Edward Fitzgerald translated them into English in 1859. Omar Khayyam died in 1131.

▲ Omar Khayyam studied the stars and the planets.

## Verses from *The Rubaiyat*

The Moving Finger writes; and, having writ,
Moves on: nor all Piety nor Wit
Shall lure it back to cancel half a line,
Nor all thy Tears wash out a Word of it. ...

For in and out, above, about, below,
'Tis nothing but a Magic Shadow-show,
Played in a Box whose Candle is the Sun,
Round which we Phantom Figures come and go.

### Analyze the Source!

1. Read the passage and tell in your own words what one of the stanzas (paragraphs of a poem) says.

2. Many believe the "moving finger" refers to time. Do you agree that once time moves on, nothing can make it go back again? Explain.

# DAMIA AL-KAHINA —
# "Queen" of the Berbers

**c. 600**
Arab armies arrive
in northern Africa

**c. 690**
Damia al-Kahina
becomes a Berber
general

**c. 701**
Arabs defeat
Damia al-Kahina

**c. 701**
Damia al-Kahina
kills herself

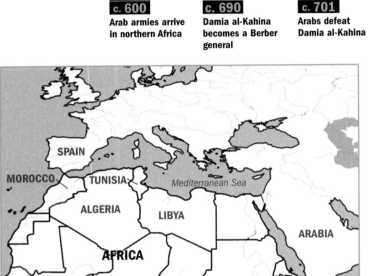

▲ Damia al-Kahina lived in the area that is present-day Libya. The Berbers lived in an area of northwestern Africa that covers present-day Libya, Algeria, Tunisia, and Morocco.

Throughout the seventh century, Arab armies advanced north and west from Arabia. As they conquered lands, they spread the Islamic faith. When the Arabs arrived in northern Africa, they tried to conquer it, but a group of people fought back.

## The Berbers

The Berbers lived in an area of northwestern Africa that covers the present-day countries of Libya, Algeria, Tunisia, and Morocco. All the Berber tribes had the same language and culture, but they did not have the same religion. Some were Christian, some Jewish, and some worshiped many different gods.

## A Common Enemy

The Berbers were not happy to see the Arabs in their land. They definitely did not want to be conquered. Seeing the Arabs as their common enemy, the Berber tribes banded together. But who would lead them? In the end, one of the Berber leaders who emerged was a woman named Damia al-Kahina.

## Damia al-Kahina

Not much is known about the early life of Damia al-Kahina. She was born to a family of nomads in North Africa, but we don't know the exact date. Some writers say she had "flashing good looks" with dark hair and skin. She also has been described as a "Moor," which is an Arabic word that means "scorched" or "black." The term *Moor* was used to describe the people of northwest Africa. Some historians think Damia al-Kahina was a member of a Jewish tribe. She was married and had two or three sons. We also know that people admired her courage and strength.

## A Natural Leader

In about 690, Damia al-Kahina took command of the Berber armies. She quickly gained a reputation as a brave and intelligent military general. For about five years, Damia al-Kahina and her armies stopped the Arabs from advancing. They even forced the Arabs to retreat. However, the Arabs were strong and would not give up. Around 701, they defeated Damia al-Kahina. After the defeat, she sent her sons to join the Arab forces. Then, she took her own life. Her sons converted to Islam and became soldiers in the Muslim army. In 756, one son crossed into Spain with Abd al-Rahman, who you will read about. Most of the Berbers became Muslims, and Arabic became the most important language.

Damia al-Kahina has been called the "queen of the Berbers," but she was never an actual queen. She was a powerful leader who raised armies to fight for political and religious freedom. 📖

### It's a FACT

Damia al-Kahina was known for her courage, but also for her powers of intuition. Some even said she could predict the future.

◄ Damia al-Kahina is sometimes called the "queen of the Berbers."

### 💡 What Do You Think?

**1.** After her defeat in battle, Damia al-Kahina sent her sons to join the Arab conquerors. Why do you think she did that?

**2.** Why did Arabic become the most important language in the region? Why do you think most people in the region converted to Islam?

# ABD AL-RAHMAN I & III —
# The Umayyad Dynasty in Spain

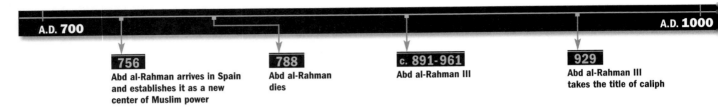

A.D. **700**

**756**
Abd al-Rahman arrives in Spain and establishes it as a new center of Muslim power

**788**
Abd al-Rahman dies

**c. 891-961**
Abd al-Rahman III

**929**
Abd al-Rahman III takes the title of caliph

A.D. **1000**

The Umayyads ruled the Islamic Empire for 90 years (661-750). They expanded and unified the empire, but their rule was filled with problems. One of the Umayyad's problems was that they were not collecting enough money in taxes. Also, people began to believe that the Umayyad leaders were more interested in worldly things than in the ideas of Islam. Some wanted to overthrow the Umayyads. In 750, members of the Abbasid family came up with a plan. An Abbasid leader invited the most important Umayyads to a feast. While the Umayyads were enjoying themselves, he ordered his men to kill them all. Only one Umayyad leader escaped. He was Abd al-Rahman.

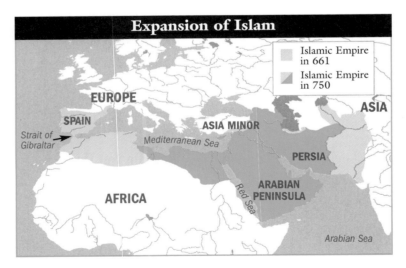

▲ The Umayyads ruled the Islamic Empire from 661-750. They expanded and unified the empire, but their rule also was filled with problems.

## Spain—A New Center of Muslim Power

Running for his life, Abd al-Rahman traveled across northern Africa and crossed the Strait of Gibraltar. He arrived in present-day Spain in 756. At that time, a large part of Spain was already under Muslim rule. Muslims living in northern Africa had crossed into Spain in about 711. Spain also was one of the few provinces that had refused to recognize the Abbasids as caliphs.

Abd al-Rahman found that the people in Spain were fighting among themselves. With help from Berber soldiers, he united the people and began a new Umayyad Dynasty in Spain. Now, there were two centers of Muslim power. One was ruled by the Abbasids in Baghdad. The other was ruled by the Umayyads in Spain. The dynasty started by Abd al-Rahman reached its greatest glory under the rule of Abd al-Rahman III.

## Independence from Baghdad

Abd al-Rahman III became ruler of much of Spain in 912. For the first 17 years he kept the title of "amir," or prince. This was the title used by the previous Muslim rulers in Spain. Over time, he extended his authority over more of the peninsula. In 929, he took the title of caliph. With this act, he declared his empire politically independent from Baghdad, the capital of the Muslim community in the East. He made the ancient Roman city of Córdoba the capital.

## A Center of Learning

Al-Rahman III was very interested in religion and science. He wanted to make the new capital city of Córdoba as great as Baghdad. He imported books from Baghdad. He also tried to convince scholars to come to Córdoba. Within a few years, Córdoba became home to poets, philosophers, historians, and musicians. Many of these were Muslims, but he also welcomed Christians and Jews. He built libraries and hospitals throughout the city.

## Making a Mark

Abd al-Rahman III earned much praise for his courage, conquests, and administrative ability. The city of Córdoba became one of the intellectual capitals of the world. People were impressed with its paved and lighted streets. It was said that a person could walk the streets for 10 miles in one direction at night and always have the light of lamps to guide the way. Cities in the rest of Europe at that time were dark and primitive in comparison.

When Abd al-Rahman III died in 961, he left an outstanding legacy of accomplishments. He also laid the foundation for some of the greatest scientific discoveries of all time. Historians believe that Europe was greatly influenced by the events and discoveries that took place in Spain under Muslim rule. 📖

▲ These are the arches in the Great Mosque at Córdoba.

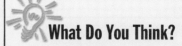

### It's a FACT

Córdoba had a population of about 200,000, making it one of the largest cities in Europe at the time.

During a feast, members of the Abbasid family killed all of the Umayyad leaders, except Abd al-Rahman.

### 💡 What Do You Think?

**1.** Spain during Abd al-Rahman III's time has been called "the brightest star in Europe." What evidence supports that statement?

**2.** How did the Umayyads transform Córdoba into a center of culture and learning?

# ABBAS IBN FIRNAS —
# Islamic Flyer

**A.D. 700**

**?-c. 888**
**Abbas ibn Firnas**

**912-961**
**Abd al-Rahman III rules Islamic Spain; Muslim culture and science reaches its highest point**

**A.D. 1000**

▲ Abbas ibn Firnas was a scholar in Córdoba, Spain. He studied the planets and even attempted to fly.

History includes many stories about people trying to fly. Some of these stories are real. Others are myths and legends. Real or not, people have always wished for wings to soar.

## Coming to Córdoba

Abbas ibn Firnas was one of the first scholars from Baghdad to arrive in Córdoba as the city was developing into a center of culture and science. The city reached its highest point during the rule of Abd al-Rahman III (912-961). Abd al-Rahman III continued to invite scholars from Baghdad to come to work in Córdoba. He wanted Córdoba to rival Baghdad.

## A Man of Many Interests

Abbas ibn Firnas came to Córdoba to teach music and tell the leaders of Spain about the latest news and thinking in Baghdad. But Abbas ibn Firnas was not a man who limited himself to one area of study. While in Córdoba, he figured out how to make glass and created a watch-like devise that kept accurate time. Abbas ibn Firnas also was interested in the movement of the planets.

## Taking to the Skies

Abbas ibn Firnas's most famous experiment was his attempt to fly. He built a pair of wings and attached them to a wooden frame. He had created a glider. Once he had built the final version, he invited the people of Córdoba to come and see him fly. Many people attended this event and watched him from a nearby mountain. Historians have recorded that he flew for a few hundred yards and then fell to earth. He was seriously injured in this fall.

## Islamic Science

Abbas ibn Firnas was one of many famous Muslim scientists who made important discoveries during the golden age of Muslim science. His attempt to fly is the earliest recorded in Western history. Many years before Leonardo da Vinci made his first drawings of a winged machine, Abbas ibn Firnas had made his own flying machine. ❏

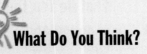
### What Do You Think?

1. Why might a scholar from Baghdad have made the trip to Córdoba?

2. Why was flying considered important? How is Abbas ibn Firnas remembered today?

Muslim scholars in Córdoba studied astronomy and other sciences. Abbas ibn Firnas was interested in the movement of the planets.

# CHARLES MARTEL —
# Another Day, Another Dynasty

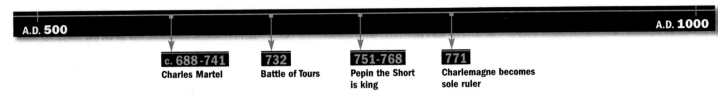

A.D. **500**                                                                                     A.D. **1000**

**c. 688-741**
Charles Martel

**732**
Battle of Tours

**751-768**
Pepin the Short
is king

**771**
Charlemagne becomes
sole ruler

Within the first few decades of the 700s, Muslims had taken control of much of Spain and set their sights on present-day France. They wanted to conquer new lands and spread Islam. A Germanic people called the Franks controlled the territory the Muslims wanted. This territory and much of Europe was Christian. The Franks had no intention of being conquered by the Arabs. They had no interest in converting to Islam.

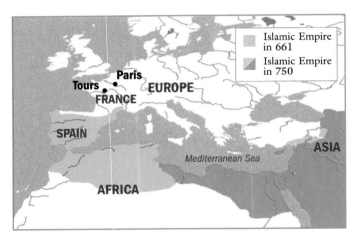

Islamic Empire in 661

Islamic Empire in 750

▲ Christian forces defeated the Muslims in the battle of Tours. Charles Martel led the battle against the Muslims.

## Christians vs. Muslims

In 732, Muslim and Christian armies faced one another at a critical battle near the city of Tours in present-day France. Would the Muslims expand the Islamic Empire throughout Europe? The Christian forces were determined to stop them, and they succeeded. The Muslim forces were defeated in the battle of Tours. In much of Arab literature, the battle of Tours is not treated as a significant event. At the time, the Muslims ruled a large area of land and there were internal problems within the part of Spain under Muslim rule. The European viewpoint of the battle is very different. For the Franks and for all Christians in Europe, the battle was extremely important.

## Charles Martel Rises to Power

A man named Charles Martel led the Franks in the battle of Tours. He was proclaimed as the man who stopped the Muslims from expanding further into Europe.

Charles Martel's victory over the Muslims and other victories made him a powerful man among the Franks. He never had the title of king, but he began to act like one. He extended Frankish rule over northern and then southeastern Gaul (present-day France). Before he died in 741, Charles made important alliances with the pope, who was the head of the Christian Church in Rome.

This illustration shows what a Carolingian king might have looked like. The name Carolingian comes from the Latin, *Carolus*, which means Charles. Charles Martel was the founder of the Carolingian Dynasty.

**It's a FACT**

Charles was given the name "Martel" after his victory at the battle of Tours. In French, *martel* means "hammer."

## The Rise of the Carolingian Dynasty

After Charles died, his son, Pepin the Short, **inherited** his power. However, he did not have the right to be king because he was not a member of a royal family. According to the system of hereditary succession, the new king had to be related to the previous king. Pepin needed a way to become king. He turned to the church for help.

**inherit:** to receive from someone who has died

## Carolingian Dynasty

### CHARLES MARTEL
### "The Hammer"

### PEPIN THE SHORT
### First Carolingian King

### CHARLEMAGNE
### "Charles the Great"

The pope declared that whoever *acts* with the power of a king should also *have* the title. In 751, Pepin the Short became king. When he died in 768, his sons, Charlemagne and Carloman, divided the lands between themselves. In 771, Carloman died.

Charlemagne was now the ruler of a vast kingdom. This is how the Carolingian Dynasty began in Europe. Even though Charles Martel never officially became king, he started a dynasty of European kings. 📖

**What Do You Think?**

1. Why do you think the battle of Tours is treated differently in Arabic and European histories?

2. Why is the battle of Tours significant for Europe?

# The Flowering of JEWISH Civilization in Spain

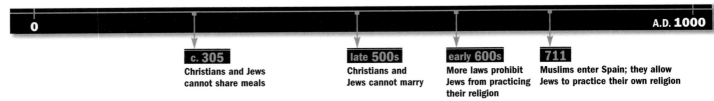

| 0 | | | | A.D. **1000** |
|---|---|---|---|---|

**c. 305**
Christians and Jews cannot share meals

**late 500s**
Christians and Jews cannot marry

**early 600s**
More laws prohibit Jews from practicing their religion

**711**
Muslims enter Spain; they allow Jews to practice their own religion

Why was there a flowering of Jewish civilization in Spain under Muslim rule? The easy answer to this question is that when Muslims ruled Spain, Jews were free to worship as they pleased and practice their own traditions. This was very different from what Jews experienced earlier in Spain or elsewhere in Europe.

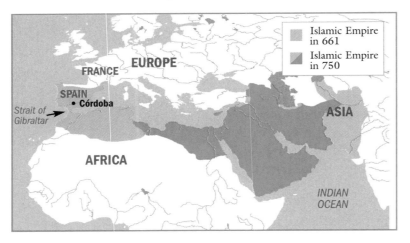

▲ **Muslims crossed the Strait of Gibraltar into Spain in 711. They allowed Jews to keep their religion.**

## From Persecution ...

Laws had been passed as early as 305 saying that Christians could not share meals with Jews. In the late 500s, laws did not allow Christians and Jews to marry. In the early 600s, more laws restricted Jews from practicing their religion. By the end of that century, Jews suffered great persecution, could not own land, were forbidden from doing certain kinds of work, and some were made into slaves.

## ... To Tolerance

When Muslims came across the Strait of Gibraltar into Spain in 711, they treated Jews differently than the Visigoths who had ruled the area before. Muslims did not force them to convert to Islam. Jews could keep their religion and be a "protected group" within Muslim society. They had to pay a special tax that was higher than the tax Muslims paid, but they were allowed to keep their traditions and worship in their own way. They lived in a separate part of Córdoba and were allowed to govern their community. They also were free to travel.

## Jewish Contributions to Islamic Spain

- **Mathematics**
- **Geography**
- **Poetry**
- **Philosophy**
- **Medicine**
- **New Discoveries**
- **Translated Books**
- **Political Ambassadors**

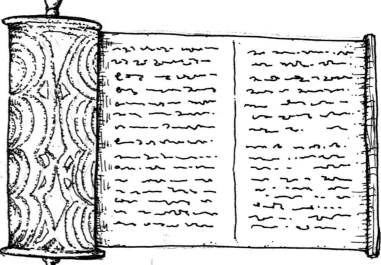

▲ The Torah contains the holy writings of the Jews.

## A Flowering of Civilization

One historian explained it this way: "Side by side with the new rulers [the Muslims] lived the Christians and Jews in peace." In this environment, free from persecution, Jewish civilization prospered. Muslim civilization prospered, too. Muslims and Jews shared a strong interest in learning. Jewish scholars played an important role in translating books. They also made contributions to mathematics, geography, poetry, and philosophy. Many of the leading doctors of the age were Jewish. Some served as representatives of Muslim rulers with other European leaders. Under Muslim rule, the city of Córdoba became one of the intellectual capitals of the world. Córdoba also boasted other examples of civilization that were quite remarkable for the time. People traveling within the city walked on paved roads. Regardless of which direction they traveled, lamps always lighted the streets. Cities in the rest of Europe were dark and primitive in comparison.

## A Community Deserving Praise

The Jewish community in Córdoba helped make it such a wonderful city as well as a cultural and intellectual center. Jewish scholars played an important role in making new discoveries and also in passing knowledge from the ancient world to Europe. The peace and tolerance of Spain under Muslim rule was fertile soil for the Jewish civilization to flower. 📖

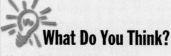

**What Do You Think?**

How did Muslims show religious tolerance? How did they treat people unequally?

# A Genoese Lady Visits the Sultan's Wife

**M**any European traders, merchants, and government representatives traveled to Istanbul, the capital city of the Ottoman Empire. On one of these trips in the mid-1500s, a lady from Genoa, Italy accompanied her husband. While there, she was invited to visit the wife of the sultan, Sulayman the Magnificent. She wrote a letter around 1550 telling about her experience. 📖

▶ **Sulayman was known to Europeans as "the Magnificent" because of his power and wealth.**

## Analyze the Source!

1. Read the passage and explain it in your own words.

2. Why do you think the Genoese lady was so interested in the sultan's wife and her culture? Why do you think the sultan's wife was so interested in the Genoese lady and her culture?

## A Genoese Lady's Letter

The Sultana ... sat upon silk cushions striped with silver. Numerous slave women, blazing with jewels, attended upon her, holding fans ... and many objects of value.

... The great lady ... extended her hand and kissed me on the brow ... . She asked many questions concerning our country and our religion, of which she knew nothing whatever ... I was surprised to notice ... that the room was full of women, who ... had come to see me, and to hear what I had to say.

The Sultana now entertained me with ... dancing girls and music ... Refreshments were served upon trays of solid gold sparkling with jewels ... .

... I made a motion of rising to leave. She immediately clapped her hands, and several slaves came forward ... carrying trays heaped up with beautiful stuffs, and some silver articles of fine workmanship, which she pressed me to accept ... .

# The Janissary Corps —
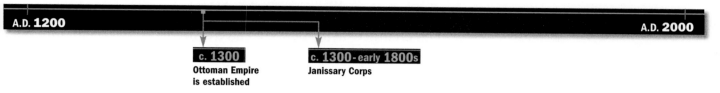
## A SLAVE ARMY

**c. 1300**
**Ottoman Empire
is established**

**c. 1300 - early 1800s**
**Janissary Corps**

From about the beginning of the Ottoman Empire until the early 1800s, a special group of Ottoman soldiers stood out from the rest. They were called the Janissary Corps. The word "janissary" comes from a Turkish word that means "new forces." Janissaries were the most skilled, experienced, and feared soldiers in the Ottoman army. They had no family ties and were loyal only to the sultan. Where did these soldiers come from? How were they trained to become the best warriors in the entire empire?

## A Slave Army Begins with Christian Boys

When Ottoman sultans fought wars in Christian territories in Europe, they captured large numbers of prisoners. Many were children. The male children were taken from their families to create a loyal slave army for the sultans. Over time, the Ottomans placed a special "tax" on the Christians in conquered territories. Each family had to provide the Ottomans with one male child. These boys usually were between eight and 15 years old.

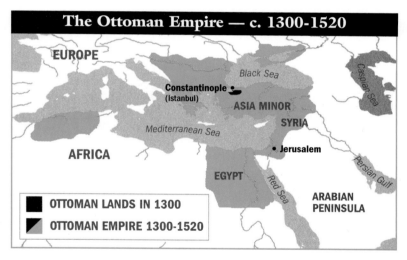

▲ This map shows the Ottoman Empire.

## Loyalty to Islam

These young boys were taught the ideas of Islam and raised in a special school far from their homes. They lost their homeland, culture, and families. They were the sultan's slaves, but generally they were well treated. They were raised as Muslims and expected to be loyal to Islam and to the sultan. If a boy showed an exceptional ability for learning, he went for additional schooling in the sultan's palace. These boys became government officials. Some even became important government officials called viziers. Boys who showed physical ability were trained as soldiers. All janissaries had rigorous military training and learned strict discipline. The Janissary Corps became known as the finest soldiers in the world.

## Janissary Corps Gains Power and Respect

Over time, the Ottoman Empire grew weaker and was unable to control all of the territory it had conquered. The sultans came to rely more on the Janissary Corps. This gave the janissaries political power. Sultans agreed that janissaries did not have to follow some of the rules other people had to follow. The janissaries did not have to pay taxes other Muslims had to pay. Many janissaries also started to make money through private businesses. People of the Ottoman Empire began to want their own children to become janissaries. The Corps changed from being a slave army to one that included soldiers from the entire Muslim population.

## The End of the Corps

In 1826, the sultan decided that major changes needed to be made in the military. The janissaries did not agree. They thought the sultan's plan was a threat to their survival. They were right. The sultan wanted to make the changes, and he did not want the janissaries to revolt. He had the Janissary Corps massacred. 📖

▲ A caldron (or pot) of soup was the symbol of the Janissary Corps. When the janissaries were unhappy with the sultan's actions, they would "overturn the cauldron." This was a symbolic gesture to reject the sultan's action and begin a rebellion.

▲ The Janissary Corps began as a slave army, but the janissaries later became known as the finest soldiers in the world. They gained political power and respect.

### What Do You Think?

1. Why would a sultan want soldiers who did not have any connection with their homeland, culture, or family?

2. What would cause a rebellion?

# MICHAEL KRITOVOULOS
## and the Fall of Constantinople

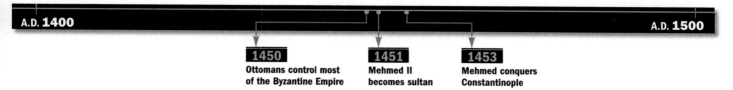

A.D. **1400**                                                                 A.D. **1500**

**1450**
Ottomans control most
of the Byzantine Empire

**1451**
Mehmed II
becomes sultan

**1453**
Mehmed conquers
Constantinople

By 1450, the Ottomans had taken over almost all of the Byzantine Empire, with one exception—Constantinople. The city was a jewel the Ottomans wanted to own. Constantinople had enormous importance. It would give the Ottomans a historic symbol of their greatness. It also would give them control of the major sea and land trading routes.

## An Aging Empire
By 1453, the Byzantine Empire was no longer a great empire. It did not control vast territories or have a strong army. Its capital, Constantinople, however, was a very hard city to conquer. It was surrounded by water on three sides. It also had city walls that were three layers thick. Constantinople had withstood attacks by many peoples, including Arabs, Persians, Bulgarians, and Russians.

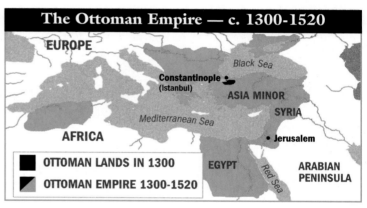

The Ottoman Empire — c. 1300-1520

■ OTTOMAN LANDS IN 1300
◪ OTTOMAN EMPIRE 1300-1520

▲ In 1453, the Ottomans conquered Constantinople. They renamed the city Istanbul.

## Mehmed II and the Siege of Constantinople
From the time he was a child, Mehmed II dreamed of capturing Constantinople. In 1451, at the age of 20, he became sultan of the Ottoman Empire. Two years later he put a plan into action. He was determined that Constantinople would fall to the Ottomans.

In April 1453, Mehmed's army of about 80,000-150,000 soldiers set up camp outside the walls of Constantinople. Following Muslim tradition, Mehmed offered the citizens of the city the opportunity to surrender. When they refused, Mehmed ordered the **siege** to begin. Cannonballs began hitting the walls of the city. There were only 7,000-10,000 Byzantine soldiers and they did not have cannons. All they could do was try to repair the walls.

The siege went on for weeks. The Byzantines began to run out of food. They hoped that western Europe would send soldiers and supplies by ship. Nothing came. Still, the Byzantines refused to surrender. Finally, on May 29, 1453, Mehmed ordered all of his best soldiers to attack. One of the main gates to the city fell open and the Muslims charged in. Constantinople fell.

**siege:** a persistent attempt to gain control

## The Aftermath of Conquest

On the afternoon of May 29, 1453, Mehmed II entered Constantinople riding a white horse. He rode down streets filled with dead bodies. One observer from Venice said, "blood flowed through the streets like rainwater after a sudden storm." An Ottoman official wrote, "The soldiers took silver and gold vessels, precious stones, and all sorts of valuable goods and fabrics from the imperial palace and the houses of the rich." Mehmed stopped one of the soldiers from taking pieces of marble from the floor of a church. He reportedly said to the soldier, "For you, the treasures and prisoners are enough. The buildings are mine."

Mehmed rode on through the streets until he reached the Hagia Sophia, the Christian church built 900 years earlier by Emperor Justinian. He got off his horse and went inside to pray to Allah. After this victory, Mehmed II also became known as Mehmed the Conqueror. 📖

▲ This is the Hagia Sophia. When Mehmed conquered Constantinople, why do you think he said, "The buildings are mine"? How do you think the function of the Hagia Sophia changed after the Ottomans took control, and how did it stay the same?

# A Witness to the Battle

At the time of the siege a Greek official, Michael Kritovoulos, wrote about what happened.

*When Sultan Mehmed saw that the companies he had sent were getting the worst of the battle ... he was furious. He decided that the situation was to be endured no longer, and he immediately sent in all of the companies he had reserved for later, his best-armed, hardiest and bravest men, who are greatly superior to the other in experience and strength ... the so-called Janissaries. He cried out ... that now was the moment to show their virtue and he led the way to the wall himself.*

*They went at it with a great terrifying cry of rage and fury, like madmen, and, as they were youthful and strong, and full of courage, they never let up. ... When the Sultan realized that the gate had been abandoned he immediately cried out ... 'The city is ours. ... The men are running from us, they cannot keep at their posts.' ... The Turks poured into the city and the army followed. ... The Sultan stood before the great wall, surveying events, for the day was beginning to dawn. ...*

## Analyze the Source!

Kritovoulos was a Greek. He was part of the Byzantine Empire that lost Constantinople. If you were a Muslim historian how might your account of the battle be different? How do you think a Muslim historian would describe the fall of Constantinople?

# Life in the ISLAMIC EMPIRE

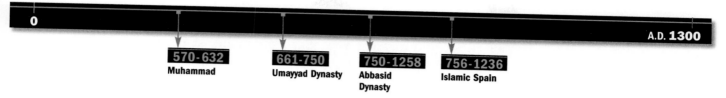

0                                                                                          A.D. **1300**

**570-632**
Muhammad

**661-750**
Umayyad Dynasty

**750-1258**
Abbasid Dynasty

**756-1236**
Islamic Spain

The people living under Muslim rule enjoyed many advancements. Muslim scholars and those working in the Muslim tradition excelled in areas from medicine to technology to developing a system for recording dates.

## Muslim Medicine— Most Advanced in the World

In the 1100s, a Muslim doctor wrote about an experience he had with a doctor in Europe. The Muslim doctor wrote that a sick man had complained about a boil—a large sore—on his leg. The doctor put medicine on the boil and the man began to get better. A European doctor later saw the same patient and said that the patient's leg had to be cut off. "Bring me an ax and a strong man," said the doctor. He told the strong man, "Strike his leg with the ax and cut it off with one blow!" The Muslim doctor had learned about the way European doctors worked in the 1100s.

Muslims were more advanced in their knowledge of medicine than other people who lived at the time. Muslim doctors were able to find out why people were sick and how to treat diseases. Their hospitals gave free medical care. Doctors had to pass tests. They knew how to use drugs to make people relax or sleep during surgery. They experimented with plants for medicine. As early as 1000, Al-Zahrarvi, a Muslim doctor in Córdoba, had learned to clean wounds so they would not become infected. In the 1200s, another Muslim doctor, Ibn an-Nafis, discovered that blood circulates through the body. A Muslim doctor in Baghdad, Al-Razi, wrote the first accurate descriptions of the diseases smallpox and measles. Ibn Sina, known in the West as "Avicenna," wrote a book that included all the information Muslims knew about diseases and how to treat them.

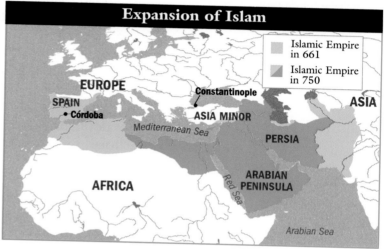

### Expansion of Islam

Islamic Empire in 661

Islamic Empire in 750

EUROPE

SPAIN
• Córdoba

Constantinople

ASIA MINOR

ASIA

Mediterranean Sea

PERSIA

AFRICA

ARABIAN PENINSULA

Red Sea

Arabian Sea

▲ This map shows the Islamic Empire in 661-750.

▲ Muslims made great advancements in the areas of science and medicine.

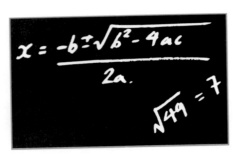

▲ A Muslim mathematician, Al-Khwarizmi, is remembered for first introducing the concept of algebra.

## Science and Technology

Muslims learned new ideas from people they came in contact with. In the mid-700s, they learned how to make paper from the Chinese. Around 825, Muslim scholar Al-Khwarizmi wrote about the system of numbers we call Arabic numerals. The system was invented in India. He used this knowledge to develop more advanced mathematics such as algebra. Muslims also learned from people who had lived before them. In Baghdad and Córdoba, scholars translated ancient Greek texts and other works into Arabic.

Muslim scholars were very good at astronomy. Mathematicians and astronomers at the House of Wisdom in Baghdad mapped stars and planets. They calculated the length of time it took the earth to go around the sun and measured the distance around the earth. They used a device called the astrolabe, invented by the Greeks, to help sailors find their way using the stars. Muslim scholar Ibn al-Haytham was interested in vision— how people see. He discovered that light travels through air and water at different speeds. His ideas eventually led to the development of the modern camera. Jabir, another Muslim scholar, made discoveries that led to the development of chemistry.

Some Muslim scholars were interested in geography. They drew maps of the world. One map, drawn in 1154, included the basic outlines of Asia, North Africa, and Europe. Scholars knew the earth was round, but they didn't know about Australia or the Americas. No one at that time knew about these continents, except the people living on them. In Spain, Muslims experimented with new crops such as rice, sugar cane, oranges, lemons, carrots, and cotton. They also experimented with new methods of growing crops, including new ways to water fields.

People today owe a great debt to these Muslim scholars, as well as Christian and Jewish scholars who worked in the Muslim tradition. They helped preserve past learning, and also created new knowledge through their experiments and discoveries. They shared knowledge with visiting scholars, merchants, and other people from all over the world.

كانت اللغة العربية في الحضارة الاسلامية اللغة الرسمية

▲ Arabic writing is read from right to left. The writing shown above says, "Arabic was the official language of the Islamic civilization."

## Language

The Umayyad caliphs ruled the Islamic Empire from 661-750. They made Arabic the official language of the empire. As the Islamic Empire expanded, Arabic became important to many more people. The primary reason for this is that the Qur'an is written in Arabic. To read their holy book, Muslims needed to know how to read Arabic. It didn't matter if they lived in Spain or India. From the beginning of the Islamic Empire to the time of the Ottoman Empire, people from many different regions lived under Muslim rule. Having a common religion and language helped unify them.

## Family Life

In the Islamic Empire, parents or other relatives arranged marriages. A marriage joined two families. Muslims believed love between a man and woman would develop as they shared the experiences of running a household. According to Islam, a man could have as many as four wives as long as he could take care of them and treat them fairly. Children, even after they became adults, were expected to obey their parents without question. Most boys did the same kind of work as their fathers. However, if a boy showed a special gift for learning, he could go to school and work in a government or administrative job. Girls did not have many opportunities for education. Wives often helped with their husband's work or sometimes did weaving at home.

Most Muslims spent their free time with family members and friends. They might enjoy food and drinks, share news, or perhaps listen to poetry or a musical performance. Muslims saw family and friends at a marketplace called a "bazaar," as well as at weddings or funerals, in mosques, or at water wells. Men and women always met as separate social groups.

▲ This is an early-1800s scene of a bazaar in Kabul, Afghanistan. It took place during the fruit season.

## The 12 months of the Islamic year

1. Muharram
2. Safar
3. Rabi' al-awwal (Rabi' I)
4. Rabi' al-thani (Rabi' II)
5. Jumada al-awwal (Jumada I)
6. Jumada al-thani (Jumada II)
7. Rajab
8. Sha'ban
9. Ramadan
10. Shawwal
11. Dhu al-Qi'dah
12. Dhu al-Hijjah

## Find Out More ...

You can find out today's date according to the Islamic calendar by going online and finding a web site that includes a "calendar converter."
Type in key words:
Islamic calendar

It's a FACT

The Gregorian calendar has 365 days. The Islamic calendar has 354 days.

▲ The Islamic calendar is based on the lunar calendar. The length of a lunar month is a little more than 29 days.

## The Islamic Calendar

In the Western world, people use a dating system based on the birth of Jesus. You use this system when you use B.C./A.D. or B.C.E./C.E. dates. However, other people based their dating systems on different dates. The starting point in the Muslim dating system is the year of the Hijra, the year Muhammad left Mecca for Medina. According to the Western calendar, the Hijra took place in A.D. 622. For Muslims, this date is AH 1. "AH" stands for *anno Hijra* or the "year of the Hijra."

Also, the Islamic calendar is based on a lunar calendar. It consists of 12 months—just like a solar calendar. A new month starts when an observer first sees the new moon (the crescent moon). The length of a lunar month, based on the motion of the moon, is a little more than 29 days. As a result, a lunar year is only about 354 days compared to 365 days in a solar calendar.

The Islamic calendar is the official calendar in Saudi Arabia and in a few other countries in the Persian Gulf. Most other Muslim countries use the Islamic calendar only for religious purposes. They use the same calendar as the Western world for business and government. 📖

# Reader's Theater Presents ...

# Ali Baba and the Forty Thieves"

IONS: Practice reading the script. When the script says, eryone in the class joins in the reading. Read with expression!

# ROLES:

- ★ SCHEHERAZADE
- ★ QUASIM
- ★ BAND OF THIEVES
- ★ ALI BABA
- ★ MURGANAH
- ★ SOUND EFFECTS
- ★ HEAD THIEF
- ★ ALL

REMEMBER: Practice reading the script. When the script says, "ALL," everyone in the class joins in the reading. Read with expression!

**SCHEHERAZADE:** This story is about Ali Baba, a poor but honest woodcutter. One day, while gathering wood in the forest, Ali Baba heard a noise.

**SOUND EFFECTS:** (*Make a noise like men coming through the forest.*)

**SCHEHERAZADE:** Fearing danger, he hid behind an old tree. He peeked out from his hiding place to see what was making the sounds.

**ALL:** What was it? Was it a wild animal?

**SCHEHERAZADE:** No, it was something more terrifying— a band of 40 thieves! Ali Baba began to say his prayers.

**ALI BABA:** Please, Allah. Save me from these thieves!

**SCHEHERAZADE:** Allah must have been looking kindly on Ali Baba because they did not see him. They were more interested in something else. Ali Baba watched the thieves stop in front of the cave. The leader shouted:

**HEAD THIEF:** Open Sesame!

**ALL:** Then what happened?

**SCHEHERAZADE:** Then the cave door opened.

**HEAD THIEF:** Come on, thieves, let's go inside.

**BAND OF THIEVES:** Yes, let's get gold, silver, pearls, rubies, and coins!

**SCHEHERAZADE:** After a while, the band of thieves left. They carried heavy bags on their shoulders. Ali Baba waited until the forest was quiet.

**ALI BABA:** I stood in front of the cave and said, "Open Sesame." The cave opened and I went inside. I couldn't believe the treasures I saw. I stuffed my pockets with gold coins. Then I ran home.

**SOUND EFFECTS:** *(Make a sound of one person running.)*

**ALI BABA:** When I got home, my brother Quasim was waiting for me.

**SCHEHERAZADE:** Quasim was a mean man with a cold and greedy heart.

**QUASIM:** Why are you late, stupid brother? Where is the wood?

**SCHEHERAZADE:** Just then, one of the coins fell from Ali Baba's pocket. Quasim forced his brother to tell him what he saw in the forest.

**ALL:** Then what happened?

**QUASIM:** The next day, I went to the forest alone. I stood in front of the cave and shouted, "Open Sesame!" The door opened just as Ali Baba had described. I hurried inside and grabbed as many riches as I could.

**SCHEHERAZADE:** When Quasim had as much as he could carry, he went to the door and said ...

**ALL:** Open Sesame!

**SCHEHERAZADE:** No, he said, "Open Door," but the door did not open. Then he said, "Open Cave," but the door still did not open. You see, in his excitement about the riches, he forgot what to say.

**QUASIM:** What am I going to do now?

**SCHEHERAZADE:** Just then, the door to the cave opened. At first, Quasim was happy. Then he saw who had opened the cave door.

**QUASIM:** Oh, no! No! No!

**SCHEHERAZADE:** It was the band of 40 thieves. And they looked very angry.

**BAND OF THIEVES:** Let's get the thief! He tried to take our treasure. Let's get him!

**HEAD THIEF:** Wait. First we have to find out if anyone else knows about the cave. How did you find out about the cave?

**SCHEHERAZADE:** The thieves found out about Ali Baba. They decided to go after him. They went to an inn and talked about how to get him.

**HEAD THIEF:** We'll make sure he doesn't get a chance to spend any of our money.

**SCHEHERAZADE:** The serving girl, Murganah, heard the thieves talking. She ran to Ali Baba's house.

**MURGANAH:** Ali Baba, you must run away. The thieves will come after you!

**ALI BABA:** Thank you for helping me. Don't worry. I'll think of something.

**SCHEHERAZADE:** And he did.

**ALL:** Then what happened?

**MURGANAH:** Ali Baba and I got married and we lived happily ever after.

**ALL:** Really? Is that the end of the story?

**SCHEHERAZADE:** Well, there's a little more, but I'm tired now. I'll finish tomorrow. 📖

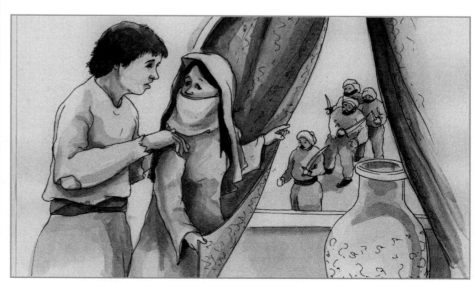

# THE NOK TRIBE —
# Ancient Ironworkers

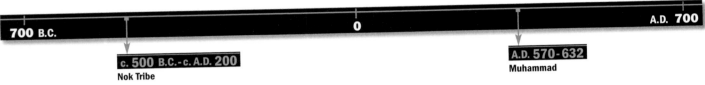

| 700 B.C. | | 0 | | A.D. 700 |
|---|---|---|---|---|

c. 500 B.C.-c. A.D. 200
**Nok Tribe**

A.D. 570-632
**Muhammad**

▲ The Nok tribe lived from about 500 B.C. to about A.D. 200 in present-day Nigeria.

The history of western Africa is the story of the coming together of many different groups of people. These people created wealthy and powerful kingdoms. But long before the rise of the kingdoms of Ghana, Mali, and Songhai, a tribe called the Nok lived in western Africa.

## A Glimpse into History

We do not have very much information about the Nok tribe. We know they lived from about 500 B.C. to about A.D. 200 in the area that is present-day Nigeria. We also know that the Nok were the first West Africans to make iron. Archaeologists have excavated sites in Nigeria and uncovered iron tools dating to about 450 B.C. Based on this evidence, we know the Nok made tools out of iron, which helped them become better farmers and hunters.

Archaeologists also have found evidence of Nok pottery making. The Nok made life-sized figures from baked clay. These figures were probably used for religious purposes. The Nok's pottery sculptures are unusual, especially because of their size.

Most of the Nok tribe lived in the cooler highlands of present-day Nigeria, north of the Niger River. Experts have traced the spread of Nok culture by tracking the path of iron making.

## A Real-life Mystery

Scholars do not know exactly when the Nok civilization ended or which modern-day Africans are their direct descendants. What we are left with is a real-life mystery. We know that the Nok were the first West Africans to make and use iron and that they made life-sized clay figures. Then, they seemed to just fade away. 📖

▶ This is an illustration of Nok pottery from around 250 B.C. It shows a seated leader.

## What Do You Think?

1. How did iron help the Nok become better farmers and hunters?

2. What clues do we have about Nok civilization? What conclusions can we make about the Nok based on these clues?

# KING TENKAMENIN
## and the Kingdom of Ghana

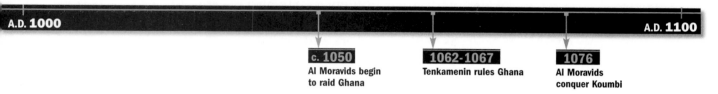

**c. 1050**
Al Moravids begin
to raid Ghana

**1062-1067**
Tenkamenin rules Ghana

**1076**
Al Moravids
conquer Koumbi

The great kingdoms of West Africa developed when camel caravans traveled across the Sahara desert carrying gold north and salt south. Trading centers developed along these routes and became important cities. Those who controlled these cities became wealthy and powerful. Ghana was one of the first great kingdoms to develop in West Africa. The Soninke tribe founded this kingdom. It had its greatest power during the rule of King Tenkamenin.

## King Tenkamenin Comes to Power

Tenkamenin came to power in 1062. From Muslim historian Al-Bakri and other sources, we have learned about the king's role during that time. Tenkamenin, like other West African kings, was the leader of the army, the religious leader, the person who served as judge in settling disagreements, and the one who punished criminals. Tenkamenin was responsible for deciding how the kingdom would be governed and who would help him. Imagine how challenging it would be to play all those different roles. However, King Tenkamenin seems to have played them well.

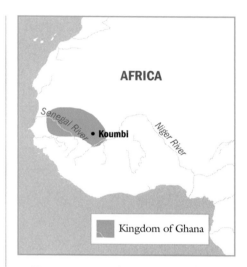

▲ Ghana was one of the first great West African kingdoms. During Tenkamenin's rule, 15,000 people lived in the capital city of Koumbi.

◄ King Tenkamenin settled disagreements and punished criminals. In this scene, you see a person kneeling in front of him asking for a favor.

## It's a FACT

The great kingdoms of West Africa were influenced by three important factors: geography, trade, and religion. Along with the trade caravans came new ideas, including ideas about the religion of Islam.

**sufficient:** as much as is needed; enough

### What Do You Think?

1. What do you think was King Tenkamenin's greatest accomplishment? Why?

2. How important are leaders in helping a society become successful? Explain.

## A Wealthy Man

As king, Tenkamenin lived in a wood and stone palace with sculptures and pictures. He had several wives and many children who lived in nearby houses. Historians think his wives were important advisors with great influence. He also had servants in his household, as well as doctors and artisans close by. He wore the finest clothes and was the wealthiest person in the kingdom. He became wealthy by taxing all the goods that came into or left the kingdom.

## A Powerful and Prosperous Empire

King Tenkamenin ruled from 1062 to 1067. During his rule, the people of Ghana enjoyed prosperity. About 15,000 people lived in the capital city of Koumbi. If they had complaints, they could pay him a visit or stop him while he walked through the city. Musicians and officials came with him on these walks. People also could kneel before him when he held court in the evening. He let local officials rule the provinces. The people in these areas were allowed to follow their own traditions and laws as long as they paid taxes to him.

King Tenkamenin was a strong military leader. He boasted that he could gather 200,000 soldiers whenever he needed them. King Tenkamenin helped to make the kingdom of Ghana a powerful and wealthy empire. At its greatest, the kingdom stretched almost from the Atlantic Ocean in the west to the great bend in the Niger River in the east.

## The Kingdom Declines

After King Tenkamenin's death, other Soninke kings ruled the kingdom of Ghana. In 1076, the Al Moravids conquered Koumbi. They ruled for 11 years, but then the Soninke defeated them. Over time, people from the Susu tribe became the kings of the kingdom of Ghana. The kingdom was never again as powerful or as wealthy as it was during the time of King Tenkamenin. 📖

### A LORD OF THE GOLD

Mahmud al-Kati was a young Soninke man who in the early 1500s became an official in the Songhai kingdom. Later in his life he wrote down some of the oral history of the kingdom of Ghana. He called the king who ruled the old kingdom of Ghana, "one of the lords of the gold." He said that before the king met in the evenings with people of his kingdom, a thousand sticks of wood "were gathered for a fire, so all might be lit and warmed." Then he said the king sat on a chair "of red-gleaming gold" and servants brought "food **sufficient** for 10,000 people."

# Life in WEST AFRICA

Africa is a continent filled with natural resources. The ancient West African kingdoms had an abundance of gold, salt, and iron. They could grow more food than they needed. People in other parts of the world began to see the riches of West Africa.

## A Golden Past

People called "griots" sang songs and told stories about West African history. They told tales about West Africa's gold and prosperous past. These stories attracted world attention. Many goods were available for traders and merchants in West Africa. However, most came for one reason—gold! They didn't know exactly where the gold came from. West African kingdoms kept the exact locations of the source of the gold a secret. The traders and merchants only knew that the gold came from a place south of Timbuktu and Gao.

▲ Modern-day griots still sing songs and tell tales of ancient days.

In the region south of Timbuktu and Gao, there was an enormous supply of gold. West Africans found it in two ways: by panning and digging. The easiest way to get the gold was to pan for it in the rivers. Basically, people took shallow pans or baskets and scooped the sediment from the bottom of the rivers. As they moved the sediment around in the pan or basket, they looked for gold nuggets.

The other way West Africans found gold was to dig for it in the earth. As they dug mines in the earth, they looked for deposits of gold. Some mines were 100-feet deep.

▲ West Africans made gold items in many different shapes. Can you see the bird, the scorpion, and the lizard?

The miners used simple hand tools to dig the mines and then get the gold out. They carried the gold out in containers. Miners today might think these methods were primitive. However, experts estimate that by 1500, West African miners had panned or dug out about 3,500 tons (or seven million pounds) of gold! It is no wonder that West Africa's gold attracted the world's attention.

## Slavery in West Africa

Gold and salt were the most important trade items in West Africa during this time, but many other goods also were traded. Traders and merchants sold horses, cloth, swords, books, honey, ivory, dates, oranges, lemons, grapefruit, baskets, jewelry, and iron tools. They also sold slaves. Slaves were usually prisoners of war or people convicted of crimes.

### What Do You Think?

**1.** What natural resource attracts world attention today? Why?

**2.** How many pounds is 3,500 tons? Think of a way to explain how much gold that is. For example, how many cars would it take to make 3,500 tons? How many students?
Hint: A car weighs 3,000 pounds. 2,000 pounds = 1 ton

West Africans did not consider slaves as property. They were human beings who were not paid for work. During this time, it was possible for slaves to earn their freedom. For example, slaves could buy their freedom through hard work or by inheriting property. Slaves also might become free through marriage. Sometimes, a male slave might marry his master's daughter. Later, when tribes traded slaves to Europeans to work on plantations and in mines in various European colonies, the idea of what it meant to be a slave changed greatly. Slaves began to be thought of as property with no rights and no possibility of becoming free.

## Yams—An Important Food Source in West Africa

Most of the Soninke, about 80%, lived on small family farms. They grew food such as rice, millet, a grain called sorghum, peas, pumpkins, watermelons, various kinds of nuts, and yams. Yams were an especially important food. Yams are native to tropical regions throughout the world and are relatively easy to grow. There are several different kinds of yams. Yams can grow as long as eight feet and can weigh as much as 100 pounds. Yams are very nutritious. They provide humans with vitamins and other healthy nutrients. They also are easy to cook. Soninke women probably boiled them in a pot of water. Because of the tropical climate, women cooked food outside. The family also ate outside.

About 20% of the people of the kingdom of Ghana lived in towns. People who lived in these towns had many choices of food. They got food from the local farmers. They also could buy food from traders who brought salt, honey, dates, oranges, and other citrus fruits. What did they use to pay the traders? Gold, of course!

## Trade in West Africa

To gain power in West Africa, a kingdom had to have a large population, a strong military, and good trade. Ghana had all three of these things, especially good trade. One of the reasons Ghana developed into a powerful trading empire was because of its location. The people of West Africa needed salt, and people in other parts of the world wanted gold. They came to Ghana to trade.

What does "trade" mean? When you trade, you exchange one thing for another thing. We trade every day in the United States. At home, you might trade your dessert to your sister for her help with your homework. Maybe you trade a friend some clothes or books for something that you want. The United States's economy is based mostly on money—we use the country's currency to buy things. But trade is still very important. Of course, some things have changed since the time of the kingdom of Ghana. Today, almost no one would be willing to trade a pound of gold for a pound of salt. This would not be considered a good deal. In America, salt is easy to get, while gold is not.

▲ Yams were an important food in West Africa.

▼ This map shows Ghana's location in relation to the salt mines in the Sahara and the gold mines in West Africa. You can also see where slaves were traded.

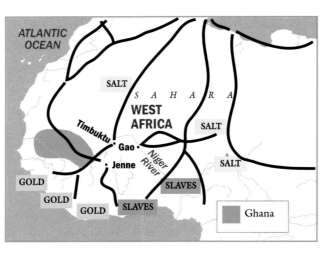

# Building a West African Kingdom

Most people who lived in the kingdom of Ghana were farmers, but some people were specialized workers. Ironworkers were some of the most important specialized workers. They made strong tools and weapons out of iron. They made iron by putting rocks filled with iron ore in a hot clay oven. The oven was so hot that the iron ore in the rocks would become soft and almost melt. Then the ironworkers would take the soft iron and shape it into tools or weapons.

Metal smiths were another group of specialized workers in West Africa. People who work with minerals such as gold or copper are called metal smiths. Metal smiths working in the kingdom of Ghana made beautiful gold jewelry, masks, and other decorations. They also used copper to make jewelry and other objects such as bowls.

Some workers helped build homes and walls in the kingdom of Ghana. They built a wall around the city of Koumbi. The people of Ghana lived in one-story houses with roofs made of straw. The walls were made of wood or mud bricks. To make mud bricks, builders took mud, formed it into the shape of bricks, and left the bricks to dry in the sun.

The people of Ghana also made baskets, clay pots, bows and arrows, and grinding stones to make flour from the grains they grew.

▲ The people of Ghana lived in one-story houses with roofs made of straw.

▲ The Sahara is the world's largest desert. It covers most of northern Africa. It is very dry, with extremely hot and cold temperatures.

## Learning about the Kingdom of Ghana

We have learned a great deal about the history of West Africa from two important men—Ibn Battuta and Al-Bakri. Ibn Battuta was an Arab traveler and historian from North Africa. He traveled to West Africa in the mid-1300s. The kingdom of Ghana was no longer powerful, but he wrote about what people remembered from earlier times. Ibn Battuta traveled across the Sahara desert with a caravan of traders giving us a first-hand account of what it was like to cross the Sahara desert.

Al-Bakri never went to Ghana. He never even went to Africa. He lived in Córdoba, Spain! However, he was interested in the stories travelers told about Ghana. He wrote a detailed description of Koumbi from the accounts travelers shared with him. He wrote about the busy market where people could buy gold, copper, cattle, fruit, ivory, and slaves. He also wrote about the people who worked here. His reports spread the news about the riches of the kingdom of Ghana. Much of the information we have about what life was like in West Africa at this time comes from these two men. 📖

## What Do You Think?

1. Why do you think West African slaves were usually prisoners of war or people convicted of crimes?

2. How did different ideas of what it meant to be a slave affect people's lives?

# AL-BAKRI—
## Views of West Africa

A great deal of what we know about the kingdom of Ghana during the time when it was most powerful comes from Al-Bakri, a man who never set foot in Africa. Al-Bakri was a Muslim historian who lived in Córdoba during the 1000s. If he didn't experience West Africa himself, what were his sources? Al-Bakri became curious about the people who lived south of the Sahara desert. He listened to the stories and accounts of travelers and traders who had been there. He wrote down their stories around 1070. One of the books he wrote about Ghana is called *The Book of Routes and Kingdoms.* You can read below some of the accounts travelers and traders told him about the kingdom of Ghana.

▲ Al-Bakri wrote down what other people said about the kingdom of Ghana.

**pavilion:** a large tent
**plait:** to weave into

## Analyze the Source!

Read the passages and tell in your own words what Al-Bakri was saying.

## Al-Bakri's Impressions

When the king gives an audience to his people, in order to listen to their complaints and set them right, he sits in a **pavilion** around which stand 10 horses with gold-embroidered trappings. Behind the king stand 10 pages holding shields and gold-mounted swords; on his right are the princes of his empire, splendidly clad with gold **plaited** in their hair. ... The door of the pavilion is guarded by dogs of an excellent breed who almost never leave the king's presence, and who wear collars of gold and silver.

❖    ❖    ❖

When a man is accused of denying a debt or having shed blood or some other crime, a headman takes a thin piece of wood, which is sour and bitter to taste, and pours upon it some water which he then gives to the defendant to drink. If the man vomits, his innocence is recognized and he is congratulated. If he does not vomit and the drink remains in his stomach, the accusation is accepted as justified.

# ABU HAMID AL-ANDALUSI —
# Views of West Africa

Spanish traveler Abu Hamid al-Andalusi visited West Africa when the kingdom of Ghana was wealthy and powerful. When he returned home, he had tales to tell about the things he saw. You can read below his impressions of the trade for gold and salt in the kingdom of Ghana.

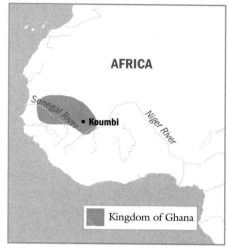

▲ Abu Hamid al-Andalusi lived in Spain, but traveled to West Africa. He wrote about the kingdom of Ghana.

## Abu Hamid Al-Andalusi's Impressions

In the sands of that country is gold, treasure inexpressible. Merchants trade with salt for it, taking the salt on camels from the salt mines. They start from a town called Sidjilmasa ... and travel in the desert as it were upon the sea, having guides to pilot them by the stars or rocks. ... They take provisions for six months, and when they reach Ghana they weigh their salt and sell it against a certain unit of weight of gold ... according to the market and the supply.

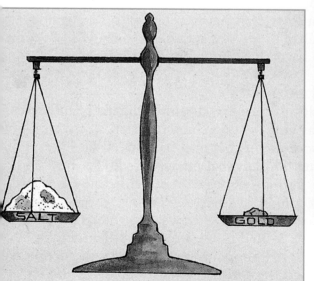

◀ Ghana had lots of gold, but the people needed salt. As a result, they traded a pound of gold for a pound of salt.

## Analyze the Source!

1. Read the passage and tell in your own words what Abu Hamid al-Andalusi was saying.

2. Abu Hamid al-Andalusi suggests that the desert is like a sea. What does he mean by that? How can a desert be like a sea?

3. Explain how traders arrive at the price of gold and salt. Abu Hamid al-Andalusi suggests it is "according to the market and the supply." What does this mean?

# SUNDIATA — An Epic Hero of Mali

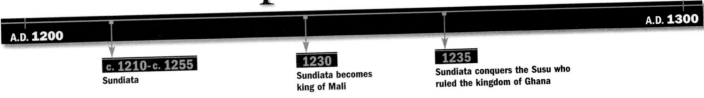

A.D. **1200**

A.D. **1300**

**c. 1210-c. 1255**
Sundiata

**1230**
Sundiata becomes
king of Mali

**1235**
Sundiata conquers the Susu who
ruled the kingdom of Ghana

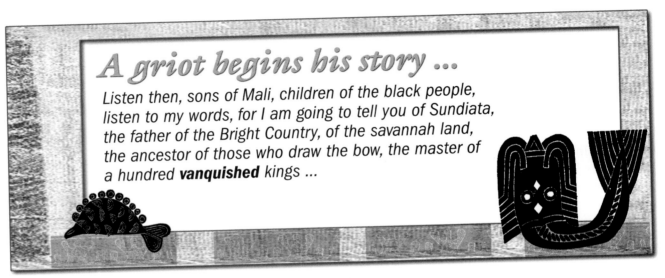

## A griot begins his story ...

*Listen then, sons of Mali, children of the black people,*
*listen to my words, for I am going to tell you of Sundiata,*
*the father of the Bright Country, of the savannah land,*
*the ancestor of those who draw the bow, the master of*
*a hundred vanquished kings ...*

**WEST AFRICA**

Senegal River

Niger River

Kingdom of Mali

▲ **Sundiata became king of Mali in 1230.**
**By 1300, the kingdom of Mali covered the**
**shaded area shown above.**

**vanquished:** conquered or
defeated
**will:** to control one's own action

For hundreds of years, West African griots have told the story of Sundiata. The details vary, but the important facts of his story are always the same. As the kingdom of Ghana broke apart, the Susu tribe challenged the other tribes for control of the gold and salt mines. According to the stories, the Susu's leader became the king of Ghana. He was said to have made the people pay high taxes and to have killed his enemies without mercy.

## The Early Life of Sundiata

Sundiata was the twelfth son of the king of Kangaba. Unlike his brothers, Sundiata was not a strong child. In fact, as a young boy he could not walk—something that may have saved his life. When the Susu conquered Kangaba, many were killed, but Sundiata was spared. Perhaps he was not killed because he was not seen as a threat to the Susu king. According to the griots' story, Sundiata saw how sad his mother was that he could not walk. He is said to have **willed** himself to walk when he was around 10 years old. Later, Sundiata was sent away by members of his family who wanted the throne of Kangaba for themselves. While he was away, he became known for his hunting skills and his ability to ride horses.

# The Rise of the Mandinke

As the Mandinke tribe expanded their territory, they became a threat to the Susu who ruled the kingdom of Ghana. The Mandinke needed a leader to help them fight the Susu. The person they turned to was Sundiata. In 1230, the leaders of the Mandinke proclaimed Sundiata king of Mali. Sundiata united the people of Mali and prepared for a battle against the Susu. The important battle between Mali and the Susu army took place in 1235 on the plains of Kirina. Sundiata won this battle of Kirina for the Mandinke. He ruled the kingdom of Mali for the next 25 years.

## Sundiata and the Kingdom of Mali

Over time, Sundiata increased the size of his kingdom and ruled over a vast area that included gold and salt mines. It also included the great cities of Timbuktu and Gao. The capital of his kingdom was the city of Niani, the place where he was born. He appointed officials to help him govern the provinces. Sundiata wanted to make certain that there was adequate food for everyone in his kingdom. He organized the people to clear land for farming. They planted crops such as onions, yams, rice, beans, and cotton.

## A Great Leader

Under Sundiata's leadership, Mali became one of the richest kingdoms in West Africa. How did he accomplish this? Part of the answer is that Sundiata was a great leader. He was a man who saw what needed to be done and made sure important things were done. Another part of the answer is that he converted to Islam. Some historians disagree on why he converted to Islam. Did he really believe in Islam? Or, did he convert to Islam because he wanted to expand the trade with his northern, Muslim neighbors? Whatever the answer, Sundiata was responsible for starting one of the greatest empires in West African history. His name and legend live on in the songs of the griots and in the written histories of West Africa. 📖

▲ Sundiata established a new capital for Mali in Niani on the Niger River. The Niger River was an easy way to transport gold and other trade items. This is what the Niger River looks like today.

## What Do You Think?

Sundiata is known as a great leader. What made him a great leader? What obstacles did Sundiata overcome?

# IBN BATTUTA — World Traveler

If you took a poll to find out who Americans think is the greatest traveler of the past, chances are most will say Marco Polo. However, based on the length of travel and the variety of places he visited, many historians might name Ibn Battuta. Accounts of his journeys vary, but he traveled for about 25 to 30 years. He visited what we would recognize as about 44 modern-day countries. When his journeys were finished, he told the story of his travels to a young Muslim scholar. Ibn Battuta's story became a book called *My Travels.*

## Who Was Ibn Battuta?

Ibn Battuta was born in 1304 in Tangier, Morocco. As a young man he studied the law. In 1325, when he was about 20 years old, he decided to make the hajj, the holy pilgrimage required of Muslims. He traveled through North Africa, Egypt, Palestine, and Syria before reaching Mecca. Rather than return directly home, in 1326, he decided to visit the area that is present-day Iraq and Iran. Some scholars believe that it was during this time that he decided to visit all of the lands ruled by Muslims.

## Traveling the Muslim World

Ibn Battuta crossed the Sahara desert in 1352. He traveled around the kingdom of Mali in West Africa for about a year. He described Taghaza, a place where salt was mined, as "an unattractive village, with the curious feature that its houses and mosques are built of blocks of salt, roofed with camel skins." He said, "There are no trees there, nothing but sand. In the sand is a salt mine; they dig for the salt and find it in thick slabs, lying one on top of the others … ." Much of the information we have about West Africa during this time comes from his accounts. According to some historians, Ibn Battuta's journeys covered more than 75,000 miles. He traveled by camel, by foot, and by ship. During his travels, he had many jobs and many adventures. For example, while in Egypt he worked as a judge for the sultan. He wrote about the customs of the ordinary citizens and described activities such as harvesting coconuts. At times he became very rich, but he ended up losing all of his money.

### It's a FACT

Ibn Battuta's story gives us a good idea of how far Islam spread at a particular point in time.

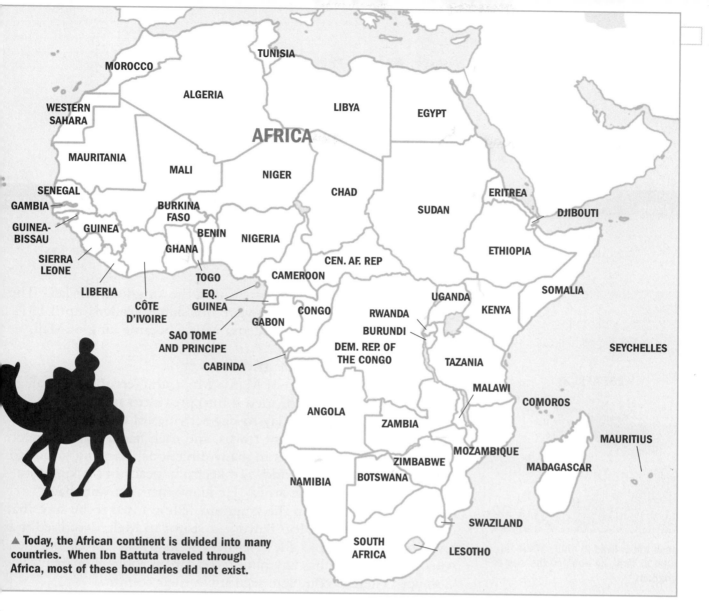

AFRICA

MOROCCO
TUNISIA
ALGERIA
WESTERN SAHARA
LIBYA
EGYPT
MAURITANIA
MALI
NIGER
CHAD
SUDAN
ERITREA
DJIBOUTI
SENEGAL
GAMBIA
GUINEA-BISSAU
GUINEA
BURKINA FASO
BENIN
NIGERIA
GHANA
TOGO
SIERRA LEONE
LIBERIA
CÔTE D'IVOIRE
EQ. GUINEA
CAMEROON
CEN. AF. REP
ETHIOPIA
SOMALIA
CONGO
GABON
SAO TOME AND PRINCIPE
CABINDA
DEM. REP. OF THE CONGO
RWANDA
BURUNDI
UGANDA
KENYA
TAZANIA
SEYCHELLES
MALAWI
COMOROS
ANGOLA
ZAMBIA
MOZAMBIQUE
MAURITIUS
MADAGASCAR
NAMIBIA
BOTSWANA
ZIMBABWE
SWAZILAND
SOUTH AFRICA
LESOTHO

▲ Today, the African continent is divided into many countries. When Ibn Battuta traveled through Africa, most of these boundaries did not exist.

## Ibn Battuta Returns Home

When Ibn Battuta finally returned home in 1355, he was about 50 years old. His parents had died. He had seen all of the world under Muslim rule. Many of the stories he told seemed unbelievable to his fellow citizens. However, toward the end of his life, the sultan of Morocco invited him to describe his journeys to a young scholar. This is the record we have of his travels. 📖

### What Do You Think?

1. Why do so few Americans know about Ibn Battuta?

2. Compare Ibn Battuta's description of the houses and mosques in Taghaza with the buildings in the place where you live. How are they similar? How are they different?

3. How can Ibn Battuta's story help historians know about the spread of Islam?

# MANSA MUSA — The Golden Age of Mali

**c. 1255**
Sundiata dies

**1312**
Mansa Musa becomes
king of Mali

**1324**
Mansa Musa begins his
pilgrimage to Mecca

**1337**
Mansa Musa dies

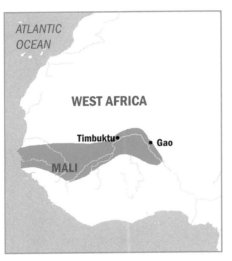

▲ Mansa Musa lived in Mali. While he was ruler of Mali, he doubled the size of the kingdom.

Sundiata is remembered for creating the kingdom of Mali. The rulers who came after him were not skillful leaders, until 1312 when Sundiata's grandson, Mansa Musa, became king of Mali.

## Mali Doubles in Size and Power

During the 25-year reign of Mansa Musa, the territory of Mali doubled. Mansa Musa divided it into provinces and appointed a governor to manage the day-to-day activities of each area. Each province also had important towns, and each had a chief. Camel caravans crossed the desert in many directions, bringing goods to Mali from all over the world. To keep the peace in his kingdom, Mansa Musa had a large army. He knew that past wars had disrupted the trading in the kingdom. He wanted to be sure that didn't happen again. Ibn Battuta, a visitor to Mali, described it as a very safe place. He said, "Neither the man who travels nor he who stays at home has anything to fear from robbers or men of violence. There is complete security in their country."

## Mansa Musa—A Devout Muslim

Mansa Musa was a devout Muslim. Like all Muslims who are financially and physically able, he planned a pilgrimage, or hajj, to Mecca, the holy city of Islam. He spent months planning for his trip. In 1324, he began his pilgrimage.

## The Journey to Mecca

According to accounts of Mansa Musa's journey, he was accompanied on this pilgrimage by as many as 60,000 people. Who were all these people? About 500 of them were slaves, each of whom carried a bar of gold weighing about four pounds. Some were friends and relatives, but he also took servants, teachers, soldiers, cooks, camel herders, blacksmiths, and other people he would need. Also on the trip were lots of animals— camels, horses, and cattle. One account says 80 camels were loaded with gold dust.

▲ Mansa Musa often walked among his subjects. People gathered to see his fine clothes and many servants. As he passed by, they listened to music played on instruments such as the ones shown above.

## Stopping in Egypt

The route Mansa Musa followed took him across the Sahara desert and into Cairo, Egypt. When he arrived, he was supposed to meet with the sultan. However, Mansa Musa refused. Mansa Musa claimed that he did not want to confuse a religious journey with any type of business trip. What Mansa Musa really did not want to do was kiss the ring of the sultan, which was the tradition. Eventually, the sultan and Mansa Musa worked out a compromise. The sultan came to visit Mansa Musa, and in turn Mansa Musa agreed to bow before the sultan.

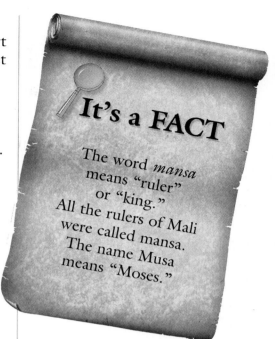

## MANSA MUSA'S CONTRIBUTIONS TO THE KINGDOM OF MALI

**Created a powerful, well-organized empire**

**Brought peace and prosperity**

**Spread Mali's fame throughout the world**

## Putting Mali on the Map

Mansa Musa was extremely generous with his wealth. He gave large sums of gold to the people he met on this pilgrimage. Soon, news of his wealth reached Europe. In 1375, Abraham Cresques, a Jewish mapmaker living in Spain, drew a map showing West Africa. Right in the middle of this map Mansa Musa is pictured holding a gold ball. Cresques had never met Mansa Musa or traveled to Mali. He probably based his map and picture of Mansa Musa on information from North African traders.

## Hostages from Songhai

On his return home, the generals that Mansa Musa had left in charge of his kingdom gave him a welcome-home gift. During his absence, they had captured the city of Gao in the Songhai kingdom. To be certain that the city would remain loyal to him, Mansa Musa stopped there and took two Songhai princes with him as hostages.

## Succession and the Fall of the Empire

Mansa Musa always dreamed of seeing his son become king and of returning to Mecca. He never accomplished either of these goals. Mansa Musa died in 1337. Following his death, various tribes raided the kingdom of Mali. Many of its schools, mosques, and marketplaces were destroyed. Just as had happened to Ghana, Mali began to break apart. A new kingdom, the kingdom of Songhai, began to gain more power.

**What Do You Think?**

**1.** The pilgrimage of Mansa Musa to Mecca brought great attention to Mali's wealth. In what ways was this attention positive? In what ways was it negative?

**2.** How would taking Songhai princes as hostages ensure that Gao would remain loyal to Mansa Musa and Mali?

# The Salt Mines

Many goods were traded in the kingdom of Ghana, but the most important were gold and salt. Many Americans today probably don't think of salt as a valuable or scarce resource, but it was very valuable and scarce in West Africa.

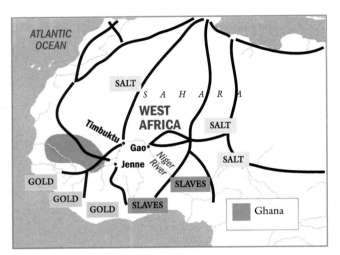

The people in southwestern Africa had lots of gold, but no salt. The salt mines were north of the kingdom of Ghana in the Sahara desert. Ibn Battuta, a scholar from North Africa, crossed the Sahara desert in 1352. He wrote his impressions of Taghaza, one of the places where salt was mined. You can read his impressions below. You also can read below the memories of Alioune, a prisoner who was forced to work in the salt mines. He told his story of working at a salt mine in the Sahara to a modern visitor to West Africa.

▲ This map shows Ghana's location in relation to the salt mines in the Sahara and the gold mines in West Africa. You also can see where slaves were traded.

**incarceration:** imprisonment
**monotonous:** having no variety
**oppressive:** causing discomfort
**transfixed:** motionless

## Analyze the Source!

1. Read the passages and tell in your own words what they mean.

2. What does each passage tell you about salt mining?

3. Which account is more powerful? Why?

## Ibn Battuta's Impressions of Taghaza

Taghaza is an unattractive village, with the curious feature that its houses and mosques are built of blocks of salt, roofed with camel skins. There are no trees there, nothing but sand. In the sand is a salt mine; they dig for the salt and find it in thick slabs, lying one on top of the other, as though they had been tool-squared and laid under the surface of the earth.

## A Modern Worker in a Saharan Salt Mine

Peering through a cloud of smoke, he told us in haunted tones of his **incarceration** in a Saharan salt mine. The brutal extremes of temperatures, the backbreaking labor, the salt that was ever-present all came into existence as he recounted his years at Taoudenni [north of Timbuktu]. Salt is mined, he informed us, and comes out as large tombstone-like slabs that are piled up and kept until the [camel] caravan arrives. Twice a year, the caravan arrives in Taoudenni; it was the only break in the spirit-deadening, **monotonous** work. ... As Alioune told his story, we sat **transfixed**. ... We could feel the **oppressive** heat of the mines, taste the grit of the Saharan sand on our tongues, and feel the sting of salt as it burned every cut and made eyes water.

# SUNNI ALI —
# Warrior and King

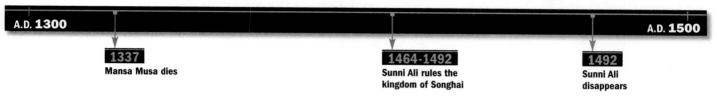

**1337**
Mansa Musa dies

**1464-1492**
Sunni Ali rules the
kingdom of Songhai

**1492**
Sunni Ali
disappears

When Mansa Musa visited the city of Gao, he brought home two princes as hostages. These princes were members of the Songhai people. They became respected members of Mansa Musa's royal family, but secretly they planned to escape back to their own people. Finally, after many years, their escape plan was ready and they fled to Gao. Mansa Musa's soldiers chased the princes all the way to Gao, but they didn't catch them. The princes made it inside of the city walls. Later, a council of elders appointed one of the princes the new king and declared Gao independent from Mali. Mali was never able to recapture the city. Over the next hundred years, Mali became less powerful. It no longer controlled the gold and salt trade through Gao. Over time, Songhai became more powerful. The Songhai king who did the most to establish the kingdom was Sunni Ali.

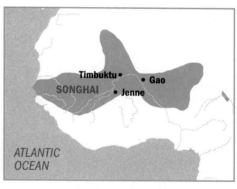

▲ Sunni Ali expanded the kingdom of Songhai (shaded) until 1492.

## Sunni Ali Comes to Power

Sunni Ali came to power in 1464. Ali was a great horseman and fearless warrior. His royal court was wherever he was at the moment. And most of the time, he was on a battlefield with his soldiers. Sunni Ali's army was different from most armies at the time. His army was made up of professional soldiers. Some of his soldiers fought on the ground and others were on horseback. His army could move quickly and always was prepared to fight.

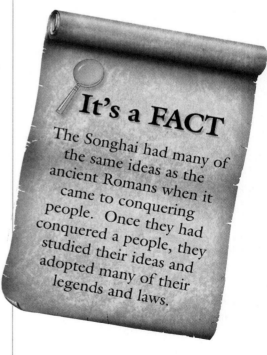

## It's a FACT

The Songhai had many of the same ideas as the ancient Romans when it came to conquering people. Once they had conquered a people, they studied their ideas and adopted many of their legends and laws.

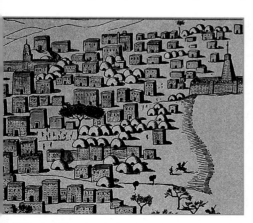

▲ This drawing shows how Timbuktu looked many years after Sunni Ali conquered it.

## Expanding the Empire—Timbuktu

After about four years as king, Sunni Ali had an opportunity to capture Timbuktu. He knew that if he captured this city, he would greatly expand the size and wealth of his kingdom. At the time, another tribe, the Tuareg, had captured Timbuktu from Mali.

The people of Timbuktu were being forced to pay taxes twice—once to the governor and a second time to the Tuareg tribe. As much as the people of Timbuktu hated Ali and the Songhai, they hated paying double taxes even more. When the current rulers saw Ali's army heading towards Timbuktu, they fled in terror. When Ali captured the city, he showed no mercy. He killed many of the Muslim leaders and everyone who had traded with the Tuareg.

## The Siege of Jenne

Sunni Ali captured another great city, Jenne. This city was located on the Niger River. It was equal to Timbuktu in wealth and was an important city on the trade routes. Jenne was built so that the river served as a natural defense. When the water level of the Niger River was high, the city became an island. When the river was low, the area around the city was swampy and full of disease-carrying mosquitoes. Ali decided to surround the city with his army and wait until the people ran out of food. He didn't think it would take too long. But he was wrong. The years passed, and finally after seven years, seven months, and seven days, the city of Jenne surrendered. The citizens feared for their lives, but Sunni Ali showed them mercy. He admired the courage he saw in the people of Jenne during the siege.

▲ Sunni Ali's victories in battle made Songhai a dominant power in West Africa.

## Conquests Continue until His Death

After Sunni Ali captured these two great cities, he decided to continue his conquests. His army raided in all directions. They won many victories. Sunni Ali continued to expand the kingdom of Songhai until 1492. During a march along the Niger River, Sunni Ali disappeared and was never seen again. People think he was thrown from his horse while crossing the river and drowned. The griots told stories of his courage and leadership. Muslim writers described him as "ruthless with his opponents, who suffered death or exile at his hands."

## Sunni Ali's Legacy

Sunni Ali united the Songhai people and established Songhai's dominance in the savannah region of the Niger River basin. However, he was not a strong supporter of Islam, and many Songhai people were Muslims. After his death, the people of Songhai wanted a ruler who would respect Islam. What they got was his son. Sunni Ali's son was not a strong supporter of Islam either. It was not long before the forces of rebellion began to gather again. ▢

### What Do You Think?

1. Why do you think the Songhai griots and the Muslim writers had different views of Sunni Ali?

2. How did geography help the city of Jenne?

3. Why do you think Sunni Ali wanted to conquer cities?

# ASKIA MUHAMMAD —
# The Askia Dynasty

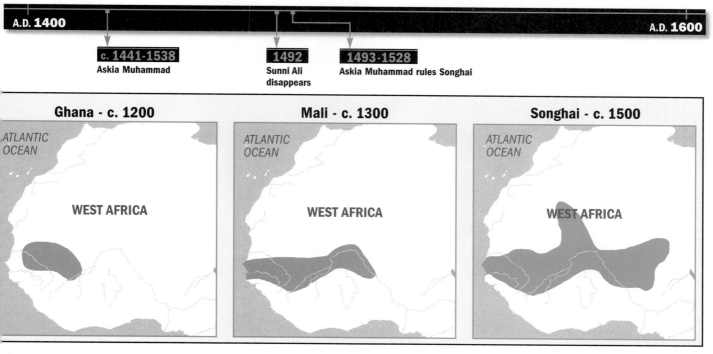

A.D. **1400**                                                                                    A.D. **1600**

**c. 1441-1538**
**Askia Muhammad**

**1492**
**Sunni Ali
disappears**

**1493-1528**
**Askia Muhammad rules Songhai**

**Ghana - c. 1200**

ATLANTIC
OCEAN

WEST AFRICA

**Mali - c. 1300**

ATLANTIC
OCEAN

WEST AFRICA

**Songhai - c. 1500**

ATLANTIC
OCEAN

WEST AFRICA

Most Americans remember 1492 as the year Christopher Columbus sailed the ocean blue. But other events occurred that year that brought important changes on another continent. In West Africa, Sunni Ali disappeared and was never seen again, leaving the people of Songhai without a leader. Sunni Ali's son was unacceptable to many of them. They wanted a leader who was a devout Muslim. They thought Askia Muhammad was a better choice. Askia Muhammad was not only a rising star in the army, but he was a devout Muslim as well. Many people thought he would be the best person to lead the kingdom. In 1493, he led a small army into battle against Sunni Ali's son. After much fighting, Askia Muhammad's army won, and he became king.

## Tolerance and Faith

One of the first things Askia Muhammad did was to invite all of the Muslims back to the cities of Gao, Timbuktu, and Jenne. Many of them had fled these cities when Sunni Ali was king. Several years later, Askia Muhammad went on a pilgrimage to Mecca. His hajj was not as spectacular as Mansa Musa's, but it was impressive. He took 300,000 pieces of gold with him. Askia Muhammad's pilgrimage lasted about two years. During that time, he studied and talked to many Muslim scholars.

▲ You can see the development of the three great West African kingdoms—Ghana c. 1200, Mali c. 1300, and Songhai c. 1500.

# It's a FACT

• In the Songhai army, the rank of general was called "askia."

• Askia Muhammad is considered the greatest Songhai king. His empire was the largest and most well organized of any West African kingdom.

Chapter 6: Mali and Songhai  **123**

He increased the size of the military.

He created a system of laws.

He encouraged new ideas about medicine, math, and science.

**Askia Muhammad**

He invited scholars to Songhai.

When Askia Muhammad returned to Gao, his faith was even stronger, and he was determined to spread the Islamic religion. He began a series of wars against the neighboring tribes. His army conquered many cities and tried to convert people to Islam. However, he did not force anyone to convert to Islam. He realized that many of his subjects continued to practice their traditional religions.

## The Songhai Kingdom under Askia Muhammad

Askia Muhammad expanded the kingdom of Songhai until it was larger than Ghana or Mali had ever been. To rule such a large area, he appointed governors to rule the provinces. He divided the government into different branches with a person in charge of areas such as navigation and fishing, and the army and the navy. He came up with a system of taxation. Although he was a devout Muslim, he tolerated other religious views. He also reestablished Timbuktu and Gao as centers of learning. He invited highly respected scholars to teach. Students came from all over the region to study there.

## A Son's Revolt

In 1528, after 35 years of rule, Askia Muhammad's son led a revolt and overthrew him. Askia Muhammad was in his mid-80s. His son was not a successful ruler and was assassinated in 1531. Other sons tried to rule, but all were unsuccessful. Finally, in 1538, when he was 97 years old, Askia died. The kingdom of Songhai declined, never again to regain the glory and golden age it had enjoyed under Askia Muhammad.

### What Do You Think?

**1.** Why do you think Askia Muhammad tolerated religious views other than Islam? Give examples to show that Askia Muhammad was a devout Muslim.

**2.** What does it mean that Askia Muhammad was "a rising star" in the army?

# LEO AFRICANUS —
# Views of West Africa

During the time that Askia Muhammad ruled the kingdom of Songhai, Hassan Ibn Muhammad, a Muslim scholar from Spain, visited West Africa. While he was returning home, however, Christian pirates in the Mediterranean attacked his ship. He was captured and taken to see Pope Leo X, the leader of the Roman Catholic Church. Pope Leo was excited to hear the stories Hassan Ibn Muhammad told about his experiences in Africa. The pope gave him a new name—Leo Africanus—and enough money so that he could spend his time writing about his African experiences. His book, *The History and Description of Africa*, provides a written account of these experiences.

SPAIN

WEST AFRICA
Timbuktu
• Gao

▲ Leo Africanus was born in Spain in the late 1400s and died in North Africa in the mid-1500s.

## Leo Africanus's Impressions of the City of Gao

Gao is a very large city ... without surrounding walls. ... Most of its houses are ugly; however, a few, in which live the king and his court, have a very fine aspect. Its inhabitants are rich merchants who travel constantly about the region with their wares. A great many Blacks come to the city bringing quantities of gold with which to purchase goods imported from the Berber country and from Europe, but they never find enough goods ... and always take half or two-thirds of it home.

The city is well-policed in comparison to Timbuktu. Bread and meat exist in great abundance, but one can find neither wine nor fruit. ... There is a place where they sell countless ... slaves on market days. A fifteen-year-old girl is worth about six ducats and a young man nearly as much; little children and aged slaves are worth about half that sum.

### Analyze the Source!

1. Read the passage and tell in your own words what Leo Africanus was saying.

2. Do you think Leo Africanus had a favorable or unfavorable view of Gao? Explain.

3. Why do you think "neither wine nor fruit" could be found in Gao?

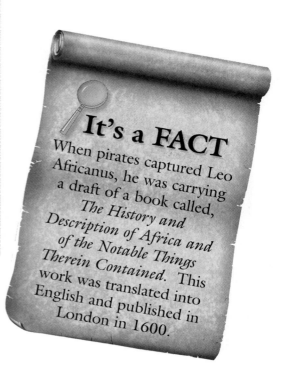

### It's a FACT
When pirates captured Leo Africanus, he was carrying a draft of a book called, *The History and Description of Africa and of the Notable Things Therein Contained*. This work was translated into English and published in London in 1600.

# How Do We Know ABOUT THE MAYA?

**c. 250-799**
Maya kingdoms flourish

**1500s**
Maya priests write *The Books of Chilam Balam*; descendants of the Maya write the *Popol Vuh*

**1500s**
Bishop Diego de Landa writes descriptions of the Maya

▲ The Maya civilization developed in an area (shaded) that is now part of five countries—Belize, El Salvador, Guatemala, Honduras, and Mexico. Sometimes this area is called "Maya country."

▲ Scholars deciphered the writing on this stela and know it was carved in 782.

Historians and archaeologists rely on three major sources of information to tell about the history of the Maya: writings from the Maya and Spaniards, Maya art, and Maya who live today.

## Written Sources

Historians and archaeologists look at writings left by the Maya who lived during the period. Maya scribes probably wrote thousands of books about history, science, trade, and family life, but only four books have survived. Historians also look at inscriptions on monuments to learn about the ancient Maya.

Another written source of information comes from both Maya and Spanish accounts of Maya life during the time when the Spanish arrived in the area. Maya priests wrote *The Books of Chilam Balam* in the 1500s about Maya life before the Spanish conquest. During this same time, the Quiche people of the Guatemalan highlands, descendants of the Maya, wrote the *Popol Vuh*. This 9,000-line poem is considered one of the finest examples of American Indian literature. The original text was lost in the 1800s, but copies have survived. In addition, a Spanish priest, Bishop Diego de Landa, also wrote descriptions of the Maya during the 1500s.

## Maya Art

Another source of information about Maya life and culture is the art they left behind. Sculptures, drawings, and paintings show Maya social classes, lifestyle, and culture. They provide details of Maya life, including information about clothing, food, animals, and rituals.

## Living Sources

A third source of information comes from the more than six million living Maya who follow the traditions of their ancestors. Historians and anthropologists study their family life, political organization, and religion for clues to the ancient Maya.

Much of the Maya's writing, art, and architecture was destroyed by weather and by the Spanish. This has made it difficult to have a complete picture of Maya history. Perhaps as experts gather more information, we will learn more about the ancient Maya. ▢

# GROWING UP:
# Childhood in Maya Society

What was it like to grow up as a Maya child during this golden age? Did children play games? How were they educated? These are difficult questions to answer. For one thing, it is impossible to describe a "typical" Maya childhood because the experience was different for boys and girls as well as for children belonging to different social classes, such as elites, commoners, and slaves. It is more accurate to think in terms of Maya *childhoods*. In addition, these questions are difficult to answer because we are missing information, and much of the information we do have is indirect—it doesn't come directly from the Maya. Still, there is a lot we do know about children of the ancient Maya.

## Maya Family Members

Historians believe the nuclear family—a mother, father, and their children—was the basic social unit of Maya society. Most men had only one wife. However, elite men sometimes had several wives.

## Beautiful Maya Babies

When a child—either a boy or girl—was born into an elite family, the mother put a board at the back of the baby's head and one against the baby's forehead. The boards were left in place for several days. This flattened and lengthened the child's head for life.

### How did the Maya view children?

From all the evidence historians have found, it seems as if Maya parents very much wanted children and welcomed them into the Maya family. One historian said, "The Maya of today love their children deeply and usually treat them very well. The same was probably true in ancient times. Children were greatly desired, and women even 'asked them of the idols with gifts and prayers.'"

▲ These are Maya children who live in Guatemala.

The Maya considered a long, flat head a sign of beauty. Evidence of this practice is found on almost every Maya picture of the human head. Historians believe all elites followed this practice.

The Maya also thought that crossed eyes were another sign of beauty. Mothers tried to achieve this effect in their children, especially boys. They placed a small ball of a sticky gum-like material in the hair that hung in the center of the child's forehead. The child would focus on this ball and end up having crossed eyes. In addition, the young child's ears, nose, and lips were pierced so that decorations could be placed there.

## Special Celebrations for Maya Children

Today, when a child is born, the family may send out announcements or have a party or a religious ceremony to celebrate the birth. The ancient Maya celebrated important events in their children's lives, too. Based on evidence from present-day Maya, historians believe that during ancient times the Maya had a ceremony for baby girls when they reached three months of age and were first carried on their mother's hip. They tied a string with a red shell on it around the baby girl's waist. The girl wore this until she reached about age 12. The Maya held a similar ceremony for baby boys when they reached four months of age. In that ceremony, a small white bead was placed in the

# Who took care of the children?

boy's hair. This bead would remain in place until the boy was about 12.

## Educating Maya Girls

There is not much written information about the education of Maya children during ancient times, but the roles of women and men in Maya society give good clues to how the children were educated. Generally, when a Maya girl reached adulthood, she was expected to become a wife and mother and to cook, clean, spin, and weave. Women also took care of chickens and other animals, sold extra cloth at the market, and traded for items the family needed at the market. Sometimes, women also helped in the fields.

Girls learned skills and responsibilities from their mothers. Part of a Maya girl's training involved religious ceremonies. Girls had to learn songs and dances so that they could participate in the ceremonies. Elite girls might have received more advanced training in weaving and embroidery and perhaps in singing and dancing. A very few

Mothers—both elite and commoner—took care of their very young children (up to the age of three or four). A Spanish priest who was in Maya country in the 1500s wrote, "They brought them up naked, except that at the age of four or five they gave them a cloak for sleeping, and some little strips to conceal their nakedness." He said that children were breastfed until they were three or four years old. He described the Maya childhood as "good and frolicsome, so that they never stopped going about with bows and arrows and playing with one another." When a boy reached the age of about five, he began to spend more time with his father. This prepared him for his role as an adult male in Maya society. A girl continued to stay close to her mother in preparation for her life as an adult female in Maya society.

elite girls went on to become rulers, called *ahaus*. For example, Lady Kanal-Ikal, the daughter of a king and member of the elite class, became ahau of Palenque on December 23, A.D. 583 and ruled Palenque for 20 years. Most ahaus, however, were male.

## Educating Maya Boys

Boys learned the duties they would be responsible for by helping their fathers. Most men had to work in the maize fields. Boys learned how to perform this role by helping their fathers in the fields. Maya boys also were expected to be warriors. The Maya kingdoms stood together against foreign enemies, but they also went to war against one another. When kingdoms fought, ahaus led the warriors in battle.

Maya boys probably learned the military skills they needed as adults from their fathers. Some elite boys also learned to become priests. This role required advanced training and education in astronomy and mathematics. Priests-in-training had to observe the movement of the stars and planets, keep track of the calendars, make predictions about the future, and conduct religious rituals. The rituals included music, dancing, and offering their blood to the gods.

Numbers were important for Maya traders and merchants which meant that the sons of traders and merchants were probably taught mathematics. These boys also would need to understand quality, value, and pricing for goods. If they were going to make good deals, they needed to know how much to trade for gold and silver, jade, obsidian, jaguar skins, cacao beans, salt, honey, and feathers. Traders carried these goods on their backs or loaded them into canoes and traveled through jungles and swamps along the region's many rivers. Boys also needed physical strength as well as geographical knowledge.

## Maya Educational System

In agricultural societies, children were taught the things they would need to know as adults in their society. The people who taught them these things were usually the close adults in their life, such as their parents. Maya children needed to know how to make a living and how to be a part of Maya life. Children learned the skills they would need as workers through a kind of apprentice system. The son of a carpenter learned woodworking skills. The son of a priest learned religious rituals. An elite daughter married an elite man and raised elite children. Children learned how to become adults through the model of adults in their community.

## Becoming an Adult

A date was chosen each year to hold a ceremony for all the boys and girls who were about 12 years of age. A priest conducted the ceremony where the children were gathered together and pieces of white cloth were put on their heads. They were asked if they had committed any sins. Then everyone was seated, prayers were said, and each child was rubbed with water. The children then gave gifts of feathers and cacao beans to the priest and his helpers. During the ceremony, the priest cut the white bead from each boy's hair. The boys got to smoke from the priest's special pipe. The mothers of all the children served food and made offerings to the gods. The girls then went with their mothers who removed the red shell tied around their waists. This formally marked the girl's passage from girlhood to womanhood. At this point, she was considered of marriageable age. Following these rituals, the parents of both the boys and girls (now "men" and women") gave more gifts, and the ceremony ended with eating and drinking well into the night. Through this ritual, Maya boys and girls were recognized as Maya men and women.📖

◀ As part of a religious ceremony, the woman in the picture is pulling a rope through her tongue. The Maya believed that blood would satisfy the gods and bring prosperity.

# MAYA Social Classes —
# Who's Who in Maya Country?

All the information we have suggests there were two major classes in Maya society—a small class of elites and a large class of commoners. There also were slaves.

## How Did Social Classes Form?

Historians think that in their early history some Maya became known for their skills as leaders or warriors. Over time, this distinction became hereditary. These elites married other elites. Their power and wealth increasingly set them apart from other people in the society—the commoners.

Slaves were another group of people in Maya society. The Maya created art showing them. Slaves were at the bottom of Maya society. People could be born slaves. They could become slaves as a punishment for stealing. Captured prisoners of war also could become slaves. Important prisoners of war and child slaves often were used as human sacrifices in Maya religious ceremonies. But, it also was possible for slaves to buy their freedom.

## How Could You Tell Classes Apart?

Historians believe the nuclear family—a mother, father, and their children—was the basic social unit of Maya society.

Most men had only one wife. However, elite men sometimes had several wives. Elite families had more and better food and resources than commoners did. You could tell elites from commoners by looking at their clothes as well as the location and size of their homes.

## Where Did People Live?

During the height of the Maya civilization, Maya cities were important political and religious centers that had control over the people living in surrounding villages. From written accounts in the 1500s, we know that elites lived in the cities. The most important elites, for example, the ahau and his or her family, lived in palaces in the heart of the city. In contrast, common people lived in one-room houses with

◄ Here you can see what commoners might have looked like in Maya society.

thatched roofs outside the city. Commoners probably only went to the city for religious ceremonies. Bishop Diego de Landa, an important Spanish priest in the 1500s, described Maya cities this way: "The Maya lived together in towns in a very civilized fashion ... in the middle of the town were their temples with beautiful plazas, and all around the temples stood the houses of the lords and priests, and then the most important people. Then came the houses of the richest ... and at the outskirts of the town were the houses of the lower class." 📖

▲ The most important elites in Maya society lived in the middle of the city where there were beautiful temples and plazas.

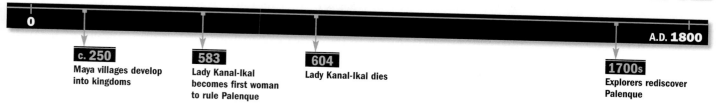

# PALENQUE and LADY KANAL-IKAL

```
0                                                              A.D. 1800

c. 250              583              604                      1700s
Maya villages      Lady Kanal-Ikal   Lady Kanal-Ikal dies    Explorers rediscover
develop            becomes first                             Palenque
into kingdoms      woman to rule
                   Palenque
```

The Maya city of Palenque came to the world's attention in the 1700s when several explorers reported its existence to people around the world. Later, in the 1800s archaeologists began to study the ruins of Palenque. It quickly became one of the most examined of all the Maya cites. People learned much about Maya life and culture from the ruins at Palenque, but many questions remained. Over time, archaeologists and other experts looked for more clues. In the early 1950s, an archaeologist working at Palenque discovered a building hidden deep inside another building. It contained many examples of Maya writing and was called the "Temple of Inscriptions." Who built this temple? Why? What did the inscriptions say?

## A List of Ancestors

By unlocking the key to Maya writing, people have been able to decipher these Maya inscriptions. One of these inscriptions was especially exciting. It told about one of the greatest rulers of Palenque—a man named Pacal. While he was ruler, he ordered the construction of many buildings. One of these buildings was the Temple of Inscriptions, which was designed to be a shrine to him. It also was to contain a tomb for his body when he died. A drawing on the cover of his tomb shows Pacal being reborn as a god. Lists of names on the sides of his tomb tell the people who ruled Palenque before him. Archaeologists report that this is the longest, intact Maya inscription they have found to date. One of the names included on this list of Palenque's past rulers was that of Lady Kanal-Ikal. She was Pacal's great grandmother.

## An Exception to the Rule

In Maya society, rulers came from a royal family. All of the Maya royal families believed they were close to the gods. They surrounded themselves with symbols of power. They also tried to gain more wealth to make them different from other people in the society. "Being different" from other members of society was important.

▲ Lady Kanal-Ikal ruled the kingdom of Palenque from 583-604. Palenque was a Maya city in the far northwest region of Maya country.

▲ Lady Kanal-Ikal's great grandson had pictures of her like this one carved on his tomb.

## It's a FACT

A board was placed on the back of Lady Kanal-Ikal's head and against her forehead when she was a baby. This created a flat, long head, which reflected the Maya's idea of beauty.

The Maya believed in hereditary succession. When a Maya king died, his son was the next in line to become king. This method of succession is called patrilineal because the succession went through male family members. But what happens if the king does not have a son or brother or other male relative? That was the problem facing Lady Kanal-Ikal's father. He had a daughter, but no sons. His brother did not have any sons either. So, they made an exception and Lady Kanal-Ikal became the ruler of Palenque.

## Lady Kanal-Ikal as Maya Ruler

Very little is known about Lady Kanal-Ikal. We know that in 583 she became the first woman to rule Palenque. We know she married a man who was not a member of the royal family, and she had at least one son. We also know that Lady Kanal-Ikal ruled for 20 years, until her death in 604. Lady Kanal-Ikal's son became king, which started another line of male descendants.

Most archaeologists and historians agree that Lady Kanal-Ikal must have been an extraordinary woman to come to the throne in Palenque. She is only one of two women we know for certain ruled in Palenque. But why is there so little known about her? Perhaps much of her history is still waiting to be uncovered in some part of Palenque that remains undiscovered. Perhaps we will find more inscriptions that tell about her life and her rule of Palenque. Until then, her past remains a mystery. 📖

### What Do You Think?

**1.** Do you think that being the first woman to rule Palenque was easy? What challenges do you think Lady Kanal-Ikal had to overcome?

**2.** How are your ideas of beauty similar to or different from the ancient Maya?

▶ **Perhaps much of Lady Kanal-Ikal's history is still waiting to be uncovered in some part of Palenque that remains undiscovered.**

# PACAL — Greatest of All Palenque Kings

A.D. **500**

A.D. **1800**

**604**
Lady Kanal-Ikal dies

**615-683**
Pacal rules Palenque

**1700s**
Explorers rediscover Palenque

The ancient Maya city of Palenque lies deep in the lush Central American rain forest. If you visit Palenque today, you can hear the sounds of howler monkeys and see the brilliant and colorful feathers of parrots and other birds. You can walk among the ruins of the splendid Maya buildings. For centuries this magnificent city was overgrown with trees and plants. It went unnoticed by the outside world until the 1700s. Since that time, however, Palenque has attracted many explorers, archaeologists, and visitors. The city has revealed an enormous amount of information about the Maya civilization.

## A Source of Information

What makes Palenque such an important source of information about the Maya? Perhaps the most important reason is that the rulers of Palenque left written records that tell about their ancestors. These records were painted on the walls of tombs and carved into stone monuments. From these written records, experts have learned about the kings, or ahaus, of Palenque, including Sun Lord Pacal (Hand-Shield) and his son, Sun Lord Chan-Bahlum (Snake-Jaguar). Pacal, and later his son, believed that it was important to record the transfer of power from one ruler to the next.

## The Rise of Palenque

Pacal was born into a royal family around the year 603. He became ruler of the Maya city-state of Palenque when he was 12 years old. During his reign, Pacal helped bring about a golden age of the Maya civilization. He was responsible for making Palenque a powerful city-state within the Maya world. He also supported the development of Maya art and architecture. Many of the extraordinary buildings in Palenque were completed during his reign. These buildings and monuments helped to make Palenque one of the most beautiful of all Maya cities.

▲ From 615-683, Pacal ruled the kingdom of Palenque, a Maya city in the far northwest region of Maya country.

▲ The ancient Maya city of Palenque lies deep in a rain forest.

It's a FACT
Pacal had pictures of his great grandmother, Lady Kanal-Ikal, carved on his tomb.

## The Temple of Inscriptions

One building in Palenque, the Temple of Inscriptions, contained many examples of Maya writing. These writings provided historians with a unique record of the history of Palenque. The Temple of Inscriptions was designed to be a shrine to Pacal and also a tomb for his body. When Pacal died in 683 at the age of 80, his body was placed in this tomb. A life-sized mask made of pieces of jade was placed over his face. A necklace was placed around his neck and jade rings were placed on his fingers. Other pieces of jade were also placed around him. Finally, a huge slab of rock was placed on top of the tomb.

## A Record of Maya Rulers

A drawing on the cover of the tomb shows Pacal being reborn as a god. On the sides of the tomb are lists of names of the people who ruled Palenque before him, including his great grandmother, Lady Kanal-Ikal. Archaeologists report that this is the longest, intact Maya inscription they have found to date. This list is considered one of the greatest archaeological records we have of the ancient Maya. Through the Temple of Inscriptions, Pacal left us an important record of the Maya and their culture. 📖

## Clothes Make A Man

All Maya men wore similar kinds of clothes. But, because he was a noble and king, Pacal's clothing was made from finer material and was more highly decorated. Maya men wore a piece of cotton cloth that was wound around the waist and passed between the legs. This kind of garment is called a loincloth. A noble Maya man's loincloth might have been decorated with beautiful embroidery and even feathers. Sometimes Maya men also wore a square piece of cotton cloth on their shoulders. This garment is called a pati. A commoner's pati would not be as fancy as a noble man's.

 **What Do You Think?**

**1.** Why do you think Pacal wanted the names of his royal ancestors on his tomb?

**2.** In what ways did Pacal display power? How does this compare with the way leaders today display power?

# DIEGO DE LANDA'S
# Account of the Maya

Diego de Landa was born in 1524 in a small town in Spain. When he was 16 years old, he began training to become a Roman Catholic friar. A friar is a type of priest whose main job is to go out into the world and tell people about Christianity. Diego de Landa wanted to share his beliefs in Christianity with people in the Americas. In 1549, he and six or seven other friars sailed to the Yucatan Peninsula. Diego de Landa traveled throughout the area we know as Maya country, learning Mayan and converting people to the Christian religion. He went back to Spain in 1563 and wrote the most detailed account we have of the ancient Maya. In 1572, he was made a bishop and returned to the Yucatan Peninsula.

Bishop de Landa lived and worked in Maya country until his death on April 29, 1579. The book he wrote about the Maya is called *Relacion de las cosas de Yucatan*, which means "History of Things of Yucatan." It is one of the most important written sources of information about the ancient Maya. In some ways, this is ironic because Bishop de Landa also was responsible for burning many Maya codices filled with Maya hieroglyphs. He said, "we burned them all, which [the Maya] regretted to an amazing degree and caused them [suffering]." You can read below an excerpt from Bishop de Landa's book.

## From Diego de Landa's Book

The Indians had potters and carpenters, and as these made idols of clay and wood ..., they earned a great deal. The business which they most favored was to take salt, clothing, and slaves to ... exchange everything for cacao and stone beads, which they used as money. With this they used to buy slaves or finer or better beads, which the lords wore like jewels during celebrations. They also used money and jewels and other beads made from certain red shells, which they carried about in bags of netting. In the markets they traded in every manner of thing found in that land. They gave credit, and made loans and purchases courteously ... The majority of the people were peasants and those who gathered in the maize and other grains ... Their mules and oxen are the people themselves ... The Indians have the good custom of helping each other in all their work at harvest time ... Whenever they go to pay a visit the Indians always take gifts with them in keeping with their position and the host repays them with another gift.

### Analyze the Source!

1. Read the excerpt and tell in your own words what it says.

2. How does this excerpt help you learn about Maya life and history? What does it tell you about Spanish culture?

3. What conclusions, if any, can you draw about the Maya's government or economy from this excerpt? Explain why you can or cannot draw conclusions.

# JOHN L. STEPHENS —
# The Father of Maya Archaeology

John Lloyd Stephens is sometimes called the "father of Maya archaeology," although judging from his early life he seems an unlikely candidate for this title. John Lloyd Stephens was born in 1805. He grew up in New York, graduated from college, and went on to law school. He started a law practice, but decided in 1834 to travel. He went to Egypt, the Arabian Peninsula, throughout southwestern Asia, and to Greece and Turkey. Then, in 1839, he was off to Central America and Mexico—Maya country.

He teamed up with Frederick Catherwood, an English artist, on this trip. In 1841, the two of them published a book called *Incidents of Travel in Central America, Chiapas, and Yucatan*. This book was very popular in America and brought public attention to the Maya civilization. Before this time, no one had written a detailed and accurate description of a Maya city. Stephens did not have any formal training in archaeology, but he left an excellent firsthand account of Maya buildings and monuments. His account and Catherwood's drawings are the only record of some Maya structures that have since been destroyed or lost. Stephens died of malaria in 1852, but his experiences live on in his writing.

Below is a passage from his book, *Incidents of Travel in Central America, Chiapas, and Yucatan*. In this excerpt, John L. Stephens tells about his feelings the first time he saw the Maya city of Copan. 

## From Stephens's Book

... America, say historians, was peopled by savages; but savages never [built] these structures, savages never carved these stones. When we asked the Indians who made them, their dull answer was *Quien sabe?* (Who knows?) ... But architecture, sculpture, and painting, all the arts which embellish life had flourished in this overgrown forest; orators, warriors, and statesmen, beauty, ambition, and glory had lived and passed away, and none knew that such things had been, or could tell of their past existence. Books, the records of knowledge, are silent on this theme.

The city was desolate. No remnant of this race hangs around the ruins, with traditions handed down from father to son and from generation to generation. It lay before us like a shattered bark [sailing ship] in the midst of the ocean, her masts gone, her name effaced, her crew perished, and none to tell whence she came, to whom she belonged, how long on her voyage, or what caused her destruction—her lost people to be traced only by some fancied resemblance in construction of the vessel, and, perhaps, never to be known at all.

### Analyze the Source!

1. Read the excerpt and tell in your own words what it says.

2. What conclusions, if any, can you draw about the Maya's political organization from this excerpt?

3. What does this excerpt tell you about American ideas in the 1840s?

# THE *POPUL VUH*:
# A Maya History of the Maya

The buildings and artifacts of the ancient Maya give us important clues to their lives. However, it is the written accounts of their way of life that help us understand what the Maya cared about and what they believed in. The *Popul Vuh*, which means "Council Book," gives us such a written account. Originally, the stories and songs that make up the *Popul Vuh* were part of the oral tradition of the Maya. The Quiche people, descendants of the ancient Maya in the Guatemalan highlands, wrote down these songs and stories 30 years after the Spanish arrived in the region. No one knows exactly who wrote the *Popul Vuh*. However, this 9,000-line poem is considered one of the finest examples of American Indian literature. The original was lost in the 1800s, but copies of it have survived. The *Popul Vuh* begins with the story of how the world began. You can read below a translation of the opening lines of this important source. 📖

## From the *Popul Vuh*

Before the world was created, Calm and Silence were the great kings that ruled. Nothing existed, there was nothing. Things had not yet been drawn together, the face of the earth was unseen. There was only motionless sea, and a great emptiness of sky. There were no men anywhere, or animals, no birds or fish, no crabs. Trees, stones, caves, grass, forests, none of these existed yet. There was nothing that could roar or run, nothing that could tremble or cry in the air. Flatness and emptiness, only the sea, alone and breathless. It was night; silence stood in the dark.

In this darkness the Creators waited ... They were there in this emptiness, hidden under green and blue feathers, alone and surrounded with light. They are the same as wisdom. They are the ones who can conceive and bring forth a child from nothingness. And the time had come. The Creators ... argued, worried, sighed over what was to be. They planned the growth of thickets, how things would crawl and jump, the birth of man. They planned the whole creation ... Then let the emptiness fill! They said. Let the water weave its way downward so the earth can show its face! Let the light break on the ridges, let the sky fill up with the yellow light of dawn! Let our glory be a man walking on a path through the trees! 'Earth!' the Creators called.

## Analyze the Source!

1. Read the excerpt and tell in your own words what it says.

2. What conclusions, if any, can you draw about the Maya's religious beliefs from this excerpt?

3. Based on this excerpt, do you agree that the *Popul Vuh* is fine literature? Why?

# How Do We Know
## ABOUT THE AZTECS?

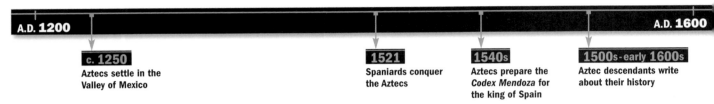

**A.D. 1200** ———————————————————————————————— **A.D. 1600**

**c. 1250**
Aztecs settle in the
Valley of Mexico

**1521**
Spaniards conquer
the Aztecs

**1540s**
Aztecs prepare the
*Codex Mendoza* for
the king of Spain

**1500s - early 1600s**
Aztec descendants write
about their history

The information we have about the Aztecs comes from two major sources. First, from the art, architecture, and artifacts the Aztecs left behind. And, secondly, from written documents about Aztec life and culture.

## Art, Architecture, Artifacts

The art images, buildings, and artifacts the Aztecs created tell us much about Aztec civilization. For example, by studying the pictures the Aztecs created, we can learn a great deal about their life and culture. We can see how people dressed, the foods they ate, what families and class structure was like, and how they interacted with the environment. Drawings and paintings show Aztec social classes, lifestyle, religious ceremonies, scientific studies, and culture. Pictures show who and what the Aztecs thought were important and provide details of Aztec life, including such things as clothing, food, animals, tribute items, and rituals.

Aztec architecture also gives us clues about the Aztecs' social organization, political structure, and technological abilities. For example, building a large temple would have required an organized work force that someone was in

▲ The Aztecs moved into the Valley of Mexico from the north. They built their capital city, Tenochtitlan, on a swampy island in the middle of Lake Texcoco. By 1519, the Aztecs controlled a large empire.

charge of directing. It would have required knowledge of mathematics to be able to cut and place stones precisely. It also would have required advanced tool making and construction techniques. In addition, the artifacts the Aztecs left behind show us examples of such things as cooking pots, jewelry, tools, weapons, calendars, bells, masks, statues, and other sculptures.

▲ Artifacts such as this calendar tell us much about Aztec culture.

## Written Accounts of Aztec History and Daily Life

Another important source of information about the Aztecs comes from written accounts of Aztec life. Aztecs created pictorial manuscripts. Unlike the Maya whose writing system allowed them to write every word that was spoken, the Aztec writing is more of an outline consisting of names and ideas. Only a few of the codices the Aztecs wrote still exist. Some tell about the history of a place or a noble family or about religious ceremonies. Others are records of tribute that individuals or city-states had to pay as a form of tax to the Aztec empire. The *Codex Mendoza* is one of the most important sources of

▲ This is a page from a codex made in about 1520. It shows Aztec people socializing and cultivating fields.

Aztec writing about Aztec life. A Spanish official had Aztecs prepare this document in the 1540s to give the king of Spain information about the Aztec empire the Spanish had conquered. Today, the *Codex Mendoza* is at Oxford University in England.

Pictorial accounts of the Aztec civilization gave archaeologists an idea of what to look for when they were excavating Aztec sites.

In addition to the Aztec accounts of their life and history, we also have gained a great deal of information about the Aztecs from Spanish conquerors, soldiers, and Christian missionaries. When the Spanish arrived in the area, men such as Hernando Cortés and Bernal Díaz del Castillo, a soldier in the Spanish army, wrote about their impressions of the Aztecs. Spanish friars such as Diego Durán and Bernardino de Sahagún wrote books about the Aztecs. They had Aztec artists draw pictures to illustrate their accounts. Their books included stories Aztecs told them about the past, as well as information about Aztec religion, the Aztec calendar, food the people ate, the way they brought up and educated their children, the kinds of work people did, and many other aspects of daily life in the Aztec empire.

Of course, the information from the Spanish conquerors, soldiers, and Christian missionaries regarding the Aztecs reflects their own experience, background, and biases. Others such as Fernando de Alva Ixtlilxochitl and Domingo de San Antón Muñón Chimalpahin Quauhtlehuanitzin, who were Aztec descendants educated by the Spanish, wrote about the Aztecs in the late 1500s and early 1600s. Their accounts help give historians a more balanced perspective of Aztec history. 📖

# BERNARDINO DE SAHAGÚN
## and the Aztecs

Bernardino de Sahagún was born in Spain in 1499—just seven years after Columbus "discovered" America. As a young man, Bernardino de Sahagún decided to become a friar in the Roman Catholic Church. A friar is a type of priest whose main job is to go out into the world and tell people about Christianity. Friar Sahagún wanted to share his beliefs about Christianity with people in present-day Mexico and Central America. The Spanish had claimed this area and called it, "New Spain." Sahagún traveled to the area in the Americas where the Aztec empire had flourished. There he helped to start a school. He taught the people Spanish and they taught him the Aztec language, Nahuatl.

Sahagún was interested in learning as much as he could about Aztec history and culture. Because he had learned Nahuatl, he could get information about these topics from the Aztecs' perspective. Over time, Sahagún wrote several accounts of the Aztec. The most important work for scholars today is called the *Florentine Codex: General History of the Things of New Spain.* You can read on the next page excerpts from Friar Bernardino de Sahagún's work. 📖

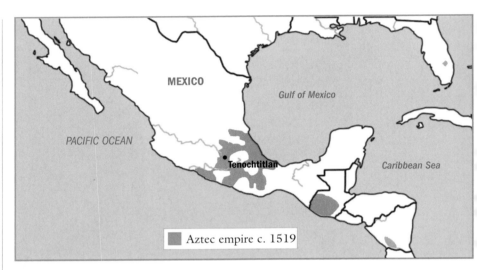

▲ The Aztecs moved into the Valley of Mexico from the north. They built their capital city, Tenochtitlan, on a swampy island in the middle of Lake Texcoco. By 1519, the Aztecs controlled a large empire.

## Analyze the Source!

1. Read the excerpts. Choose one and tell what it means in your own words.

2. How does the excerpt you chose help you learn about Aztec life and history? What does it tell you about Spanish culture?

3. What conclusions, if any, can you draw about Aztec culture from this excerpt? Explain why you can or cannot draw conclusions.

## ON FARMERS

The farmer ... is bound to the soil; he works—works the soil, stirs the soil anew, prepares the soil; he weeds, breaks up the clods, hoes, levels the soil, makes furrows ... he makes holes; he plants, hills, waters, sprinkles; he broadcasts seed; he sows beans, provides holes for them ... fills in the holes; he hills [the maize plants], removes the undeveloped maize ears, discards the withered ears ... gathers the maize, shucks the ears, removes the ears ...

## ON JEWELERS

Their creations were lip pendants, lip plugs, and ear plugs, ear plugs of obsidian, rock crystal, and amber; white ear plugs; and all manner of necklaces; bracelets.

## ON MERCHANTS

As they traveled the road, they went [dressed] for war. They bore their shields, their obsidian-bladed swords, [and] their devices, because they passed through the enemy's land, where they might die [and] where they took captives.

## ON SCRIBES

The scribe: writings, ink [are] his special skills. [He is] a craftsman, an artist, a user of charcoal, a drawer with charcoal; a painter who dissolves colors, grinds pigments, uses colors. The good scribe is honest ... a judge of colors, an applier of colors, who makes shadows, forms feet, face, hair. He paints, applies colors, makes shadows, draws gardens, paints flowers, creates works of art.

## ON DOCTORS

The true doctor. He is a wise man; he imparts life ... He has worked with herbs, stones, trees, and roots. His remedies have been tested; he examines, he experiments, he alleviates sickness. He massages aches and sets broken bones. He administers [medicine] and potions; he bleeds his patients; he cuts and he sews the wound; he brings about reactions; he [stops] the bleeding with ashes.

## ON RULERS

The good ruler [is] a protector; one who carries [his subjects] in his arms, who unites them, who brings them together. He rules, takes responsibilities, assumes burdens. He carries [his subjects] in his cape; he bears them in his arms. He governs; he is obeyed.

# DIEGO DURÁN and the Aztecs

Diego Durán was born in Spain around 1537. When he was a boy, he was brought to the area in the Americas the Spanish had claimed. They called this area, "New Spain." Diego Durán grew up in this region where the Aztec empire had flourished. In 1556, he decided to become a friar in the Roman Catholic Church. Friar Durán wanted to share his beliefs about Christianity with people in New Spain. As he traveled throughout the area, however, he became more and more interested in Aztec culture and history. He read what other Spaniards had to say about the Aztecs, but he also interviewed Aztecs and looked at Aztec codices. He tried to look at the Aztecs' culture from their perspective. Based on the information he gathered, Durán wrote three books about the Aztecs, including *The History of the Indies of New Spain*. You can read on the next page excerpts from Friar Diego Durán's work. 📖

▲ Diego Durán tried to look at the Aztecs' culture from their perspective. Based on the information he gathered, Durán wrote three books about the Aztecs, including *The History of the Indies of New Spain*.

## DIEGO DURÁN ON TRIBUTE PAID TO TENOCHTITLAN

The conquered people gave themselves as vassals, as servants, to the Aztecs and they paid tribute in all things created under the sky ... There were such vast quantities of all these things that came to the city of Mexico [Tenochtitlan] that not a day passed without the arrival of people from other regions who brought large amounts of everything, from foodstuffs to luxury items, for the king and the lords.

## ON MUSIC AND DANCE

Young people took great pride in their ability to dance, sing, and guide the others in the dances. They were proud of being able to move their feet to the rhythm and of following the time with their bodies in the movements the natives used, and with their voice the tempo. The dances of these people are governed not only by the rhythm but by the high and low notes in the chant, singing and dancing at the same time.

Thus these differences in songs and dances existed: some were sung slowly and seriously; these were sung and danced by the lords on [serious] and important occasions ... others [were] less sober and more lively. These were dances and songs of pleasure ... during which they sang songs of love and flirtation, similar to those sung today on joyful occasions. There was also another dance ... with all its wriggling ... It is highly improper.

## ON MERCHANTS

Buying and selling, going forth to all the markets of the land, bartering cloth for jewels, jewels for feathers, feathers for stones, and stones for slaves, always dealing in things of importance, of renown, and of high value. These [men] strengthened their social position with their wealth.

## Analyze the Source!

1. Read the excerpts. Choose one and tell what it means in your own words.

2. How does the excerpt you chose help you learn about Aztec life and history? What does it tell you about Spanish culture?

3. What conclusions, if any, can you draw about Aztec culture from this excerpt? Explain why you can or cannot draw conclusions.

# The Spaniards Describe Women in Aztec Society

We have learned about women's lives in Aztec society from both Aztec and Spanish sources. For example, Aztec codices show mothers teaching their daughters the skills they would need in order to carry out their responsibilities as women. We also have learned about the lives of Aztec women from accounts left by the Spaniards who conquered and then ruled the Aztec people. Of course, the perspective of the Spaniards comes with their own biases and interpretations and will be different from that of the Aztecs. Below are accounts from three Spaniards: Friar Diego Durán, Friar Bernardino de Sahagún, and Alonso de Zorita.

**Speaking about women and the importance of markets to them, Friar Diego Durán said:**

*The markets were so inviting, pleasurable, appealing, and gratifying to these people that great crowds attended, and still attend, them ... I suspect that if I said to a market woman accustomed to going from market to market: "Look, today is market day in such and such a town. What would you rather do, go from here right to Heaven or to that market?" I believe this would be her answer: "Allow me to go to the market first, and then I will go to Heaven."*

**Writing about the advice to an Aztec bride during the Aztec wedding ceremony, Friar Bernardino de Sahagún said:**

*Forever now leave childishness, girlishness; no longer art thou to be like a child ... Be most considerate of one; regard one with respect, speak well, greet one well. By night look to, take care of the sweeping, the laying of the fire. Arise in the deep of night [to begin your house work].*

**Friar Bernardino de Sahagún described Aztec women who also worked outside their homes:**

*[S]he would become very rich. She would produce well, make her wares well, and bargain [cleverly]. She would be of good birth, and would arrange and distribute her merchandise and her people. [S]he would become rich and wealthy; courageous, strong ... She would give honor as a man. And [among] her gifts, she would speak well ... give good counsel, and arrange her conversation and manner of speaking well in her home.*

**Alonso de Zorita, an early Spanish governor of New Spain, which included the area of the Aztec empire, summarized the duties of an Aztec wife:**

*When your parents give you a husband, do not be disrespectful to him; listen to him and obey him, and do cheerfully what you are told. Do not turn your face from him ... Do not insult him or say offensive words to him in front of strangers or even to him alone; for you will harm yourself thereby, and yours will be the fault.*

## Analyze the Source!

1. Read the excerpts. Choose one and tell what it means in your own words.

2. How does the excerpt you chose help you learn about Aztec life and history?

3. How do ideas about women today compare with ideas about women in Aztec society?

# HUITZILOPOCHTLI and QUETZALCOATL —
# Gods of the Aztec Spirit World

To the Aztecs, gods were invisible spirits or forces. The Aztecs thought each god had a different role and form. They also thought their gods could change roles and forms. The stories about the Aztec spirit world are sometimes inconsistent, so it is often difficult for us to understand who was who. Generally, however, the Aztecs seemed to worship four different kinds of gods.

▲ **The Aztecs built their capital city, Tenochtitlan, on a swampy island in the middle of Lake Texcoco.**

## Four Kinds of Aztec Gods

The first category includes gods involved with the creation of the world. Ometeotl is an example of this kind of creation god. Ometeotl is at the center of one of the Aztecs' creation myths. The second category includes gods related to water and agriculture. Tlaloc is an example of this category of gods. Mesoamerican people had worshipped Tlaloc since ancient times. The third category includes gods of war, sacrifice, blood, and death. Huitzilopochtli is an example of this kind of god. A fourth category of gods includes spirits associated with creation, water and agriculture, and also with war, sacrifice, blood, and death. Quetzalcoatl is an example of this kind of god.

## Huitzilopochtli—
## "Hummingbird of the Left or South"

In 1250, the people we know as the Aztecs settled near a swamp in the Valley of Mexico. They believed in many gods that had been important to other Mesoamerican people. However, Huitzilopochtli, which means "Hummingbird of the Left or South," was a special God to them. The Aztecs persuaded the king of the Culhua, another group living in the area, to let them settle on land no one else wanted. They lived on this land for many years, but then were forced to leave.

According to Aztec accounts, Huitzilopochtli told them they should worship a Culhua princess as a goddess. The king agreed to send his daughter to the Aztecs. Later, the Aztecs invited the king of Culhua and his nobles to see the ceremony honoring the Culhua princess. Imagine their horror when they found the princess had been killed and her skin removed. An Aztec priest was wearing it as he danced during the ceremony.

The Aztecs were driven out of the area by the angry Culhua king and his warriors. As they fled, they carried with them the image of Huitzilopochtli.

Eventually, the Aztecs moved into the area around the lakes in the Valley of Mexico. They stayed there for weeks. Then, according to legend, Huitzilopochtli visited one of the priests in a **vision**. The priest said Huitzilopochtli told him, "Go where the cactus grows, on which the eagle sits happily." When they came to such a place, they believed it was to be their new home. They began to build their great city, Tenochtitlan, there in the year 1325. The first structure they built was a shrine to Huitzilopochtli. Historians and archaeologists believe this was the earliest phase of a huge temple structure called the Templo Mayor. They believe that each new Aztec leader (or "tlatoani") stood before the image of Huitzilopochtli and made offerings and sacrifices. They have concluded that each new tlatoani who came to power also added to or improved this temple structure.

Huitzilopochtli remained one of the Aztecs' most important gods. Huitzilopochtli was a god of warfare, blood, sacrifice, and the sun. The Aztecs believed that all their gods, especially Huitzilopochtli, required human blood to maintain the cycle of life. The Aztecs' religious beliefs gave them a strong desire to expand their empire and conquer other peoples. Why? Because most of the people who were sacrificed to the gods were prisoners of war.

## Quetzalcoatl—"Quetzal-Feathered Serpent"

Mesoamerican people had worshiped Quetzalcoatl since ancient times. "Quetzalcoatl" means quetzal-feathered serpent. Quetzalcoatl was the god associated with Aztec creation myths. He also could change forms to become the god of wind and the god of learning and knowledge. In addition, Quetzalcoatl was considered a special god to priests. It was very common in Aztec society that different groups of workers had their own special gods. And, since Aztec priests were such an important social group, their god was considered very important. The most important priests in Tenochtitlan were given the title of "Quetzalcoatl."

According to one of the Aztecs' myths, Quetzalcoatl gave his own blood to create human life. Like other Mesoamerican people, the Aztecs came to believe that blood was the most important sacrifice they could make to the gods. They believed they owed a debt to the gods who had sacrificed themselves for human beings. They thought it was their duty to repay the gods by offering their own blood sacrifices. ☐

**vision:** an experience in which someone sees something that is out of the ordinary; a mystical or supernatural experience

▲ The Aztecs believed that an eagle and snake on top of a cactus led them to their new home.

## What Do You Think?

1. What did Huitzilopochtli and Quetzalcoatl have in common? How were they different?

2. How did the Aztecs adapt the religious beliefs of earlier Mesoamerican peoples?

# AHUITZOTL —
# "Supreme King" of the Aztecs

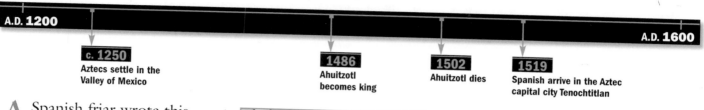

**c. 1250**
Aztecs settle in the Valley of Mexico

**1486**
Ahuitzotl becomes king

**1502**
Ahuitzotl dies

**1519**
Spanish arrive in the Aztec capital city Tenochtitlan

A Spanish friar wrote this about Aztec rulers: "The good ruler [is] a protector; one who carries [his subjects] in his arms, who unites them, who brings them together. He rules, takes responsibilities, assumes burdens. He carries [his subjects] in his cape; he bears them in his arms. He governs; he is obeyed."

## Becoming King

The men who led the Aztecs were called *tlatoani*, a word that means "first speaker." Aztec nobles elected these tlatoani or kings. Ahuitzotl is known as the eighth Aztec tlatoani. We do not know much about his early life. His name appears in the Aztec historical record when he became king. Archaeologists have found many stone monuments and also accounts of his becoming king. The *Codex Mexicanus*, for example, gives a chronology of Ahuitzotl's rise. First there is a date and picture showing the death of one ruler and the appointment of Tizoc as Aztec king. Then there is a later date and picture telling about a terrible defeat of the Aztec armies. The next date and picture show Ahuitzotl as king.

▲ The Aztecs moved into the Valley of Mexico from the north. They built their capital city, Tenochtitlan, on a swampy island in the middle of Lake Texcoco. By 1519, the Aztecs controlled a large empire.

Some people suspect that Tizoc was assassinated, but no one knows for sure. What we do know is that Ahuitzotl was Tizoc's younger brother and Ahuitzotl was made king in the Aztec year 7 Rabbit. From our understanding of the Aztec calendar, this is the date we refer to as 1486.

▶ This illustration of Ahuitzotl is modeled after a drawing in the Templo Mayor Museum in Mexico. The Templo Mayor was the first structure the Aztecs built in Tenochtitlan in 1325. Each king added onto or improved the structure. Ahuitzotl completed the Templo Mayor in 1487.

▲ Each year, Aztec priests sacrificed thousands of people during religious ceremonies. Priests cut open the victim's chest and ripped out the person's beating heart. Ahuitzotl dedicated a temple to Huitzilopochtli and Tlaloc, the god of rain and agriculture, with ceremonies that lasted four days and included the sacrifice of as many as 20,000 people. When Ahuitzotl died, 200 of his slaves were sacrificed to the gods.

## From Tlatoani to Huehuetlatoani

Some nobles thought Ahuitzotl was too young to take on the responsibilities of king. However, Ahuitzotl proved them very wrong. By the time Ahuitzotl became king, the Aztecs were the most powerful group in the Valley of Mexico and the most powerful member of the Triple Alliance. It seemed only fitting that he have a more important title than "king." Instead of being a tlatoani, Ahuitzotl was considered a huehuetlatoani or "supreme king." He was crowned king in an elaborate ceremony that included sacrifices to Aztec gods, such as Huitzilopochtli, the god of war.

## Expanding the Empire

As an Aztec ruler, it was Ahuitzotl's responsibility to lead the military. One of the first problems he had to face was a rebellion among a group of conquered people. The king of the Huaxtec people who lived on the Gulf Coast decided he no longer wanted to pay tribute to the Aztecs. He thought his army was strong enough to resist the armies of the Triple Alliance. Ahuitzotl stopped this rebellion. However, Ahuitzotl was not interested in simply putting down rebellions. He wanted to conquer new lands and peoples. He began to expand the Aztec empire through military campaigns and through trade. These traders were heavily armed and if they were attacked, Ahuitzotl's armies would come to their aid. Ahuitzotl built fortresses in areas he conquered and then sent loyal subjects from the Valley of Mexico to protect and settle these conquered areas. As a result of his efforts, the Aztec empire nearly doubled in size.

## A Brave and Popular Leader

Ahuitzotl was a popular leader among his people. He fought alongside his armies in battle and rewarded brave soldiers with special privileges. He also encouraged merchants to travel all over the empire. Not only did these merchants bring exotic goods back to Tenochtitlan, but they also brought Ahuitzotl information about what was going on in the empire. Ahuitzotl made it possible for talented commoners to advance in Aztec society. They could become government officials. This created new opportunities for commoners.

## Growth and Prosperity

During Ahuitzotl's reign, the Aztec empire grew in size and wealth. The Aztecs had become dominant over the other two city-states that made up the Triple Alliance. Over time, Ahuitzotl took responsibility for managing the entire empire. When he died in 1502, Ahuitzotl's nephew, Moctezuma II, became the new king of the Aztecs. Moctezuma inherited a large, prosperous empire. Who could have known that within 20 years the Aztec empire would be conquered? 

### What Do You Think?

1. How does knowing the chronology of Aztec history help us understand Aztec politics?

2. What do you think was Ahuitzotl's greatest accomplishment? Explain your answer.

3. How did Ahuitzotl's actions demonstrate the themes of continuity and change?

# MOCTEZUMA II —
# The Last King of the Aztecs

A.D. **1400**        A.D. **1600**

**c. 1480**
Moctezuma
Xocoyotzin is born

**1502**
Moctezuma
becomes king

**1519**
Hernando Cortés lands
in the New World

**1520**
Moctezuma
is killed

**1521**
Spaniards conquer Tenochtitlan
and the Aztec empire

Moctezuma II was not the Aztecs' greatest leader, but he is certainly the most well known. He was the king of the mighty Aztec empire when the Spaniards arrived. Moctezuma Xocoyotzin was born around 1480. He was named after his great grandfather, Moctezuma, a great warrior and earlier Aztec king. That is why the historical record calls him Moctezuma II. His father, Axacayatl, also was an Aztec ruler who became king in 1469. When Axacayatl died, however, his son Moctezuma did not become king. Instead, Moctezuma's uncle Ahuitzotl was chosen to be the ruler. During Ahuitzotl's reign the Aztec empire grew in size and wealth. Ahuitzotl took responsibility for managing the entire empire, and under his leadership the Aztecs dominated the other two Triple Alliance powers.

## Becoming an Aztec King
When Ahuitzotl died in 1502, his nephew Moctezuma was chosen to become the new king of the Aztecs. An account in the *Codex Mendoza* described Moctezuma as "well versed in all the arts, military as well as

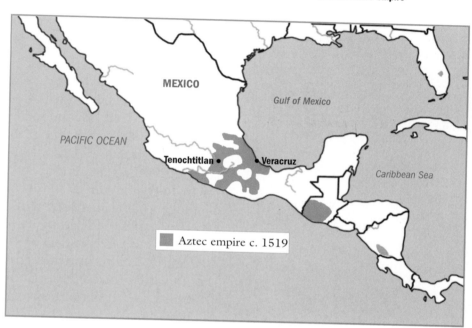

MEXICO

Gulf of Mexico

PACIFIC OCEAN

Tenochtitlan •  • Veracruz

Caribbean Sea

■ Aztec empire c. 1519

others ..., in comparison with his ancestors none of whom had as much power or majesty as Moctezuma. ..." Bernal Díaz del Castillo, a Spanish soldier who accompanied Hernando Córtes, described Moctezuma this way: "He was of medium height, well-proportioned, thin, not very dark ... his hair was not long... his face was somewhat long and happy. ... He was neat and clean. He bathed once every day."

## Experienced Leader
Moctezuma inherited a large, prosperous empire, and he seemed well prepared to lead it.

▲ **Moctezuma inherited a large, prosperous empire.**

As a young man, he had taken part in many of his uncle Ahuitzotl's wars of conquest. Because of this, he had become an experienced military leader. As Aztec king, he led many military campaigns to stop rebellions in regions the Aztecs already had conquered. He reconquered the areas and forced the people to pay a heavy price for their rebellion. Not surprisingly, these actions made the people the Aztecs conquered hate them even more.

Moctezuma also led the Aztecs in battles against the people of Tlaxcalla, but was unable to conquer them. As king, Moctezuma changed his uncle Ahuitzotl's practice of rewarding brave soldiers with special privileges. It was no longer possible for talented commoners to advance in Aztec society. Moctezuma decided that important positions in the military and government should go only to nobles.

▲ **Moctezuma consulted the Aztec calendar when making decisions.**

## Consulting the Calendar

Moctezuma had trained to become king since he was born. He studied ancient Aztec myths and stories. He studied the stars and consulted the calendars when making decisions. Like other Mesoamerican peoples, the Aztecs believed there were lucky and unlucky times to do things. That is one reason why calendars were so important in their lives. They consulted their calendars to help them make good decisions about traveling, planting, and even marrying. It was almost like checking a horoscope today, but they took the information much more seriously.

## Legend of Quetzalcoatl

In spring 1519, Hernando Cortés and his army of 550 soldiers landed in the New World near present-day Veracruz. Word of their arrival spread across the Aztec empire. Cortés was described as a bearded, fair-skinned man. Some people believe that the Aztecs thought he was Quetzalcoatl. The legend of Quetzalcoatl told how he made the first people, taught them to grow corn, weave cloth, polish jade, study the stars, and calculate the days of the year. The legend also promised that Quetzalcoatl would return in the Aztec year Ce Acatl (1519) as a bearded, fair-skinned man. Was this the promised return of Quetzalcoatl? It is not possible to know what Moctezuma believed. However, the decisions Moctezuma made about how to deal with the Spaniards seem to suggest that he had his doubts.

## "Welcome to Tenochtitlan"

Some of Moctezuma's advisors counseled him to conquer the strangers. Others thought the strangers should be welcomed. In the end, Moctezuma decided to send a group of Aztec officials with gifts to meet with Cortés. Moctezuma's strategy was to gain information about the strangers and also to give them fabulous gifts as a bribe to leave the area. Of course, the fabulous gifts gave Cortés an idea of the riches of the Aztec empire. He was not going to settle for a few gifts. Moctezuma's officials tried to persuade Cortés to leave, but Cortés insisted he must not leave without meeting with Moctezuma.

Finally, Moctezuma agreed that Cortés and his men could enter Tenochtitlan. On November 12, 1519, with many of the city's 300,000 people looking on, the Spaniards entered the city. Bernal Díaz del Castillo later wrote, "These great towns and ... buildings rising from the water, all made of stone, seemed like an enchanted vision ... . Indeed, some of our soldiers asked whether it was not all a dream ... . It was all so wonderful that I do not know how to describe this first glimpse of things never heard of, seen, or dreamed of before."

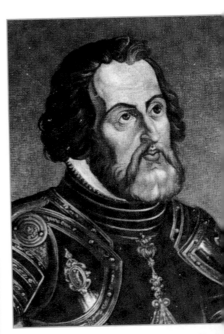

▲ **Cortés and his army landed in the New World in 1519.**

▲ This is a scene from an ancient Aztec drawing. It shows the Spanish defeating the Aztecs.

## Noble Hostage

Moctezuma allowed Cortés and some of his men to stay in his palace. The Spaniards quickly decided to make Moctezuma their hostage. The Spaniards made themselves comfortable and took charge. Moctezuma spent his days with the Spaniards, following their orders. When Cortés left Tenochtitlan on business, he put his senior officer Pedro de Alvarado in charge.

During one of these times, Alvarado was responsible for killing 3,400 Aztecs who were participating in an Aztec religious ceremony. This was more than the people of Tenochtitlan could stand, and they decided to take action. Cortés returned in time to

**chaotic:** extremely confused and disorderly

organize the Spaniards' defense. Cortés and the Spaniards boarded themselves up in the palace for protection and sent Moctezuma out to calm the crowd. However, by this time the people no longer respected Moctezuma as their leader. They did not respond to him and the scene became even more **chaotic**. People were throwing things and shouting. Somehow, an object hit Moctezuma. He did not appear to be hurt badly, but he died several weeks later.

## A New Aztec King

The Spaniards knew they needed to leave Tenochtitlan. They made a secret plan to escape, but the Aztecs discovered their plan. A great battle took place. Many Spaniards died, but Cortés and many of his men escaped during what has been called "the sad night." Cortés and the other survivors went back to the Spanish colony in Cuba for more men and

supplies. Meanwhile, the Aztecs selected a new king, Moctezuma's nephew Cuitláhuac. However, this new leader died within a few months. Like many other Aztecs, he had become sick from a disease brought by the Spaniards. The Aztecs then selected another one of Moctezuma's nephews, Cuauhtémoc, to be their king.

## The Conquest

Cuauhtémoc fought bravely against Cortés and his larger army when they returned to Tenochtitlan months later. Courage, however, was no longer enough. When the Spanish returned, they had trained soldiers, better weapons, and horses. They also had the help of many of the people the Aztecs had conquered or tried to conquer, such as the people of Tlaxcalla. The population of Tenochtitlan was sick and dying from European diseases. On August 13, 1521, the Spaniards conquered Tenochtitlan and took control of what had been the mighty Aztec empire. When Moctezuma became the king of the Aztecs in 1502, who could have known that within 20 years the empire he ruled would no longer exist? 📖

### What Do You Think?

Put yourself in Moctezuma's place. You believe that a god is going to return as a bearded, fair-skinned man. You then hear about the arrival of a bearded, fair-skinned man. What would you have done?

# MALINCHE — The Key to the Spanish Conquest of the Aztecs?

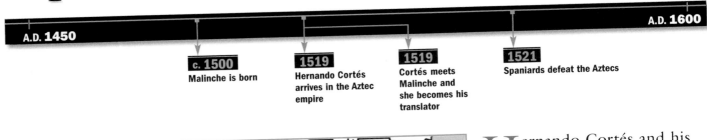

A.D. **1450**

A.D. **1600**

**c. 1500**
Malinche is born

**1519**
Hernando Cortés
arrives in the Aztec
empire

**1519**
Cortés meets
Malinche and
she becomes his
translator

**1521**
Spaniards defeat the Aztecs

▲ Malinche was born in the coastal city of Coatzacualco. She later was a slave to a group of people in Tabasco where she learned to speak Mayan.

Hernando Cortés and his army of 550 soldiers arrived in the Aztec empire in 1519. By the year 1521, the Aztecs were defeated and the Spanish took control of the area. The Spaniards called the area "New Spain" and began what would be a long period of rule over the people in the region.

It seems puzzling to people today that the Aztecs—who had a large, powerful empire—could be defeated in such a short period of time by such a small group of Spaniards.

One reason for the defeat was that many of the native people in the city-states controlled by the Aztecs helped the Spanish conquerors. These native people were unhappy with the harsh Aztec rule. In addition to the help they received from the native people, the Spaniards also had better weapons and horses in battle. Also, many of the native people became extremely sick and died of diseases that the Spaniards brought to the Americas. The Spanish were also very lucky. Perhaps the biggest piece of luck was meeting a woman named Malinche.

## A Noblewoman, Then a Slave

Malinche was born around 1500 near the coastal city of Coatzacualco. She was born into a noble Aztec family. Her family spoke Nahuatl, and she was educated as a noble Aztec girl. Her life changed dramatically, however, after her father died. Her mother remarried and had a son with her new husband.

According to an account by the Spanish soldier Bernal Díaz del Castillo, Malinche's family gave her to a group of Indians passing by and told everyone that she had died. These Indians, in turn, gave Malinche to another group of people in Tabasco. Born the daughter of an important nobleman, she now had become a slave to a Tabascan chief. It was during this time that Malinche learned to speak Mayan.

## A Gift to Cortés

When Hernando Cortés and his army landed on the eastern coast of Central America in 1519, he came face to face with the group of people in Tabasco who held Malinche as a slave. The two groups fought in a brief battle, but the Tabascans soon withdrew. Instead of fighting another battle, they gave gifts to Cortés. Among the gifts were Malinche and about 19 other young women. Bernal

> "Doña Marina ... heard every day how the Indians were going to kill us and eat our flesh with chili and had seen us surrounded in the late battles, and knew that all of us were sick and wounded, yet never allowed us to see any sign of fear in her, only a courage passing that of a man."
>
> —A Spanish soldier under Cortés

Díaz del Castillo described Malinche as "good looking and intelligent and without embarrassment." He reported, "Cortés allotted one of the women to each of his captains." However, when Cortés recognized Malinche's education and language abilities, he took her for himself. Malinche and the other young women were baptized and converted to Christianity. Her Christian name was "Marina," and as a sign of respect she was called "Doña Marina."

## The Benefits of Knowing Two Languages

A short while before meeting young Malinche, Cortés had had another lucky break. He had come upon Gerónimo de Aguilar, a Spaniard who several years earlier had been shipwrecked off the coast of the Gulf of Mexico.

During that time, Aguilar learned to speak Mayan. Now everything fit into place! Cortés could speak Spanish to Aguilar, Aguilar could speak Mayan to Malinche, and Malinche could speak Nahuatl to the Aztecs. It was Malinche who translated Cortés's words to Moctezuma. One historian commented, "Without her it would have been Cortés who was conquered." He also credited Malinche's knowledge of the Aztecs' language and customs for helping the Spanish more than once get themselves out of embarrassing and dangerous situations.

HOW CORTÉS COMMUNICATED WITH THE AZTECS

Cortés — Spanish — Aguilar — Mayan — Malinche — Nahuatl — Aztecs

It's a FACT

People sometimes call Malinche the "Mexican Eve" because she gave birth to a child that was both Spanish and Indian. Her child with Cortés was the first "Mexican."

## What Do You Think?

1. What advantages did Malinche have in life? What obstacles did she have to overcome?

2. Do you think Malinche was a hero or a traitor? Why?

3. One historian commented, "Without her it would have been Cortés who was conquered." Do you agree or disagree with this statement? Why?

## A Talented, Kind, and Brave Woman

Eventually, Malinche learned to speak Spanish as well as Nahuatl and Mayan. Over time, she became more than a translator to Cortés and his soldiers.

One Spanish soldier spoke of her courage: "Doña Marina, although a native woman, possessed such manly [bravery] that, although she heard everyday how the Indians were going to kill us and eat our flesh with chili and had seen us surrounded in the late battles, and knew that all of us were sick and wounded, yet never allowed us to see any sign of fear in her, only a courage passing that of a man."

In 1523, Cortés took Doña Marina with him to stop an uprising in one of the provinces. Along the way, they stopped in Coatzacoalco. While there, she saw her mother and her half brother. Bernal Díaz del Castillo said, "Both she [Malinche's mother] and her son [Malinche's half-brother] were very much afraid of Doña Marina; they feared that she had sent for them to put them to death, and they wept." However, that is not what happened. Instead, as Castillo described it, Doña Marina "comforted them ... and gave them many golden jewels and some clothes." Eventually, Doña Marina and Cortés had a child together—a son named Martín.

## Gifts and a Marriage

Cortés gave Doña Marina gifts of land, including a piece of land that had belonged to Moctezuma. Later, Cortés, who had a wife in Spain, arranged for Doña Marina to marry a man named Juan Jaramillo. Not much is known about her after that. She died at the age of 24. Some people think of Doña Marina as a traitor to her people. However, others believe she saved many lives by convincing people to give up peacefully rather than fight against the better armed Spaniards. ⬚

# Collision of Two Worlds —
# The Aztecs and the Spanish

A.D. **1500**　　　　　　　　　　　　　　　　　　　　　　　　A.D. **1550**

**1519**
Cortés lands on the
Yucatan Peninsula

**1521**
Spaniards defeat the Aztecs

After Columbus's voyages, the Spanish began to colonize the area they claimed in the New World. They called this area "New Spain." At first, they explored islands in the Caribbean Sea and set up a base in Cuba. From there, they sent out expeditions to explore the Mexican and Central American coasts. They were especially interested in finding a kingdom that they heard was rich and powerful. In 1519, Hernando Cortés and 550 men set sail from Cuba to find this kingdom.

## A Lucky Break
The 11 ships carrying Cortés and his men landed on an island just off the Yucatan Peninsula. They met a Spanish sailor who

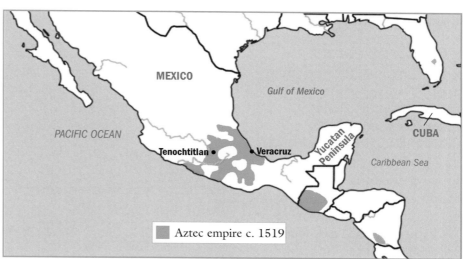

MEXICO

Gulf of Mexico

PACIFIC OCEAN

Tenochtitlan •　　• Veracruz

Yucatan
Peninsula

CUBA

Caribbean Sea

■ Aztec empire c. 1519

had been shipwrecked on the island several years earlier. His name was Gerónimo de Aguilar. While he was on the island, he had learned to speak the language of the Maya. This was a lucky break for Cortés—now he had an interpreter on the expedition who could speak both Spanish and Mayan.

## Another Lucky Break
Cortés and his men continued their journey along the Yucatan coast. At one point, a small Maya army tried to kill the Spaniards, but they were not successful. The leaders of this group then offered gifts to Cortés. One of the gifts was a young woman. Her name was

▲ Cortés and his army set sail from Cuba to explore Mexico and Central America.

Malinche, but after she became a Christian the Spanish called her Doña Marina. She was the daughter of a noble, but had been sold into slavery. She knew how to speak both Mayan and Nahuatl, the language of the Aztecs. This was another lucky break for Cortés—now he had an interpreter on the expedition who could speak both Mayan and Nahuatl. This gave Cortés a way to communicate with the Aztecs. Cortés could speak to Aguilar in Spanish, Aguilar could speak to Doña Marina in Mayan, and Doña Marina could speak to the Aztecs in Nahuatl.

▲ Malinche was Cortés's translator.

## Enemies or Gods?

Moctezuma had been hearing about Cortés from messengers in the Aztec empire. He had many questions about Cortés and was not sure if Cortés was an enemy or a god. It's easy to understand how Moctezuma would see Cortés as an enemy, but why did he think Cortés might be a god? According to an Aztec legend, Quetzalcoatl, the powerful feathered serpent god, was going to return to Tenochtitlan in 1519. This god was said to have fair skin and a beard. Cortés was fair skinned and had a beard. Could he be Quetzalcoatl?

## The First Meeting

Moctezuma decided to get more information. He sent messengers to meet Cortés and his expedition when they landed at what is present-day Veracruz. These messengers brought gifts. Moctezuma thought this would help him to know whether the men were enemies or gods. How would the strangers react to these gifts?

▶ Imagine you were one of the Spanish soldiers that entered the Aztec city of Tenochtitlan. How would you have felt?

## "They Thirsted Mightily for Gold"

An Indian who saw this meeting later told a Spanish friar, Bernardino de Sahagún, what he observed:

> [The Aztec messengers] laid before them golden streamers, quetzal feather streamers, and golden necklaces. And when they have given them the gift, they appeared to smile, to rejoice exceedingly, and to take great pleasure. Like monkeys they seized upon the gold … . For in truth they thirsted mightily for gold; they stuffed themselves with it, and starved and lusted for it like pigs.

Before the messengers returned to Tenochtitlan, they saw the Spaniards fire a cannon which greatly frightened them. They took this news back to Moctezuma. He decided to wait before taking any action against Cortés and his men.

## Making "Friends"

Cortés and his men spent the next few months exploring the region. The Spaniards went to battle against some of the local people. The Spaniards had better weapons, including guns. They also wore armor and had horses and fighting dogs. The local groups quickly saw the Spaniards as a powerful force. They also were tired of paying high tribute and taxes to the Aztecs. It didn't take them long to decide to help Cortés. More and more groups of people who had been under the Aztecs' rule decided to join Cortés.

Moctezuma sent more gifts to Cortés and asked him to go back to Spain. He did not want Cortés to visit Tenochtitlan. However, the gifts only made Cortés more eager than ever to see the city he had been hearing so much about. He was determined to go to Tenochtitlan.

## Moctezuma Welcomes Cortés

Cortés and his men continued on to the city of gold and riches. When they crossed the causeway into Tenochtitlan, Moctezuma came out to welcome them. His servants were carrying him on a raised platform. This is how a Spanish friar, Diego Durán, described the first meeting.

*On seeing Cortés, he descended [from the raised platform]. When Cortés saw this, he climbed down from his horse and went to embrace the Aztec [king], treating him with much [honor]. Moctezuma did the same, paying homage to the other with humility and words of welcome. From one of his noblemen he took a splendid necklace of gold, inlaid with precious stones, and placed it around Cortés's neck.*

## Cortés in Tenochtitlan

Moctezuma invited Cortés and his men to stay with him in his palace in Tenochtitlan. Increasingly, Cortés took charge of Tenochtitlan. He held Moctezuma hostage and told him what to say and do. The Spaniards were impressed with many of the things they saw in Tenochtitlan, but they were horrified when they saw human sacrifice as part of the Aztecs' religious rituals. This was very much against their Christian beliefs. They thought it was their responsibility to stop this practice. The Aztecs thought the Spaniards should not get involved.

▲ **The Spanish defeated the Aztecs in 1521.**

## The Night of Sorrows

The situation in Tenochtitlan was very difficult and tense. However, when Cortés left the city to handle a problem on the coast, the situation exploded. The man Cortés put in charge killed many Aztecs involved in a religious ritual. This was the last straw for the Aztecs. They decided they would have no more of the Spaniards. The Aztec army attacked the palace. Cortés, who had just returned to Tenochtitlan, and the other Spaniards tried to fight back, but it was useless. They tried to have Moctezuma calm the people, but he was wounded and later died. No one knows for sure whether it was an Aztec or Spaniard who killed him. The Spaniards knew, however, that they needed to leave Tenochtitlan quickly. They made plans to leave the city in secret on the night of June 30, 1520. Many of the Spaniards wanted to take their gold and treasures with them. When the Aztecs found out about their plan, a great battle took place. Many Spaniards and Aztecs were killed that night. Since that time, it has been known as the *noche triste* or "night of sorrows." Some call it the sad night.

## Escape and Then Return

Cortés escaped and returned to Tenochtitlan several months later. This time he had 700 Spanish soldiers and help from groups of people in the region who were tired of the Aztecs' rule. The Spaniards also were helped by an unintentional weapon—disease. People in Europe had built up resistance to diseases such as smallpox and measles. But people in the Americas did not have any resistance to them. As a result, when Cortés returned, the Aztecs were greatly weakened. In time, millions died. Here is how an observer described to Friar Sahagún what happened:

*A great plague broke out here in Tenochtitlan. It ... lasted for seventy days, striking everywhere in the city and killing a vast number of our people. Sores erupted on our faces, our breasts, our bellies; we were covered with agonizing sores from head to foot.*

*The illness was so dreadful that no one could walk or move. The sick were so utterly helpless that they could only lie on the beds. ... A great many died from this plague, and many others died of hunger. They could not get up to search for food, and everyone else was too sick to care for them, so they starved to death in their beds.*

## The End of Tenochtitlan

It took Cortés and his army and supporters several months, but they defeated the Aztecs and took over the city of Tenochtitlan on August 13, 1521. Many of the people of Tenochtitlan were killed. The Aztec civilization was destroyed. ▢

# A Spaniard's Perspective —
# BERNAL DÍAZ DEL CASTILLO

Bernal Díaz del Castillo was born in Medina del Campo, Spain in 1492. Around 1514, he decided to go to the New World. He was looking for adventure and riches. His first expedition was not very successful. He said of that experience, "Oh! What a troublesome thing it is to go and discover new lands and the risks we took it is hardly possible to exaggerate." However, he must not have been too discouraged because he went on a second expedition and then a third in 1519. Hernando Cortés led this expedition into Tenochtitlan. Bernal Díaz del Castillo was a soldier in this army and observed firsthand the Spanish conquest of the New World.

From 1541 until his death in 1584, Bernal Díaz del Castillo lived and worked as an official of the Spanish government in what is present-day Guatemala. There, in the 1560s, he wrote a book about his experiences and observations. Historians generally agree that he wrote it to correct the historical record. His book, *The True History of the Conquest of Mexico*, was not printed until 1632, long after his death. It gave historians important information about the people, events, and places of this time in history. Bernal Díaz del Castillo's original manuscript is kept in the national archives of Guatemala. Here are some excerpts from this book.

## CASTILLO ON SEEING TENOCHTITLAN FOR THE FIRST TIME

Next morning, we came to a broad causeway and continued our march ... And when we saw all those cities and villages built in the water, and other great towns on dry land, and that straight and level causeway leading to Mexico [Tenochtitlan], we were astounded. These great towns and ... buildings rising from the water, all made of stone, seemed like an enchanted vision. ... Indeed, some of our soldiers asked whether it was not all a dream. It is not surprising therefore that I should write in this vein. It was all so wonderful that I do not know how to describe this first glimpse of things never heard of, seen or dreamed of before.

## ON THE MARKET IN TENOCHTITLAN

We were astounded at the great number of people and the quantities of merchandise, and at the orderliness and good arrangements that prevailed, for we had never seen such a thing before ... You could see every kind of merchandise to be found anywhere in New Spain [present-day Mexico and Central America].

## ON THE STATUE OF HUITZILOPOCHTLI, THE AZTECS' GOD OF WAR AND THE SUN

He had a broad face and huge terrible eyes. And there were so many precious stones, so much gold, so many pearls stuck to him that his whole body was covered with them. He was wrapped with huge snakes made of gold, and he held a bow and arrows. The walls and floor of his shrine were so splashed and caked with blood that they were black.

## Analyze the Source!

1. Read the excerpts. Choose one and tell what it means in your own words.

2. How does the excerpt you chose help you learn about Aztec life and history?

3. What do these excerpts tell you about Spanish culture?

# A Spaniard's Perspective —
# HERNANDO CORTÉS

A.D. **1450**
A.D. **1550**

**1485-1547**
Hernando Cortés

**1519**
Cortés lands on the Yucatan Peninsula

**1520**
Moctezuma dies

**1521**
Cortés conquers Tenochtitlan and the Aztec empire

Hernando Cortés will forever be linked with the fall of the Aztec civilization. He was born in Spain in 1485. Thirty-four years later, in 1519, he landed on the Yucatan Peninsula and led a small army into Tenochtitlan. By 1521, Cortés had defeated the Aztecs and begun to build Mexico City on the ruins of their capital city. He wrote five letters to the king of Spain, Charles I. These letters are a good source of information about his impressions of the Aztecs.

Hernando Cortés and other Spanish conquistadors—conquerors—helped Spain become the richest and most powerful country in Europe—at least for a while. Cortés had other adventures, but later in life he was forgotten by the king he had made so wealthy. Legend says that one day Cortés saw the king's carriage and ran up to it. He threw himself in front of the carriage and asked to speak to the king. According to the legend, King Charles asked, "Who is this man?" Cortés said, "I am the man who brought you a kingdom beyond all your dreams." The story says that the king's carriage simply drove away.

Cortés died peacefully in bed at the age of 62. You can read below some of his impressions of the Aztecs and their culture.

## CORTÉS ON THE MARKET IN THE AZTEC CITY OF TLATELOLCO

... Markets are continually held and the general business of buying and selling proceeds. One square in particular ... [has] daily more than sixty thousand folk buying and selling. ... There is a street of game where they sell ... rabbits ... deer and small dogs, which they breed especially for eating. There is a street of herb-sellers where there are all manner of roots and medicinal plants that are found in the land ... There are barbers' shops where you may have your hair washed and cut. There are other shops where you may obtain food and drink. There are street porters such as we have in Spain to carry packages ... Each kind of merchandise is sold in its own particular street and no other kind may be sold there: this rule is very well enforced. All is sold by number and measure, but up till now no weighing by balance has been observed. A very fine building in the great square serves as a kind of audience chamber where ten or a dozen persons are always seated, as judges ... and pass sentence on evildoers. In the square itself there are officials who continually walk amongst the people inspecting goods ... on certain occasions I have seen them destroy measures which were false.

### Analyze the Source!

1. Read the excerpt and tell in your own words what it means.

2. How does the excerpt help you learn about Aztec life and history? What does this excerpt tell you about Spanish culture and Spanish ideas?

# A Spaniard's Perspective —
# FRANCISCO LOPEZ DE GÓMARA

Francisco Lopez de Gómara served as Hernando Cortés's loyal secretary for many years. About 30 years after the Spanish conquered present-day Mexico, Gómara wrote about Cortés, the places they conquered, and the events that had occurred. He emphasized Cortés's greatness. Other Spaniards at the time thought his account was biased. You can read here some of what he wrote. 📖

---

**spoils:** goods or property taken after a conflict, especially a war

---

## Analyze the Source!

1. Read the excerpts. Choose one and tell what it means in your own words.

2. What does the excerpt you chose tell you about Spanish culture, technology, and ideals?

3. Do you think any of these excerpts reflect bias? Explain. Give examples to explain your answers.

## GÓMARA ON CORTÉS

Cortés was a conqueror ... Beauty was of interest to him only when it was exchangeable for gold, and greatness only as something against which to measure his own. He was concerned with profit for himself and his Hispanic Majesty [King Charles I of Spain], and at most with furthering the supremacy of the Cross [the Roman Catholic Church], but certainly not the advancement of knowledge.

## ON THE AZTECS' IMPRESSIONS OF THE SPANIARDS' WEAPONS

... They had been dazzled by the flashing swords ... and they found the roar and flames of the guns more stunning than thunder and lightning from the skies ... They also were astonished and frightened by the horses, whose great mouths seemed about to swallow them, and also by the speed with which the horses overtook them. ... Since they had never before seen a horse, the first one that attacked them terrified them ...

## ON THE SPANIARDS' IMPRESSION OF TENOCHTITLAN

Mexico was a city of sixty-thousand houses ... The main part of the city was surrounded by water. ... Mexico had many temples with towers ... [The main temple] resembled a pyramid of Egypt, save that it [ended] in a square platform. ... From it one had a fine view of the city and the lake with all its towns, the most beautiful sight in the world.

## ON THE CONQUEST OF MEXICO

The Conquest of Mexico and the conversion of the peoples of New Spain ... should be included among the histories of the world ... because it was very great ... in the fact that many and powerful kingdoms were conquered with little bloodshed or harm to the inhabitants, and many millions were baptized ...

## ON DISTRIBUTING THE RICHES

The **spoils** of Mexico were melted down and ... distributed [to the men of the expedition] ... The Emperor [King Charles I of Spain] was ... given many precious stones, among them a fine emerald as big as the palm of one's hand ... a great table service of gold and silver, cups, pitchers, plates, bowls, and pots ... Besides this, he was sent ... three tigers [jaguars], one of which broke loose on shipboard and scratched six or seven men, killed two of them, and then jumped into the sea. A second tiger was killed to prevent another such accident ...

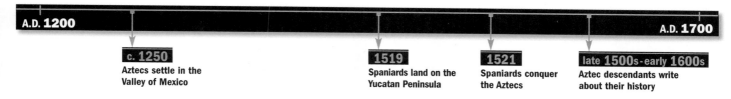

# AZTEC POETRY

| A.D. **1200** | | | | A.D. **1700** |
|---|---|---|---|---|

**c. 1250**
Aztecs settle in the Valley of Mexico

**1519**
Spaniards land on the Yucatan Peninsula

**1521**
Spaniards conquer the Aztecs

**late 1500s-early 1600s**
Aztec descendants write about their history

**B**elow are two poems and a passage that were written during different parts of Aztec history and have been translated into English. While you read, keep in mind what was happening in the Aztec empire during the time period when each piece was written.

**TENOCHTITLAN** (c. early 1500s)
Proud of itself
Is the city of Mexico-Tenochtitlan.
Here no one fears to die in war.
This is our glory.
This is Your Command,
Oh Giver of Life! ...
Do not forget it.
Who could conquer Tenochtitlan?
Who could shake the foundation of heaven?

**Analyze the Source!**

1. Read the three selections. Choose one and tell in your own words what it says.

2. How does the selection you chose help you learn about Aztec life and history?

3. What conclusions, if any, can you draw about Aztec culture from this piece? Explain your answer.

**AZTEC POEM** (c. mid-1500s)
Nothing but flowers and songs of sorrow
are left in Mexico and Tlatelolco,
where once we saw warriors and wise men.

We wander here and there
in our **desolate** poverty.
We are **mortal** men.
We have seen bloodshed and pain
where once we saw beauty and **valor**.

We are crushed to the ground;
we lie in ruins.
There is nothing but grief and suffering
in Mexico and Tlatelolco,
where once we saw beauty and valor.

Have you grown weary of your servants?
Are you angry with your servants,
O Giver of Life?

**UNTITLED PASSAGE** (c. mid-1600s)
*by Fernando Alvarado Tezozomoc*

Thus they have come to tell it,
thus they have come to record it in their narration,
and for us they have painted it in their codices,
the ancient men, the ancient women.

Thus in the future
never will it perish, never will it be forgotten,
always we will treasure it,
we, their children, their grandchildren,
brothers, great-grandchildren,
great-great-grandchildren, descendants,
We who carry their blood and their color,
we will tell it, we will pass it on
to those who do not yet live,
who are yet to be born,
the children of the Mexicans,
the children of the Tenochcans.

**desolate:** lonely
**mortal:** something that eventually dies
**valor:** courage; bravery

# FOODS that Changed the World

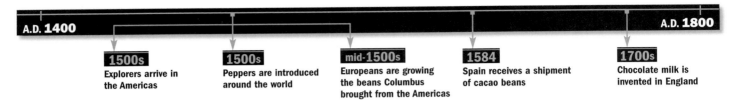

A.D. **1400**

**1500s**
Explorers arrive in
the Americas

**1500s**
Peppers are introduced
around the world

**mid-1500s**
Europeans are growing
the beans Columbus
brought from the Americas

**1584**
Spain receives a shipment
of cacao beans

**1700s**
Chocolate milk is
invented in England

A.D. **1800**

When the Spaniards arrived in the Americas, they were eager to find gold, claim new territories for Spain, and convert the native people to Christianity. Their arrival, which had many consequences, brought together two different parts of the world.

Some consequences have had an important effect on world history. For example, people from Europe brought animals such as horses and cows to the Americas. They also brought crops such as wheat and barley to plant in American soil. More importantly, perhaps, they learned about plants that were native to the Americas and introduced them to other parts of the world, including Europe, Asia, and Africa. Over time, these plants, especially beans, peppers, peanuts, tomatoes, and chocolate, changed the diets of people all over the world.

## Beans—New Varieties

When the Spaniards arrived, many of the trees, plants, and foods they saw were completely foreign to them. However, they were not at all surprised when they saw the beans grown by the Aztecs and other Mesoamerican people. Beans, peas, and lentils grow as seeds inside a covering called a pod.

Aztec empire c. 1519

▲ Europeans found new varieties of beans in the Americas.

The group of plants that includes beans, peas, and lentils are called legumes. People in other parts of the world, including Europe, grew several varieties of legumes, such as fava beans, lentils, and chickpeas. However, the varieties of beans grown in the Americas—pinto beans, kidney beans, black beans, wax beans, and lima beans—were native to the

▲ Europeans found foods native to the Americas and introduced them to other parts of the world.

Americas. They were not grown in other parts of the world until after the time of Christopher Columbus. These legumes were important to the Aztecs and other Mesoamerican peoples. Friar Bernardino de Sahagún reported that the Aztecs had 12 kinds of beans including ones that were "big, long and flat" and others that were "chili-red, blood colored." People in Mesoamerica paid their taxes in beans. Beans also were an important part of people's diet. Sahagún described one way the people prepared beans: "It can be cooked in a olla [clay pot]; it can be baked. ... Grains of maize can be added."

Historians believe that Columbus probably brought some of these American varieties of beans with him on his return to Europe. By the mid-1500s, Europeans knew about and were growing some of these new varieties. People in Italy began using white kidney beans (which they called cannellini) in soup. People in France added beans to meat to create a dish called "cassoulet." American varieties of legumes did not become as popular in Asia or Africa.

▲ Peppers from the Americas quickly became popular throughout the world.

# Peppers—Mild, Hot, Spicy

Christopher Columbus kept a journal during his voyages of discovery. This gives us much information about his travels, including information about the people he met, their customs, and the food they ate. On January 15, 1493, he wrote a journal entry about peppers. He compared the peppers he found in the New World to black pepper. Europeans already knew about black pepper, which was a valuable seasoning imported from Asia. They ground peppercorns into what we would call black pepper. However, the peppers we know of as hot peppers, sweet peppers, green peppers, and chile peppers were unknown to people outside the Americas. These peppers were all native American plants that were introduced to Europe, Asia, Africa, and other parts of the world in the 1500s.

Peppers quickly became very popular throughout the world. Europeans liked sweet peppers or varieties of peppers that were not too hot and spicy. People in regions of Asia and Africa, in particular, went wild over hot peppers. They became a very important part of their cooking. It is difficult to think about some kinds of Chinese food or Indian food without thinking about "hot and spicy" food. The peppers that make this cooking so distinctive came from the Americas. Today, people all over the world eat peppers and pepper products—things like salsa, hot sauce, paprika, and chili powder.

# Peanuts—Delicious and Nutritious

Have you been to a baseball game and munched on a bag of peanuts? Do you like peanut butter sandwiches? Do warm peanut butter cookies melt in your mouth? Many people do not realize that peanuts were one of the gifts of the New World. They are not only delicious, but also an important addition to the world's menu. Peanuts were first grown in South America, but soon spread to Central America and then North America. Peanuts puzzled Columbus and the Europeans who arrived after him. They certainly had seen nuts before, but they were used to nuts that grew on trees. Peanuts grow under the soil. Europeans were interested in the peanut plant, but the climate in Europe was too cold for peanuts to grow there successfully. However, the peanut plant became a popular and important food crop in Africa and Asia. The people of Africa, in particular, welcomed the peanut plant. It was easy to grow and provided a needed source of food and oil for cooking.

▼ Peanuts were first grown in South America.

Today, the peanut is an important ingredient in African cooking, particularly West African cooking. Peanuts also are important in many parts of Asia, including Indonesia. One of the most famous Indonesian dishes is called saté. It consists of small pieces of grilled meat served with a spicy peanut sauce. Of course, peanuts are still important in the Americas, particularly in the southeastern region of the United States. In addition to peanut butter sandwiches and peanut butter cookies, we eat peanut brittle, peanut candy bars, peanut butter ice cream, and salted peanuts.

## Tomatoes—Red Gold?

If someone invited you for an Italian dinner, what food would you expect to eat? Many people would answer "spaghetti" or some kind of

▲ Did you know that tomatoes are native to the Americas?

### What Do You Think?

1. Why do you think some people were suspicious of new foods from the Americas?

2. In the long run, which do you think was more important, the gold Spain got from the Americas or the new foods they learned about? Explain your answer.

3. How did the foods of the Americas affect people in other parts of the world?

pasta and spicy tomato sauce. However, Italians did not know about the tomato until after Columbus's voyage to the Americas. People in other parts of the world did not know about or grow tomatoes. Tomatoes are native to the Americas.

Friar Bernardino de Sahagún described how the Aztecs used tomatoes for sauces. He also wrote about the tomatoes on display at the market in Tenochtitlan: "large tomatoes, small tomatoes ... those which are yellow, very yellow, quite yellow, red, very red, ... bright red, reddish, rosy dawn colored." The Aztecs and other Mesoamerican peoples grew and used many different varieties of tomatoes. Spaniards brought tomato seeds back to Spain, but at first tomatoes were not very popular. People did not know what to do with them. Some

people were suspicious that tomatoes might be dangerous to eat. Others thought tomatoes might stir up feelings of love. They even called it the "love apple." People in Spain and other countries in southern Europe began to grow and use tomatoes in their cooking. Over time, it became an essential ingredient in soups and sauces. Tomatoes were cooked and spread over a thin crust of bread to make pizza. In Africa and Asia, tomatoes were used in stews and soups and in sauces served with meat and rice.

Today, tomatoes are eaten every day by many Americans—in sauces, in soups, in salads, on pizza, bottled as ketchup, in salsa, and sliced fresh with a little oil and salt.

## Chocolate— Food of the Gods

The Maya, Aztecs, and other Mesoamerican peoples placed a high value on cacao beans. Throughout Mesoamerica, people used cacao beans as a form of currency to pay taxes and tribute. Why were cacao beans so valuable? They could be ground into a paste and mixed with other spices, honey, and water to make a slightly bitter, very foamy drink. This beverage was only served to nobles, wealthy traders, and important warriors. Friar Bernardino de Sahagún called it "the drink of nobles" and described what happened when he observed an Aztec woman pouring it from one cup to another: "She makes it form a head, makes it foam." Cacao beans only grow in tropical lowland areas. Cacao seeds (often called "beans") grow in pods on the trunk and branches of the cacao tree. There are about 20-40 beans in each pod. The Aztecs' subjects sent the beans to Tenochtitlan as tribute. It took a while to process the beans so that they could be used. The covering on them was removed. The beans were dried, washed, and then roasted. The meat inside the bean was ground into a paste.

The first record we have of Europeans learning about chocolate comes from Bernal Díaz del Castillo, one of Hernando Cortés's soldiers. He wrote that Moctezuma "was served, in cup-shaped vessels of pure gold, a certain drink made from cacao." When Cortés returned to Spain, he took some of the cacao beans with him. In 1584, Spaniards in the Americas sent a shipment of these beans to Spain. The Spaniards must have valued cacao beans because they kept them a secret for about 100 years. Over time, however, people in Italy, France, and other European countries began to enjoy the chocolate beverage from the Americas. Places where people could go to drink this beverage popped up in

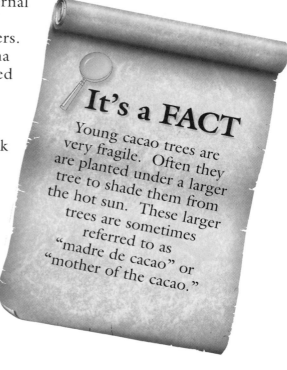

## It's a FACT

Young cacao trees are very fragile. Often they are planted under a larger tree to shade them from the hot sun. These larger trees are sometimes referred to as "madre de cacao" or "mother of the cacao."

London in the late 1600s. It was not until the 1700s, however, that the queen of England's doctor had the idea to mix chocolate with milk. Later, the Cadbury brothers began to use chocolate in a candy bar. The name plant scientists have given to the cacao tree is *Theobroma cacao*, which means "food of the gods." Americans today enjoy chocolate made from cacao beans in many forms—in candy, cookies, brownies, ice cream, and cake. Like the Aztecs, we drink a beverage made from the cacao bean—hot chocolate.

◄ Chocolate is made from cacao beans.

# PACHACUTI —
# The Greatest King of the Inca

A.D. **1400**                                                                                    A.D. **1500**

**c. 1438**
Pachacuti becomes
ruler of the Inca

**1471**
Pachacuti names one
of his sons ruler

**1471**
Pachacuti dies

◀ **Until the early 1400s, the Inca controlled only a small area around Cuzco, their capital. At the height of its power in the early 1500s, the Inca empire covered parts of present-day Ecuador, Peru, Bolivia, Argentina, and Chile.**

early 1400s
early 1500s

▲ **The Inca sent observers to learn about a region they wanted to conquer. Then they tried to persuade the people of the region to give up without a fight. If the people refused, the Inca sent a huge army of soldiers to defeat them. They made some of the leaders of the defeated people live in Cuzco.**

Until the 1400s, the people we call the Inca were just one of a number of small kingdoms in the northwest region of South America. They raided neighboring kingdoms and made them pay tribute. Their first king was Manco Capac. His title was "Inca," a Quechua word that means "lord" or "king." Today, we refer to all the people of the kingdom he ruled as the Inca. When Viracocha Inca, the eighth Inca (or ruler), came to power in the early 1400s, he controlled a 20-mile area around Cuzco. He wanted to expand the size of his kingdom and was successful in increasing it another five miles. However, it was one of his sons, Pachacuti, who would be the man most responsible for creating the huge empire of the Inca.

## Battling the Chanca

Viracocha Inca led his warriors to victory in a battle against the Chanca people. Then there was a second battle. One source said, "Pachacuti captured two Chanca captains in battle, cut off their heads, and put the heads at the tips of lances. At the sight, the Chanca troops fled."

Another source reported, "Pachacuti was merciless with the Chanca captives ... [but] he was generous in rewarding the people who had ... joined his ranks, and their captains offered to serve him and pleaded with him to wear the **fringe** which signified kingship."

As king, Viracocha had the right to the spoils—all the land and riches—of the conquered kingdom. Would Pachacuti take these spoils and become king himself? According to one historical account, "Pachacuti politely declined, saying that his father was still alive, but asked them to go to his father and do whatever Viracocha commanded." Pachacuti's followers went to Viracocha and asked him to make Pachacuti the new king. Viracocha was impressed with their loyalty and with his son's behavior. Not long after, in 1438, Viracocha went to Cuzco. According to the story, "When he met his son, he declared him to be truly a son of the Sun and took the fringe and put it on his head." This act made Pachacuti the new king.

## A Political Leader

Pachacuti has been described as "the most [brave] and warlike, wise and statesmanlike of all the Incas." He created an orderly society that was governed by laws. One account says, "He injected order and reason into everything ..." He reorganized Cuzco and directed the people to build terraces for crops. He also wanted a count—or census—of all the people in his empire. He used the information from this census to distribute land. He directed the construction of canals to irrigate the crops, storehouses to hold the surplus food and other supplies, and bridges to make travel possible throughout the kingdom. One account says he "married the young unmarried men and women of Cuzco ... giving to each man and woman two costumes ... food and dishes and everything they need for a household."

**fringe:** a line of threads hanging loose

▼ Pachacuti directed the people to build terraces. Terraces gave the Inca more agricultural land for planting crops.

▼ Pachacuti directed the construction of bridges to make travel possible throughout the kingdom.

▲ Pachacuti built religious temples such as this. He made sure that sacrifices were made to Inca ancestors and gods. You can see here the symbol of the Inca god Inti.

**It's a FACT**

"Pachacuti" means "change of time" or "earth turned upside down." People thought the changes he made were so important that they seemed to have turned the world around.

## What Do You Think?

1. Why do you think Pachacuti is remembered as the greatest Inca king?

2. Some of the accounts of Pachacuti's life tell about his military campaigns in great detail. Others hardly mention them. How do people decide what information to include or leave out in factual accounts of events?

3. Symbols are important in every culture. Fringe was placed on the head of the new Inca king. What symbols of power and authority are given to new leaders in the United States?

## A Religious Leader

As religious leader, Pachacuti made sure that temples were rebuilt and that religious ceremonies were performed. He made sure sacrifices were made to the Inca's ancestors and gods. One account says, "Sacrifices were made to each mummy, and so they were transformed into gods ..." It also was written that he "eliminated and added rites and ceremonies ... enlarged ... the temples with magnificent structures ...; reformed the calendar; divided the year into twelve months ... ."

## A Military Leader

As a military leader, Pachacuti added much new territory to the Inca empire. Many kingdoms fought back courageously, but some had heard of the Inca army's strength and gave up peacefully. When Pachacuti returned to Cuzco after victorious battles, there were great celebrations. One account says, "Having enlarged his empire with so many and such vast provinces, during the remainder of his life this king devoted himself to improving the provinces by building in the major towns of each one magnificent temples and palaces and some strong castles ..."

## A Ruling Family

Pachacuti lived a long life and had many children—some say he had 200 sons and 100 daughters. After ruling the Inca for almost 35 years, he "placed the fringe" on the head of his son Topa Inca Yupanqui in 1471. Pachacuti died soon thereafter. According to several accounts, "After he died, a song was sung through the town: I flowered like a flower in the garden, I gave order and reason to the best of my ability, and now I am dust."

# Honoring the Gods

Cristobal de Molina was a Spaniard who learned Quechua, the Inca language. He was interested in the religious beliefs and rituals of the Inca. He was able to talk to important Inca people about how they organized their calendar and why they celebrated festivals. He learned that most of the important events took place around the agricultural cycle—the first rain, planting time, the harvest. The Inca believed they had to pray to their gods for help and that they had to make sacrifices to satisfy the gods. Molina gathered all the information he learned and published a book, *The Fables and Rites of the Incas*, in 1573. You can read below an excerpt from his book. In this excerpt, he describes an Inca festival held in the month called Coya-raymi (our month of August). The Inca performed this ceremony to ask the gods to keep the people healthy. ▢

## Cristobal de Molina on an Inca Festival

At about eight or nine in the morning the principal lord Inca [the king], with his wife, and the lords of the council who were in his house, came forth into the great square of Cuzco, richly dressed. They also brought out the image of the Sun called Apupunchau, which was the principal image among those in the temple. They were accompanied by all the priests of the Sun, who brought the two figures of gold, and their women called Inca-Ollo and Palla-Ollo. There also came forth the woman called Coya-facssa, who was dedicated to the Sun. She was either the sister or the daughter of the ruler. The priests carried the image of the Sun, and placed it on a bench prepared for it in the square ... . At this feast they brought out all the [mummies] of their lords and ladies, very richly adorned. The bodies were carried by the descendants of the respective [families], and were deposited in the square on seats of gold, according to the order in which they lived.

### Analyze the Source!

1. Read the excerpt and tell in your own words what it says.

2. How does this excerpt help you learn about the Inca's religious beliefs? How does it help you learn about their social organization and economy?

3. What conclusions could you draw about the Inca's view of their ancestors? What evidence in the excerpt supports your position?

# GARCILASO DE LA VEGA —
## "El Inca" Tells about Everyday Life

▲ The shaded area shows the Inca empire during the 1400s and 1500s.

early 1400s
early 1500s

Garcilaso de la Vega was born in 1539 in Cuzco in present-day Peru. His father was a Spanish captain and governor of Cuzco. His mother was a member of an Inca noble family. Garcilaso de la Vega, who is sometimes referred to as "El Inca," grew up in the Americas. However, he moved to Spain when he was 21 years old. He wrote about daily life in the Inca empire before the Spanish conquered it. He also wrote about the time after the Spaniards came to power.

Part One of Garcilaso de la Vega's written account, *Royal Commentaries of the Incas*, was published in 1609. This first volume focuses on the history of the Inca and their culture. It ends with the civil war between the brothers Atahualpa and Huascar, which happened just before the Spanish arrived. Part Two of his work was published in 1616-1617, after he died in 1616. This second volume tells about the Spanish rule of the area. Garcilaso de la Vega's work continues to be an important source of information about the Inca. It describes an Inca civilization that was orderly and stable and people who were hard-working, honest, and moral. His *Royal Commentaries* provides a more positive view of the Inca civilization than the accounts left by Spanish conquerors. You can read on the next page several excerpts from Garcilaso de la Vega's account. ▢

◀ This is a photograph of Cuzco today.

Families were given farm land based on their needs. The nobles redistributed the land if a family's needs changed.

## GARCILASO DE LA VEGA WRITES ABOUT INCA CHILDREN ...

As soon as a child was born, they bathed the little creature with cold water before wrapping it in a blanket; and each morning, before it was wrapped up, they washed it with cold water, generally in the open air. And when the mother would show unusual tenderness, she took the water in her mouth and washed the whole of the child's body with it, except the head, and particularly the crown of the head, which they never touched. They said that they did this to accustom the children to the cold and to hard work, and also to strengthen their limbs.

## ABOUT USING STRINGS AND KNOTS ...

Quipu means to knot, or a knot, and it was also understood as an account, because the knots supplied an account of everything. The Indians made strings of various colors. Some were all of one color, others of two combined, others of three, others more; and these colors, whether single or combined, all had a meaning ... . The thing to which a string referred was understood by its color: for instance, a yellow string referred to gold, a white one to silver, and a red one to soldiers ... . Although there was, at that time, little difference of character among the Indians, because owing to their gentle dispositions and excellent government all might be called good, yet the best, and those who had given the longest proofs of their fitness, were selected for [being in charge of the quipu] ... and other offices. They were not given away from motives of favoritism, because these Indians were never influenced by such considerations, but from considerations of special fitness.

## ABOUT PREPARING AND DIVIDING THE AGRICULTURAL LAND ...

Having dug the channels [for irrigation], they leveled the fields and squared them so that the irrigation water could be adequately distributed. They built level terraces on the mountains and hillsides. ... If there were rocky places, the rocks were removed and replaced by earth brought from elsewhere to form the terraces, so that the space should not be wasted ...

Having thus extended the cultivable land, each settlement in each province measured all the land assigned to it and divided it into three parts, one for the Sun, one for the king, and one for the inhabitants. In the division care was taken that the inhabitants should have enough to sow for themselves, and rather too much than too little. When the population of a town or province increased, part of the area assigned to the Sun or the Inca [the king] was transferred to their subjects.

## ABOUT PACHACUTI, THE INCA RULER ...

[His name] means "Reformer of the World." That title was confirmed afterwards by his distinguished acts and sayings, insomuch that his first name was entirely forgotten. He governed his empire with so much industry, [caution] and resolution, as well in peace as in war, that not only did he increase the boundaries ... but also he enacted many laws, all which have been confirmed by our Catholic kings, except those relating to idolatry and to forbidden degrees of marriage. This Inca [Pachacuti] above all things [dignified] and increased ... the schools that were found in Cuzco.

## Analyze the Source!

1. Read the excerpts and tell in your own words what one of the excerpts says.

2. What conclusions, if any, can you draw about the Inca's political organization or government from this excerpt? Explain why you can or cannot draw conclusions.

3. Do you think Garcilaso de la Vega showed a bias toward the Inca or the Spanish? Explain your answer.

# ATAHUALPA and HUASCAR — War between Brothers

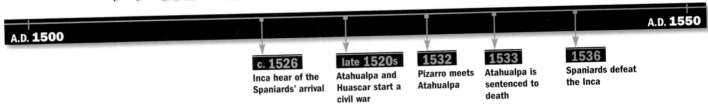

| A.D. **1500** | | | | | A.D. **1550** |

**c. 1526**
Inca hear of the Spaniards' arrival

**late 1520s**
Atahualpa and Huascar start a civil war

**1532**
Pizarro meets Atahualpa

**1533**
Atahualpa is sentenced to death

**1536**
Spaniards defeat the Inca

▲ The shaded area shows the Inca empire during the 1400s and 1500s. While he was king, Huayna Capac expanded the borders of the Inca empire into present-day Ecuador and southern Colombia.

**doctrine:** ideas taught

After ruling the Inca for almost 35 years, Pachacuti was more than 70 years old and no longer felt able to govern the large empire he had created. He "placed the fringe" on the head of his son Topa Inca Yupanqui in 1471. This gave the empire its new ruler—the tenth Inca. Upon being crowned king, Topa Inca Yupanqui followed the model his father had set. The record says, "he decided to continue with the conquests of his father, and since he found the military so well prepared ... very little was necessary in order to put his desire into effect." He led military campaigns and successfully expanded the Inca empire. He ruled the Inca until 1493.

## Huayna Capac and the Arrival of the Spanish

The next ruler was Topa Inca Yupanqui's son, Huayna Capac. Huayna Capac also achieved many military victories. He expanded the borders of the Inca empire into present-day Ecuador and southern Colombia. The empire he ruled stretched nearly 2,500 miles from north to south. It was late 1526 or early 1527 when Huayna Capac heard about the arrival of the Spaniards. The Spaniards had landed at the coastal town of Tumbes (in present-day Ecuador)—about 100 miles from where Huayna Capac was staying. One account says the king's messengers were very frightened by the Europeans. They reported "how some strange people never seen before who preached new **doctrines** and laws had shown up on the beach of Tumbes." The messengers said the men were "stuffed into their clothes, which covered them from head to foot; they were white and had beards and a ferocious appearance." When Huayna Capac asked where the strangers came from, he was told "the strangers traveled across the sea in large wooden houses."

| INCA KINGS |
|---|
| Pachacuti |
| Topa Inca Yapanqui |
| Huayna Capac |
| Huascar and Atahualpa |

◄ **This scene shows the murder of Huascar by order of Atahualpa.**

Later there were reports of the strangers robbing treasures from Inca palaces. Not long after the Spanish arrived, many people in the region began to become sick and die. They had become infected with a disease the Europeans unknowingly carried with them to the New World. Some think it was smallpox; others believe the disease was **typhus**. Whichever it was, the Inca ruler Huayna Capac died from the disease in 1527.

**typhus:** a disease that causes fever and skin rash

## An Empire Divided

Before he died, Huayna Capac divided the Inca empire between two of his sons—Huascar and Atahualpa. Although Atahualpa was said to be his favorite son, Huascar was given the larger half of the empire as well as the title of Inca. Huascar ruled from the capital city of Cuzco. Atahualpa's kingdom was centered in Quito.

Atahualpa is described as a "noble youth" and one who was "well received by the old captains and soldiers." Accounts tell us that he was born in Cuzco and often went with his father on military expeditions. This meant that he had "more than average experience in matters of war," and the Inca's captains knew him and loved him. Huascar was not as popular or as experienced as his brother in military matters. Some believed he was a spiritual man, but others thought he was crazy. He ordered people be put to death for breaking very minor laws.

## An Empire at War

The war between these two brothers was sparked in the late 1520s when Huascar invited his brother to come to Cuzco. Huascar wanted Atahualpa to attend the ceremony making Huascar ruler of the Inca. Atahualpa refused the invitation. Huascar asked again, but again Atahualpa refused. Huascar asked a third time, and a third time was refused. Instead of coming in person, Atahualpa sent some of his officials with gifts for his brother. Huascar was furious. He burned the gifts and had several of the officials killed. The others were sent back dressed as women.

A series of battles followed. Huascar sent his army to fight his brother. However, Huascar's army was no match for the skill and experience of Atahualpa and his generals. It is estimated that between 15,000-16,000 warriors were killed in one of these battles between the brothers. Soon the entire Inca empire became involved in this bloody civil war, which continued from the late 1520s until 1532. In that year, the brothers' armies met in a great battle outside the city of Cuzco. At first, it seemed as if Huascar would win the battle. However, Atahualpa's men were clever and determined. They also were ferocious fighters. As many as 150,000 people died at the battle.

In the end, Atahualpa's forces were victorious. Atahualpa's generals sent word that Huascar had been captured. This prompted Atahualpa to make himself the sole ruler of the Inca empire. He had anyone who claimed to be the new ruler killed, including all of Huascar's children. He allowed Huascar to live for a while longer.

## It's a FACT

The Inca ruler was considered so holy that he was not supposed to touch the ground. As a result, he was carried on a litter (a raised platform) from place to place. If one of the men who carried the litter stumbled or fell, the man was killed.

► Atahualpa first met Pizarro at Cajamarca in 1532. The Spaniards were not planning for a peaceful meeting. They intended to capture Atahualpa. They took him hostage and massacred most of the 6,000 men who came with him.

Atahualpa celebrated his victory and his kingship in Cajamarca, a town of about 10,000 people. Atahualpa enjoyed the hot springs there and planned the ceremony that would make him king. However, his celebration was interrupted by a message telling him that the Spaniards had returned to Tumbes. Although no one knows why, Atahualpa decided to meet with the Spaniards.

## Meeting at Cajamarca

Francisco Pizarro, head of the Spanish expedition, led his men to meet Atahualpa. As they crossed the Andes Mountains and looked down on Cajamarca in the valley below, one of the Spanish soldiers, Juan Ruiz de Arce, reported, "The Indians' camp looked like a very beautiful city. So many were the tents that we were filled with fright ... It filled all us Spaniards with confusion and fear. But we dared not show it, much less turn back, for if they sensed the least weakness in us, the very Indians we brought with us would have killed us."

Pizarro sent a message to Atahualpa asking for a meeting. They agreed to meet face to face on November 16, 1532. The Spaniards were not planning a peaceful meeting. They intended to capture Atahualpa. They took him hostage and massacred most of the 6,000 men who came with him. While he was being held captive, Atahualpa ordered that Huascar be killed. Pizarro promised to release Atahualpa if he paid a huge ransom. Gold and silver poured in from all over the Inca empire, but later Pizarro had Atahualpa put to death anyway.

Historical accounts say that the Spaniards buried Atahualpa and "put a cross on top of him because he had become a Christian before his death." Reports also say that "Indians dug him up secretly and took him to be buried" in the Inca way.

## The End of the Inca

The Inca empire did not end immediately. An Inca army fought against the Spaniards, but was defeated in 1536. A few Inca fled to settlements high in the Andes. They struggled against the Spanish until 1572, when the last Inca leader was killed. This marked the end of the Inca empire. 📖

### What Do You Think?

**1.** How did the war between the brothers contribute to the downfall of the Inca empire?

**2.** Describe the method the Inca used for selecting new leaders. What were the advantages and disadvantages of this method?

**3.** Think about the way the Inca government was organized. Who had the power in the government? How would capturing Atahualpa give Pizarro control over all the Inca?

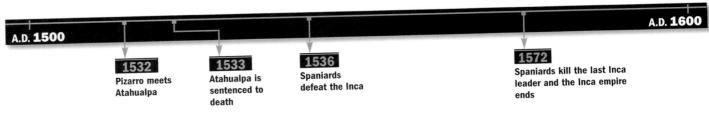

# Collision of Two Worlds —
## The Inca and the Spanish

A.D. **1500**

**1532**
Pizarro meets Atahualpa

**1533**
Atahualpa is sentenced to death

**1536**
Spaniards defeat the Inca

**1572**
Spaniards kill the last Inca leader and the Inca empire ends

A.D. **1600**

▲ The shaded area shows the Inca empire during the 1400s and 1500s.

**privation:** the lack of basic needs

▲ The Spaniards wanted gold and cloth that came from the wool of llamas like this.

After Columbus's voyages to the New World, the Spanish began to colonize the area they called, "New Spain." At first, they explored islands in the Caribbean Sea and set up a base in Cuba. From there, they sent out expeditions to explore the Mexican and Central American coasts. In 1519, Hernando Cortés and 500 men set sail from Cuba to find the rich and powerful kingdom of the Aztecs. Francisco Pizarro was another Spanish explorer interested in finding a city of gold. He set sail with two ships in 1524, but he was not successful. However, he was a determined man. He led a second expedition in 1526 to find the rich and powerful kingdom he had heard so much about. Pizarro and his expedition made their base in the area that is present-day Panama.

## An Interesting Encounter

Pizarro sent one ship to travel down the coast to find out about the land. Members of the expedition met some native people who wore clothes made of fine cloth. The Spaniards thought the cloth was as excellent as cloth in Europe. The native people told the Spaniards that the cloth came from the wool of llamas. They said the people who lived to the south had great herds of llamas. The Spaniards also learned that the people to the south had great amounts of gold.

## Poverty or Wealth?

Some of Pizarro's men wanted to go home. They were tired and uncomfortable. Pizarro drew a line in the ground and said to them, "Comrades and friends, on this side [of the line] lies poverty, hunger, effort, ... and **privation**. On that side lies pleasure. On this side we return to Panama and poverty. On that side, we become rich." Twelve men agreed to go with Pizarro. At first, the group sailed south. They looked out from the deck of their ship at the land of gold. Then they reached a busy port city where something remarkable happened.

## "Big Ears"

While they were walking among the people in the busy port city, a man stepped up to them. He was a representative of the Inca king, Huayna Capac. He was responsible for keeping the king informed about what was happening in the empire. As a representative of the king, he wore huge ornaments in his earlobes. The Spaniards called such men *orejónes*—"big ears." The king's representative asked the Spaniards why they had come and what they wanted. Pizarro told him about the king of Spain. Pizarro also gave him an iron ax as a gift. This was quite remarkable because iron was unknown to the Inca. "Big Ears" sent a messenger to Huayna Capac telling him about these strangers.

## More Exploring

Pizarro and his men continued their expedition along the southern coast of present-day Peru. They thought the people of the region were very friendly toward them. They didn't know that many of these people were angry with the Inca who ruled them. Huayna Capac was busy stopping rebellions against his authority. In 1528, Pizarro returned to Spain. He wanted the king to give him money so he could conquer the Inca empire.

▲ Atahualpa met Pizarro at Cajamarca in 1532.

## An Unintentional Weapon ...

Meanwhile, the Spaniards were already conquering the region with an unintentional weapon—disease. People in Europe had built up resistance to diseases such as smallpox, measles, and typhus. But the people of the Americas did not have any resistance to these diseases. Huayna Capac had never met a European, but the diseases they carried spread through the population. Huayna Capac died in 1527 from one of these diseases, probably smallpox or typhus.

**squadron:** a unit of soldiers

## ... And a Civil War

Huayna Capac's two sons, Huascar and Atahualpa, argued about which one of them should become king. Their argument caused a civil war in the Inca empire. Thousands died as these brothers struggled for power. Eventually, Atahualpa defeated his brother. He took his troops to the small town of Cajamarca.

## Pizarro Returns

Francisco Pizarro finally convinced the king to support another expedition to the Americas. He arrived back in 1532 with 63 cavalrymen and 200 foot soldiers. He was surprised that the por city they had stopped at on their last visit was no longer a busy port city. Most of the people were sick, dying, or already dead. Pizarro and his men left quickly. They decided to go to Cajamarca. They had learned that Atahualpa was there.

## "Let's Meet"

Pizarro sent a message to Atahualpa asking for a meeting. Atahualpa was curious about these strangers and decided to meet with them. Atahualpa was probably about 30 years old at the time. He wore beautiful clothes and jewels. He offered Pizarro a drink made out of maize. At first, Pizarro refused this drink, but Atahualpa would not begin discussions until this custom was honored. They agreed to meet the next day—November 16, 1532—for more serious discussions.

## A Peaceful Meeting?

Atahualpa thought the meeting with Pizarro would be peaceful. His servants carried him on a raised platform called a litter to the main plaza of the town. Francisco de Xeres, Pizarro's secretary, wrote about the meeting in 1534. He described Atahualpa's entrance this way:

> First came a **squadron** of Indians dressed in ... different colors, like a chess board. They advanced, removing the straws from the ground, and sweeping the road. Next came three squadrons in different dresses, dancing and singing. Then came a number of men with armor, large metal plates and crowns of gold and silver. Among them was Atahualpa in a litter lined with plumes of macaws' feathers, of many colors, and adorned with plates of gold and silver. Many Indians carried it on their shoulders on high. Next came two other litters and two hammocks, in which were some principal chiefs; and lastly, several squadrons of Indians with crowns of gold and silver.

Pizarro asked Vicente de Valverde, the priest on the expedition, if he wished to speak with Atahualpa. Father Valverde said that he did. He held a cross in one hand and a Christian Bible in the other and said to Atahualpa, "I am a priest of God, and I teach Christians the things of God, and in like manner I come to teach you. What I teach is that which God says to us in this book."

According to Xeres, Atahualpa asked for the book, looked at it, and then he threw it on the ground. Pizarro was furious and grabbed his arm. Then he tried to pull him off the litter. The Inca were shocked. No one was allowed to touch the king. Then, according to Xeres, Pizarro cried out, "Santiago," which in English means "St. James."

## Atahualpa Held Hostage

All this time, Pizarro's men had been hiding. At the moment they heard Pizarro call out "Santiago," they rode into the crowd and shot their guns. Everything was very confusing. Within an hour, the plaza was calm again, but dead bodies were everywhere. Here is what Xeres wrote about this event:

> *During the whole time no Indian raised his arms against a Spaniard. So great was the terror of the Indians at seeing the Governor [Pizarro] force his way through them, at hearing the fire of the artillery, and beholding the charging of the horses, a thing never before heard of, that they thought more of flying to save their lives than of fighting.*

▲ The Spaniards seized Atahualpa and held him hostage in Cajamarca.

Atahualpa's clothes were torn. The Spaniards tied his hands and held him hostage. Atahualpa knew that Pizarro wanted gold, so he promised him a room filled with gold if they released him. Pizarro also wanted a room filled with silver. Soon gold and silver poured in from all over the Inca empire. Historians estimate that the Inca gave Pizarro more than six tons of gold and more than 12 tons of silver so that he would set Atahualpa free.

## Atahualpa's Death

Pizarro received news that one of Atahualpa's generals was going to rescue him. Pizarro decided that Atahualpa had to die. In 1533, he put him on trial on trumped up charges and sentenced him to death.

## The End of the Inca

An Inca army fought against the Spaniards, but the army was defeated in 1536. A few Inca fled to settlements high in the Andes. They struggled against the Spanish until 1572, when the last Inca leader was killed. This was the end of the Inca empire. 📖

### What Do You Think?

1. Describe the factors that contributed to the Inca's defeat. Which factor do you think was most important?

2. Examine the meeting between Pizarro and Atahualpa from both perspectives. How do you think the Spanish justified their actions?

3. Find the current value of gold the Inca gave Pizarro. What would be the value of this ransom today?

# A Peruvian Chief's "Letter to a King"

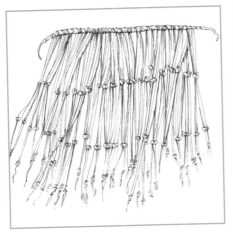

▲ Some historians believe the Inca used knotted, colored strings called "quipus" to record events.

Unlike the Maya and the Aztecs, the ancient Inca did not have a writing system. Some historians believe the Inca used knotted, colored strings called "quipus" to record events, but no one has been able to decipher the "language" of these strings. The lack of a written language means that most of the writing about the Inca is from the perspective of the Spanish. That is why modern historians were very excited to learn about a document written by an Inca noble, Huamán Poma. He wrote this account between 1567 and 1615 when he was about 90 years old. He described life in the Inca empire before and after the arrival of the Spanish. Somehow, however, this "document" was lost in the historical record. It was not until the 1960s that Christopher Dilke rediscovered it in a library in Copenhagen, Denmark. He described the moment when the document was finally in his hands:

*An attendant brought a big bundle of keys, of which the last but one unlocked the case. A few minutes later I was turning the pages, which until re-discovery had been lying untouched for 300 years, and were as thin and light as a spider's web. The ink, originally black ... had turned to a reddish-brown.*

The book, called *The First New Chronicle and Good Government,* was written by hand in broken Spanish and Quechua. The book included more than 1,400 pages, many of which were beautifully illustrated showing scenes of Inca life. It took Dilke five and a half years to translate and edit the book. When he was through, it was clear that Huamán Poma's purpose was to describe for the Spanish king the suffering of the native peoples under Spanish rule. He wrote about Inca culture, customs, government, and history. He also wrote about the Spanish rule. There is no evidence to tell whether the king of Spain ever read Huamán Poma's account. On the facing page, you can read what Huamán Poma had to say about Inca children. 📖

## ABOUT INCA BOYS AND GIRLS BETWEEN THE AGES OF 9-12

*The boys were employed in trapping small birds which were sometimes brilliantly colored, like hummingbirds ... . The skins of these birds were treated as leather, the flesh was prepared for eating and the feathers were used to decorate shields or ... lances for the Inca and his warriors.*

*Boys got their education in the fields and were not sent to any other school. It was considered inadvisable to train them for a job, since they would only have treated the job as a game until they were grown up. Only small tasks like watching the flocks, carrying wood, weaving and twisting thread were entrusted to them.*

*The main occupation of the girls in this category was picking the large variety of wild flowers in the countryside. These flowers were used for dyeing the fine cloth ... among other purposes. The girls also gathered nutritious herbs, which were dried and stored for a period of up to one year.*

## ABOUT INCA BOYS AND GIRLS BETWEEN THE AGES OF 13-18

*The boys' main duty was to watch the flocks of mountain sheep. Whilst so occupied, they learned to catch or kill a wide variety of animal life ... boys of this age were employed in the personal service of the rulers and their divinities [gods].*

*The young girls with cropped hair, who belonged in this age-group, performed various useful jobs in and out-of-doors for their parents and grandparents, such as cooking and cleaning the house or helping about the farm. Being submissive and respectful, they quickly learned whatever was expected of them. Along with their short hair they went barefoot and wore short dresses ... until they reached the age of marriage.*

*... They continued to lead the same life of poverty and service until the change from the single to the married state was ordered by the Inca or someone acting in his name.*

## Analyze the Source!

1. Read the excerpts and tell in your own words what one of them says.

2. How do these excerpts help you learn about Inca life and history?

3. How were the lives of young Inca like and unlike young Americans today?

# Setting the Story Straight —
# MANCIO SERRA DE LEGUIÇAMO

▲ Inca society included a king, nobles (shown here), and commoners.

**adulterous:** having relations with a man or woman who is not your husband or wife

**idle:** useless; unemployed; lazy

In Part Two of *Royal Commentaries of the Incas*, Garcilaso de la Vega, El Inca, told of the Spanish conquistadors who conquered the Inca empire. One of these Spanish conquerors was a man named Mancio Serra de Leguiçamo. According to Garcilaso de la Vega, Mancio Serra de Leguiçamo received the gold disk from the Temple of the Sun as his share of the Inca riches. Mancio Serra de Leguiçamo, like many other Spanish conquerors, told stories of the wealth of the Inca empire. However, the Spanish conquistadors did not tell about the remarkable achievements of the Inca people. In fact, they made it sound as if the Inca culture was inferior to the Spanish. When he was an old man about to die in 1589, Mancio Serra de Leguiçamo wanted to set the story straight about the Inca.

You can read below what he said in a letter to the king of Spain about the Inca and their culture. 📖

## Analyze the Source!

1. Read the excerpt and tell in your own words what it says.

2. How does this excerpt help you learn about Inca life and history before and after the Spaniards arrived?

3. Why do you think it was important to Mancio Serra de Leguiçamo to "set the story straight" before he died?

## MANCIO SERRA DE LEGUIÇAMO SETS THE STORY STRAIGHT

*We found these lands [of the Inca] in such a state that there was not even a robber or a vicious or **idle** man, or **adulterous** or immoral woman: all such conduct was forbidden ... Everyone had honest and profitable occupations ... . Everything from the most important to the least was ordered ... with great wisdom. The Incas [kings] were feared, obeyed, respected ... by their subjects, who considered them to be most capable lords ... I desire his majesty [King Philip II of Spain] to understand why I have set down this account; it is to unburden my conscience and confess my guilt, for we have transformed the Indians who had such wisdom and committed so few crimes ... that the owner of 100,000 pesos of gold or silver would leave his door open placing a broom fixed to a bit of wood across the entrance to show that he was absent: this sign was enough to prevent anyone from entering or taking anything ... . This kingdom has fallen into such disorder ... it has passed from one extreme to another. There was no evil: now there is almost no good ...*

Inca (king)

# When Worlds Meet

pomegranate: a hard, red fruit with many seeds

The Spanish conquest brought together the New World— the Americas—and the Old World—Europe. Spaniards brought their beliefs, values, and ideas with them. They also brought along animals and plants and introduced them into this new environment. You can read below an excerpt from a Spaniard's account of the environment of the Inca empire (in present-day Peru). Pedro Cieza de León wrote this description in 1553.

# Pedro Cieza de León Describes the Inca Empire

Many places in this kingdom, such as the coast valley and the land on the banks of rivers, are very fertile, and yield wheat, maize, and barley in great quantities. There are also not a few vineyards at San Miguel, Truxillo, the City of the Kings, Cuzco, and Guamanga ... There are orange and **pomegranate** trees, and other trees brought from Spain, besides those of the country ... . There is only one thing that has not yet been brought to this country ... the olive tree ... . If young plants were brought from Spain, and planted in the coast valleys, and on the banks of rivers in the mountains, there would soon be as large olive woods as there are at Axarafe de Sevilla. For if they require a warm climate it is here; if they want much water, or none, or little, all these requirements can be found here ... My opinion is that the conquerors and settlers of these parts should not pass their time in fighting battles and matching in chase of each other; but in planting and sowing, which would be much more profitable.

## Analyze the Source!

1. Read the excerpt and tell in your own words what it says.

2. How does this excerpt help you learn about the Inca's natural environment? How does this excerpt help you learn about Spain's natural environment?

3. Do you think the Spanish conquerors and settlers took Pedro Cieza de León's advice? Why or why not?

▼ This is a view of a valley in Cuzco today.

# A Food that Changed the World — The Potato

4000 B.C.

0

A.D. 2000

**c. 3000 B.C.**
Potatoes become domesticated in present-day Peru

**late A.D. 1500s**
Spaniards bring potatoes to Europe

▲ The Andes in South America are the second tallest mountains in the world. Potatoes can grow on the Andes at higher than 10,000 feet.

**domesticate:** to tame for human use

When the Spaniards arrived in the Americas, they were eager to find gold, claim new territories for Spain, and convert the native people to Christianity. Their arrival brought together two different parts of the world. This had many consequences, some of which were negative, especially for the people of the Americas. For example, the Spaniards unknowingly brought diseases that were deadly to the native people who had no resistance to them. Some consequences had an important affect on world history. For example, people from Europe brought animals such as horses and cows to the Americas. They also brought plants such as wheat and barley to the New World. More importantly, perhaps, they learned about plants that were native to the Americas and introduced them to other parts of the world, including Europe, Asia, and Africa. Over time, these plants, including potatoes, changed the diets of people all over the world.

## Papas—Strange, but Tasty!

The Spaniards who arrived in the New World saw many trees, plants, and foods that were completely unknown to them. When Francisco Pizarro led his expedition to South America and the land of the Inca, Europeans encountered the potato for the first time. Potatoes, called *papas* in Quechua, were not part of the diet of Mesoamerican people. It was not a food that Hernando Cortés and his men found on the tables or markets of Tenochtitlan. When Pizarro and his men saw potatoes, they thought they were quite strange. However, when they tried some, they thought they were very tasty.

## Colorful "Buried" Treasure

Experts estimate that people living in present-day Peru had **domesticated** the potato by around 3000 B.C. Potatoes grew well in the Andes Mountain region. Inca farmers grew potatoes in the soil of the terraces they carved out of the mountainsides. Their potatoes were not the smooth brown or gold potatoes we buy in markets today. Inca farmers grew many different kinds of potatoes— some were brown, but others were red, pink, orange, and purple. Some were small and others large. Many had lumps on them.

Gold and silver from the land of the Inca made Spain one of the richest countries in Europe in the 1500s and 1600s. However, in the long run, potatoes were a much more valuable gift to the world.

## First, Fear and Confusion ...

Historians believe that Spaniards brought potatoes to Europe in the late 1500s. Europeans liked the potato flower, but they were suspicious about the potato itself. Some believed it caused disease, perhaps because the potatoes they saw were lumpy. Europeans also were somewhat confused by these potatoes. They were different from the potatoes that Columbus and his men brought back from the West Indies. The native peoples of these islands grew a plant they called *batatas*, which today we call sweet potatoes. Europeans thought the two plants must be related. Today, we know that the plants are not part of the same plant family.

## Then, Wide Acceptance ...

Over time, Europeans began to grow large potato crops. Potatoes became popular for several reasons. First, they were easy to grow in the cool climates of northern Europe. Since potatoes grow underground, farmers did not have to worry about seeds blowing away or rain or hail hurting the plant. In addition, potatoes did not take a lot of land or much work to grow. Perhaps most importantly, potatoes were a good source of nutrition. In some regions of Europe, the potato became the single most important crop. The population in many parts of Europe grew at a rapid rate because of this source of food. Eventually, the potato became an important food crop in cooler areas of Asia and Africa, too.

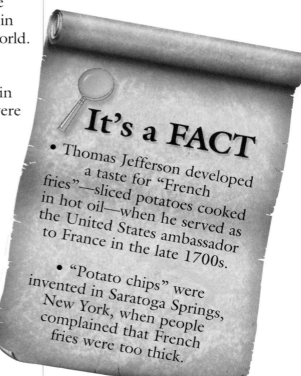

## It's a FACT

- Thomas Jefferson developed a taste for "French fries"—sliced potatoes cooked in hot oil—when he served as the United States ambassador to France in the late 1700s.

- "Potato chips" were invented in Saratoga Springs, New York, when people complained that French fries were too thick.

### Potatoes Today

It is difficult for many people today to think of a diet that does not include potatoes. On average, the people of Germany probably eat the most potatoes. However, people all over the world enjoy such potato treats as baked potatoes, potato chips, French fries, potato salad, potato pancakes, and potato soup. 📖

### What Do You Think?

**1.** Why do you think some Europeans were at first suspicious of the potato?

**2.** In the long run, do you agree that new foods such as the potato were more valuable than silver or gold? Explain your answer.

**3.** How did the potato, a native plant of the Americas, affect people in other parts of the world?

# HIRAM BINGHAM
# and the Lost City of the Inca

Have you seen any of the Indiana Jones movies? Indiana Jones is a fictional archaeologist who seems to spend most of his time in action adventures. That character could have been modeled after Hiram Bingham. Bingham was born in 1875 to missionary parents living in Hawaii. As a boy, he attended school in Hawaii, but later moved to the mainland United States. After graduating from Yale University in New Haven, Connecticut in 1898, he worked in various jobs—at a mission in Hawaii and then at a sugar company. Bingham decided to go back to school, and he earned a doctorate from Harvard University in 1905. At Harvard he studied history.

**gourd:** the dried shell of a fruit used as a cup

## BINGHAM DISCOVERS MACHU PICCHU

The morning of July 24th dawned in a cold drizzle. Arteaga shivered and seemed inclined to stay in his hut ... When asked just where the ruins were, he pointed straight to the top of the mountain. No one supposed that they would be particularly interesting. And no one cared to go with me ... . So, accompanied only by Sergeant Carrasco, I left camp at ten o'clock. Arteaga took us some distance upstream ... . Shortly after noon, just as we were completely exhausted, we reached a little grass-covered hut 2,000 feet above the river where several good-natured Indians ... welcomed us with dripping **gourds** full of cool delicious water ... . Through Sergeant Carrasco I learned that the ruins were "a little further along." ... Arteaga had "been there once before," so he decided to rest and gossip ... . They sent a small boy with me as a "guide."

... On top of this particular ledge was a semicircular building ... . Owing to the absence of mortar, there were no ugly spaces between the rocks. They might have grown together ... . It seemed like an unbelievable dream. Dimly, I began to realize that this wall and its adjoining semicircular temple over the cave were as fine as the finest stonework in the world. It fairly took my breath away. What could this place be?

... Then the little boy urged us to climb up a steep hill over what seemed to be a flight of stone steps. Surprise followed surprise in bewildering succession ... . Suddenly we found ourselves standing in front of the ruins of two of the finest and most interesting structures in ancient America ... . The sight had me spellbound ... . I could scarcely believe my senses ...

## Analyze the Source!

1. Read the excerpt and tell in your own words what it says.

2. How does this excerpt help you learn about the people of the ancient Inca civilization?

3. Why do you think Hiram Bingham was interested in finding the Inca's lost city? Are people today interested in solving mysteries? Give examples to explain your answer.

He became very interested in South America and went on several trips there. It was on his 1911 expedition that Bingham made the discovery for which he became famous—the "lost city" of Machu Picchu. Later he became interested in politics and was elected to the U.S. Senate. Hiram Bingham died in 1956, but people still remember his account of finding Machu Picchu. You can read on the previous page an excerpt from the book he wrote about that experience. This book is titled *Lost City of the Incas: The Story of Machu Picchu and Its Builders.*

# LAOZI, BUDDHA, and CONFUCIUS —
# The Age of Philosophers

650 B.C.                                                                              450 B.C.

c. 601-531 B.C.          c. 563-483 B.C.          551-479 B.C.
Laozi                    Buddha                   Confucius

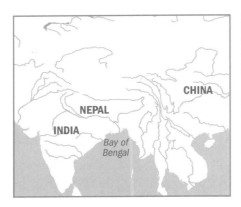

▲ Confucius and Laozi lived in China. Buddha lived in Nepal. These men are considered three of the world's greatest philosophers.

▲ The Dao symbol of yin and yang represents balance in the universe.

What is the meaning of life? Why do people suffer? How can people find happiness? Philosophers have discussed these questions for centuries and continue to talk about them even today. Three of the world's greatest philosophers—Laozi, Buddha, and Confucius—thought about these questions more than 2,500 years ago. The time when they lived is sometimes called the "age of philosophers."

## Laozi—The Founder of Daoism

Scholars know very little about Laozi, the person credited with founding Daoism. Historians think Laozi was born around 601 B.C. This was a time of great social disorder in China. Many people were distrustful of religion. Because life in China had become so unpredictable, many people were eager to escape from everyday life. They found this escape in a return to a simpler life. Our ideas about Laozi are shaped by a book he is credited with writing. The name of this book is *Dao Te Ching*, which means "the way and its power." Dao (pronounced "dow") is translated into English as "the way" or "the path."

## The History of Daoism

The early Chinese, like many other peoples, believed that rocks, mountains, the sun, stars, animals, and other things in nature had spirits. This is sometimes called nature worship. Laozi took the ancient Chinese tradition of nature worship and made it into a way of life. He developed the idea that the Dao was the beginning of all things. He also taught that the Dao was the force behind all changes in the natural world. According to Laozi, the Dao is a force that surrounds everything and everyone. However, while the Dao flows through all living and non-living things, Laozi said it was not possible to see it. Only people living in harmony with nature could experience the Dao. Laozi's ideas about the importance of nature influenced the way people thought about their bodies. They believed there was a connection between living in harmony with nature and having a healthy lifestyle. Many people who believed in Daoism became interested in herbal medicine and a healthy diet. They also developed systems of physical exercise to keep their bodies strong and healthy.

## Laozi's Legacy

Daoism became one of the three main belief systems of China. However, during his life, Laozi never preached to large groups of people or organized groups of followers. He really never did anything to promote his ideas. Whether it is a historical fact or a myth, it is said that Laozi was so unconcerned with the success of his philosophy that he never even stayed to answer questions from those who came to find him. Perhaps his attitude is best understood by the Daoist saying: "Those who know do not speak; those who speak do not know." There are many things about Daoism that are very different from other belief systems or religions you may know about. However, there are also many things in Daoism that are easily understood by all people. For example, Daoists believe that each person's most important responsibility is to develop moral **virtue**. Daoists believe the most important moral virtues are compassion, **moderation**, and humility.

▲ Laozi took the ancient Chinese tradition of nature worship and made it into a way of life.

**moderation:** balance; avoiding extremes
**outspoken:** open and sincere in expression; straightforward
**virtue:** goodness; honesty; worth

## Confucius—The Founder of Confucianism

Confucius was born in 551 B.C. in the state of Lu in present-day northeastern China. Modern historians are not certain about some of the details of his life. For example, they are not sure exactly where he worked, the particular job he held, or when he lived in certain places. However, they have pieced together general information about his life. Confucius was from a poor family, but he may have been part of the noble class at one time. Confucius's father died when he was young. As a boy, Confucius traveled widely and studied in the city of Zhou. For most of his early life, he wanted an appointment to an important government position. However, he was only partly successful in achieving this goal. Generally, he was able to get only minor government positions. He was a tax collector for a while and later was an official responsible for keeping track of the cattle. He usually only held these positions for short periods of time. During these years, he was an **outspoken** teacher. Many students (or "disciples") gathered around him to hear his ideas. On at least two occasions, he wandered the Chinese countryside with his disciples going from one royal court to another. Eventually, he gave up on ever finding a permanent government position. He decided to return to his home to teach and write.

**It's a FACT**
Some historians think Laozi was not one man, but several people.

## It's a FACT

Laozi never preached to large groups or organized groups of followers. He did not promote his ideas. Confucius, on the other hand, was eager to have government positions from which he could teach his ideas.

**righteousness:** acting in a just and moral way

**subordinate:** below another person in rank and importance

### What Do You Think?

**1.** How is Daoism like the belief systems of other civilizations you have read about?

**2.** What are the advantages of a Confucian system where relationships in society are clearly defined? What are the disadvantages?

## The Teachings of Confucius

During his life, Confucius was not a famous or powerful man. He was like other men of his time. The message that Confucius taught was simple: To have peace and order in the world, people must return to the traditional values of virtue. Virtue for Confucius included such qualities as kindness, goodness, respect, and "proper conduct." Proper conduct focused on the way people should act in their relationships with others. Confucius believed society would be stable and orderly if people understood and performed their roles. He said, "Riches and honor are what men desire; if not obtained in the right way, they do not last. Poverty and penny-pinching are what men hate, but are only to be avoided in the right way."

## Confucianism—A Belief System

Confucius did not teach about God or life after death. He was more concerned with practical and earthly subjects such as treating people fairly, good manners, and improving family relations. His ideas are considered a belief system, which we call Confucianism. Confucianism is concerned with how to live in this world. Confucius felt that each person must have five qualities: integrity, **righteousness**, loyalty, selflessness, and goodness. He believed the world would be a better place if all people, both men and women, tried to achieve these ideals.

## Order in the Family and Society

Confucius believed that the family, not the individual, is the basic unit of society. He emphasized order in the relationships among family members. Confucius described five social relationships that must always be honored: father and son; ruler and subject; husband and wife; elder brother and younger brother; and older friend and younger friend. Confucius taught that the people in these relationships had a responsibility to each other. For example, a father, who is always superior to his son, has a responsibility to care for the well-being of the son. The son, in turn, is always **subordinate** to his father and must show his father unquestioned loyalty. These same, well-defined roles between people in superior and subordinate positions held for each of the social relationships. This meant that a ruler was responsible for caring for his subjects and subjects owed the ruler their loyalty. Confucius believed that if each person performed a role in society with sincerity and understanding, there would be no need for laws and punishments. The society would be orderly.

## Education and Bureaucracy

As people learned more about Confucius's ideas, they began to place a higher value on education. Through education, people could learn how to perform their role in society. Confucius said, "Men are born pretty much alike, it's practicing something that puts distance between them." Schools were established to teach Confucian ideas. Men attended these schools to prepare themselves for government jobs.

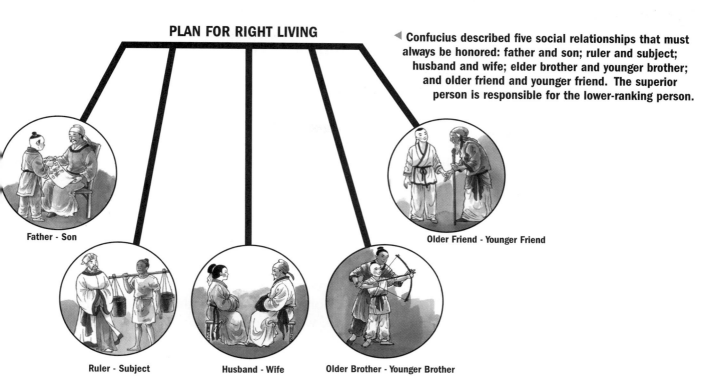

**PLAN FOR RIGHT LIVING**

◄ Confucius described five social relationships that must always be honored: father and son; ruler and subject; husband and wife; elder brother and younger brother; and older friend and younger friend. The superior person is responsible for the lower-ranking person.

Father - Son

Older Friend - Younger Friend

Ruler - Subject

Husband - Wife

Older Brother - Younger Brother

Previously, the emperor had appointed nobles to these government jobs. Over time, however, men who were educated in these Confucian schools became important government officials. They began to form a group we sometimes refer to as the Confucian bureaucracy—men educated in Confucian thinking who served as officials in the government.

## Confucian Ideas Today

When Confucius died in 479 B.C., he did not leave books or writings to explain his ideas. The information we have about his teachings comes from books his disciples wrote. One of the most famous of these books is called the *Analects* or *Conversations*. This book consists of many statements by Confucius. It also contains conversations Confucius had with his disciples. Not everyone agrees that all the information reflects accurately Confucius's ideas, but it provides a reference that tells us about Confucius and his ideas. Today, Confucius is known as one of China's most influential and important teachers. Confucius developed a way of thinking about the world that has been followed by more people, for a longer period of time, than any other person in the history of the world. In addition to China, almost every other Asian country uses some parts of Confucius's teachings as a guide.

## IDEAS CONFUCIUS SHARED WITH HIS STUDENTS

*Silence is a friend who will never betray.*
*Don't do unto others what you yourself would not like.*
*In education, there are no class distinctions.*

royalty: a king, queen, or other person in a ruling family

## A Prince Becomes the Buddha

Gautama Siddhartha, the man we call Buddha and the founder of Buddhism, was born around 563 B.C. Most people agree that Siddhartha was born into a royal family. His family lived in an area that is now the southern edge of Nepal, just north of India, in the foothills of the Himalayas. As the child of **royalty**, Siddhartha led a very safe, secure, and privileged life. His parents wanted to shelter him from ugliness and unhappiness. As a young boy, he never left the palace. He never came into contact with everyday people or saw how they lived their lives. His parents did everything they could so that he would never be bored or lonely or want for any material things. However, as Siddhartha grew older, he became curious about life outside his palace walls.

## Seeing Life for Himself

As the traditional story is told, Siddhartha decided he had to see for himself what life was like outside the palace. For several nights in a row, Siddhartha left his privileged surroundings and walked in the nearby streets. While on these walks, he saw things he had never seen or heard of before—people who were sick, people who were old, people who were poor, and people who had died. Siddhartha had never seen illness, old age, poverty, or death. This experience changed his life entirely. He could not understand how such a wonderful life he lived in the palace could exist at the same time that there was sickness, old age, poverty, and death. He decided he would abandon all of his worldly pleasures to look for answers to his questions about the world. He wanted to understand how the beauty of his palace life existed at the same time as all of the suffering he saw in the world.

## A Blinding Flash and Enlightenment

One night, Siddhartha left the palace on horseback. He rode to a place far away from everyone. For days, he sat under a tree and tried to understand what life and suffering meant. His followers believe that after many days the "answer" came to him in a blinding flash. His followers say that he became enlightened—free from wanting material things or power. In that moment, his followers say that he became Buddha, a name that means "enlightened one." Another name for enlightenment is "nirvana." Over time, Buddha developed a way of talking about his enlightenment. He also began to talk about how others could reach enlightenment. Buddha said that the first thing a person must do is to accept what he called "The Four Noble Truths." (See the chart to the left.)

What do these noble truths mean? Think about the ideas they express. Suppose you want a new toy or game or pair of shoes. Buddhists believe that the more you want something, the unhappier you become. Buddha's solution to this unhappiness is for people to learn to stop wanting things. This is not necessarily an easy thing to do. In fact, it is a very difficult thing to do.

# THE FOUR NOBLE TRUTHS

*1. Life is filled with suffering.*

*2. Desire for material things and power causes suffering.*

*3. Suffering can end.*

*4. Suffering ends when people no longer desire material things and power.*

To help people stop wanting things, Buddha developed a way to guide his followers. This is called the Eightfold Path. It called upon people to have right views, right intentions, right speech, right action, right livelihood, right effort, right mindfulness, and right concentration.

Buddha's followers thought they would find enlightenment if they followed the standards of behavior set forth in the Eightfold Path.

◄ Buddhism became especially popular during the Tang period (618-907). Buddhist monks played important economic roles and supported the arts.

## Buddhism during the Tang Dynasty

Buddhism became extremely popular in China during the Tang Dynasty. Empress Wu was a strong believer in Buddhism. During her reign, she insisted that Buddhist temples be built throughout China. She made Buddhism the favored state religion. Buddhism also flourished in China during this time because Buddhist monks were important in China's economy. They operated mills to grind grain, performed banking services, and provided medical care. They used money they earned to build temples and also supported the arts.

## Different Types of Buddhism

As it often happens with belief systems or religions, people interpreted Buddhism in different ways. Throughout Asia, different kinds of Buddhism began to be practiced by sects or groups of followers. Some of these sects are more likely found in China. Others are more likely to be found in India or Japan. While each major sect has a different method of teaching the principles of Buddhism, all have the same goal—for each person to reach enlightenment—what Buddhists think of as a state of "eternal bliss." 📖

### What Do You Think?

Buddha taught that the more people want material things, the unhappier they become. Do you agree or disagree with this idea? Why?

# Buddhist Influences on Chinese Literature

During the Tang Dynasty, Buddhism became extremely popular in China. Like Daoism, Buddhism emphasized living a simple life, meditating, and having self-discipline. Buddhists tried to free themselves from wanting material things or power. They thought that by freeing themselves from these wants, they could escape human suffering and reach enlightenment. Buddhist ideas had a strong influence on Chinese literature during the Tang period. You can read some of the Chinese poems (translated below) that were influenced by Buddhist ideas. 📖

▲ Tang scholars are eating, drinking, and discussing ideas. They may even be composing poetry, which was a common party game. This watercolor painting is based on a 12th century Chinese silk painting.

## Analyze the Source!

1. Read the poems and tell in your own words what they mean. How does each poem make you feel?

2. How do the poems reflect Buddhist ideas?

3. What do these poems have in common? What important differences do you see?

## Chinese Poetry

### UNTITLED POEM

I didn't know where the temple was,
pushing mile on mile among cloudy peaks;
old trees, peopleless paths,
deep mountains, somewhere a bell.
Brook voices choke over craggy boulders,
sun rays turn cold in the green pines.
At dusk by the bend of a deserted pond,
a monk in meditation, taming poison dragons.
—By Wang Wei

### SPRING WATERS RISE

One night, water rises two feet and more;
Several days, not possible that banks can
      withstand, hold.
Southern Market, at ferry head, there are
      boats for sale;
Have not a coin that I may buy, and bind one
      To my fence.
—By Du Fu

### IN THE MOUNTAINS

Why do I live among the green mountains?
I laugh and answer not, my soul is serene:
It dwells in another heaven and earth belonging to no man.
The peach trees are in flower, and the water flows on ...
—By Li Bo

# EMPEROR WEN —
# Founder of the Sui Dynasty

| 300 B.C. | 0 | | | | A.D. 1000 |
|---|---|---|---|---|---|

**c. 200 B.C.-A.D. 220**
The Han Dynasty

**c. A.D. 581-604**
Emperor Wen rules China

**581-618**
Sui Dynasty

**618-907**
Tang Dynasty

The Han Dynasty ruled China more than 400 years, from about 200 B.C. to A.D. 220. After the Han leaders lost power, China divided into many smaller states and kingdoms. Non-Chinese people took control of large parts of northern China and adopted a Chinese way of life. Throughout other parts of China, families fought each other as they tried to control larger amounts of territory. Several dynasties ruled one after another, but none of them lasted very long. The period after the fall of the Han Dynasty was a time of great change and chaos in China.

## The Sui Come to Power

Then, in the late 500s, a northern Chinese general, Wen, unified the northern provinces under his control. Next, General Wen turned his attention to the southern part of China. In 589, he defeated the last of the southern provinces. With both the northern and southern provinces unified, Emperor Wen had succeeded in reunifying China. He became the first ruler of a new dynasty—the Sui Dynasty. The Sui Dynasty is remembered for restoring many Chinese traditions. The Sui leaders also were known for their religious tolerance, building strong economic ties between the northern and southern parts of China, developing a new legal code and rules for state government, and using their military forces effectively.

## A Different Approach to Ruling China

Emperor Wen took a very different approach to ruling China than previous emperors. Wen did not force people in the northern and southern areas into entirely new patterns of living and working. Although Wen was a Buddhist, he was tolerant of other religions and used Daoist and Confucian traditions to gain acceptance from people throughout China. He also created a legal code that blended ideas from legal traditions in northern and southern China.

## Building a Canal

One of the most important accomplishments of the Sui Dynasty was the building of a canal linking China's two great rivers, the Yellow River and the Yangtze River. It was 1,100 miles long.

▲ After the Han dynasty, there was a time of chaos in China. Emperor Wen restored many Chinese traditions during the Sui Dynasty.

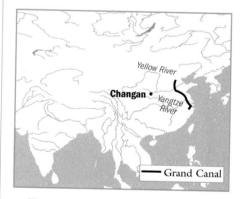

▲ The Grand Canal was one of the most important accomplishments of the Sui Dynasty. The canal linked the Yellow and Yangtze rivers.

The Grand Canal connected the southern part of China, rich in natural farm land, with the north where money was available to invest in agriculture. Emperor Wen also began to build storehouses for surplus grain, which helped to develop a strong economy.

## A Changing Government

Emperor Wen changed the way the government was managed. In the past, the government had many levels of officials. Wen wanted the government to be able to manage activities from a central location, so he eliminated one of the levels of local management. Wen also put into place rules and regulations that forbid government officials from working in their home areas. These rules made it much more difficult for government officials to cheat. It also made the officials more responsible to the central government.

## Expanding the Empire

Emperor Wen and his son who succeeded him were the only emperors in the Sui Dynasty. They effectively used the military to expand the empire. They sent soldiers to many distant parts of the empire, as well as to places as far away as present-day Vietnam. On three separate occasions the Sui armies were defeated in their attempts to gain control over the provinces of northern Korea. These military expeditions were costly in terms of money and human life and before long, the Chinese peasants began to revolt. Eventually, the Sui government could no longer control the rebellion, and the Sui Dynasty was overthrown.

## The Legacy of Emperor Wen and the Sui Dynasty

The Sui Dynasty was responsible for restoring many Chinese traditions. The Sui leaders also were known for religious tolerance, building strong economic ties between north and south, developing a new legal code and rules for state government, and for building a canal linking the Yangtze and Yellow rivers.

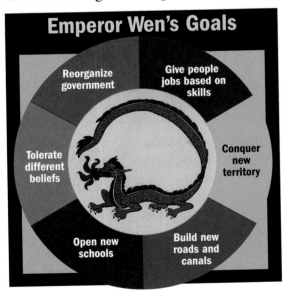

Emperor Wen's Goals

Historians depict Emperor Wen and his son as being very ambitious—they tried to do too much, too soon. Their military campaigns were more costly than the empire could support. By 618, their rule of China had ended. However, the Tang emperors who succeeded the Sui adopted many of their ideas and policies.

### What Do You Think?

1. To govern effectively, Emperor Wen believed it was better to allow people to keep many of their own traditions rather than to force them to do something completely different. What are the advantages and disadvantages of this approach?

2. How did Emperor Wen unify China?

3. Why do you think Tang emperors adopted many of the ideas of the Sui Dynasty?

# EMPEROR TAIZONG —
# Powerful Leader of the Tang Dynasty

A.D. **200**                                                                                    A.D. **1000**

| 581-618 | 599-649 | 618-907 |
| --- | --- | --- |
| Sui Dynasty | Taizong | Tang Dynasty |

Emperor Wen and his son had restored many of China's traditions during their ambitious leadership in the Sui Dynasty. When their rule ended in 618, the Tang Dynasty came to power. The top general in the Sui Dynasty founded the Tang Dynasty, and many of the Tang Dynasty's officials had worked in the Sui Dynasty. It is not a surprise, then, that there were not many significant changes in government policies and ideas when the Tang Dynasty came to power. After the first Tang emperor died, his sons fought over who would be his successor. The winner was Taizong. In 626, he made himself emperor.

▲ Emperor Taizong expanded China by conquering land in Tibet, Vietnam, and almost to the border of what is now North Korea. He lived in Changan (modern-day Xian).

◄ Taizong became one of China's most admired rulers.

## A Man of Many Skills

Emperor Taizong is one of the most admired rulers in Chinese history. He is best remembered for his political ability. Taizong was very good at matching the right person with a particular job. He wisely chose people to guide him on moral questions, as well as on issues such as agriculture, education, and law. He followed many of the Sui's policies and ideas. For example, Taizong blended ideas from the three major belief systems—Buddhism, Daoism, and Confucianism—to gain acceptance from the people he ruled. As emperor, Taizong supported activities for the good of all people. For example, he built new schools and encouraged men from all parts of China to work in government jobs.

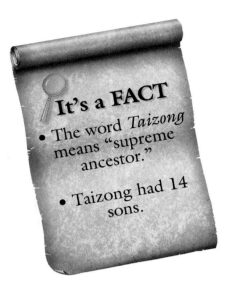

plot: a plan

## What Do You Think?

1. Taizong is admired for his military skills, physical strength, and political ability. Of these, which do you think is most important? Why?

2. How important is it for a leader to pick the right person for a particular job? Explain your answer.

3. How might blending ideas from the three major Chinese belief systems have helped Taizong gain acceptance from the people of China?

## Reforming China

Taizong appointed important government officials to oversee taxes, war, government workers, public works, and other important areas of government. He created a new code of law, which included permanent laws, as well as laws that could be adjusted according to changing conditions and local customs. Taizong wanted to expand China's boundaries to the west and east. He conquered land in areas such as present-day Tibet and Vietnam. Taizong's government enjoyed a strong economy. He encouraged trade with people in other lands. Exotic goods and foods flowed into the capital city of Changan. During Taizong's reign, foreign trade increased, and many visitors from other areas came to China.

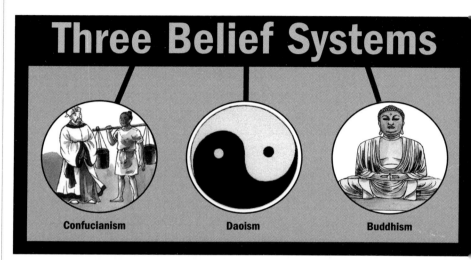

## Three Belief Systems

Confucianism        Daoism        Buddhism

▲ Emperor Taizong blended ideas from the three major belief systems in China—Confucianism, Daoism, and Buddhism.

## In Later Life

Taizong is regarded as one of the most successful Chinese emperors. He ruled for 23 years and brought peace and prosperity to China. As he grew older, Taizong began to think about who would succeed him as emperor. Many people thought his eldest son was very odd because he chose to live as a nomad. This son was not an acceptable choice as emperor. Another of Taizong's 14 sons became involved in a **plot** to take over as emperor. He was not an acceptable choice either. When Taizong died in 649, his son Gaozong, a young prince, was selected to succeed him. As it turned out, Gaozong was not a strong leader. 📖

# EMPRESS WU —
# First Woman to Rule China Officially

A.D. **200**

**599-649**
Taizong

**618-907**
Tang Dynasty

**c. 625-c. 705**
Empress Wu

A.D. **1000**

Empress Wu was an important ruler in China. To understand her significance, it is necessary to understand Chinese society. China was (and is) a society dominated by men. Men make the important decisions about law, government, and how people will be treated. This has been part of the Chinese culture for thousands of years. Also, Chinese society is based on the teachings of Confucius. According to the teachings of Confucius, relationships between people are based on the idea that one person is superior (or has a higher place in society) and the other person is subordinate (or has a lower position in society). Think about these two concepts, then consider that Empress Wu was the first woman to rule China officially. For a woman to achieve the position of emperor in a society dominated by the idea of men as rulers is quite remarkable. How did she achieve this powerful position?

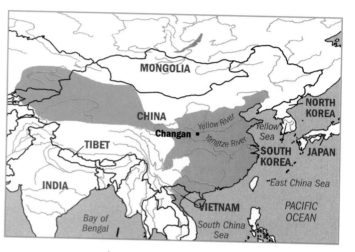

▲ **During the Tang Dynasty, Empress Wu ruled a unified China (shaded area) from the capital city of Changan. You can see the outlines of present-day countries and regions in this part of Asia.**

► **Chinese rulers sometimes toured the country. Many nobles, officials, and servants went with them. It almost looked like a parade. This scene shows an artist's idea of Empress Wu on such a tour.**

### It's a FACT

Empress Wu had statues of Buddha carved into the 1,000 Buddha Caves at Luoyang, China.

▼ Empress Wu lived in Changan. It was a busy city. Many visitors came to trade, study, and visit. More than one million people lived there. Another million people lived outside the city walls.

## From Concubine to Outcast ...

When she was 14 years old, Mei-Niang (later, Wu Zetian) was chosen to be one of Emperor Taizong's concubines. However, when Taizong died, Mei-Niang and the other concubines were sent away from the emperor's royal court. Once a woman had served as a concubine, she could no longer marry. She was expected to live quietly with the other concubines until her death. However, things changed for Mei-Niang. Very soon after she was sent away, she received a message from Gaozong, Taizong's son and the man who had become the new emperor. Gaozong had seen Mei-Niang and wanted her to return to the palace. Two months later she returned. She soon became one of the new emperor's favorite concubines.

## ... To Empress

Court life was uncertain. Mei-Niang quickly understood that to survive she would have to gain power. She soon gave birth to Gaozong's son. In contrast, the emperor's wife had not been able to have any children with him. After the emperor's wife visited Mei-Niang's son, Mei-Niang strangled the baby and then convinced Gaozong that his wife was the murderer. The emperor threw his wife out of the palace. Soon after, Mei-Niang became the new empress.

## Mei-Niang Increases Her Influence

Over the next few years, Mei-Niang helped Gaozong make many decisions that helped the Chinese people. At the same time, she increased her own influence at the royal court. When the emperor died in 683, Mei-Niang took over the administrative duties of the court. This was a position equal to that of the emperor. Once she was in this position, she ruthlessly eliminated anyone who stood in her way. One of her sons became emperor, but she forced him out and made her youngest son emperor. He was ruler in name only because she held all the power.

## Empress Wu—Ruler of China

Around 690, Mei-Niang had herself declared emperor. She took the name of Wu Zetian. During her reign, Wu Zetian accomplished many things for the Chinese people. She found the best people to help her run the government. She treated the people she trusted in a fair manner. She started a new system for entry into government service based on examinations rather than on family ties. She also lowered the taxes peasants had to pay, developed more public services, and increased agricultural production.

## A Strong Believer in Buddhism

Empress Wu was a strong believer in Buddhism. During her reign, she insisted that Buddhist temples be built throughout China. She also tried to limit the influence of Confucianism in China. She removed (sometimes violently) Confucian scholars from the government. She made Buddhism the favored state belief system. Buddhism became very popular in China during the Tang Dynasty.

## The End of Her Reign

After ruling China for almost 15 years, Wu Zetian was old and very fearful of those around her. In 705, she was pressured to give up her throne. She no longer had the power to keep her position. Her third son took her place. During her reign, women enjoyed more freedom than ever before in China. Empress Wu was responsible for helping to create a golden age in Chinese history.

### What Do You Think?

1. The authors wrote, "For a woman to achieve the position of emperor in a society dominated by the idea of men as rulers is quite remarkable." Do you agree or disagree with this statement? Why?

2. What personal qualities helped Mei-Niang become empress of China? Do you admire these qualities? Why or why not?

3. What do you think was Empress Wu's most important accomplishment? Why?

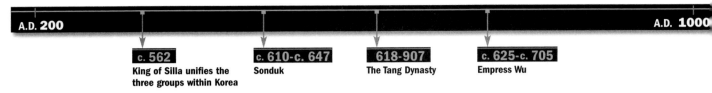

# QUEEN SONDUK of Korea

A.D. **200**

**c. 562**
King of Silla unifies the three groups within Korea

**c. 610-c. 647**
Sonduk

**618-907**
The Tang Dynasty

**c. 625-c. 705**
Empress Wu

A.D. **1000**

▲ Queen Sonduk lived in the kingdom of Silla (present-day South Korea).

Emperors of both the Sui and Tang dynasties tried to extend their control over the peninsula of Korea. Generally, their attempts ended in failure. Three major groups of people within Korea—the Koguryo, the Paekche, and the Silla—also tried to control the entire peninsula, but they failed as well. Then, around 562, the king of the Silla was able to unify the three groups in Korea.

► This is a model of what Queen Sonduk might have looked like sitting in her palace.

## An Observant Young Girl

When it was time for the king of Silla to choose the next ruler, he chose his daughter Sonduk. He knew that Sonduk was very intelligent and observant. There is a story about Sonduk that demonstrates these qualities. According to the story, when Sonduk was about seven years old, her father received a gift from another king. The gift was a box of peony seeds along with a painting of peony flowers. Her father was very impressed with the gift and asked his daughter if she liked it, too. Sonduk studied the painting for a long while. Then she replied that the flowers were pretty, but they must not smell very sweet. Her father was puzzled by her comment. Sonduk told him that if the flowers smelled sweet, the painting would show bees and butterflies around them. The people who heard her comment were confused. What should they do? How could they tell if she was correct? Her father had an idea. He ordered the gardeners to plant the peony seeds. When the flowers bloomed, the king brought them to his nose and smelled them deeply. Sonduk was right—the peonies had no smell. Her father knew that she was a very observant young girl.

## Sonduk Becomes Queen

In 634, Sonduk became queen. She ruled for the next 14 years. During her reign, there were many rebellions and much fighting in Korea. Sonduk used her considerable intelligence to keep her kingdom unified. During her reign, she strengthened her kingdom's ties with China. She even started an educational exchange program. Many Korean students went to China to study. One of these students became very interested in Buddhism and brought Buddhist ideas to Korea. This made Buddhism more important in Korea. As a Buddhist herself, this made Sonduk very proud.

## Studying the Stars

Sonduk also was responsible for building a tower from which people could study the stars. This kind of building is called an observatory. The tower she had built, called the Tower of the Moon and Stars, was one of the first observatories in Asia. The tower still stands in the old Silla capital in present-day South Korea.

## Much Remains Unknown

While historians know some of the details of Queen Sonduk's early life, much of her later life remains a mystery. Did she ever marry? Did she ever have children? Did she step down from her throne or was she forced out? We do not know. What we do know is that in 647, her cousin Chinduk followed her to the throne and became the second queen to rule Silla. What happened to Queen Sonduk is still a mystery.

### What Do You Think?

**1.** Sonduk was an intelligent and observant young girl. How important are intelligence and the power of observation to a leader?

**2.** What conclusions can you draw about Sonduk and the qualities she possessed from reading this brief biography of her?

**3.** Why do you think Sonduk started an exchange program with China? Why do countries have exchange programs today?

# GENGHIS KHAN

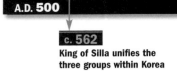

A.D. 500                                                                                    A.D. 1300

**c. 562**
King of Silla unifies the
three groups within Korea

**c. 1167-1227**
Temujin (Genghis Khan)

**late 1100s**
Temujin begins to bring
together the Mongols

**1206**
Temujin is given the
title of Genghis Khan

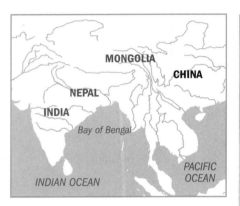

▲ Genghis Khan conquered parts of China.

▲ The men in Genghis Khan's army gave up their ties to all other tribes or clans.

At the height of their reign, the Mongols ruled one of the largest empires that ever existed, including all of central Asia, China, and Korea. They also controlled large parts of eastern Europe and Asia, including Russia and Persia. In the West, their power extended all the way to the Adriatic Sea. But the Mongols were nomads—moving, fighting, and living day-to-day. How did a group of nomads, who fought their neighbors and even one another, come to rule such a vast territory?

## The Father and the Son

Yesukai, a Mongol chief who ruled a large region in northern Mongolia, killed his rival, Temujin, in battle. To honor this rival warrior, Yesukai named his newborn son Temujin. When young Temujin was about 13, his father was killed. Temujin tried to lead his father's tribe, but the men would not accept him as their leader. For several years, Temujin wandered the steppes of Mongolia. Eventually, he returned to his tribe and convinced them of his ability to lead. Over time, he gained greater power and prestige among the various tribes of Mongols.

## Genghis Khan

In the late 1100s, Temujin began to bring together the Mongols. He recognized talented people and was a leader that others would follow. After winning several key battles, he established a reputation as a strong military leader. In 1206, when he was about 40 years old, Temujin was given the title of Genghis Khan. This title means "universal ruler." The Mongols believed they lived in the center of the universe. They saw their leader's conquests as being the actions of a man who was entitled to rule the world.

▶ The Mongols were mighty warriors. Here, Mongol cavalry soldiers are fighting a battle. This painting is based on a Persian painting that hangs in the Edinburgh University Library in Scotland.

## Ability to Organize and Lead

Genghis Khan created a set of laws that required obedience and unity from the tribes. He used this unity to establish an organization that the Mongols had never before had. With his ability to organize and lead, he created a powerful and successful army.

## The Conquests of Genghis Khan

Once he had united the Mongol tribes, Genghis Khan turned his attention to China. He had made the Mongol army into one of the greatest fighting forces of its time. The Mongols were tough soldiers who could fight hard and travel long distances. Within just a few years, Genghis Khan and his army conquered parts of China, turned north to conquer Russia, and then turned south again to capture Beijing. Genghis Khan showed no mercy. People who resisted the Mongol army were killed. People who surrendered became slaves. The Mongols burned down towns and cities. They destroyed anything they could not use. One of the Mongols' greatest weapons was the fear they **instilled** in people. Even the Europeans, who considered themselves strong warriors, had never seen anything like the Mongol army.

## The Foundation for an Empire

By his death in 1227, Genghis Khan ruled one of the largest empires that ever existed. He also had put into place the foundation for an empire that could be passed to his sons and grandsons. When he died, the empire was divided into four parts. Later, his grandson, Kublai Khan, would rule the Mongol empire.

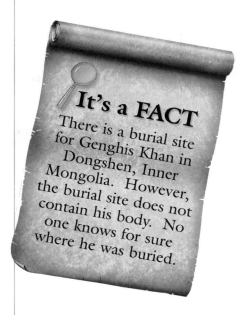

It's a FACT

There is a burial site for Genghis Khan in Dongshen, Inner Mongolia. However, the burial site does not contain his body. No one knows for sure where he was buried.

**instill:** to put an idea into

### What Do You Think?

**1.** Genghis Khan was able to unify Mongol tribes that were very independent and had resisted orders from previous leaders. What qualities would a leader have to have in order to unify such tribes?

**2.** Why do you think the Mongols believed they lived at the center of the universe? What place would you say is the center of the universe? Explain your answer.

**3.** How can fear be a powerful weapon?

# KUBLAI KHAN —
# A Mongol Chief Rules China

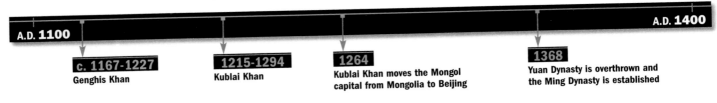

**c. 1167-1227**
Genghis Khan

**1215-1294**
Kublai Khan

**1264**
Kublai Khan moves the Mongol capital from Mongolia to Beijing

**1368**
Yuan Dynasty is overthrown and the Ming Dynasty is established

By 1280, Kublai Khan had defeated the Song Dynasty and become ruler of China. For the first time in history, a foreigner ruled China. Who was this man? How did he rise from being a Mongol chief to emperor of China?

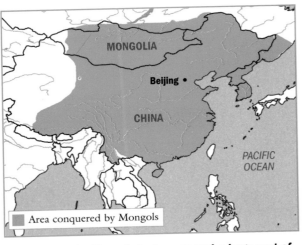

▲ By 1279, the Mongols had conquered a huge part of Asia. You can see the outline of present-day China.

◄ Kublai Khan dressed as a traditional Chinese emperor. He even gave his ruling dynasty a Chinese name—Yuan.

## Early Rise to Power

Kublai Khan, the grandson of Genghis Khan, leader of the Mongols, was born in 1215. After his father's death, his mother raised him and his three brothers. In 1227, when Kublai was about 12 years old, Genghis Khan died. Then the Mongol empire was divided into four parts, each ruled by one of his sons.

The Mongol empire had grown so large that is was hard to govern. The Mongols had never written any formal rules about how leaders should be chosen. As a result, the death of a leader set off a war among the men who wanted to rule. In 1260, Kublai gained the title of "Khan" after defeating his rivals, including one of his brothers.

## The Reign of Kublai Khan

During his reign, Kublai Khan was responsible for great changes in government, commerce, and social policy. One of his most important accomplishments was moving the Mongol capital from Mongolia to Beijing in 1264. In 1271, he named his ruling dynasty the Yuan Dynasty. Over the next few years, Kublai Khan completed what his grandfather had begun. By defeating the Song Dynasty in 1279, he reunited northern and southern China.

## Governing China

In most ways, Kublai Khan continued the basic system of government established during the Tang Dynasty. However, he did make changes. For example, he ordered a census—a counting—of the entire population. Then he divided the population into four groups. He placed Mongols in the highest position and the people of the Song Dynasty at the bottom. After unifying China, he was more dependent on the Chinese to help him rule, but this was difficult for him to accept. He did not trust the Chinese government officials and replaced them with Mongol or non-Chinese officials, including Muslims. Kublai Khan also made changes in the area of commerce. He created an office to oversee the production of grain. He had storage areas built in case there were food shortages. He organized a system to collect taxes. He used tax money to complete a canal so that grain could be shipped from southern China to northern China. In addition, he used tax money to improve the postal service. Kublai Khan adopted the use of paper currency, which had been in use in China for some time. He was the first person to make paper currency the only legal way to buy and sell goods in China.

## Religious Tolerance

Like most Mongols, Kublai Khan was Buddhist. Kublai Khan was very interested in and tolerant of different religions. During his reign, there was much discussion and debate about religion and belief systems at the royal court. He gave economic privileges to all religions. For example, religious groups did not have to pay taxes.

## The Decline of the Yuan

Kublai Khan also faced many problems during his rule. While the economy was generally good, Kublai Khan sent armies to conquer Japan in 1274 and again in 1281. Both times he was defeated. These wars were costly. He raised the money to pay for them by increasing taxes. The peasant farmers suffered greatly and over time began to rebel. Kublai Khan's government made some other bad economic choices, which caused a general decline in economic activity. As the Mongols learned, once this decline starts, it is very hard to stop.

## The End of the Yuan Dynasty

Adding to his problems, Kublai Khan had never really adopted Chinese customs. The Chinese saw him and all other Mongols as foreigners in their land. When things became difficult, the Chinese were not very eager to help solve the problems. When Kublai Khan died in 1294, there was a fight to see who would succeed him. Within the next 40 years, eight different emperors ruled. None lasted very long, and all of them died young. At a time when China needed a strong government, the Mongols simply fought among themselves. Finally, in 1368, a rebellion overthrew the Yuan Dynasty and the Ming Dynasty was established. 📖

## It's a FACT

- Kublai Khan's postal service had about 1,400 postal stations and relied on about 50,000 horses.

- One of the most famous visitors to Kublai Khan's court was Marco Polo, who traveled to China from his home in Venice.

### What Do You Think?

1. How do you think the Mongols were able to get the Chinese to accept their rule?

2. What are the advantages of having a set of formal rules about how leaders should be chosen? What are the disadvantages?

3. How do you think the Confucian scholars felt about Kublai Khan? Explain your answer.

# MARCO POLO'S Observations of Kublai Khan's China

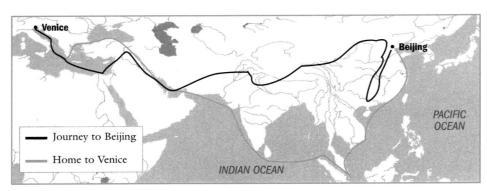

◄ This map shows Marco Polo's journey from Venice to Beijing. When he returned to Venice in 1295, Marco Polo wrote a book about the time he spent in China.

Kublai Khan became leader of the Mongols in 1260. Four years later, in 1264, he moved the Mongols' capital to Beijing. By 1280, he was the ruler of China. Kublai Khan encouraged trade and travel. He also welcomed visitors to his royal court. Perhaps his most famous visitor was Marco Polo, the son of a merchant from Venice, Italy. Marco Polo spent almost 20 years in China. When he returned to Venice in 1295, he wrote a book about his experiences and the sights he saw. As a result of his book, many European traders and explorers became interested in seeing China themselves. His book also left us with vivid descriptions of the Great Khan's power and might. You can read here some of Marco Polo's observations of Kublai Khan's palace and his power.

## MARCO POLO OBSERVES KUBLAI KHAN

Kublai Khan built a huge palace of marble and other ornamental stones. ... The whole building is marvelously embellished and richly adorned. At one end ... [is] sixteen miles of parkland well watered with springs and streams and diversified with lawns. Into this park there is no entry except by way of the palace. Here the Great Khan keeps game animals of all sorts ... .

In the midst of this enclosed park ... the Great Khan has built another large palace ... decorated with beasts and birds of very skillful workmanship. It is reared on ... pillars, on each of which stands a dragon, entwining the pillar with his tail and supporting the roof on his outstretched limbs. ...

All the rulers, and all the provinces and regions ... bring him costly gifts of gold and silver and pearls and precious stones and abundance of fine white cloth, so that throughout the year their lord may have no lack of treasure and may live in joy and gladness. ...

... On this day the Great Khan receives gifts of more than 100,000 white horses, of great beauty and price ... A great lion is led into the Great Khan's presence; and as soon as it sees him it flings itself down ... before him with every appearance of deep humility and seems to acknowledge him as lord. There it stays without a chain, and is indeed a thing to marvel at.

## Analyze the Source!

1. Read the passage and tell in your own words what it means.

2. How does this passage help you learn about Chinese life and history during this period?

3. What does this passage reveal about Marco Polo and his culture?

# EMPEROR TAIZU —
# Founder of the Ming Dynasty

**A.D. 1200**

**1294**
Kublai Khan dies

**c. 1328-1398**
Zhu Yuanzhang (Taizu)

**c. 1368**
Taizu becomes a military commander and begins to rule as emperor

**A.D. 1400**

After Kublai Khan died in 1294, eight different Mongol rulers held power in China. Most of these men ruled for only a few years. The lack of strong and consistent leadership weakened the Mongols' hold over China. A combination of several factors led to the decline of the Mongol rule. One factor relates to Kublai Khan's practice of grouping people into four categories. The Chinese bitterly disliked this practice. Another factor was the lavish lifestyle enjoyed by the Mongol emperors while the peasants suffered. Local rebellions began in the late 1340s. By the 1350s, they had become widespread. The Chinese looked upon the Mongols as barbarians. While the Mongols were excellent warriors, they were not very successful farmers. Many Mongols became homeless. In addition, the Mongol leadership tried to control the countryside from a few military bases. However, the Chinese population greatly outnumbered the Mongol population.

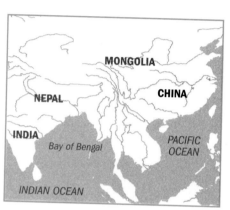

▲ Zhu Yuanzhang, known as Taizu, established the Ming Dynasty and ruled China for 30 years.

## The Opposition Grows
As the opposition to the Mongols grew, a secret society, the White Lotus, began to organize a revolution. A Buddhist monk named Zhu Yuanzhang decided to join this group. Within a few years, he became a military leader for the White Lotus. By 1368, Zhu's army was unstoppable. He had captured the city of Nanjing and made it his capital. The Mongol ruler fled to the Mongols' former capital in Mongolia. Zhu, who became known as Taizu after his death, established the Ming Dynasty. He ruled China for the next 30 years.

**divine:** being or having the nature of a god

## Governing China
As a soldier, Taizu fought to bring back a traditional Chinese society. This meant a strong, central government where he was the leader. Taizu had seen for himself what could happen when the Mongols' government lost control. He wanted to make sure this did not happen to him. He created new ceremonies that gave him an almost **divine** position in society.

To guard against possible Mongol uprisings, Taizu strengthened the military. Taizu sent groups of soldiers to different places in the empire. He told them they always needed to be ready for war. He made the commanders of this military into a class of nobles. He also ordered the men who had fought alongside him, the new Chinese nobility, to live at his court. He insisted that the army could never abuse the Chinese citizens. Anyone guilty of this offense or anyone suspected of plotting against him was killed.

## Strengthening the Economy and Legal System

Taizu also wanted to strengthen China's economy. Under his rule, more farm land was cultivated. He gave new land to farmers who had faced a difficult situation under the Mongols. Taizu had the canals and irrigation systems repaired, and he started a program to replant many areas with trees. Like the Mongols, he ordered a census. However, he used the information to adjust taxes and manage the growing population. Taizu also wrote a new legal code for China. This legal code was made up of two parts: The first part of the code dealt with permanent laws. The second part of the code included rules that might have to be changed depending on circumstances. However, Taizu made it clear that if officials changed the laws too quickly, people would lose confidence in them. In addition to these actions, Taizu also established the Imperial University and once again instituted civil service examinations. Under Taizu, Confucianism again became the official belief system of the state.

## It's a FACT

One way that Taizu controlled people in the countryside was by organizing them into groups. Each group was called a "li." If someone in a li did something wrong, everyone in the group was punished.

▲ This is a photograph of the Great Wall today.

## Taizu's Legacy

The picture of Taizu would not be complete without mention of his reputation as a harsh ruler. He wanted to make almost all of the decisions in government himself. He also was very suspicious and distrustful of people. He formed a secret police force so that he could get information about people in the empire. This secret police force sometimes tortured prisoners to get information. Emperor Taizu was perfectly willing to put thousands of people to death to make sure people respected his authority. Despite this, he is thought of as one of the greatest of all Chinese rulers. During the Ming Dynasty, there was stability and prosperity for the Chinese people. Perhaps another part of Taizu's legacy is that emperors who ruled after him were more autocratic and authoritarian than Chinese emperors who had ruled earlier. 📖

### What Do You Think?

1. Why was the "li" an effective way to control people in the countryside? Do you think it is fair for everyone in a group to be punished for one person's action? Why or why not?

2. Why do you think the emperors who ruled after Taizu were more autocratic and authoritarian than Chinese emperors who had ruled before? What lesson could you draw from this example?

# ZHENG HO — Chinese Explorer and Commander of the Treasure Fleet

**A.D. 1300**                                                    **A.D. 1500**

**c. 1381-1433**
Zheng Ho

**1405-1433**
Zheng Ho embarks on maritime
expeditions around Asia and Africa

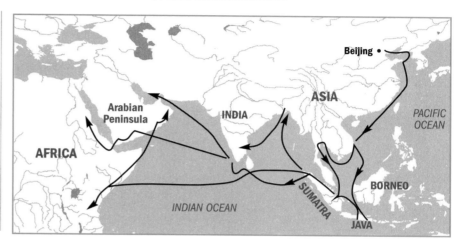

Almost 100 years before Columbus sailed to America, Zheng Ho commanded a fleet of Chinese ships that went on maritime expeditions around Asia and Africa. He and his men sailed seven different voyages. They battled pirates and used a compass for navigation. Who was Zheng Ho? What did he and the Chinese hope to find on these voyages of discovery?

▲ This map shows some of the places Zheng Ho visited on his voyages. He led almost 30,000 men on seven separate expeditions. To find his way around, he used the compass, which the Chinese had invented hundreds of years earlier.

## China Under Ming Rule

In 1403, after a long civil war, Chengzu became emperor of China. He had several goals in mind. He wanted to rebuild the capital city of Beijing and the Grand Canal. He also decided to build a great navy. With a strong navy, Chengzu could control the pirates who sailed along the coast of China. Chengzu also wanted to use the navy to explore other parts of the world. The person he chose to build the navy and command the fleet of ships was Zheng Ho.

## Zheng Comes to China

Historians do not know many details about Zheng's early life. He was born around 1381 in the area of China known as the Yunan Province. This province is in the southwestern part of China, just north of present-day Laos and Myanmar. Zheng came from a Muslim family. When Zheng was about 13, the Chinese invaded the Yunan region and took him captive. Along with other boys, Zheng was brought to Beijing and became a servant in Chengzu's household. This was before Chengzu had become emperor. As Zheng grew older, he became an excellent warrior. He was also very tactful and polite, which helped him become an able diplomat. When Chengzu became emperor, he appointed Zheng as the admiral of his navy. Chengzu's orders to Zheng Ho were clear—build a navy, control the pirates, and explore the seas around China.

▶ Zheng Ho was a famous Chinese explorer.

## The Treasure Fleet

Zheng Ho built a fleet of 62 ships. These ships were called the Treasure Fleet. The ships were very large and made of wood. The four largest ships were about 400-feet long and about 160-feet wide at the beam (the widest point of a ship). Each ship had a specific task. One was the "horse ship" and carried nothing but horses. Another was the "water ship" and carried only fresh water. There was a supply ship with food and other supplies. And of course, there also was a combat ship—this ship was used for fighting. All of the other ships were filled with Chinese goods to trade with people Zheng Ho and his sailors met on their voyages. In 1405, Zheng Ho set sail on his first voyage as commander of the Treasure Fleet. He had about 30,000 men with him.

## Travels to Distant Lands

The Treasure Fleet's first destination was the city of Calicut on the Indian coast. Zheng and his men also stopped in Vietnam and Java. They battled pirates along the coast of Sumatra, and then in 1407, returned to China. The Chinese had been trading with Arabs since the early Middle Ages, and they had sailed to the South China Sea and eastern Africa. Based on this information, historians conclude that Zheng had at least a general idea of where he was going and what he might find. The Treasure Fleet used a compass for navigation and burned specially marked sticks of incense to tell them how much time had passed.

### What Do You Think?

1. Why do you think the name "Treasure Fleet" is a good way to describe this group of ships?

2. The Chinese believed that their civilization was the "perfect civilization" under heaven. The voyages of the Treasure Fleet showed China's riches and greatness to other peoples. What were the benefits of other people finding out about China's riches and greatness?

3. What advantages did Zheng Ho have in life? What obstacles did he face?

## Zheng Ho Completes His Mission

Between 1405 and 1433, the Treasure Fleet sailed on seven separate voyages. Zheng commanded all but one of them. After he returned from the seventh voyage in 1433, Zheng Ho died. Over the next years, other emperors were not as interested in voyages of exploration. They no longer spent money to build large ocean-going ships.

◀ Zheng Ho brought back many exotic animals to China. He brought tigers, ostriches, zebras, and giraffes (shown here).

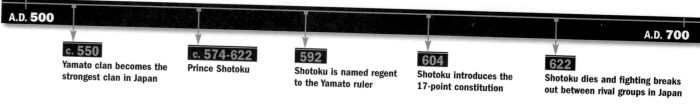

# Prince SHOTOKU and Japan's First Constitution

A.D. **500**                                                                                                A.D. **700**

**c. 550**
Yamato clan becomes the
strongest clan in Japan

**c. 574-622**
Prince Shotoku

**592**
Shotoku is named regent
to the Yamato ruler

**604**
Shotoku introduces the
17-point constitution

**622**
Shotoku dies and fighting breaks
out between rival groups in Japan

A number of clans ruled Japan between 500 and 550. Each clan tried to claim more territory from the other groups. Wars and feuds were common. Gradually, however, the Yamato clan began to gain control. By 550, the Yamato were the strongest clan and controlled the territory that had some of the best agricultural land. This made it possible for them to grow more food, which played an important role in their development.

## Outside Influences on Japan

During this time, Japan was influenced by foreign countries, especially China and Korea. The Chinese and Koreans who came to Japan brought along their traditions in art and writing. They also brought belief systems such as Confucianism and Buddhism. Most likely, the Japanese learned of Buddhism before 550. However, we know that in 552, a Korean king sent some Buddhist priests, writings, and statues to the Yamato royal court. This started a bitter battle in Japan.

## A Battle over Buddhism

On one side of the battle were people who did not want a new belief system. They thought that accepting a foreign religion would bring Japan bad luck. They also thought a new religion would limit their influence. Others, especially the Soga clan, accepted Buddhism. They supported the Yamato ruler who was eager to accept Buddhism. The disagreement between these two groups led to a battle in 587. The Soga won this battle and became the most powerful clan. They recognized the Yamato clan as the rightful rulers over Japan, but the Soga became "the power behind the throne." Suiko, a member of the Yamato clan, was made ruler. However, because of her young age, in 592, the Soga clan leader named his nephew, Prince Shotoku, as regent. Prince Shotoku was a young man with great promise. He, not Suiko, was the real decision-maker.

▲ The shaded area shows where the Yamato clan lived. Prince Shotoku lived in Asuka (south of present-day Nara).

▶ Prince Shotoku made great achievements in the areas of religion, government, and foreign relations with China.

Chapter 12: Japan **213**

▲ At first, some people in Japan did not accept Buddhism. However, over time, Buddhism became a major belief system in Japan.

**It's a FACT**

Prince Shotoku's constitution said, "Any person of any age should revere Buddhist law."

## An Extremely Capable Man

There is a great deal of information about Prince Shotoku. However, it is a mix of myth and fact. For example, there are stories claiming that Shotoku could speak at birth, was able to understand 10 conversations at one time, and knew what was going to happen before it took place. These are myths. Historians are more certain about other parts of Prince Shotoku's life and recognize him as a man who made great achievements in three areas: the development of Buddhism in Japan, the beginning of a more formalized Japanese government structure, and the opening of foreign relations with China.

## The Development of Buddhism

Buddhism had started to take a firm hold in Japan since 552. When Shotoku became regent, he already was a devout Buddhist. As the most powerful man in Japan, he gave strong support to Buddhist practices. Through his efforts, many Buddhist temples were built. During his time as regent, the number of Buddhist monks and nuns greatly increased. For these reasons, many people refer to him as the "father" of Japanese Buddhism.

## A More Formalized Japanese Government Structure

As regent, Prince Shotoku put into place a more structured central government. His thinking in this regard was greatly influenced by Confucian ideas. For example, in 603 he established 12 court ranks. Each man was placed in one of these court ranks. Each wore a different colored cap which signified his rank. This "hat rank" was more than just a way to improve court organization. Each of the colors for the hats was named for a different Confucian value, such as virtue, faith, righteousness, and knowledge.

## The 17-Point Constitution

One of Prince Shotoku's greatest achievements was the 17-point constitution he introduced in 604. In this document, Shotoku outlined ideals for government and rules for human conduct. Although Shotoku was a devout Buddhist, Confucian ideas are clearly evident in this constitution. For example, the first point is a statement about the importance of Confucian harmony in society. The second point said, "Few persons are really bad. If they are well taught, they will be obedient."

The third point said, "The emperor is Heaven and his ministers are Earth. ... ministers must accept imperial commands: When actions are taken on high, those below must comply. So edicts handed down by the emperor must be ... obeyed."

This document was the first in Japan to describe the duties and the rights of the ruler, government officials, and the people. It was Japan's first constitution.

## Relations with China

Prince Shotoku wanted Japan to have a closer relationship with China. Before he came to power, Japan had to deal with China from the position of being a less powerful nation. Prince Shotoku took a different approach. His letter to the Sui Dynasty supposedly shocked the Chinese emperor because it referred to the Chinese emperor as the ruler of "where the sun sets," and to Prince Shotoku as the ruler of "where the sun rises." Prince Shotoku was suggesting that the two countries were equal in power. He supported many diplomatic exchanges between China and Japan. He also sent many Japanese students to China to learn about Chinese culture.

## After Prince Shotoku's Death

After Prince Shotoku's death in 622, fighting broke out between rival groups. The clans fought to gain influence over the emperors. Finally, in 645, the Fujiwara clan gained control and formed a new government. However, Prince Shotoku's constitution continued to give Japan standards and values to guide its government. 📖

**What Do You Think?**

**1.** What Chinese ideas influenced Prince Shotoku? Which do you think was the most important? Why?

**2.** Why do you think Prince Shotoku wanted Japan to be seen as an equal with China? Why do you think the Chinese emperor was shocked by the letter Prince Shotoku sent him?

▼ Prince Shotoku was responsible for the building of the Buddhist temple Horyuji. This wooden temple was largely destroyed by fire in 670. Later it was rebuilt. Visitors today can see some of the oldest wooden buildings left on earth.

# Lady MURASAKI SHIKIBU —
## A Glimpse into Japanese History

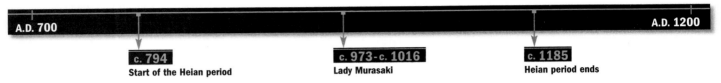

A.D. 700                                           A.D. 1200

**c. 794**
Start of the Heian period

**c. 973- c. 1016**
Lady Murasaki

**c. 1185**
Heian period ends

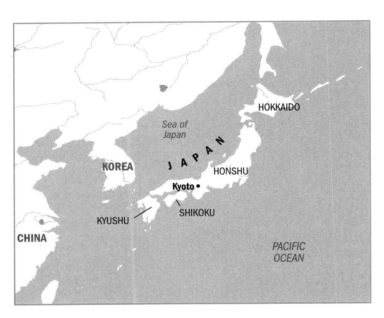

Many people say that the Heian period is one of the most interesting times in Japanese history. This period lasted from about 794 to 1185. During this time, the Japanese aristocracy, not the emperor, had the most influence on society. The aristocracy lived in the city of Kyoto and created a refined culture that continues to influence Japanese culture today. Historians have learned a great deal about the events of the Heian period by studying the literature written during that time. The diaries, poetry, and prose of Japanese aristocrats give us detailed information about the daily lives of the upper classes. During the Heian period, Murasaki Shikibu wrote the world's first novel, *The Tale of Genji*.

▲ During the Heian period, Japanese aristocracy lived in the city of Kyoto. They created a refined culture.

## Early Life

The woman we call Lady Murasaki Shikibu was born between 973 and 978. Her real name is not known. The name, Murasaki Shikibu, is made up of two parts: "Shikibu" is the office her father held, and "Murasaki" is a character in her book. We know that Murasaki Shikibu's father was a minor government official and a scholar of Chinese language and literature. We also know that he hired a tutor to teach his son Chinese literature, calligraphy, and etiquette. At the time, it was not considered proper for women to learn these subjects. However, Murasaki Shikibu's father allowed her to attend the lessons unofficially. She appears to have been a better student than her brother. She wrote in her diary that she helped her brother "whenever he got stuck." On these occasions, her father would sigh and say, "If only you were a boy, how proud and happy I should be." Some historians believe that Murasaki gained so much knowledge that later in life she had to hide much of what she knew.

◄ This is a modern drawing of Lady Murasaki. During the Heian period, a perfect lady was beautifully dressed, had lovely handwriting, and appreciated music, poetry, art, and the beauty of nature.

## Marriage and Court Life

Murasaki Shikibu married when she was in her late teens. She had one daughter, and it appears that her marriage was happy. However, in 1001, just a few years after her marriage, her husband died. Her father then arranged for her to become an attendant to the Empress Akiko, who was only about 16 at the time. Most historians agree that Lady Murasaki had begun writing *The Tale of Genji* by the time she entered the royal court. Historians believed she finished writing this book by about 1002.

## Life at Court

Murasaki Shikibu wrote about the things she observed at the royal court. For example, she described how others dressed and how they behaved. She kept track of stories about the various court festivals, parties, and other activities. She also described people's feelings and was interested in knowing why people acted the way they did. Although there is some disagreement about exactly when she started writing *The Tale of Genji*, how long it took her, and when she finished, no one disagrees that the story of Genji, the shining prince, is a wonderful story filled with vivid details about court life in Japan during this time.

## *The Tale of Genji*

*The Tale of Genji* tells the story of a prince. Genji's father is an emperor and his mother is the emperor's favorite concubine. To protect his son, the emperor makes the boy a member of the "Genji" clan. This meant the boy could not be a threat to anyone who wanted to be emperor. Genji grows up to be a very handsome young man. The novel tells about his romantic adventures with a number of women—some married, some unmarried, and some who were part of the royal court. Murasaki Shikibu describes these women in detail. The characters are probably based on people she knew at court. Her novel reveals the women's talents in art, music, and poetry. It includes Buddhist teachings and themes. For example, there is always a strong sense that material things do not last. This is a basic teaching of Buddhism. She also tells about the beauty of nature—the change of seasons, the sounds of birds, and the clap of thunder. In this way, she reveals a great deal about Japanese culture during the Heian period.

*The Tale of Genji* is a very long novel. It has 54 chapters and is more than 1,100 pages long. It is also a complicated novel. The action takes place over a 75-year period and there are more than 400 characters to follow! However, *The Tale of Genji* represents Murasaki Shikibu's gift to the modern world—a wonderful story that captures the image of a unique period in Japanese history.

▲ This type of rich, silk fabric has a 1,300-year-old history in Japan. Clothing for the Japanese aristocracy during the Heian period was made from material such as this.

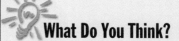

**What Do You Think?**

1. Why do people write diaries, poems, and novels?

2. Why do you think Murasaki Shikibu decided that Genji, the main character in her story, would have no claim to be emperor?

3. Why do you think Murasaki Shikibu may have had to hide her knowledge?

# Lady MURASAKI SHIKIBU and
## *The Tale of Genji*

Lady Murasaki Shikibu wrote stories about court life in Kyoto in the early 1000s. These stories became the novel, *The Tale of Genji*. This book is divided into 54 chapters and is more than 1,100 pages long. There are more than 400 characters in the novel, many of whom are related to one another. In these many pages and through these many characters, Lady Murasaki Shikibu reveals the story of a very handsome young prince, Genji. Her novel tells about Genji's romantic adventures with a number of women—some married, some unmarried, and some who were part of the royal court. Genji enjoys both happy and sad times. You can read below a translation of the opening of Lady Murasaki Shikibu's novel. You will read how the emperor loved Genji's mother. This sets the stage for the story of Genji. 📖

### From *The Tale of Genji*

At the Court of an Emperor (he lived it matters not when) there was among the many gentlewomen of the Wardrobe and Chamber one, who though she was not of very high rank was favoured far beyond all the rest ... . Thus, her position at Court ... exposed her to constant jealousy and ill will; and soon ... she fell into a decline, growing very melancholy and retiring frequently to her home. But the Emperor, so far from wearying of her now that she was not long well or gay, grew every day more tender ... till his conduct became the talk of all the land. They whispered among themselves that in the Land Beyond the Sea such happenings had led to riot and disaster ... . Yet, for all this discontent, so great was the sheltering power of her master's love that none dared openly **molest** her.

Her father, who had been a Councillor, was dead. Her mother, who never forgot that the father was in his day a man of some consequence, managed despite all difficulties to give her as good an upbringing as generally falls to the lot of young ladies whose parents are alive and at the height of fortune. It would have helped matters greatly if there had been some influential guardian to busy himself on the child's behalf. Unfortunately, the mother was entirely alone in the world and sometimes, when troubles came, she felt very bitterly the lack of anyone to whom she could turn for comfort and advice. But to return to the daughter.

## Analyze the Source!

1. Read the excerpt and tell in your own words what it says.

2. How does this excerpt help you learn about Japanese culture and history?

3. What advantages in life did Genji have? What obstacles do you think he had to overcome?

**enmity:** the feelings of an enemy; hostility
**molest:** to annoy or bother
**qualm:** doubt; uncertainty
**vie:** to compete

In due time she bore him a little Prince who ... turned out as fine and likely a man-child as well might be in all the land. The Emperor could hardly contain himself during the days of waiting. But when, at the earliest possible moment, the child was presented at Court, he saw that rumour had not exaggerated its beauty. His eldest born prince was the son of Lady Kokiden, the daughter of the Minister of the Right, and this child was treated by all with the respect due to an undoubted Heir Apparent. But he was not so fine a child as the new prince; moreover the Emperor's great affection for the new child's mother made him feel the boy to be in a peculiar sense his own possession. Unfortunately she was not of the same rank as the courtiers who waited upon him in the Upper Palace, so ... it was not without considerable **qualms** that he now made it his practice to have her by him not only when there was to be some entertainment, but even when any business of importance was afoot ... .

Seeing the Emperor's preference for his mistress and their son, Lady Kokiden began to fear that the new prince might become heir instead of her son. Everyone knew that the Emperor would protect his mistress from harm, but he could not protect her from the mean tricks people played to embarrass and humiliate her. Over time, this made the Emperor's mistress very ill. She repeatedly asked the Emperor to let her go home, but he could not bear to let her go. Finally, when the young prince was about three years old, she died. The Emperor was very sad and agreed that it would be better for the young prince to return to his home to be raised by his grandmother. Still, as time went on, he missed the young prince very much. He sent servants to bring him news of how the boy was doing. Eventually, he asked the boy to come back to the palace to live with him. The Emperor made sure that Genji had the best education. The Emperor thought about making the boy his heir. However, he decided against it because of the problems it would create in the court and the land. Instead, he made the boy a member of the "Genji" clan. That meant he had an important position in society, but could not become emperor.

Genji ('he of the Minamoto clan'), as he was now called, was constantly at the Emperor's side. He was soon quite at his ease with the common run of Ladies in Waiting and Ladies of the Wardrobe, so it was not likely he would be shy with one who was daily summoned to the Emperor's apartments. It was but natural that all these ladies should **vie** eagerly with one another for the first place in Genji's affections, and there were many whom in various ways he admired very much. But most of them behaved in too grown-up a fashion; only one, the new princess was pretty and quite young as well ... . Kokiden had never loved this lady too well, and now her old **enmity** to Genji sprang up again; her own children were reckoned to be of quite uncommon beauty, but in this they were no match for Genji, who was so lovely a boy that people called him Hikaru Genji or Genji the Shining One ... .

# SEI SHONAGON and the
## *Pillow Book*

Lady Murasaki Shikibu is probably the most famous person to write during the Heian period in Japan, but she was not the only writer. Sei Shonagon was born around 966 and became a member of Empress Sadako's court. Like Lady Murasaki, Sei Shonagon wrote about the people she knew at court and the experiences she and others had there. Her descriptions are contained in the *Pillow Book*. You can read below a translated excerpt from Sei Shonagon's *Pillow Book*. ▢

**bevy:** group
**malady:** illness

### FROM THE *PILLOW BOOK*

A girl is wearing an unlined robe of soft white stuff, full trousers, and a light purple mantle thrown across her shoulders ... . But she has some terrible **malady** of her chest. Her fellow ladies-in-waiting come in turns to sit with her, and outside the room there is a crowd of very young men inquiring about her with great anxiety: How terribly sad! Has she ever had such an attack before? And so on ...

The lady binds back her beautiful, long hair and raises herself on her couch. Even now there is a grace in her movements that makes them pleasurable to watch. The empress hears of her condition and at once sends a famous reciter of the Scriptures, renowned for the beauty of his voice, to read at her bedside. The room is very small, and now to the throng of visitors is added a number of ladies who have simply come to hear the reading. At this exposed **bevy** of young women the priest constantly glances as he reads, for which he will certainly suffer in the life to come.

## Analyze the Source!

1. Read the excerpt and tell in your own words what it says.

2. How does this excerpt help you learn about Japanese culture and history?

3. Can you draw any conclusions about Japanese beliefs about health from this excerpt? Explain why you can or cannot.

4. Why do you think Sei Shonagon says the priest "will certainly suffer in the life to come"?

# The Tales of the Heike —
# SAMURAI WARRIORS

From 1188-1333, an era known as the Kamakura period, the samurai class was gaining power in Japan. The literature of this time reflects the growing importance of the samurai—fearless soldiers. Storytellers told tales of samurai in battle. Historians believe that at first these stories were chanted and accompanied by music. These tales of war and warriors were very popular with all classes in Japanese society. Later, the stories were written down in books such as *The Tales of the Heike*, which tells about a samurai priest who fought with the Minamoto clan. You can read below translated excerpts from this book. The first excerpt describes the samurai warriors in heroic terms. The second excerpt describes Tomoe, a samurai woman who was a member of the Minamoto clan. 📖

## FROM *THE TALES OF THE HEIKE*

[He] sprang forward alone onto the bridge and shouted in a mighty voice, "Let those at a distance listen; these that are near can see; I am Tsutsui Jomyo Meishu, the priest; who is there in Miidera who does not know me, a warrior worth one thousand men? Come on anyone who thinks himself someone, and we shall see!" And loosing off his 24 arrows like lightning flashes he slew 12 of the Heike soldiers and wounded 11 more ... . [He took off his shoes] and springing barefoot onto the beams of the bridge he strode across. All were afraid to cross over, but he walked the broken bridge as one who walks along the street Ichijo or Nijo of the capital. With his "naginato" [pole sword] he mowed down five of the enemy, but with the sixth [the pole sword broke and he took out] his sword, wielding it in the zigzag style ... cross, reversed dragonfly, waterwheel, and eight-sides-at-once styles of fencing, and cut down eight men.

---

Tomoe had long black hair and a fair complexion, and her face was very lovely; moreover she was a fearless rider whom neither the fiercest horse nor the roughest ground could dismay, and so dexterously did she handle sword and bow that she was a match for a thousand warriors and fit to meet either god or devil. Many times had she taken the field, armed at all points, and won ... in encounters with the bravest captains, and so in this last fight, when all the others had been slain or had fled, among the last seven there rode Tomoe.

▲ Only samurai were permitted to carry swords.

## Analyze the Source!

1. Read the excerpts and tell in your own words what they say.

2. How do the excerpts help you learn about Japanese culture and warfare?

3. What conclusions, if any, can you draw about the role of samurai women in Japanese society during this time? Explain why you can or cannot draw conclusions.

# JAPAN — Then and Now

Japan adapted ideas from the Chinese to create its own unique culture. Japan had a strong military force, a government ruled by shoguns and samurai, and a distinct class system. Many of the traditions and much of the culture developed during ancient times continue today.

▲ This map shows the Japanese archipelago. Many of the Japanese traditions developed hundreds of years ago continue in Japan today.

## Samurai

Samurai were Japanese warriors and members of the ruling class. Samurai were the most powerful group of people in Japan from the 1100s until the 1700s. Both samurai men and women had weapons. A samurai woman kept a short knife in a piece of silk material she wrapped around her waist. Before guns were introduced, a samurai man's main weapons were his swords, lance, and bow and arrow. His most important weapon and the symbol of his class was his pair of matching swords. Samurai believed swords had special powers. Swordmaking was a sacred art in Japan. The people who made swords were considered master craftsmen and artisans. Even today, people can tell a particular swordmaker's sword because of the way the blade was made.

A samurai warrior also treasured his armor. Not only was it a work of art, but it also could save his life in battle. Lower-ranking samurai wore armor made of small metal plates. Higher-ranking samurai wore armor made of large pieces of iron. Samurai also wore helmets and face guards. The face guard sometimes was painted with colors and pictures to frighten the enemy.

◄ This photograph shows a modern-day parade in Japan. The men are dressed as traditional samurai. In ancient times, only samurai were allowed to carry swords.

### Lasting Influences ...

Hundreds of years ago, samurai spent a great deal of their time training for war. They learned and practiced ways of fighting, or what we call "martial arts." Japan continues to be known for its martial arts. Martial arts today represent a continuation of the samurai fighting traditions that began much earlier in Japanese history. There are many different kinds of Japanese martial arts. Kendo began in the Ashikaga period, and jujitsu began in the Edo period. Judo is an outgrowth of jujitsu. The word *jujitsu* means "the gentle art." Jujitsu, like other martial arts traditions, emphasizes flexibility rather than strength. Karate, which may be the most well-known martial art, actually was a method of fighting that the Japanese borrowed from China.

## Noh Drama and Kabuki

Throughout Japanese history, people enjoyed hearing stories and seeing plays. Japanese nobles enjoyed a special kind of entertainment called Noh drama. In Noh drama, all the actors are men. They wear masks when they play female roles. They also wear masks to demonstrate a character's feelings—happiness, sadness, jealousy, or anger. The actors wear beautiful costumes. Usually, a traditional program of Noh theater includes both serious and funny plays. Most Noh plays deal with topics such as gods and devils, the ghosts of samurai, and Buddhist ideas. Some people sit to one side of the stage and recite poetry while the actors are dancing. The audience sits on two or three sides of the stage, and usually there is little scenery on the stage.

At the end of the 1400s, a new kind of entertainment called Kabuki theater became popular. Kabuki plays were presented in large theaters. The plays often were adapted from puppet theater. In puppet theater, people made puppets move, sing, and speak. In Kabuki, however, there was more emphasis on acting, music, dance, and beautiful scenery. Kabuki theater was almost the opposite of Noh drama. It was packed with action, fight scenes, loud songs and speeches, brave women and men, and evil villains. At first, shoguns tried to stop Kabuki theater, but it was too popular with the people.

▲ Kabuki theater has acting, music, dance, and beautiful scenery.

### Lasting Influences ...

Noh drama and Kabuki theater are still very popular in Japan today. Just as it was hundreds of years ago, Noh drama is presented on a simple stage without special scenery. The play is accompanied by the music of flute and drums. Kabuki theater attracts many Japanese who go to see the beautiful costumes, elaborate make-up, rhythmic music, artful dance, and compelling drama. The most famous Kabuki play, *Sukeroku*, is still performed in the traditional way. It tells about the conflict between a young commoner and a samurai bully.

▲ Performers in a Noh play wear masks to demonstrate a character's feelings.

## Lasting Influences ...

Today, when Japanese businessmen and women go home after a hard day's work, they often change into the same kind of clothing Japanese people have worn for hundreds of years. Many Japanese today wear kimonos for special occasions as well as when they visit friends. Women also carry fans. Most Japanese women today can't put special occasion kimonos on without help because they are accustomed to wearing Western clothing. Married and unmarried women wear different types of kimonos. These elements of dress—kimonos and fans—continue to be influenced by nature and its beauty. Kimonos also reflect the simplicity of Zen Buddhist teachings.

▲ Wealthy women carried fans.

### COUNTING IN JAPANESE

| Arabic Numeral | Japanese Character | Pronunciation |
|---|---|---|
| 1 | 一 | (ee-CHEE) |
| 2 | 二 | (nee) |
| 3 | 三 | (sahn) |
| 4 | 四 | (shee) |
| 5 | 五 | (goh) |
| 6 | 六 | (roh-KOO) |
| 7 | 七 | (shee-CHEE) |

▲ The Japanese counting system developed from the Chinese language.

## Kimonos and Fans

The kimono is the traditional clothing of Japan. A kimono is a long, loose robe that is tied at the waist with a piece of material. Traditionally, men, women, and children all wore kimonos. Before 300, kimonos were made of a rough cloth and tied loosely around the waist. When the Yamato clan came to power, people began to wear kimonos that consisted of two pieces. The piece worn on the upper body had tight sleeves. The part worn on the lower body was loose and flowing.

By 792, kimonos had become more elaborate. They were longer, fuller, and made of colored cloth. Wealthy people had different clothes to wear at court on special occasions, as well as everyday. People showed their love of color, beauty, and art in their clothes. Women at court sometimes wore kimonos with 10, 15, or 20 layers of cloth. This helped them keep warm in the winter. Sometimes, however, the kimonos were so heavy that women had difficulty moving in them.

Wealthy women often carried fans as accessories. They used the fans to cool themselves in the heat. Fans might include a picture of a cherry blossom or a bird on a branch. These scenes expressed inner peace. Some fans were made out of paper. Others were carved from wood or ivory. ▢

# JAPAN TODAY—THE ESSENTIALS

| | |
|---|---|
| **COUNTRY NAME:** | Japan |
| **NICKNAME:** | Land of the Rising Sun |
| **CAPITAL:** | Tokyo |
| **LOCATION:** | Archipelago in the Pacific Ocean off the northeastern coast of Asia |
| **AREA:** | 142,811 square miles; Japan has approximately 5,900 miles of coastline |
| **HIGHEST ELEVATION:** | Mount Fuji (12,388 feet)—an inactive volcano |
| **CLIMATE:** | Hokkaido, the northern island, has cold, snowy winters and short, cool summers; the northern part of Honshu, the middle island, is cold, but in the south the winter is mild and the summer is warm and wet; Kyushu and Shikoku, the southern islands, have long, hot summers and mild winters |
| **POPULATION:** | 126,281,000; less than 1% of the population is non-Japanese |
| **FORM OF GOVERNMENT:** | Constitutional monarchy; the emperor is the head of state and the prime minister is the head of government |
| **UNIT OF MONEY:** | Yen |
| **LANGUAGE:** | Japanese |
| **MAJOR RELIGIONS:** | Shinto, Buddhism, Christianity |
| **FLAG:** | Red sun against a white background |
| **IMPORTANT PRODUCTS:** | Rice, soybeans, tea, fish, computer and electronic devices, motor vehicles, ships, steel, textiles, financial services |

# The Development of Buddhism in Japan

600 B.C.

0

A.D. 1300

c. 563-483 B.C.
Guatama Siddhartha

552 B.C.
Buddhism spreads to
Japan

A.D. 1200s
Zen Buddhism becomes
established in Japan

▲ The man we call Buddha and the founder of Buddhism was born in what is now Nepal. Buddhism spread to China and many other parts of the world.

▲ This Japanese statue shows Buddha, the founder of Buddhism. This statue was completed in 749. It is located in the Great Buddha Hall in Nara, Japan.

Gautama Siddhartha, the man we call Buddha and the founder of Buddhism, was born around 563 B.C. and died in 483 B.C. Most people agree that Siddhartha was born into a royal family. His family lived in an area that is now the southern edge of Nepal, just north of India, in the foothills of the Himalayas. As a young prince, Siddhartha lived a life of luxury. One day he left the royal palace where he lived. While he was outside the palace walls, he met an old man, a poor man, and a sick man. For the first time in his life, he also saw a dead man. From these experiences, Siddhartha learned that death happened to all human beings. From that moment on, he decided to give up worldly pleasures and spend his life in search of religious truth.

At first, his life was extremely difficult. In fact, he did without basic necessities and almost died. Later, he found a "middle way." He realized that it was important to live with just enough to get by. After a long period of meditation, he gained a state of spiritual understanding. His followers say that he became enlightened—free from wanting material things or power. In that moment of revelation, his followers say that he became Buddha, a name that means, "enlightened one." Another name for enlightenment is "nirvana." Buddha spent the rest of his life teaching others about how they might gain enlightenment. His followers became known as Buddhists. Buddha's ideas and teachings became known as Buddhism.

## Buddhism Spreads

Over time, Buddhism spread throughout India and across China. Generally, the spread of Buddhism followed the trade routes that crisscrossed the Asian continent. Buddhism appealed to the Chinese because it dealt directly with human suffering in a way that their own religious traditions did not. In 552, Buddhism spread to Japan. In that year, a Korean king sent a statue of Buddha, some Buddhist priests, and Buddhist writings to the Yamato ruler. Some people thought Buddhism was in conflict with Japan's traditional Shinto religion. They did not think it was a good idea to welcome a foreign religion.

Others, however, thought Buddhism and Shintoism supported each other. They thought Buddhism met spiritual needs that Shintoism did not, but that Shintoism gave them a very important connection to Japanese history and traditions. The disagreement between the two groups was not settled until the two sides went to war and Prince Shotoku became regent to the young Yamato ruler in 592. Prince Shotoku was a devout Buddhist. He supported the building of many Buddhist temples and brought Buddhist priests from the Asian mainland. Within a short time, Buddhism and Shintoism existed side by side. Over the next 700 years, new ideas about Buddhism were introduced into Japan. Different groups of Buddhists with slightly different ideas about Buddhism began to form. These different groups are sometimes called sects.

## Buddhism in Early Japan

From about 710 to 784, people were drawn to Buddhism for two major reasons. First, they liked the spiritual message in Buddhism. Second, they were attracted to the beauty of Buddhist rituals. During this time, the Japanese built many beautiful Buddhist temples, including the Todaiji monastery in the city of Nara.

## New Buddhist Sects

During the period from 794 to 897, two new Buddhist sects formed in Japan. The first was the Tendai sect. The followers of the Tendai sect brought new Buddhist ideas from China to Japan in 805. They founded the Tendai sect on Mt. Hiei, which is northeast of Kyoto. The followers of the Tendai sect believed that enlightenment was possible for everyone through a strict life of religious devotion. Another new Buddhist sect that developed during this time was the Shingon sect. Followers of the Shingon sect insisted on very secret and complicated rituals. They also believed in the Ten Stages of Religious Development. This was a ranking of the various types of Buddhism. Of course, Shingon ranked first. The teachings of the Shingon were difficult to understand, and over time this sect died out.

## More Buddhist Sects

Beginning around 1185, a new Buddhist group formed. Founded by a monk named Honan, this sect was called Pure Land Buddhism. The followers of Pure Land Buddhism were interested in finding happiness in an afterlife, not finding enlightenment on earth. They believed they could be reborn in a paradise or "pure land" by reciting, over and over, the name "Amida." They believed Amida was an Indian prince who became enlightened and then established a pure land or paradise in the West. In 1224, one of Honan's followers, a monk named Shinran, had a different idea about how people could find enlightenment. He founded the True Pure Land sect. He taught that people could not gain enlightenment through their own efforts. Instead, they had to depend on the power of Amida. Once people had gained enlightenment, they could marry and enjoy life on earth.

▲ Prince Shotoku, a devout Buddhist, became regent to the young Yamato ruler in 592.

▲ The Great Buddha Hall in Nara was built in 745. The Japanese city of Nara was modeled after Changan in China.

---

Around this same time, another monk, a man named Nichiren, thought the other Buddhist sects were hurting Japan. He believed that the only truth came from the Lotus Sutra, a very old Buddhist writing from India. He said disaster would befall Japan if people did not follow his teachings. Nichiren's followers wanted people to accept his teachings, even if they had to use force. They armed themselves with weapons and burned the temples and monasteries of other religious sects.

## Zen Buddhism

Zen Buddhism also became established in Japan in the 1200s. Some Japanese knew about Zen practices in China before this time. However, it was during the 1200s that two Buddhist monks, Eisai and Dogen, spread the teachings of Zen Buddhism. Zen Buddhism was different from other forms of Buddhism. It emphasized strict discipline, very simple living, and meditation. The word *Zen* comes from an Indian word meaning "meditation." Unlike other Buddhist sects that believed enlightenment took years of study and prayer, Zen Buddhists believed that enlightenment occurred suddenly. They thought it came as a result of strong physical or mental discipline. Some Zen Buddhists believed they could gain enlightenment by meditating on riddles. For example, one Zen riddle asks, "What is the sound of one hand clapping?" Other Zen Buddhists sat silently mediating without a specific goal.

Zen Buddhism became very popular among Japan's samurai class, including its shoguns, because many of its teachings supported the samurai ideas. Samurai also were attracted to Zen Buddhism because it required a great deal of sacrifice and difficult physical training. Zen Buddhism focused on the present, not the past or future. It emphasized the importance of the way things are done. You can see this idea reflected in a Japanese tea ceremony. Every part of the ceremony—from the placement of the cups to the steps in preparing the tea—has great meaning. You also can see this idea in a Zen garden where every rock is carefully placed. Zen Buddhist ideas greatly influenced Japanese rituals, art, and drama.

▼ The traditional Japanese tea ceremony began as a Zen Buddhist ritual.

# European Impressions of Japan

Portuguese traders and religious missionaries first arrived in Japan in 1543. Some of the traders wrote about their experiences, but it is Christian missionaries who wrote the most about their observations. They wrote about the geography, language, everyday life, and culture of Japan. You can read here the impressions some Europeans had of the Japanese during the mid-1500s and early 1600s.

▲ Portuguese traders and religious missionaries first arrived in Japan in 1543.

## JORGE ALVARES

Jorge Alvares, a Portuguese merchant and sea captain, visited southern Kyushu in 1547, and wrote about the natural environment:

*It is a beautiful and pleasing country and has an abundance of trees, such as the pine, cedar, plum, cherry, peach, laurel, chestnut, walnut, oak ... . There is also much fruit not to be found in our country; they grow the vegetables which we have in Portugal, except lettuces, cabbages ... and even mint; all the rest they have. They also cultivate roses, carnations and many other scented flowers, as well as both sweet and bitter oranges, citrons (although I did not see any lemons), pomegranates and pears ...*

## LUIS DE ALMEIDA

Luis de Almeida went to Japan in 1556 as a Portuguese merchant, and later returned as a Jesuit priest. He wrote about the elaborate Japanese tea ceremony in the 1560s:

*There is a custom among the noble and wealthy Japanese to show their treasures to an honored guest at his departure ... . These treasures are made up of the utensils with which they drink a powdered herb called cha [tea], which is a delicious drink once one becomes used to it. To make this drink, they pour half a nutshell of this powdered herb into a porcelain bowl, and then adding very hot water they drink the brew. All these utensils used for this purpose are very old ... all these make up the treasures of Japan, just as rings, gems, and necklaces of precious rubies and diamonds do with us ...*

notable: important
Orient: Asia

▶ **Father Lourenço Mexia wrote about Japanese music in the 1560s.**

## FATHER LOURENÇO MEXIA

Father Lourenço Mexia, a Jesuit priest from Portugal, worked in both Japan and China. He wrote about Japanese music in the 1560s:

*Their natural and artificial music is so dissonant and harsh to our ears that it is quite a trial to listen to it for a quarter of an hour; but to please the Japanese we are obliged to listen to it many more hours. They themselves like it so much that they do not think there is anything to equal it in the wide world ... . They put on many plays and dramas about various wholesome and joyful things during their festivals, but they are always accompanied by this music.*

## BERNARDINO DE AVILA GIRÓN

Bernardino de Avila Girón, a Spanish trader, arrived in Japan around 1594. He traveled in other parts of Asia, but returned to Japan in 1607. He wrote about how the Japanese kept track of history:

*They count the years by eras in the following manner. They remember the past eras (of which there are a great many) by the various events, the good and bad fortune, and the **notable** happenings which occurred, for the eras both begin and end with these. But as regards the present era, they know neither how long it will last nor when the next one will begin ...*

## JOÃO RODRIGUES

João Rodrigues sailed from his home in Portugal to Japan in 1576 when he was only about 15 years old. While in Japan, he became a Jesuit priest. Rodrigues became so fluent in Japanese that he worked as an interpreter for Hideyoshi and Tokugawa. He lived in Japan until he was forced to leave in 1612. He wrote about many aspects of Japanese society, including their paper:

*They make various kinds of paper from the bark of certain trees which they cultivate for this purpose, for paper is one of the things which they use most in Japan. Its antiquity is not certain but it appears that they learnt about it from their neighbors, the Koreans, who make paper from the same material. The Koreans received it from the Chinese, who seem to have been the first to invent it in the **Orient**, or indeed in the whole world ... .* 📖

## Analyze the Source!

1. Read the excerpts on pages 229 and 230. Choose one and tell in your own words what the excerpt says.

2. How does the excerpt you put in your own words help you learn about Japanese culture and history?

3. How does this excerpt help you learn about European culture?

# TOKUGAWA IEYASU —
# Japanese Shogun

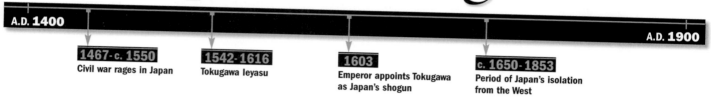

**1467-c. 1550**
Civil war rages in Japan

**1542-1616**
Tokugawa Ieyasu

**1603**
Emperor appoints Tokugawa as Japan's shogun

**c. 1650-1853**
Period of Japan's isolation from the West

Civil war raged in Japan between 1467 and 1550. Dozens of aristocrats known as daimyo competed with one another for control of larger territories. Then, around 1590, a great general, Hideyoshi, conquered all the daimyo. He ordered all the peasants to give up their metal weapons. He passed laws forbidding farmers to leave their fields, and made it illegal for a samurai to leave his master without permission. His actions brought order to Japan. It was his hope that his son would succeed him as leader, but instead another powerful and ambitious daimyo, Tokugawa Ieyasu, became shogun—the military leader of Japan.

## Early Life

Tokugawa Ieyasu was born in 1542 in the Okazaki Castle. His father was a military leader who governed an area in the central part of Japan. As a young boy, Ieyasu was kept as a hostage by a rival warlord. The rival did this so that Ieyasu's father would protect the rival's property and members of his clan. Eventually, Ieyasu was released. As he grew up, Tokugawa Ieyasu became a samurai warrior himself. He rose to power by joining the military forces of the shogun, Nobunaga.

## A Plan to Seize Power

When Nobunaga died, one of his generals, Hideyoshi, carried out Nobunaga's plan to unify Japan. Tokugawa watched what happened very carefully. Hideyoshi made all the daimyo pledge allegiance to him. Before he died 1598, Hideyoshi also made the daimyo pledge allegiance to his five-year-old son. But a five-year-old boy could not rule without help. Tokugawa was one of several men chosen to rule on the boy's behalf until he came of age. However, almost immediately after Hideyoshi's death, Tokugawa began to plan how he would take over all of Japan. In 1600, at the battle of Sekigahara, he defeated all of his rivals and became the most powerful warlord in Japan. In 1603, the emperor appointed Tokugawa as Japan's shogun.

▲ Tokugawa Ieyasu lived in Edo (present-day Tokyo).

### It's a FACT

Members of Tokugawa's clan ruled Japan for 250 years, until the mid-1800s. This period in Japanese history is often known as the Edo period.

**Samurai**

**Artisans**

**Farmers**

**Merchants**

▲ There were four distinct classes in Japan—samurai, artisans, farmers, and merchants. The shogun and daimyo were members of the samurai class.

## Governing Japan

Tokugawa established his government in Edo (present-day Tokyo). As shogun, Tokugawa made considerable changes in Japan. He emphasized Confucian thinking in his view of government and society. This meant that there would be rigid social grouping, or classes, of people. These classes were samurai, artisans, farmers, and merchants. Samurai were at the top of society. Over time, samurai spent less time on war and more time on government work. Merchants were at the bottom of society. Some merchants ran small shops, while other merchants were responsible for storing rice and other foods. Artisans were responsible for making and repairing weapons, tools, pots, and other items needed in everyday life. Japanese farmers were always at the mercy of the weather. However, during this period, they grew more food than in earlier times and life improved for them. In keeping with Confucian thinking, these classes of people were ranked according to their moral importance to society, not on their wealth.

Under Tokugawa's leadership, Japan became wealthy and made many cultural advances. Tokugawa was interested in expanding Japan's foreign trade with other Asian countries. Cities such as Edo and Osaka became large trading centers. Almost half the male population could read. Samurai men and women learned martial arts and studied literature.

## Controlling the Daimyo

Tokugawa controlled the Japanese daimyo through a system called "sankin-kotai" or "alternate attendance." According to "alternate attendance," each daimyo was required to live at the shogun's palace in Edo for 12 out of every 24 months. This gave the shogun a chance to keep his eye on the daimyo. In addition, because it cost a lot of money for the daimyo to move back and forth from their own homes, they had less money. This meant that Tokugawa reduced the possibility that any daimyo could try to raise an army to overthrow him. Tokugawa also required the daimyo to leave many of their relatives in his castle when the daimyo returned home. This system helped keep peace in Japan among the daimyo for almost 250 years.

## An Enduring Dynasty

Tokugawa died in 1616 at the age of 75. He had passed the title of shogun to his son years earlier, so his death did not create a crisis. The dynasty continued for hundreds of years. Although there was peace in Japan during the Tokugawa Dynasty, his successors had to deal with important challenges, including the arrival of Western traders and Christian missionaries. By the time of Tokugawa's death, there was already a strong feeling against foreigners. By 1650, Japan was isolating itself from the West. This isolation continued until 1853. □

# BASHŌ — Haiku Master

Matsuo Bashō is considered one of Japan's greatest poets. He was born in 1644 to a samurai family. It is said that a friend gave him a bashō—a banana tree—when he was a boy. He liked it so much that he decided to change his name to Bashō. Bashō traveled throughout Japan, but lived most of his life in Kyoto and Edo. Bashō was interested in writing a very special kind of poem called haiku. Most haiku poems describe a moment in nature. A haiku poem has 17 syllables, and these syllables are arranged in lines of five syllables, seven syllables, and five syllables. This is a very strict form. The haiku poet had to express important ideas in a few words.

Below you can read a translation of one of Bashō's most famous haiku. A modern poet described the haiku as being a celebration of life. In other words, when a poet such as Bashō describes the moment when a frog jumps in a pond and there is the sound of a splash of water, he is reaffirming that he was alive at that moment and saw that scene. Bashō wrote haiku until his death in 1694. ▯

## Analyze the Source!

1. How does this haiku help you learn about Japanese culture and history?

2. Using critical thinking skills, explain why Bashō's haiku does not seem to follow the haiku form of having exactly 17 syllables.

**Old pond:
Frog jump-in
Water-sound.**

*—By Matsuo Bashō, 1686*

◄ **Kanji, which are the characters of Japanese writing, often look like forms out of nature. This is the kanji character for "rain." Can you see the rain drops?**

# The Rule of ST. BENEDICT

A.D. 400

A.D. 700

**c. 480-547**
St. Benedict

**c. 590-604**
Pope Gregory I is
bishop of Rome

EUROPE

Nursia •
• Rome
ITALY

Mediterranean Sea

▲ Pope Gregory I lived in Rome. St. Benedict was born in Nursia, Italy.

Most of what we know about St. Benedict comes from the writings of Pope Gregory I (Gregory the Great). Benedict was born around 480 to a wealthy family in Nursia, a small village in north central Italy. He went to school in Rome, but was not happy there. He had trouble fitting in with the other students. He thought most of them were only interested in leading a life of fun and pleasure. He decided to join a religious community and become a monk. Living the life of a monk was an important calling in medieval Europe. Benedict lived a life of discipline and prayer, and he developed a reputation as a man of God. During his life, people considered him a very holy person as well as someone who had common sense. Benedict started many monasteries, including Monte Cassino, which is near Naples in southern Italy.

St. Benedict is best remembered for the rules he set forth to govern the lives of monks. Monks had to make three promises—to spend their entire lives in the monastery, to try to become closer to God, and to obey the head of the monastery. St. Benedict died in 547. However, over time, his rules were followed by many orders of monks and nuns, which helped to standardize practices within the church. You can read below an excerpt from *The Rule of St. Benedict*. In this excerpt, Benedict describes the kind of man an abbot—the head of a monastery—should be. 📖

▲ St. Benedict is remembered for the rules he set to govern the lives of monks.

## Analyze the Source!

1. How does this excerpt help you understand how religion influenced the people of Europe during this time?

2. Do you think St. Benedict's ideas about the head of a monastery are fair? Why or why not?

### From *The Rule of St. Benedict*

The abbot who is worthy to rule over a monastery should always remember what he is called and suit his actions to his high calling. For he is believed to take the place of Christ in the monastery. ... The abbot ought not to teach, ordain, or command anything which is against the law of the Lord. ... Let him make no distinction of person in the monastery. Let no one be loved more than other. ... Let not the free-born monk be put before the man who was born in slavery unless there is some good reason for it. But if the abbot, for some reason, shall see fit to do so, he may fix anyone's rank as he will; otherwise let all keep their own places, because whether slave or freeman, we are all one in Christ and we must all alike bear the burden of service under the same Lord.

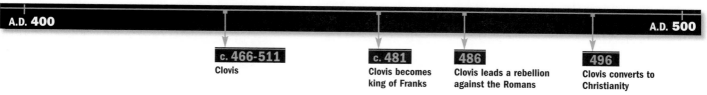

# CLOVIS the FRANK

A.D. **400**

A.D. **500**

**c. 466-511**
Clovis

**c. 481**
Clovis becomes
king of Franks

**486**
Clovis leads a rebellion
against the Romans

**496**
Clovis converts to
Christianity

The Roman Empire was facing many different problems in the 400s. One of the most critical problems was the Germanic tribes to the north and east of Italy. Many of these Germanic tribes lived along the Rhine River. Over time, they became known as the Franks, a word that means "fierce" or "free." In the late 400s, one group of Franks attacked the Roman soldiers at a nearby fort. The Romans defeated these Franks and then forced them to move to present-day Belgium. Over time, many Franks became soldiers and even officers in the Roman army. However, the Franks never developed a strong loyalty to the Roman army. In 486, Clovis, a Frank in the Roman army, led a rebellion against the Roman commander in this area. After his victory, Clovis made himself ruler of a territory that included land south and west of the Rhine River.

▲ The shaded area shows Clovis's empire around 511. He lived in what is present-day northwestern France. Paris was his capital.

## Becoming a Christian King

Clovis ruled as king of the Franks. He thought that by having the support of leaders in the Christian Church, he would be a stronger ruler, especially in his dealings with other Germanic tribes. Although he was not a Christian himself, in 493 he married a Christian woman named Clothilde. Throughout their marriage, Clothilde repeatedly asked Clovis to become a Christian. He refused, although he allowed their children to be baptized. In 496, however, during a battle he thought his army would lose, he prayed to God. He promised God that if he won the battle, he would become a Christian. His army won, and Clovis was immediately baptized. Many of his followers also converted to Christianity.

## Building a Kingdom

During his reign, Clovis selected the city of Paris as his capital. By doing this, he strengthened his ties to Christianity because Paris was linked to St. Denis. St. Denis was greatly admired by the people of the region.

▲ Clovis ruled as king of the Franks. He was a fierce warrior.

Chapter 13: The Making of Europe **235**

▲ This image shows the baptism of Clovis. Clovis strengthened his power to rule by converting to Christianity.

---

### What Do You Think?

**1.** Clovis's sons inherited the kingdom he built. However, like many other rulers you have read about, the sons were much less successful than their father. Why do you think that is so?

**2.** Why do you think Clovis's conversion to Christianity was so important?

**3.** What qualities do you think Clovis needed in order to be a leader during this period? How does this compare with the qualities needed by leaders today?

---

St. Denis also was believed to be a disciple of St. Paul, the man most responsible for spreading Christian ideas in the early days of Christianity. By linking himself with St. Denis and St. Paul, Clovis became more closely identified with Christianity. Clovis expanded his territory and built a kingdom that included much of present-day France and Germany.

## A Kingdom Divided

After Clovis died in 511, his kingdom was divided among his four sons. However, none of these men turned out to be very good rulers. The entire kingdom became caught up in a civil war until only one son survived. While Clovis's sons were busy fighting, the family of Charles Martel came to power. The dynasty Clovis founded came to an end. The power to rule passed to a new group of Franks and a new dynasty of kings. 📖

# CHARLEMAGNE —
# Emperor of the Romans

A.D. **700** ──────────────────────────────────────────── A.D. **1000**

**c. 742-814**
Charlemagne

**800**
Pope Leo III declares
Charlemagne "Emperor
of the Romans"

**late 800s-900s**
Carolingian empire
declines

Charles the Great, the man we know as Charlemagne, is one of the most important figures of the Middle Ages. Throughout his reign, he placed great importance on Christianity, the rule of law, and education. He unified much of western Europe and laid the foundation for a modern European civilization.

## Early Life

Charlemagne was most likely born in 742. He was the son of Pepin the Short and the grandson of Charles Martel. Charlemagne's father, Pepin, was a Frankish leader. At first, Pepin served as "mayor of the palace," a position that was chief advisor or prime minister to the king. Pepin also provided support for the pope, the man who served as leader of the Western Christian Church. Later, with help from the pope, Pepin became king of the Franks. When he died, the empire was divided, according to custom, between his two sons—Carloman and Charlemagne. These two brothers shared rule of the empire for a few years. However, when Carloman died unexpectedly, Charlemagne quickly took control of his brother's territory.

## Early Reign and Territorial Expansion

When Charlemagne became king, he followed his father's example. Like Pepin, Charlemagne developed a relationship of mutual support with the pope. Soon after he became king, Charlemagne was involved in the first of many wars. In 772, when Pope Adrian I asked for his protection against the Lombards, Charlemagne conquered the Lombards. He also agreed that he would keep his father's promise to protect the Papal States—land in the north central part of Italy. For many decades to come, Charlemagne continued to fight and expand his empire.

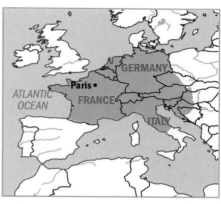

▲ This map is shaded to show Charlemagne's empire around 890. It covered roughly the areas that are modern-day France, Germany, and Italy.

◄ Charlemagne unified much of western Europe and laid the foundation for a modern European civilization.

It's a FACT

It's a FACT

The name Carolingian comes from the Latin *Carolus* meaning "Charles."

**count:** a nobleman; the word *count* comes from the Latin word *comes*, meaning "companion"

▲ This picture shows Charlemagne in the city of Jerusalem. It was created in the 1400s.

**What Do You Think?**

1. Why do you think leaders at this time were expected to have strong military skills? Do we expect leaders today to have these kinds of skills?

2. Why do you think Charlemagne sent officials to check on the counts? Who are government officials responsible to in our government today?

Charlemagne fought battles in the north against the Saxons, in the east against the Bavarians, and in northwestern Spain against the Basques. The only battle he ever lost was in Spain against the Muslims. His journey home after this defeat inspired the medieval epic poem, *The Song of Roland*, which was written hundreds of years after the events had taken place.

## Government of the Carolingian Dynasty

Charlemagne's empire was organized as a loose grouping of people. Most of the people in the empire were farmers. The only people who did not spend most of their time farming were the aristocrats, professional soldiers, and members of the clergy. As Charlemagne traveled throughout the empire, he would take land from the local lord and give it to other nobles who had pledged to support him. Because the empire was so large, Charlemagne appointed men called "**counts**" to govern local areas. Charlemagne sent out other people called *missi dominici*, which means "agents of the lord king," to make sure the counts were doing a good job. It was the responsibility of these officials to make certain that Charlemagne's rules and wishes were being carried out.

## The Importance of Education

Charlemagne's royal court in Aachen was filled with intellectuals from Spain, England, and Italy. Charlemagne placed Alcuin of York, an English member of the clergy, in charge of his education program. During his reign, Charlemagne established a palace school and supported other schools throughout his empire. He sent people throughout the empire to look for books. Works by Virgil, Horace, Tacitus, and others were first copied during the reign of Charlemagne. Another outcome of Charlemagne's emphasis on education is a form of writing called "Carolingian minuscule" or "Caroline minuscule." This type of writing uses capital letters and small letters. It was developed specifically for copying—so that it would be easier to read the ancient Roman texts. Most books today, including the one you are reading now, are printed in a version of Carolingian minuscule.

## Charlemagne and Pope Leo III

In A.D. 800, Charlemagne received a letter from Pope Leo III, head of the Western Christian Church. In this letter, the pope told Charlemagne that enemies had attacked him. Like his father, Charlemagne had pledged to provide support for the pope. He led his army to Rome and fought the pope's enemies. These events took place in the late fall and early winter. On Christmas Day 800, before Charlemagne returned home, Pope Leo III placed a crown on Charlemagne's head as Charlemagne knelt before him in St. Peter's Basilica. The pope declared him "Emperor of the Romans." An account written at the time this event took place reported that Charlemagne was surprised when the pope placed the crown on his head. For the first time in several hundred years, a large part of western Europe was united under one ruler.

**It's a FACT**
Before the invention of Carolingian minuscule, writing consisted of all capital Roman letters with no spaces:
THISISWHATITWOULD
LOOKLIKEINENGLISH.

## The Carolingian Empire Declines

Charlemagne died in 814. His empire went to his only surviving son, Louis the Pious. Louis was well educated and very religious, but he was not a soldier. He did not have the respect of the military or the aristocracy. Without their respect and help, the empire was too difficult to govern. After Louis died, the empire was divided among his male heirs. They were dissatisfied with the territory they received and fought among themselves. In the late 800s and 900s, invaders attacked the divided empire. Travel, trade, and farming were disrupted. The population declined. By 870, the empire Charlemagne created had collapsed. Each of the separate kingdoms had a ruler. Eventually, the king of the German territory took the title of Roman emperor. Over time this title became "Holy Roman Emperor." 📖

# EINHARD —
# Charlemagne's Biographer

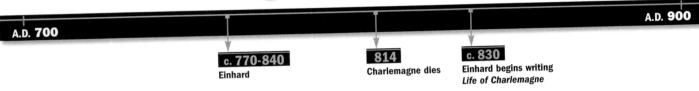

A.D. **700**

c. **770-840**
Einhard

**814**
Charlemagne dies

c. **830**
Einhard begins writing
*Life of Charlemagne*

A.D. **900**

▲ **Einhard portrayed Charlemagne as a hero and a family man.**

**distaff and spindle:** a stick holding wool for spinning and a slender rod on which thread is twisted
**enervate:** to lose energy or vitality; become weak
**liberal studies:** subjects such as reading, mathematics, music, Latin, and philosophy; not technical subjects

Einhard, a member of the Christian clergy, was born around 770 and died in 840. During his life, he served as a secretary to Charlemagne and eventually became his biographer. Einhard obviously admired Charlemagne greatly. He wrote about Charlemagne in heroic terms, often comparing him to Augustus, the first Roman emperor. However, Einhard's writing also reveals Charlemagne as a very human man who deeply loved his family. You can read below an excerpt from Einhard's biography, *Life of Charlemagne*. In this excerpt, Einhard is describing the importance Charlemagne placed on education.

## From *Life of Charlemagne*

The King [Charlemagne] thought so much about the education of his children that he caused both sons and daughters to be early instructed in those **liberal studies** which attracted his own attention. As soon as his sons were old enough he caused them to ride on horseback, as was the Frankish custom, and to practice themselves in arms and hunting. He bade his daughters should learn wool-spinning and the use of the **distaff and spindle**, and be taught to employ themselves industriously in very virtuous occupation, that they not be **enervated** by idleness ...

Charles was so careful in the bringing up of his sons and daughters that when at home he never dined without them, and they always accompanied him on his journeys, his sons riding by his side, and his daughters following close behind, attended by a train of servants appointed for that purpose. His daughters were very fair, and he loved them passionately. Strange to say, he would never consent to give them in marriage, either to any of his own nation or to foreigners; but he kept them all at home and near his person at all times until his death ...

## Analyze the Source!

1. How does this excerpt help you learn about the culture and history of Europe during Charlemagne's time?

2. Why do you think Charlemagne educated his sons and daughters in different ways? Do parents today do this? Why or why not?

# ALCUIN of YORK on CHARLEMAGNE

A.D. 700

A.D. 800

c. 735-804
**Alcuin**

c. 742-814
**Charlemagne**

c. 781
**Charlemagne starts the palace school and places Alcuin in charge**

Charlemagne was not well educated, but he was intelligent and he valued learning. His royal court in Aachen was filled with intellectuals from Spain, England, and Italy. During his reign, Charlemagne established a palace school and supported other schools throughout his empire. Charlemagne placed Alcuin (AL-kwin) of York, an English member of the clergy, in charge of his education program. He also made Alcuin head of the palace school. Alcuin was born around 735 and died in 804. Below is an excerpt from his writings. In this excerpt, Alcuin is describing Charlemagne as a leader. 📖

▲ Alcuin of York was in charge of Charlemagne's palace school in Aachen.

## ALCUIN DESCRIBES CHARLEMAGNE

... Most beloved and honorable defender and ruler of the churches of Christ, let ... your most holy wisdom encourage some with **admonitions**, chastise others with punishment, and instruct others with the learning of life. Thus, when all has been done, you, among the rest, shall deserve to have a perpetual reward ...

Behold, on you alone rests the entire safety of the churches of Christ. You are the avenger of crimes, you are the guide of the **erring**, you are the consoler of the grieving ...

Nothing can be concealed from your wisdom: for we know that you are exceedingly well-learned both in the holy Scriptures and in secular histories. In all these things you have been given full knowledge of God, so that through you the holy Church of God might be ruled, exalted, and preserved for the Christian people.

### Analyze the Source!

1. Read the excerpt and tell in your own words what it says.

2. What do you think Alcuin of York admired about Charlemagne?

3. Do you think there was a close relationship between religion and politics during this time? Give examples to support your answer.

**admonition:** sharp criticism or warning
**err:** to make a mistake or commit a sin

# The Song of ROLAND

The heroic French story, *The Song of Roland*, was written around 1100. It tells of an incident where Charlemagne was fighting in northern Spain in a war against the Muslims in the late 700s. Charlemagne decided to withdraw his armies, but in order to get back to France, he had to lead his men through the Pyrenees. This was dangerous territory because enemies could attack the soldiers by surprise as they were marching away. Charlemagne asked his nephew Roland and some of his men to form a rear guard. This meant they had to ride at the end of the entire army. At one of the mountain passes, a Muslim army attacked Roland's rear guard. Roland waited a long time before he raised the alarm for help because he did not want anyone to think he lacked courage. Below is a translated excerpt from *The Song of Roland*. In this excerpt, Charlemagne has just heard the alarm call signaling that Roland is in trouble. 📖

---

**gonfalon:** banner-like flag carried on a long pole
**hauberk:** armor made of links of chains; "chain mail"
**indignant:** feeling angry because of something thought to be unfair

## Analyze the Source!

1. Read the excerpt and tell in your own words what it says.

2. How does this excerpt help you learn about the culture and history of Europe in the 1100s? How does it help you learn about the culture and history of Europe in the late 700s when the event took place?

3. The *Song of Roland* is often described as a heroic story. From this excerpt, who would you say is a hero in the story? Why?

### From *The Song of Roland*
It is the end of day and full of light,
arms and armor are ablaze in the sun,
and fire flashes from **hauberks** and helmets,
and from those shields, painted fair with flowers,
and from those lances, those gold-dressed **gonfalons**.
The Emperor rides on in rage and sorrow,
the men of France **indignant** and full of grief.
There is no man of them who does not weep,
they are in fear for the life of Roland. ...

The Emperor rides on, rides on in fury,
the men of France in grief and indignation.
There is no man who does not weep and wail,
and they pray God: protect the life of Roland
till they come, one great host, into the field
and fight at Roland's side like true men all.
What does it matter what they pray? It does no good.
They are too late, they cannot come in time.

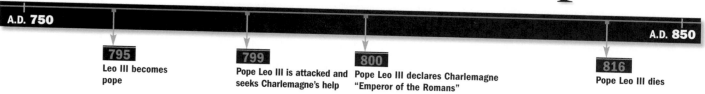

# POPE LEO III —
## "Charlemagne's Pope"

A.D. **750**                                       A.D. **850**

**795**
Leo III becomes pope

**799**
Pope Leo III is attacked and seeks Charlemagne's help

**800**
Pope Leo III declares Charlemagne "Emperor of the Romans"

**816**
Pope Leo III dies

Pope Leo III created an alliance with Charlemagne that strengthened the relationship between the Western Christian Church and the Franks. To understand this relationship, it is important to know something about the events that brought them together.

## The Background
Beginning in the late 300s and continuing for several hundred years, various Germanic peoples invaded the Italian peninsula. By the mid-700s, the Lombards had taken possession of a large portion of northern Italy. The Roman people disliked the Lombards and did not want to be a part of their kingdom. When the Lombards broke their peace treaty with Rome and began to march on the city, Pope Stephen III decided to find help to defend Rome. Stephen asked Pepin, king of the Franks, to come to the defense of Rome and the territory controlled by the pope. Pope Stephen gave Pepin the title of "protector of the Roman church." Pepin, in turn, marched his army into Italy and defeated the Lombards. Several years later, Pepin again came to the defense of Rome and once again defeated the Lombards. Pepin also made a gift to the pope of a large amount of territory in north central Italy. This territory became known as the Papal States. The relationship of mutual support between the Frankish leader and pope continued after both Stephen and Pepin had died.

## Continuing Mutual Support
Pepin's successor was his son, Charlemagne. Pope Stephen's successor was Pope Adrian. One of Pope Adrian's first acts was to ask the Franks to help protect the church from the Lombards. In 773, Charlemagne marched his army to Italy and defeated the Lombards once and for all. He captured the Lombard king and sent him to a monastery for the rest of his life. Then, Charlemagne declared himself, "king of the Lombards." In 795, Pope Adrian died and a successor was elected to be the new pope—Leo III. Pope Leo sent Charlemagne a letter letting him know that he was now pope. Leo also wanted Charlemagne to know that he considered Charlemagne protector of the church.

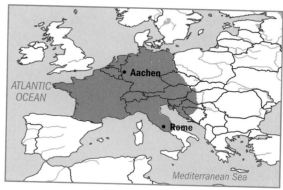

▲ Pope Leo III named Charlemagne "Emperor of the Romans." The shaded area shows the area Charlemagne ruled.

▲ Pope Leo III helped create an alliance between Charlemagne and the Western Christian Church.

## A Call for Help

In 799, as Pope Leo was returning from a church service, a large group of men attacked him. The men tried to scratch out his eyes and cut out his tongue. He was left bleeding in the street. After some time, he was taken to a nearby monastery. While there, he recovered the use of his eyes and was able to speak again. However, he realized the danger he faced and decided that he needed Charlemagne's help. He traveled to Charlemagne's court where he was greeted warmly. After a few months, the pope returned to Rome under Charlemagne's protection.

## An Eventful Christmas

In 800, Charlemagne arrived in Rome to clear up charges made against Pope Leo by people who did not want him to be pope. The nobility, bishops, and other clergy who attended the meeting said they had no right to judge the pope's guilt or innocence. Nevertheless, Pope Leo stood before them in St. Peter's Basilica and declared his innocence. His accusers were unable to prove that Pope Leo had done any wrong and were sent away. On Christmas Day, two days after he had declared his innocence, Pope Leo conducted church services at St. Peter's Basilica. As Charlemagne was praying during this church service, Pope Leo approached him and placed a crown on his head. Leo declared, "Long life and victory to Charles, the most pious Augustus, the great and peace-giving emperor of the Romans." With this act, Pope Leo made Charlemagne the Christian ruler of a Christian empire. People believed it showed that God had blessed Charlemagne's authority to rule.

## Strengthening the Church

For the next 14 years, until he died in 814, Charlemagne did many things to strengthen the church. For example, he recovered some of the church's land and property and defended church territory. Charlemagne donated a great deal of money to the church. Pope Leo used this money to help the poor and to repair many churches. By strengthening the church, Charlemagne also helped strengthen his own rule. Most of the people in his empire were Christians. The pope was the leader of their church and he supported Charlemagne. In 816, Pope Leo III died and was buried in St. Peter's Basilica. He was declared a saint in 1673.

### It's a FACT
Historians sometimes call Pope Leo III "Charlemagne's pope" because Charlemagne used Leo to help him create his empire.

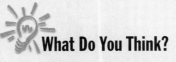

### What Do You Think?

1. Do you agree that Pope Leo III was "Charlemagne's pope"? Why or why not?

2. How did the events that took place before Charlemagne became king and before Leo became pope affect their relationship?

3. Why do you think Pope Leo compared Charlemagne to Augustus?

# Beowulf — The Struggle Between Good and Evil

**A.D. 400** **A.D. 850**

**476**
Fall of the Western
Roman Empire

**c. 500**
The events in the story
*Beowulf* take place

**800**
Charlemagne is crowned
"Emperor of the Romans"

**c. 800**
*Beowulf* is written

During the Middle Ages, many monks spent their lives copying religious manuscripts and producing beautifully detailed illuminated manuscripts. Other monks wrote new books during this period. One such book is the epic story of *Beowulf*.

## An Ancient Legend about Heroic Virtues

People living in the British Isles probably had heard the story of *Beowulf* for centuries. It was an ancient legend about a Scandinavian king and the struggle between good and evil. Beowulf was the heroic warrior of this story. He had great courage and was strong and loyal—all heroic virtues. When Beowulf was victorious in battle, his people also were victorious. They shared in the spoils of war—the treasure that a winner can claim. *Beowulf* is a long tale that was told in a serious way. This kind of story or poem is called an epic. The storyteller probably told the story while playing a lute, a guitar-like instrument. This story was passed down orally for generations.

Sometime around 800, a monk decided to write down the story. He set the events of the story around 500. What was going on in Europe in 500? The most important event was the fall of the Roman Empire. Roman legions had left Britain. Many groups of people were moving into Europe and settling in various parts of what had been the Roman Empire.

## Including New Ideas

The monk who wrote *Beowulf* used a language called Old English. Today, only people with special training can read Old English. Old English was the language of the Anglo-Saxons, Germanic peoples who streamed into Britain in the 400s. These Germanic groups were each ruled by a powerful warrior who was king or chief. The groups fought one another to gain more power. If the leader was successful in battle, the entire group was successful.

▲ The events of *Beowulf* take place in Europe around 500. Clovis the Frank had built a kingdom that included much of present-day France and Germany.

▲ The hero, Beowulf, fought an evil dragon in the epic poem *Beowulf*.

The victors in battle enjoyed the spoils of war and could rule over the defeated people. Of course, if the leader failed in battle, the entire group would become the subjects of another people. The monk who wrote *Beowulf* included ideas from the legend that had been passed down orally. However, he also included ideas from the Germanic tradition and from the Christian religion of his own day in writing down the epic story.

## Why Is *Beowulf* Important Today?

*Beowulf* remains one of the most important works of literature in the English language. One scholar said: "The poem *Beowulf*, which [expresses ideas of] Anglo-Saxon culture and language more completely and intensely than any other work of literature, still stands as a great fountainhead of our culture and our language. To understand and appreciate this great epic is to be more intimately acquainted with our culture and ourselves."

*Beowulf* is more than 100 pages long. Below is an excerpt that has been translated from Old English. Beowulf has just killed the fire-breathing dragon known as "the destroyer of people." One of Beowulf's warriors, Wiglaf, bravely came to his aid during the battle. Beowulf lays dying from the dragon's poisonous bite and the burns from its fiery breath. Beowulf has just asked Wiglaf to get the treasures in the dragon's cave—the spoils of war.

**barrow:** a heap of rocks or earth marking a grave; a mound
**headland:** a peak of high land that juts out into a body of water
**venom:** poison that some snakes and other animals inject with their bites

### From *Beowulf*

Now Wiglaf gathered all that he could hold:
The standard; dishes, jewels, cups, a sword;
Then strung his arms with rings of twisted gold
And hurried, wondering if he'd find his lord
Alive. He found him slumped, his eyes half glazed,
His breathing hoarse. He splashed his burns then raised,

Gently, his head. The dying hero spoke,
Looking on the treasures: "I thank the Lord
That I could get these goods and look at them
Before I died, can give them to my folk.
They're bought with life; I cannot be here long.
The **venom** bites my blood, my limbs are crisp.
But even if my brain had burned, at last
I would have thrust my longspear through those teeth!

Tell them to make a mound atop the **headland**,
After my body-burning, overlooking
The sea ... .
So that forever after, sailing men
Will call it Beowulf's **Barrow**, when the longships
Come from afar across the mist-hung seas."

## Analyze the Source!

1. How does this excerpt help you learn about the culture and history of Europe in 500? In 800?

2. Why do you think the author included ideas from the ancient legend, Germanic traditions, and Christianity in *Beowulf*?

3. How does the story of Beowulf and the short excerpt you read compare with Japanese haiku?

# The Legend of KING ARTHUR

**0** — — — — **A.D. 1500**

**c. 475-500**
When some historians believe Arthur is born

**476**
Fall of the Western Roman Empire

**1100s**
Geoffrey of Monmouth writes the first reference of the man who could have been Arthur

**1450**
Sir Thomas Mallory writes one of the most famous stories about King Arthur, *The Death of Arthur*

After the Romans left Britain in the early part of the fifth century, Anglo-Saxon tribes from northern Germany invaded. The Anglo-Saxons pushed their way westward through Britain, and the people there were terrified. All the order and organization of the Roman Empire had disappeared when the Romans left the provinces. Outlaws roamed the land. They attacked and robbed people, and no one seemed to be able to stop them. Out of this chaos emerged the stories and legend of King Arthur. There is conflicting evidence about whether a man named King Arthur really lived, and historians are not certain if he was a real person. Questions remain about the accomplishments for which he is given credit.

## Good and Evil

The legend of Arthur was passed orally from generation to generation. Whether the story is true or not is less important than what it tells us about the people who lived during the time that the events of the story takes place. From the story of Arthur, we know that people living in the chaos after the Romans left the area were desperate for good to triumph over evil. They wanted their leaders to be strong and fair. It is also important to consider what the legend of Arthur tells us about the people who lived in the ninth century and later Middle Ages, which was when stories about King Arthur were written down. The people of these times wanted their leaders to live by a code of honor or chivalry. They included these ideas in the legend of Arthur.

## What We Know about Arthur

As historians examine ancient records, they have found references to a person who may have been King Arthur. He is not identified clearly or specifically mentioned by name. However, these references have led many historians to believe that parts of the legend of King Arthur may be true. If so, then Arthur was most likely born between A.D. 475 and 500. He came to power as a young man of only 15 and proved himself worthy to be king through an extraordinary set of events. These events and the people surrounding Arthur make up most of the legendary tales.

▲ After the Romans left Britain in the early part of the fifth century, Anglo-Saxon tribes from northern Germany invaded.

▲ In the 1100s, a monk named Geoffrey of Monmouth wrote *The History of Kings of England*. This document seems to be the first reference to the man who could have been Arthur.

# The Legend of King Arthur

The legend of Arthur has been passed down through the generations. He is said to have gathered all his knights around a round table so that all would be equal. King Arthur and the Knights of the Round Table gathered in Camelot, a legendary English town. According to the legend, Arthur and his knights lived by a strict code of behavior. They were expected to show respect for the church, pity for the poor, bravery, and courtesy. The legend continues to be popular even today. In modern times, people have told and retold the story of King Arthur in books, cartoons, television shows, plays, and movies. The figure of Arthur has come to represent hope, courage, and fair play. Today, the word *Camelot* is also used to describe any time or place that is exciting, purposeful, and has a high level of culture. Below is an excerpt from one of the most famous stories written about King Arthur. It was written by Sir Thomas Mallory in 1450 and is called "The Death of Arthur." Mallory takes different parts of the legend and weaves them together into a tale of uncommon bravery. He emphasizes the triumph of good over evil and the eventual end to the golden age of Camelot.

▲ This 14th-century illustration shows King Arthur and the Knights of the Round Table. King Arthur is presenting Sir Galahad to the other knights.

*You were the most courageous knight that ever bore a shield. And thou were the truest friend that ever bestrode a horse. And thou were the kindest man that ever struck with sword. And thou were the goodliest person that ever came among a group of knights, and thou were the meekest man and gentlest who ever ate in hall among ladies.* 📖

## What Do You Think?

**1.** How does the code of behavior followed by King Arthur and his Knights of the Round Table compare with the Japanese idea of bushido?

**2.** How would seating people around a round table make them all equal?

# WHO'S WHO in History —
# Curious Minds Want the Facts!

GORIVS·I·MAGNVS·ROMANVS

**Q.** **Who made it popular to use the birth of Christ to date events in history?**

**A.** Bede the Venerable. He was born around 673 in England. At the age of 19, he became a monk. He lived in a monastery and spent much of his time writing. He wrote about religion, science, and history. One of his most important works is *History of the English Church and Its People*. It tells how various groups of people in Europe converted to Christianity. He is the person who made it popular to use the birth of Christ (B.C./A.D.) to date events in history. He died in 735.

**Q.** **Why do people call Pope Gregory I, Gregory the Great?**

**A.** In 590, Rome was in a state of chaos. People were dying from disease, and there was not enough to eat. The Lombards were on the attack. That's when Gregory established his reputation for greatness. Gregory was born around 540 to a wealthy Roman family, but he was not interested in living a life of luxury. He wanted to help the poor and to lead a life of service. He became the abbot of a monastery in Rome. Later, after he became pope, he organized Rome's defenses against the Lombards. He also gave food and money to the poor. The church thought he did other great things, too. For example, he sent St. Augustine of Canterbury to convert the people of England to Christianity. Gregory died in 604. To this day, people refer to him as Gregory the Great.

**Q.** **Is St. Augustine of Hippo the same person as St. Augustine of Canterbury?**

**A.** No. They are different people who lived at different times in different parts of the world. What they have in common is that they were both strong and influential Christian leaders.

**Q.** **Why do people remember St. Augustine of Hippo?**

**A.** He wrote important books about religion. One of his most influential books was *The City of*

▼ St. Augustine of Canterbury

▲ St. Augustine of Hippo

*God*, which was written during the time when the Roman Empire was crumbling. In this book, he argued that Christianity would survive the fall of earthly empires. Charlemagne greatly admired this book. One of St. Augustine of Hippo's most famous sayings is, "Love the sinner, hate the sin." He was born in 354 in present-day Algeria, North Africa. Augustine was an exceptionally intelligent boy. His parents sent him to school in Carthage where he studied law and philosophy. He became a university teacher and gained a reputation as a brilliant scholar. As a young man, he traveled to Milan, Italy. While there, he felt called to the Christian faith and was baptized. Then he returned to Africa where he spent his days in study and prayer. In 395, he became the bishop of Hippo. He died in 430. 📖

# WILLIAM THE CONQUEROR

A.D. **700**

**late 800s-1100s**
*The Anglo-Saxon Chronicle* is written

**1028-1087**
William the Conqueror

**1066**
William the Conqueror is crowned king of England

A.D. **1100**

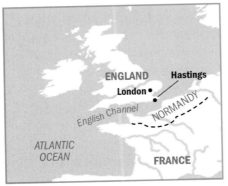

▲ **William the Conqueror was born in Normandy.**

How did a boy named William become a man known as "William the Conqueror"? To answer this question, it is important to know where he came from and how he came to power.

## The Vikings, Normandy, and England

Normandy is an area on the northern coast of France. It had been part of Charlemagne's empire—part of the Frankish kingdom. In the 900s, Normandy was a wealthy region with many small towns and many monasteries. The wealth in Normandy made it an inviting target for Viking raiders from the north. Around 911, one of the Viking leaders, Rolf, made an offer to the people who lived in Normandy. If they agreed to make him duke of Normandy, Rolf promised that he would defend the area against other Viking raiders. Rolf also promised that he and his men would become Christians. The agreement was made and the Vikings settled in Normandy. The people already living there referred to the Vikings as "North Men" or "Norsemen." The land given to these "North Men" was called Normandy. Although Rolf was now duke of Normandy, Viking raids on the area continued. But the Vikings were not only interested in Normandy, they also attacked and raided England. By the early 1000s, three different groups had power in England—the Vikings, the Saxons (who had come from Germany), and the ancient Celts. Of the three groups, the Saxons had the largest population and controlled most of the territory.

## William's Early Life

In 1028, Robert I, duke of Normandy and a descendant of Rolf the Viking, had a son, William. Although William's mother and father were not married when he was born, Robert recognized William as his son. This meant that William was also a descendant of the first duke of Normandy, Rolf the Viking. When William's father died, William was declared duke.

◀ **Duke William of Normandy was crowned king of England on Christmas Day in 1066.**

◄ **William's conquest of England is sometimes called the Norman Conquest. The story of the Norman Conquest is embroidered on a piece of cloth called the Bayeux Tapestry. This is an illustration of a segment of the Bayeux Tapestry.**

William was only eight years old and had **guardians** to help him govern Normandy. Many other nobles in the region wanted to become duke themselves. For 10 years, William and his guardians fought off various plots to kill the young duke. Finally, when William was 18, he became duke "officially" without any guardians.

## Duke William of Normandy

In his early years as duke of Normandy, William fought many wars with his neighbors. He was victorious in all of these battles. He also formed an alliance with a powerful family in his region by marrying the daughter of the count of Flanders. William was very clever. He gave much of the territory he conquered to the men who had helped him win the battles. These pieces of land were called fiefs. These gifts of land made the men very loyal to William. They were willing to fight with him in other battles in other places.

## Meanwhile, Back in England

After years of attacking England, the Vikings finally conquered the area held by the Saxons. Edward the Confessor, the Saxon king, fled across the English Channel to Normandy. William was only 14 when Edward went back to England from Normandy to reclaim the throne, but he understood the situation in England. He also recognized the close ties between the Normans and the Saxons. When Edward returned to England, he tried to control the nobles, many of whom wanted to become king when Edward died. Edward realized that his only true friends were the Normans. They had given him a safe place to live when he had to flee England. Edward decided he needed a peaceful way to solve the problem of who would succeed him. He sent one of his nobles, Harold Godwinson, to Normandy to tell William he was to be the next king of England.

**guardian:** a person legally in charge of a young person

## Who Would Become England's King?

When Edward the Confessor died, Harold decided that he did not agree with the decision to make William king. He wanted to be king himself. The Saxons agreed with him and named him king of England. William was furious. He realized that the only way he could claim the throne of England would be through war. During the fall of 1066, William began building a fleet of ships to take his army from Normandy to England. In England, Harold also began to gather an army. Toward the end of September, Harold had to deal with another crisis. A group of Vikings had invaded northern England. Harold led his army north and defeated the Vikings in a decisive battle. However, while Harold was fighting the Vikings, William's army set sail for England. William's ships landed near the town of Hastings. His army immediately began to build forts where they could defend themselves. By the time Harold had returned to the south of England, William's army was well established in the area around Hastings.

## The Battle of Hastings

Historians do not know many of the details of the actual battle of Hastings. We know that Harold's army arrived in Hastings and took up a position on some low hills. William's army attacked on October 14, 1066. The battle lasted almost the entire day. As Saxon soldiers tired, they began to leave the field of battle. Late in the day, Harold was killed and the battle was lost. By the next morning there were no more Saxon soldiers left to fight against William's army. William had conquered England. For the next few days after the battle, William hoped the Saxon nobles would recognize him as the king of England. None did. So William and his army began to march on London. By December of 1066, he had captured London. Duke William of Normandy was crowned king of England on Christmas Day in 1066. For the next several years, William fought small rebellions by the Saxon nobility. He crushed them all and established Norman rule. Finally, in 1073, William the Conqueror returned to Normandy. He died in 1087.

## William's Conquest of England

William's conquest of England had many consequences. The English nobles who had supported Harold lost both power and wealth. William claimed ownership of about one-fifth of England. Because the Normans spoke French, French became the language of the government and the nobility. William collected a huge amount of information about England so he could figure out how much to tax the people. He emphasized the importance of building stone castles, which had not really existed in England before William. Perhaps most important of all, William brought feudalism, a new kind of political and economic system, to England. ⬚

### What Do You Think?

1. What advantages did William have in life? What obstacles did he face?

2. How did past events affect William's life?

3. William rewarded his supporters with pieces of land called "fiefs." Why did this practice make his supporters more loyal to him? Why were they more willing to fight for him?

# The BAYEUX Tapestry

A.D. **1000**                                                                    A.D. **1100**

**1066**
William's army defeats Harold
and his forces; William is
crowned king of England

**c. 1077**
The Bayeux Tapestry
is completed

The Bayeux Tapestry is a piece of cloth on which the story of the Norman Conquest appears in embroidered scenes. This tapestry is one of the most important pictorial works that has survived from the Middle Ages. The tapestry is 230-feet long—about the length of a football field—but only about 20-inches wide. Historians do not know much about its origins. Some experts believe English women in the city of Winchester, England created the tapestry. Others think Queen Matilda, William the Conqueror's wife, and her ladies stitched these scenes of the Norman Conquest.

**ENGLAND**
London •     Hastings
English Channel   NORMANDY

▲ **This map shows the location of the
battle of Hastings.**

NERVNT

▲ **This illustration shows a segment of the Bayeux Tapestry. Many web sites focus on its history, facts, and pictures. Some of these
sites show the entire 230 feet of tapestry, panel by panel. Log on with the key search terms: Bayeux Tapestry.**

## Importance of the Tapestry

It may have been completed in 1077 in time for the opening of the new cathedral in Bayeux. Historians argue about the date and other details, but they agree on the importance of this tapestry. It not only tells us about events of the time of the Norman Conquest, but it also reveals how people of the time interpreted these events.

## The First 100 Feet

The first half of the Bayeux Tapestry shows the adventures of Harold Godwinson. Harold went to Normandy to tell William, the duke of Normandy, that Edward the Confessor had named William as his successor. That meant that when Edward died, William would become the king of England. Harold's boat was shipwrecked off the Normandy coast, and he was captured. William paid his ransom and, in return, Harold swore allegiance to him. However, when Edward the Confessor died, Harold ignored the oath he had pledged to William. This set the stage for the battle of Hastings—the battle that would decide who would be the next king of England.

## The Second 100 Feet

The second half of the Bayeux Tapestry shows William and his army getting ready to go to England. It shows the battle of Hastings and ends with the defeat of Harold and his forces. The last 20-25 feet of the tapestry is incomplete. Historians can only guess what it might have shown. Perhaps it would have depicted William being crowned king in Westminster Abbey, near London.

## Historical Perspective and Clues to the Past

It is important to remember when examining an artifact like the Bayeux Tapestry that it is "written" from a particular point of view. In this case, the story is told from the perspective of the victorious Norman conquerors. In other words, the tapestry shows the Norman version of events. In addition to showing at least one side's view of events, the Bayeux Tapestry also provides important historical information. For example, it shows how a castle was built. It also traces the construction of warships, beginning with the cutting down of the trees to the launching of the ships. Many of the places that are depicted on the tapestry still exist. This gives us the opportunity to compare how these places look today with how the people who created the tapestry saw them. For example, the monastery at Mt. St. Michele appears on the tapestry and can be easily compared with the monastery today. This kind of comparison gives us a glimpse into the way people in the middle of the 11th century saw their world. 📖

### What Do You Think?

1. Why do you think women of this time created this tapestry showing the story of the Norman Conquest?

2. Examine a picture of a section of the Bayeux Tapestry (e.g., see page 216 of the *Explore World History* textbook). What information can you find about food, tableware, clothing, hairstyles, animals, and social class?

3. If you were asked to decide what should go on the last section of the Bayeux Tapestry, what would you suggest?

# DOMESDAY BOOK — The Normans Calculate their Conquest

Historians have learned a great deal about the period known as the Norman Conquest from *The Anglo-Saxon Chronicle*, a set of documents relating to English history. These documents were written beginning in the late 800s and continuing through the 1100s.

After William the Conqueror won the battle of Hastings, he could claim England as his own. What did this mean? What did he own in England? William wanted to tax his new subjects, but he needed to know how much they should pay. He came up with a plan to find out about the region and its wealth. In 1086, he sent officials to every part of England. He had them make a listing of all the property held by the people of England. In every village, a group of local people and a priest had to swear to answer honestly the king's questions about property ownership. This information was collected in a book that became known as the *Domesday Book*. The information recorded in the *Domesday Book* was the most complete listing since the Roman tax rolls and the most extensive land survey of the Middle Ages.

The first excerpt below is from *The Anglo-Saxon Chronicle*. It tells about William the Conqueror and his plan to collect information about England. The second excerpt is from the *Domesday Book*. 📖

## Analyze the Source!

1. Read the excerpts and tell in your own words what one of them says.

2. In the first excerpt, how would you describe the writer's general evaluation of William the Conqueror?

---

**gainsay:** challenge
**hide:** a measure of land varying from 80-120 acres
**sagacity:** wisdom
**villein:** serf

## FROM *THE ANGLO-SAXON CHRONICLE*

... the king [William] had a great council ... [and asked his advisors] about this land, how it was peopled, or by what men; then he sent his men over all England ... [to find out] what land the king himself had, and cattle within the land, or what dues he ought to have. ... there was not ... one yard of land, nor even—it is shame to tell, though it seemed to him no shame to do—an ox, nor a cow, nor a swine, left that was not set down in his [document]. ... King William, about whom we speak, was a very wise man, and very powerful, more dignified and strong than any of his predecessors were. He was mild to the good men who loved God, and beyond all measure severe to the men who **gainsaid** his will. ... Among other good things is not to be forgotten the good peace that he made in this land. ... He reigned over England, and by his **sagacity** so thoroughly surveyed it that there was not a **hide** of land within England that he knew not who had it, or what it was worth, and afterwards set it in his [document].

## FROM THE *DOMESDAY BOOK*

Peter de Valence holds in domain Hechen, which Haldane a freeman held in the time of King Edward as a manor, and 5 hides. ... At that time there were 8 **villeins**, now 10; [there are] ... woods for 300 swine, 18 acres of meadow. There were two fish ponds and a half, now there are none ... When we received this manor he found only 1 ox and 1 planted acre. Of the five hides spoken above, one was held in the time of King Edward by 2 freeman, and was added to this manor in the time of King William ...

# POPE URBAN II and the Call for a Religious Crusade

In 1054, the Christian Church split into two churches: the Eastern Christian Church (or Greek Church) in the East and the Western Christian Church (or Roman Catholic Church) in the West. However, when Muslim Turks captured the holy city of Jerusalem in 1071, Christians in the East asked for help from Christians in the West. By the 1090s, the pope decided that he needed to do something. What he did greatly affected world history. In 1095, at a meeting in Clermont, France, Pope Urban II gave a powerful speech urging Christians to go to battle against the Muslims or "infidels" as Europeans called them. During this speech, Pope Urban II called on Christians to begin a holy war against the Muslims.

Pope Urban II was born Odo de Lagery in the French province of Champagne. He became pope in 1088 at the age of 46 and served until 1099. Below is an excerpt from Pope Urban II's speech—the speech that started the Crusades. In this speech, Pope Urban II compliments the Europeans' background or "race," urges Christians to stop fighting against other Christians (as they had been doing in Spain), and encourages them to free Jerusalem from the Muslims. 📖

## Analyze the Source!

1. Read the excerpt and tell in your own words what it says.

2. How does this excerpt help you learn about religious intolerance during the Middle Ages?

3. Why do you think Pope Urban II's speech had such a great influence on the people of Europe during this time?

▶ In the 1095 meeting in Clermont, Pope Urban II called Christians to the First Crusade.

remission: forgiveness
render: to give

## FROM POPE URBAN II'S SPEECH THAT STARTED THE CRUSADES

O, race of the Franks, race from across the mountains, race beloved and chosen by God! As is clear from your many works you are a race set apart from all other nations by the situation of your country as well as by your catholic faith and the honor which you **render** to the holy church. ... It has been reported that a race from the kingdom of the Persians ... has violently invaded the lands of those Christians. ... Let your quarrels end, let wars cease ... [Jerusalem] is now held captive by the enemies of Christ. ... Undertake this journey for the **remission** of your sins, with the assurance of the imperishable glory of the kingdom of heaven.

# Views of the Crusades

**1095**
Pope Urban II calls for a
crusade against the Muslims

**1096**
The First Crusade
begins

**1170**
William of Tyre writes a
description of the First Crusade

When Pope Urban II spoke at a meeting of Roman Catholic Church leaders in 1095, he called for a holy war—a crusade—against the Muslims. In 1096, the First Crusade started toward Jerusalem. The group included about 4,000 knights and about 26,000 soldiers, clergy, and others. Some went on the First Crusade because they believed it was a holy cause. Some thought it was a way to have their sins forgiven. Some peasants saw it as a way to free themselves from working on their lord's manor. Other crusaders were looking for adventure, new lands to conquer, and wealth.

▲ **Christians in the First Crusade traveled through Constantinople and then to Jerusalem.**

◀ **This painting shows knights conquering Jerusalem during the First Crusade.**

Chapter 14: The Middle Ages  **257**

Despite the problems the crusaders faced, the First Crusade accomplished its goal of conquering Jerusalem. But many people were killed in the process. Below is an excerpt from a description of the crusaders' capture of Jerusalem. William of Tyre, a Christian bishop, wrote this description many decades after the event. He was not an eyewitness to the event, but relied on descriptions told to him by crusaders who were there. William of Tyre told how the crusaders succeeded in getting inside the city walls and what they found in the city.

## WILLIAM OF TYRE DESCRIBES THE CAPTURE OF JERUSALEM

The greater part of the people had taken **refuge** in the court of the Temple because it ... was very strongly defended by a wall, towers, and gates. ... A crowd of knights and foot soldiers was introduced, who massacred all those who had taken refuge there. No mercy was shown to anyone, and the whole place was flooded with the blood of the victims ...

... It was impossible to look upon the vast numbers of the slain without horror; everywhere lay fragments of human bodies, and the very ground was covered with the blood of the slain. ... Still more dreadful was it to gaze upon the victors themselves, dripping with blood from head to foot ...

Each **marauder** claimed as his own ... the particular house in which he had entered, together with all it contained. For before the capture of the city the pilgrims had agreed that, after it had been taken by force, whatever each man might win for himself should be his forever by right of possession. ... Consequently the pilgrims searched the city most carefully and boldly killed the citizens. ... At the entrance of each house, as it was taken, the victor hung up his shield and arms, as a sign to all who approached not to pause there but to pass by that place as already in possession of another.

**marauder:** robber; referring to "crusader"
**refuge:** shelter from danger

## Analyze the Source!

1. Read the excerpt and rewrite it in your own words.

2. How does this excerpt help you learn about the culture and history of Europe during the Middle Ages?

3. Compare the perspectives of this event. What do you think the crusaders thought about the actions they took? What do you think the Muslims in the region thought about the actions the crusaders took?

4. From this excerpt, how would you describe William of Tyre's perspective of these actions?

# ANNA COMNENA — One of the World's First Female Historians

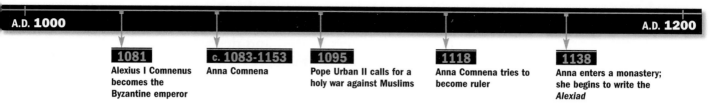

A.D. **1000**                                                                                                    A.D. **1200**

**1081**
Alexius I Comnenus
becomes the
Byzantine emperor

**c. 1083-1153**
Anna Comnena

**1095**
Pope Urban II calls for a
holy war against Muslims

**1118**
Anna Comnena tries to
become ruler

**1138**
Anna enters a monastery;
she begins to write the
*Alexiad*

Anna Comnena was a king's daughter, but history remembers her as one of the world's first female historians. How did this little girl who lived a royal life in Constantinople, the capital of the Byzantine Empire, achieve such fame and distinction?

## An Eastern Empire under Attack

In 1054, the Christian Church split into two parts. The Western Christian Church was centered in Rome. The Eastern Christian Church was centered in the Byzantine city of Constantinople. In the late 1000s, the Byzantines were having trouble controlling their empire. The Normans took control of many Byzantine cities located in Italy. In 1071, an army of Turks attacked the eastern part of the Byzantine empire. The Byzantine emperor was defeated in battle and captured. The next Byzantine emperor was Alexius I Comnenus. For a short time he was successful in holding off the advance of the Turks. However, the Turks continued toward Constantinople. This Turkish advance toward Constantinople along with reports of Christians being persecuted by Muslims in the Holy Land alarmed the people of western Europe. Alexius I realized that to hold his empire together he would need help.

## A Call for Help

Alexius I decided to ask Pope Urban II, the head of the Western Christian (or Roman Catholic) Church, for help. In response to his request, in 1095, Pope Urban II made a famous speech. During this speech, Urban II called for a Christian holy war against the Muslims. Thousands of people went on a crusade to the Holy Land in order to reclaim this land from the Muslims. Some of the crusaders were knights and professional soldiers, but many were just peasants. When they arrived in Constantinople, the crusaders were reported to have acted more like conquerors than people who had come to fight the Turks.

▲ Anna Comnena lived in Constantinople. She wrote about the crusaders that passed through Constantinople on their way to Jerusalem.

▲ Anna Comnena is known as one of the world's first female historians.

**loot:** to steal

## What Do You Think?

**1.** We know that the *Alexiad* is very one-sided or biased. What could historians learn from a biased work such as Anna Comnena's book?

**2.** Why do you think the emperor, Alexius I, kept silent when the "rude Frank" sat on his throne? What would you do if someone you had asked to help you did something rude?

# Anna Comnena and the *Alexiad*

Historians have looked at various sources to understand the events that took place at this time. One of these sources is a book written by Anna Comnena, the daughter of Alexius. She is one of the world's first female historians. The book she wrote about her father's reign is called the *Alexiad*. It is a 15-volume history of her family. Anna wrote about how her father was generous and kind to the crusaders. From her viewpoint, the crusaders were rude and barbaric. She wrote that the crusaders **looted** and destroyed much of Constantinople. In one part of her book, Anna wrote about a particular incident involving a crusader's manners.

*When the Franks [the crusaders] had all gathered together and taken an oath to the emperor [Alexius, Anna's father], there was one count who was so bold as to sit on the emperor's throne. The emperor, knowing the pride of the Latins, kept still. But another Frank, Baldwin, approached the man sitting on the throne and said to him, "You should not sit on the emperor's throne, that is an honor reserved for him and he permits no one else to sit there. You are in a different country, why don't you observe its customs?" The rude count gave no reply to Baldwin, but said in his own language, "this must be a rude man [referring to the emperor] who would sit when so many warriors are standing up." The Emperor Alexius saw the man's lips move and asked his interpreter what had been said. When he had been told the translation, the emperor did not comment, but he did not forget either. Later, when the crusaders were on their way to battle, the emperor asked the man who had been sitting on his throne who he was. The rude count said, "I am a Frank of high and ancient nobility. And I know one thing—I have awaited any man to challenge me to single combat but no one would do so." The emperor was alert to not accepting this challenge. Instead, the emperor said, "You now have a chance to fight, and I want to give you a piece of advice. Do not put yourself at the front or the rear of the army, but in the middle. I have had experience with these Turks and I am convinced this is the best place." The count was later killed in battle.*

After her father died, Anna's brother became emperor. She tried unsuccessfully to become the ruler herself. After her failed attempt to seize power, Anna was forced to leave the royal court. She entered a monastery when she was 55 years old. It was then that she began to write the *Alexiad*. She died in 1153. 📖

# POPE GREGORY VII — A Hero of the Roman Catholic Church

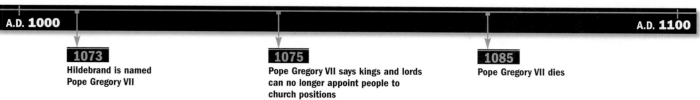

A.D. **1000**                                           A.D. **1100**

**1073**
Hildebrand is named
Pope Gregory VII

**1075**
Pope Gregory VII says kings and lords
can no longer appoint people to
church positions

**1085**
Pope Gregory VII dies

Heroes come in all shapes and sizes and from all walks of life. Physically, Pope Gregory VII was a small man, but his determination to reform the Roman Catholic Church was great. During the Middle Ages, the church had a strong disagreement with the kings and nobles about how a person became pope. Should a king appoint the bishops and pope? Or should the bishops of the church choose the pope? Gregory VII spent most of his life fighting for the church's right to appoint religious leaders without the influence of any king.

## Early Life

Pope Gregory VII did not always have that name. When he was born, his parents called him Hildebrand. Historians know only a few details of his early life. He was born in a region of Italy called Tuscany, which is north of Rome, sometime between 1020 and 1025. Hildebrand's parents were poor. His father, Bonizo, may have been a carpenter. We have no record of his mother's name. As a boy, Hildebrand was sent to Rome to study at a monastery where his uncle was abbot. He decided to become a monk. Later, he became the assistant to the man who became Pope Gregory VI.

## A Respected Church Leader

Pope Gregory VI gave Hildebrand many important responsibilities. One of his jobs was to restore law and order to the city of Rome. The city had become a very difficult and unsafe place to live because of increasing crime. Hildebrand did this job and others very well. He was an important help to Pope Gregory VI. After Pope Gregory VI died, Hildebrand left Rome and went to live in a monastery in France. However, he was there only a short time when the next pope, Leo IX, called him back to Rome. Pope Leo IX wanted Hildebrand to help reform the church. By 1073, Hildebrand had become a highly respected person in the church. He had a reputation as a man who fought against evils in the church. Hildebrand had served as an advisor to six different popes. When Pope Alexander II died, church leaders wanted Hildebrand to become pope himself. He was named Pope Gregory VII in June 1073.

▲ Hildebrand was born in Tuscany, Italy. He later became Pope Gregory VII.

▲ Pope Gregory VII fought for the church's right to appoint religious leaders without the influence of kings.

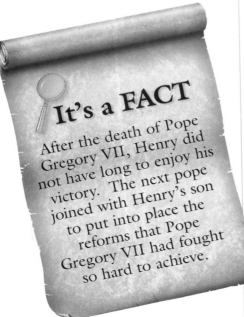

**It's a FACT**

After the death of Pope Gregory VII, Henry did not have long to enjoy his victory. The next pope joined with Henry's son to put into place the reforms that Pope Gregory VII had fought so hard to achieve.

## Gregory VII Battles Henry IV

Gregory thought one of the greatest problems facing the church was that kings and lords appointed bishops and abbots. Once appointed, these church officials had great power in the areas where they lived. The kings and lords who had appointed them wanted loyalty from these church officials. Pope Gregory VII was determined to stop this practice, which was called "lay investiture." "Lay" means non-church or secular. "Investiture" is the act of appointing a person to a position. But Pope Gregory VII had a strong opponent—King Henry IV. Henry ruled most of present-day Germany. He was determined to appoint church officials. He wanted to remain deeply involved in running the church, so he challenged the pope's order to stop appointing bishops and abbots. In fact, Henry went so far as to send soldiers to kidnap Gregory during a Christmas church service. The next day, however, the people of Rome rushed to where Gregory was being held. When the kidnappers saw how much support Gregory had, they released him.

## A Call to Rome

Gregory called Henry to Rome to answer the charges against him, but Henry refused. Henry called a meeting of the bishops he had appointed. He wanted them to criticize Gregory and call for his removal. After this, Pope Gregory VII did not feel that he had many choices left. He decided that King Henry had to be excommunicated. This was a very bold move. Excommunication was a serious matter.

## Asking for Forgiveness?

What happened next was that Henry promised to obey the pope. Then the pope forgave him. But Henry did not keep his promise. He did not want to give up his authority to appoint bishops and abbots. Finally, after much negotiation and the involvement of many other nobles, Henry decided to bring an army to Rome. He also brought along his own choice for pope. When Gregory heard that Henry was marching on Rome, his advisors told him to leave the city. Gregory decided to stay. Henry arrived, conquered the city, and made his own choice the new pope—Clement III.

## In Exile

Pope Gregory VII was rescued by an army of Norman soldiers who were in the southern part of Italy. Reluctantly, Gregory left Rome. He went into exile in a town called Salerno in southwestern Italy. He continued to fight for church reforms and appointed 12 new church leaders—men called cardinals—and put them into important church positions. Before he died in 1085, Pope Gregory VII forgave all the people he had excommunicated except for Henry and the man he had named as the new pope. He may have died thinking he had failed to reform the church. One of the last statements he made was, "I have loved justice and hated inequity." Historians recognize Pope Gregory VII's role in making the church independent of kings and lords. He was declared a saint in 1728. □

### What Do You Think?

**1.** At the time Pope Gregory VII lived, kings and nobles had authority to decide who would be bishops and abbots. Church leaders also were involved in political life. What are the dangers of this close relationship between church and state?

**2.** What advantages did Pope Gregory VII have in life? What obstacles did he face?

# HENRY IV —
# Emperor of Germany

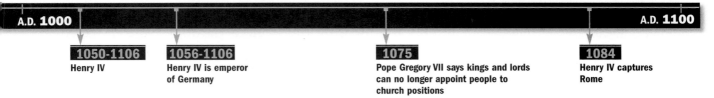

| A.D. **1000** | | | | A.D. **1100** |

**1050-1106**
Henry IV

**1056-1106**
Henry IV is emperor
of Germany

**1075**
Pope Gregory VII says kings and lords
can no longer appoint people to
church positions

**1084**
Henry IV captures
Rome

One of the most dramatic events of the Middle Ages was the conflict between Henry IV and Pope Gregory VII. Henry thought he had the right to control important church matters. The pope strongly disagreed. This quarrel changed history.

## A Holy Roman Empire

Charlemagne had the idea of a "Holy Roman Empire" in 800, but historians usually do not use that name to describe his empire. After Charlemagne died, his empire gradually broke apart. In 936 a man named Otto I became king of Germany. He wanted to restore the old Roman Empire that had been so powerful 1,000 years earlier. In 962, the pope crowned Otto I Emperor Augustus. Otto and his vassals conquered a large amount of territory in western and central Europe. At its center was present-day Germany. This empire became known as the Holy Roman Empire. It lasted in some form until 1806. Henry IV was emperor of this empire from 1056 to 1106.

▲ Pope Gregory VII lived in Rome. Henry IV was born in Germany in 1050 and later became the king of Germany.

◀ Henry IV said Pope Gregory VII was "a false monk" and was "no longer pope."

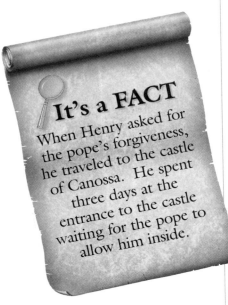

It's a FACT
When Henry asked for the pope's forgiveness, he traveled to the castle of Canossa. He spent three days at the entrance to the castle waiting for the pope to allow him inside.

## Henry—Roman Emperor

Henry was born in Goslar, Germany in 1050. He was the son of Henry III and Agnes of Poitou. At this time, the emperor was elected by a group of German nobles. These nobles were very powerful, but the emperor had figured out ways to control them. Because most of the empire's wealth came from northern Italy, the emperor also had found a way to control the Roman Catholic Church. The emperor had a difficult challenge. He had to find a balance between pleasing the nobles and pleasing the Roman Catholic Church. Henry became emperor when he was just six years old. Because he was a child, his mother was his regent—she ruled on his behalf until he was old enough to do it himself. However, his mother did not have a good understanding of the political part of her job. The powerful nobles of Germany were angry that the queen favored the church. To stop her, they kidnapped Henry. Then they began to serve as his regent in ruling the German empire.

## Henry's Problem with the Pope

During the time that Henry was growing up, many efforts were made to reform the church. Henry's father had strongly supported these reform efforts. Many people felt the church had become corrupt. They did not think it was right that the popes gave emperors their blessings in exchange for land.

Henry IV finally became emperor in his own name around 1070. He found himself in the middle of a fight with the pope. The argument was over who had the right to appoint local bishops and other church officials. Much of Henry's power came from his ability to make these appointments. He was determined to keep this power, but Pope Gregory VII saw things very differently.

## Lay Investiture

Under Pope Gregory VII, church reform began to have serious consequences. Pope Gregory VII wanted to solve two major problems. First, he wanted to rid the church of its corruption. For example, he wanted priests to live their lives according to the promises they made when they joined the clergy. Second, he wanted rulers such as Henry IV to stop interfering in church affairs. For centuries, rulers appointed officials to church positions in their territories. Rulers used these church officials to help them govern. Often, these church leaders were more loyal to the ruler who appointed them than to the church in Rome. This practice of rulers' appointing church officials is called "lay investiture."

# Excommunication

When Pope Gregory ordered Henry to end the practice of lay investiture, Henry ignored the pope's order. In response, Pope Gregory VII excommunicated Henry. Henry, in turn, with the support of his German bishops, declared that Pope Gregory VII was "no longer pope, but a false monk." But this was not the end of the conflict. Pope Gregory VII said that all the Christians living in Germany were released from any oath they had sworn to Henry. He threatened to excommunicate any of the emperor's vassals who supported Henry. This was terrifying to Christians in the Middle Ages. They believed people who were excommunicated would go to hell. Finally, Henry seemed to back down. He begged the pope to allow him back in the church. The pope agreed, but Henry did not keep his word. He soon began appointing church officials again.

# A Civil War

In Germany, people who supported the pope against Henry conveniently ignored the fact that the pope had forgiven Henry. The pope's supporters decided to name a new ruler. When a new king was named, Henry started a civil war. The pope wanted to end the war. Henry insisted that the pope excommunicate the new king. Henry declared that if the pope did not take this action, Henry would name a new pope! Henry called a meeting of his supporters—mostly bishops he had previously appointed. Henry convinced them to call for the removal of Pope Gregory VII. When the pope found out what Henry had done, he again excommunicated Henry. Henry's newly elected pope, Clement III, then crowned Henry emperor. After much negotiation and the involvement of many other nobles, Henry decided to bring his army to Rome. Gregory left Rome for Salerno in southern Italy. Henry marched his army against Rome several times. He finally captured the city in 1084. Gregory died in Salerno in 1085.

# What It All Means

Historians generally agree that the "investiture" argument between Henry IV and Pope Gregory VII changed political history in Europe. This fight was more a battle of words than of swords. Public opinion had become important. Both sides used carefully worded statements to defend their positions. Over time, the idea of separate areas of influence between church and government began to be more common. The church continued to have a strong influence over people's lives in Europe for the next 200-300 years. However, the church's influence began to become more limited to spiritual matters. The rise of the nation-states such as France and England began to have more influence on people's lives in political and economic terms. 📖

▲ Pope Gregory VII (above) wanted the church to be independent of kings. King Henry IV did not want to lose his influence over the church.

## What Do You Think?

1. During the Middle Ages, people were terrified of excommunication from the church. Are people terrified of being excluded from church today? Are people terrified or concerned about being excluded from other groups? Why?

2. What penalties for wrongdoing terrify people today?

# ABBOT SUGER and the Invention of the Gothic Cathedral

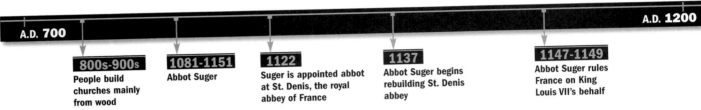

| A.D. 700 | | | | | A.D. 1200 |
|---|---|---|---|---|---|

**800s-900s**
People build churches mainly from wood

**1081-1151**
Abbot Suger

**1122**
Suger is appointed abbot at St. Denis, the royal abbey of France

**1137**
Abbot Suger begins rebuilding St. Denis abbey

**1147-1149**
Abbot Suger rules France on King Louis VII's behalf

▲ The man we know as Abbot Suger was born in 1081. His family lived in a small village near Paris. Suger dedicated his life to the abbey at St. Denis, France.

What difference does one person make in history? Can an individual really change the way the world looks? One man did. His name was Abbot Suger (SOO-zhair). He dramatically influenced the way European churches looked for hundreds of years.

## Abbot Suger and a New Kind of Architecture

Throughout the 800s and 900s, people built churches mainly from wood. During the Viking invasions, many of these churches were destroyed. When they were rebuilt, people used stone to make the structures stronger. The stone also made it less likely for buildings to catch on fire.

▶ Historians know a great deal about the building of the cathedral at St. Denis because Abbot Suger wrote three short works about its construction and decoration.

However, these new stone churches were very dark inside. Builders thought the walls had to be thick to support the heavy ceiling. They thought having large spaces for windows might make the ceiling fall. As a result, the only windows in these stone churches were very small. However, due to the influence of one man, Abbot Suger, the architectural style in Europe changed dramatically in the 1100s.

## Abbot at St. Denis

The man we know as Abbot Suger was born in 1081. His family lived in a small village near Paris. From a very early age, people could see that he was extremely intelligent. His village priest helped him enter the abbey at St. Denis so he could receive a good education. While there, Suger made friends with a fellow student, a boy who grew up to be King Louis VI of France. Suger dedicated his life to the abbey at St. Denis in France. Eventually, in 1122, he was appointed abbot at St. Denis. The position of abbot was a very important job. By the time Suger became head of St. Denis, it had become the royal abbey of France.

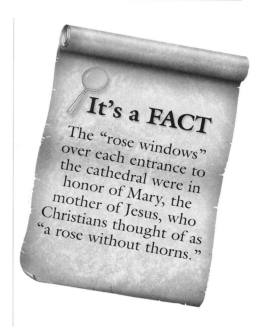

It's a FACT

The "rose windows" over each entrance to the cathedral were in honor of Mary, the mother of Jesus, who Christians thought of as "a rose without thorns."

## An Important and Influential Person

As head of the royal abbey, Abbot Suger was an important and influential person. He used his influence and power in religious as well as political matters. For example, he tried to bring the king and the nobles closer together by emphasizing their Christian faith. When lands belonging to the king of France were invaded in 1124, Abbot Suger offered the king the banner from St. Denis to carry into battle. When Louis VI's son became king, Abbot Suger took on more important duties. In fact, when King Louis VII went away to war from 1147-1149, he asked Abbot Suger to rule France on his behalf.

▶ Gothic cathedrals were built in the shape of a cross. The pointed arches shown here are a special feature of the Gothic style. This and other Gothic features let in a lot more light. Suger thought light was a symbol of heaven. Some people thought the pointed arches in Gothic cathedrals looked like praying hands.

It's a FACT

The National Cathedral in Washington, D.C. is an example of Gothic architecture in the United States.

## What Do You Think?

1. Do you agree that Abbot Suger is an example of the interdependence of religious leaders and political leaders during this time? Why or why not?

2. What do you think is Abbot Suger's greatest accomplishment? Why?

3. Do you think that people invest their time and money in things they believe are important? Explain why or why not. Give examples to support your position.

# Light and Heaven

Abbot Suger is best remembered as the man who helped invent the Gothic cathedral. The church at St. Denis had been built in 775. After standing for more than 350 years, it was in need of serious repair. In 1137, Abbot Suger decided to begin rebuilding it. He thought light was a symbol of heaven. His idea was that the new church should have more light inside. To accomplish this goal, the builders of the time had to develop techniques allowing large windows to be placed in the walls. They accomplished this with new inventions such as the flying buttress, pointed arches, and ribbed vaulting. With these new techniques, a new style of architecture was born. Today, this style of building is called Gothic architecture. By 1144, much of the work Abbot Suger started on the new cathedral at St. Denis was completed. In June of that year, the French king, Louis VII, along with many bishops and other church leaders, took part in a ceremony to dedicate the first Gothic cathedral. Abbot Suger said the new cathedral of St. Denis was filled "by a wonderful and continuous light." Abbot Suger died in 1151. He had achieved his goal of building a church that was filled with "heavenly" light.

# The Gothic Style Spreads

People in other areas began to copy the Gothic style. It spread to other European countries. Each country adapted the Gothic style to meet its own tastes, but they all kept the central features. For example, all Gothic churches had high ceilings and stained glass windows (called "rose windows") over each of the entrances. Many French architects were invited to travel to places throughout Europe to supervise the design and building of other cathedrals. The construction of a Gothic-style cathedral was a major undertaking for the city in which it was located. Hundreds of craftsmen were needed to complete the cathedral. Each cathedral needed stone cutters, sculptors, masons, mortar makers, carpenters, blacksmiths, glassmakers, and roofers. Many times the work was passed from one generation of craftsmen to their sons. Almost no cathedrals were completed during the lifetimes of the workers who started the project. Because many Gothic cathedrals took more than 200 years to build, the style of many glassmakers or masons often is represented in the same church. 📖

# ELEANOR of Aquitaine

**c. 1122-1204**
Eleanor of Aquitaine

**1137**
Eleanor marries Louis VII
and becomes queen of
France

**1152**
Louis and Eleanor divorce

**1154**
Eleanor becomes queen of
England

Eleanor of Aquitaine is one of the most remarkable people of the Middle Ages. Her life began at a time when feudal lords, such as her father, ruled large provinces. As she grew older, the world began to change. Kings and queens became powerful and marriages between royal families concentrated power in a few families. Eleanor was very accomplished in this new world. She was a woman who knew what she wanted and was not afraid to go after it.

## Heir to Aquitaine

When Eleanor of Aquitaine was born, dukes and duchesses ruled large areas throughout France. These large areas were called duchies. Aquitaine was the most important French duchy during the late Middle Ages. Eleanor's father, William X, was the powerful duke of Aquitaine. When Eleanor was young, both her mother and brother died. Her father made sure she received an excellent education to prepare her for her role as a duchess. Eleanor developed a love for music, literature, and travel. When she was only 15, her father died while making a religious pilgrimage. Eleanor became the duchess of the huge and wealthy territory of Aquitaine.

## Queen of France

Before William died, he had asked the king of France to look after his daughter. The king arranged for his son Louis to marry Eleanor. Shortly after, the king died. Louis then became the new king of France, Louis VII, and Eleanor became queen of France. Eleanor was not like most royal women of the time. She was very active. She frequently gave advice to her husband on political matters. And, much to the disappointment of the king's advisors, he often took her advice. During the first years of their marriage, Eleanor gave birth to a daughter, Marie, in 1145. However, Eleanor did not think motherhood was a reason to settle down and become a "traditional" wife.

## The Second Crusade

Christians had controlled the city of Edessa (in modern-day Turkey) since about 1100. However, in 1144, Muslims captured it. The citizens of Edessa had been either massacred or sold into slavery. In response, the French and the Germans launched the Second Crusade. Eleanor decided that she would go with her husband on this crusade. At first, her husband said "no," but he later agreed.

▲ The Second Crusade went through cities such as Vienna, Constantinople, and Antioch.

◀ This is a portrait of Eleanor of Aquitaine.

Eleanor gathered together 1,000 men and about 300 women from Aquitaine. Eleanor said the women were there to nurse the wounded. All of the women wore armor and carried lances, but they did not do any fighting.

## Queen of England

The goal of the Second Crusade was to reach Jerusalem. However, by the time they arrived in Antioch, a city in modern-day Syria, the crusaders could not agree on how to proceed. The arguments became so heated that the crusaders decided to go home. When Louis announced he was returning to France, Eleanor made her own announcement. She said she wanted to divorce the king. In 1152, the pope granted Eleanor a divorce.

Within two months of her divorce from King Louis of France, Eleanor married Henry Plantagenet. Henry was the grandson of King Henry I of England. Henry was only 18 at the time of their marriage, 11 years younger than Eleanor. By 1154, Henry had become Henry II, king of England, and Eleanor was again a queen.

## Problems in the Marriage and the Kingdom

Eleanor and Henry had seven children. As their children grew older, however, Eleanor and Henry were not as close. Henry started having secret love affairs. After a while, he allowed these relationships to become public knowledge. Eleanor was very unhappy and decided to return to Aquitaine. In Aquitaine, Eleanor's court became a center of culture. She encouraged discussion of chivalry and literature. Her court was filled with minstrels who sang about fair ladies and brave knights. In Aquitaine, Eleanor also reunited with her first daughter, Marie. But these activities were not enough for Eleanor. She wanted a role in the political world and started plotting against Henry with her three eldest sons, Henry, Richard, and Geoffrey. In 1173, with Eleanor's support, the three sons started an open rebellion against their father. They were not successful and had to flee. Eleanor tried to follow, but Henry's army captured her. For the next 16 years, Eleanor was a prisoner.

## A New King

The battles between Henry and his sons continued until 1189 when Henry II died. Henry's eldest son had already died, so the next son, Richard, became king of England. He later became known as Richard the lion heart. Richard spent most of his life away from England. When Richard died, his younger brother, John became king of England. John had great respect for his mother's ability and took her advice on many things. In return for his loyalty, Eleanor supported John against his enemies. Although Eleanor was quite old by the standards of the time, she continued to be involved in many activities. However, she was happiest in Aquitaine and returned there to live the last days of her life. She died in 1204 at the age of 82. Eleanor is buried at Fontevrault Abbey. ▢

**What Do You Think?**

**1.** Why do you think the king of France arranged for his son Louis to marry young Eleanor?

**2.** How is Eleanor of Aquitaine like modern women? How is she different?

**3.** What contributions did Eleanor of Aquitaine make to England? To France? To women?

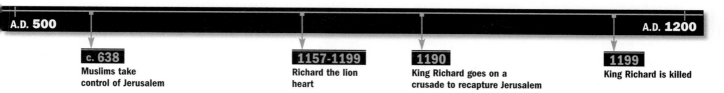

# RICHARD the Lion Heart

| A.D. 500 | | | | A.D. 1200 |
|---|---|---|---|---|

**c. 638**
Muslims take
control of Jerusalem

**1157-1199**
Richard the lion
heart

**1190**
King Richard goes on a
crusade to recapture Jerusalem

**1199**
King Richard is killed

Other nobles were named "Richard" during the Middle Ages, but only one became known as "Richard the lion heart." What courageous deeds did he do? Why is he a figure in so many stories about chivalry and honor?

## William the Conqueror's Great, Great Grandsons

William the Conqueror had two very famous great, great grandsons. One was King John, the English king who signed the Magna Carta. This great charter gave the nobility basic rights and privileges. It also included the idea that the king must obey the law. The other famous great, great grandson was Richard, John's older brother. Richard was the English king who went off to the Crusades and became known as Richard the lion heart.

## Eleanor of Aquitaine's Son

Richard was born in September 1157 in Oxford, England. His father was the English King Henry II and his mother was the queen, Eleanor of Aquitaine. While he was growing up, Richard spent most of his time in France at his mother's court. Richard was closer to his mother than his father. He also was much more interested in his mother's possessions. Henry was unwilling to give Richard or his brothers any real authority. However, Henry did give them land. Richard and his brothers spent much of their early lives rebelling against their father. Oftentimes, their mother helped. When Henry died, Richard became king of England. Soon, he decided to lead a crusade to the Holy Land. Richard led what has become known as the Third Crusade.

## King Richard and the Third Crusade

Richard left the administration of England to his assistants, and in 1190 he set out for the Holy Land. His goal was to recapture the city of Jerusalem from the Muslim leader, Saladin. King Philip II of France traveled with him on this Crusade. Richard and Philip disliked one another intensely. As they traveled towards Jerusalem, they captured Cyprus and Messina. Soon after this, the arguments between them increased. Finally, Philip decided to return to France.

▲ In 1190, Richard the lion heart left England on the Third Crusade. King Philip II of France traveled with him. On their way to Jerusalem, they captured Cyprus and Messina.

▲ Richard the lion heart was born in September 1157 in Oxford, England. He died in April 1199 in Aquitaine, France. He spent many years traveling to and from the Holy Land.

◀ Richard is saying farewell as he leaves for the Holy Land. To raise funds for the Third Crusade, Richard made the English people pay a special tax, called a "Saladin tithe."

When Richard arrived in the Holy Land, his mission was not entirely successful. He did not recapture Jerusalem. However, he signed a treaty with Saladin, which allowed Christians to have easier access to the region.

## Meanwhile, Back in England ...

As Richard was fighting Saladin, Philip, who had returned to France, joined with Richard's brother John to remove Richard as king. When Richard found out about this plot, he immediately started for home. On the way, however, he was captured in Austria and held hostage. Richard was finally released after his mother arranged to pay a huge ransom. Richard returned to England and received a hero's welcome. He also put down the revolt led by his brother. But Richard's problems were not over. The cost of the Crusade and the ransom paid for his release left England in very poor financial condition. There was no money to run the government or to fight new wars. To raise money, Richard created a new "great seal" that had to appear on all official documents. Any documents with the old seal were not legal. This meant everyone had to pay for the use of this new seal. With the money he raised, Richard returned to France and took up his battle with Philip. The armies of the two men fought off and on for several years. In the end, the French were defeated.

## The Death of Richard

Historians' writing at the time reported that Richard died in a curious manner. A peasant plowing a field in Aquitaine happened to dig up a box filled with gold statues and coins. The feudal lord who owned the land claimed the treasure from his vassal. Richard claimed the treasure from the lord, but the lord refused to give it to him. This prompted Richard to attack the lord's castle. According to the story, Richard was riding close to the lord's castle one day and saw an archer aim an arrow at him. Richard was not wearing his entire armor, but stopped to applaud the archer. The story says that Richard was hit with the arrow, refused treatment, and died shortly after from infection. Richard's great military ability and his bravery earned him the name Richard the lion heart.

### What Do You Think?

1. The Crusades meant long journeys far from home and bloody battles. Why do you think rulers like King Richard of England went on the Crusades?

2. Why did writers include Richard the lion heart in their stories?

3. What do you think Muslim leaders such as Saladin thought of Richard and the other crusaders?

# The MAGNA CARTA —
# A Great Charter!

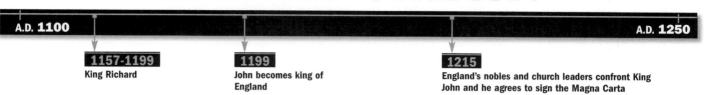

| A.D. **1100** | | | A.D. **1250** |
|---|---|---|---|

**1157-1199**
**King Richard**

**1199**
**John becomes king of England**

**1215**
**England's nobles and church leaders confront King John and he agrees to sign the Magna Carta**

In June 1215, many of England's nobles and church leaders confronted King John of England. After days of arguing, the king finally agreed to approve a treaty called the Magna Carta. Magna Carta means "great charter." The Magna Carta gave the nobility basic rights and privileges that the king could not take away. One of the most important ideas in this treaty was that the king must obey the law. Another was that a person accused of a crime had to be treated fairly and given a speedy trial. Over time, these rights and privileges were extended to others in society. People in England began to see the Magna Carta as a written statement of their liberties. This great charter became the foundation of English law and justice. Below are some parts of the Magna Carta. 📖

▲ This stone carving shows King John sitting on the throne signing the Magna Carta. It also shows the first words of the Magna Carta: "The Church of England shall be free." This carving is displayed in the National Cathedral in Washington, D.C.

## From the Magna Carta

... We have granted, moreover, to all free men of our kingdom, for us and our heirs forever, all the liberties written below, to be had and holden by themselves and their heirs from us and our heirs.

**28.** No constable or other bailiff of ours shall take any one's grain or other chattels [property] without immediately paying for them in money, unless he is able to obtain a postponement at the good will of the seller.

**30.** No sheriff or bailiff of ours, or any one else, shall take horses or wagons of any free man, for carrying purposes, except on the permission of that free man.

**39.** No free man shall be taken, or imprisoned, or dispossessed, or outlawed, or banished, or in any way injured, nor will we go upon him, nor send upon him, except by the legal judgment of his peers or by the law of the land.

**40.** To no one will we sell, to no one will we deny or delay, right or justice.

## Analyze the Source!

1. Read the excerpts and tell in your own words what they say.

2. How do you think these ideas might have affected the feudal system?

3. How do you think American colonists were influenced by these ideas? How do these ideas continue to influence Americans today?

# HILDEGARD of Bingen —
## "Know the Way"

A.D. **1000**                                                                              A.D. **1200**

**1098-1179**
Hildegard of Bingen

**1141**
Hildegard has a vision in which she
believes God orders her to write down
her visions

GERMANY

Mediterranean Sea

▲ Hildegard lived in what is present-day
Germany.

Hildegard of Bingen was born in 1098 to a noble in what is present-day Germany. As a very young child, she reported having visions in which God spoke to her. When she was just eight years old, she went to live with a group of nuns. Her aunt was the abbess, or leader, of this community. When her aunt died, Hildegard became abbess. Throughout her life, Hildegard continued to have visions. In 1141, she reportedly had a vision in which she believed God ordered her to write down her visions. These writings were collected in a book called *Scivias*, which means "know the way." Hildegard also illustrated this book with her own paintings. Many people during the Middle Ages read this book. Hildegard wrote other books—some were religious, some were scientific, and some were medical. She also wrote a symphony of hymns. Hildegard established a religious community in Bingen and was active as its leader until she died in 1179. Today, Hildegard is admired by many people who think of her as a medieval feminist—someone who called for greater equality of women in society. Below is an excerpt from her book *Scivias*. In this excerpt, Hildegard is describing what she said God told her in one of her visions. 📖

## Hildegard Describes a Vision From God

You [human beings] have been given great intelligence; and so great wisdom is required of you. Much has been given to you, and much will be required of you. But in all these things I [God] am your Head and your helper. For when Heaven has touched you, if you call on Me I will answer you. If you knock at the door, I will open to you. You are given a spirit of profound knowledge, and so have in yourself all that you need. And, this being so, My eyes will search you closely and remember what they find.

## Analyze the Source!

1. Read the excerpt and tell in your own words what it says.

2. What is the difference between intelligence and wisdom?

3. Do you agree that much is required of those to whom much has been given?

# FRANCIS of Assisi

A.D. **1000**                                   A.D. **1250**

**c. 1181-1226**
St. Francis of Assisi

**c. 1208**
Francis begins preaching

**1228**
The Roman Catholic Church
declares Francis a saint

Umbria is a region in the center of the Italian peninsula that is known for its green, rolling hills and rich soil for farming. People built walled cities on the tops of many of the tallest hills. One of these walled cities on a hill is named Assisi. It was here that the man we have come to know of as St. Francis of Assisi was born.

## Growing Up

Francis Bernadone was born into a wealthy family around 1181. His father, Pietro, was a successful cloth merchant. Like many fathers, Pietro wanted his son to follow him into the family business. As a child and young man, Francis lived a life of luxury. His family's wealth provided him with money and lots of leisure time. By all accounts, people liked Francis very much. He was charming, full of fun, and almost always happy. If he didn't do well in school, no one seemed to mind. If he offended someone, he was quickly forgiven. Francis was the kind of person that others just liked to be around. Because of his money and his personality, he became the leader of a group of young people who went from one party to the next.

## On the Battlefield

Despite his wild ways, Francis was good at business. This made his father happy, but Francis was not that interested in business. He wanted adventure. He also wanted to be a knight. He had his chance for both when Assisi declared war against the nearby town of Perugia. Francis volunteered to fight. Assisi lost the battle and Francis was captured. He spent a year as a prisoner before he was finally released. Then he returned to a life of parties and wild nights. When a call was issued for knights to join the Fourth Crusade, he volunteered. He bought a custom-made suit of armor and a good horse, and he left with the crusaders. But then everything changed.

## A Message from God

On his first night away from home, Francis reported that he had a dream in which God told him to return to Assisi. When he woke up, that's exactly what he did. The young man who had bragged about being a knight returned after only one day.

▲ Francis lived in Assisi, Italy.

▲ This picture of St. Francis of Assisi is based on a picture created by a famous Italian painter named Giotto di Bondone. There is a story that a wolf was terrorizing the people of a nearby town. Francis is said to have walked up to the wolf and asked it to stop hurting people. According to the story, everyone in the town was amazed to see the wolf walk up to Francis and then lay down at his feet. St. Francis is often pictured surrounded by animals.

The people of Assisi laughed at him. Imagine the humiliation he must have felt. But Francis was certain he had done what God had asked him to do. He helped his father in his business, but Francis also began to spend more time in prayer. More and more he became filled with what he described as "God's grace."

## Meeting a Leper

One day as Francis was returning home, he came face-to-face with a leper. Lepers were people who suffered from a terrible disease called leprosy that caused sores to form all over their bodies. Francis's first reaction was to turn away—the leper was covered in sores and horrible to look at. However, Francis overcame his first reaction and kissed the hand of the leper. His gesture of kindness was returned, and it is reported that Francis was filled with overwhelming joy. As he continued home, he turned to look at the leper. The man had disappeared. Francis saw this event as a test from God.

## "Repair My Church"

As Francis was praying one day at an old church in Assisi, he believed he heard the voice of Jesus. The voice told Francis, "Repair my church." Francis believed Jesus was telling him to repair the church he was praying in. So Francis took some of his father's cloth and sold it. This gave him the money he needed to fix the old church. When his father found out what Francis had done, he was furious! He charged Francis with theft and made him go before the bishop of the town. His father wanted Francis to return the money and give up his right to any inheritance. During this conflict, Francis removed all of his clothing except for his shirt. He turned to his father and said that from that moment on his only father was, "Our Father who art in heaven." Francis never owned anything for the rest of his life.

## What Do You Think?

**1.** During the past 50 years, St. Francis has become one of the most popular and respected saints. Why do you think people today admire St. Francis?

**2.** What advantages did Francis enjoy in life? What obstacles did he face?

**3.** What people today exhibit the character traits of St. Francis of Assisi?

## The Founding of the Friars

Francis repaired the old church himself. Shortly after this, he also started to preach. He spoke to people about the need to live simply and return to the ways of living as written in the Bible. He taught the importance of obeying the church and returning to God. Slowly, people began to listen to him and to follow his example. Francis went to the pope in Rome and asked permission to preach. He also asked permission to begin a new religious order. At first, the pope would not agree. However, when he saw the tremendous influence Francis had on people, the pope gave his permission. Francis called his order the Friars Minor. Today they are called the Franciscans.

▲ The famous Dutch painter Rembrandt created this picture in the 1600s. It shows an older Francis praying beneath a tree.

## The Growth of the Order

Francis wrote a "rule" that all members had to follow. This rule said that all of the brothers must live in poverty and work to help the poor. Within 10 years, there were more than 5,000 Franciscan friars. Some church leaders and members of his own community thought Francis's rule to live in complete poverty was too harsh. Francis realized that he could no longer control what he had started, so he gave up his authority in the organization. He became just another brother—as he had started. He spent the rest of his life quietly in the hills above Assisi. He died in 1226. Two years later, in 1228, the Roman Catholic Church declared him a saint. 📖

# CLARE SCIFI of Assisi

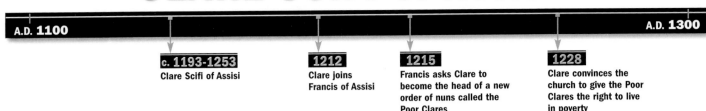

A.D. **1100**

**c. 1193-1253**
Clare Scifi of Assisi

**1212**
Clare joins
Francis of Assisi

**1215**
Francis asks Clare to
become the head of a new
order of nuns called the
Poor Clares

**1228**
Clare convinces the
church to give the Poor
Clares the right to live
in poverty

A.D. **1300**

EUROPE

ITALY
• Assisi
• Rome

Mediterranean Sea

AFRICA

▲ Clare Scifi lived in Assisi, a small hill
town in central Italy. She dedicated her
life to the church.

Francis of Assisi attracted many followers to his order. Often he was asked to visit the local churches around the town of Assisi, Italy. It was at one of these visits to a local church that 18-year-old Clare heard Francis express his ideas and teachings. From that moment on she knew she wanted to devote her life to prayer and to helping others. Clare secretly met with Francis to ask for his help in living a holy life.

Historians do not know very much about Clare's early life. It is generally accepted that she was the eldest daughter of Ortolama and Favorino Scifi, Count of Sasso-Rosso. Her family was a wealthy, old Roman family that owned a large palace in Assisi. Clare's mother was a deeply religious person. As a young girl, Clare was also very religious. As she grew older, most accounts of her life indicate that she grew less interested in worldly possessions and even more interested in a spiritual life.

## A Turning Point
On the day celebrating Palm Sunday in 1212, Clare attended Mass in the cathedral in Assisi. At one point in the Palm Sunday service, people went forward to accept a palm leaf from the bishop conducting the service. The bishop performing the ceremony in Assisi noticed that Clare did not join the others in moving forward. Accounts of the incident say the bishop left the altar and placed the palm leaf in Clare's hand. The other people present are reported to have said that Clare appeared to be in some type of happy dream. That night, Clare secretly left her family home. She made her way to the place where Francis was living with the members of his community.

▼ This is a sketch of Assisi, Italy. St. Clare
was first buried in the church of San
Giorgio (St. George) in Assisi. Later, her
body was moved to Santa Chiara, a
church in Assisi built in her honor. In
Italian, *Santa Chiara* means "St. Clare."

## Joining a Religious Community

Francis and his followers welcomed her. Clare exchanged her expensive dress for a rough cloth tunic. Francis cut off her hair, and Clare made a promise to live a life in the service of God. When Clare's father discovered that she had joined this religious community, he did everything he could to bring her home. Despite his best efforts, Clare was determined to keep her promise to serve God. Finally, her father agreed to honor her decision. Within days, Clare moved to a community of nuns. After about two weeks, Clare's sister, Agnes, decided to join her. During the next several years, other women, including her mother, joined Clare. All of these women felt a strong desire to give up their personal wealth. Like Clare, they took vows of poverty.

## Beginning a New Order

Francis helped these women move to a small building next to the church of San Damian in Assisi. In 1215, Francis asked Clare to become the head of a new order of nuns. This new order was called the Poor Clares. Within a few years, similar religious communities of women developed in many Italian cities and in parts of France and Germany.

## A Short History of the Poor Clares

Clare and her followers lived with as few worldly things as possible. The Poor Clares went without shoes, slept mostly on the ground, ate no meat, and spoke only when it was absolutely necessary. Clare felt these sacrifices were important because they helped the women focus on God. On several occasions, a church leader tried to "soften" these rules. In 1219, Cardinal Ugolino wrote a new rule for the Poor Clares that said they could have some worldly goods. The church wanted to give the poor Clares some money every year. However, Clare argued that taking any money went against Francis's teachings. After Francis died, Cardinal Ugolino had become Pope Gregory IX. He came to Assisi to declare Francis a saint and again tried to convince Clare to accept some money every year. He thought the women should have something in case of an emergency. Again, however, Clare was determined not to give in. Eventually, the pope agreed with her. In 1228, the church gave the Poor Clares the right to live in poverty.

## Clare's Death and Legacy

As Clare grew older, the difficult life she led was very hard on her health. She became very ill and called the other nuns to her bedside. She reminded them of the gifts God had given to them. She encouraged them to work hard to keep their faith and never to give up their vow of poverty. As she lay dying, her sister Agnes and three of the earliest companions of St. Francis surrounded her. As they had done for St. Francis 27 years before, they read aloud from the Bible. Clare died in 1253 and was declared a saint two years later.

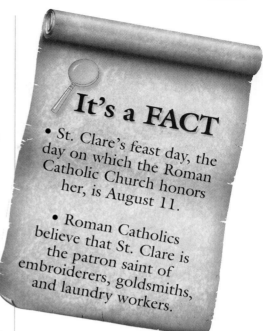

**It's a FACT**

- St. Clare's feast day, the day on which the Roman Catholic Church honors her, is August 11.

- Roman Catholics believe that St. Clare is the patron saint of embroiderers, goldsmiths, and laundry workers.

## What Do You Think?

1. Clare made a promise to live a life of poverty and service to God. You could say that she had the courage of her convictions. What do we mean by the phrase, "having the courage of one's convictions"?

2. Why do you think Clare's father wanted her to come home? Why do you think he finally accepted her decision to become a nun?

3. Why do you think Clare refused to take money every year from the church? Do you admire this decision? Why or why not?

# THOMAS AQUINAS — The Man Who Wrote about Reason and Faith

| A.D. **1000** | | | | A.D. **1300** |
|---|---|---|---|---|

**c. 1225-1274**
St. Thomas of Aquinas

**c. 1245**
Thomas starts his studies
with St. Albert the Great

**1273**
Thomas receives a
life-changing vision

**1274**
Thomas falls ill and dies
on the way to see the pope

EUROPE

ITALY

Rome
• Monte Cassino
NAPLES

Mediterranean Sea

AFRICA

▲ Thomas Aquinas was born around 1225 to a noble Italian family. His father was the count of Aquino and his mother Theodora was a noble woman from Naples.

Thomas Aquinas is best known for bringing together two areas of knowledge that often had been thought of as separate: reason and faith. His work became the approved teaching of the church, and his ideas continue to influence people even today.

Thomas grew up in his family's castle in southern Italy. He went to school at the monastery at Monte Cassino and later at the University of Naples. His teachers called him brilliant. His parents thought he would become an important man in society. They were quite unhappy to learn that he wanted to join the Dominican order of monks. It took some time for his parents to accept his decision.

## A Dominican Monk

The Dominican order attracted brilliant thinkers. Dominicans were trained to ask and answer questions, particularly about the Christian faith. They also took a vow of poverty. Thomas would never be rich.

▲ This is a reproduction of a picture called "The Triumph of St. Thomas Aquinas." St. Thomas is sitting (second from the left) in front of Pope Alexander IV. He is defending the attacks made on the church.

Thomas would distinguish himself in another way. When he was about 20, Thomas traveled to Paris to study with a great Dominican scholar, Albertus Magnus (St. Albert the Great). Thomas was a tall and heavyset man. He did not say much in class, but he listened. Some students thought Thomas was stupid. They called him a "dumb ox." But his teacher was impressed with his abilities and promised that the world would hear the "**lowing**" of this particular "dumb ox." He was right.

## Reason and Faith—Two Paths to the Same End

Before Thomas, medieval scholars such as St. Anselm (1033-1109) and Peter Abelard (1079-1142) used both reason and faith to understand the world. As far back as ancient Greece, philosophers such as Aristotle had used reason to describe the way the world worked. Some thought that faith, specifically Christian faith, was the best way to understand the world. Like Anselm and Abelard before him, however, Thomas thought reason and faith were both important. He pointed out that Aristotle used reason to identify a "supreme being" who started the world. Aristotle and other ancient philosophers did not have faith in God or a supreme being. They used their intellects to reason that someone created the world. Thomas argued this was consistent with the Christian faith that God created the world. Christians did not use reason to come to this understanding. They had faith. Thomas said reason and faith were two paths to the same end. You could reason that there was a supreme being or God. You also could have faith that there was one. Both reason and faith bring one to a belief in God. Thomas argued that without God, there could have been no universe. In this way, he showed how reason and Christian faith could be combined. His ideas about how logic explains a belief in God are contained in a book called *Summa Theologica*.

## Natural Law

Thomas also spent time thinking about the purpose of law. He argued that the purpose of law is the common good and universal happiness. He thought that all laws made by human beings should agree with natural law and divine law. Natural law refers to rules of conduct based on the morals that human beings are born with or have naturally. Thomas said natural law is what we use to decide "what is good and what is evil." Divine law refers to the rules of conduct that have been revealed by God or a higher power. He said that since God's ideas are eternal, "this kind of law must be called eternal. ..."

## A Vision, Joy, and Death

In 1273, Thomas Aquinas reportedly had a vision. It left him joyful, and no longer interested in writing. He said, "All I have written seems to me like so much straw compared with what I have seen and what has been revealed to me." In 1274, he began a journey to see the pope, but he fell ill and later died. His philosophy became the church's approved teaching. In 1323, he was declared a saint. □

**lowing:** the sound made by oxen

## What Do You Think?

1. What does the phrase "different paths to the same end" mean?

2. In your own words, describe Thomas Aquinas's view of law (or natural law). Do you agree or disagree with his position? Why or why not?

3. Why do you think the church approved Thomas Aquinas's philosophy?

# KING EDWARD I's Invitation to Discuss Important Matters

| A.D. **1100** | | | A.D. **1400** |
|---|---|---|---|

**1239-1307**
Edward I

**1272-1307**
King Edward I rules
England

**1295**
King Edward I calls together several groups in England to
discuss the issue of taxes for a war with France

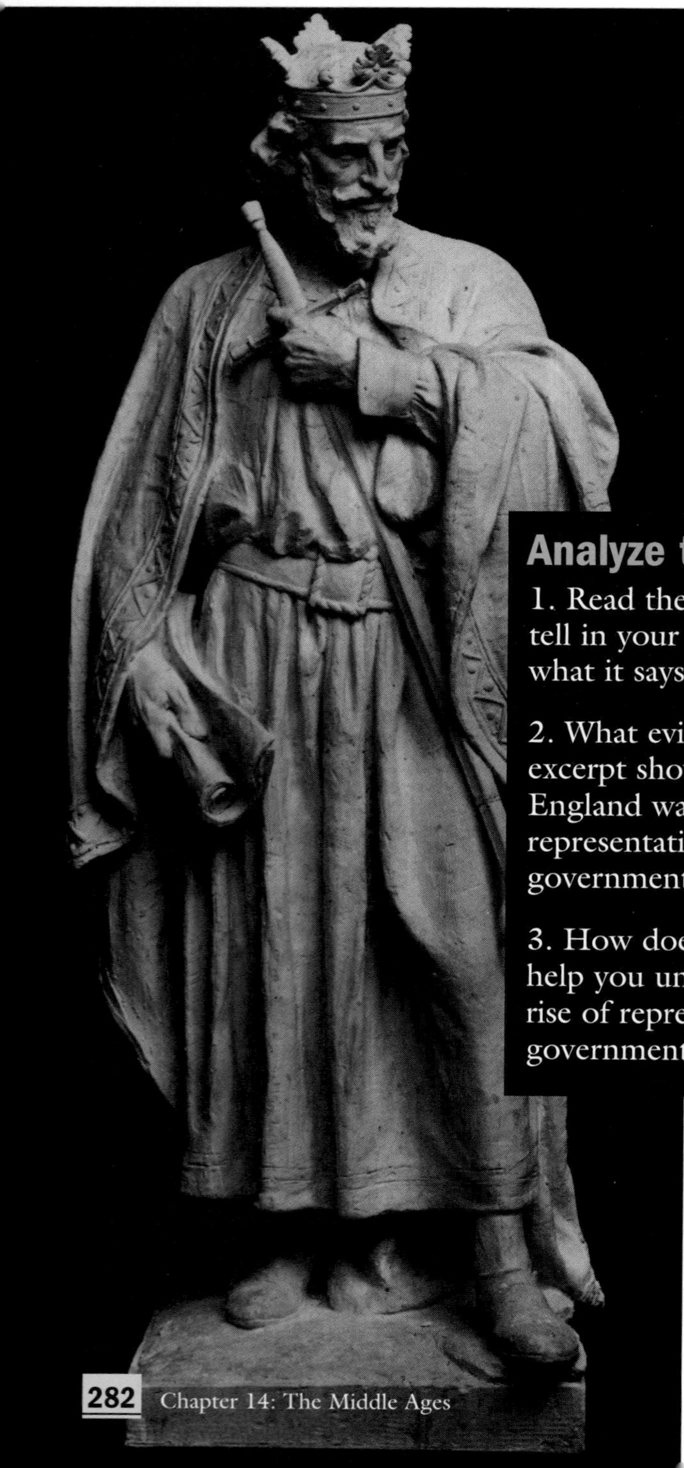

In 1295, King Edward I of England invited nobles, bishops, knights, and town leaders to meet with him. He wanted to discuss with them the issue of taxes for a war with France. The groups represented at this meeting established the general model that Parliament would follow in the future. Below is an excerpt from the king's letter inviting the sheriff from one of the counties to this meeting. ☐

## Analyze the Source!

1. Read the excerpt and tell in your own words what it says.

2. What evidence in this excerpt shows that England was developing a representative form of government?

3. How does this excerpt help you understand the rise of representative government in England?

## King Edward I's Invitation to the Sheriff of Nothamptonshire

Since we intend to have ... a meeting with the earls, barons, and other principal men of our kingdom with regard to providing **remedies** against the dangers which are in these days threatening the same kingdom [England], and ... do as may be necessary for the avoidance of those dangers, we strictly require you to cause two knights from the aforesaid county, two citizens from each city in the same county, and two burgesses ... to be elected without delay, and to cause them to come to us at the aforesaid time and place.

Moreover, the said knights [and citizens and burgesses] are to have full and sufficient power for themselves and for the community ... for doing what shall then be **ordained** according to the common council. ... Witness the king, at Canterbury, on the 3rd of October [1295].

---
**ordain:** to appoint or establish
**remedy:** something to correct a wrong

# THE DIVINE COMEDY

Many consider *The Divine Comedy* the greatest piece of literature of all time. It is both a description of the state of man's soul after death and a story of how human beings search for **salvation**. In the poem, Dante the Pilgrim represents humanity as he journeys through the three levels of the afterlife. He travels through hell—a place Christians think very sinful people go after they die. He also visits purgatory. At that time, Christians thought some people would go to a place called purgatory for a little while after they die. They would spend time in purgatory to pay for their sins. After they did this, Christians believed they could go to heaven or "paradise," which is the third level of the afterlife. Heaven is where Christians think people who live good lives go after they have died.

## Dante Aligheri

The author of *The Divine Comedy*, Dante Aligheri, was an Italian poet and one of the greatest figures in all of literature. Dante was born in Florence in 1265. The period of time in which he lived was filled with conflict. Dante was greatly influenced by these conflicts. He was both a cavalryman and a politician in defense of his native Florence. At the time, there was no central government in Italy. Cities such as Florence and Venice were independent city-states, each with its own governments and laws. As Dante viewed the situation in Italy, he was angered by the corruption of the Roman Catholic Church and the political fighting in Florence. By 1301, Dante's political rivals had forced him into exile from Florence.

## *The Divine Comedy*

Dante began writing *The Divine Comedy* around 1307, during his exile from Florence. The poem is set in the year 1300 and tells the story of Dante's imaginary journey as he travels through the afterlife in the *Inferno* (hell), *Purgatorio* (purgatory), and *Paradiso* (heaven). One purpose of the poem was to describe the condition of human souls after their death. Another purpose was to describe the process of religious conversion and salvation. Because the church was central in almost everyone's life during the Middle Ages, seeking religious salvation was important. Virgil, a famous ancient Roman poet, serves as the guide on most of the journey through the afterlife. Virgil lived from about 70 to 19 B.C. His most famous work was the epic poem, *The Aeneid*. This poem was very popular with Romans because it told the story of the founding of Rome in a way that glorified the city, emperor Augustus, and the citizens of Rome.

▲ Dante Aligheri was an Italian poet and one of the greatest figures in all of literature.

**salvation:** saving of the soul from sin and its consequences; the state of being saved

Dante thought highly of Virgil, and *The Divine Comedy* is similar to a part of Virgil's *The Aeneid*. In *The Divine Comedy*, Virgil represents "human reason" as he guides Dante through the first two-thirds of his journey.

## Other People in *The Divine Comedy*

Dante's poem is full of many people he knew in Florence, many people from the Western Christian Church, and figures from ancient mythology. Throughout the poem, Dante placed these people in different levels of hell, purgatory, or heaven. As Virgil and Dante travel through the different levels of hell and purgatory, they see the souls of sinners being given various punishments. In the last part of the poem, a woman named Beatrice meets Dante and becomes his guide through heaven. Dante knew Beatrice when he was a boy. Beatrice had died at a young age, and Dante had written about her in his other works before his death in 1321. In *The Divine Comedy*, Beatrice represents God's love. Accompanied by Beatrice, Dante at the end of his story meets God.

*The Divine Comedy* begins on **Good Friday** of 1300. The story covers seven days and is written in three parts or cantos (Inferno, Purgatorio, and Paradiso). *The Divine Comedy* was one of the first books to be printed when the new movable type was introduced into Italy from Germany during the 1460s and 1470s.

Translated below are the opening lines of the first canto of *The Divine Comedy*. Dante wrote *The Divine Comedy* in Italian and he invented a rhyming pattern called "terza rima" in which the middle line of the first three lines rhymes with the first and third line of the next three lines. For example, the word "dark" rhymes with "embark" and "stark." (You can see the line numbers to the left of the poem.) It was unusual during this time for a work of literature to be written in Italian. Most works of literature were written in Latin, which was the common language of scholars.

**embark:** to begin
**Good Friday:** the Friday before Easter

## Analyze the Source!

1. Read the excerpt and tell in your own words what it says.

2. How does this excerpt help you learn about attitudes toward death during this period?

3. Why is a common language(s) for scholars important? Why is Latin no longer the language of scholars? Is there a language of scholars today? Explain your answer.

## Opening Lines of *The Divine Comedy*

1 In the middle of our life's way
  I found myself in a wood so dark
That I couldn't tell where the straight path lay
4 Oh how hard a thing it is to **embark**
  Upon the story of that savage wood,
For the memory shudders me with fear so stark
7 That death itself is hardly a more bitter fruit
  Yet whatever I observed there I'll convey
In order to tell what I found that was good.

# PIERS PLOWMAN—
# A Poem by William Langland

A.D. **1300**

A.D. **1400**

c. **1332**-c.**1400**
**William Langland**

c. **1369**-c.**1400**
**William writes *Piers Plowman***

Throughout the Middle Ages in Europe, the Christian Church held an important place in almost everyone's life. However, as it became stronger and wealthier, it also became more corrupt. Some Europeans began to express their concerns about the church. William Langland was one such person. He wrote a famous poem in which he criticized the church and church authorities for their behavior. In his poem *Piers Plowman*, Langland wrote about life from the point of view of a peasant—a life that was extremely hard and that had not improved for hundreds of years.

William Langland was born around 1332 in Ledbury, England. His mother was not married to his father. During this period, this meant that he could not take his father's name or inherit any of his father's property. By all accounts, Langland grew up poor and remained poor during his lifetime. He did attend school, but he worked on a farm at the same time. He knew from his own experience how hard farming was and always praised the work of farmers.

▲ **William Langland was born in Ledbury, England.**

◄ **William Langland wrote *Piers Plowman* from a peasant's point of view.**

### Creating *Piers Plowman*

In his book, Langland used a style of writing called allegory or dream allegory. This is a type of writing in which the author uses one story to tell the reader two things. On one level, the writer will tell what is going on in the story. For example, Piers Plowman is a farmer who helps a group of people look for a nobleman. On a second level, however, the writer's story has a meaning that is deeper.

The meaning of the story goes beyond what is actually taking place. For example, the story of *Piers Plowman* is also a way of telling people how a Christian could be saved and go to heaven. By using dream allegory, Langland was able to criticize the church without saying anything directly against it. This was a very popular style of writing during the Middle Ages. During that time, many people believed that God sent messages to people through dreams. *Piers Plowman* is told in 10 dreams.

Below are a few lines from Langland's poem. On one side of the page is the original language. On the other side is the modern translation. 📖

**habit:** costume; clothes
**hermit:** one who lives alone away from people

## Original Language from *Piers Plowman*

In a somer sesun, whon softe was the sonne,
I schop me into a shroud, as I a scheep were;
In habite as an hermite unholy of werkes
Wente I wyde in this world wondres to here;
Bote in a Mayes morwnynge on Malverne hulles
Me bifel a ferly, of fairie, me-thoughte.
I was wery, forwandred, and wente me to reste
Undur a brod banke bi a bourne side;
And as I lay and leonede and lokede on the watres,
I slumbrede in a slepynge, hit swyed so murie.

## Modern Translation

In a summer season, when soft was the sun,
I clothed myself in a cloak as I shepherd were,
**Habit** like a **hermit's**, unholy in works,
And went wide in the world, wonders to hear.
But on a May morning, on Malvern hills,
A marvel befell me, a fairy, methought.
I was weary with wandering, and went me to rest
Under a broad bank, by a brook's side,
And as I lay and leaned over, and looked into the waters
I fell into a sleep, for it sounded so merry.

### Analyze the Source!

1. Why do you think writers such as William Langland used allegory during this time?

2. What can you tell about European life and culture during the Middle Ages from the story of William Langland and his poem, *Piers Plowman*?

3. Do writers today still write allegories? Why or why not? What would be examples of modern-day allegories?

# The BLACK DEATH

A.D. **1200**

**c. 1300**
The "Little Ice Age" begins

**1347**
Asian ships bring the Black Death to Italy

**1351**
Black Death weakens

A.D. **1500**

Beginning around 1300, Europe experienced what geographers call the "Little Ice Age." The climate changed, bringing endless rains. Crops were destroyed, and there wasn't enough food for everyone. Many died of starvation. Then, when everyone thought things could not get worse, they did. In 1347, ships from Asia carrying a terrible disease docked in Italy. This disease came to be called the Black Death.

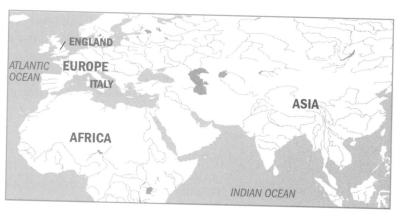

▲ In 1347, ships from Asia brought the Black Death to Europe.

## How Did the Plague Spread?
During the Middle Ages, Europeans were terrified of the Black Death. And there was good reason for their terror. The disease, which we now know was the bubonic plague, caused a horrible and painful death. At the time no one knew what caused the disease. People did not know where the disease started or how it was spread. Today, we know the plague probably began in central Asia and then was carried to China. From China, it spread to southwestern Asia, and then to Europe.

◄ In some parts of Europe, the Black Death killed half the population. The Black Death was spread by infected fleas on rats.

Once in Europe, the disease quickly spread north from Italy along the trade routes. Doctors had no cure for it. They did not even have any medicine to help ease a person's pain. As this plague spread across Europe, millions of people died. Experts believe that almost 35% of England's population (1.4 million people) died of the plague. In other parts of Europe, the Black Death killed almost half of the population. Imagine what this would be like. A huge part of the population was sick and dying. Who would take care of all these sick people? Who would work on the farms to grow food? Who would take care of the children? No one had answers to these questions. It was a terrible time. Many of the people who survived the plague lost their faith and confidence in the feudal lords.

## A Punishment from God?

Some people thought the Black Death was a punishment from God. Some believed Jews had caused the plague by putting poison in the water. Others thought something in the air carried the disease. Today, we understand more about illnesses. We know there were rats with fleas infected with bubonic plague aboard the ships. The bite of one of these fleas could infect a person, and that person could infect other family members, neighbors, or others with whom they came into contact. At first, the infected person felt a bump in the neck or on another part of the body. Black spots soon appeared all over the person's skin. The sick person's face became red, and they began sneezing, coughing, and spitting up blood. Finally the person died.

## No Cures or Medicines

Today, we have medicines to cure diseases such as the plague. During that time, however, doctors had no cure and no medicines to ease a person's pain. Hospitals were overcrowded. Nuns nursed people who had the plague. Sometimes they put two patients in the same bed not knowing that this helped to spread the disease. Some people thought oranges covered with cloves or peeled onions would cure them. Some people tried to protect themselves from the plague by carrying little bags filled with flower petals. "Ring Around the Rosie," a song children still sing today, tells what happened to the victims of the plague.

## "Ring Around the Rosie"

Ring around the rosie,
A pocketful of posie,
Ashes, ashes
All fall down.

(the "rosie" is the sick person whose face becomes very red)
(the "posie" is the bag filled with flower petals)
("ashes, ashes" is the sneezing sound the sick person makes)
(the sick person falls down in death)

## Consequences of the Plague

By 1351, the Black Death weakened. However, there were many consequences of the Black Death for the people who had survived. People began to have different ideas about life and death. There were fewer people to do the work and conflicts grew between peasants and the nobles. Many people also lost respect for the church. The time was right for big changes in European society. In the end, millions of Europeans died of the Black Death. Agnolo di Tura, a man from the Italian city-state of Siena, wrote about how the plague affected his community between May 1348 and September 1348. He reported that 52,000 people died in Siena and another 28,000 people died in the outlying areas. Below you can read how he described the events.

**mortality:** death
**stupefy:** to stun or astonish

### Agnolo di Tura Describes the Plague

The **mortality** began in Siena in May [1348]. It was a cruel and horrible thing; and I do not know where to begin to tell of the cruelty and the pitiless ways. It seemed to almost everyone that one became **stupefied** by seeing the pain. And it is impossible for the human tongue to recount the awful thing. ... And the victims died almost immediately. They would swell beneath their armpits and in their groins, and fall over dead while talking. Father abandoned child, wife husband, one brother another, for this illness seemed to strike through the breath and sight. And so they died. And none could be found to bury the dead for money or friendship. Members of a household brought their dead to a ditch as best they could, without priest. ... Nor did the death bell sound. ... And they died by the hundreds both day and night, and all were thrown in those ditches and covered over with earth. And as soon as those ditches were filled more were dug ... . And I ... buried my five children with my own hands ... There was no one who wept for any death, for all awaited death. And so many died that all believed that it was the end of the world. ...

### Analyze the Source!

1. Read the excerpt and tell in your own words what it says.

2. How does this excerpt help you learn about the culture and medical technology of Europe during the Middle Ages?

3. How do you think the plague affected the economy of Europe?

# The Persecution of the Jews

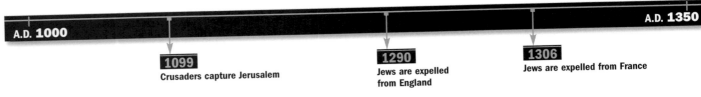

**A.D. 1000** ———————————————————————————————— **A.D. 1350**

**1099**
Crusaders capture Jerusalem

**1290**
Jews are expelled
from England

**1306**
Jews are expelled from France

▲ Jews were forced out of England in 1290, and then forced to leave France in 1306. During this period in European history, most people were Christian.

**exempt:** to be freed from an obligation or duty
**magistrate:** an officer of the law

When things go wrong, people often try to blame someone. Throughout history, different peoples have blamed Jews for many of the world's problems. How and why the Jewish population has been the object of prejudice is a complex subject. Jews have had no more to do with any particular problem than other groups. However, this fact has not stopped people from placing blame for problems on Jews. From the time of the crusaders' capture of Jerusalem in 1099 to the beginning of the Black Death in Europe around 1347, Jews in Europe suffered increasing persecution. They were forced out of England in 1290, and then forced to leave France in 1306. Their property also was taken from them. When the bubonic plague spread to Germany, people in many German cities expelled and even killed Jews. Some Christian Church officials tried to save them, but people blamed Jews for the spread of the plague. In the later Middle Ages, greed, fear, and ignorance all played a part in the rise of anti-Jewish feelings.

Below is an excerpt from a document written during the mid-1300s. The writer reported that a group of Jews had "confessed" that they put poison into the town wells. At the time no one knew what caused the plague. Doctors thought it was spread through the air and that a person could catch it by taking a bath. 🕮

## Analyze the Source!

1. Read the excerpt and tell in your own words what it says.

2. How does this excerpt help you learn about the culture and history of Europe during the Middle Ages? How does it help you learn about law and justice during this period?

3. During the Middle Ages, people in Europe became more intolerant of other religious ideas. Is intolerance of different religious ideas still a problem today? Explain your answer.

## A Report that Jews Poisoned the Town Wells

To the Noble and prudent **Magistrates**, Council and Community of the Town of Strasbourg [a town on the border of France and Germany], from the Deputy of the Lord Magistrate at Chablias. I am given to understand that you are desirous of being made acquainted with the confession of the Jews and with the evidence brought against them ... I therefore inform you by this present communication that ... [we] have received a copy of inquisitions and confessions of the Jews who were recently in their territory and were accused of having placed poison in the wells and in many other places, and that these accusations have proved quite true, as many Jews have been submitted to torture and some were **exempted** because they confessed and were brought before another court and burnt.

# The Peasant Revolts

A.D. **1300**

A.D. **1500**

**1337-1453**
The Hundred Years' War

**1358**
French peasants revolt

**1380**
English peasants oppose a tax on all adult males

**1381**
English peasants revolt

During the Middle Ages, a peasant's life was a hard life. Peasants had to pay the lord of the manor special fees to grind their grain. They had to work on his land. They needed his permission to marry. They had to pay taxes to support the wars that nobles became involved in. When crops were bad, peasants did not have enough to eat. Diseases that periodically spread across Europe sickened some and killed others. The Black Death was particularly deadly. Peasants had always looked to the nobles for protection, but the lords did not protect them from famine, disease, and war. Over time, they became tired of paying high taxes to the lords. They had had enough.

## Peasant Revolts in France

Throughout Europe, but especially in France and England, peasants sometimes rose up against the nobles. These uprisings are called peasant revolts. French peasants became very unhappy when the French nobles raised their taxes to pay for the Hundred Years' War. In 1358, French peasants revolted. Large groups of peasants rioted in the countryside. At first, the nobles were on the defensive. Eventually, they organized themselves and crushed the revolt. However, that did not end the revolts in France. Over the next 75 years, other serious revolts sprang up throughout different parts of France.

## The Peasants' Revolt of 1381

In 1381, a group of almost 100,000 English peasants revolted. Historians think it was the largest single uprising during the Middle Ages. The Peasants' Revolt of 1381 took place over a large portion of southwest England. The economic consequences of the Black Death contributed greatly to the revolt. After the Black Death, fewer peasants were available to work. They demanded higher pay for their labor. Not surprisingly, wealthy landlords tried to pay as little as possible. Another factor that contributed to the revolt was that the upper classes tried to keep the peasants from gaining higher social status in the society. Since the late 1200s, English peasants had seen an improvement in their living and working conditions. They were frustrated to be told that they could not earn higher pay or gain higher social status.

▲ French and English peasants revolted against the nobles in the 1300s.

▲ Peasants grew more food during medieval times, but often they did not have enough to eat.

Chapter 14: The Middle Ages **291**

When things seemed as if they could not get worse, the English government imposed a head tax on all adult males. In 1380, peasants strongly opposed this tax. In 1381, when the government called again for the tax, the peasants began to revolt. It started with attacks on the tax collectors, and then peasants began to rob and burn castles and manors. Many nobles were murdered, including the archbishop of Canterbury who had ordered the collection of the tax.

## Ending the Revolt

England's King Richard II, who ruled from 1377-1399, met with the leaders of the revolt. He agreed to many of the peasant's demands, including granting their freedom. However, he did not keep his word. He quickly crushed the uprising with his strong army. After the revolt was over, the nobility gave little thought to what had led to this violent revolt. Below is an excerpt from a document written at the time of the Peasants' Revolt of 1381. We do not know who wrote this document, but it appears to be a government or church official in London.

▲ After the Black Death, fewer peasants were available for work. Since the supply of labor was smaller, peasants thought they could demand higher pay for their work.

## Analyze the Source!

1. Read the excerpt and tell in your own words what it says.

2. How does this excerpt help you learn about law and justice during this period?

3. During the Middle Ages, peasants rebelled against nobles for many different reasons. Which do you think is the most important? Why? Why do you think peasants turned to violence?

### About the Peasant Revolt of 1381

[The peasants] went to various towns and raised the people, whether they wished to do so or not, until they had gathered together fully 60,000. And as they journey towards London they encountered various lawyers and twelve knights of the king and the countryside, and they took them and made them swear to support them, or otherwise would be beheaded. And they wrought much damage in Kent [an English city] and especially to Thomas Haselden, a servant of the Duke of Lancaster, because of their hatred for the duke. They **rased** his manors to the ground and all his houses, and sold his beasts—his horses, oxen, cows, sheep, and pigs—and all his stores of corn, at cheap rates. ... And when the king heard of their doings he sent his messengers to them ... to ask them why they were behaving in this fashion and why they were raising a rebellion in the land. And they returned answer by his messengers that they were rising to deliver him and to destroy the traitors to him [the nobles] and to his kingdom.

**rase:** to tear down

# The Trial of JOAN OF ARC

**A.D. 1400**                                                  **A.D. 1450**

**1412-1431**
Joan of Arc

**1429**
Joan leads an army to victory
in the battle of Orleans

**1431**
Joan is burned at the stake

Joan of Arc was born to a religious French family in 1412. As a young girl, she felt called by God to drive the English out of France. She also believed it was her duty to help the dauphin— the man in line to become the French ruler—become king. In 1429, the 17-year-old Joan cut her hair short, dressed like a man, and went to see the dauphin. She convinced him to let her lead an army into battle. It seemed almost a miracle that she led the French to victory in the battle of Orleans. She later led the French to four other victories before English allies in France captured her. Church and government leaders tried her as a heretic and a witch. They put her on trial for these crimes and executed her in 1431. The evidence for these crimes was the way she dressed and the voices she reported hearing. Below is an excerpt from the trial of Joan of Arc where this evidence was revealed.

▲ In 1920, the pope declared Joan of Arc a saint. This picture of St. Joan of Arc shows her as a soldier and a saint. She is a national hero in France.

## From the Trial of Joan of Arc
On Monday following, the day after Holy Trinity Sunday, we the said judges repaired to Jeanne's [Joan's] prison to observe her state and disposition.

Now because the said Jeanne was wearing a man's dress, a short mantle, a hood, a doublet, and other garment used by men (which at our order she had recently put off in favor of woman's dress), we questioned her to find out when and for what reason she had resumed man's dress and rejected woman's clothes. ... she answered that she ... preferred man's to woman's dress. ...

Asked for what reason she had assumed male costume, she answered that it was more lawful and convenient for her to wear it, since she was among men, than to wear woman's dress. She said she had resumed it because the promises made to her had not been kept, which were to permit her to go to Mass and ..., and to take off her chains.

... we asked her whether she had not since Thursday heard the voices of St. Catherine and St. Margaret. She answered yes. ... Asked if she believed the voices to be St. Catherine and St. Margaret, she answered "Yes, and they came from God."

... If the judges wished, she would once more wear woman's dress, but for the rest she would do no more.

### Analyze the Source!
1. Read the excerpt and tell in your own words what it says.

2. How does this excerpt help you learn about the culture and history of Europe during the Middle Ages?

3. Why do you think the judges considered her dressing like a man as evidence that she was a witch? Why do you think the judges considered her hearing the voices of saints as evidence that she was a heretic?

# Medieval Meals

What did you have to eat today? A hamburger? Burrito? Spring roll? Oatmeal? Did you buy the food you ate at a fast food restaurant or did you have it at home? Did you enjoy the food, or was it just fuel to put in your body to keep you going? Today, many Americans see meals as pleasurable events. Many Americans also have tremendous choices in terms of the foods that are available. "What do you want to eat?" is a question most of us ask or answer every day. Was this always the case? For most people in the past and many people living in parts of the world today, the more relevant question is:

"Will I have anything to eat?" People have not always had a choice about what to eat. However, during the Middle Ages, food and different ways to prepare it were becoming important topics. We have many clues about what some groups of people ate during the Middle Ages. We see these clues in paintings as well as in written accounts of life during the time. We also have clues to food during the Middle Ages by reading recipes people wrote down so they would remember how to make medieval favorites. Here are several recipes from an English cookbook that was written in the 1400s.

## Pork Pie

Take fresh pork, cut it and grind it on a mortar [a very hard bowl in which softer substances are ground], and put it into a fair vessel [container]. Take the white and the yokes of eggs, and strain into a vessel through a strainer, and mix with the pork. Then take pines [seeds of fir or pepper pines], currants [berries], and fry them in fresh grease, and add powdered pepper, ginger, cinnamon, sugar, saffron [a spice], and salt; and put all in a pie crust, and set on the crust lid above it, pines, cut dates, raisins, and small birds, or hard yokes of eggs; and if you use birds, fry them in a little grease, before you put them on the pie crust, and gild [make golden] with yokes of eggs, and saffron. Bake the pie until it is done and then serve.

# Fruit Pudding

Take strawberries, and wash them, in season, in good red wine; then strain through a cloth, and put them in a pot with good almond milk; cover it with wheat flour or rice flour, and make it thick, and let it boil, and add currants [berries], saffron [a spice], pepper, plenty of sugar, powdered ginger, cinnamon, galingale [a spice like ginger]; make it acid with vinegar, and add a little white grease; color it with alkanet [a red dye made from plant roots], and mix it together, sprinkle it with the grains of pomegranate, and then serve it up.

# Fritters

Take the yolks of eggs, put them through a strainer, add fair flour, yeast, and ale; stir in together until it is thick. Take pared [peeled] apples, cut them thick like sacramental wafers [bread given at communion], lay them in the batter; then put them into a frying pan, and fry them in fair grease or butter until they are golden brown. Then put them in dishes and strew [sprinkle] sugar on them enough, and serve.

## What Do You Think?

**1.** How do these recipes help you learn about the culture and history of Europe during the Middle Ages?

**2.** Based on these recipes, compare the food people ate during the Middle Ages with the food Americans eat today.

# FRANCESCO PETRARCH —
# The Father of the Renaissance

**A.D. 1200**            **A.D. 1500**

**1304-1374**
Petrarch

**c. 1350**
The Renaissance begins

EUROPE

ITALY

Mediterranean Sea

▲ Petrarch was one of the greatest writers of the Italian Renaissance.

Francesco Petrarch, the man many people call the "father of the Renaissance," was born in 1304. He was one of the greatest writers of the Italian Renaissance. Petrarch believed human beings could make choices in their lives and ask questions. His ideas were very different from others who thought people should simply follow the teachings of the church.

In addition to writing, Petrarch was very interested in learning, and he liked to collect and read books. Petrarch thought people of his time were entering a new age of rediscovery and learning. In the paragraph below, you can read what Petrarch wrote about the importance of books in his life. 📖

## Petrarch Describes the Importance of Books

I cannot get enough books. It may be that I have already more than I need, but it is with books as it is with other things: success in **acquisition spurs** the desire to get still more. Books, indeed, have a special charm. Gold, silver, gems, ... a house of marble, a well-tilled field, paintings, a **steed** with splendid trappings—things such as these give a silent and superficial pleasure. Books delight us through and through, they talk with us, they give us good counsel, they enter into a living and intimate companionship with us.

## Analyze the Source!

1. Read the excerpt and tell in your own words what it says.

2. How does this excerpt help you learn about education in this period?

3. Do you agree or disagree with Petrarch's feelings about books? Why or why not?

**acquisition:** gaining
**spur:** to urge
**steed:** horse

# JOHANNES GUTENBERG —
# The Father of Modern Printing

A.D. **1300**                                                                                                                          A.D. **1500**

**c. 1394-1468**
Johannes Gutenberg

**1455**
Gutenberg prints
the Gutenberg Bible

**1456**
Gutenberg loses
his printing press

**1457**
Gutenberg starts a new
printing business

Today, most people don't think that reading a book is a very unusual thing to do. But 600 years ago, reading a book was very uncommon for most people. Books were so expensive that only universities, churches, or very wealthy people could buy them. One of the reasons books were so expensive is that they were produced by woodcarving or had to be copied by hand. Just think how long it would take you to copy an entire book by hand!

## A Revolution in Printing

Why did people stop copying books by hand and start printing them using machines? Who was the leader of this revolution in printing? Many people say that Johannes Gutenberg is the person most responsible for beginning the modern age of printing.

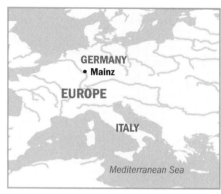

▲ Johannes Gutenberg was born in Mainz, Germany sometime between 1394 and 1399.

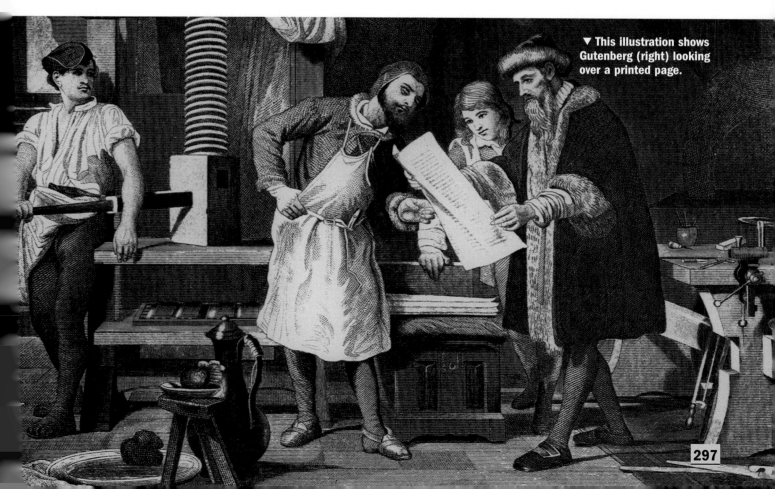

▼ This illustration shows Gutenberg (right) looking over a printed page.

**frame:** a structure, such as pieces of wood nailed together, to hold something inside

**mold:** a form into which something is poured

**parchment:** the skin of a sheep or goat prepared for writing or painting upon

**trinket:** any small ornament, such as a small piece of jewelry

**vellum:** the skin of a calf or lamb prepared for writing or painting upon

Gutenberg did not invent the first printing press. Hundreds of years earlier, the Chinese had invented a printing press. But no one in Europe knew about it, so we could say that Johannes Gutenberg was the first person in Europe to develop the printing press. This was the beginning of modern printing in the Western world.

## Gutenberg's Life

We don't know very much about Johannes Gutenberg. We know he was born in Mainz, Germany. Historians think he was born sometime between 1394 and 1399. We also know his parents were members of the upper class. As a young man, he learned how to work with gold and other metals. At first, he made **trinkets** by pouring melted metal into **molds**. When the metal cooled, he took the object out of the mold. Many of these objects had religious symbols and designs. People were very interested in buying these religious objects.

## A Bright Idea

As Gutenberg was making these trinkets, he had a wonderful idea. If he could make trinkets this way, why couldn't he make molds for each of the letters in the alphabet? He could arrange the letters into words and place the words together to make sentences. Then he could put the sentences together to make an entire page of writing. He started to work on this idea around 1436. He decided to make all the letters the same size so that they would fit easily into a **frame**. After all the letters were set in the frame, he put ink on them and then pressed **parchment**, **vellum**, or paper against the letters. Later he could take the letters apart and make a different page of writing. It was a lot of work to set a page of writing. However, once the work was done, he could print many pages. It took a long time and many different experiments for Gutenberg to get the letters, the ink, and the printing press just right. It also took a lot of money—more money than he had. Gutenberg had to borrow money to pay for his work.

## The Gutenberg Bible

Historians think that between 1450 and 1455, Gutenberg printed many small books and even a calendar using his printing press and movable type. However, his greatest achievement was the book he printed in 1455. He did not write or translate this book, but it is called the Gutenberg Bible. We think he printed about 200 copies of the Gutenberg Bible. They are sometimes called the "42-line Bibles" because there are two columns of type on each page and almost every page has 42 lines of type. Only about 20 copies of the original Gutenberg Bible remain. One copy of the Gutenberg Bible is in the Library of Congress in Washington, D.C.

This printing press is one person's idea of what Gutenberg's invention looked like. The printing press made it possible for more people to read the Bible and many other written texts.

## Obstacles to Success

The story of Johannes Gutenberg and his printing press is the story of a man who faced many hardships. In 1456, when he could not pay back the money he borrowed to finish printing the Gutenberg Bible, he lost everything. He had to give his printing press and all his other printing equipment to the men who had lent him the money. The Gutenberg Bible was one of the most beautiful books of this age, but Gutenberg did not make any money from it. However, he did not give up. He started a new printing business in 1457 and printed another Bible, a dictionary, calendars, and other materials until his death in 1468.

That was almost 600 years ago. We still remember Johannes Gutenberg today because his invention made it much easier to print books and other writings. By 1500, about 1,000 European printers had printed more than nine million books. For the first time in history, it was possible for average people to buy books on many different subjects. This made more people want to learn to read. You could say that Johannes Gutenberg was one of the leaders of the new information age. 📖

### What Do You Think?

1. What advantages did Johannes Gutenberg have in life? What obstacles did he face?

2. How did Gutenberg get ideas? How do people today get ideas?

3. Thomas Edison, a famous American inventor, said, "There is no substitute for hard work." What does this mean? Do you think Gutenberg would have agreed or disagreed with this statement? Why?

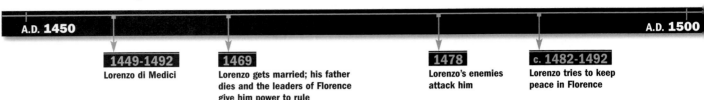

# LORENZO DI MEDICI —
# A Magnificent Patron of the Arts

A.D. **1450**                                                                 A.D. **1500**

| **1449-1492** | **1469** | **1478** | **c. 1482-1492** |
|---|---|---|---|
| Lorenzo di Medici | Lorenzo gets married; his father dies and the leaders of Florence give him power to rule | Lorenzo's enemies attack him | Lorenzo tries to keep peace in Florence |

EUROPE

• Florence

**ITALY**

*Mediterranean Sea*

▲ **Lorenzo di Medici invited artists such as Michelangelo, Sandro Botticelli, and Domenico Ghirlandaio to spend time in Florence. He commissioned Sandro Botticelli to paint "The Birth of Venus."**

---

**represent:** to stand for; to serve as the spokesperson or agent for
**tutor:** a person who teaches only one or two students at a time

---

During the Renaissance, Florence was one of the most important cities in the world. It was ruled by about 800 of the city's richest families. One of the richest and most powerful families in Florence was the Medici family. One of the most important members of this family was Lorenzo di Medici.

## Early Life

Lorenzo di Medici was born on January 1, 1449. His family had a rich and successful banking business. They lived in a palace and had everything they wanted. His father hired **tutors** to teach young Lorenzo about many different subjects. Lorenzo was a very good student and learned quickly. He studied history, politics, art, and science. When he was 15 years old, Lorenzo began to **represent** his family at important events in Florence. He even represented his family in meetings with important people in other rich Italian city-states such as Milan, Naples, and Venice.

## Becoming a Powerful Leader

It is said that Lorenzo di Medici was tall and strong, but not very handsome. People said he had a "joyful nature," was very kind, and he liked to sing, tell jokes, and write poetry. He enjoyed hunting and going to parades and dances with his friends. He also liked to go to the many festivals that were held in Florence. In 1469, several events changed his life. First, he got married. Then, six months later, his father died. Two days after his father's death, the leaders of Florence visited him with an important request. They wanted Lorenzo to take over his father's position of power in Florence. They did not want Lorenzo to have an official title such as king or prince, but increasingly he would gain the power to rule like one.

## Plots against Lorenzo di Medici and His Family

The Medicis had enemies. Many rich Florentine families were jealous of Lorenzo di Medici and his family's power and money. One of these enemies tried to kill Lorenzo and his brother Giuliano. They planned their attack for Sunday, April 26, 1478.

◀ In 1459, Renaissance artist Benozzo Gozzoli was chosen to decorate the chapel walls in the Medici family's palace. One picture is called "The Procession of the Magi." The youngest of the Magi—wise men—is shown here. He is said to look like Lorenzo di Medici as a young boy.

As the two brothers, Lorenzo and Giuliano, entered the cathedral to attend church services, some men grabbed them. The men began stabbing Lorenzo and Giuliano with **daggers**. Lorenzo got away, but his brother was not as quick. Giuliano was stabbed many times and died almost immediately.

Lorenzo, his family, and the people of Florence were very angry about this attack. The people of Florence admired Lorenzo and his family. Within a few days, the killers were captured and killed. The following years were difficult for Lorenzo and his family. The family began to have financial problems. There always seemed to be some threat to peace in the city. Men tried to kill Lorenzo again and other families tried to ruin him financially. However, during the last 10 years of his life, Lorenzo tried to keep peace in Florence, with the other Italian city-states, and with people from other regions.

## A Tyrant or Admired Leader?

During this time, Lorenzo became more powerful. His enemies called him a tyrant. One person said, "If Florence was to have a tyrant, she could never have found a better or more delightful one."

**dagger:** a short, pointed knife used as a weapon

Many of the poor people of the city agreed with this view because Lorenzo made sure they had enough food to eat. Artists and scholars also admired Lorenzo. First, he treated the artists who worked for him with respect and kindness. He saw artists and scholars as people with special gifts. He did not treat them like common workers. Another reason why artists and scholars admired Lorenzo was because he used his wealth and the wealth of Florence to support their work.

## Supporting Promising Artists

Lorenzo started a school for promising young artists. One of the first students at this school was the young artist Michelangelo who went on to become one of the greatest sculptors who ever lived. Michelangelo is also remembered for his paintings on the ceiling of the Sistine Chapel in Rome. Leonardo da Vinci was another artist Lorenzo supported and encouraged. Today, people consider Leonardo da Vinci one of the greatest artists, inventors, and thinkers of all time. In addition to supporting artists directly, Lorenzo encouraged other wealthy Florentines to hire artists to create sculptures, paintings, and other works of art. Some of these wealthy patrons wanted artists to make art in honor of God. Some wanted art to make their city a more beautiful place. Other patrons wanted art to glorify themselves. Lorenzo also supported writers and scholars. He spent a great deal of money on books for his private library. He also gave money to support the University of Florence.

## Lorenzo the Magnificent

When Lorenzo died in April 1492, all the people of Florence came to his funeral. He was buried next to his brother Giuliano. Other men in the family were named Lorenzo di Medici, but this Lorenzo is the one history books refer to as "Lorenzo the Magnificent."

### What Do You Think?

1. What advantages did Lorenzo di Medici have in life? What obstacles did he face?

2. Lorenzo di Medici could have used his wealth for any purpose. Why do you think he used it to support the arts?

3. What do you think is Lorenzo di Medici's greatest achievement? Give reasons for your answer.

▼ Artists and scholars admired Lorenzo because he used his wealth and the wealth of Florence to support their work. A Florentine architect who lived during the Renaissance, Filippo Brunelleschi (broo-nuh-LES-kee), built a beautiful dome on the city's cathedral, which is called the Duomo. It was considered an engineering marvel.

# LEONARDO DA VINCI —
# Artist, Inventor, and Thinker

A.D. **1300**                                                                                                    A.D. **1550**

**1452-1519**
Leonardo da Vinci

**c. 1463**
Leonardo becomes an apprentice
to artist Andrea del Verrocchio

**1482**
Leonardo
goes to Milan

**1516**
Leonardo goes to
live in France

Leonardo da Vinci is one of the greatest artists, inventors, and thinkers who ever lived. He was born on April 15, 1452 in the small town of Vinci, about 20 miles from Florence. Leonardo was born in an exciting time in art history—during the Renaissance. And he was born in the area where the Renaissance began. Leonardo's father was a leading citizen of the community of Vinci.

## Lots of Advantages?

You might think that Leonardo was a very lucky boy to have such advantages. However, he faced problems, too. His mother was only a peasant girl, and she was not married to his father. There were strict rules for children whose parents were not married. For example, they could not go to the university. Nor could they become doctors or lawyers or bankers. However, Leonardo had great talents. People said he could sing beautifully, but his greatest skill seemed to be drawing.

▲ Leonardo da Vinci is remembered as one of the greatest artists, inventors, and thinkers of all time.

◄ One of da Vinci's most famous paintings is the "Mona Lisa." It shows a woman with a curious smile on her face.

## Becoming an Apprentice

When Leonardo was about 11 or 12, his father took him from the little town of Vinci to the city of Florence. Leonardo became an **apprentice** to a famous artist named Andrea del Verrocchio. At first, Leonardo ran errands, swept the floor, and did other little jobs around the artist's workshop. Later he learned to make colors and brushes.

**apprentice:** a person who goes to work for another person for a specific period of time; in return for this work, the apprentice learns a trade, art, or business

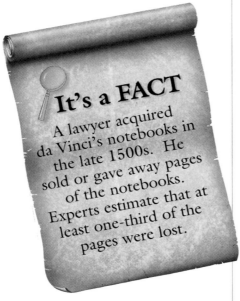

Da Vinci practiced drawing and helped with the paintings and sculptures Verrocchio was making. When he was about 20, Leonardo joined the painters' guild in Florence and worked there for 10 years. When he was 30, Leonardo decided to go north to Milan. Leonardo sent a letter to the powerful ruler of Milan, Duke Ludovico Sforza, asking for work. In the letter, he did not focus on his artistic skills. Instead, he talked mostly about his ideas for "machines of war" and about architecture.

## Different Ideas

The duke did not answer Leonardo's letter—at least not right away. So Leonardo began to paint a picture for a local church in Milan. The monks who hired him were very clear about the kind of picture they wanted. They said it should be very traditional, like all the pictures they had ever seen. But Leonardo had other ideas. He painted people in the picture who looked like real people. They were not stiff and serious figures. The monks and others were surprised at this new way of painting, and many admired his work. One of the admirers was the duke, who decided to become Leonardo's patron. Leonardo stayed in Milan and worked for the duke until 1499. Leonardo designed costumes, thought of a way to heat bath water, designed new weapons, and painted pictures of important people and other subjects.

## "The Last Supper"

One of the most famous pictures Leonardo painted during this time is called "The Last Supper." The duke wanted a picture painted for a local church. Leonardo decided to paint the picture on a wall in the room where the monks ate. "The Last Supper" showed Jesus and his followers at dinner the night before Jesus was killed. The way Leonardo painted the picture on the wall almost made it seem as if Jesus and his followers were eating with the monks! Leonardo used a new way of painting for this picture. Unfortunately, his experiment was not a success. The paint started to chip off almost right away. Still, many people say it is one of the most beautiful pictures in the world.

## Leonardo's Notebooks

Leonardo wrote pages and pages of notes about his work and about the things he saw around him. He wrote notes about what he learned about the human body. He wrote notes about experiments he conducted. He also wrote notes about his inventions, including such things as a flying machine. He drew pictures to illustrate many of these ideas. He wrote his notes backwards, which led some to think that he was trying to keep others from stealing his ideas. Sometimes he wrote his notes in code, which was a much more effective way to keep his secrets.

### What Do You Think?

**1.** What advantages did Leonardo da Vinci have in life? What obstacles did he face?

**2.** Why do you think Leonardo's letter to the duke of Milan talked mostly about "machines of war" and architecture?

**3.** What do you think is Leonardo da Vinci's greatest achievement? Give reasons for your answer.

## Meeting Other Renaissance Masters

Leonardo's years in Milan ended in 1499 when a French army attacked and took the duke prisoner. Leonardo traveled all over Italy for the next 16 years working for different patrons. One of the people he met during this time was Niccolo Machiavelli, a **diplomat** from Florence. Machiavelli helped Leonardo get work in Florence. Leonardo was asked to paint a battle scene in a government building. A young artist named Michelangelo was asked to paint a second picture in the same building. Leonardo and Michelangelo did not like each other very much. They often argued and insulted each another. In the end, for different reasons, neither man finished his painting.

## Facing Many Problems

During this time, Leonardo had to face many problems. After his father and uncle died, the family fought about who would get their money. In the end, Leonardo did not get anything because his father and mother never married. Leonardo also was getting old and was often sick. He had never married and did not have children to take care of him. Then, around 1516, something wonderful happened. The king of France invited Leonardo to come to France. The king promised to pay him well and to give him a place to live. Leonardo agreed happily and set out for France. He took his notebooks and several paintings along with him. One of these paintings is probably the most famous painting in the world. It is a picture of a woman smiling. Did you guess the "Mona Lisa"? If so, you are right! This painting now hangs in the Louvre, a museum in France.

Leonardo lived as the king's honored guest until he died at the age of 67 on May 2, 1519. Today when people hear the name "Leonardo da Vinci," they remember one of the greatest artists, inventors, and thinkers of all time. 📖

▲ **This statue of da Vinci stands in front of the Uffizi Gallery in Florence.**

**diplomat:** a person who represents a government in relations with other governments

# Reader's Theater Presents ...

# "What Will Becon of This Boy?"

**DIRECTIONS:** Practice reading the script. When the script says, "ALL," everyone in the class joins in the reading. Read with expr

## ROLES:

★ NARRATOR 1
★ NARRATOR 2
★ ALL
★ TOWNSWOMEN
★ TOWNSMEN
★ UNCLE FRANCESCO
★ LEONARDO

**NARRATOR 1:** On April 15, 1452 a boy named Leonardo was born. His father was a leading citizen of the community. He was responsible for preparing legal documents. This was an important job.

**NARRATOR 2:** But Leonardo's mother was only a peasant girl. And she was not married to Leonardo's father.

**ALL:** What difference did that make?

**NARRATOR 2:** Well, that meant Leonardo could not go to the university. He could not become a doctor or lawyer or a banker.

**NARRATOR 1:** This might have been a terrible problem for other boys. However, young Leonardo was quite different.

**TOWNSWOMEN:** Nothing good will become of that boy. He is too curious! Yesterday, he asked why the rainbow had so many colors.

**TOWNSMEN:** Last week he spent an entire morning building a castle out of mud. This was

no ordinary castle. It had towers and gates!

**TOWNSWOMEN:** What about all the time he spends watching ants and bees?

**TOWNSMEN:** And drawing pictures?

**TOWNSWOMEN:** Why does he collect rocks and leaves and stare at the clouds?

**TOWNSMEN:** Why does he draw pictures of tools, jars, and bundles of straw?

**ALL:** What will become of this boy?

**UNCLE FRANCESCO:** Stop it! I am proud of Leonardo. He is a bright and curious boy. Some day you will see how wrong you are about him!

**LEONARDO:** Thank you, Uncle Francesco, for believing in me. Come quick. I want to show you the flying machine I made. I am going to fly like a bird!

**ALL:** Oh no. A flying machine?

**NARRATOR 1:** Some people thought Leonardo would never become successful.

**NARRATOR 2:** They thought he would never choose one thing and become really good at it.

**ALL:** Were they right?

**NARRATOR 1:** Yes and no.

**NARRATOR 2:** Leonardo did not choose to do one thing. He decided to do many things—engineering, architecture, painting, and inventing. He even designed costumes!

**NARRATOR 1:** And he became very good at all these things. He wrote pages and pages of notes about his ideas. And he drew lots of pictures of his ideas.

**ALL:** Can we read his notes?

**NARRATOR 2:** You can if you have a mirror and know Italian.

**ALL:** Why do we need a mirror?

**NARRATOR 1:** Because Leonardo wrote his notes backwards.

**ALL:** What a bright idea!

**NARRATOR 2:** Today, when you hear the name "Leonardo da Vinci," think of the curious and bright little boy who became one of the greatest artists, inventors, and thinkers of all time. 📖

# ISABELLA D'ESTE —
# Renaissance Princess

A.D. **1400**

A.D. **1550**

**1452-1519**
Leonardo da Vinci

**1474-1539**
Isabella d'Este

**1504**
Isabella writes to
Leonardo da Vinci

▲ **This is a drawing of a young woman during the Renaissance. Isabella helped educate young women for nontraditional roles in society.**

Isabella d'Este was born in 1474 to one of the oldest ruling families of Italy. In fact, her father was the Duke of Ferrara. Isabella lived a privileged life and was highly educated. By the time she was 16, she spoke Latin and Greek and was an accomplished musician and dancer. When she married the Duke of Mantua, she was well prepared to be a noble Renaissance wife. After her husband died, she became a patron of the arts. She also showed great leadership in governing the state of Mantua.

Isabella was concerned about the role of women during this time. She opened a school to help educate young women for nontraditional roles in society. During her lifetime, Isabella wrote more than 2,000 letters on many different subjects. One person she wrote to was Leonardo da Vinci. Leonardo had stopped at Isabella's home one day. While he was there, he drew a quick picture—a sketch—of Isabella. Below you can read part of the letter she wrote to Leonardo after he left. Isabella never received her painting from Leonardo. □

**cherish:** to hope for
**consent:** to agree
**affirmative:** a "yes" answer

## Isabella's Letter to Leonardo da Vinci

To Master Leonardo Vinci, the painter: Hearing that you are settled in Florence, we have begun to hope that our **cherished** desire to obtain a work by your hand may be at length realized.

... if you will **consent** to gratify this our great desire, remember that apart from the payment, which you shall fix yourself, we remain so deeply obliged to you that our sole desire will be to do what you wish, and from this time forth we are ready to do your service and pleasure, hoping to receive an answer in the **affirmative**.

—Mantua, May 14, 1504

## Analyze the Source!

1. Read this excerpt and tell in your own words what it says.

2. How does this excerpt help you learn about the culture and history of Europe during the Renaissance?

3. Why do people want to have pictures of themselves?

# "It Is Not Seemly for a Woman ..." The Role of Women During the Renaissance

Do men and women have different roles in life? Should women be able to do the same jobs as men? Throughout history, people have thought about these questions. However, the answers they came up with may be very different from the answers people might give today.

The excerpt below is from *The Courtier*, one of the most important books of the Renaissance. Baldassare Castiglione wrote this book around 1516. It was intended to be a guide for men who wanted to become gentlemen. The book said gentlemen should be able to sing, play a musical instrument, and speak and write well. Gentlemen also should dress well, be guided by reason, know how to fight, and ride a horse well. *The Courtier* also described a woman's role in Renaissance society. Below is an excerpt from *The Courtier* about the role of women. 📖

### From *The Courtier*

It is not **seemly** for a woman to handle weapons, ride, play tennis, wrestle, and do many other things that are **suited** to men. A woman if married should have the ability to manage her husband's **property** and house and children.

... it is well for a woman to have a certain soft and delicate tenderness, with an air of feminine sweetness in her every movement. ... It also seems to me that good looks are more important to her than to the courtier, for much is lacking to a woman who lacks beauty.

**property:** all things a person owns
**seemly:** proper; socially acceptable
**suited:** acceptable; appropriate

### Analyze the Source!

1. How does this excerpt help you learn about men and women during this period?

2. Do you agree with Castiglione's view of the proper role of a woman? Explain your answer.

# NICCOLO MACHIAVELLI —
# Father of Political Science

A.D. **1400**       A.D. **1600**

**1449-1492**
Lorenzo di Medici

**1469-1527**
Niccolo Machiavelli

**1513**
Machiavelli is arrested
and sent to prison

T oday, when people hear the word "Machiavelli," they think of a person who wants power and who will do anything to get it. Who was this man called Machiavelli? Why do people have the idea of a power-hungry person when they hear his name?

### Early Life

Niccolo Machiavelli was born on May 3, 1469 in Florence, Italy. His family was wealthy and made sure he had a good education in the arts and literature. During the Renaissance, Florence was one of the most important cities in the world. Like other Italian city-states, rich families ruled Florence. The leaders of the city-states fought other families and other city-states to keep their power and to get more power.

### A Government Career

Florence was an exciting place to be during this time, especially for a young man who loved his city and wanted to see it become more powerful. Niccolo Machiavelli was such a young man. He was patriotic and wanted to serve Florence, his city-state. Machiavelli began his **career** by working as a **clerk** in the government of Florence. During this time, the Medici family was very important and powerful. But after Lorenzo di Medici, one of the most powerful Medici leaders, died in 1492, Florence had many problems. It no longer had as much power as it once did. Machiavelli continued to work for the government and his jobs became more important. In 1498, he was asked to be one of the leaders of a council responsible for Florence's military. This council also was responsible for Florence's diplomacy—its relations with other governments. As a leader in the group, Machiavelli became one of Florence's most important diplomats.

▲ Machiavelli wrote his ideas about politics and power. His most famous book is *The Prince*.

**career:** a person's chosen life work
**clerk:** a person who works in an office, files papers, and does other office work

He went on diplomatic missions to visit the king of France and the emperor of Germany. He also visited the pope, who was head of the Roman Catholic Church. These diplomatic missions gave Machiavelli a chance to see how rulers gained power, kept it, and used it.

## Problems in Florence

Men fought about who would have the power to rule Florence. In 1512, some members of the Medici family tried to regain power. They hired a Spanish army to help them. The following year, Machiavelli was arrested and sent to prison. The Medici rulers said Machiavelli had **plotted** against them. Machiavelli, who said he was wrongly accused, eventually was allowed to go free. But he never worked for the government again. He spent his time at his home outside Florence writing his ideas about politics and power. His most famous book is *The Prince*. In this book, he wrote about how a ruler should get power, keep power, and get more power. He thought the book would help new rulers understand how to rule effectively. He said in *The Prince*: "... Those who read what I have to say may the more easily draw those **practical** lessons which one should seek to obtain from the study of history."

### It's a FACT
Machiavelli said that in order for a republic to survive it had to encourage its citizens to be patriotic.

**plot:** to plan
**practical:** able to be used or put into effect

◄ After Lorenzo di Medici died, Florence had many problems. In 1512, members of the Medici family tried to regain control. They saw Machiavelli as a threat and had him arrested the following year.

LORENZO IL MAGNIFICO

**political science:** the study of government and government organizations

## What Do You Think?

1. How does the story of Niccolo Machiavelli help you understand Europe during the Renaissance?

2. Niccolo Machiavelli is famous for the idea that "the ends justify the means." Do you agree or disagree with this idea? Explain your answer.

3. What do you think is Niccolo Machiavelli's greatest achievement? Give reasons for your answer.

## Ideas about Government

Machiavelli thought that good governments had to be effective. This means that they had to set goals and meet those goals. In *The Prince*, Machiavelli answered the question of whether it is better for a ruler to be loved or feared. He said, "... It would be desirable to be both ... but as it is difficult to be both at the same time, it is much more safe to be feared than to be loved." He thought it was the ruler's job to make sure the government's goals were met. Machiavelli did not think it mattered how a ruler achieved his goals. The only thing that was important is that he achieved them. Machiavelli is famous for the idea that "the ends justify the means." Some people thought he meant that rulers should do bad things to stay in power. Niccolo Machiavelli was never able to change the negative ideas many people had about him. He was never given the chance to work for Florence again. He died at his home in 1527.

## The Father of Political Science

Today, many people think Machiavelli's ideas about government are misunderstood. They don't think he wanted rulers to do bad things at all. In fact, in *The Prince*, Machiavelli says that the best way for rulers to stay in power, keep power, and get more power is to rule well. Niccolo Machiavelli is sometimes called the "father of **political science**" because he was one of the first people to write about government and society. ▢

▼ During the Renaissance, Florence was one of the most important cities in the world. Today, it remains known for its fine art and culture.

# Who's Who in Renaissance Art History

**Q: Which Renaissance artist painted those cute little angels?**

**A:** Renaissance artist **Raphael**. The cupids are only part of Raphael's painting called "Sistine Madonna." Raffaello Sanzio was born in Urbino, Italy in 1483. Raphael learned how to paint from his father. In 1504, he went to Florence and studied the work of Leonardo da Vinci and Michelangelo. Raphael was a favorite painter of both Pope Julius II and Pope Leo X. Pope Leo X made Raphael the chief architect of St. Peter's Basilica in Rome. Raphael painted pictures with religious themes as well as portraits. Raphael is known as one of the world's greatest painters. He died in Rome on his 37th birthday in 1520.

**Q: Who was Lorenzo di Medici's favorite painter?**

**A:** Many say it was **Sandro Botticelli**. Botticelli spent most of his life working for Lorenzo di Medici and other important Florentine families. He painted portraits and religious subjects. One of his most famous paintings is "The Birth of Venus." The original hangs in the Uffizi Gallery in Florence. Botticelli died in 1510.

**Q: Can you name a great Renaissance artist outside Italy?**

**A: Albrecht Dürer.** He was born in 1471 in Nuremberg, Germany. Dürer was a painter, writer, and perhaps the greatest printmaker of his time. His work is known for its attention to detail. Like other Renaissance artists, Dürer's work reflected both religious and secular themes. One of his most important works is a woodcut print called "The Four Horsemen of the Apocalypse," which he created in 1497-1498. It shows the coming of a Day of Judgment described in the Bible. Four horsemen ride out. One symbolizes conquering power, the second represents war, the third is famine, and the fourth is death. The original print hangs in the Metropolitan Museum of Art in New York. Dürer died in 1528.

# LAURA CERETA —
# Renaissance Scholar

A.D. **1400**

**1469-1499**
Laura Cereta

**1485**
Cereta gets married

**1488**
Cereta publishes a book of letters

A.D. **1500**

▲ Laura Cereta was born in Italy.

**accomplished:** skilled; expert
**adorn:** to decorate or make beautiful
**coiffure:** hairstyle

## What Do You Think?

1. What advantages did Laura Cereta have in life? What obstacles did she face?

2. Why was her husband's death a turning point in her life?

3. Laura Cereta wrote harshly about women who spend all their time on fashion and clothes. Do you agree or disagree with her position? Explain your answer.

Most Renaissance scholars and artists were men, but there were important women artists and scholars in the Renaissance, too. One such woman was Laura Cereta.

Laura Cereta was born in 1469 to a noble family. Her family lived in Brescia, a city about 70 miles east of Milan in northern Italy. Like many other girls of noble birth, she went to school at a convent. She loved learning and was a good student. She studied reading, writing, and Latin at the convent until she was 11 years old. Then she was called home to help care for her younger brothers and sisters.

### A Turning Point

When she was 15, Laura faced a decision that noble girls faced. She had to decide to marry or to spend the rest of her life in a convent. She chose marriage. In 1485, Laura Cereta married Pietro Serina. After just 18 months, however, Pietro died. Laura was still only a teenager, and this was a turning point in her life. She decided that she would dedicate her life to learning.

### A Book of Letters

In 1488, Laura Cereta published a book of letters. This was very unusual for a Renaissance woman. In fact, it was unheard of! Her letters point out that there have been many **accomplished** women throughout history. She said, "All history is full of such examples." Her letters also show that she strongly believed women have a right to be educated. She wrote harshly about women who spend all their time on fashion and clothes. She described them as "empty women, who strive for no good but exist to **adorn** themselves." She said, "These women of majestic pride, fantastic **coiffures**, outlandish ornament, and necks bound with gold or pearls bear the glittering symbols of their captivity to men."

Many men and women criticized Laura Cereta's book of letters. She was hurt by this criticism and never published another book. She died when she was only 30 years old. Still, she left an important legacy. Today, almost everyone agrees that women should have the same rights to education as men. Think of Laura Cereta, however, and remember that was not always true! □

# MICHELANGELO —
## "Many Kings but Only One Michelangelo"

A.D. **1400**
A.D. **1600**

**1475-1564**
Michelangelo Buonarroti

**c. 1488**
Michelangelo becomes an apprentice with painter Ghirlandaio

**1501-1504**
Michelangelo creates "David"

Michelangelo Buonarroti was born in a small village near Florence, Italy in 1475. He was born during the Renaissance—one of the greatest periods of artistic accomplishment in the history of the Western world. During his early life, he struggled to convince his father that he wanted to be an artist. When he was about 13 years old, he became an apprentice with Ghirlandaio, a well-known Florentine painter. He didn't remain an apprentice for long. Ghirlandaio recognized Michelangelo's talent for drawing and painting. However, Michelangelo's true love was sculpture.

## An Invitation from Lorenzo di Medici

Lorenzo di Medici, the most important leader in Florence, invited Michelangelo to study sculpture. Lorenzo di Medici became his patron, and for the next four years Michelangelo spent almost all his time learning the art of sculpture. He began to study the human body, which helped him make sculptures that looked like real people. By the time he was 16 years old, Michelangelo had created two important sculptures. When Lorenzo di Medici died, Michelangelo traveled to other Italian city-states such as Bologna and Rome looking for new patrons to support his work. In Rome, he carved two more sculptures in the years between 1496 and 1501. One of these sculptures, the "Pieta," is one of the most famous works of art in history. You can see it today in St. Peter's Basilica in Rome. Michelangelo was only about 25 or 30 years old when he finished these works. He then went home to Florence.

## Florence and David

People knew of the work he had done in Rome. Michelangelo wrote in his diary, "When I returned to Florence, I found myself famous." To Michelangelo's delight, the leaders of the city asked him to carve a statue. He wrote in his diary, "I locked myself away in a workshop behind the cathedral, hammered and chiseled at the towering block for three long years." He took a huge piece of marble and carved the figure of David. David is the boy described in the Bible who fought with only a slingshot against the larger and stronger Goliath.

▲ On the day Michelangelo was born—March 6, 1475—his father wrote: "A child of the male sex has been born to me and I have named him Michelangelo. He was born on Monday between 4 and 5 in the morning, at Caprese." Caprese is a small village near Florence. Michelangelo thought of himself as a Florentine.

▲ You can visit Florence to see the art Michelangelo created during the Renaissance. Michelangelo's "David" stands in the Galleria dell'Accademia in Florence.

▲ Giorgio Vasari wrote a book called *Lives of the Artists* in 1550. In the book, he described the "Pieta," Michelangelo's famous sculpture: "It would be impossible for any craftsman or sculptor ... to surpass the grace or design of this work ... It is certainly a miracle that a formless block of stone could ever have been reduced to a perfection that nature is scarcely able to create in the flesh."

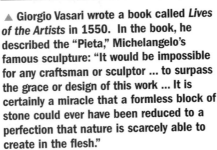

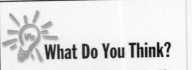

## What Do You Think?

How does Michelangelo's life help you understand Europe during the Renaissance?

Some people say Michelangelo's "David" is the most beautiful statue ever created. It was placed in the center of Florence as a symbol of the republic. Michelangelo wrote, "Archways were torn down, narrow streets were widened ... it took forty men five days to move it. Once in place, all Florence was astounded."

### Then, the Sistine Ceiling and St. Peter's Basilica

In 1505, after Michelangelo finished the statue of "David," Pope Julius II asked him to come to Rome. The pope and Michelangelo had a difficult relationship. Despite their problems, however, Michelangelo completed several of his greatest works, including the frescoes on the ceiling of the Sistine Chapel. During the last part of his life, Michelangelo also designed buildings. He was asked to be the chief architect for St. Peter's Basilica in Rome, which previously was Renaissance artist Raphael's job. When Michelangelo finished this work, he went back to the sculpting that he loved so much. In his final days, he spent most of his time alone. He worked with his chisels and his pieces of marble. One person said, "The world has many kings but only one Michelangelo." He died in 1564 when he was 88 years old.

# SOFONISBA ANGUISSOLA —
# Artist and Role Model

A.D. **1400**

**1475-1564**
Michelangelo
Buonarroti

**c. 1532-1625**
Sofonisba Anguissola

**1560**
Philip II of Spain asks
Sofonisba to paint pictures
of the Spanish royal family

A.D. **1650**

During the Renaissance, girls did not have many choices about what they would do when they grew up. Most girls of noble birth were expected to marry. While waiting for marriage, most of these girls spent their time doing things such as sewing and embroidering. Only a few exceptional girls became well educated or went on to become important artists. Sofonisba Anguissola is one such woman. She did not follow the traditional role of women in Renaissance society. She became well known as an excellent portrait painter.

## Early Life

Sofonisba Anguissola was born around 1532 in Cremona, Italy. She was the oldest of six sisters. Her father was a wealthy nobleman. When his daughters were young, he decided to educate them as if they were his male heirs. Sofonisba and her sisters received an excellent education and each was an accomplished painter and musician. Early in her training, Sofonisba was sent to study painting.

▶ Sofonisba Anguissola became an exceptional painter during the Renaissance. Most artists at the time made people in their portraits look serious. The people in Anguissola's paintings smiled.

innovative: creative
international: involving two or more nations
recognition: favorable attention or notice

It's a FACT

• Sofonisba was born around 1532 and died in 1625—at age 94!

• Sofonisba was married twice. After her first husband died, she went on a sea voyage. The captain of the ship took good care of her. She eventually married him!

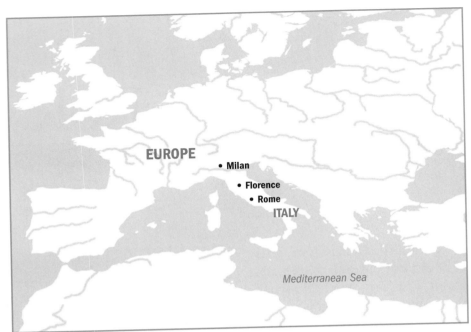

▲ Sofonisba Anguissola was born in Cremona, a city in northern Italy about 40 miles southwest of Milan.

## An Innovative Painter

As a young woman, Sofonisba Anguissola painted pictures of herself and her sisters. Even at an early age, she was an **innovative** painter. One of her most famous paintings shows three of her sisters playing chess. What is very different about this picture is that the sisters are smiling. Most other artists of the time painted pictures of people with very serious looks on their faces. Another innovative painting was the one she painted of her teacher, Campi. In this painting, Campi is shown painting a picture of Sofonisba Anguissola herself. Over time, her importance as an artist grew. In 1560, King Philip II of Spain asked her to come to his court. He wanted her to paint pictures of the Spanish royal family.

## A Role Model

For the next 10 to 20 years (historians are not exactly sure), Sofonisba Anguissola lived and worked in Spain. She became a role model for other women artists. Other Renaissance artists, including Michelangelo, knew of her work. Her father sent one of her drawings to Michelangelo who was reported to have been impressed with it. Sofonisba Anguissola lived to a very old age and enjoyed **international recognition**. During her life, Sofonisba Anguissola painted more than 50 pictures. Today, her paintings are considered excellent examples of Renaissance portraits. ▢

## What Do You Think?

1. What is a "role model"?

2. Why do you think Sofonisba Anguissola became a role model for women?

3. Who are role models for women today?

# MIGUEL CERVANTES —
## *Don Quixote de la Mancha*

**A.D. 1500** ———————————————————————— **A.D. 1650**

**1547-1616**
Miguel Cervantes

**1571**
Cervantes loses the
use of his left hand

**1580**
Cervantes is
captured by pirates

**c. 1605-1616**
Cervantes writes *Don
Quixote de la Mancha*

Miguel Cervantes was born in Alcála de Henares, Spain in 1547. As a young man, he traveled to Italy, the place where the Renaissance began. Cervantes was interested in reading literature, but he also wanted action and adventure. He became a soldier and fought with a Spanish army. He was wounded at the battle of Lepanto (in Greece) in 1571 and lost the use of his left hand. That did not stop him from fighting in another battle, this time against Muslims in North Africa. In 1580, as he was returning to Spain, pirates captured him and demanded a ransom for his release. After his ransom was paid, Cervantes returned to Madrid, Spain. He had various government jobs, but was not very successful at any of them. His personal life was not very happy or successful either.

▲ **Miguel Cervantes lived in Spain.**

Then in his late 50s and throughout his 60s, Cervantes seemed to find his own personal "rebirth" or Renaissance. He wrote the story *Don Quixote de la Mancha*, which became hugely successful throughout Europe. His story was a parody—a comic imitation— of the romantic tales of chivalry that had been very popular. In Cervantes' story, the chivalrous knight was out of his mind, but he was extremely sincere. The effect is that the story is tragic, but funny. On the following page, you can read an excerpt from the story. In this passage, Cervantes is giving the reader some background information to explain why the main character, the gentleman who eventually named himself Don Quixote, went mad and began to roam the countryside like the knights of the Middle Ages. 📖

▶ **Miguel Cervantes wrote during the Renaissance.**

◄ *Don Quixote de la Mancha* is a story of a knight. This scene shows Don Quixote in one of his many adventures. He is attached to a line held by another man and is preparing to enter a cave.

## Analyze the Source!

1. Read the excerpt and tell in your own words what it says.

2. How does this excerpt help you learn about the culture and history of Europe during the Renaissance?

3. Why do you think the main character in the story became so involved in books of chivalry and created his own fantasy world? Do people today become involved in times past or future? Do they create their own fantasy worlds? Explain your answer.

◄ Here Don Quixote is sitting under a tree with shepherds. One of the shepherds is playing an instrument and one is cooking.

## From *Don Quixote de la Mancha*

This gentleman of ours was close to fifty, of a **robust constitution** but with little flesh on his bones and a face that was lean. ... On those occasions when he was at leisure, which was most of the year round, [he] was in the habit of reading books of chivalry with such pleasure and devotion as to lead him almost wholly to forget ... even the administration of his estate. So great was his curiosity and **infatuation** in this regard that he even sold many acres of tillable land in order to be able to buy and read the books that he loved, and he would carry home with him as many of them as he could obtain ...

In short, our gentleman became so **immersed** in his reading that he spent whole nights from sundown to sunup and his days from dawn to dusk in **poring** over his books, until, finally, from so little sleeping and so much reading, his brain dried up and he went completely out of his mind. He had filled his imagination with everything that he had read, with enchantments, knightly encounters, battles, challenges, wounds, with tales of love and its torments, and all sorts of impossible things, and as a result had come to believe that all these fictitious happenings were true; they were more real to him than anything else in the world.

**immersed:** deeply involved
**infatuation:** an intense, temporary love
**pore:** to read or study carefully
**robust constitution:** healthy body

# WILLIAM SHAKESPEARE —
# The World's Greatest Playwright

A.D. **1500**                                                      A.D. **1650**

**c. 1564-1616**
William Shakespeare

**1582**
Shakespeare marries
Anne Hathaway

**1588**
Shakespeare arrives in
London and begins to
write poetry

**c. 1595**
Shakespeare writes
*Romeo and Juliet*

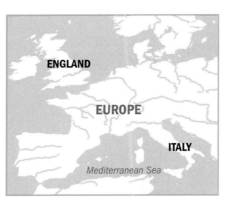

▲ **William Shakespeare lived in England during the time of the Renaissance.**

**playwright:** a person who writes plays

▲ **William Shakespeare was an actor and playwright.**

Throughout the Western world, William Shakespeare is often considered the greatest **playwright** who ever lived. You probably have heard of some of the 38 plays he wrote. They include *Romeo and Juliet, Hamlet, Othello, Julius Caesar,* and *MacBeth.*

## Early Life

We don't know much about Shakespeare's early life. We know he was born in a little town in England called Stratford-upon-Avon, about 65 miles northwest of London. People say Shakespeare was born on April 23, 1564, but no one knows for sure. We know he was baptized on April 24, 1564 because there is a church record of this event. William was the third of eight children and the oldest son in the Shakespeare family. His father, John Shakespeare, was an important merchant in the town. His mother, Mary, was from a wealthy, land-owning family. We think young William went to school in town where he learned to read and write.

## A Merchant?  Butcher's Apprentice?  Hunter?

As he got older, William probably began to learn something about business. During that time, a boy often trained to do the same kind of work as his father. William was probably expected to become a merchant like his father. However, we don't know this for sure. Some people believe he became a teacher. Another story says he became an apprentice to a butcher, a person who sells meat. The plays he wrote later in his life include a lot of information about hunting, so historians think he must have had free time when he was growing up. Church records tell us that William Shakespeare married Anne Hathaway, the daughter of a farmer, in 1582. They soon began their family. They had a daughter in 1583 and twins (a boy and a girl) in 1585.

## Performing for London Audiences

Shakespeare left Stratford-upon-Avon without his family and arrived in London in 1588. He began to write poetry that people greatly admired. He also joined a group of actors called the King's Men. This acting group often performed plays in front of the English royalty. However, Shakespeare's greatest talent was writing plays.

Some of his plays were about people and events in history. For example, he wrote a play about Julius Caesar, a ruler of ancient Rome. He also wrote about rulers in English history.

## Tragedies

Many of Shakespeare's plays are tragedies. They tell stories about the struggle between good and evil. Tragedies usually end with the death or downfall of the main character. These plays are often very sad, but they can help us understand how not to make the same mistakes the characters made. One of Shakespeare's most famous tragedies is *Romeo and Juliet*. In this play, two young people fall in love. But their families are bitter enemies. Romeo and Juliet are caught in the middle of this family fight. One of the most famous scenes in this play is when Juliet is standing on the **balcony** of her house. She looks out and says to herself, "Romeo, Romeo, wherefore art thou Romeo?" Juliet doesn't know that Romeo is on the ground below the balcony. She is in love with him, but knows that their love is impossible.

▲ Shakespeare joined an acting group that performed plays in front of the English royalty. This drawing shows him performing before Queen Elizabeth and her court.

**balcony:** a platform that sticks out of the wall of a building and is surrounded by a railing

▶ This is a scene from Shakespeare's comedy *A Midsummer Night's Dream*. Some of the educated people of his day did not think Shakespeare's plays were proper entertainment. But his plays were very popular with most people.

---

**foolish:** silly; lacking good judgment or common sense

---

### What Do You Think?

**1.** How does the story of William Shakespeare help you understand Europe during the Renaissance?

**2.** Do you think plays—comedies and tragedies—can teach us lessons about life? Explain your answer.

**3.** What do you think is William Shakespeare's greatest achievement? Give reasons for your answer.

---

She says she wishes he were from a different family and that he had a different last name. She asks, "What's in a name? That which we call a rose by any other name would smell as sweet." In the end, both Romeo and Juliet die. We are left with the idea that hatred only causes sadness.

## Comedies

Not all of Shakespeare's plays are tragedies. He also wrote many plays that are comedies. For example, *As You Like It* and *Much Ado about Nothing* are two of his comedies. A comedy is a funny play. The characters in comedies usually act **foolishly**, but the plays always have a happy ending. Most of Shakespeare's comedies end with the boy and girl getting married. Like tragedies, comedies can teach us lessons about life. They can help us avoid the foolish behavior we saw in the play!

## Back in Stratford-upon-Avon

Around 1608, when Shakespeare was in his mid-40s, he began to spend more time at his home in Stratford-upon-Avon. He was an important person in the town. He built a beautiful home for his family and lived there until his death on April 23, 1616. He was buried at the Stratford church. Today, people still enjoy going to see Shakespeare's plays or movies that are based on his plays. William Shakespeare is often considered the greatest playwright who ever lived. 📖

---

# JOHN WYCLIFFE — "Morning Star of the Protestant Reformation"

**c. 1320-1384**
John Wycliffe

**1372**
John Wycliffe earns a doctoral degree
in theology at Oxford University

Historians sometimes call John Wycliffe the "**morning star** of the **Protestant Reformation**" because he shared his ideas about what he saw as **abuses** and false teachings in the Roman Catholic Church. And he did this almost 200 years before Martin Luther published his ideas that began the Protestant Reformation.

We don't know very much about John Wycliffe's early life. Some historians believe he was born in 1320. We know he lived in the little town of Hipswell in northern England. As a young man, he went to school at Oxford University. He earned a doctoral degree in **theology** there in 1372.

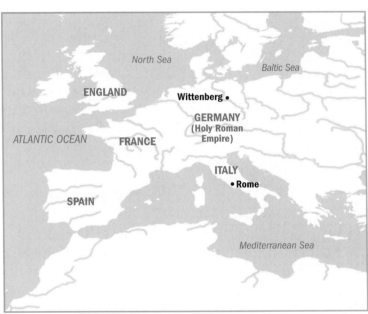

▲ The Protestant Reformation began in Germany in the early 1500s, but soon spread throughout northern Europe. John Wycliffe lived 200 years before the Reformation. Some believe his ideas led to that movement.

◄ The main point of John Wycliffe's writing was that the Bible was the most important source of authority. The Roman Catholic Church disagreed. Men such as Martin Luther and John Calvin later adopted Wycliffe's position.

**abuse:** a corrupt practice or custom; wrongdoing
**morning star:** a planet visible in the east just before sunrise; something that happens first
**Protestant Reformation:** a movement to reform the Roman Catholic Church
**theology:** the study of religious ideas and questions

It's a FACT

About 30 years after John Wycliffe died, the church ordered that his body be dug up and his bones burned.

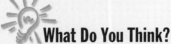

**heresy:** a religious idea or opinion that is not approved by the church

### What Do You Think?

**1.** John Wycliffe was not afraid to express his ideas even though they were unpopular. Do you agree or disagree with his decision to express unpopular ideas? Why or why not?

**2.** Are people today afraid to express ideas that are unpopular? Why or why not? Give examples to justify your answer.

**3.** From reading this information about John Wycliffe's life, what can you conclude about the influence of religion on society during this time?

## Correcting Church Abuses

People began to pay attention to Wycliffe. He was a popular teacher at Oxford University and openly shared his ideas about problems that he saw in the Roman Catholic Church. He also questioned the church's sacraments, including the Eucharist. He thought the English government also had a responsibility to correct the church's abuses. He believed the English government had a responsibility to remove church leaders if they were not doing their jobs the way they should. He also thought the government should even be able to take the church's property.

## An Angry Response from Church Leaders

The pope was very angry about John Wycliffe's ideas. However, Wycliffe continued to criticize the Roman Catholic Church and the power of the pope. He believed that the Bible was the most important authority for all church teachings. In contrast, most Roman Catholics at that time believed the church's authority came from both the church's teachings and from the Bible. Later reformers, including Martin Luther and John Calvin, shared Wycliffe's idea that the Bible was the most important authority.

## A Different View

Wycliffe's ideas were very different from other people's at that time. Eventually, he ended up without many supporters at Oxford. The leaders of the university did not approve of his teachings, and he no longer was allowed to give lectures about his ideas. To make matters worse, the archbishop of Canterbury, one of the most powerful religious leaders in England, said Wycliffe's ideas were **heresy**.

## Translating the Bible into English

Throughout these difficult times, John Wycliffe continued to write. He worked on translating the Bible from Latin to English. Parts of his translated Bible were very different from the traditional Bible.

## Wycliffe's Legacy

John Wycliffe spent his last days living quietly and peacefully. He died in 1384. It would be 133 years before Martin Luther issued his *Ninety-Five Theses* that spelled out his disagreements with the Roman Catholic Church. Many people see that action as the beginning of the Protestant Reformation. However, it is important to remember that John Wycliffe shared many of the same concerns. That is why people say that John Wycliffe was a man before his time. That is why they call him the "morning star of the Protestant Reformation."

# CATHERINE OF SIENA
## and the Great Schism

| A.D. **1300** | | | | A.D. **1400** |
|---|---|---|---|---|

**1347-1380**
Catherine of Siena

**1370**
Catherine has many visions

**1376**
Pope Gregory XI decides to make
Rome the city of his official residence

The woman we know of today as St. Catherine of Siena was a cloth dyer's daughter. No one would have predicted that she would become a central figure in one of the most difficult problems the Roman Catholic Church ever faced.

## Early Life

Catherine was born in 1347 in Siena, an Italian city-state northeast of Rome. She was the youngest of 25 children. Her father's job was to **dye** cloth, and the family was part of Siena's lower-middle class. When she was a young girl, Catherine reported that she began to have visions. For example, when she was six, she reported that she had a vision of Jesus Christ surrounded by saints.

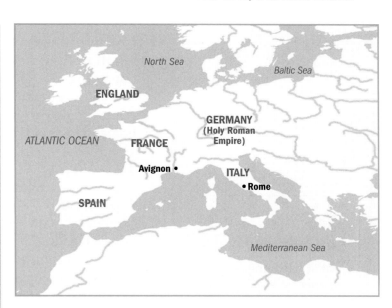

▲ Catherine lived in Italy during the time of the Great Schism—the split in the Roman Catholic Church. Don't be confused! Earlier in history (1054 to be exact), the Christian Church split into two churches. One was centered in Rome in the West. The other was in Constantinople in the East. This split is called a schism.

**dye:** to color

◄ Catherine did not learn how to write until the end of her life, but that did not stop her from expressing her ideas. She often dictated letters to others to write down for her.

As she grew older, Catherine's parents hoped that she would be like other girls in their neighborhood. However, Catherine had other ideas. When she was 16 years old, she went to work with the religious order of St. Dominic. Her job was to care for sick people, especially those suffering from **leprosy** and other deadly diseases.

## A Holy Woman

Over time, many people began to think of Catherine as a person with great insight. People began to ask her for spiritual advice. Catherine started to write to many different people. Some were ordinary people, while others were bishops and kings. During the summer of 1370, Catherine reported many visions. During one of these visions, Catherine said she was commanded to enter into a more public life. One of the first public actions she took was to try to convince the pope, Gregory XI, to leave Avignon, France and return to Rome. Starting in 1309, popes had been living in France, not Rome. French cardinals and French popes controlled the church. Catherine believed the pope should live in Rome. In 1376, Pope Gregory decided to make this change, a change that made the French king angry.

## Two Popes?

Soon after he returned to Rome, Gregory died. Another man— Pope Urban VI—was chosen as the new pope. The French did not like Pope Urban VI. The leaders of the Roman Catholic Church in France decided to choose their own pope. They selected a man known as Clement VII to become pope. Now the Roman Catholic Church had two popes! Pope Urban VI in Rome and Pope Clement VII in Avignon.

## The Great Schism

This split in the Roman Catholic Church is called the Great **Schism**. Catherine supported Pope Urban VI. She thought he was the true pope and that the pope should live and work in Rome. She supported Pope Urban's claim as pope by writing to many important people. Catherine said she "was chosen and sent on this earth in order to right a great scandal."

## St. Catherine of Siena

During this time, Catherine continued her work with the sick and the poor, but this did not stop her from taking strong stands about the social issues of her day. She died in 1380 at the age of 33. Catherine was known for her visions and the importance she placed on prayer. The Roman Catholic Church remained divided in her lifetime. However, in 1417 a group of church leaders got together and recognized one pope in Rome. This brought the Roman Catholic Church back together under one leader. The Roman Catholic Church named Catherine a saint 81 years after her death. Today, we know this lower-class daughter of a cloth dyer as St. Catherine of Siena. ▢

---

**leprosy:** a deadly disease that causes sores on the skin

**schism:** a separation, division, or split, especially within a Christian church

---

## What Do You Think?

**1.** What advantages did Catherine of Siena have in life? What obstacles did she face?

**2.** Who do you think that Catherine believed chose her "to right a great scandal"? What does this tell you about religious ideas during this period of history in Europe?

**3.** From reading this information about Catherine of Siena's life, what can you conclude about the role of women in society during this time?

**4.** What do you think is Catherine of Siena's greatest achievement? Give reasons for your answer.

---

# MARGERY KEMPE —
# A Woman of Her Time

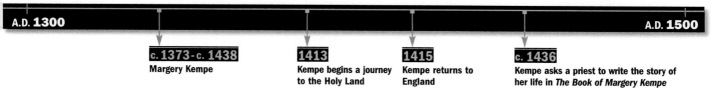

A.D. **1300**                                              A.D. **1500**

**c. 1373- c. 1438**
Margery Kempe

**1413**
Kempe begins a journey to the Holy Land

**1415**
Kempe returns to England

**c. 1436**
Kempe asks a priest to write the story of her life in *The Book of Margery Kempe*

During the time when Margery Kempe lived, many people were trying to correct the abuses they saw in the church. However, that was not Margery Kempe's goal in life. Instead, she wanted to express her religious ideas and feelings in her own way.

## Early Life

Around 1373, a baby girl—Margery—was born to Mr. and Mrs. John Burnham in Bishops Lynn, a small town northeast of London, England. The Burnham family was part of the growing middle class in England. Like most other middle-class girls of her time, Margery spent her early life preparing for her future role in society. She learned to cook, clean, and sew. She never learned to read or write.

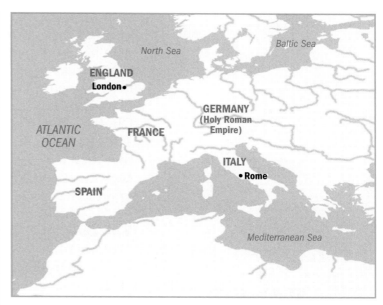

▲ Margery Kempe lived in England. She wrote a book about the story of her life. It contained ideas about religion that the Roman Catholic Church did not like.

▼ Margery went with a small group of other travelers on her journey to the Holy Land. They stopped in the Netherlands, Germany, Italy, and Greece on their way to the city of Jerusalem.

**autobiography:** a book written by a person about that person's life

## Marriage, Family, and Religious Visions

When she was 20 years old, Margery married John Kempe, a successful merchant. Soon Margery became pregnant with the first of her 14 children. After Margery gave birth to her child, she said she had a vision of Jesus Christ. Throughout her life, she reported many more such visions. Margery decided she should visit the Holy Land and in 1413 began a journey there. She went on this trip with a small group of other travelers. The journey lasted almost two years. Often during this time, Margery meditated for long periods.

## Experiencing God through Prayer

When she returned to England in 1415, Margery Kempe talked with others about her spiritual experiences and feelings. She believed that through prayer she could experience God. People who believe this way are sometimes called "mystics." Margery Kempe, like other mystics, did not think she needed priests to help her experience God. This was an unusual idea during this time. It was certainly not a popular idea with the Roman Catholic Church. But Margery Kempe was different from other mystics. The church thought many of Margery's ideas were strange and that they were inconsistent with approved church teachings. In fact, she spent much of the last part of her life defending herself against charges of heresy.

## The Book of Margery Kempe

Around 1436, Margery Kempe asked a priest to write down the story of her life. She felt strongly that she wanted a written record of her life and religious experiences. At first, the priest was afraid, but finally he agreed to write her story as she told it to him. The priest wrote what Margery told him in what has come to be called *The Book of Margery Kempe*. Sometimes this book is called the first **autobiography** in English, which was beginning to be considered the national language of England.

## What Does the Book Tell Us?

This book tells us about her visions, her struggles, her travels, and her trial for heresy. *The Book of Margery Kempe* begins this way: "Here begynnyth a schort tretys and a comfortably for synful wrecchys, wherein thei may have gret solas and comfort to hem and undyrstondyn the hy and unspeacabyl mercy of ower sovereyn Savyowr Cryst Jehusu. ..." Does this seem difficult to read and understand? If so, one reason is that it is written in a kind of English that is different from what we use today. And to make matters more difficult for readers today, writers during that time spelled words any way they wanted! Today, we would probably write the sentence this way: "Here begins a short story for sinners. It is intended to give them comfort and help them understand the great mercy of Jesus Christ. ..."

### What Do You Think?

1. What advantages did Margery Kempe have in life? What obstacles did she face?

2. One of the points Margery Kempe wanted to make was that God's mercy is more important than money or belongings. Why might this position have been unpopular at the time?

3. From reading this information about Margery Kempe's life, what can you conclude about the influence of religion on society during this time?

| How Margery Kempe's Story Was Written ... | How We Might Write It Today ... |
|---|---|
| *Here begynnyth a schort tretys and a comfortably for synful wrecchys, wherein thei may have gret solas and comfort to hem and undyrstondyn the hy and unspeacabyl mercy of ower sovereyn Savyowr Cryst Jehusu. ...* | *Here begins a short story for sinners. It is intended to give them comfort and help them understand the great mercy of Jesus Christ. ...* |

## The Life of a Middle-Class Woman

Throughout the book, Margery Kempe refers to herself in the third person as "this creature." The book describes her life as a middle-class woman in England in the 1400s. It tells about the people she met and the places she visited. She wrote about her pride and love of fine things. She said she "wore gold pipes [as decoration] on her head" and that "her desire was ... to be worshiped ..." Margery said, "she ever desired more and more." Margery Kempe also wrote about how she wanted to make a lot of money as "one of the greatest **brewers** in town ..." However, the point of her story is that she finally began to see that God's mercy was more important than money or belongings. She said, "And when this creature was thus graciously come again to her mind, she thought she was bound to God and that she would be his servant." Today, we probably would write the sentence this way: "And when I came to my senses, I remembered that I believed in and was a servant of God." Margery Kempe wanted to share these ideas with others.

## Margery Kempe's Legacy

It is not certain when or how Margery Kempe died, but historians think it was around 1438. During the time when she lived, other people tried to reform the abuses they saw in the church. However, Margery Kempe did not try to reform the church. Her goal was to express her religious ideas and feelings in her own way and to tell other people about these ideas and feelings.

**brewer:** a person who makes beer

## It's a FACT

• When Margery's husband could not provide her with all the luxuries she wanted, she decided to go into business for herself as a brewer making beer and ale.

• As a young girl, Margery committed what she called a "secret sin." She did not leave any details about what she had done wrong. She was too afraid to tell anyone about it.

# MARTIN LUTHER — The Little Boy with His Finger in the Dam

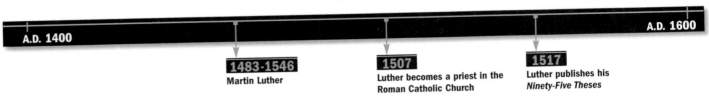

A.D. 1400                                                                  A.D. 1600

**1483-1546**
Martin Luther

**1507**
Luther becomes a priest in the
Roman Catholic Church

**1517**
Luther publishes his
*Ninety-Five Theses*

Martin Luther was born on November 10, 1483 in Saxony, an area in Germany. His family did not have much money, but they thought education was important. They sent Martin to school, where he was a very good student. One day as he was walking home from school, there was a terrible storm. Martin was afraid he would be killed. It is reported that he began to ask for God's help to save him from death. As he prayed, he promised that if he were allowed to live, he would begin a life of religious service. Martin Luther lived through the storm and kept his promise. He became a priest in the Roman Catholic Church in 1507. He also continued his studies and earned a doctoral degree.

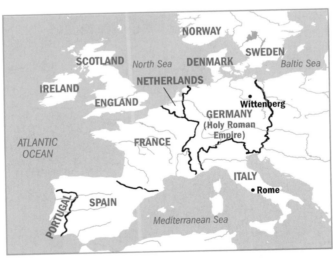

▲ The Protestant Reformation began in present-day Germany, but soon spread throughout northern Europe.

## Luther Publishes his *Ninety-Five Theses*

Over time, Luther began to disagree with some of the ideas and practices in the Roman Catholic Church. For example, he thought the Bible was the most important authority for all church teachings. In contrast, most Roman Catholics believed the church's authority came from both the church's teachings and from the Bible. Luther also opposed the sale of papal **indulgences**. In addition, he was critical of the pope's wealth. Martin Luther published these ideas—his *Ninety-Five Theses*—on October 31, 1517. At that time, scholars would post their ideas on a church door so that others could read and discuss the ideas. Luther thought his ideas would begin a reform in the church.

**dam:** a barrier made to hold back the flow of water
**indulgence:** a document sold by the Roman Catholic Church to reduce or cancel punishment for a person's sins

## The Protestant Reformation

Many people supported Luther and agreed with his ideas. They became known as Protestants because they were protesting against some of the ideas and practices in the Roman Catholic Church. Their movement to reform the Roman Catholic Church is called the Protestant Reformation. Do you know the old story of the little boy who put his finger in the **dam**?

According to the story, the boy saw a crack in a dam that was holding back the sea. By placing his finger in the crack, he saved the entire area from a huge flood. Some people sometimes think of Martin Luther as the little boy with his finger in the dam. However, they say that Martin Luther "pulled his finger out" and let "the floods" come. Below is one of the ideas that started the Protestant Reformation. This is one of Martin Luther's *Ninety-Five Theses*. Martin Luther wrote these theses in Latin, but they were soon translated into German and then other languages. 📖

▲ Luther thought his ideas would bring a reform in the church.

## From Martin Luther's *Ninety-Five Theses*

Why does not the Pope, whose riches are at this day more ample than those of the wealthiest of the wealthy, build the one Basilica of St. Peter's with his own money, rather than with that of poor believers ...?

## Analyze the Source!

Read the excerpt and tell in your own words what it says.

◀ St. Peter's Basilica is the main Roman Catholic Church in Rome named after Peter, one of Jesus's 12 followers. Early Christians believed Jesus gave Peter the power to govern the church.

▶ This drawing shows Martin Luther burning a letter from the pope. You can see a little of the town of Wittenberg, Germany in the background.

# ANNA BIJNS — Poet

NETHERLANDS

GERMANY
(Holy Roman Empire)

Mediterranean Sea

▲ Anna Bijns was born in 1493 in the Netherlands. She disapproved of Martin Luther and the Protestant Reformation.

Anna Bijns was born in 1493 to a Roman Catholic family in Antwerp in the Netherlands. Her father was a city leader. Anna became known for her dislike of Martin Luther and the Protestant Reformation. Her poems expressed her strong feelings. Below is one part of a translated poem in which she compares Martin Luther with a man named Martin Rossom. Martin Rossom was deeply hated by people of the Netherlands because he was believed to have killed 200 peasants. How does Anna Bijns think Martin Rossom, the criminal, compares with Martin Luther, the man who started the Protestant Reformation? Read an excerpt from her poem and decide for yourself. 📖

**lay waste:** to destroy
**rack:** to hurt or inflict pain
**spawn:** to produce or bring forth
**weary fancy:** tired imagination

## A Poem by Anna Bijns

What was there to brighten up my mood
With nothing but sorrow to spare—and I was sad.
And then my **weary fancy** in its rambling
Called forth a pair of men
With names the same but not much else.
One, Martin Luther, whose error **spawns** and spreads;
The other, Martin Rossom, whose cruel sword
Proved far too sharp for many far and near.
Rossom **racks** the body, Luther **lays waste** the soul.

So what's up! "Evil creature" fits them both.
To choose between these two? Waste of time.
Still, since Luther through his error kills your soul,
When compared, Martin Rossom comes out best.

## Analyze the Source!

1. Read the excerpt and tell in your own words what it says.

2. Why do you think Anna Bijns concluded that "Martin Rossum comes out best" in the comparison with Martin Luther?

# THOMAS MORE and HENRY VIII —
# A Conflict of Power and Values

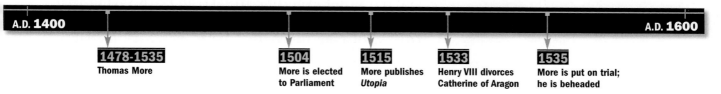

A.D. **1400**                                                    A.D. **1600**

**1478-1535**
Thomas More

**1504**
More is elected
to Parliament

**1515**
More publishes
*Utopia*

**1533**
Henry VIII divorces
Catherine of Aragon

**1535**
More is put on trial;
he is beheaded

Thomas More was born in London, England on February 7, 1478. His father was a judge from a wealthy and important family. As a boy, Thomas received an excellent education and continued on to Oxford University. He wanted to study Greek, but his father wanted him to study law. He did as his father wanted and eventually became a lawyer. However, Thomas never gave up his love of Greek. He read all the Greek books he could find and began to translate many of them into English. More continued his legal career, too, and was elected to Parliament in 1504.

## *Utopia* and Powerful Positions

In 1515, More's most famous book, called *Utopia*, was published. *Utopia* tells about More's ideas of a perfect world. More was very active in government, and his work began to attract the attention of the king of England, Henry VIII. In 1523, the king made him "Speaker of the House of Commons," an important leadership position in Parliament. In time, More became the most powerful judge in all of England.

## Good Relations End

The good relations between Thomas More and Henry VIII did not last. The problems began around 1532 when Henry decided to divorce his wife, Catherine of Aragon. Catherine was the daughter of Isabella and Ferdinand, king and queen of Spain. Catherine's nephew was Charles V, king of Spain, who opposed the divorce. But Henry was determined to divorce Catherine and marry another woman, Anne Boleyn. The problem was that divorce was against the teachings of the Roman Catholic Church, and the pope would not agree to let Henry divorce Catherine. Henry decided he was going to get a divorce anyway. Henry decided to start his own church called the Church of England (or Anglican Church). In 1533, the Church of England let him divorce Catherine so he could marry Anne.

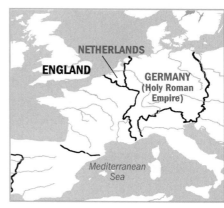

▲ Thomas More was born in England. He later was elected to Parliament.

▲ Thomas More refused to take an oath saying that Henry VIII was supreme ruler of the world. He was put on trial and then killed for this refusal.

# Defender of the Roman Catholic Church

▲ Henry VIII started the Anglican Church because the pope would not allow him to divorce his wife.

Thomas More was a strong supporter of the Roman Catholic Church. He did not approve of Henry's actions and did not attend the wedding of Henry VIII and Anne Boleyn, even though Henry invited him. This made the king very angry. When Henry VIII passed a law requiring everyone to take an **oath** saying that Henry was supreme ruler of the world, More said he could not take this oath. More was put on trial in May 1535 because he would not take this oath. Eventually, he was found guilty of treason and sentenced to die. The judge could not understand why More would not take this oath. He reminded More that many church leaders and scholars had already taken the oath. He asked More why he was not willing to do so, too. Thomas More responded in this way:

> *I am able to produce against one bishop which you can produce, a hundred holy and Catholic bishops for my opinion; and against one* **realm***, the consent of Christendom for a thousand years. ... Your lordships have been my judges to condemnation, yet we may hereafter meet joyfully together in Heaven to our everlasting salvation.*

**behead:** to separate the head from the body
**execute:** to kill
**oath:** a formal promise or pledge
**realm:** a kingdom

Thomas More was **beheaded** on July 6, 1535. His head was placed on London Bridge for all to see. Eventually, his daughter took it down. Reportedly, King Henry VIII was playing cards when he was told that Thomas More was dead. It is said that he left the card game right away to find his wife, Anne Boleyn. He is reported to have said to her, "Thou art the cause of this man's death."

Henry VIII took all of Thomas More's property. Eleven months later he accused Anne Boleyn of adultery, and she was beheaded. Henry married four more wives before he died in 1547. While he was king, almost 120 people a month were **executed** in England. The Roman Catholic Church made Thomas More a saint in 1866. ▢

## What Do You Think?

**1.** How does this reading help you learn about the culture and history of Europe during the Reformation?

**2.** How does the statement by Thomas More help you learn about the influence of religion during this period?

# JOHN CALVIN —
# New Ideas about Christianity

| A.D. **1500** | | | A.D. **1570** |
|---|---|---|---|

**1509-1564**
John Calvin

**1533**
Calvin comes to believe that God has chosen him to reform the Roman Catholic Church

**1536**
Calvin publishes his ideas about Christianity

John Calvin was born in 1509 in the small town of Loyon in northwestern France. As a young man, he went to school to study law. However, in 1533, he came to believe that God had chosen him to reform the Roman Catholic Church. He was interested in the ideas of Martin Luther, the founder of the Protestant Reformation, and became a Protestant himself. His ideas, however, did not agree with Martin Luther's teachings. John Calvin left France in 1534 because Protestants were being persecuted there. Two years later, in 1536, he published his ideas about Christianity. He taught that God already had chosen the people who would be saved and go to heaven. He did not think that doing good works and living a good life could help a person get to heaven. But he did think these were signs that the person was probably among those already chosen to go to heaven.

Other Protestant groups disagreed with John Calvin's ideas and his Calvinist Church. Protestant groups even persecuted one another. However, Calvin's ideas became widely accepted among many Protestants. For example, the group we call the Puritans followed his ideas. The Calvinist Church had strict laws. Calvinists wore plain clothing and were not allowed to play cards or dance. In the paragraph below, you can read what John Calvin had to say about Christianity and suffering. ⬚

## John Calvin on Christianity and Suffering

Are we so **delicate** as to be unwilling to endure anything? Then we must renounce the grace of God by which He has called us to the hope of salvation. For there are two things which can not be separated—to be members of Christ, and to be **tried** by many **afflictions**.

### Analyze the Source!

How does this excerpt help you learn about the culture and history of Europe during the Reformation?

**affliction:** pain or suffering
**delicate:** easily hurt or damaged
**try:** to test

▶ People who accepted John Calvin's ideas are called Calvinists.

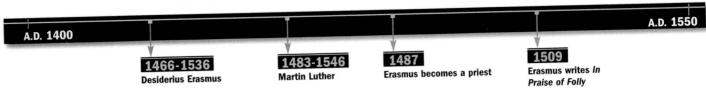

# DESIDERIUS ERASMUS —
# Scholar and Critic

A.D. 1400 ——————————————————————————————————————————————————— A.D. 1550

**1466-1536**
Desiderius Erasmus

**1483-1546**
Martin Luther

**1487**
Erasmus becomes a priest

**1509**
Erasmus writes *In Praise of Folly*

Erasmus was a man who became caught up in the Protestant Reformation. Leaders of both the Roman Catholic Church and Protestant Reformation disliked him. Who was Erasmus? Why is he an important figure of the time?

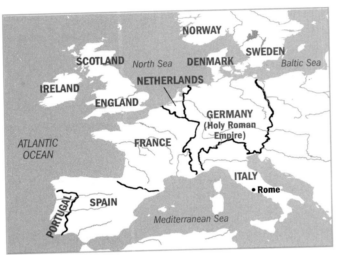

▲ Desiderius Erasmus was born in the present-day Netherlands and attended many important universities in Europe. He wrote about the abuses of the Roman Catholic Church.

**independent:** free from the influence, guidance, or control of others; self-reliant

## Early Life

Desiderius Erasmus was born in Rotterdam in the Netherlands in 1466. There are only a few accounts of his early life. We know that his parents were not married. We also know they made a good life for him until they died when Erasmus was about 14 years old. After his parents' death, Erasmus attended schools supported by the church. These schools had a lifelong influence on him.

## A Priest, Scholar, and Writer

Erasmus became a priest when he was about 21. Two years later, he decided to study at the University of Paris. From that time on, he spent most of his life writing and learning. He traveled to many of the important universities in Europe. For a short period of time, he taught at Cambridge University in England. However, Erasmus did not like university life. He liked being an **independent** scholar and writer.

## Criticizing Abuses in the Church

Erasmus was known as one of the most important and most outspoken scholars of his time. Long before the beginning of the Protestant Reformation, Erasmus wrote about the abuses of the Roman Catholic Church. He was especially angered by the church's sale of indulgences.

## *In Praise of Folly*

While visiting a friend in England in 1509, Erasmus wrote his most famous work, *In Praise of Folly*. In this book, Erasmus made fun of what he thought were the foolish practices of the church. The book attacked superstitious religious practices.

It criticized religious leaders who lived like kings. In this book, he also suggested that things might not necessarily be the way they look. He asked, "Who would not **avow** that the king is a rich and great lord? Yet let the king be **unfurnished** in goods of the spirit, let him find satisfaction in nothing, and you see in a **trice** that he is the poorest of men." Today, we might say: "Who wouldn't agree that a king is a rich and great person? But what if you found out that the king didn't believe in spiritual things or that he didn't enjoy anything. Wouldn't you agree that he was a very poor man?"

▲ Erasmus made fun of what he thought were foolish practices of the church.

## The Crisis of the Protestant Reformation

For about the next 10 years, Erasmus criticized the abuses of the Roman Catholic Church. He also translated the New Testament of the Bible into Greek. His work made him famous and rich. During this same time, Martin Luther was publishing his own criticisms of the Roman Catholic Church. Because Erasmus was such a well-known scholar, he was asked to take sides on the question of church reform. Martin Luther wanted Erasmus to agree with him. The leaders of the Roman Catholic Church wanted Erasmus to support their position.

## Pleasing No One

In the end, Erasmus agreed with Luther's position that the Roman Catholic Church must be reformed. However, he wanted the church to reform itself. He did not want to see the church split up. At the end of his life, Protestants and Catholics alike disliked Erasmus. He died in 1536. Shortly after his death, the Roman Catholic Church placed his writings on the *Index of Prohibited Books*. But this did not stop people from wanting to read what he had to say. In fact, his books have been reprinted many times since his death. Today, Erasmus is remembered as one of the Roman Catholic Church's strongest critics, but also as one of its most loyal members. 📖

**avow:** to declare as true
***Index of Prohibited Books:*** a listing of books and writings that Roman Catholics were forbidden to read
**trice:** a very short time; an instant
**unfurnish:** to strip

### What Do You Think?

How would you describe the problem that Erasmus faced during the Protestant Reformation? Do you agree or disagree with the position he took? Why?

# IGNATIUS OF LOYOLA —
# Founder of the Jesuits

| A.D. 1400 | | | A.D. 1560 |
|---|---|---|---|

**1491-1556**
Ignatius of Loyola

**1521**
Ignatius is wounded
in the leg

**1541**
The Society of Jesus begins and
Ignatius is elected the leader

▲ Ignatius of Loyola lived in Spain. After recovering from an injury, he started on a journey to Jerusalem.

**wounded:** hurt; injured

The year was 1491. The location was northern Spain. At this time and in this place, the man we know of as Ignatius of Loyola was born.

## Early Life
He was born Iñigo López de Recalde, the last of 12 children. His family was part of the Spanish nobility. As a young man, Ignatius was mostly interested in having a good time and enjoying himself. He lived a wild life as a soldier fighting for Spain. Things changed for Ignatius when he reached the age of 30. He was seriously **wounded** in the leg during a battle defending the Spanish city of Pamplona against the French. This leg injury forced him to rest for a long time. While he was resting and getting well, he began to read about the life of Jesus and the lives of various saints. The more that he read, the more peaceful he began to feel. This was the beginning of his religious life.

## A Journey toward Jerusalem
After he recovered from his injuries, Ignatius started on a journey toward Jerusalem. He decided that he wanted to live where Jesus had spent his life on earth. After Ignatius left his home, he came to a small Spanish town called Manresa. While he was there, Ignatius reported that he had a vision. In this vision, Ignatius believed he saw God. Later, Ignatius said that this experience made him believe that God was present in everyone's life. Ignatius soon decided that he wanted to become a priest.

▶ Ignatius journeyed to Jerusalem to live where Jesus had spent his life on earth.

Over the next few years, Ignatius studied to become a priest and also spent time helping people. After he became a priest, Ignatius traveled to Rome to see the pope. On his journey, he reported that he had another vision.

## The Society of Jesus—The "Jesuits"

The following year, 1539, Ignatius invited several of his friends who were priests to come to Rome. After much discussion and prayer, they decided to start a religious community. This new community would be dedicated to education and missionary work. They also promised complete obedience to the pope. Officially, the Society of Jesus (or Jesuits) began in April 1541. The members elected Ignatius as the leader of the new religious community. He was called the Superior of the Jesuits. As Superior, Ignatius had many responsibilities.

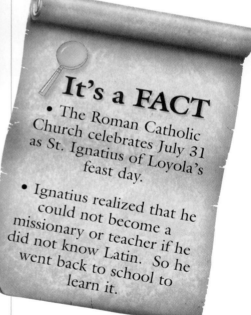

## It's a FACT

- The Roman Catholic Church celebrates July 31 as St. Ignatius of Loyola's feast day.

- Ignatius realized that he could not become a missionary or teacher if he did not know Latin. So he went back to school to learn it.

▲ In this picture, Pope Paul III is confirming the Society of Jesus (Jesuits). St. Ignatius of Loyola is the patron saint of soldiers and the Jesuits.

## What Do You Think?

1. What advantages did Ignatius of Loyola have in life? What obstacles did he face?

2. What lessons could you draw from reading about the life of Ignatius of Loyola?

3. What qualities of Ignatius of Loyola do you admire? Give examples to justify your answer.

4. Ignatius of Loyola was greatly influenced by reading about the lives of saints. Does reading about people's lives influence you? Why or why not?

He wrote the rules for the Society of Jesus. He also spent a great deal of time writing to members of the Society who had been sent by the pope to faraway places. More than 7,000 of his letters have survived.

## The Growth of the Jesuit Order

Over time, the membership of the Society of Jesus grew. The work Jesuits did in the name of Jesus became well known. Perhaps Jesuits are best known for starting new schools. In each place where the Society's members were sent, they began a school. These Jesuit schools were places to educate new priests as well as faithful followers of the church. The Jesuits spread across Europe and many also went as missionaries to Asia and to the New World.

## St. Ignatius of Loyola

As Ignatius grew older, he suffered from many physical problems. In the summer of 1556, he became ill and died a short time later. Ignatius had dedicated his life to God. Recognizing this dedication, in 1622 Pope Gregory XV made him a saint. Today, people refer to Ignatius as St. Ignatius of Loyola. 📖

# WILLIAM TYNDALE
# and the English Bible

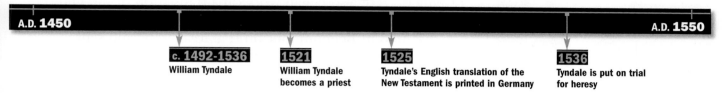

A.D. **1450**            A.D. **1550**

**c. 1492-1536**
William Tyndale

**1521**
William Tyndale
becomes a priest

**1525**
Tyndale's English translation of the
New Testament is printed in Germany

**1536**
Tyndale is put on trial
for heresy

William Tyndale translated a book that people lined up for hours to read—the book was the Bible.

## Early Life
No one knows for sure when William Tyndale was born. Some believe he was born in 1492. Others think he was born in 1494 or 1495. We know that he was born in a little town in western England. As a young man, Tyndale was a student at both Oxford University and Cambridge University. He became a priest in 1521. Around that time, he began to talk about his goal in life. More than anything else, Tyndale wanted to translate the Bible into English. Up until that time, no one had ever translated the Bible into English from the original Greek or Hebrew.

## Few Encouraging Words
Many powerful religious leaders tried to discourage him from this goal, but Tyndale was **persistent**. He said, "If God spare my life, ere many years I will cause a boy that driveth the plow to know more of the Scripture than thou dost." Tyndale was saying that if God let him live, he would translate the Bible into English. This would mean that a simple farm boy would be able to know more about the Bible than an educated religious leader. However, Henry VIII, the powerful king of England, did not think an English version of the Bible was a very good idea.

## A Life in Exile
Tyndale decided to go to Germany. While he was there, he met Martin Luther, the man who started the Protestant Reformation. Tyndale's life in exile was very hard. He did not have much money and often faced persecution and danger.

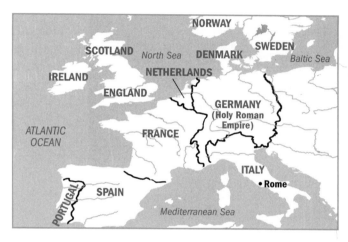

▲ William Tyndale attended Oxford University and Cambridge University in England. He traveled to other parts of Europe.

▲ William Tyndale wanted to translate the Bible into English.

**persistent:** refusing to give up or let go

▲ One of Tyndale's bitterest enemies was Thomas More, the man who eventually was caught up in a power struggle with King Henry VIII.

**credit:** an acknowledgment of work done

Despite these difficulties, Tyndale worked diligently on his translation of the Bible. Finally, in 1525, 18,000 copies of his English translation of the New Testament were printed in Germany. Many of these copies were smuggled to England.

## The English Bible

Tyndale continued to revise his English translation of the New Testament. He also began work on a translation of the Old Testament. However, before he completed this work, Tyndale was captured in Belgium, put on trial for heresy, and sentenced to die in 1536. While waiting for the death sentence to be carried out, he asked for a warm coat and "to have my Hebrew Bible, Hebrew Grammar, and Hebrew Dictionary, that I may spend my time with that study."

Tyndale's work did not end with his death. Miles Coverdale, a friend of Tyndale's from Oxford, continued Tyndale's translation of the Bible. An entirely English version of the Bible was published in 1537. Several copies of this Bible were placed in a London Church where people lined up all day long to see it and read from it. William Tyndale was not given **credit** for his work on this Bible, but it was his translation. It also reflected his ideas about what words and phrases to leave out and which ones to insert. Some people say that other English Bibles have been influenced by William Tyndale's original translation. 📖

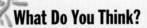

### What Do You Think?

**1.** What advantages did William Tyndale have in life? What obstacles did he face?

**2.** What qualities of William Tyndale do you admire? Give examples to justify your answer.

**3.** Why do you think some people in England did not want the Bible translated into English?

## It's a FACT

• Of the 18,000 copies of Tyndale's translation of the New Testament, only two survive today.

• King Henry VIII approved of Miles Coverdale's Bible in English.

# NICOLAUS COPERNICUS —
# The Man Who Moved the Earth

A.D. **1400**  A.D. **1600**

**1473-1543**
**Nicolaus Copernicus**

**1543**
**Copernicus is given a copy of his published work**

Did a scientist from Poland really move the earth in the 1500s? Some people say that he did!

## Early Life

Nicolaus Copernicus was born in February 1473 in Poland, a country in northern Europe. His father died when he was a young boy, so he went to live with his uncle. His uncle thought education was important and helped Nicolaus get into the University of Krakow. This school was famous for its courses in mathematics and astronomy. As he studied these subjects, Nicolaus discovered what he thought were mistakes in people's ideas about how the sun and planets moved in the sky.

## How Do Planets Move?

After several years at the university, Copernicus traveled to Italy to study at an Italian university. While he was there, Copernicus became more interested in how the planets moved in the sky. He became so interested in this topic that he began to draw the positions of the stars and planets. Telescopes had not been invented yet, so he drew sketches based on what he could see with his own eyes. Before leaving Italy to go home, he wrote a short report about the movement of the planets.

## Developing a Theory of Planetary Movement

When Copernicus returned to Poland, his uncle helped him get a job in the church. This job allowed Copernicus to earn a living as well as to continue working on his theory of how the planets moved. His theory was that the earth moves in an orbit around the sun. This idea was very, very different from what everyone believed at the time. For thousands of years, everyone had accepted the ancient Greeks' teaching that the sun and all of the planets moved around the earth. In addition, the Christian Bible said that God stopped the sun. Because Copernicus's theory went against both traditional thinking and church teaching, Copernicus waited a long time before he made a public announcement about his ideas. He was afraid that the church would call him a **heretic**. It took a long time for anyone to pay attention to what he had said.

▲ Copernicus studied law at the University of Bologna and studied medicine at the University of Padua. However, he became interested in how the planets moved in the sky.

**heretic:** a person who has religious ideas and opinions not approved by the church

Finally, people began to talk about his ideas. One story says that Copernicus was given a copy of his published work as he lay on his deathbed in 1543.

## A Leader of the Scientific Revolution

Copernicus was one of the leaders of the scientific revolution. His thinking about astronomy was different from what almost everyone else at the time believed was true. Many scientists became interested in his ideas and began to study his theory. Using new inventions, including the telescope, they found evidence to support the idea that the earth moves around the sun. This helped prove that Copernicus was right. It may be correct to say that Copernicus was the man who moved the earth! □

### It's a FACT

There are many monuments and buildings named after Copernicus, including an orbiting space laboratory on display at a museum in Washington, D.C.

▶ In this picture, Copernicus is studying the stars using an instrument called an astrolabe.

### What Do You Think?

1. What advantages did Nicolaus Copernicus have in life? What obstacles did he face?

2. Copernicus waited a long time before he published ideas about his new theory. What was he afraid of? Do you agree or disagree with his decision to wait? Why?

3. Are people today afraid to express ideas that are different? Why or why not? Give examples to justify your answer.

4. From reading this information about Nicolaus Copernicus's life, what can you conclude about the role of science and religion in society during this time?

# ANDREAS VESALIUS —
# A New Kind of Doctor

Andreas Vesalius was born in Brussels in 1514. When he was about 20 years old, he went to study at the University of Paris. He was interested in learning about medicine. In 1537, he went to the University of Padua. He earned a degree in medicine and got a job teaching. Vesalius changed the way medicine was taught at the university. He asked his students to come close to the **operating** table so they could see what was happening. He thought it was important to observe the human body in order to understand how it works. One way he learned about the human body was by **dissecting cadavers**. Up to this time, most other doctors only dissected animals.

Vesalius showed that what other doctors had been teaching was incorrect. It took great courage for Vesalius to speak out against these earlier teachings. Vesalius wrote about what he learned through his research. His most famous book, *De Humani Corporis Fabricai*, was published in 1543. This was the most accurate and complete book on human **anatomy** up to this time. Below is some of what Vesalius wrote about the human brain. In the first part, he tells the easiest way to get brains for study. Then he tells how to open the skull to look at them.

▲ **Vesalius was born in present-day Brussels, Belgium, in 1514. He studied in France and Italy.**

**anatomy:** shape and structure of an organism
**cadaver:** dead body
**dissect:** to cut apart, especially for study
**operate:** to perform surgery
**orbital region:** the area where the eyes are located

### Vesalius Describes the Human Brain

Heads of beheaded men are the most suitable since they can be obtained immediately after execution with the friendly help of judges ... Whatever way the head has fallen, its bone must be divided with the saw. Begin the dissection with the razor or knife in the **orbital region**, a thumb's breadth above the eyebrows ...

## Analyze the Source!

1. Read the excerpt and tell in your own words what it says.

2. How does this excerpt help you learn about the influence of science during the scientific revolution?

3. Why does it take courage to speak out against accepted teachings?

# FRANCIS BACON —
## "Knowledge is Power"

A.D. 1500

**1561**
Francis Bacon is born

**1603**
James I becomes king of England and gives Bacon many honors and titles

**1605**
Bacon publishes *Novum Organum*

**1626**
Bacon becomes ill and dies

A.D. 1650

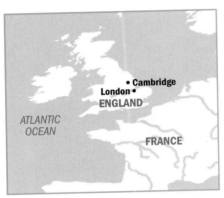

▲ Francis Bacon lived in England. He was born in London and attended Trinity College in Cambridge.

**House of Commons:** one of the two branches of Parliament, England's law-making body

▲ Francis Bacon entered Trinity College in Cambridge at the age of 12.

As a boy, Francis Bacon asked lots of questions. His favorite question seemed to be, "Why?" History remembers him as the man who showed the power of inductive reasoning.

## Early Life
Francis Bacon was born in London in 1561. His father was an advisor to the queen of England. Francis was the youngest of six sons. He was educated at home until he was about 12. Then he entered Trinity College in Cambridge, England. Even at this early age, Francis questioned many ideas about science that everyone else accepted. His doubts about how people looked at scientific ideas became an important part of his later writings. When Francis was 18 years old, his father died. As the youngest son, he had no inheritance, so he had to think about earning a living. He decided to study law and become a lawyer. By the time he was 23, he had entered the **House of Commons**.

## A Flourishing Career
When James I became king of England in 1603, Bacon's career began to flourish. The king gave Bacon many honors and titles, including making him a knight. In addition to practicing law and working in the government, Bacon also spent time thinking and writing about science and nature. He believed that he could develop a better system to organize information.

## Experiment!
Francis Bacon wanted people to know all about nature. He thought the best way to understand nature was through experimentation. He did not think people could simply trust their judgment. He insisted that to understand nature, people should use inductive reasoning. Inductive reasoning begins with observations and experiments and leads the scientist to develop a theory. Bacon wrote about his ideas in a famous book called *Novum Organum* (in English this means "new tools"). Bacon's writing became one part of the new scientific method called "inductive reasoning."

◀ Francis Bacon was the first to say, "knowledge is power."

**bribery:** the act of giving, taking, or offering money (or something valuable) to influence or persuade

## What Do You Think?

**1.** What advantages did Francis Bacon have in life? What obstacles did he face?

**2.** What lessons could you draw from reading about the life of Francis Bacon?

**3.** In what ways was Francis Bacon's life remarkable?

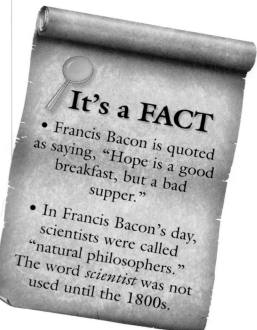

## It's a FACT

• Francis Bacon is quoted as saying, "Hope is a good breakfast, but a bad supper."

• In Francis Bacon's day, scientists were called "natural philosophers." The word *scientist* was not used until the 1800s.

## ersonal Troubles

year after the publication of *Novum Organum*, Bacon got into ouble with the law. He was charged with **bribery** and admitted at he was guilty of this crime. He had to pay a fine and lost his les, but he continued to think and write about science. In 26, Francis Bacon was conducting an experiment about the ect of cold temperatures on meat. He became ill and died a ort time later in March 1626. ◻

# LETTERS OF LOVE —
# Galileo and Suor Maria Celeste

A.D. 1450                                                                A.D. 1650

**1473-1543**
Nicolaus Copernicus

**1564-1642**
Galileo Galilei

**1600**
Suor Maria Celeste
is born

**1632**
Galileo publishes a book that says the
earth moves around the sun

▲ Galileo lived his entire life in Italy, but
he was famous all over the world because
of his inventions and discoveries.

---

**house arrest:** being confined to
one's house, instead of a jail
**recant:** to take back something
that was said earlier

Galileo Galilei was born in 1564 in Florence, Italy. He was a
talented musician and painter, but he is best known as a
brilliant scientist. Galileo lived his entire life in Italy, but was
famous all over the world because of his inventions and
discoveries. People were especially excited about the telescopes he
made. These telescopes allowed him to see stars and planets more
clearly and accurately than ever before. Using these telescopes,
he gathered evidence to support Copernicus's theory that the
earth moves around the sun.

## The Earth Isn't the Center of the Universe?

In 1632, Galileo published a book about his theory. At this time,
both the Roman Catholic Church and Protestant churches taught
that the sun moved around the earth. This idea had been accepted
since the time of the ancient Greeks. Church leaders said Galileo's
idea that the earth moves around the sun was heresy. Galileo was
put on trial for his ideas. He was disappointed and surprised that the
church leaders did not accept his logic and evidence. Later, Galileo
**recanted** his ideas about the movement of the planets, but he was
put under **house arrest**. Galileo spent the last eight years of his life
conducting scientific experiments until he died in 1642.

▼ Galileo was born in 1564
in Florence, Italy.

◀ Galileo was a talented musician and painter, but he is best known as a brilliant scientist.

## A Daughter's Love

Galileo never married, but he loved a woman named Marina Gamba. They had three children together—two daughters and a son. Because Galileo and Marina were not married, their children had fewer opportunities in life. For example, his daughters were considered "unmarriageable." Galileo decided that the only alternative they had was to become nuns. Galileo's older daughter, Virginia, who was born in 1600, was 13 years old when she became a nun. Galileo and Virginia (who changed her name to "Suor Maria Celeste" when she became a nun) kept in touch with each other through letters. We do not have any of the letters that Galileo sent to his daughter. However, historians have found many letters that Suor Maria Celeste sent to her father.

Today, Suor Maria Celeste's letters are bound together with cardboard and leather covers. They are kept in Florence's National Central Library. You can still read the handwriting (if you can read Italian!), but the black ink has faded to brown. Some of the letters have water marks on them. Maybe the letters got wet when they were carried through the rain. Or maybe, as some people think, tears made the water stains. If this is true, were they Suor Maria Celeste's tears or Galileo's tears? We will never know. Below is part of one of the letters Suor Maria Celeste wrote to her father in 1633. At this time, Galileo was waiting to be questioned by the Roman Catholic Church for his idea that the earth moves around the sun. 📖

**It's a FACT**
Suor Maria Celeste was a Poor Clare nun.

**confide:** to tell in private
**jeopardize:** to risk or endanger
**torment:** great physical or mental pain

## Analyze the Source!

1. Read the excerpt and tell in your own words what it says.

2. How does this excerpt help you learn about the culture and history of Europe during the scientific revolution?

3. How does this excerpt help you learn about children's relationships with their parents during this period?

## Suor Maria Celeste Writes to Her Father

The only thing for you to do now is to guard your good spirits, taking care not to **jeopardize** your health with excessive worry, but to direct your thoughts and hopes to God, Who, like a tender loving father, never abandons those who **confide** in Him and appeal to Him for help in time of need ... I wanted to write to you now, to tell you I partake in your **torments**, so as to make them lighter for you to bear ...

# JOHANNES KEPLER — Supporter of Copernicus's Theory

A.D. 1450                                                                    A.D. 1650

**1473-1543**
Nicolaus Copernicus

**1564-1642**
Galileo Galilei

**1571-1630**
Johannes Kepler

▲ **Kepler used mathematics to support Copernicus's theory that the planets orbit the sun. He also supported Galileo in his discovery of new planets and moons.**

**disparage:** to belittle or insult
**equanimity:** calm
**jeer:** mocking; insult
**rash:** acting without thinking

Johannes Kepler was born on December 27, 1571 in a small town in southwest Germany not far from France. Johannes became very ill when he was still a baby and suffered from poor health most of his life. As a young man, he studied mathematics and astronomy at a German university. His teachers could see that Kepler was extremely intelligent. Even as a student, Kepler was very interested in Nicolaus Copernicus's theory that the earth revolves around the sun. At the time, this theory was not very popular. In fact, both Roman Catholic and Protestant leaders condemned the idea.

Kepler used mathematics to show that the planets travel at different speeds. He showed that their speed has to do with their distance from the sun. His work supported Copernicus's theory. In coming to this conclusion, Kepler communicated with other great scientists who lived and worked in Europe during this time. One of the greatest of these scientists was Galileo, a Florentine mathematician. Below is part of a letter Kepler sent to Galileo in 1610. Galileo had just published a book announcing his discovery of new planets and moons. In this letter, Kepler recognizes Galileo's achievement. Kepler died in 1630. 📖

## Analyze the Source!

1. Read the excerpt and tell in your own words what it says.

2. How does this excerpt help you learn about the culture and history of Europe during the scientific revolution?

3. How does this excerpt help you learn about the influence of science during this period?

### Kepler Recognizes Galileo's Achievement

I may seem **rash** in accepting your claims so readily with no support from my own experience. But why should I not believe a most learned mathematician. ... He has no intention of practicing deception in a bid for vulgar publicity, nor does he pretend to have seen what he has not seen. Because he loves the truth, he does not hesitate to oppose even the most familiar opinions, and to bear the **jeers** of the crowd with **equanimity**. Does he not make his writing public? ... Shall I **disparage** him, a gentleman of Florence, for the things he has seen?

# RENE DESCARTES —
# Mathematician and Philosopher

A.D. **1500**      A.D. **1700**

**1596-1650**
Rene Descartes

**1628**
Descartes meets a cardinal who encourages him to spend his life studying mathematics and philosophy

**1647**
Descartes is given a pension by the French government in honor of his work in mathematics

**1649**
Queen Christina of Sweden invites Descartes to come to her country

"I think, therefore, I am." This is one of the most famous quotations in philosophy. It reflects the ideas and the approach to understanding the world of Rene Descartes.

## Personal Life
Rene Descartes was born in Tours, France in 1596. His family was an important part of the community, and his father was a member of the local city government. At the age of eight, Rene was sent to a Jesuit school. Because of his delicate health, he stayed in bed most mornings. He continued this habit throughout his life. From paintings of Descartes, we know that he was a small man with a large head and big nose. We know a few details of his personal life. He never married. He did not have a warm personality. Sometimes he was described as selfish.

## A Mathematical Challenge
Descartes was generally displeased about the quality of his education. Most of the subjects he studied did not give him the knowledge he wanted. There was one exception—mathematics! Descartes thought the knowledge he gained from mathematics was very important. In 1612, Descartes went to Paris and studied mathematics. Then, around 1617, he joined the army and was sent to the Netherlands. While there, Descartes had an unexpected opportunity to use his mathematical ability. Because Descartes could not speak the local language, he asked a man on the street to translate a sign hanging in a store window. The man told him that the sign challenged people to solve a difficult mathematical problem. No one had been able to solve this problem, but Descartes solved the problem quickly.

**NETHERLANDS**

**FRANCE**

*Mediterranean Sea*

▲ **Rene Descartes was born in France in 1596.**

▶ **Descartes said, "I think, therefore, I am." This drawing shows Descartes in Amsterdam, an important city in the Netherlands.**

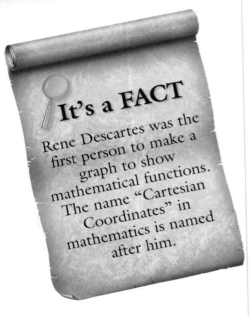

## It's a FACT

Rene Descartes was the first person to make a graph to show mathematical functions. The name "Cartesian Coordinates" in mathematics is named after him.

## Three Dreams

In 1619, while still in the army, Descartes reported that he had three dreams. He claimed these dreams were signs that he would develop a way to study the world based on mathematics. In 1621, Descartes left the army and began traveling. Then, in 1628, Descartes's life changed when he met a cardinal, an important church leader, in Paris. This cardinal encouraged Descartes to spend his life studying mathematics and philosophy. Descartes agreed and moved back to the Netherlands where for the next 20 years he worked on his ideas.

## Describing How the World Works

During the first few years in the Netherlands, Descartes wrote *Le Monde* (in English this means "the world"). This book was his attempt to describe the **physical laws** of the universe. However, at just about the time his ideas were going to be published, Descartes learned about Galileo's trouble with the Roman Catholic Church for writing about similar ideas. Not wanting to be called a heretic, Descartes decided to wait many years before publishing his book.

## Deductive Reasoning and the Scientific Method

During the rest of his time in the Netherlands, Descartes wrote many other books about the physical laws of the universe. He also wrote about his discovery of how to measure angles and curves. He believed scientists should start with basic ideas and then conduct experiments to see if the ideas are correct. This approach is called deductive reasoning. Descartes believed that only ideas that could be proven by evidence or reasoning were true. This approach to science based on observation and experimentation is called the "scientific method." Descartes's ideas helped improve the scientific method. In 1647, Descartes was given a **pension** by the French government in honor of his work in mathematics.

**pension:** money paid regularly as a retirement benefit or as support

**physical laws:** general rules about the nature of energy and nonliving things

▲ In 1649, Queen Christina of Sweden invited Descartes to come to her country as her mathematics tutor. Rene Descartes believed that the best way to do good work in mathematics was not to get out of bed in the morning until he felt like it. Queen Christina did not share Rene Descartes's view of sleeping in. She insisted that he give her lessons in mathematics at 5 A.M.

## What Do You Think?

1. What advantages did Rene Descartes have in life? What obstacles did he face?

2. What lesson could you draw from reading about the life of Rene Descartes?

3. Rene Descartes is famous for the statement, "I think, therefore, I am." What does this statement mean? What does it prove?

## Rene Descartes's Legacy

In 1649, Queen Christina of Sweden invited Descartes to come to her country. He accepted the queen's invitation. However, the cold climate in Sweden was not good for his delicate health. Descartes became ill and died in Stockholm, Sweden in 1650. More than 300 years later, people remember him as one of the leaders in developing modern mathematics and the use of the scientific method.□

# ISAAC NEWTON —
# A Scientific Giant

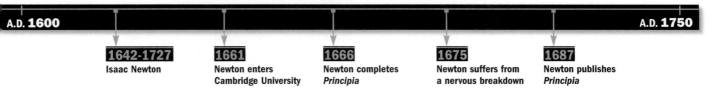

| A.D. 1600 | | | | | A.D. 1750 |
|---|---|---|---|---|---|

**1642-1727**
Isaac Newton

**1661**
Newton enters
Cambridge University

**1666**
Newton completes
*Principia*

**1675**
Newton suffers from
a nervous breakdown

**1687**
Newton publishes
*Principia*

Isaac Newton said, "If I have seen farther, it is by standing on the shoulders of giants." He may have stood on the shoulders of giants, but he remains one of the most important men in the history of science. Isaac Newton was a scientific giant in his own right.

## Early Life

On Christmas Day in 1642, Isaac Newton was born in Grantham, England, a small farming town about 100 miles northwest of London. His father died before he was born. His mother soon remarried and Isaac's grandmother raised him. As a young boy from a poor farming family, Isaac did not show much ability as a farmer. However, he was very bright and his uncle suggested that he go to college. In 1661 he entered Cambridge University. His family wanted him to become a minister in the Church of England.

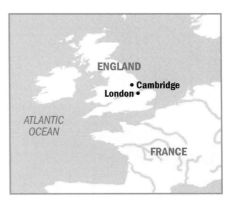

▲ Isaac Newton lived in England.

◄ Isaac Newton's approach to science was very logical and based on reason. However, he believed deeply in the existence of God. He said the natural world could only have come from "an intelligent and powerful Being."

▶ This drawing shows Newton analyzing a ray of light. Newton studied light, the laws of motion, and mathematics.

## It's a FACT

In addition to his scientific work, Isaac Newton was active politically. He was elected to Parliament in 1689. Later he was appointed as the official in charge of the Royal Mint.

## Intellectual Influences

As a young boy and throughout his life, Newton kept almost everything he wrote. From reading these notebooks, historians know what he studied at school and how his ideas changed as he grew older. For example, we know that at college Newton studied the teachings of Aristotle, an ancient Greek thinker. We also know he wrote about the great thinkers of his own time. These thinkers included men such as Copernicus, Galileo, and Descartes, who were among the first to question Aristotle's thinking. When Newton read these new ideas, he realized that the study of science had to change.

## A Creative Time

Isaac Newton was forced to leave Cambridge from 1665-1666 because of the threat of the plague. Later, Newton said this period away from Cambridge was extremely creative for him. During this time, he wrote one of his most famous works—*Philosophiae Naturalis Principia Mathematica*. In English this means "mathematical principles of natural philosophy," but the book is more commonly known simply as *Principia*. In this work, Newton described three laws of motion, which have become known as Newton's Laws of Motion. These laws define the actions of forces such as **gravity**. Newton's work put into practice what he had come to believe. He thought theories had to be tested before they could be accepted as true. He did not think it was enough to just observe an experiment and try to think about why it happened. Throughout his life, Newton was hesitant to publish his ideas. In fact, even though he completed *Principia* in 1666, he did not publish it until 1687.

## Facing Criticism and Accepting Admiration

Newton's ideas were very different than other scientists' ideas, and his work was not immediately accepted in Europe. In fact, several of his rivals criticized his ideas and published articles saying that Newton's experiments could not be duplicated. Disagreements between Newton and European scientists continued for more than 10 years. Eventually, however, Newton's ideas became more widely accepted throughout Europe. Scientists began to respect and admire him.

Throughout his life, Newton lived very simply. He was generous to his friends, but he could respond harshly to people who challenged his ideas. During his lifetime, scientists and other educated people admired Newton. Alexander Pope, a famous English poet, wrote this **rhyme** in honor of Isaac Newton:

> *Nature, and nature's laws lay hid in night.*
> *God said, "Let Newton be!" and all was light.*

Many people considered Isaac Newton a genius, but Newton was modest about his fame. He said, "If I have seen farther, it is by standing on the shoulders of giants."

## Newton's Legacy

In the last years of his life, Isaac Newton spent much of his time revising his major writings. He never married and his personal life was not always happy. He suffered from a nervous breakdown in 1675. Throughout his life, criticism hurt him very much. Though he was a man of simple tastes, after his death in 1727, he was buried with great **ceremony** in London. Scientists today still think of Isaac Newton as a genius. His contributions in mathematics and chemistry formed the foundation of the modern **physical sciences**. 📖

**ceremony:** an act or set of acts performed according to tradition or custom; ritual

**gravity:** a force that tends to pull all bodies in the earth's sphere towards the center of the earth

**physical science:** any of the sciences that have to do with the nature and property of energy and nonliving things; physics, chemistry, astronomy, and geology are all physical sciences

**rhyme:** a poem in which the ending lines have the same sound

### What Do You Think?

1. What advantages did Isaac Newton have in life? What obstacles did he face?

2. What qualities of Isaac Newton do you admire? Give examples to justify your answer.

3. Throughout his life, Isaac Newton was very sensitive to criticism and could be greatly hurt by it. How is criticism a harmful thing? How can it be a good thing?

# HENRY THE NAVIGATOR —
# The Man Who Began Europe's Age of Exploration

A.D. **1300**                                                                                        A.D. **1550**

**1394-1460**
Henry of Portugal

**1434**
One of Henry's expeditions
sails around Cape Bojador

**1458**
Henry's sailors establish
colonies in Africa

**1459**
Fra Mauro completes his world map based
on information from Henry's explorers

▲ Henry the Navigator lived and died in Portugal. He
sent out important expeditions to Africa.

When Henry the Navigator was born, Portugal was a small kingdom on the Iberian Peninsula. Henry's parents, King John I and Queen Philippa, were the rulers of Portugal. King John had been fighting against invading armies from other kingdoms, including the kingdom of Castile. He also had been trying hard to unify the people in his own kingdom. In 1385, he succeeded in unifying Portugal.

## Early Life

King John and Queen Philippa had six children—five boys and one girl. Henry was the third son. He was born in March 1394 in the city of Oporto, Portugal. All of the boys were very well educated. They studied Greek, Latin, Portuguese, and French. By 1411, when Henry was about 17, Portugal was a prosperous kingdom. There were no wars, everyone in the royal family was healthy, and the three older boys, including Henry, had become knights.

## Not a Tournament, A War

King John wanted to celebrate his good fortune, so he decided to hold a jousting tournament. A jousting tournament was a sporting event where two knights on horseback—each knight carrying a lance—try to knock one another to the ground. People came to watch and to cheer for their favorite knights. King John's plan was to invite knights from all over Europe. He was going to award great prizes to the winners of the tournament. However, the king's sons were not interested in a sporting event. It would be better, they thought, if they could have a real fight.

The sons convinced their father that Portugal should capture the North African city of Ceuta (SAY-oo-tah). Arab traders ruled this city. If Henry and his brothers were successful, they would gain control of Ceuta's trade routes.

▲ Henry insisted that all his ships carry
a compass. At his home, he had a
compass face built into his courtyard to
help train his sailors.

For three years they prepared to fight. Then, in 1415, the Portuguese fleet sailed to Ceuta and captured the city. However, Portugal did not become wealthy and gain control of the trade routes. The Arab traders of Ceuta simply moved their trading business to another city they controlled. But this was Henry's first fight and the beginning of Portuguese expansion in Africa.

## Henry's School of Navigation

After the capture of Ceuta, Henry returned to Portugal. He decided that if he could not force the Arabs to trade, he would try to bypass them completely. To do this he had to sail along the African coastline farther south than any Europeans had ever done. But how? To learn how to make this kind of trip, he invited sailors and shipbuilders to come to Portugal where he started a school of navigation. At this school, sailors, shipbuilders, mapmakers, astronomers, and others interested in and knowledgeable about sea travel could share information.

Henry gathered every map he could find. He encouraged the men at the school to develop new sailing tools to help sailors determine their exact position at sea. When Henry thought that his students were ready to explore the unknown coastline, he sent them off on expeditions. Each sea captain was told to write down what he saw and to make drawings of the land and other geographical features. Henry was interested in knowing about the tides, reefs, channels, landmarks, harbors, the color of the water, and other information that would help future expeditions. Sailors had not done this before in a systematic way.

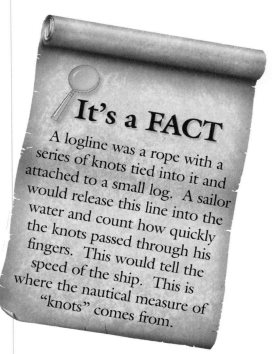

## It's a FACT

A logline was a rope with a series of knots tied into it and attached to a small log. A sailor would release this line into the water and count how quickly the knots passed through his fingers. This would tell the speed of the ship. This is where the nautical measure of "knots" comes from.

# New Information about Africa

By 1434, one of Henry's expeditions sailed around Cape Bojador. This was an important milestone because legends said the water would boil red with blood after rounding Cape Bojador. The expedition did not find red, boiling blood!

With each trip, Henry's explorers sailed farther south down the African coast. On one trip, the sailors left their ship and went inland by horseback. They were attacked. They returned to Portugal and reported this to Henry. Henry told his sailors to go back and make friends with the Africans they had encountered. When the sailors went back, they captured about 10 Africans and brought them back to Portugal. Henry listened to these people tell about their land. He began to realize that Africa was a very large continent and that there was land farther south. He released the prisoners and sent them home.

# Bypassing Arab Traders

Henry's explorers discovered uninhabited islands off the western coast of Africa. They set up trading posts along the coast. They traded cloth, wheat, iron knives, and other manufactured goods for African gold. Henry realized that his ambition of trading directly with Africans for gold—bypassing the Muslims—was possible.

This also was the beginning of the African slave trade. When an African ruler had no more gold to trade, he offered prisoners as slaves. In 1441, Portuguese explorers brought their first cargo of African slaves to Portugal. Soon, slaves were in demand in Europe.

# Henry the Navigator's Legacy

By 1458, Henry's sailors had established many colonies on the western coast of Africa. At his school in Portugal, mapmakers were using the information from the many voyages to draw new maps and charts. Astronomers and instrument makers were finding ways to improve navigational tools that were critical to Henry's sailors. In 1459, one of the greatest Venetian mapmakers, **Fra** Mauro, completed a large map of the world based on the information Henry's explorers had gathered. This map showed the world using information carefully gathered by explorers. There were no sea monsters, just the physical geography of the earth drawn with precise mathematics. Superstition was being replaced by scientific facts.

Henry died in 1460 when he was 66 years old. Although he was called "the Navigator," Henry never commanded a ship and only sailed on three voyages. While Henry died in debt, Portugal became a very rich country because of the explorations he sponsored. In many ways, Henry is the man who began Europe's age of exploration—a time which had far-reaching consequences. □

▲ Henry the Navigator is remembered all over the world as the man who began Europe's age of exploration. This statue of Henry stands in New Bedford, Massachusetts.

**Fra:** brother; a title given to an Italian friar or monk; abbreviation of the Italian word *frate*

## What Do You Think?

1. Henry the Navigator could have done many different things with his life. Why do you think he started a school of navigation and encouraged exploration?

2. What were some of the unintended consequences of Henry's exploration?

3. What do you think is Henry the Navigator's greatest accomplishment?

# GOMES EANES DE ZURARA —

# An Account of the Portuguese Slave Trade

Much of what we know about Prince Henry of Portugal, known as "Henry the Navigator," comes from the written accounts of Gomes Eanes de Zurara. Zurara served as the official chronicler, or reporter, of Prince Henry's experiences. Because he depended on Prince Henry's support, historians consider Zurara a biased observer. Often, Zurara's accounts portray Prince Henry as a perfect Christian prince without any flaws. Still, Zurara's writings give us a glimpse of the historical events of the time. Zurara's two most important reports are the *Chronicle of the Capture of Ceuta*, written around 1450, and the *Chronicle of Guinea*, written around 1457-1465. The *Chronicle of the Capture of Ceuta* describes Henry's experiences in North Africa during the Crusades. The *Chronicle of Guinea* describes Portugal's exploration of western Africa between 1434 and 1447.

In 1441, Portuguese explorers brought their first cargo of African slaves to Portugal. In 1444, the first major expedition was organized with the main purpose of getting African slaves. Two hundred and forty men, women, and children were loaded onto six Portuguese caravels. On the next page is an excerpt from the *Chronicle of Guinea*. In this excerpt, Zurara describes what happened to these African slaves when they arrived at a Portuguese port in August 1444. The slaves were divided into five groups. One of the groups would go to Prince Henry, who had given approval for the expedition. It was traditional for the royal Spanish ruler to take one-fifth of any wealth or riches gained in exploration. This was called the "royal fifth." Henry gave two slaves to local churches. The other slaves were sold and the profits divided among the captain and his men. 📖

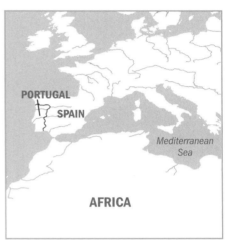

▲ Gomes Eanes de Zurara wrote about Portugal's exploration of western Africa.

► This drawing shows Africans who were forced into slavery.

# From Chronicle of Guinea

These people, assembled together on that open place, were an astonishing sight to behold. Among them were some who were quite white-skinned, handsome, and of good appearance; others were less white, seeming more like brown men ... . What heart, however hardened it might be, could not be pierced by a feeling of pity at the sight of that company? Some held their heads low, their faces bathed in tears as they looked at each other; some groaned very piteously ... others struck their faces with their hands and threw themselves full length on the ground; yet others **lamented** in the form of a chant, according to the custom of their native land, and though the words of the language in which they sang could not be understood by our people, the chant revealed clearly enough the degree of their grief. To increase their **anguish** still more, those who had charge of the division then arrived and began to separate them one from another so that they formed five equal lots. This made it necessary to separate the sons from their fathers and wives from their husbands and brother from brother. No account was taken of friendship or relationship, but each one ending up where chance placed him ... . Who could carry out such a division without great difficulty for as soon as the children who had been assigned to one group saw their parents in another they jumped up and ran towards them; mothers clasped their other children in their arms and lay face downwards on the ground, accepting wounds ... rather than let their children be torn from them.

**anguish:** suffering
**lament:** to express grief or sadness

## Analyze the Source!

1. Read the excerpt and tell in your own words what it says.

2. How does this excerpt help you learn about European attitudes toward the people of Africa during the age of exploration?

3. Based on this excerpt, do you think Zurara was simply describing what he saw as an observer or do you think he was touched by the human misery of slavery? Give examples to explain your answer.

**362** Chapter 17: The Age of Exploration

# Who's Who in Europe's Age of Exploration

**Q.** **Who was the first European to explore the Americas?**

**A.** It was probably **Leif Ericson**, a Viking. His father, Eric the Red, had established a settlement in Greenland. Leif Ericson heard stories of land southwest of his father's settlement. In 1001, he left Greenland with a crew of 35 to explore the land he had heard about. Historians think he probably got as far as Newfoundland, which is on the eastern coast of North America. The Vikings did not establish a permanent settlement there, and Europeans did not explore North America again until the late 1400s.

▲ This drawing shows Leif Ericson, Eric the Red, and other Vikings.

**Q.** **Who was the first European to sail around the Cape of Good Hope at the tip of Africa?**

**A.** **Bartolomeu Dias.** He led an expedition from Lisbon, Portugal in the summer of 1487. The goal of this voyage was to sail around the southern end of Africa—the Cape of Good Hope. The men on the expedition also wanted to find the country of a legendary Christian African king called Prester John. Dias commanded two caravels and a supply ship. Among the people who accompanied him were six Africans—two men and four women. Their job was to go ashore at various places to explain the purpose of the expedition to the people who lived there. While on this voyage, Dias rounded the southern tip of Africa. He called the land there the Cape of Torments because of the strong currents, forceful winds, big waves, and many storms. Then and now this cape is a very difficult area for ships to navigate. However, because of the success of Dias's expedition, the king of Portugal suggested that it be renamed the Cape of Good Hope, and that's the name that stuck. Thirteen years later, on May 29, 1500, Dias died at sea, not far from the Cape of Good Hope. Today, a maritime museum in Mossel Bay, South Africa includes a life-size replica of the caravel Bartolomeu Dias sailed into Mossel Bay in 1488.

## Q. Spain sent out so many explorers. How can I keep them straight?

A. This is a challenge! Spain enjoyed early success in the exploration business which encouraged men to make more expeditions. You can organize Spain's explorers by the area they explored. For example, in 1540-1542, **Francisco Coronado** explored areas of southwestern North America, including parts of present-day Colorado, northern Texas, Oklahoma, and eastern Kansas.

You also can organize Spain's explorers chronologically with **Christopher Columbus** first, **Amerigo Vespucci** second, and so on. Another way to organize Spain's explorers is alphabetically. Here is a creative use of the ABCs to account for some of Spain's explorers:

| Spain's Explorer | Dates of Exploration | Area Explored (Present-Day Name) |
|---|---|---|
| **A**merigo Vespucci | 1497-1498 | South America and the West Indies |
| Vasco Nuñéz de **B**alboa | 1513 | Pacific Ocean |
| Juan Rodríguez **C**abrillo | 1542 | California |
| Hernando **C**ortés | 1519-1521 | Southern North America and Central America |
| Álvar Nuñéz **C**abeza de Vaca | 1536 | Texas and northern Mexico |
| Juan Ponce **d**e Leon | 1513 | Florida |
| Pánfilo **d**e Nárvaez | 1528 | Florida and Mexico |
| Hernando **d**e Soto | 1539-1542 | Mississippi River and the American Southeast |
| **E**steban and Father Marcos | 1539 | American Southwest; Quebec, Canada; and New Mexico |
| **F**rancisco Pizarro | 1533 | Northwestern Coast of South America |
| **F**rancisco Coronado | 1540-1542 | American Southwest |
| **F**erdinand Magellan | 1519-1522 | Sailed around the world |

## Q. What about French explorers? Are there any important French explorers?

A. France was not very interested in expeditions across the Americas until 1524. In that year, the French sent an expedition across the Atlantic Ocean. It was led by **Giovanni da Verrazano**. That doesn't sound like a French name, does it? Well, Verrazano was not born in France. He was born around 1485 to a wealthy family who lived just south of Florence, Italy. However, when he was about 21, Verrazano moved to France to begin a maritime career. He joined one expedition to North America before he led his own expedition there in 1524. He left port that year with four ships, but only one actually made it to North America. He explored the northeastern coast of North America and "discovered" New York Harbor. This was a part of North America other Europeans had not explored.

**Jacques Cartier** is another famous French explorer. In 1535, he led an expedition to find a Northwest Passage—a sea route from the Atlantic Ocean to the Pacific Ocean through Canada and north of Alaska. Cartier was born in 1491 in St. Malo, a seaport town on the northwestern coast of France. We don't know much about Cartier's life until 1534 when he took his first voyage across the Atlantic. It took him only about 20 days to make this crossing.

After landing on an island off the coast of Newfoundland, Cartier sailed north

▲ Jacques Cartier was a French explorer who searched for a Northwest Passage.

into the Bay of St. Lawrence and along the western coast of Newfoundland. After exploring the area, he headed back to France. He took with him two Huron Indians he had met on the expedition. He led a second expedition the following year. This time, however, he reached the St. Lawrence River and sailed all the way up to the location of the present-day city of Quebec. Cartier returned to France and had to wait until 1541 to sail on a third expedition to North America. This was not an especially successful expedition. Indians who did not want the French to settle in the region killed many of Cartier's men. Cartier returned to his home in St. Malo and died in 1557 at the age of 66. He never found the Northwest Passage he was looking for, but he gave France a claim to land in the northern part of North America.

A third French explorer you might have heard of is **Samuel de Champlain**. He was born around 1567. He made several expeditions to North America, beginning in 1603. He is most famous for founding the city of Quebec in 1608. In 1609, he came upon a large lake between what is now eastern New York and western Vermont. This body of water is now known as Lake Champlain. Champlain explored the northern area of present-day New York, the Ottawa River, and the eastern Great Lakes. He died in Quebec in 1635.

▲ **Samuel de Champlain is most famous for founding the city of Quebec in 1608.**

### Q. Did England send out any famous explorers during this time?

A. Yes. Have you heard of **John Cabot**? John Cabot was born near Naples, in southern Italy, around 1455. His father and mother named him Giovanni Caboto. He became a merchant like his father and moved to Venice. He married a Venetian woman around 1482, and they had three sons. He sailed throughout the eastern Mediterranean Sea trading for spices, silks, and other goods from Asia. In 1490, Giovanni Caboto and his family moved to Spain. We aren't sure why he moved there, but perhaps like other seamen of the time, he wanted to be closer to where the action was in terms of European exploration—crossing the Atlantic Ocean. However, by the time he got settled, Spain and Portugal already had their important explorers. So, around 1495, Caboto and his family moved again—this time to England. There he became known as John Cabot. English merchants decided to support him on an expedition to find a trade route to Asia by sailing across the Atlantic. The king of England even gave him a letter authorizing him to explore "whatsoever islands, countries, regions or provinces ... which before this time were unknown to all Christians." John Cabot set off in 1497 and landed in North America on the coast of present-day Canada. He claimed the land for England. Cabot went on another expedition the following year, but he never returned. He probably died at sea.

**Sir Francis Drake** is another well-known English explorer. He was born around 1540 to a farming family in southwestern England. When he was still a boy, his family moved to the coast. Francis was only a boy when he went to sea for the first time as a seaman's apprentice. However, he learned quickly and eventually became a captain in his own right. In 1577, he left England with five ships. People thought he was going on a trading expedition, but he had decided to sail around the world. His expedition experienced many problems, and two of the ships were lost. However, Drake was not discouraged. He renamed one of the ships, his flagship, the *Golden Hind*, and continued on the journey. He faced many obstacles, but kept going. As he traveled around South America, he raided Spanish possessions. He sailed up the coast of North America and then crossed the Pacific Ocean. He finally made it home to England in the fall of 1580. His journey had covered about 36,000 miles. The voyage had taken him nearly three years. He and his crew were the first Englishmen to travel around the world. The English considered him a great sea captain and a hero. The Spanish feared but respected him. Drake died in 1596 while he was on an expedition in the Caribbean. He was buried at sea off the coast of Panama.

▼ This is a drawing of Henry Hudson's ship and the flag of the Dutch East India Company.

**Q. That's it, right? There can't be any more famous explorers!**

**A.** Well, there is at least one more famous explorer—**Henry Hudson**. Hudson explored North America on behalf of both England and the Netherlands. The Dutch East India Company wanted him to find a Northwest Passage. In 1609 he set sail to find this passage, but he ran into terrible storms. So, he sailed up the Atlantic coast to a large river, now called the Hudson River. Then he returned home. He set sail again in 1610 for North America and came upon a huge bay, now named Hudson Bay. This voyage was very difficult, and Hudson's men were unhappy with him. On the way home, they put Hudson on a small boat by himself. He was never heard of again and almost certainly died at sea. The Dutch greatly benefited from Hudson's explorations along the Hudson River. The English benefited from his explorations in Canada. 📖

# Life on the High Seas

During the European age of exploration, explorers sailed across the oceans looking for a quicker route to China and India. The sailors on these expeditions created new technology to overcome some of the problems they faced. The life of a sailor was hard work. Read on ...

## The Life of an Ordinary Sailor

A sailor's life was difficult and uncomfortable. Usually, sailors did not know how long they would be at sea. It could be months or even years. Their work was hard and dangerous. They often had to work when the weather was terrible—winds or waves could blow them into the sea. Sailors took turns "on watch." They looked for landmarks, changes in weather, and other ships.

Sailors spent most of their time working. However, they had some free time when they could enjoy their hobbies or even play tricks on the other sailors! A few read, but most sailors did not know how to read. Often sailors spent their spare time gambling. Some sailors knew how to play musical instruments. These instruments were mainly used in signaling other ships. Sometimes, however, sailors played the instruments for the ship's crew.

▲ Sailors used special instruments to navigate at sea.

Sailors did not have beds or special places to sleep. Many sailors kept their belongings in a sea chest. They didn't have many clothes, and the ones they did have were not waterproof. There was no way to keep food fresh. As a result, the food on board the ship was not fresh or very tasty. The sailors did not have fresh water and there were no bathrooms on board. Rats and roaches were everywhere. Many sailors died during voyages. An ordinary sailor's life was difficult and uncomfortable, but it offered a life of travel and adventure and the possibility of becoming rich.

## The Life of a Ship's Captain and Officers

The leaders on a sea voyage were the captain and his officers. The captain was responsible for the ship and made all the important decisions. His officers—the pilot and first mate—gave him information about the position of the ship. They also supervised the sailors. The captain and officers kept detailed notes about the voyage. Each day they would write information about how far they had traveled, the direction they had taken, other ships they had seen, or landmarks they had passed.

▲ The captain and his officers were the leaders on a sea voyage.

▲ Explorers used a comfortable, hanging bed called a hammock. Hammocks did not weigh very much or take up much room.

The captain and officers also would include information about the weather, the ship's supplies of food and drink, and any sickness among the crew. Officers were responsible for taking regular sightings of the sun and stars.

The captain and ship's pilot usually had beds, but they weren't very comfortable. The food they ate on board might have been better than what ordinary sailors ate, but it was still terrible. There was no fresh water or any bathrooms on board ship. Rats and cockroaches were everywhere. Sometimes sailors became frightened and wanted to turn back. Many sailors became sick and some died. It was the captain and officers' job to keep the ship on course. They had to deal with emergencies and make decisions. They did not have easy jobs. However, a ship's captain and ship's officers lived a life of adventure and travel and had the possibility of becoming rich.

## A New Bed for Sailors!

During the age of exploration, European explorers learned about many new ideas from the people they met in the lands they explored. They used some of these ideas to makes their lives better and more comfortable. One thing explorers learned about from American Indians was a comfortable, hanging bed called a hammock. People make hammocks by weaving together pieces of rope or heavy cord. When it is completed, a hammock looks like a big fish net. Each end is tied to a post (or other heavy object). A person can sleep comfortably in the netting.

Sailors thought the hammock had many advantages. First, it did not weigh very much or take up much room on board a tiny ship. It could be folded up and placed in a bag until the sailors were ready to use it. Second, the hanging beds meant the men did not have to sleep on cold, damp wood. Third, a sailor would not fall out of bed even in rough seas because a hammock swings from side to side.

## What's for Dinner?

One of the biggest problems European explorers faced during the age of exploration was food. There were no refrigerators on ships to keep food fresh. Canned food had not been invented yet. Voyages usually started out with cheese and fresh fruits and vegetables, but this food rotted quickly. Sailors knew this would happen, so they brought along barrels of salted meat and fish, and lots of hard biscuits, rice, dried peas, and beans. They also brought along barrels of water and wine. However, the barrels often leaked and supplies usually ran low. The crew collected rain water to drink, but they could not count on that. Oftentimes, they went thirsty.

Sailors didn't have to ask, "What's for dinner?" They knew the answer. They had the same food every day. And the food that made up their diet was not very healthy. On long voyages where sailors could not get fresh fruits or vegetables, many got a disease called scurvy. This disease is caused by having a diet lacking in vitamin C. A long voyage was considered lucky if only one out of every five men died of scurvy.

▲ Explorers brought barrels of food on their voyages.

# The Caravel—The Best Ship that Sailed the Sea

During the age of exploration, one sailor described the caravel as "the best ship that sailed the seas." It was better than other ships that came before it for several reasons. First, it was smaller, lighter, and stronger. The wooden planks of the ship were nailed directly to the frame. In older ships, these planks overlapped, making the ship slower in the water. In contrast, the caravel could glide quickly through the ocean water, even in rough seas. This meant it could sail faster, which was important because it was difficult to store food without it spoiling on voyages.

The second reason the caravel was better than older ships was that it was easier to sail and could be sailed into shallower water. The older ships had one large square sail. The caravel had three smaller triangular sails, an idea copied from Arab sailing ships. The smaller sails were easier to handle and could be moved quickly. Caravels also had a rudder in the middle at the back of the ship. This meant the caravel could make sharp turns and steer more easily. A lighter, easier-to-handle ship could be sailed closer to land. This was something the older, bigger ships could not do.

▲ Caravels were called the best ships that sailed the seas.

# How Much Longer Until We Get There?

If you decided to go to Europe today, your travel agent could tell you the exact day and hour when you would arrive. During the age of exploration, however, it was very difficult to know how long a voyage would take. Columbus thought his voyage would take about a month. It ended up taking him more than three months. And he didn't end up in China, the destination he planned to visit. Columbus and other explorers were highly skilled sailors, but they did not have the information or the technology we have today. Accurate maps of the world were not available. They had to rely on simple instruments, their knowledge of the sea, and their experience.

Improvements to navigational instruments during the 1400s helped sailors go farther on ocean voyages. For example, improvements were made to the astrolabe, an instrument that measures the distance of the sun and stars above the horizon. The Portuguese also made improvements to the compass that made it more accurate. Later, sailors began to use magnetic compasses. This instrument helped navigators figure out the course their ship should take. It also helped them decide which direction to steer the ship. 📖

**MAKE A COMPASS**

## Try making your own compass by following the directions below.

1. Rub a needle with a magnet (20-30 times).
2. Stick the needle through the middle of a piece of cork.
3. Float the cork in a shallow bowl of water. The needle will point towards magnetic north.

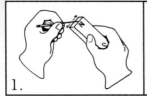
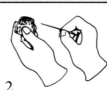
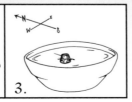

# FERDINAND AND ISABELLA —
# The Beginnings of a
# Spanish Empire

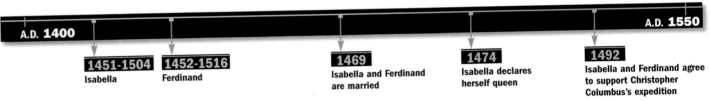

A.D. **1400**

**1451-1504** Isabella

**1452-1516** Ferdinand

**1469** Isabella and Ferdinand are married

**1474** Isabella declares herself queen

**1492** Isabella and Ferdinand agree to support Christopher Columbus's expedition

A.D. **1550**

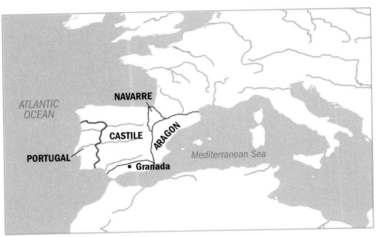

▲ Isabella was born in Castile, the largest kingdom in Spain in the 1450s. Ferdinand was born in Aragon, the second largest kingdom. Muslims ruled only the area around Granada.

In the 1400s, Spain was not a united country with one ruler. Christian armies had conquered Córdoba in 1236, but there was still an Islamic kingdom in Granada. The rest of Spain was divided into Christian kingdoms. Castile, the largest kingdom, and Aragon, the second largest kingdom, ruled northern and central Spain. When these two kingdoms were united politically through marriage, a powerful new Spanish empire began to emerge.

## Isabella of Castile—Early Life

Princess Isabella of Castile was born on April 22, 1451. It seemed unlikely that she would ever actually rule Castile because she had an older brother. At the time, females became rulers only if there were no male heirs. When Isabella's father died, her older brother Henry became king. Almost immediately, he forced Isabella and their younger brother to leave the king's court. She went to live in a cold and dreary castle. She spent her days learning to read and write. Priests taught her about the Roman Catholic religion. Isabella studied history, poetry, and music. She also learned to sew and how to act like a Spanish noblewoman. In her spare time, she liked to ride horses and hunt rabbits and deer. When she was about 11, her brother, the king, invited her to come back to his court in Castile. She did not have many friends there, but became very close to a priest called Father Tomás de Torquemada. He had a strong influence on her. She became convinced that Christianity was the only true religion.

Isabella became queen of Spain in 1474.

## Arranging a Marriage

By the time Isabella turned 13, her brother the king was looking for a husband for her. It was traditional among nobles, especially princesses, to have arranged marriages. These marriages were intended to bring together important noble families or political territories. It did not matter if the people loved one another or even liked one another. The first person chosen for Isabella was very old and not someone she thought she could possibly marry. Happily for her, the man died before the marriage could take place. She received many other proposals from noble families. Everyone was eager it seemed to make an alliance with the princess of the most powerful kingdom in Spain. Isabella, however, had decided on the man she wanted to marry. He was her first cousin, Ferdinand II of Aragon.

## Ferdinand II of Aragon

Ferdinand II of Aragon was born on March 10, 1452. He received an excellent education and learned about government and history as well as the arts. It is said that he was especially fond of music. In addition to formal schooling, Ferdinand's father strongly believed in the importance of learning through experience. Ferdinand observed and participated in the business of the royal court, but he also was trained and served as a soldier. As a young man, Ferdinand had many girlfriends. Several of these girlfriends gave birth to his children. Ferdinand often is described as a man with a commanding personality who could be very emotional. It does not appear that he was warm and friendly, but he had integrity and was brave and wise. He certainly was wise enough to know that marrying the princess of the largest kingdom in Spain would be a good move.

## It's a FACT

By the late 13th century, Christian kingdoms dominated most of the Iberian Peninsula. Muslims ruled only a small area by that time.

## A Simple Wedding

While both Isabella and Ferdinand thought their marriage was a great idea, Isabella's brother—the king—did not share their enthusiasm. With help from an archbishop, Isabella sent a message to Ferdinand telling him to meet her at a palace in Castile at once. Isabella quickly rode to the palace and waited for Ferdinand to arrive. Since Ferdinand knew the king's soldiers would stop him if they could, he came up with a plan to disguise himself. He dressed as a servant and ordered some of his knights to dress as merchants. Then the "merchants and their servant" headed for Isabella's palace. Ferdinand arrived on October 15, 1469. He was not happy when he read the marriage agreement because it gave Isabella most of the power to rule. Isabella, however, said that they would rule as equals. With this settled, the two teenagers married on October 19, 1469. It was not a very fancy wedding, but it united two people who would create a Spanish empire.

Not surprisingly, Isabella's brother, King Henry, was furious when he heard about Isabella's marriage. He decided that she had to give up her right to be queen. When Henry died in 1474, however, Isabella declared herself queen. She was just 26 years old. The archbishop who had helped her marry Ferdinand crowned her queen in a ceremony in Castile. At the time, Ferdinand was away fighting a war with the French. When he returned home, he was angry that she had not waited for him to be included in the ceremony. He understood, however, that if she had not taken this quick action, Isabella's younger sister might have declared herself queen.

## King and Queen

Their early years as king and queen were spent training an army and then fighting wars to protect and expand their territory. One of their most important goals was to force an army of invading Portuguese soldiers out of Castile. On March 1, 1476, Isabella and Ferdinand won an important battle. While the war continued, Isabella gave birth to their first child, John, on June 30, 1478. The war ended the following year. The king of Portugal agreed to leave their territory forever. Then Isabella and Ferdinand began to take actions to rebuild and strengthen their kingdom. They set up a system of law and order. They also traveled throughout the kingdom to hear about problems people were facing. During these years of rebuilding, Isabella gave birth to four more children.

## A Christian Kingdom

Spain had been home to Muslims, Christians, and Jews for hundreds of years. Throughout this time, there were periods when different religious beliefs were tolerated. However, this began to change in the late 1000s, especially with Pope Urban II's call for the Crusades. Christians in Europe began to hate non-Christians. At first, this hatred was directed at Muslims, but it also rekindled old hatreds toward Jews.

**It's a FACT**

Isabella and Ferdinand's daughter Catalina was the first wife of King Henry VIII of England. In England, she was called Catherine of Aragon.

By the 1400s, Christians in Spain did not tolerate non-Christian beliefs. Some of this intolerance stemmed from economic issues. Poor Christians were jealous of the wealth and success of Jews. Some Jews decided to become Christians to keep from being killed. However, some Christians thought the Jews who converted to Christianity were still practicing the Jewish religion in secret. Isabella and Ferdinand decided to address this problem by setting up a special court called an Inquisition. It was the job of this court to decide if anyone was secretly practicing the Jewish religion. Isabella asked the priest she had befriended as a child, Father Tomás de Torquemada, to be in charge of this court. The Inquisition was a sad chapter in Spanish history. Many people were tortured and killed because of religious intolerance and suspicion.

## Driving Muslims out of Spain

With the issue of Jews now in Father Torquemada's hands, Ferdinand and Isabella turned to another issue they wanted to address—Muslims in Spain. In December 1481, a Muslim army attacked a castle in Ferdinand and Isabella's kingdom. They killed the men and sold the women and children into slavery. As revenge, Ferdinand led an army into a Muslim city, killed more than 1,000 Muslims, and released all the Christians being held as prisoners. Ferdinand and Isabella then moved to Córdoba and made plans to drive all the Muslims out of Spain. It took them almost 10 years to accomplish this goal, but in January 1492, the leader of the Muslims surrendered. Ferdinand's army marched triumphantly into Granada, the last Muslim city in Spain. His men placed a silver cross on the highest tower of the Alhambra palace. That same year, Isabella and Ferdinand signed a law that required every Jew in Castile to become Roman Catholic or to leave the kingdom forever. Most decided to leave even though it meant giving up their property and the only home their families had known for more than a thousand years. Many of those who fled went first to Portugal and then settled in the Netherlands.

## Explorations and the Beginnings of a World Empire

The year 1492 was momentous for other reasons as well. For a long time, Christopher Columbus had tried to interest Queen Isabella and King Ferdinand of Spain in his plan to sail west across the Atlantic to reach Asia. However, when he first approached them in 1485, they were busy trying to drive all the Muslims out of Spain.

**It's a FACT**

Christian knights began what is called the "Reconquest" of the Iberian Peninsula from the Muslims in the 11th century. This Reconquest was completed in 1492 when Ferdinand and Isabella conquered Granada.

▼ **Columbus first presented his plan to the queen in 1485. In 1492, Isabella and Ferdinand agreed to support his expedition. That was the same year the Muslims were driven out of Spain.**

## It's a FACT
When Isabella died in 1504, Ferdinand is reported to have described her as "the best and most excellent wife a king ever had."

**mismanagement:** wrong or bad management

### What Do You Think?

**1.** What qualities of Isabella and Ferdinand do you admire?

**2.** How did Isabella and Ferdinand's religious beliefs affect their actions? Give examples to support your answer.

**3.** How did events in Europe such as wars and religious intolerance affect the age of exploration?

**4.** What helped Spain become the richest country in the world at that time?

Columbus presented his plan to the queen in 1486. She listened to him and appointed a group of advisors to study his plan, but nothing seemed to happen. Columbus decided to go back to Portugal, but returned to Spain in 1492 because things had changed. For one thing, the Portuguese had found a sea route to Asia. Isabella and Ferdinand did not want Portugal to become richer or more powerful than Spain. So, in 1492, they agreed to support Columbus's expedition.

On August 3, 1492, with three ships and 88 men, Christopher Columbus set sail for Asia. It was a long and difficult journey across the Atlantic. On October 12, 1492, about two months after they had left Spain, Columbus and his crew sighted land. Columbus returned to Spain and informed the king and queen of his voyage. They treated Columbus like a hero and conqueror. They were pleased to see the gifts he had brought them—gold jewelry, exotic plants, tools they had never seen before, and people dressed in strange clothes decorated with feathers. They were interested in hearing about the plants, animals, and the people he met on this voyage. Isabella and Ferdinand were delighted to hear about the conquests Columbus had made for Spain. They were so pleased, in fact, that they gave Columbus support for three more voyages.

## "Unchristian" Behavior
Before Columbus returned from his third voyage, Isabella and Ferdinand had heard disturbing stories about problems in the new colonies. There were reports of **mismanagement** of the colony and mistreatment of the Indians. Columbus was arrested and brought back to Spain in chains. Isabella, in particular, was angry that Columbus brought people from the New World to sell as slaves. She wanted the people of the New World to become Christians.

## The Last Years of Their Reign
The end of Queen Isabella's life was filled with unhappiness. Her only son died in 1497, and the next year her oldest daughter died. Then the grandson who was to become king also died. Isabella became ill during the summer of 1504 and died several months later on November 26, 1504. Columbus had just returned to Spain from his last voyage, but the king would have nothing to do with him. Ferdinand married again in 1505 for political reasons. His health began to give out in 1513, and he died on January 23, 1516.

Columbus did not find a sea route to Asia, but his "discoveries" had a much more significant effect. The land claims Spain made in the New World as a result of Columbus's explorations and those of other Spanish explorers led to riches beyond Spain's imagination. Gold and silver and other New World treasures poured into Spain. It became the richest country in the world in the 1500s.

Isabella was angry that Columbus brought people from the New World to sell as slaves. She wanted the people of the New World to become Christians.

# CHRISTOPHER COLUMBUS —
# Curious about the
# Secrets of the World

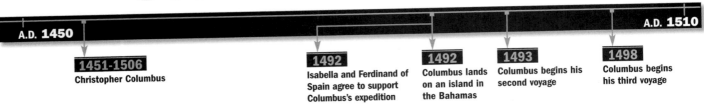

A.D. **1450**

**1451-1506**
Christopher Columbus

**1492**
Isabella and Ferdinand of
Spain agree to support
Columbus's expedition

**1492**
Columbus lands
on an island in
the Bahamas

**1493**
Columbus begins his
second voyage

**1498**
Columbus begins
his third voyage

A.D. **1510**

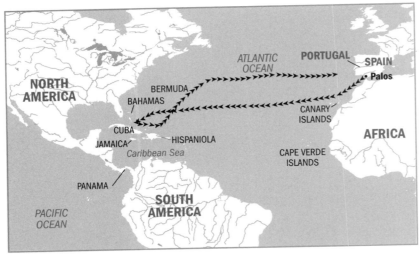

▲ Christopher Columbus tried to find a
new route to China. Instead, he landed in
Hispaniola.

The man we call Christopher
Columbus was born in 1451. His
parents, Domenico and Susanna, named
him Cristoforo Colombo. They raised
Cristoforo, his three younger brothers,
and a younger sister in the bustling
Italian port city of Genoa. Because the
family was not wealthy, it is unlikely that
any of the children went to school. The
boys probably spent most of their time
in their father's weaving shop. If he
had any time to spare, Cristoforo
probably rushed to the docks to see the
ships coming and going.

Genoa was a busy trading center. Sometime before he
turned 20, Cristoforo went to sea. He was a sailor on cargo
ships that sailed throughout the Mediterranean. After five years
in the calm waters of the Mediterranean, he was ready to sail on
the Atlantic. He joined a crew that was headed for northern
Europe. Everything went well until the ship was passing by
Portugal's coast. Another ship sank the one on which
Columbus was sailing.

## Safety in Portugal

Columbus swam six miles to the shore of Portugal. After he
recovered his strength, he joined a Portuguese crew and sailed to
England. He taught himself to read and write the language used
by educated people in Portugal. He married and began a family.
During this time, he sometimes worked in his brother's
mapmaking shop in Lisbon, Portugal. It also was during this
time that he began to think about finding a sea route to Asia by
sailing west across the Atlantic Ocean. Most people knew the
world was round at this time, so Columbus's idea was not crazy.

◀ American historians writing about Christopher Columbus in the late 1800s described him in heroic terms. They wrote about his "discovery of a New World." They praised his determination and courage. They called him the man who discovered America. Today, historians are interested in presenting a more balanced view of Columbus. They write about his exploration of a world that was new to Europeans, but not to the people of the Americas. They emphasize the meeting of two worlds.

It made sense to Columbus that he could reach Asia by sailing toward the west rather than the east, especially because one of the most respected mapmakers of the time, Paolo Toscanelli, supported this view.

## Toscanelli's Map Influences Columbus

Paolo Toscanelli was an Italian mathematician and considered an expert in understanding and describing the earth. Toscanelli had read the work of Ptolemy, an ancient Greek scholar, and studied the travels of people such as Marco Polo. Toscanelli carefully and methodically gathered all the information he could find about the earth. Then, in 1474, he used this information to produce a map of the world. His map showed a round earth with Europe and Asia covering nearly two-thirds of the earth's surface. Toscanelli tried, but failed, to convince the Portuguese that they could reach Asia by sailing west. Columbus, however, was greatly influenced by Toscanelli's ideas.

▲ This drawing shows Columbus landing at San Salvador.

As we know today, Toscanelli's theory was correct, but his map had a serious flaw. As much geographical knowledge as he and other Europeans had gained by that time, they still did not know about the existence of North and South America. Toscanelli's map showed the distance between Europe and Asia was about 3,000 or 4,000 miles. Today, we know the distance is about 10,000 miles. Columbus, of course, was completely unaware of this problem.

## Looking for Support

Columbus needed support for what would be an expensive and risky voyage. Who could and would support such an expedition? The place to look for support was among people who were wealthy. And, at that time, the people who had the most money were kings and queens. Columbus started with the king of Portugal. However, the king's counselors advised against providing support for the expedition. In 1485, his wife now dead, Columbus sailed to Spain with his young son, Diego. Queen Isabella and King Ferdinand of Spain were quite busy at that time. They were fighting a war to force all the Muslims out of Spain. Columbus finally got to present his plan to the queen in 1486. She listened to him and appointed a group of advisors to study his plan, but nothing seemed to happen. Columbus decided to go back to Portugal and ask the king of Portugal for support a second time.

Just as Columbus arrived, Bartolomeu Dias returned from his successful voyage around the Cape of Good Hope. The Portuguese had their sea route to Asia. They had no need to find another route sailing across the Atlantic. Columbus decided to go back to Spain. He did not receive an immediate "yes" from Ferdinand and Isabella. But in 1492, they agreed to support his expedition.

## The Voyage

On August 3, 1492, with three ships and 88 men, Christopher Columbus set sail for Asia. Columbus commanded the large flagship, the *Santa María*. The other ships, the *Niña* and the *Pinta*, were smaller but faster caravels. Columbus kept a journal of the voyage and wrote in it almost every day. It was a long and difficult journey across the Atlantic. Part of his crew wanted to turn around and go home. He wrote in his journal, "I am having trouble with the crew … complaining that they will never be able to return home." But Columbus was determined that they would go on. He promised a reward—a coat—to the first man to see land. The men looked out across the water searching for any sight of land. On October 12, 1492, about two months after they had left Spain, a sailor called out *tierra*, the Spanish word for "land."

▲ It was a long and difficult journey across the Atlantic. Some of Columbus's crew wanted to go home. He wrote in his journal, "I am having trouble with the crew … complaining that they will never be able to return home." In this picture, you can see Columbus calming angry sailors on his ship.

## Landing in a New World

The three ships landed on an island in the Bahamas, just off the southern coast of present-day Florida. Columbus called the island San Salvador and claimed it for Spain. He believed he was in the Indies and called the friendly people who greeted him "Indians." He wrote in his journal that the Indians did not have any weapons and "brought us parrots and cotton thread and many other things." In return, Columbus and his men gave the people red caps and beads and other small trinkets. The expedition then sailed to other islands. One in particular reminded him of Spain. This island became known as Hispaniola. When the *Santa María* wrecked off the shore of Hispaniola, the people who lived on the island—the Arawaks—helped the Europeans gather all the wood. Columbus's crew, with help from the Arawaks, built a fort on the island. Columbus named the fort La Navidad.

**vessel:** a container

### From Columbus's Journal from October 13, 1492

*As soon as it dawned, many of these people came to the beach ... very handsome people, with hair not curly but straight and coarse, like horsehair; and all of them very wide in the forehead and head, more so than any other race that I have seen so far. And their eyes are very handsome and not small; and none of them are black, but of the color of the Canary Islanders. ... I was attentive and labored to find out if there was any gold; and I saw that some of them wore a little piece hung in a hole that they have in their noses. And by signs I was able to understand that, going to the south or rounding the island to the south, there was there a king who had large vessels of it and had very much gold. ...*

**It's a FACT**

Christopher Columbus wrote in his diary, "I went sailing upon the sea and have continued to this day ... to learn the secrets of the world."

## Heading Home to a Hero's Welcome

Some of Columbus's crew stayed at the fort. The others returned to Spain with Columbus in the two remaining ships. It was a difficult voyage home. The two ships became separated, but both made it back to the port of Palos, Spain. Columbus immediately sent a letter to the king and queen of Spain telling them of his voyage. When they wrote back, they addressed the letter to their "Admiral of the Ocean Sea, Viceroy and Governor of the Islands." They invited Columbus to their court in Barcelona. When he reached their palace, he was treated like a hero and conqueror. They were delighted to see the things he had brought them—gold jewelry, exotic plants, tools they had never seen before, and people dressed in strange clothes decorated with feathers. He told them about the birds and animals he saw and about the food the people ate and their manners. He also told them that the people could become good Christians. The king and queen were thrilled to hear about the conquests Columbus had made for Spain.

## More Voyages

It was easy for Columbus to get support for a second voyage. He left Spain in the fall of 1493. However, when he arrived at Hispaniola, he found that the fort had been destroyed and the crew he had left there were gone. Later, Columbus found out that the crew had badly mistreated the Arawaks. The Arawaks fought back and eventually killed the crew. Columbus rebuilt a settlement there and began to explore other islands. When he returned to Hispaniola before heading back to Spain, he found that the settlement was having problems. He returned to Spain, but this time he did not receive a hero's welcome. Other explorers had made new discoveries and Columbus's voyage did not seem as fantastic as it once did. He still insisted he had found the Indies, but others were less sure. He went on a third voyage in 1498 and explored more islands, but he did not find China or Japan or India. Moreover, the colony on Hispaniola was in terrible trouble.

Isabella and Ferdinand were concerned when they heard charges of government mismanagement and mistreatment of the Indians. They sent an official to look into the matter.

▲ Here you can see Columbus among the native people of Hispaniola. Experts estimate that the native population of the island of Hispaniola was about 100,000 in 1492. By 1570, experts estimate the native population had dropped to about 300.

▲ After Columbus's first voyage, Isabella and Ferdinand welcomed him back as a hero. They were delighted to see the things he had brought them—gold jewelry, exotic plants, tools they had never seen before, and people dressed in strange clothes decorated with feathers. However, later they were concerned when they heard charges of government mismanagement and mistreatment of the Indians.

The official ended up arresting Columbus and bringing him back to Spain in chains. The king and queen released him from his chains, but they were no longer very interested in him. However, Isabella and Ferdinand did support Columbus on one last voyage. In 1502, he headed back across the Atlantic. Unfortunately, the ships he had were old and not very seaworthy. Columbus and his crew were forced to stay on an island near Jamaica for almost a year before they were rescued. Columbus went back to Spain, an old and sick man.

## Home Alone

Queen Isabella died shortly after Columbus returned home for the last time. Columbus wanted to have the titles and riches that he thought belonged to him, but King Ferdinand would have nothing to do with him. Christopher Columbus died on May 20, 1506, with only his family and close friends at his bedside. No important people came to pay their last respects. There was no large public funeral to honor his passing. It seemed as if he was completely forgotten.

# Christopher Columbus's Legacy

Christopher Columbus's voyage in 1492 is one of the most famous voyages in history—at least in the English-speaking world. What would Christopher Columbus think of his place in history? On the one hand, he has his very own holiday. He also has cities, rivers, and even a country named after him. Schools, libraries, art galleries, and a film company bear his name. Many Roman Catholic men in the United States belong to a group called the Knights of Columbus. But not everyone honors Christopher Columbus or considers him heroic. Some criticize him for sailing to a place he did not intend to go and then never realizing his mistake. Others see Columbus as a symbol of Europe's superior attitude toward and mistreatment of the people of the New World. They point out that when Columbus could not find enough gold on the islands of the West Indies, he captured local people and sent them to be sold as slaves in Spain. Perhaps the only thing that everyone agrees on is that Christopher Columbus played a critical role in world history.

## What Do You Think?

**1.** How have American historians changed the way they tell the history of Christopher Columbus? How and why can history change over time?

**2.** Do you think Columbus was a hero or a villain or somewhere in between? Explain your answer. How do you think your background and values affect your response?

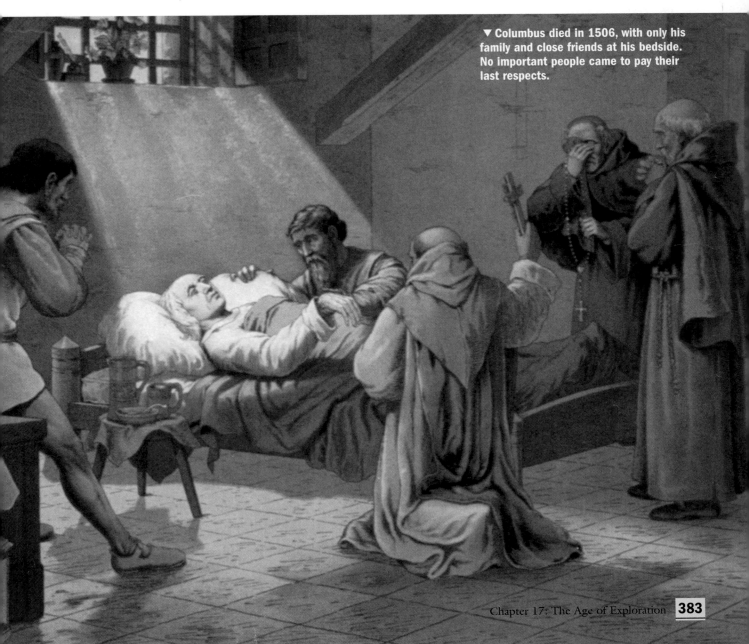

▼ Columbus died in 1506, with only his family and close friends at his bedside. No important people came to pay their last respects.

# Reader's Theater Presents ...

# "Land Ho!"

**DIRECTIONS:** Practice reading the script. When the script says, "ALL," everyone in the class joins in the reading. Read with expression!

## ROLES:

★ NARRATOR 1
★ NARRATOR 2
★ ATTENDANT
★ QUEEN ISABELLA
★ KING FERDINAND
★ COLUMBUS
★ SAILORS' WIVES
★ JUAN RODRIGUEZ BERMEJO
★ SAILORS
★ ALL

**NARRATOR 1:** It is the spring of 1486. A young sea captain is sure he can find a new route to China, but he needs money to pay for the expedition.

**NARRATOR 2:** You must be very rich to pay for voyages of exploration. The richest people in Europe are the kings and queens.

**NARRATOR 1:** Our story begins in the royal court of Spain.

**ATTENDANT:** Your majesty Queen Isabella, a young sea captain is here to see you. He says he must see you and the king.

**QUEEN ISABELLA:** What business would a sailor have with the king and queen of Spain? What is the name of this salty sailor?

**ATTENDANT:** He calls himself Columbus. Christopher Columbus. He is only the son of a weaver in Genoa, but he has an exciting idea.

**KING FERDINAND:** Let this young man tell us about his idea.

**COLUMBUS:** I can give Spain its own route to the riches of the East. The earth is round, so I will sail westward to reach China and its treasures of gold, silk, and spices.

**NARRATOR 2:** Isabella and Ferdinand listened to Columbus's idea, but they were busy fighting the Muslims in Spain. They did not have time for voyages to the unknown.

**NARRATOR 1:** However, several years later—in 1492—they had driven the Muslims out of Spain.

**NARRATOR 2:** Now they listened to Columbus's idea with great interest. They heard his demands.

**COLUMBUS:** I need experienced sailors, many supplies, and three ships.

**SAILORS' WIVES:** Isabella and Ferdinand gave Columbus what he wanted.

**SAILORS:** Two of the ships, the *Niña* and *Pinta*, were caravels—beautiful ships! They were about 70-feet long and could hold 25 men.

**SAILORS' WIVES:** The *Santa María*, the flagship, was larger and prettier.

**SAILORS:** But it wasn't a caravel!

**KING FERDINAND:** We hope Columbus will find gold and new trade routes.

**QUEEN ISABELLA:** We hope he will claim new land for Spain and spread Christianity.

**SAILORS:** On the morning of August 3, 1492, we set sail.

**SAILORS' WIVES:** As the three ships sailed away, we shouted, "We will miss you."

**SAILORS:** We were frightened, but also excited.

**COLUMBUS:** My friend Toscanelli, the famous geographer, figured out how far it was from Europe to China by sea. I calculated that we should arrive in China in a month.

**SAILORS:** We'll be drinking Chinese tea in early September.

**ALL:** But that didn't happen. The distance was much farther than Columbus thought.

**COLUMBUS:** It was September. I wrote in my journal, "We have been sailing for a month, but there is no sight of land. We are running out of supplies. Some men are sick. Others are afraid!"

**SAILORS:** Let's go home! We're all going to die if we don't turn back.

**COLUMBUS:** Have faith. We will soon see land. Have faith.

**NARRATOR 1:** But Columbus was worried, too. The voyage was taking longer than he thought it would.

**NARRATOR 2:** That's because the world was larger than Columbus realized.

**ALL:** Finally, on Friday, October 12, 1492, a voice rang out:

**JUAN RODRIGUEZ BERMEJO:** Tierra, tierra!

**ALL:** Land, ho. Land, ho.

**NARRATOR 1:** Columbus and his men had sighted land.

**ALL:** But the land was not China.

**NARRATOR 2:** No, the land was not China, but Columbus's voyage changed the history of the world in ways he would never know. 📖

# AMERIGO VESPUCCI —
# The Namesake of Two Continents

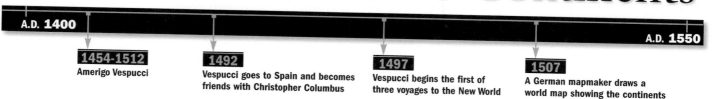

A.D. **1400**

A.D. **1550**

**1454-1512**
Amerigo Vespucci

**1492**
Vespucci goes to Spain and becomes friends with Christopher Columbus

**1497**
Vespucci begins the first of three voyages to the New World

**1507**
A German mapmaker draws a world map showing the continents of North and South America

◄ America is named after the explorer Amerigo Vespucci.

▲ Vespucci made three voyages to the New World, beginning in 1497.

▲ Vespucci met and became friends with Columbus in Spain. He helped Columbus prepare his ships for voyage.

Christopher Columbus gets most of the credit for being the first European to "discover" America. Some people think it was an unfair twist of fate that the continents he explored are named after someone else. We do not live on the continent of North Columbus. We live in North America. America? Where did that name come from? The answer is "Amerigo Vespucci," an Italian explorer born in Florence in 1454. He moved to Seville, Spain in 1492, which was a center of activity for European explorers. There he met and became friends with Christopher Columbus. Vespucci made three voyages to the New World, beginning in 1497. Italian Lorenzo di Pierfrancesco di Medici, cousin of Lorenzo the Magnificent, supported these expeditions. However, Vespucci's home became Spain.

On his first voyage, Vespucci explored the mouth of the Amazon River. While he was on this trip, he realized that the landmasses we call South America and North America were separate continents. Vespucci wrote to his patron about his voyages. The news spread across Europe. In 1507, a German mapmaker named Martin Waldseemüller drew a new map of the world showing these two continents. He wrote the name "America" across the area of present-day Brazil. The Spanish resisted the use of "America" as the name of this land, but clearly it caught on. Amerigo Vespucci eventually became a Spanish citizen. He died in Seville in 1512. Below is an excerpt from a letter that Amerigo Vespucci wrote to Lorenzo di Pierfrancesco di Medici in March or April 1503. Vespucci was on his third voyage to the New World during this time. 📖

**bore:** to make a hole
**clemency:** mercy
**countenance:** face
**perforation:** hole

# Vespucci Describes the New World

... I found a continent in the southern part [of the Atlantic Ocean]; more populous and more full of animals than our Europe, or Asia, or Africa, and even more temperate and pleasant than any other region known to us. ... We knew that land to be a continent, and not an island, from its long beach extending without trending round, the numerous tribes and people, the numerous kinds of wild animals unknown in our country, and many others never seen before by us. ... The **clemency** of God was shown forth to us by being brought to these regions; for the ships were in a leaking state, and in a few days our lives might have been lost in the sea. ... [the people] have large, square-built bodies, and well-proportioned. Their color reddish, which I think is caused by their going naked and exposed to the sun. Their hair is plentiful and black. They are agile in walking, and of quick sight. They are of a free and good-looking expression of **countenance**, which they themselves destroy by **boring** the nostrils and lips, the nose and ears: nor must you believe that the borings are small, nor that they have one, for I have seen those who had no less than seven borings in the face, each one the size of a plum. They stop up these **perforations** with blue stones, bits of marble, of crystal, ... also with very white bones and other things ... if you could see, it would appear a strange and monstrous thing. ... They have no cloth, either wool, flax, or cotton, because they have no need of it; nor have they any private property, everything being in common. They live amongst themselves without a king or ruler, each man being his own master, and having as many wives as they please. The children cohabit with the mothers. ... They have no temples and no laws. ... What more can I say! They live according to nature. ... They live for 150 years, and are rarely sick. ... These are the most noteworthy things I know about them. ...

## Analyze the Source!

1. Read the excerpt and tell in your own words what it says.

2. How does this excerpt help you learn about European attitudes toward people of the New World during this period?

3. Do you think this account is entirely factual? Why or why not? Give examples to explain your answer.

# The Pope Who Drew a Line in the Ocean

**c. 1431-1503**
Pope Alexander VI

**1493**
The pope draws an imaginary line through the Atlantic Ocean

**1494**
The line in the Atlantic Ocean is moved 1,100 miles west

Almost as soon as Christopher Columbus returned from his voyage to the New World, Ferdinand and Isabella wrote to the pope. They wanted the pope to give Spain control of all the lands Columbus had "discovered" or would discover in the future. Most of all, they did not want the Portuguese to benefit from Columbus's exploration of the New World. At the same time, the Portuguese wanted to protect their trade route to Africa, which they thought was threatened. The rulers of Spain and Portugal argued for almost 18 months about where to draw a "line of **demarcation**" marking the boundary between Spanish and Portuguese claims.

In May 1493, Pope Alexander VI decided to stop the arguing and clear up the confusion. At Spain's urging, he drew an imaginary line running north and south through the middle of the Atlantic Ocean. This line was a little more than 298 miles from the Cape Verde Islands. According to Pope Alexander's plan, Spain would have any unclaimed territory west of this line and Portugal would have any unclaimed territory east of it. The pope presented Spain and Portugal with this plan in 1494. They agreed in principal, but Portugal argued that the line should be moved farther west. They met in the Spanish town of Tordesillas. After discussions, on June 7, 1494, they agreed to move the line about 1,100 miles from the Cape Verde Islands. They signed the Treaty of Tordesillas agreeing to the change. Pope Alexander's line of demarcation became known as the line of Tordesillas. He became known as the pope who drew a line in the ocean.

Although they did not realize it at the time, by moving the line farther west, Portugal gained control over part of South America. Over the next 200 years, Portuguese explored the interior of South America and established settlements beyond the limits of the treaty. Eventually, the land of North and South America was divided among Spain, Portugal, France, Holland, and Great Britain. 📖

▲ Pope Alexander VI is known for drawing an imaginary line down the middle of the Atlantic Ocean.

**demarcation:** the setting or marking of boundaries or limits

**What Do You Think?**

**1.** Why do you think the pope became involved in settling an international political problem?

**2.** Why do you think European countries believed it was their right to claim land in North and South America?

# VASCO DA GAMA —
# Beginnings of European Colonial Empires

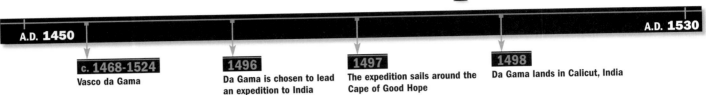

A.D. **1450**                                                                                                                   A.D. **1530**

**c. 1468-1524**
Vasco da Gama

**1496**
Da Gama is chosen to lead
an expedition to India

**1497**
The expedition sails around the
Cape of Good Hope

**1498**
Da Gama lands in Calicut, India

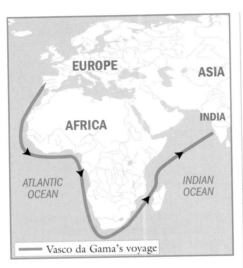

▲ **Vasco da Gama used the most modern navigational instruments available at the time, including the astrolabe. Using measurements from the astrolabe, he could figure out how far south he had traveled. This told him his latitude.**

Every American seems to know something about Christopher Columbus. However, far fewer know very much about Vasco da Gama. Who was Vasco da Gama? What did he do that was important enough for people to remember him?

Vasco da Gama was born in the small Portuguese coast town of Sines around 1468. His was a wealthy and important family. His father held an important position in the court of the Portuguese king. He grew up at a time and in a place where the sea was important in every aspect of his life. He fished, swam, and sailed from an early age. He learned to become a disciplined soldier and also studied navigation. As a young man, he shared the dream of other Portuguese men to find a sea route to India for Portugal. He got his chance to pursue this dream in 1496 when the king of Portugal chose him to lead an expedition to India. Vasco da Gama was only 27 years old.

## Preparations for the Voyage

The king provided Vasco da Gama with four ships. Two of them were large merchant ships. These ships had cannons. The king also provided a caravel and a supply ship. The ships had enough supplies so that the men could be at sea for months. They also would be able to stop along the way and get more supplies. Besides supplies, the ships were filled with goods to trade, including cotton, sugar, honey, olive oil, jackets, hats, caps, glass beads, bells, rings, and bracelets. In addition to Vasco da Gama, the captain, and officers and sailors, the expedition also included interpreters, priests, an historian, and men who could do carpentry work and make ropes.

## The Voyage Begins

On July 8, 1497, Vasco da Gama set sail for Asia. Church leaders were there to bless the voyage. Wives and children waved good-bye, not knowing if they would see their loved ones again.

The ships sailed south to the Madeira Islands, but then went west toward South America. At the equator, the ships turned south again and then east to round the southern tip of Africa. It is not clear why Vasco da Gama followed this course, but it turned out to be the best sea route around the Cape of Good Hope. It is possible that he used knowledge that earlier captains had brought back to Portugal. Whatever the reason, historians believe Vasco da Gama was the first European sea captain to use the southeast trade winds to sail across the South Atlantic.

## It's a FACT
Vasco da Gama's body was returned to Portugal in 1531, where he was buried on his estate. In 1898, his remains were moved to the Church of the Jerónimos near Lisbon.

## Landing in Southern Africa
On November 4, 1497, after more than three months at sea, one of the sailors sighted land. The four ships landed on the coast of southern Africa in a place they called St. Helena Bay. They made some repairs to their ships and looked for fresh water. They also met some of the people who lived in the region—a group of people called Hottentots. At first, they seemed friendly. However, when a fight broke out between the Europeans and Africans, da Gama and his men set sail. They rounded the Cape of Good Hope on November 22, 1497—10 years since Bartolomeu Dias had first sailed around it. Then they landed at Mossel Bay, where another group of Hottentots greeted them and brought items to trade. The Africans traded an ox for bracelets and played music on their flute-like instruments. However, after this friendly beginning, things did not go well. The expedition left, but they did not leave on good terms.

## Landing in Eastern Africa
Vasco da Gama made the decision to get rid of the supply ship. He wanted the other three ships to be as strong and well supplied as possible in case they lost touch with one another. The three remaining ships sailed north along the eastern coast of Africa. No Portuguese had ever sailed this far before. They landed again on January 11, 1498 and were met by friendly Bantu people. The crew repaired their ships, but many members of the expedition died of scurvy or became very sick with this disease. The Bantu gave the men who were still alive some fruit. This helped them to get well and continue their journey on February 24. In early March 1498, the sailors saw white buildings, the domes of mosques, and minarets in the Muslim coastal city in Mozambique. Unfortunately for Vasco da Gama, the Muslim merchants and the sultan were not impressed with the trading goods he brought. In fact, the Muslim merchants and sultan were insulted by the bells and bracelets and refused to trade with Vasco da Gama and his men. Da Gama and his men sailed north to Mombassa, but they were not welcomed there either.

▲ One account described Vasco da Gama as a man "strong enough to be feared in any dispute."

fast: tied or held so as not to fall
lurch: to sway

## Welcome to Malindi

Finally, Vasco da Gama and his men were welcomed at the Muslim port city of Malindi, which is about 60 miles north of Mombassa on the eastern coast of Africa. The sultan of Malindi gave the Portuguese food and spices such as cloves, ginger, nutmeg, and pepper in exchange for their trinkets. The sultan also gave Vasco da Gama a skilled seaman who could show the Portuguese the way to India. Vasco da Gama set sail for India on April 22, 1498.

## India at Last!

With expert assistance from the Indian seaman the sultan of Malindi had provided, Vasco da Gama landed in Calicut on May 20, 1498. It became immediately clear to da Gama that Arabs were important trading partners with India. The ruler of Calicut agreed to sell Vasco da Gama food, but he did not want to insult his Arab trading partners by trading with the Portuguese. Moreover, the cheap trinkets of the Portuguese did not impress him.

### FROM GASPAR CORREA'S JOURNAL

Some of the information we have about Vasco da Gama's voyage comes from a man named Gaspar Correa. He took part in the expedition and wrote a journal about his experiences. Historians think the journal contains many errors, but it still provides valuable information about the people, time, and place. Here is how Gaspar Correa described one of the storms the sailors faced on the voyage:

> The seas rose towards the sky and fell back in heavy showers which flooded the ships. The storm raging thus violently, the danger was doubled, for suddenly the wind died out, so that the ships lay dead between the waves, **lurching** so heavily that they took in water on both sides; and the men made themselves **fast** not to fall from one side to the other; and everything in the ships was breaking up, so that all cried to God for mercy.

## A Long Trip Home

Vasco da Gama proved there was a sea route to India. However, he concluded that the Portuguese would have to use force to get India to trade with Portugal. On August 29, 1498, the Portuguese started their long voyage home. Without the help of an expert Indian seaman, the voyage back to eastern Africa took three months. It was a long and terrible trip. Food and water ran out. Many crew members died. Da Gama decided there were not enough men for three ships, so he burned one of the ships and divided the surviving crew among the two remaining ships. Then the crew headed south along the eastern coast of Africa for the Cape of Good Hope, the Atlantic Ocean, and Portugal.

## Back Home

Vasco da Gama sailed into Portugal at the end of August or the first of September in 1499. Da Gama had traveled more than 27,000 miles. They were greeted by cheering crowds. The spices they brought with them were worth a fortune. However, of the 160-170 men who started the trip, only about 50 made it home. Vasco da Gama went on another voyage and earned many honors, but then he retired to his estate just east of Lisbon. When the king of Portugal asked him to come out of retirement to help settle problems in India, he agreed. Vasco da Gama died on December 24, 1524, just after he had landed in India.

## Vasco da Gama's Legacy

Vasco da Gama's first voyage is not as well known as Columbus's expedition in 1492—at least in the English-speaking world—but it was an important milestone in world history. Soon after the voyage, the Portuguese began to establish permanent trading settlements along the coasts of East Africa, Arabia, India, and southern and southeastern Asia. This was the beginning of European colonial empires in Africa and Asia. 📖

## It's a FACT

To thank da Gama for his efforts on behalf of Portugal, the king of Portugal made him lord of the town of Sines, awarded him many titles, and also gave him a yearly allowance.

◀ This illustration shows one of Vasco da Gama's ships.

## What Do You Think?

**1.** Why do you think the English-speaking world knows much more about Christopher Columbus than about Vasco da Gama?

**2.** Why do you think the Hottentots were happy with the bracelets and bells the Portuguese brought in trade? Why do you think the Muslim traders and merchants were insulted by these items?

**3.** How did permanent trading settlements along the coasts of East Africa, Arabia, India, and southern and southeastern Asia become the beginnings of European colonial empires?

# FERDINAND MAGELLAN —
## The First Man to Sail Around the World

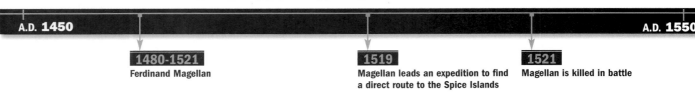

A.D. **1450**                                                                                     A.D. **1550**

**1480-1521**
Ferdinand Magellan

**1519**
Magellan leads an expedition to find a direct route to the Spice Islands

**1521**
Magellan is killed in battle

▲ Magellan discovered the passage around South America on November 1, 1520. November 1 is the day on which the Christian Feast of All Saints is celebrated. In honor of this holiday, Magellan called the passage the "Strait of All Saints." Many years later, mapmakers renamed this passage the Strait of Magellan.

Throughout the 1400s and 1500s, many men set sail to explore the world and find new trade routes to Asia. Ferdinand Magellan was one of these men. Inspired by Henry the Navigator and Christopher Columbus, he became the first man to lead an expedition that sailed around the world.

## Early Life
Magellan was born in 1480 in Oporto, Portugal to a noble family. Ferdinand was the third child in his family. When he was about 12, his parents sent him to Lisbon, the capital of Portugal, to work as a page in the court of the queen of Portugal. This was a great honor and also offered many privileges. Most importantly, all royal pages received an excellent education. Magellan studied geography, navigation, and astronomy. In 1505, Magellan joined the Portuguese navy and sailed the Indian Ocean for several years. He spent many hours studying sea charts and maps. Over time, he decided that he wanted to find a sea route to the Spice Islands from Portugal by sailing west. This would be an important discovery for Portugal. One Portuguese sea captain, Vasco da Gama, already had found a sea route to the islands by sailing around the southern tip of Africa. This discovery had made Portugal a wealthy country. Magellan's dream was to sail around the world by heading west. He wanted to succeed where Columbus had failed.

## Seeking Support
Magellan asked the king of Portugal for money to buy ships and supplies. However, since Portugal already controlled the southern trade route around Africa to the Spice Islands, Magellan's request was refused. Magellan then turned to the king of Spain and made the same request. Spain had no direct route to the islands. The Spanish king decided to support Magellan's expedition to find a new route. If Magellan were successful, Spain would become as rich as Portugal.

◀ Ferdinand Magellan was born in 1480 in Oporto, Portugal. He died in 1521 in the Philippines.

## A Bad Beginning

In 1519, Magellan left Spain in command of five ships and about 250 sailors. His troubles began almost immediately. Portugal did not want him to succeed. They had hired workers to load empty water barrels on the ships. These workers also provided false information about how much food was loaded on board the ships. Magellan believed he had much more than he actually did!

Over the next several months, Magellan and his ships sailed south and west across the Atlantic Ocean to present-day Brazil. Several times, his crew tried to take over his command. It was not an easy crossing! When Magellan and his crew arrived at what is present-day Rio de Janeiro, they rested and got fresh supplies from the local people before heading south along the South American coast. After several weeks of trying to sail south through heavy seas and cold weather, Magellan finally found the passage around the tip of South America. Many of his crew began to argue that they should return to Spain, but Magellan said they must go on. As they sailed through the straits and into uncharted water, Magellan named the body of water *Mar Pacifico*, which means calm or peaceful sea. The name stuck and people have since called this body of water the Pacific Ocean.

## Sailing Across the Pacific

Now that they were sailing in the Pacific Ocean, Magellan thought it would be a short trip to the Spice Islands. The "short trip" turned out to be almost four months. Many of the crew became sick and died. Finally, the ships landed on the present-day island of Guam. The men rested and got more supplies before sailing to a chain of islands known today as the Philippines. Instead of continuing towards the Spice Islands, Magellan insisted on exploring the Philippines. The king of Spain had given him orders to try to convert new groups of people he encountered to Christianity. On the first island, he was successful at this, so he went to the next island. Unfortunately for Magellan, a battle was raging on this island between two rival groups. One of the groups was ready to convert, but the other was not. Magellan decided to use force to make this second group convert. In the battle, Magellan was killed. The year was 1521.

## The End of the Exploration

After Magellan's death, his expedition experienced even greater problems. The remaining men and ships decided to go in different directions. Some sailed home, retracing the way they had come from Spain. When this did not work, they were forced to sail back to the Spice Islands. Most of these men never made it home. Others sailed toward the Cape of Good Hope. Finally, in 1522, the only caravel remaining from the original five ships returned to Spain. Only 18 men had survived the journey. The Spanish forgot about Magellan and made a national hero of the captain who had brought home the last ship. It was only years later that the world became aware of Ferdinand Magellan and his achievement as the first man to sail around the world. 📖

▲ This is a photograph of the Strait of Magellan. Magellan discovered this passage around South America.

## It's a FACT

Ferdinand Magellan did not return to Spain, but he is given credit for "circumnavigating" (sailing completely around the world) because he passed the easternmost point he had visited on an earlier journey.

## What Do You Think?

1. What qualities do you admire in Ferdinand Magellan?

2. Should Magellan be recognized as the first man to sail around the earth?

3. How did world politics play a role in Europe's age of exploration?

# BARTOLOMÉ DE LAS CASAS —
# In Defense of the Indians

We have gained a great deal of information about the people who lived in the Americas when the Spanish arrived from accounts written by Spanish conquerors, soldiers, and Christian missionaries. One of these Spanish missionaries was a man named Bartolomé de las Casas.

He was born in Seville, Spain in 1474 and went to Cuba in 1502. He had a large estate there with Indians living on this estate as his serfs. Around 1513, Bartolomé de las Casas became a priest. Historians think he was the first person in the Americas to become a Roman Catholic priest. The next year, 1514, he decided to set free the Indians who were serfs on his estate. He traveled to Spain on many occasions. He tried to convince Spanish leaders that the Indians should be treated as human beings. He encouraged the passage of laws in Spain that would protect the rights of Indians in the Americas. Later, he became a Dominican missionary and then a bishop in present-day Guatemala. He wanted to convert the people of the Americas to Christianity, but believed it should be introduced peacefully. Bartolomé de las Casas returned to Spain for the last time in 1547.

▲ **Bartolomé de las Casas wrote about the injustices of conquistadors such as Hernando Cortés and Francisco Pizarro and their soldiers.**

Before he died in 1566, de las Casas worked to improve the treatment of Indians. He wrote to the king of Spain about the terrible injustices that were being done in the Americas by conquistadors such as Hernando Cortés and Francisco Pizarro and their soldiers. For example, this is how he described the behavior of Pedro de Alvarado, an officer in Cortés's army: "He advanced killing, ravaging, burning, robbing, and destroying all the country wherever he came." Bartolomé de las Casas's writing was translated into English and read throughout Europe. Below is an excerpt from Bartolomé de las Casas's "In Defense of the Indians." Bartolomé de las Casas wrote this document in 1552.

▲ Bartolomé de las Casas tried to convince Spanish leaders that the Indians should be treated as human beings. This statue shows de las Casas and an Indian. It stands in Madrid, Spain.

## From Bartolomé de las Casas's "In Defense of the Indians"

... What man of sound mind will approve a war against men [referring to the natives of the New World that the Spanish called "Indians"] who are harmless, ignorant, gentle, **temperate**, unarmed, and **destitute** of every human defense? For the results of such a war are very surely the loss of the souls of that people who perish without knowing God and without the support of the sacraments, and, for the survivors, hatred and loathing of the Christian religion. ... What will these people think of Christ, the true God of the Christians, when they see Christians venting their rage against them with so many massacres, so much bloodshed without any just cause? ...

... How will they become our friends (which is necessary if they are to accept our religion), when children see themselves deprived of parents, wives of husbands, and fathers of children and friends? When they see those they love wounded, imprisoned, plundered, and reduced from an immense number to a few? When they see their rulers stripped of their authority, crushed, and afflicted with a **wretched** slavery? All these things flow necessarily from war. Who is there who would want the gospel preached to himself in such a fashion?

... "So always treat others as you would like them to treat you." This is something that every man knows, grasps, and understands by the natural light that has been **imparted** to our minds. ... Consider that war and the massacre of this timid race [the Indians of the Americas] has lasted, not for one day or a hundred days, but for ten or twenty years, to the incredible harm of the natives; that as they wander about, hidden and scattered through the woods and forests, unarmed, naked, deprived of every human help, they are slaughtered by the Spaniards. ... In the absolutely inhuman things they [the Spaniards] have done to those nations [the native people of the Americas] they have surpassed all other barbarians.

**destitute:** lacking
**impart:** to teach
**temperate:** moderate
**wretched:** terrible

## Analyze the Source!

1. How does this excerpt help you learn about the culture and history of Europe during the age of exploration? How does it help you learn about the culture and history of the Americas at this time?

2. How does this excerpt help you learn about European attitudes toward the people of the New World during this period?

# CATALINA DE ERAUSO —
## The Lieutenant Nun

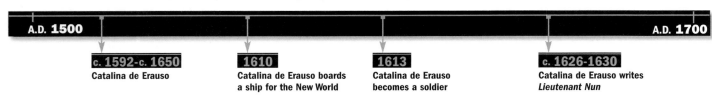

A.D. **1500**　　　　　　　　　　　　　　　　　　　　　　　　　　　　A.D. **1700**

**c. 1592-c. 1650**
Catalina de Erauso

**1610**
Catalina de Erauso boards
a ship for the New World

**1613**
Catalina de Erauso
becomes a soldier

**c. 1626-1630**
Catalina de Erauso writes
*Lieutenant Nun*

The New World attracted average Spaniards who wanted adventure and riches, even if it meant facing danger and risking their lives. Historical accounts are filled with stories of such men. But women also went to the New World for adventure and riches. One such woman was Catalina de Erauso.

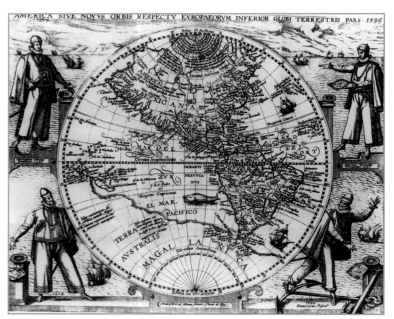

▲ This map shows the New World around 1600.

▲ The story of Catalina de Erauso has interested the Spanish-speaking world for hundreds of years. In Spanish, her book is called *La Monja Alférez*.

### Early Life

Catalina de Erauso was born in San Sebastian, on the northern coast of Spain, around 1592. Her family was Basque, a group of people who lived in the region between Spain and France. At that time, this region was part of the Spanish empire. Catalina's father was Captain Miguel de Erauso. Both he and Catalina's older brother had served as Spanish soldiers in the Americas. Later, three other brothers also went to South America to find their fortunes. This was considered appropriate for boys, but definitely not for girls. Girls were sent to convents where they were educated and prepared to become nuns or to marry a suitable man of their parents' choosing. Catalina and her four sisters were no exception. They were sent to San Sebastian's Dominican Convent, where their aunt was in charge. One of Catalina's sisters married. The other three became nuns. Catalina had a different idea about what she wanted to do with her life.

### Breaking Free

When she was 15 years old, Catalina decided to escape from the convent. One moonlit night, she cut her hair, dressed in men's clothes she had made from her own dresses, and fled from the convent. She started walking south. She worked doing odd jobs at various households. She told people her name was Antonio Ramirez. She was large for a girl, strong, energetic, and very daring. She traveled throughout Spain for several years, sometimes getting into fights. She even went to prison for a month. Then, in 1610, she decided to board a ship for the New World.

## A New Life in a New World

Catalina de Erauso stayed on the ship until it reached Panama. Then, she stole the purse of one of the other passengers, got off the ship, crossed the isthmus, and sailed south down the western coast of South America. She arrived at a small coastal town and got a job in a shop. At first things went well, but then she began to get into fights and went to jail again. When her employer asked her to open a new shop 250 miles to the south, she jumped at the chance. The change of scenery, however, did not change her personality. Again, she began to get into fights and even killed a man. In 1613, she and some of her friends decided to go to Cuzco and become soldiers. She was 21 years old and everyone she knew was convinced she was a very tough young man. She became a soldier in the army of Gonzalo Rodriguez. Word arrived about two months after her arrival of an Indian revolt south of Cuzco. This meant the Spanish army in Cuzco was going into battle. By her own account, the Spanish fought badly and were close to disaster. She was covered with blood, but she refused to give up and began shouting, "Santiago! Santiago and attack!" The Indians were frightened by the sight and sound and left the battlefield. Later, she was given a promotion to lieutenant. She continued to get into all kinds of trouble and soon headed for Chile.

### It's a FACT
- During one of her "scrapes," Catalina de Erauso killed her brother. She said she did not know it was him and she did not mean to do it.
- Santiago (St. James in English) is the patron saint of Spain.

## Marriage? Hanging? The Truth?

A widow who owned a large estate in Chile let her stay with her. The widow thought young Antonio (who was actually Catalina) would make a good husband for her daughter. Just before the wedding was to take place, Catalina slipped away. She ended up in a small Peruvian town where her past caught up with her. She was going to be hanged for her crimes. First, however, the bishop wanted to speak with her. Catalina de Erauso admitted that she was a woman. The bishop wrote to the pope for advice. After two years, the bishop got an answer. The king of Spain and the pope would deal with her. She boarded a ship for Spain on November 1, 1624.

## The Lieutenant Nun

When she landed in Europe, Catalina de Erauso met with the king of Spain and later with the pope. The king listened to her story and gave her an allowance for the rest of her life. The pope also was very interested in her story. He gave her permission to wear men's clothes and allowed her to return to the New World after she wrote the story of her life. Sometime between 1626 and 1630, Catalina de Erauso wrote a book about her adventures called *Lieutenant Nun*. Then she traveled to the New World. No one knows much about her life after that time. A friar reported seeing her in 1645. Some say she died around 1650. Others think she lived to be an old woman. Whatever is the truth, Catalina de Erauso lived an exciting life—one that was very different from most women of the time. 📖

### What Do You Think?

**1.** How would you describe the opportunities that were available to European women at this time?

**2.** Why do people want adventure?

**3.** Do you think Catalina de Erauso was a hero or a villain or somewhere in between? Explain your answer. How do you think your perspective, background, and values affect your response?

# JOHN HARRISON —
# The Search for Longitude

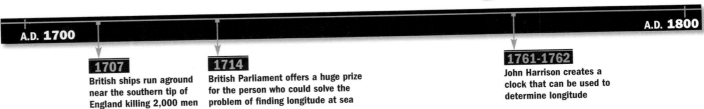

A.D. **1700**

**1707**
British ships run aground near the southern tip of England killing 2,000 men

**1714**
British Parliament offers a huge prize for the person who could solve the problem of finding longitude at sea

**1761-1762**
John Harrison creates a clock that can be used to determine longitude

A.D. **1800**

What is the greatest scientific problem people today face? Finding the cure for a disease such as cancer or AIDS? Figuring out how people can travel through time to explore distant planets? One of the most important scientific problems people faced during the age of exploration and through to the early 1700s was how to determine longitude.

ENGLAND
Greenwich •

Mediterranean Sea

▲ In 1852, scientists at the Royal Observatory in Greenwich, England used a telegraph signal to come up with time zones. They started the signal at Greenwich and called that Greenwich Mean Time. A group of 25 nations gathered in Washington, D.C. in 1884 and approved Greenwich as 0 degrees longitude. This made it the "prime meridian." The only nation that did not vote for this was France, which thought the prime meridian should go through Paris. This agreement created the worldwide time zones that we use today.

## Latitude—Easy!

By 300 B.C., the Greeks had figured out how to determine their latitude by studying the angle of the sun and stars. From about A.D. 150, mapmakers used grid lines to show different points on the earth's surface. The set of parallel lines drawn from east to west are called the lines of latitude or "parallels." Lines of latitude are always the same distance apart. There are 180 lines of latitude and they are each 69 miles apart. During Europe's age of exploration, Christopher Columbus sailed a straight path—or parallel—across the Atlantic Ocean on his voyage in 1492. Sailors of that time understood and could find their latitude. They used instruments such as the astrolabe and later the sextant to help them. It was longitude that created problems for them.

## Longitude—Very Difficult!

Finding longitude was much more difficult. As the earth rotates, the sun and stars appear to be moving. So, finding the angle of the sun and stars does not help find longitude in the same way they help determine latitude. Instead, to figure out their longitude, sailors needed to know the time on board the ship and the time at a specific location on land. Knowing the time on board the ship was relatively easy—as long as it was not a cloudy day! All sailors did was reset their ship's clock every day at noon when the sun reached its highest point in the sky. However, knowing the time at the specific location on land was problematic. But even if it were not a problem, you may be asking yourself, "How would the time on land and the time on the ship help find the ship's longitude?" It gets back to a basic scientific principle. The earth rotates 360 degrees every 24 hours. If you do the division, you will find that $360 \div 24 = 15$. In other words, the earth rotates 15 degrees per hour.

So, for example, if the time of the starting point on land is 12 noon and the time on the ship's clock is 1:00 P.M., the sailors know there is an hour's difference, which means they have traveled 15 degrees longitude (east or west). This information is critical because lines of longitude, unlike lines of latitude, are *not* parallel. At the equator, for example, 15 degrees of longitude is almost 1,000 miles. However, positions north or south of that line are less than 1,000 miles. In fact, as you get closer to the North and South Poles, the distances are almost nothing.

## The Consequences of Not Knowing Longitude

Not knowing longitude may seem like a small problem. The truth is that thousands of sailors were killed when their ships were lost or wrecked because the sea captains did not know their positions. On October 22, 1707, for example, four British ships ran aground near the southern tip of England—an accident in which almost 2,000 men were killed. Of course, another problem of not knowing longitude was that ships could easily sail into waters where enemies could sink them or take their cargo or both. Rulers throughout Europe understood the enormous cost of sailors not knowing their longitude. They encouraged scientists to come up with a solution. In Spain, the Netherlands, and some of the Italian city-states rewards and prizes were promised to the person who could solve the problem. The British Parliament attracted the greatest attention, however, when it offered the largest prize ever for a practical way to determine longitude.

## The Longitude Act of 1714

In 1714, the British Parliament said it would give the person who could solve the problem of finding longitude at sea a huge prize—£20,000. Today, this would be more than several million dollars. Do you think this attracted a great number of proposals? If so, you would be right. And some of the proposals seem quite ridiculous today. For example, one idea involved a knife, a dog, and a powder believed to have special powers. This is how the plan worked. Someone would cut a dog with a knife in London. Then the dog would be brought aboard a ship that sailed on its journey. Each day at noon in London, someone would sprinkle the special powder on the knife used to cut the dog. When this happened, it was believed that the dog at sea would somehow "feel" this powder and begin yelping. Sailors on board the ship would then know that it was 12 noon in London. Not surprisingly, this was not the winning solution to the problem of longitude. The prize ultimately would go to John Harrison, the son of a carpenter, a man who had no formal education.

▲ John Harrison came up with a solution for finding longitude at sea. Latitude comes from a Latin word that means "wide" or "broad." Longitude comes from a Latin word that means "long."

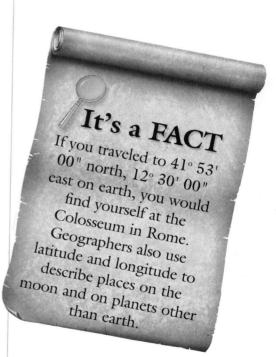

## It's a FACT

If you traveled to 41° 53' 00" north, 12° 30' 00" east on earth, you would find yourself at the Colosseum in Rome. Geographers also use latitude and longitude to describe places on the moon and on planets other than earth.

# John Harrison and His Clocks

As you read, the problem with determining longitude was not figuring out the time at sea. All sailors had to do was reset their ship's clock every day at noon when the sun reached its highest point in the sky. That was easy. The hard part was figuring out what the time was at the specific location on land. People today might shake their heads about this "problem." After all, today for only a few dollars we could buy two wristwatches. We could set one at the time of the specific location on land and reset the other every day by watching the sun. Yes, this is an easy problem to solve today. However, in the 1700s, wristwatches had not been invented. In fact, clocks at the time were mechanical devices with long pendulums that swung at regular intervals to keep time. Can you imagine, however, how the motion of the sea would affect these pendulums? The water and temperature changes also greatly affected the accuracy of these timepieces. No, pendulum clocks would not do. In order to determine longitude exactly, sailors needed to know the precise time.

John Harrison was an English clockmaker who was something of a genius when it came to mechanical devices. No one gave him much chance to win the longitude prize, especially when you consider all the important scientists of the day who worked on the problem. The people in charge of reviewing the proposals seemed to want to give the prize to one of the great scientists, not to an uneducated "mechanic." They changed the rules of the competition to favor the great scientists. However, as much as they discouraged his efforts, John Harrison submitted a proposal they could not ignore. They gave him a small amount of money to test his device—a clock that had springs in it instead of a pendulum. This kind of highly accurate clock used for scientific purposes is also called a chronometer. The test was carried out on a five-week voyage to Lisbon and back. The test on Harrison's chronometer went well, but the clock still lost about 10 seconds a day—too many seconds lost to win the prize.

## More Tests and a Smaller Clock

John Harrison was pleased about the test, but started working on improvements to his clock right away. He worked on his second clock for two years. When he found a problem with that clock, he put it aside and started work on a third one. That's when he got the idea that he should be focusing on a small time piece, not a large clock. So, he put aside his third clock, and started on a fourth one, which was only about five inches wide and weighed only about three pounds. His son tested this clock on a voyage in 1761-1762. The ship with Harrison's timepiece sailed from Great Britain to Jamaica, a journey that took almost seven weeks. On this test, Harrison's timepiece lost only about five seconds. This was an amazing result. Still, Harrison was denied the longitude prize. The officials demanded another test before finally giving him half the prize.

---

## What Do You Think?

**1.** Do you think it was fair that the officials changed the rules of the competition to favor great scientists rather than uneducated "mechanics"? Why or why not?

**2.** Study a map showing latitude and longitude. How many miles are there between 15 degrees of longitude at 15 degrees latitude? How many miles are there between 15 degrees of longitude at 60 degrees latitude?

# LATITUDE AND LONGITUDE ... DO YOU KNOW?

| | Latitude | Longitude |
|---|---|---|
| What's the trick to remembering the difference between them? | Think about the lines of latitude as rungs on a ladder—"ladder-tude." | Think about the lines of longitude as all being very long. |
| Are the lines the same length? | No. The lines of latitude are different lengths. The equator—the imaginary line around the middle of the earth that is the same distance from both poles—is the longest line of latitude. | Yes. The lines of longitude are all the same length. |
| How many are there? | Most maps show only a few lines of latitude, but geographers actually have divided the earth into 180 lines of latitude. | Most maps show only a few lines of longitude, but geographers actually have divided the earth into 360 lines of longitude. |
| What is the distance between lines called? | The distance between each line of latitude is called a "degree." The symbol for degree is (°). Each degree of latitude is exactly 69 miles apart. | The distance between each line of longitude is called a "degree." The symbol for degree is (°). The distance between degrees of longitude ranges from 0 to 69 miles. |
| How is time measured between latitude and longitude? | Each degree of latitude is divided into 60 minutes. The symbol for minute is ('). Each minute is then divided into 60 seconds. The symbol for second is ("). | Each degree of longitude is divided into 60 minutes. The symbol for minute is ('). Each minute is then divided into 60 seconds. The symbol for second is ("). |
| How do you write the position of a place using latitude and longitude? | You always write the position of a place with latitude first. For example, in **41° 53' 00" north**, 12° 30' 00" east, the bold face part is the latitude. | You always write the position of a place with longitude second. For example, in 41° 53' 00" north, **12° 30' 00" east**, the bold face part is the longitude. |

## Justice at Last

It was not until 1772 that King George III of England granted John Harrison's son a meeting. The king was extremely displeased to hear how John Harrison had been treated. It was reported that the king pounded his fist on the table and shouted, "By God, Harrison, I shall see you righted." And finally, at age 80, Harrison was "righted." He was given the other half of the prize as well as money to cover all the expenses of his work. John Harrison died a few years later, on March 24, 1776. Today he is regarded as a hero among clockmakers and sailors who know their history. 📖

# "What an Exciting Time"
# EDWARD WINTHROP'S STORY

As a result of the explorations of the 1400s and 1500s, trade increased dramatically. Many traders and merchants became wealthy from trade, but the cost of overseas trade was high. There was great competition to get the best ships, crews, and ports. Overseas trade also was dangerous. Ships were lost to storms. Pirates raided ships and stole all the goods. There was much money to be made, but traders and merchants also could lose everything they had. Some men had an idea they thought would help traders and merchants. Their idea was to organize companies that would share the costs and profits of trade among many people. The men who started these companies thought they could make a lot of money. This is a fictional story of one such man, Edward Winthrop. 📖

## THE STORY OF EDWARD WINTHROP

I couldn't believe what my friend Jonathan was telling me. He was crazy with fear. At first, he shouted, "Shipwreck, shipwreck, shipwreck." Then he only moaned, "Shipwreck, shipwreck." Poor Jonathan. A year ago he had sold his land and all his animals. There were stories throughout the country about the money to be made in overseas trade. I can remember Jonathan's visit to see me last year. "Come on, Edward," he roared. "Let's become rich men. It will be easy, quick money. And more of it than we have ever seen in our lives!" I could not decide what to do. I ended up doing nothing, but Jonathan put all his money into a trading expedition to India. But the ship he invested in sunk. And now poor Jonathan's life was ruined. He had no money, no way to start over.

I have always been a cautious man, but I have a touch of greed, too. Yes, my friend Jonathan had lost everything, but I knew other men who had become fabulously rich. I wanted to get rich, too. But I did not want to risk my family's future. It seemed unfair that some got everything and some got nothing. Then I had an idea. I'll get a group of people who want to make some money and can afford to lose a little money. If we put our money together we can finance a trading expedition overseas.

It turned out to be much easier than I thought. Goodness, people are so interested in making money! There were 25 investors in all. Two of us put in $2,500. Three friends put in $1,000 and 20 friends put in only $100. But we all had a share in the company. If we made money on the trading expedition, we would share the profits. If we lost money, we would share the loss. We named our company the Claremont West Indies Company.

I took the stockholder's money—$10,000 in all—and spent my days getting the expedition ready. I hired a ship, captain, and crew. I bought cloth, wheat, and iron tools to trade. I bought food and supplies for the crew. Finally, on November 23, 1543, the captain and crew set off on the voyage. On the outside, I was confident and happy. Inside, however, I was filled with fear and questions. We wondered if there would be storms. We wondered if the crew would stay healthy. We wondered if the ship would make it back safely. I'm happy to report that with God's help, the expedition was successful beyond our wildest dreams. After paying all our expenses, we made $100,000. We all got a share of this money. We went to our church to thank God for this good fortune. Then, all the investors went to a nearby inn and ate a fine meal. I gave my loving wife a large piece of silk cloth to celebrate our success.

# CARDINAL RICHELIEU —
# The Power Behind the Throne

A.D. **1500**                                                            A.D. **1650**

**1585-1642**
Cardinal Richelieu

**c. 1624**
Richelieu becomes
a cardinal

**1628**
Cardinal Richelieu becomes
King Louis XIII's chief advisor

Cardinal Richelieu (RISH-uh-loo) was the dominant force in French politics from 1628 until his death in 1642. He continued to have an impact on politics even after his death. He strongly influenced the king to implement his ideas and policies, which resulted in a monarch with absolute power in government.

## Early Life
The man we know as Cardinal Richelieu was born in 1585 to a noble family. His parents named him Armand Jean du Plessis. He took the name Richelieu from one of the estates his family owned. As the younger son in his family, he first trained for a career in law. In 1607, he became a bishop in the Roman Catholic Church. Richelieu was a hard worker and a successful bishop. In 1614, he was chosen as a leader of the clergy in the French government. He did so well in this job that the king's mother had him appointed to the Royal Council, a group that advised Louis XIII, the young king of France. By 1624, the pope had made Richelieu a cardinal in the Roman Catholic Church. Four years later, in 1628, Cardinal Richelieu became president of the Royal Council.

## Three Main Goals
When Richelieu became the king's chief advisor or prime minister, he and the king were almost a perfect match. The king, Louis XIII, did not like governing, and Cardinal Richelieu liked nothing better. Cardinal Richelieu had three main goals. First, he wanted to strengthen the monarchy. Second, he wanted to control the noble class. Third, he wanted to extend the king's control over local government. Richelieu promoted the idea of *raison d'etat*, which means "reason for state." According to this idea, the needs of the state are more important than the needs of any individual group.

## Strengthening the Monarchy
To help the king have a stronger monarchy, Richelieu fought a series of battles against the French Protestants, called Huguenots. The Huguenots were a group of people who wanted to have their own state and self-rule within France. Richelieu defeated them and disbanded their army.

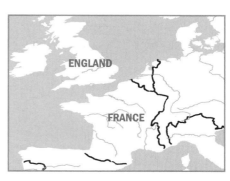

▲ Cardinal Richelieu was the chief advisor to France's king, Louis XIII.

▲ To control the French nobility, Cardinal Richelieu decided he had to make an example of nobles who plotted against the king. To punish these nobles, he ordered the destruction of their castles and fortresses.

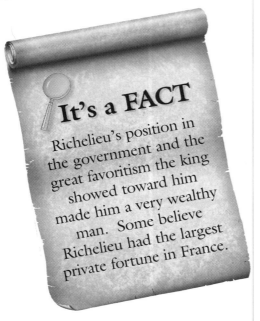

## It's a FACT

Richelieu's position in the government and the great favoritism the king showed toward him made him a very wealthy man. Some believe Richelieu had the largest private fortune in France.

**absolve:** to clear of guilt or blame; to pardon

### What Do You Think?

**1.** Historians sometimes say that Cardinal Richelieu is a perfect example of an individual who acted as "the power behind the throne." What does this mean?

**2.** Why do you think Cardinal Richelieu's policies were followed even after his death? How do you think these policies might lead to a revolution in France—what group or groups might be unhappy with his policies?

**3.** Do leaders today handpick their successors? Why or why not?

## Controlling the Nobles

To control the French nobility, Cardinal Richelieu decided he had to make an example of nobles who plotted against the king. To punish these nobles, he ordered the destruction of the castles and fortresses they controlled. Anyone who rebelled or plotted against the king was executed or exiled. Cardinal Richelieu demanded that all groups in France, including the nobility, submit completely to the king's authority.

## Controlling Local Government

Cardinal Richelieu was known as a very effective administrator. To extend the king's authority in France, Cardinal Richelieu developed a system to control local government. He handpicked men to control the 32 districts within France. These men were called "intendants." They were responsible for recruiting men for the army, collecting taxes, and managing the economic activity within their districts. These intendants also served as spies for Cardinal Richelieu. They quickly sent word to him about any plots against the king or Richelieu's authority.

## Absolute Power

Cardinal Richelieu played a key role in making sure the French king had absolute power in government. He also helped develop the French navy and established French colonies in Africa, Canada, and the West Indies. Working to build a strong monarchy, Cardinal Richelieu took extreme measures against groups in France who had different ideas than he did. He also took harsh action against any countries that he thought were a threat to the French monarchy. As a bishop and cardinal he did many things that would seem to go against the principles of the church. However, to justify his actions, Richelieu wrote, "... where the interests of the state are concerned, God **absolves** actions which, if privately committed, would be a crime."

## Cardinal Richelieu's Legacy

Cardinal Richelieu took a great interest in the arts and made sure the government invested in this area. He rebuilt part of the University of Paris and founded the French Academy, an organization of the leading writers in France, which still exists. However, he did not pay much attention to many problems facing the French people. King Louis XIII died in 1643, bringing the child king Louis XIV to the throne. Six months earlier, Richelieu had died, but he continued to influence France. Before his death, he made sure that the new king would be influenced by his handpicked successor, a man named Cardinal Mazarin. The policies Richelieu had established continued to be followed. Cardinal Richelieu is the man some think is most responsible for creating the absolute power of the French monarchy. 📖

# LOUIS XIV —
# The Sun King

Historians point to King Louis XIV as the best example of an absolute ruler—a monarch who believed he ruled by divine right. This is how Louis XIV described the role of a king in a letter to his son: "In a well-run state, all eyes are fixed upon the monarch alone. ... Nothing is undertaken, nothing is expected, nothing is done except through him alone." Louis XIV dominated the age in which he lived. Some observers referred to the time as the "Age of Louis XIV." Below are translated excerpts that reveal what others at the time thought of Louis and his self-confidence.

## About Louis XIV and the Divine Right of Kings

**Anne-Marie Louise, duchess of Montpensier, was known in Louis's court as La Grande Mademoiselle. This is how she described Louis XIV:**

*He has an elevated, distinguished, proud, **intrepid**, agreeable **air** ... a face that is at the same time sweet and majestic. ... His manner is cold; he speaks little except to people with whom he is familiar. ... He has natural goodness, is charitable, liberal, and properly acts out the role of king.*

**The duke of Saint-Simon, a noble in Louis's court, said this:**

*[Louix XIV] brought to his court those persons he cared least about ... It was still another device to ruin the nobles by accustoming them to equality and forcing them to mingle with everyone ... Upon rising, at bedtime, during meals, in his apartments, in the gardens of Versailles, everywhere the courtiers had a right to follow, he would glance right and left to see who was there; he saw and noted everyone; he missed no one, even those who were hoping they would not be seen. ... Louis XIV took great pains to inform himself on what was happening everywhere, in public places, private homes, and even on the international scene. ... Spies and informers of all kinds were numberless. ... But the King's most vicious method of securing information was opening letters.*

> **air:** manner
> **intrepid:** brave

## Analyze the Source!

1. Read the excerpts and tell in your own words what they say. Based on these excerpts, how would you describe Louis XIV?

2. How do these excerpts help you learn about the culture and history of Europe during the age of absolutism?

# PHILIPPE DUPLESSIS-MORNAY —
# Defending Liberty Against Tyrants

Philippe Duplessis-Mornay was a French nobleman and Huguenot. By 1573, he had become an important advisor to Henry of Navarre. He continued to serve in this role until Henry of Navarre became king of France and converted to Roman Catholicism. Duplessis-Mornay wrote an important essay called *A Defense of Liberty Against Tyrants*. This is considered one of the first writings that justified the idea that it was acceptable for people to resist lawful authority. In this essay, Duplessis-Mornay asks and answers three questions. First, do people have to obey rulers if they give orders that are against the law of God? Second, may people resist rulers with force and weapons? And third, can people resist a ruler who hurts the state? Below is a translation of part of Duplessis-Mornay's responses to these questions. 📖

**brute:** animal
**commonwealth:** the people of a nation or state
**convention:** rule
**fallible:** imperfect
**iniquitous:** wrong
**presumptuous:** conceited

▲ Philippe Duplessis-Mornay was an important advisor to Henry of Navarre (shown above) who later became king of France.

### From *A Defense of Liberty Against Tyrants*

Since a man does not govern other men as a god, as men do with oxen, but rather as a human being born to the same lot as they, it is not only **presumptuous** of a prince to mistreat human beings as though they were **brutes**, but also **iniquitous** of the people to look for a god in their prince, and a divinity in his **fallible** nature. If the prince, however, overturns the **commonwealth** on purpose, if he ... demolishes the laws, if he cares not a bit about promises, **conventions**, justice, and piety, if he becomes an enemy to his people, and finally if he exercises all or the most important tyrannical skills ... , then he can really be judged a tyrant, that is ... an enemy of God and man.

## Analyze the Source!

1. How does this excerpt help you learn about the culture and history of Europe during the age of absolutism?

2. Do you think Philippe Duplessis-Mornay believes people have a right to protest against an unjust ruler? Explain your answer.

# QUEEN ELIZABETH I —
## Queen of an Age

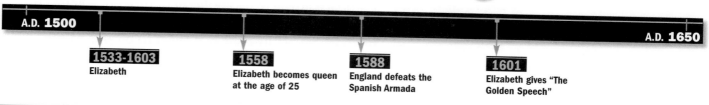

| A.D. **1500** | | | | | A.D. **1650** |
|---|---|---|---|---|---|

**1533-1603**
Elizabeth

**1558**
Elizabeth becomes queen
at the age of 25

**1588**
England defeats the
Spanish Armada

**1601**
Elizabeth gives "The
Golden Speech"

▲ Elizabeth was born in September 1533
and died in March 1603. She is buried in
Westminster Abbey, London. She ruled
England for 44 years.

◄ Elizabeth became queen of England at
the age of 25.

When Elizabeth was born, no one could have guessed what lay ahead for her. Her life was complicated and sometimes full of danger. The story of how she became queen is full of twists and turns, much like a work of fiction.

Elizabeth was born between three and four in the afternoon at the king's palace in Greenwich, England on September 7, 1533. She was a healthy baby, but her father King Henry VIII was terribly disappointed. He had wanted a son.

▲ Elizabeth was a healthy baby, but her father King Henry VIII was disappointed that she was not a boy.

In order to marry Elizabeth's mother, Anne Boleyn, Henry had broken away from the Roman Catholic Church and created his own church in England—the Anglican Church. Henry had disobeyed the pope and lost the Roman Catholic Church he had once defended. He also lost many friends, destroyed abbeys and monasteries, and put men to death whose only crime was their Roman Catholic faith. He had done all of this, but still had no son and heir. Elizabeth's mother, Anne, now feared for her own life because she had failed to produce a son.

## A Childhood Filled with Problems

Within the next few years, Anne was accused of adultery and witchcraft. She was put on trial, found guilty, and then executed. Elizabeth was two years old. Elizabeth had many problems as a child. Her father married a series of four more wives. These marriages left Elizabeth with a half brother and many half sisters, all of whom had some claim on the throne of England. In many cases, Henry's wives and children saw Elizabeth as a threat to their chances to become ruler. Elizabeth lived with various relatives at different times in her life. Despite this, she received a wonderful education and was a gifted student. She studied literature and mathematics. She also developed a strong bond with her half-brother Edward, who would later become king of England.

## The Line of Succession

During her early 20s, Elizabeth faced many difficulties. First, she was falsely accused of trying to overthrow her brother, King Edward. She defended herself and was cleared of the charges. When Edward became ill and died, powerful people in England began plotting who would be the next ruler of England. Edward's sister, Mary, was the rightful heir to the English throne. Although Mary was a Roman Catholic, she was crowned queen in 1553. When Mary became queen, she started to bring back Catholicism to England. English nobles were not pleased with this idea.

## Myths about Queen Elizabeth

- *King Henry VIII did not pay much attention to Elizabeth when she was a baby. She had to wear clothes that were too small.* **True**

- *Queen Elizabeth was bald.* **False**

- *Queen Elizabeth would sometimes disguise herself as an ordinary woman.* **True**

- *Sir Walter Raleigh laid his cape on the ground so that Elizabeth did not have to step in the mud.* **False**

There was a plot to overthrow her. Again, Elizabeth was named as a suspect. Elizabeth was arrested and taken to the Tower of London—the same place her mother had been executed. Elizabeth's strong denial of any involvement saved her. She was taken from the Tower and placed under house arrest for the next year. When Queen Mary died in 1558, Elizabeth, who was 25 years old, became queen of England.

▲ Francis Bacon, Ben Jonson, and William Shakespeare all wrote during this period. Here you see Shakespeare performing for Queen Elizabeth.

## Queen Elizabeth

From the moment Elizabeth became queen, everyone wanted to know when she would marry. Europe's royal families almost always married their sons and daughters to other powerful families to create alliances. Elizabeth had numerous offers of marriage, all of which she respectfully declined. How long could she stay single? She needed a male heir to continue her family's reign. All of her advisors reviewed each marriage proposal and tried to decide who would be best for Elizabeth and for England. But as the years went by, Elizabeth never chose a man to marry. No one knows whether she wanted to marry or not. We do know, however, that when England needed help from another country, Elizabeth offered the possibility of marriage as a way to create an alliance.

## England Fights Spain

One of the most important events of Elizabeth's reign was the battle between the English and the great Spanish Armada. At the time, the Americas had just been discovered. As men seeking adventure and wealth sailed back and forth from the New World to Europe, fortunes were made and lost. Spain, as the most powerful country in Europe, had the most to gain from trade with the New World. But Elizabeth was concerned that if Catholic Spain became too rich, the Spanish would be able to afford an invasion of Protestant England. To avoid a Spanish invasion of England, Elizabeth encouraged her sailors to raid Spanish ships returning from the New World. Elizabeth also sent troops to the Netherlands to help the Protestants there who were fighting against Spain. King Philip II of Spain decided to settle the question of control over the New World and stop the attacks on his ships. In 1588, the Spanish Armada, a huge fleet of warships, sailed into the English Channel. The Spanish fleet had 130 ships—all of which were bigger and stronger than the English ships. However, the English ships were faster and easier to sail. They also could fire and reload their cannons more quickly. In July 1588, the English defeated the Spanish Armada. England's power grew after this victory. It went on to become the most important world power for the next several centuries.

**It's a FACT**
Queen Elizabeth is reported to have said, "Better beggar woman and single, than Queen and married."

## FROM ELIZABETH'S "GOLDEN SPEECH" TO PARLIAMENT

"It is not my desire to live or reign longer than my life and reign shall be for your good ... While you have had and may have many mightier and wiser princes sitting in this seat, yet you never had, nor shall have, any that will love you better."

## Life during Elizabeth's Reign

Elizabeth's reign was a time when great English literature was written. Francis Bacon, Ben Jonson, and William Shakespeare all wrote during this period. Nobles liked to have a good time, and there were great parties with music, dancing, games, and sports. Queen Elizabeth also enjoyed many of these same pastimes. She loved to ride horses and hunt for deer. During this time, English women could not attend universities, but tutors could educate them. Women were not allowed to vote, but not all men could vote either. Women could not become doctors or lawyers. They could become writers, but few books written by women were actually published. Women could not appear on stage. Instead, young boys played the roles of women in plays. In some cases, women could inherit land.

**flattery:** praise or compliments
**scold:** to find fault with; to be angry with

## Queen Elizabeth's Legacy

Queen Elizabeth's reign was filled with many challenges. For example, in the 1590s, English farmers suffered a series of poor harvests. In addition, as the cost of government increased, she found it necessary to raise taxes. This was an issue that created conflicts between the crown and Parliament. Elizabeth was an expert, however, at dealing effectively with members of Parliament. Sometimes she would use **flattery** to get her way. Other times she would **scold** them. She developed close friendships with people such as Sir Walter Raleigh and Robert the Earl of Essex. However, these friendships sometimes were very costly to her.

In the final years of her life, Elizabeth was tired and discouraged. In November 1601, she gave what has become known as "The Golden Speech" to Parliament. She said, "It is not my desire to live or reign longer than my life and reign shall be for your good." She continued by saying, "While you have had and may have many mightier and wiser princes sitting in this seat, yet you never had, nor shall have, any that will love you better." Queen Elizabeth's last act was to name her cousin James as her successor. She died on March 24, 1603. She was 69 years old. During her 44-year reign, England developed a strong navy and became a world power. After her death, people looked back at her extraordinary reign and called it the Elizabethan Age. □

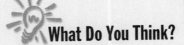

### What Do You Think?

1. What advantages did Queen Elizabeth I have in life? What obstacles did she face?

2. How does Queen Elizabeth compare with other rulers you have learned about?

3. What lessons can you learn from Queen Elizabeth's life?

# SIR WALTER RALEIGH — Queen Elizabeth's Favorite Courtier

A.D. **1500**

A.D. **1620**

**1552-1618**
Walter Raleigh

**1558-1603**
Elizabeth is the queen of England

Queen Elizabeth I never married, but if she had, many believe she would have chosen Walter Raleigh. Raleigh was born in 1552 to a noble family. As a boy growing up, he was well educated, but he wanted a life of adventure. He became a military commander in his mid-20s and then at age 29 found himself in the court of Queen Elizabeth. Raleigh was tall, strong, intelligent, self-confident, and by all accounts a thoroughly dashing man. There is a myth that says he threw his cape over a mud puddle that was in the queen's path. Historians do not believe this actually happened, but they agree that it is the kind of thing that Walter Raleigh would do. He certainly caught the queen's eye almost immediately.

Walter Raleigh's relationship with Queen Elizabeth became extremely close. He had great influence over her. She agreed that he could form an expedition to explore the Americas, but only if he agreed not to go himself. She made him a knight, appointed him captain of her personal guards, and awarded him vast land holdings and titles. When he asked her to give the poet Edmund Spenser a pension, she agreed. At one point, however, Queen Elizabeth asked him, "When will you cease to be a beggar?" He is reported to have replied, "When your Majesty ceases to be a benefactor." In other words, as long as she was willing to grant him favors and requests, he was going to keep asking for them. Their relationship became strained when the queen found out that Raleigh had fallen in love with another woman and was planning to marry her. On the next page is a poem Raleigh wrote in 1603 to his wife describing his ideas about love. 📖

▲ Sir Walter Raleigh lived in England and was part of Queen Elizabeth's court. He had great influence over her.

▶Queen Elizabeth never married, but if she had, many believe she would have chosen Walter Raleigh. Raleigh had an extremely close relationship with the queen.

## Description of Love
By Walter Raleigh (1593)

Now what is love? I pray thee, tell.
It is that fountain and that well
Where pleasure and repentance dwell.
It is perhaps that saucing bell
That tolls all into heaven or hell:
And this is love, as I hear tell.

Yet what is love? I pray thee say.
It is a work on holy-day;
It is December matched with May;
When lusty bloods, in fresh array,
Hear ten months after of the play:
And this is love, as I hear say.

Yet what is love? I pray thee sain.
It is sunshine mixed with rain;
It is tooth-ache, or like pain;
It is a game where none doth gain;
The **lass** saith no, and would full fain:
And this is love, as I hear sain.

Yet what is love? I pray thee say.
It is a yea, it is a nay,
A pretty kind of sporting **fray**;
It is a thing will soon away:
Then take the **vantage** while you may:
And this is love, as I hear say.

Yet what is love, I pray thee show.
A thing that creeps, it cannot go;
A prize that passeth to and fro;
A thing for one, a thing for **mo**;
And he that proves must find it so:
And this is love, sweet friend, I **trow**.

▲ Raleigh's relationship with Queen Elizabeth (shown above) became strained after she found out he had fallen in love with another woman.

## Analyze the Source!

1. Read the excerpt and tell in your own words what it says.

2. Raleigh compares love to many different things in this poem. Pick one of his comparisons and explain what it means. Do you agree with Raleigh? Why or why not?

**fray:** conflict
**lass:** girl
**mo:** more
**trow:** to think
**vantage:** advantage; better position

# JAMES I —
# The Divine Right of Kings

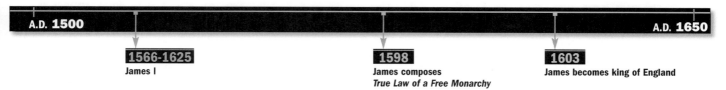

A.D. **1500** — A.D. **1650**

**1566-1625**
James I

**1598**
James composes
*True Law of a Free Monarchy*

**1603**
James becomes king of England

When Queen Elizabeth I died in 1603, her cousin James became king of England. He believed strongly in the divine right of kings. He told the House of Commons that he answered only to God. King James I believed he had authority over the English people, their liberties, and their property. His ideas about the divine right of kings are contained in a document called *True Law of a Free Monarchy*. He composed this document in 1598, about five years before he was crowned king of England. You can read below some of his ideas about the divine right of kings.

▲ King James I wrote a document called *True Law of a Free Monarchy.*

## From *True Law of a Free Monarchy*

By the Law of Nature the King becomes a naturall Father to all his **Lieges** at his **Coronation**: And as the Father of his fatherly duty is bound to care for the nourishing, education, and ... government of his children; even so is the king bound to care for all his subjects. ... As the kindly father ought to foresee all ... dangers that may arise towards his children ... so ought the King towards his people. As the father's wrath and correction upon any of his children that offendeth, out to be by a fatherly **chastisement** seasoned with pitie ... so ought the King towards any of his Lieges that offend in that measure. ...

... The duty and allegiance, which the people swearth to their prince, is not only bound to themselves, but likewise to their lawful heires and posterity. ... [The prince] is their heritable over-lord, and so by birth, not by any right in the coronation, commeth to his crown; ... For at the very moment of the expiring of the king reigning, the nearest and lawful heire entereth in his place. ...

[I do not mean that a king should escape punishment] ... but by the contrary, by **remitting** them to God (who is their onely ordinary Judge) I remit them to the sorest and sharpest schoolmaster that can be devised for them: for the further a king is preferred by God above all other ranks & degrees of men, and the higher that his seat is above theirs, the greater is his obligation to his maker. ...

**chastisement:** discipline
**coronation:** the ceremony in which a monarch is crowned
**liege:** subject
**remit:** to send

## Analyze the Source!

King James argues that a king answers only to God. Why? To whom do leaders today answer?

# THOMAS HOBBES —
# Ideas about Government during the Age of Absolutism

| A.D. **1500** | | | A.D. **1700** |
|---|---|---|---|

**1588-1679**
Thomas Hobbes

**1608**
Hobbes graduates from
Oxford University

**1651**
Hobbes writes *Leviathan*

▲ Hobbes entered Oxford University
at the age of 15.

▲ Thomas Hobbes argued that an
absolute monarchy, which gave all power
in government to a king or queen, was
best. Charles I (shown above) was king
of England at the time.

Thomas Hobbes thought and wrote a great deal about
government. To him, government was quite simple. Rulers
ruled, and subjects obeyed. When this agreement was honored,
people stopped fighting among themselves. When this agreement
was broken, human beings returned to what Hobbes thought was
their natural state of fighting for power.

## Early Life

Thomas Hobbes was born near London, England in 1588. His
father was the local Anglican priest in the village where he was
born. Generally, Hobbes had a happy boyhood, filled with more
free time than most other children had in that day. When he was
only 15 years old, he enrolled at Oxford University and graduated
five years later in 1608. Shortly after his graduation, Hobbes
became a tutor. Over the next 30 years, Hobbes traveled
throughout Europe. During these trips, he met with scholars
such as Francis Bacon and Galileo and others who greatly
influenced his thinking.

## His Writing

Hobbes wrote several books about science, philosophy, and politics. However, he is most identified with one topic—government. He wanted to understand why people allow themselves to be ruled. He also wanted to determine the best form of government for England. In 1651, Hobbes wrote his most famous book, *Leviathan*. In this book, Hobbes argued that an absolute monarchy, which gave all power in government to a king or queen, was best. Hobbes believed there were several reasons to support this argument. In *Leviathan*, Hobbes wrote that people are naturally wicked and therefore cannot be trusted to govern. People, he said, were basically selfish. If left to themselves, Hobbes thought people would act only in their own interests. Therefore, they could not and should not be trusted to make decisions on their own. Hobbes also believed that nations, like individuals, were selfishly motivated.

## Hobbes's View of Government

According to Hobbes, governments were created to protect people from their own selfishness. Therefore, he argued that the best government was one that had great power. For Hobbes, this meant that a king was best suited to rule a nation. Hobbes believed that democracy—giving citizens the right to elect government leaders—would not work. Hobbes wrote that all people are in a "**perpetual** and restless desire for power" that ends only when people die. He thought that giving power to the individual would create a dangerous situation. Why? Because if individuals had power, there would be a "war of every man against every man ... making life **solitary**, poor, nasty, brutish, and short."

**perpetual:** constant
**solitary:** lonely

## Voice of the People

Even though Hobbes distrusted democracy, he believed a group of people with different points of view should represent the common people. This would prevent a king from being unfair or cruel. Hobbes used the phrase "voice of the people" to describe how one person could be selected to represent a group of people with similar views. Of course, even though the views of many people would be heard, it was the final decision of the king that counted. When rulers ruled and subjects obeyed, people were not pitted against another. When this agreement was broken, people returned to their natural state of fighting for power.

## Thomas Hobbes and His Legacy

Throughout his life, Thomas Hobbes continued to write on the topic of politics. He also wrote about the history of the English Civil War and published his autobiography, in Latin verse, when he was 84. He left London in 1675 to live with friends in the English countryside. He died four years later. He was one of the strongest voices for an absolute form of government. 📖

### What Do You Think?

**1.** What qualities of Thomas Hobbes do you admire?

**2.** How does Thomas Hobbes compare with other scholars you have learned about? What lessons can you draw from Thomas Hobbes's life?

**3.** What ideas did Hobbes contribute to ways of governing? How did these ideas influence American democracy?

# The English Civil War, Oliver Cromwell, and Parliament's Role in English Government

▲ This picture shows Oliver Cromwell as Lord Protector in 1657. Cromwell ruled England during a very troubled time. He helped bring order to what had been a very confused and violent situation. At times, Cromwell used force to keep things from getting out of control. However, historians also agree that Cromwell was a tolerant man, and he continuously spoke of his love for a constitutional government.

**dissolve:** to make something go away
**traitor:** one who betrays his or her country

When Charles I became king of England in 1600, he wanted to continue the traditions of the Church of England. In 1637, Charles appointed a new archbishop of Canterbury. The archbishop wanted to support Charles and strengthen the rule of the church. To do this, the archbishop insisted that one group of English citizens, the Scots, use a different prayer book. The Scots rebelled against the archbishop and the church. In 1640, the Scots invaded England. Charles needed a larger army to fight back, but he did not have the money to pay for it. He needed support from the English Parliament. However, Parliament refused. The king was furious. In 1641, he tried to arrest the leaders of Parliament. His attempt was unsuccessful, and he was forced to flee London. In 1642, Charles declared that the leaders of Parliament were **traitors**. England was swept into a civil war. Charles and his followers, the Royalists or Cavaliers, were on one side. On the other side were the Parliamentarians, who were also known as the Roundheads because of their close-cropped hair style.

## Why They Fought

Royalists fought to defend the king, their church, and general social stability. Parliamentarians believed they were fighting for the rule of law, their civil liberties, and their religious rights. After several years of war, the king's army was defeated. But, ending the war was not as easy as defeating the king's army in battle. The king's army had not been paid for years. Now the soldiers demanded payment. When they did not get their money, they kidnapped the king and demanded that Parliament pay their back wages. This started another round of fighting. As long as the armies were fighting, Charles was still the king. However, in 1647, Parliamentary forces under the direction of Oliver Cromwell crushed the Royalist army and ended the rebellion. Any members of Parliament who had supported the king were killed. The remaining members of the Parliament were called the Rump Parliament. They brought King Charles to trial and then executed him on a cold day in January 1649.

## The Role of Oliver Cromwell

Cromwell was first elected to Parliament in 1628. This Parliament was **dissolved** by Charles I in 1629. The king did not call another Parliament for 11 years. When the next elections were held, in 1640, Cromwell was reelected to represent the area in which he lived.

Cromwell was unhappy with the Anglican Church's emphasis on church ritual. When the English Civil War started, he sided with Parliament and took a strong position against the king. After the execution of Charles, Cromwell remained a leader in Parliament. He and members of Parliament tried to find a solution to the crises in England. However, Cromwell did not think Parliament could solve the problems. In 1653, with the support of the army, Cromwell forced Parliament to disband. He then became leader of a revolutionary government. For a short time, Cromwell tried to rule with help from members of the disbanded Parliament. When this was unsuccessful, he took the title of Lord Protector and ruled as a military dictator.

## Holding England Together
Oliver Cromwell held the government together through the force of his own personality. He had experience in the army as well as in Parliament. This helped him resolve conflicts between these two groups. For years he had opposed King Charles's policies that he thought were unfair. Under his leadership, England enjoyed more religious tolerance. Jews were welcomed back to England during this time. Cromwell was a strict Puritan, but he tolerated all religious beliefs, except Roman Catholicism.

## A Short Military Dictatorship and then the Restoration
Some of Oliver Cromwell's supporters wanted him to become king of England. However, he did not want to begin a new monarchy. He believed that the English Parliament should have fundamental authority in England. He ruled England as a military dictator from 1653 to 1658. When he died in 1658, the different groups that he had held together began to argue again. For a short time Cromwell's son, Richard, was named Lord Protector. However, Richard did not have his father's sense of purpose, and things began to come apart quickly. Two years later, England restored the monarchy and Charles II became king. Historians call this the Restoration. During the reign of Charles II, some members of Parliament began to act as advisors to the king.

## Lasting Effects
The English Civil War had lasting effects on England's form of government. Although the government remained a monarchy, Parliament's role in governing England could not be ignored. Parliament had become a permanent part of the government. During this time, the absolute monarchy in England was moving toward a constitutional monarchy. 📖

▲ The British House of Parliament was built sometime between 1840-1850. About 200 years earlier, Oliver Cromwell had forced Parliament to disband. He then became leader of a revolutionary government.

### What Do You Think?

1. How does Oliver Cromwell compare with other rulers you have learned about?

2. Does the need for an orderly society ever outweigh the right of people to express their views on religion or politics? Give reasons to explain your answer.

3. Why do you think Oliver Cromwell believed in a constitutional government?

# REMBRANDT in the Golden Age of the Netherlands

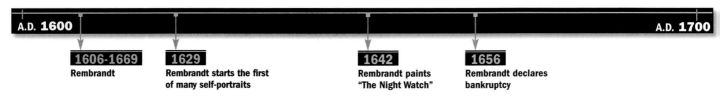

A.D. **1600**      A.D. **1700**

**1606-1669**
Rembrandt

**1629**
Rembrandt starts the first
of many self-portraits

**1642**
Rembrandt paints
"The Night Watch"

**1656**
Rembrandt declares
bankruptcy

In 1609, King Philip III of Spain ended his country's long war with the Netherlands. He signed a treaty recognizing the independence of the United Provinces of the Netherlands. During this period the Dutch made great achievements in science, literature, and art. This was the world in which Rembrandt Harmenszoon van Rijn lived. Today, we usually refer to this great artist by only one name—Rembrandt.

## Early Life

Rembrandt was born in 1606 in the town of Leiden, which was known as one of the country's most important intellectual and artistic centers. His father was a successful miller and his mother was the daughter of a baker. Although his parents were not wealthy, they placed great importance on education. As a boy, Rembrandt studied mathematics, Greek, classical literature, and history. Later, he attended Leiden University where he studied science. He also took great interest in anatomy courses, where he learned about the skeletal structure of the human body. As he and the other students dissected bodies of people who had died, they gained knowledge about the human form. Later, Rembrandt would put this knowledge of the human form to great use in his art.

## Rembrandt Learns His Craft

Rembrandt became an artist's apprentice in Leiden around 1620. While there, he was influenced by the work of his teachers who had spent time in Italy and studied the work of the Italian Renaissance painters. After three years, he moved from Leiden to Amsterdam and began to study with another artist. Rembrandt then returned to Leiden in 1625 to start his own art studio. In 1629, he started the first of many self-portraits. It was at this time that Rembrandt began to become known as a gifted painter.

## Amazing Work

Around 1632, Rembrandt completed a work called "The Anatomy Lesson of Dr. Tulp." This painting was different from anything that had been painted before. Rembrandt arranged the subjects in in this painting in the form of a triangle.

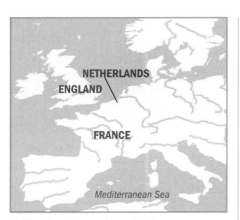

▲ Rembrandt was born in the Netherlands in 1606. During his life, he lost four children and two wives. However, he was able to produce great works of art still admired today.

▲ Rembrandt created this self portrait in 1640. You can see many reproductions of Rembrandt's works by going on the Internet and using the keyword "Rembrandt." His pictures show life in the Netherlands during its golden age.

Before this, other painters had shown people arranged only in a straight line. People responded with amazement to this painting. Over the next 10 years, Rembrandt's reputation and wealth grew. He married a beautiful and wealthy Dutch woman, and they began a family. He also purchased a large, expensive house. Everything seemed to be going his way. However, his happiness did not last very long. Between 1635 and 1641, three of his children died.

## A Life of Sorrow

Then, in 1642, Rembrandt's wife died suddenly. This changed him forever as a man and as an artist. Grief and hopelessness overcame him. However, during this same year, he painted the most important work of his career, a painting called "The Night Watch." People today greatly admire this work. When it was first shown, however, most people who saw it were not impressed. Why? One reason was probably because of the way Rembrandt used light. In "The Night Watch," the light seems to come from within the people in the painting. He also painted the figures looking out past where someone looking at the painting would be standing. These new developments in portrait painting were not popular at first. The negative response to this work did not help Rembrandt's **morale**. He was still deeply upset by his wife's death, and even though he was a successful artist, his financial problems worsened. For one thing, the payments on his large house were becoming too expensive for him.

## Starting Over

In 1652, Rembrandt remarried. In 1654, he and his new wife had a baby girl. However, his financial troubles did not improve. Finally, in 1656, he was forced to declare bankruptcy. He had to sell all of his paintings and his art collection. In 1663, Rembrandt suffered another personal loss when his second wife died. Five years later, in 1668, his beloved son died of the plague. Through all of his troubles, however, Rembrandt continued to paint. His self-portraits painted during this time show a man who was deeply troubled. Rembrandt died in 1669.

## Rembrandt's Legacy

Rembrandt was a painter willing to explore new techniques. In his paintings, he tried to show both the physical person as well as the person's feelings. His work greatly influenced European painting. His courage as an artist inspired later generations of artists. 📖

▲ Some of Rembrandt's pieces have a religious theme. This drawing made in 1635 is called "Christ Driving the Money Changers from the Temple." During his life, Rembrandt produced more than 600 paintings and nearly 2,000 drawings.

**morale:** how a person or a group is feeling

### What Do You Think?

1. What advantages did Rembrandt have in life? What obstacles did he face?

2. How does Rembrandt's life and approach to art compare with other artists you have learned about?

3. What lessons can you draw from Rembrandt's life?

# CHRISTINA OF SWEDEN

A.D. **1550**                                                                                   A.D. **1700**

**1626-1689**
Christina of Sweden

**1644**
Christina crowns herself
queen at the age of 18

**1648**
Christina signs the Peace
Treaty of Westphalia

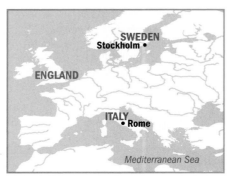

▲ Christina was born in Stockholm,
Sweden. She died in 1689 in Rome, Italy.

Great joy filled Stockholm, Sweden in 1626. News went out that King Gustav's wife, Maria, had given birth to a baby boy—a baby boy who would become king of Sweden one day. Everyone began to celebrate the birth until they realized a mistake had been made. The news was wrong. The baby was not a boy. It was a girl.

## Early Life

King Gustav and Queen Maria decided to bring up their daughter in the same way as they would have raised a son. As Christina grew up, the young princess learned to hunt and ride horses, as well as study art, music, language, and philosophy. When Christina was only six years old, her father died. Christina became the queen, but a group of five men were appointed to govern the country until she was older. According to most accounts, by the time she was 13 years old, Christina was a bold and fearless young woman. She had so much self-confidence that in 1644, the 18-year-old Christina had herself crowned queen of Sweden. Soon after, she began to have strong disagreements with the men who had helped rule Sweden when she was growing up. Their major disagreement was whether or not to end Sweden's involvement in the Thirty Years' War. Christina believed it was necessary for this war to end. She signed the Peace Treaty of Westphalia in 1648.

## Naming a Successor

It was the custom of the time for monarchs to name their successors during their lifetime. Since Christina was not at all interested in marriage and children, she decided to name her cousin, Charles Gustavus, as her successor. Having named a successor, Christina now could turn her attention to the things that mattered to her—studying literature and science and supporting artists, musicians, and the arts in general. She invited important scholars to her royal court. The most popular visitor was Rene Descartes. Descartes was a French philosopher, artist, scientist, and mathematician. He was the queen's favorite guest.

▲ Christina made herself queen of
Sweden when she was 18 years old.

▲ Christina wanted to make Stockholm the "Athens of the North." She invited important scholars to her royal court. The queen's favorite guest was Rene Descartes (shown above).

According to an often-told story, while Descartes was visiting Christina during the winter, she demanded that he begin their tutoring sessions at 5 A.M. The early morning hour and extreme cold did not suit Descartes, who quickly developed pneumonia and died.

## Giving Up Her Royal Position

By 1650, Christina began to think about letting her successor become the new ruler of Sweden. By 1651, she decided to step down. However, several advisors persuaded her to continue as queen for a little while longer. In 1653, Christina decided she was going to leave Sweden. In March of that year, Gustavus became king. A few days later, Christina left Sweden. She traveled toward Rome, talking to many Roman Catholic clergy along the way. She intended to convert to the Roman Catholic religion.

## Rome and Sweden

After arriving in Rome, Christina had a difficult time adjusting to the fact that she was no longer a queen. At one point she even tried to convince French authorities to take over the Kingdom of Naples (an area that covered the southern part of the Italian peninsula) so that she could become queen there. The plot failed in 1657. During the last years of her life, Christina returned to Sweden twice. On the second trip, she tried to regain her crown. She was unsuccessful, but did not seem to be too upset about this failure. She returned to Rome and became involved in church politics. Christina died in Rome in 1689 and was buried in St. Peter's Basilica.

## Christina's Legacy

Christina's life was very different from most women who lived during this time. It was even very different from the lives of other royal women of the period. Christina refused to marry, gave up her throne, and converted to Catholicism. Her legacy includes helping to end the Thirty Years' War and giving strong support to the arts and sciences. 📖

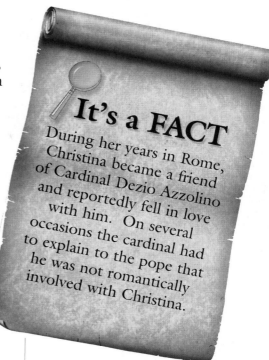

It's a FACT

During her years in Rome, Christina became a friend of Cardinal Dezio Azzolino and reportedly fell in love with him. On several occasions the cardinal had to explain to the pope that he was not romantically involved with Christina.

## What Do You Think?

**1.** Which of Christina's qualities do you admire?

**2.** How does Christina's life and the choices she made compare with other monarchs you have learned about?

**3.** What does it mean that Christina wanted to make Stockholm the "Athens of the North"?

# JOHN LOCKE'S
## *Treatise on Government*

A.D. **1600**

A.D. **1750**

**1632-1704**
John Locke

**1690**
Locke publishes *Second Treatise on Government*

▲ The Enlightenment began in France. Enlightenment ideas soon spread throughout Europe and across the Atlantic Ocean.

ENGLAND
FRANCE
NORTH AMERICA
ATLANTIC OCEAN
AFRICA

The great thinkers of the Enlightenment believed people could create better societies if they understood how societies worked. These Enlightenment thinkers were influenced by ideas of people who lived in earlier times. All those earlier thinkers believed the world could be understood and that human beings should try to find answers that would lead to this understanding. Some of the most important Enlightenment ideas came from John Locke.

John Locke was born in the small English village of Bristol on August 29, 1632. His parents wanted him to become a minister, but Locke had other ideas. He enrolled at Oxford University with the idea of becoming a doctor. However, while there he encountered many ideas that were new to him, including the idea of religious freedom and the rights of citizens. Later he became a teacher and writer. In 1690, Locke published essays on his ideas about **civil** government. He argued that people had the ability to govern themselves. He attacked the concept of the divine right of kings.

**civil:** relating to the people and citizens of a state

◄ John Locke believed that people had the ability to govern themselves. He said people had certain natural rights such as life, liberty, and the right to own property.

Locke argued that governments needed the consent of the people they governed. He said people had certain natural rights such as life, liberty, and the right to own property. Locke died in 1704. His ideas greatly influenced other Enlightenment thinkers. They also had a tremendous influence on the founders of the United States of America. Below is an excerpt from Locke's *Second Treatise on Government*. □

**contrary:** different from
**execute:** to carry out
**exempt:** to excuse
**frailty:** weakness

# From Second Treatise on Government

The legislative power is that which has a right to direct how the force of the commonwealth shall be employed for preserving the community and the members of it. Because those laws which are constantly to be **executed**, and whose force is always to continue, may be made in a little time, therefore there is no need that the legislative should be always in being, not having always business to do. And because it may be too great temptation to human **frailty**, apt to grasp at power, for the same persons who have the power of making laws to have also in their hands the power to execute them, whereby they may **exempt** themselves from obedience to the laws they make, and suit the law, both in its making and execution, to their own private advantage, and thereby come to have a distinct interest from the rest of the community, **contrary** to the end of society and government. Therefore in well-ordered commonwealths, where the good of the whole is so considered as it ought, the legislative power is put into the hands of divers persons who, duly assembled, have by themselves, or jointly with others, a power to make laws, which when they have done, being separated again, they are themselves subject to the laws they have made; which is a new and near tie upon them to take care that they make them for the public good ...

## Analyze the Source!

1. Read the excerpt and tell in your own words what it means.

2. How does this excerpt help you learn about the culture and history of Europe during the Enlightenment?

3. Why does Locke think it is a mistake for the people who make the laws to also carry them out? Do you agree or disagree with his position?

# BARON DE MONTESQUIEU
## and *Spirit of Laws*

▲ Baron de Montesquieu thought people should use reason to create the best form of government.

Baron de Montesquieu was born in 1689 to a noble French family. He was well educated and achieved great distinction as an intellectual in the Paris salons of Enlightenment thinkers. He thought people should use reason to create the best form of government. In 1748, after 14 years of work, he published his most important work, entitled *Spirit of Laws*. In this book, he argued that the best government encouraged liberty and opposed tyranny. In it, he agreed with John Locke's idea of the three branches of government. However, he said that the three branches should be equal and separate. Baron de Montesquieu died in Paris in 1755. His ideas continued to have a strong influence, particularly on America's founders. Montesquieu's idea of separate and equal branches of government is a central part of the United States Constitution. Below is an excerpt from *Spirit of Laws*. ▫

**assiduous:** diligent; persistent
**capacity:** ability

### From *Spirit of Laws*

In a democracy the people are in some respect the sovereign, and in others the subject. ...

The people are extremely well qualified for choosing those whom they are to entrust with part of their authority. They can tell when a person has been often in battle, and has had particular success; they are therefore capable of electing a general. They can tell when a judge is **assiduous** in his office, when he gives general satisfaction, and have never been charged with bribery. These are all facts of which they can have better information in a public forum, than a monarch in his palace. But are they able to manage an affair, to find out and make a proper use of places, occasions, moments? No, this is beyond their **capacity**.

## Analyze the Source!

What does Montesquieu say the people of a democracy can do well? What does he say they do not do well? Do you agree or disagree with his position?

# JEAN-JACQUES ROUSSEAU
## and *The Social Contract*

Jean-Jacques Rousseau was born in 1712 in Geneva, Switzerland. He did not have a happy family life and received very little formal education. He became an apprentice for a short while, but then began traveling throughout Europe. Eventually, he made his home in Paris where he became involved with other intellectuals of the day. His most important political writing was a book called *The Social Contract*. Even though he did not have a very happy life, he had a positive view of human beings. He thought people were basically good and that a ruler should govern according to the people's needs and interests. He thought the people should take part in their government. Rousseau died in 1778, just 11 years before the French Revolution. Many of his ideas, however, were central to that revolution. In *The Social Contract*, Rousseau asked and answered the question, "How do you know whether people are governed well or badly?" You can read part of his response in the excerpt below.

▲ Jean-Jacques Rousseau's most important political writing is a book called *The Social Contract*.

### From *The Social Contract*

Subjects **vaunt** public **tranquility**; citizens, individual liberty; one prefers the safety of property, and the other that of the person; one thinks that the best government is the most severe, the other maintains that it is the most gentle; this one wishes that crimes be punished, and that one that they be prevented; one finds it delightful to be feared by his neighbors, another prefers to be unknown to them; one is content when money circulates, another requires that the people have bread.

... What is the object of political association? The preservation and prosperity of its members. And what is the surest sign that they are preserved and prospered? It is their number and population. Do not look elsewhere for this much disputed sign. Other things being equal, the government under which ... the citizens increase and multiply most, is invariably the best. That under which a people diminishes and perishes is the worst. Statisticians, it is now your affair; count, measure, compare.

### Analyze the Source!

1. Read the excerpt and tell in your own words what it means.

2. Do you agree or disagree with Rousseau's idea as to the surest sign of a good government? Explain your answer.

tranquility: peace
vaunt: to brag

# VOLTAIRE and *Candide*

▲ **Voltaire is known as one of the greatest Enlightenment thinkers. He was born in France and traveled throughout England.**

The man we know as Voltaire was born François-Marie Arouet to a middle-class Parisian family in 1694. Growing up, he received an excellent education in Jesuit schools and made plans to become a lawyer. However, he began writing plays and poetry and eventually became known as one of the greatest Enlightenment thinkers. Voltaire has been called "the wittiest writer in an age of great wits." His life was not always easy. In fact, when he criticized the Roman Catholic Church and the French government, he was put in jail and forced to leave Paris. He traveled to England where he saw the rights enjoyed by English citizens in their government. Eventually, he returned to France with new ideas and a growing reputation as an enlightened thinker. He died in 1778, but his ideas had far-reaching effects.

Voltaire wrote about many different topics, including religion, science, and politics. However, his most famous work is *Candide*. Voltaire wrote this book in 1758 when he was 64 years old. He was living in Geneva, Switzerland at the time. He said he felt safe there from attacks by the Roman Catholic Church and the French government.

*Candide* tells a satirical story of an inexperienced young man who learns about intolerance and cruelty in the world. Candide's mother and father were not married. Candide wanted to marry the young and beautiful Cunégonde, the sister of a powerful baron. However, the baron refused because Candide was not of noble birth. Later in life Candide finds Cunégonde again. She is no longer young and beautiful. Still, Candide agrees to marry her. On the next page is a translated excerpt from *Candide* that tells what happened next. 📖

▲ Voltaire wrote *Candide* in 1758.

# From Candide

In the neighborhood there was a small farm which the old woman suggested that Candide should take, while waiting for the party's fortunes to improve. Cunégonde did not know she had grown so ugly, since no one had told her; but as she now reminded Candide of his promises with the utmost firmness, the good man did not dare to refuse her. He then informed the Baron that he was going to marry his sister.

'I shall never allow her to disgrace herself so meanly,' said the Baron, 'and I shall not permit such insolence from you. With that disgrace at least I shall never be reproached. My sister's children could never enter the highest ranks of German society. No, my sister shall marry none but a baron of the Holy Roman Empire.

Cunégonde threw herself at his feet and bathed them with her tears, but the Baron was inflexible.

[Candide was very angry and thought him ungrateful. He said:] 'I have taken you from the galleys and paid your ransom, and I have paid your sister's too. I found her washing dishes, and she's as ugly as a witch. Yet when I have the decency to make her my wife, you still pretend to raise objections. I should kill you again, if my anger got the better of me.'

'You can kill me again, if you like,' said the Baron, 'but while I live, you shall never marry my sister.'

## Analyze the Source!

1. Read the excerpt and tell in your own words what it means.

2. How does this excerpt help you learn about the culture and history of Europe during the Enlightenment? How does it help you learn about class distinctions at this time?

3. Why do you think *Candide* was a popular book during the Enlightenment?

# MADAME DU CHÂTELET —
# A Woman of the Enlightenment

A.D. **1600**

**1694-1778**
Voltaire

**1706-1749**
Madame du Châtelet

**1725**
Emile marries at
the age of 19

A.D. **18**

The woman we call Madame du Châtelet was born Gabrielle Emile Le Tonnelier de Breteuil in 1706. Her family was part of the elite French aristocracy. Known to her friends as Emile, her family expected that she would marry a French nobleman and live a traditional aristocratic life. As it turns out, her life was anything but traditional! Emile was an intellectual during a time when it was very difficult for women to be accepted as intellectuals.

▲ In a letter to Frederick the Great of Prussia, Madame du Châtelet wrote, "Judge me for my own merits, or lack of them, but do not look upon me as a mere appendage [part] to this great general or that great scholar ... I am in my own right a whole person, responsible to myself alone for all that I am, all that I say, all that I do."

## Early Life
Emile's parents owned a country house, but when she was nine her family moved Paris. They realized that Emile was a bright young girl, and by the age of 12 s was being tutored in English, Latin, and Italian. She was an awkward teenager, larger than most girls her age and a bit clumsy. Her greatest passion was learning and her strong desire was to receive a serious education. Emile was good at mathematics and science. She loved to listen to the many intellectuals and schola who came to visit her father.

## Marriage and the Philosophes
In 1725, at the age of 19, Emile married a military officer from a prominent family. He was often away from home for long periods on military assignments. Emile, alon in Paris, began to spend her spare time involved in social activities. She became interested in opera and the theater. She beg to spend time in Parisian cafes discussing ideas with the intellectuals of her time. These intellectuals were called *philosophe*

The philosophes were mostly people from the middle and upper class of French society. One of the most famous philosophes was a man named Voltaire. Voltaire and other thinkers of the Enlightenment believed that human beings could use reason to develop a better society. Voltaire convinced Emile to live her life as an intellectual.

▲ Although she remained married to her husband, Emile had a long, loving relationship with Voltaire.

### Emile and Voltaire

Voltaire was already a famous writer by the time he and Emile met. Although she remained married to her husband, Emile had a long, loving relationship with Voltaire. For many years, Emile and Voltaire lived and worked in the French countryside. This is where she did most of her writing. It also was during this period of almost 16 years that Voltaire wrote many of his most important works. Their relationship was not a secret, and it caused a great deal of gossip in the French royal court. Towards the end of her life, Emile stopped living with Voltaire, but they continued to be close friends.

### Emile and the Philosophes

Emile was an extremely intelligent woman and very well educated. Under Voltaire's influence, however, she became a serious student of science and philosophy. As Voltaire's student and friend, she was at the center of Enlightenment thinking. Being an active intellectual during this time was very difficult for women because women generally were not accepted as intellectuals. Emile's greatest accomplishments came from her work in translating many of the most important writings of the Enlightenment from English into French. For example, without her translation, the work of Isaac Newton would not have been known so quickly in France. Emile also influenced Voltaire to take up the study of physics begun by Newton.

### Madame du Châtelet's Legacy

Many historians have written about Madame du Châtelet's life with Voltaire, sometimes neglecting mention of the important work she did in her own right. Madame du Châtelet died in 1749. While she will always be associated with Voltaire, she also deserves her own place in the history of Enlightenment thinkers. 📖

## It's a FACT
- Madame du Châtelet's husband was a descendant of Charlemagne.
- Madame du Châtelet loved to gamble. Throughout her life, she bet large amounts of money.

## What Do You Think?

**1.** What advantages did Madame du Châtelet enjoy in life? What obstacles did she face?

**2.** Historians have sometimes paid more attention to Madame du Châtelet's relationship to Voltaire than to her own work. Why do you think that is so?

**3.** Do you agree that Madame du Châtelet deserves her own place in the history of Enlightenment thinkers? Why or why not?

# WOLFGANG AMADEUS MOZART —
# He Will Play!

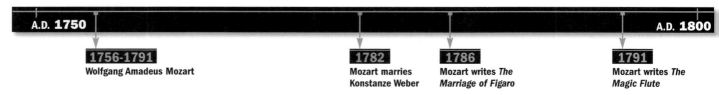

| A.D. **1750** | | | | A.D. **1800** |

**1756-1791**
Wolfgang Amadeus Mozart

**1782**
Mozart marries
Konstanze Weber

**1786**
Mozart writes *The
Marriage of Figaro*

**1791**
Mozart writes *The
Magic Flute*

▲ Wolfgang Amadeus Mozart was born in
1756 in Salzburg, Austria. He died in
1791 in Vienna, Austria.

▲ Wolfgang Amadeus Mozart is one of the
most famous composers of all time.

Wolfgang Amadeus Mozart is one of the most famous composers of all time. His passion was writing music. However, his short life was often sad and filled with problems.

Mozart was born in Salzburg, Austria in 1756. His father, Leopold, was a well-known musician and composer. Leopold was a violinist in the orchestra of the archbishop of Salzburg. By the time Wolfgang was three, Leopold knew that his son had great talent. Historians refer to Mozart as a "precocious child." This means that he could do things that other children his age could not do. By the time Mozart was three, for example, he could sit at the harpsichord, an early type of piano, and play musical chords. At the age of four, his father began to give him music lessons. By the time he was six, Mozart already had written a large number of musical compositions.

## Mozart's First Tour

When Mozart was six, he went on his first European concert tour. He played at royal courts and in concert halls. The tour was a great success. People admired Mozart's great ability and were fond of his boyish charm. In Frankfurt, Germany, Mozart gave a type of circus performance in which he did musical "tricks." For example, an announcement in the local newspaper said: "He will play a concerto for violin … on harpsichord and organ for as long as may be desired and in any key." Mozart's concert tour went to Frankfurt, Paris, and London. He enjoyed success in each place he performed. After four years, however, Mozart returned to Salzburg. The tour had provided Mozart with much praise, but it did not result in a permanent position in one of Europe's royal courts.

## A Tour Crowned in Glory

In 1769, Mozart made his first trip to Italy. In the cities of Mantua and Milan, Mozart was greeted warmly. He was asked to write an opera. Mozart also went to Rome. During his visit there, one of the most amazing events in his life took place. Each year during the Easter holiday, the papal choir performed a special musical composition. The pope said this composition could not be played at any other time of year. He also said no one could copy the music.

The only existing written copy of the music was closely guarded. Anyone who copied the music would be excommunicated. After hearing the composition only once, however, Mozart returned home and wrote the entire work on paper from memory. No one else has ever been able to do this. Hearing what had happened, the pope invited Mozart back to Rome. Instead of punishing him, the pope praised Mozart and gave him a special medal.

▲ As a child, Wolfgang Amadeus Mozart often performed with his older sister, Maria Anna, who also was an accomplished pianist. In this painting, the seven-year-old musical genius, Mozart, and his sister are entertaining a royal court.

## Mozart—The Young Man

During the next few years, Mozart's life was filled with both success and personal difficulty. He wrote an opera that was to be performed on Christmas 1770. It was very successful, but his life in Salzburg was disappointing. He did not like the members of the orchestra, and he was paid a small salary. In 1777, he went on another European tour. By 1781, he had written his first great opera, *Idomeneo*. Mozart's personal life also changed during this time. In 1782, he married Konstanze Weber. In May 1786, Mozart's next great opera, *The Marriage of Figaro*, was performed to immediate success. Soon after this professional triumph, however, his first child died. Despite his musical success, Mozart and his wife were extremely poor and did not have enough to eat. He pleaded with his friends for financial help, but no one helped him. His wife became ill and died.

## Mozart's Greatest Works and the End of His Life

Despite his personal troubles, Mozart continued to compose. In 1787, he wrote the opera *Don Giovanni*. Many people think this is the greatest opera ever written. In 1791, he wrote another famous opera called *The Magic Flute*. While writing these operas, he also was composing his three final symphonies. Mozart's last work was written under mysterious circumstances. As the story goes, a stranger asked Mozart to compose a requiem, which is a musical work composed for the dead. Mozart had been ill and thought this request was a sign that he would soon die. He worked on the symphony night and day at a tremendous pace. He did not sleep and ate very little as he tried to finish this work as quickly as possible. One day his friends found him unconscious at his work desk. They placed him in his bed and called a doctor. Mozart knew he was dying. He called one of his students to his bedside and with his last few breaths tried to sing the notes that would finish his requiem. He died shortly after that on December 5, 1791. He was so poor that his body was thrown into a pauper's grave unmarked and unidentified.▢

### What Do You Think?

1. What advantages did Mozart have in life? What obstacles did he face?

2. What qualities of Mozart do you admire?

3. What lessons can you draw from Mozart's life?

# BENJAMIN FRANKLIN —
# An Enlightened American

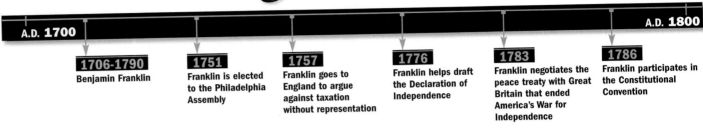

| A.D. 1700 | | | | | A.D. 1800 |
|---|---|---|---|---|---|

**1706-1790**
Benjamin Franklin

**1751**
Franklin is elected to the Philadelphia Assembly

**1757**
Franklin goes to England to argue against taxation without representation

**1776**
Franklin helps draft the Declaration of Independence

**1783**
Franklin negotiates the peace treaty with Great Britain that ended America's War for Independence

**1786**
Franklin participates in the Constitutional Convention

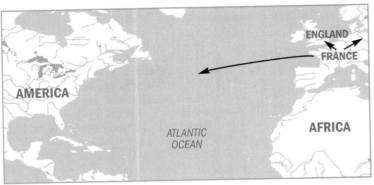

▲ The Enlightenment began in France. It soon spread throughout Europe and across the Atlantic Ocean. Benjamin Franklin helped put Enlightenment ideas into practice in America.

▲ Benjamin Franklin married Deborah Read Rogers in 1730, and they had several children.

From a very young age, Benjamin Franklin showed great talent. At 12 he was a printer's apprentice. By 16 he was writing a newspaper column using the name "Silence Dogood." Later, he became a publisher, public servant, inventor, and diplomat. Franklin represented the spirit of America, the new country he helped create. Franklin's accomplishments took place during a time when people believed they were living in a new age—an age of Enlightenment. During this period, great thinkers were interested in science, reason, and humanity. Franklin's various jobs reflect these interests. He was self-educated and read the works of John Locke and other great thinkers of the Enlightenment. Franklin believed in the Enlightenment idea of the possibility of progress. When the Declaration of Independence was written, Benjamin Franklin and other American leaders signaled that people were not just talking about Enlightenment ideas—they were putting them into practice.

## Early Life

Benjamin Franklin was born on January 17, 1706 in Boston. His father had come to Massachusetts from Oxfordshire, England. In Boston, he made and sold candles and soap. When Franklin was born, Boston was a city of about 20,000 people. It was a place where an ambitious and bright boy could make his mark. However, after just a few years as a printer's apprentice, Franklin left Boston for Philadelphia where he gained more experience as a printer. Franklin traveled to England and bought printing equipment. After returning to Philadelphia he began to publish *The Pennsylvania Gazette*, which quickly became a success. By 1732, he also was publishing the first of 24 annual editions of *Poor Richard's Almanack*. These books contained advice on how to lead a better and healthier life, weather forecasts, and other educational and practical information. Franklin knew that this was the only book that some citizens of Philadelphia ever bought. He saw it as a chance to help educate them.

## Franklin—Public Servant

As he grew older, Franklin became well known and moderately wealthy. In 1737, he was appointed postmaster of Philadelphia. In 1753, he was named deputy postmaster for all of North America. He also helped establish the Philadelphia hospital, police force, volunteer fire service, and the Philadelphia Academy. This academy later became the University of Pennsylvania.

## Taxation without Representation

When Benjamin Franklin was elected to the Philadelphia Assembly in 1751, he voiced his strong disapproval of the tax system Great Britain enforced on the American colonies. He did not think people in the Pennsylvania colony should pay taxes to the British government without having someone who represented their point of view in the government. In 1757, Franklin went to England to argue against taxation without representation. By the time he left in 1762, he had convinced the British that Pennsylvania should be allowed to impose its own taxes. Franklin returned to England in 1764 and stayed until 1775. During this visit, he asked the king to make Pennsylvania a royal colony. The colonists wanted the British to help defend the Pennsylvania frontier. The British gave the colonists a choice—either defend the frontier yourselves or pay for 10,000 British soldiers. The colonists said no to both choices. Soon after, the British Parliament passed the Stamp Act of 1765. This forced the colonists to pay to defend their frontiers. Franklin spoke to the British Parliament and convinced them to repeal this act.

By 1767, the relationship between Great Britain and the colonies had become very strained. The British had imposed taxes on the Americans for things like paper, glass, and tea.

▲ In this picture, Franklin is standing before the Lord's Council in Whitehall Chapel in London in 1774. He is presenting the concerns of the American colonists.

**It's a FACT**
One of Benjamin Franklin's greatest interests was science. He discovered that lightning is a form of electricity. He also invented bifocal glasses and the odometer.

**eradicate:** to wipe out; destroy
**universal:** pertaining to all people

Despite America's growing opposition to the British government, Franklin tried to find a way for Great Britain and the colonies to remain united. He warned, however, that "the seeds of liberty are **universally** found and nothing can **eradicate** them." This statement reveals the influence of Enlightenment thinking—the idea of individual rights, democracy, and the need for limited government.

## Defender of American Rights

By 1773, Franklin and others recognized that there was going to be a split between Great Britain and the American colonies. To help calm the tensions of the times, Franklin published his *Rules by Which a Great Empire May be Reduced to a Small One.* This publication angered British government leaders because they thought it made them look foolish. Around this same time, Franklin came into possession of some letters from a British general. These letters said the civil liberties enjoyed by the colonies might have to be taken away. Franklin sent copies of the letters to other colonists, who became outraged. Franklin could not stop the war between Great Britain and the colonies and, in 1775, sailed home to America. During the next two years, he served in the Continental Congress and submitted articles of confederation for the united colonies. In 1776, he helped draft the Declaration of Independence. Much of Franklin's thinking about the declaration had been influenced by essays on civil government written by the Enlightenment writer John Locke in 1690.

### What Do You Think?

**1.** What advantages did Benjamin Franklin have in life? What obstacles did he face?

**2.** What lessons can you learn from Benjamin Franklin's life?

**3.** Benjamin Franklin wrote, "Hide not your talents. They for use were made. What's a sundial in the shade?" What do you think Franklin meant by this statement?

## Franklin's Final Acts

Benjamin Franklin sailed on his last trip to Europe in 1778. He had been asked to be an ambassador to France. While in this position, he negotiated the peace treaty with Great Britain in 1783 that ended America's War for Independence. Two years later, Thomas Jefferson succeeded him in this position. After his return from France, Franklin participated in the Constitutional Convention of 1786. In 1790 he died. Benjamin Franklin was a man of great business skill, a gifted politician and diplomat, and a person who left an everlasting and "enlightened" mark on the history of America. 📖

▼ Benjamin Franklin helped write America's Declaration of Independence. At the age of 70, Franklin was the oldest delegate to sign the Declaration of Independence.

# THOMAS JEFFERSON and the Declaration of Independence

A.D. **1650**
A.D. **1850**

**1706-1790**
Benjamin Franklin

**1743-1826**
Thomas Jefferson

**1776**
Thomas Jefferson writes the Declaration of Independence
with Benjamin Franklin and John Adams

Most Americans immediately recognize the name Thomas Jefferson. Born into one of Virginia's leading families in 1743, Jefferson is one of our country's most celebrated founding fathers. He served in the Virginia colonial assembly and was a delegate to the Second Continental Congress. He also served as governor of Virginia, secretary of state, vice president, and president of the United States. Later in his life, he established the University of Virginia. Today, many people consider him one of the greatest American thinkers of all time.

Thomas Jefferson played a central role in writing America's Declaration of Independence, one of the most important documents in the history of democratic government. At the request of the Second Continental Congress, Thomas Jefferson, Benjamin Franklin, and John Adams wrote the Declaration of Independence, which Congress approved on July 4, 1776. Below is an excerpt from this document. 📖

▲ Thomas Jefferson helped write America's Declaration of Independence.

## From the Declaration of Independence

When in the course of human events, it becomes necessary for one people to dissolve the political bands which have connected them with another, and to assume among the Powers of the earth, the separate and equal station to which the Laws of Nature and of Nature's God entitle them, a decent respect to the opinions of mankind requires that they should declare the causes which **impel** them to the separation.

We hold these truths to be self-**evident**, that all men are created equal, that they are endowed by their Creator with certain **inalienable** Rights, that among these are Life, Liberty and the pursuit of Happiness. That to secure these rights, Governments are instituted among Men, deriving their just powers from the consent of the governed, That whenever any Form of Government becomes destructive of these ends, it is the Right of the People to alter or to abolish it, and to institute new Government, laying its foundation on such principles and organizing its powers in such form, as to them shall seem most likely to effect their Safety and Happiness ...

**evident:** easy to see; clear
**impel:** to urge
**inalienable:** not transferable

## Analyze the Source!

1. How does this excerpt help you learn about the culture and history of Europe during the Enlightenment?

2. How does it help you learn about the culture and history of America during this time?

# MARIE ANTOINETTE —
# Let Them Eat Cake!

Many people think of Marie Antoinette as a spoiled, selfish queen mainly interested in clothes and jewelry. It's hard to believe that she didn't know what was going on with the citizens of France while she enjoyed such luxuries. Did she realize that French citizens were starving? Was she simply trying her best in a difficult situation? Read about her life and decide for yourself.

▲ Marie Antoinette was born in November 1755 in Vienna, Austria.

▲ Marie Antoinette became the queen of France and lived in Versailles and Paris.

## Early Life

Marie Antoinette was born on November 2, 1755 in Vienna, Austria. Her parents were Maria Theresa and Francis I, rulers of the Holy Roman Empire. Marie Antoinette was baptized as Maria Antonia Josephina Johanna. It was the practice of the time that every archduchess—the title held by each daughter of the royal couple—was given the first name Maria. Her mother referred to her as Antonia. It was only later when she lived in France that she became known as Marie Antoinette. As a child, Marie Antoinette lived a carefree life with her many brothers and sisters. Although her mother ruled a vast empire, she paid close attention to her children. The children had their own doctor who looked after their diet and their health. Her father paid close attention to his children's education, but he thought education was more important for his sons than his daughters. Marie Antoinette did not care much for school. She convinced her tutor to shorten her hours of study.

## Marriage to the King of France

Marie's life was very pleasant until 1765 when her father died. Her mother became very sad and withdrew from society and her family. Marie Antoinette spent less and less time with her mother. However, as her mother recovered, she began to think about marriage for her daughters. She made arrangements for Marie Antoinette to marry the great grandson of Louis XIV of France. In 1770, Marie Antoinette married the crown prince of France. Four years later, her husband was crowned King Louis XVI and Marie became queen of France. Their marriage strengthened the relationship between France and Austria, but it was not popular with the French people.

## An Unpopular Queen

Marie Antoinette was unpopular because she tried to interfere with France's foreign policy. She wanted to do things to help Austria. French diplomats, however, were not interested in helping Austria.

France was their primary concern. In addition, many people did not approve of Marie Antoinette's lifestyle. A queen was expected to do things as they had always been done. But Marie Antoinette did things her own way. She seemed to be very bored by life and used France's wealth to create excitement and fun for herself. For example, she had a life-size village built on the grounds of Versailles. Then she and her friends dressed as peasants and played "villagers." She also was involved in a number of scandals. Some were her own fault, but others were just blamed on her. For example, it was reported that when she heard that the common people of France did not have enough bread to eat, she replied, "Let them eat cake." She did not really say this, but people believed the rumor. Why? Many people did not think she knew or cared much about the problems facing French commoners. They thought this statement sounded like something she would say.

▲ Marie Antoinette was arrested on suspicion of treason. She was executed in 1793.

## Marie Antoinette and the French Revolution

By 1789, the French monarchy was in serious trouble. The French economy was very bad, people were out of work, and there was rioting in the streets. Marie Antoinette tried to get Austria to help France, but Austria did not help. In 1791, a mob marched to Versailles. The king and queen were forced to move to Paris. In 1791, the royal family tried to flee Paris, but failed. When Austria and Prussia declared war on France, Marie Antoinette was accused of passing military secrets to the enemy. In 1792, the royal family was arrested on suspicion of treason. In 1793, King Louis XVI was convicted and executed. Marie Antoinette also was executed later that same year.

## A Woman Caught in the Changes of the Times

By all accounts, Marie Antoinette was brave in the days before her death. Many portraits of her execution show her looking calm and dignified. Historians agree that she was unprepared for her life when she married Louis. They also agree that her actions during her marriage did not win her any friends. However, the political situation in France was changing in the late 1700s. The Enlightenment brought a new way of thinking, especially in terms of government. Marie Antoinette was caught up in changing times. She had been raised to be a queen of a country led by an absolute ruler. She was not prepared for the changing views of government brought on by the Enlightenment. 📖

# Scandal!

As queen of France, Marie Antoinette was involved in many scandals, including one known as the "Affair of the Diamond Necklace." Some French nobles convinced a cardinal of a way to gain the queen's favor. They persuaded him to buy a very expensive diamond necklace for the queen. After the cardinal bought the necklace, he gave it to the nobles who took it to England and sold it. Then they faked a series of letters between the cardinal and the queen. These letters made it appear that the queen had received the necklace. However, Marie Antoinette knew nothing about the necklace or the cardinal. Marie had never asked for the necklace. She did not even know the cardinal. When the story came out, however, she had to suffer the accusations of the public. This scandal added to her unpopularity.

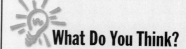

**What Do You Think?**

1. What lessons can you learn from Marie Antoinette's life?

2. How was the political situation in France changing?

# France's *Declaration of the Rights of Man*

▲ **The people who wrote France's *Declaration of the Rights of Man* were influenced by the English Bill of Rights.**

On August 27, 1789, the National Assembly of France published the *Declaration of the Rights of Man*. It included many Enlightenment ideas, including the idea that "men are born and remain free and equal in rights" and that liberty is a natural right. The people who wrote this document were influenced by the English Bill of Rights as well as America's Declaration of Independence and the statements of rights contained in American state constitutions. Below is an excerpt from this document. 📖

## Analyze the Source!

1. How does this excerpt help you learn about the culture and history of Europe during the Enlightenment?

2. How do these rights compare with those rights Americans have today?

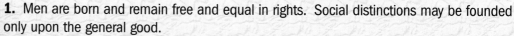

### From the *Declaration of the Rights of Man*

*The representatives of the French people, organized as a National Assembly ... have determined to set forth in a solemn declaration the natural, inalienable, and sacred rights of man. ... The National Assembly recognizes and proclaims, in the presence and under the auspices of the Supreme Being, the following rights of man and of the citizen:*

**1.** Men are born and remain free and equal in rights. Social distinctions may be founded only upon the general good.

**2.** The aim of all political association is the preservation of the natural and imprescriptible rights of man. These rights are liberty, property, security, and resistance to oppression.

**4.** Liberty consists in the freedom to do everything which injures no one else; hence the exercise of the natural rights of each man has no limits except those which assure to the other members of the society the enjoyment of the same rights. These limits can only be determined by law.

**5.** Law can only prohibit such actions as are hurtful to society. Nothing may be prevented which is not forbidden by law, and no one may be forced to do anything not provided for by law.

**6.** Law is the expression of the general will. Every citizen has a right to participate personally, or through his representative, in its formation. It must be the same for all, whether it protects or punishes. All citizens, being equal in the eyes of the law, are equally eligible to all dignities and to all public positions and occupations, according to their abilities, without any distinction, except that of their virtues and talents.

**7.** No person shall be accused, arrested, or imprisoned except in the cases and according to the forms prescribed by law. ...

**8.** The law shall provide for such punishments only as are strictly and obviously necessary. ...

**11.** The free communication of ideas and opinions is one of the most precious of the rights of man. Every citizen may, accordingly, speak, write, and print with freedom, but shall be responsible for such abuses of this freedom as shall be defined by law.

# France's *Declaration of the Rights of Woman*

In 1789, the National Assembly of France published the *Declaration of the Rights of Man*. It included many Enlightenment ideas, such as the idea that "men are born and remain free and equal in rights" and that liberty is a natural right. The people who wrote this document were influenced by the English Bill of Rights and also by America's Declaration of Independence and the statements of rights contained in American state constitutions. In 1791, the daughter of a French butcher, Olympe de Gouges, wrote the *Declaration of the Rights of Woman*. In this document, she argued for social and political rights for women. She began the document by asking a question, "Man, are you capable of being just?" Then she asked what gave men the right to dominate women. Olympe de Gouges argued that "in a century of enlightenment and wisdom," men claimed their rights of equality, but did not address the issue of equality when it came to women. She then listed what she thought should be the rights of women. Below is an excerpt from this document. 📖

▲ **Olympe de Gouges, the woman who wrote France's *Declaration of the Rights of Woman*, was influenced by the English Bill of Rights and France's *Declaration of the Rights of Man*.**

**rigor:** strictness; harshness

## From the *Declaration of the Rights of Woman*

### Article I
Woman is born free and lives equal to man in her rights. Social distinctions can be based only on the common utility [usefulness].

### Article VI
The law must be the expression of the general will; all female and male citizens must contribute either personally or through their representatives to its formation; it must be the same for all: male and female citizens, being equal in the eyes of the law, must be equally admitted to all honors, positions, and public employment according to their capacity and without other distinctions besides those of their virtues and talents.

### Article IX
Once any woman is declared guilty, complete **rigor** is [to be] exercised by the law.

### Article XVII
Property belongs to both sexes whether united or separate. ...

## Analyze the Source!

1. Read the articles and tell in your own words what they mean.

2. How does this excerpt help you learn about the culture and history of Europe during the Enlightenment?

3. Which of the rights in this excerpt from the *Declaration of the Rights of Woman* do you think is most important? Why?

# FRANCE —
# After the Revolution

Louis XIV, the Sun King, built a palace of breathtaking beauty at Versailles. It took almost 50 years to complete and included hundreds of exquisitely decorated rooms. There were lovely gardens, fountains, and works of art everywhere. How was this symbol of the French monarchy treated during the French Revolution? How did life change for the common people of France after the revolution? Below is part of an account by a man named Richard Twiss. He wrote these observations while he was on a trip to Paris during the summer of 1792. 📖

## Analyze the Source!

1. How does this excerpt help you learn about the culture and history of Europe during the Enlightenment?

2. How would you describe the writer's perspective toward the French Revolution? Give examples to support your answer.

### Observations of Paris after the Revolution

I went once to Versailles; there is hardly anything in the palace but the bare walls, a very few of the looking-glasses [mirrors], tapestry, and large pictures remaining, as it has now been near two years uninhabited. I crossed the great canal on foot; there was not a drop of water in it. ...

The common people are in general much better clothed than they were before the Revolution, which may be ascribed [credited] to their not being so grievously [badly] taxed as they were ... All those ornaments, which three years ago were worn of silver, are now of gold. All the women of the lower class, even those who sit behind green-stalls [vegetable stands], etc., wear gold ear-rings, with large drops, ... and necklaces of the same. Many of the men wear plain gold ear-rings. ... Even children of two years old have small gold drops in their ears.

► Here you see Louis XIV's palace at Versailles before the French Revolution.

# EDMUND BURKE on the Death of Marie Antoinette

Edmund Burke was born in Dublin, Ireland in 1729. He became a member of the British Parliament in the late 1700s. He criticized the French Revolution and spoke out about the passing of an era in history. Below is part of a speech he gave in 1793 where he expressed his sadness about Marie Antoinette's death and also about the "death" of an age. Burke died in 1797.

▶ Edmund Burke was sad about Marie Antoinette's death and the passing of an era.

**cavalier:** a gentleman who fights skillfully
**scabbard:** container for a sword

### From Edmund Burke's Speech
### About the Death of Marie Antoinette

... Little did I dream that I should have lived to see such disaster fallen upon her, in a nation of gallant [heroic] men, in a nation of men of honor, and of **cavaliers**! I thought ten thousand swords must have leaped from their **scabbards**, to avenge even a look that threatened her with insult.

But the age of chivalry is gone ... the glory of Europe is extinguised [gone] forever. Never, never more, shall we behold [see] that generous loyalty to rank and sex, that proud submission, that dignified obedience. ...

## Analyze the Source!

1. Read the excerpt and tell in your own words what it says.

2. How does this excerpt help you learn about the culture and history of Europe during the Enlightenment?

3. From reading this excerpt, what would you say Edmund Burke missed about an earlier time in history?

# GLOSSARY

## A

**absolve:** (ab-ZAHLV) *v.* To clear of guilt or blame; to pardon.

**abuse:** (uh-BYOOS) *n.* A corrupt practice or custom; wrongdoing.

**accomplished:** (uh-KAHM-lisht) *adj.* Skilled; expert.

**acknowledge:** (ak-NAHL-ij) *v.* To recognize or to accept responsibility.

**acquisition:** (ak-wi-ZIH-uhn) *n.* Gaining.

**admonition:** (ad-moh-NISH-un) *n.* Sharp criticism or warning.

**adorn:** (uh-DOHRN) *v.* To decorate or make beautiful.

**adulterous:** (uh-DUL-ter-uhs) *adj.* Having relations with a man or woman who is not your husband or wife.

**affirmative:** (uh-FUHR-ma-tiv) *n.* A "yes" answer.

**affliction:** (uh-FLIK-shun) *n.* Pain or suffering.

**air:** (ayr) *n.* Manner.

**anatomy:** (uh-NAT-uh-mee) *n.* Shape and structure of an organism.

**anguish:** (ANG-gwish) *n.* Suffering.

**apprentice:** (uh-PREN-tis) *n.* A person who goes to work for another person for a specific period of time; in return for this work, the apprentice learns a trade, art, or business.

**aqueduct:** (AK-we-dukt) *n.* A structure that helps move water in a certain direction.

**assiduous:** (uh-SIJ-oo-us) *adj.* Diligent; persistent.

**astronomy:** (uh-STRAHN-uh-mee) *n.* The study of the universe, including the stars and planets.

**autobiography:** (aw-toh-biy-AHG-ra-fee) *n.* A book written by a person about that person's life.

**avenge:** (uh-VENJ) *v.* To take revenge; to get back at someone for wrong or injury.

**avow:** (uh-VOW) *v.* To declare as true.

## B

**balcony:** (BAL-kuh-nee ) *n.* A platform that sticks out of the wall of a building and is surrounded by a railing.

**barrow:** (BAR-oh) *n.* A heap of rocks or earth marking a grave; a mound.

**behead:** (bi-HED) *v.* To separate the head from the body.

**bevy:** (BEV-ee) *n.* Group.

**bore:** (bohr) *v.* To make a hole.

**brewer:** (BROO-er) *n.* A person who makes beer.

**bribery:** (BRIYB-ur-ee) *n.* The act of giving, taking, or offering money (or something valuable) to influence or persuade.

**brute:** (broot) *n.* Animal.

## C

**cadaver:** (kuh-DAV-ur) *n.* Dead body.

**capacity:** (kuh-PAS-i-tee) *n.* Ability.

**career:** (kuh-REER) *n.* A person's chosen work in life.

**cavalier:** (kav-uh-LEER) *n.* A gentleman who fights skillfully.

**ceremony:** (SER-e-moh-nee) *n.* An act or set of acts performed according to tradition or custom; ritual.

**chaotic:** (kay-AHT-ik) *adj.* Extremely confused and disorderly.

**chastisement:** (chas-TIYZ-munt) *n.* Discipline.

**cherish:** (CHER-ish) *v.* To hope for.

**civil:** (SIV-ul) *adj.* Relating to the people and citizens of a state.

**clemency:** (KLEM-un-see) *n.* Mercy.

**clerk:** (klerk) *n.* A person who works in an office, files papers, and does other office work.

**coiffure:** (kwah-FYOOR) *n.* Hairstyle.

**commonwealth:** (KAHM-un-welth) *n.* The people of a nation or state.

**confide:** (kuhn-FIYD) *v.* To tell in private.

**consent:** (kuhn-SENT) *v.* To agree.

**contrary**: (KAHN-trer-ee) *adj.* Different from.

**convention**: (kuhn-VEN-shun) *n.* Rule.

**conversion**: (kuhn-VUR-shun) *n.* A change where one adopts a new religion.

**coronation**: (kohr-UH-nay-shun) *n.* The ceremony in which a monarch is crowned.

**council**: (KOWN-sil) *n.* A group of people called together for discussion.

**count**: (kownt) *n.* A nobleman; the word *count* comes from the Latin word *comes*, meaning "companion."

**countenance**: (KOWN-te-nans) *n.* Face.

**credit**: (KRED-it) *n.* An acknowledgment of work done.

**creditor**: (KRED-i-tor) *n.* A person or organization to whom money is owed.

# D

**dagger**: (DAG-ur) *n.* A short, pointed knife used as a weapon.

**dam**: (dam) *n.* A barrier made to hold back the flow of water.

**defaulter**: (dee-FAWLT-ur) *n.* A person or organization that fails to pay money that is owed.

**delicate**: (DEL-i-kit) *adj.* Easily hurt or damaged.

**demarcation**: (di-mahr-KAY-shun) *n.* The setting or marking of boundaries or limits.

**descendant**: (di-SEN-dunt) *n.* A person related to someone who lived in the past.

**desolate**: (des-UH-lit) *adj.* Lonely.

**destitute**: (DES-ti-toot) *adj.* Lacking.

**diplomat**: (DIP-luh-mat) *n.* A person who represents a government in relations with other governments.

**disparage**: (di-SPAR-ij) *v.* To belittle or insult.

**dissect**: (di-SEKT) *v.* To cut apart, especially for study.

**dissolve**: (di-ZAHLV) *v.* To make something go away.

**distaff and spindle**: (DIS-taf and SPIN-del) *n.* A stick holding wool for spinning and a slender rod on which thread is twisted.

**divine**: (di-VIYN) *adj.* Being or having the nature of a god.

**doctrine**: (DAHK-trin) *n.* Ideas taught.

**domesticate**: (duh-MES-ti-kayt) *v.* To tame for human use.

**dye**: (diy) *v.* To color.

# E

**embark**: (em-BAHRK) *v.* To begin.

**enervate**: (EN-ur-vayt) *v.* To lose energy or vitality; become weak.

**enmity**: (EN-mi-tee) *n.* The feelings of an enemy; hostility.

**epic**: (EP-ik) *n.* A long poem, usually celebrating heroic actions.

**equanimity**: (ee-kwuh-NIM-i-tee) *n.* Calm.

**eradicate**: (i-RAD-i-kayt) *v.* To wipe out; destroy.

**err**: (ayr) *v.* To make a mistake or commit a sin.

**evident**: (EV-i-dunt) *adj.* Easy to see; clear.

**execute**: (EK-se-kyoot) *v.* 1. To kill; 2. To carry out.

**exempt**: (ig-ZEMPT) *v.* 1. To be freed from an obligation or duty; 2. To excuse.

# F

**fallible**: (FAL-i-bul) *adj.* Imperfect.

**fast**: (fast) *adj.* Tied or held so as not to fall.

**flattery**: (FLAT-uh-ree) *n.* Praise or compliments.

**foolish**: (FOO-lish) *adj.* Silly; lacking good judgment or common sense.

**Fra**: (fraw) *n.* Brother; a title given to an Italian friar or monk; abbreviation of the Italian word *frate*.

**frame**: (fraym) *n.* A structure, such as pieces of wood nailed together, to hold something inside.

**frailty**: (FRAYL-tee) *n.* Weakness.

**fray**: (fray) *n.* Conflict.

**fringe**: (frinj) *n.* A line of threads hanging loose.

# G

**gainsay**: (GAYN-say) *v.* To challenge.

**geography**: (jee-AHG-ruh-fee) *n.* The study of the earth's surface and features.

**gonfalon**: (GAHN-fuh-lun) *n.* Banner-like flag carried on a long pole.

**Good Friday**: (gud FRIY-day) *n.* The Friday before Easter.

**gourd**: (gohrd) *n.* The dried shell of a fruit used as a cup.

**gravity**: (GRAV-i-tee) *n.* A force that tends to pull all bodies in the earth's sphere towards the center of the earth.

**graze**: (grayz) *v.* To feed on growing grasses and other plant materials.

**guardian**: (GAHR-di-un) *n.* A person legally in charge of a young person.

**guardianship**: (GAHR-di-un-ship) *n.* Legal responsibility for the care of a person or property.

# H

**habit**: (HAB-it) *n.* Costume; clothes.

**hauberk**: (HAW-burk) *n.* Armor made of links of chains; "chain mail."

**headland**: (HED-land) *n.* A peak of high land that juts out into a body of water.

**heresy**: (HER-i-see) *n.* A religious idea or opinion that is not approved by the church.

**heretic**: (HER-i-tik) *n.* A person who has religious ideas and opinions not approved by the church.

**hermit**: (HUR-mit) *n.* One who lives alone away from people.

**hide**: (hyd) *n.* a measure of land varying from 80-120 acres.

**house arrest**: (hows uh-REST) *n.* Being confined to one's house, instead of a jail.

**House of Commons**: (hows uv KAWM-uns) *n.* One of the two branches of Parliament, England's law-making body.

# I

**idle**: (IY-dul) *adj.* Useless; unemployed; lazy.

**immersed**: (i-MURST) *v.* Deeply involved.

**impart**: (im-PAHRT) *v.* To teach.

**impel**: (im-PEL) *v.* To urge.

**inalienable**: (in-AYL-yuh-nuh-bul) *adj.* Not transferable.

**incarceration**: (in-kahr-suh-RAY-shun) *n.* Imprisonment.

**independent**: (in-di-PEN-dunt) *adj.* Free from the influence, guidance, or control of others; self-reliant.

*Index of Prohibited Books*: (IN-deks uv proh-HIB-i-tud buks) *n.* A listing of books and writings that Roman Catholics were forbidden to read.

**indignant**: (in-DIG-nant) *adj.* Feeling angry because of something thought to be unfair.

**indulgence**: (in-DUL-jens) *n.* A document sold by the Roman Catholic Church to reduce or cancel punishment for a person's sins.

**infatuation**: (in-fach-oo-AY-shun) *n.* An intense, temporary love.

**inherit**: (in-HER-it) *v.* To receive from someone who has died.

**iniquitous**: (i-NIK-kwa-tus) *adj.* Wrong.

**innovative**: (in-uh-VAY-tiv) *adj.* Creative.

**inscribe**: (in-SKRIYB) *v.* To mark or carve into stone or other material.

**instill**: (in-STIL) *v.* To put an idea into.

**intercept**: (in-tur-SEPT) *v.* To stop or cut off.

**international**: (in-tur-NASH-uh-nul) *adj.* Involving two or more nations.

**intrepid**: (in-TREP-id) *adj.* Brave.

# J

**jeer**: (jeer) *n.* Mocking; insult.

**jeopardize**: (JEP-ahr-diyz) *v.* To risk or endanger.

**Judaism**: (JOO-dee-iz-um) *n.* The religion of the Jewish people.

# L

**lament**: (la-MENT) *v.* To express grief or sadness.

**lass**: (las) *n.* Girl.

**lay waste**: (lay wayst) *v.* To destroy.

**leprosy**: (LEP-roh-see) *n.* A deadly disease that causes sores on the skin.

**liberal studies**: (LIB-uh-ral STUD-ees) *n.* Subjects such as reading, mathematics, music, Latin, and philosophy; not technical subjects.

**liege**: (leej) *n.* Subject.

**loot**: (loot) *v.* To steal.

**lowing**: (LOH-ing) *n.* The sound made by oxen.

**lurch**: (lurch) *v.* To sway.

**luxury**: (LUG-zhuh-ree) *n.* Something extra that makes life more comfortable and enjoyable.

# M

**magistrate**: (MAJ-i-strayt) *n.* An officer of the law.

**malady**: (MAL-uh-dee) *n.* Illness.

**marauder**: (muh-RAWD-ur) *n.* Robber; referring to "crusader."

**merchant**: (MUR-chunt) *n.* A shopkeeper; a person who buys and sells things.

**mismanagement**: (mis-MAN-ij-munt) *n.* Wrong or bad management.

**missionary**: (MISH-uh-ner-ee) *n.* A person who goes to a foreign country to do religious work.

**mo**: (moh) *adj.* More.

**moderation**: (mahd-uh-RAY-shun) *n.* Balance; avoiding extremes.

**mold**: (mohld) *n.* A form into which something is poured.

**molest**: (muh-LEST) *v.* To annoy or bother.

**monotonous**: (muh-NAHT-uh-nus) *adj.* Having no variety.

**morale**: (muh-RAL) *n.* How a person or group is feeling.

**morning star**: (MOHR-ning stahr) *n.* A planet visible in the east just before sunrise; something that happens first.

**mortal**: (MOHR-tul) *n.* Something that eventually dies.

**mortality**: (mohr-TAL-i-tee) *n.* Death.

# N

**notable**: (NOH-tuh-bul) *adj.* Important.

# O

**oath**: (ohth) *n.* A formal promise or pledge.

**operate**: (AHP-uh-rayt) *v.* To perform surgery.

**oppressive**: (uh-PRES-iv) *adj.* Causing discomfort.

**orbital region**: (OR-bi-tul REE-jun) *n.* The area where the eyes are located.

**ordain**: (or-DAYN) *v.* To appoint or establish.

**Orient**: (OHR-i-ent) *n.* Asia.

**outspoken**: (owt-SPOH-kun) *adj.* Open and sincere in expression; straight forward.

# P

**parchment**: (PAHRCH-munt) *n.* The skin of a sheep or goat prepared for writing or painting upon.

**pavilion**: (puh-VIL-yun) *n.* A large tent.

**pension**: (PEN-shun) *n.* Money paid regularly as a retirement benefit or as support.

**perforation**: (pur-fuh-RAY-shun) *n.* Hole.

**perpetual**: (pur-PECH-oo-ul) *adj.* Constant.

**persistent**: (pur-SIST-unt) *adj.* Refusing to give up or let go.

**physical laws**: (FIZ-i-kul) *n.* General rules about the nature of energy and nonliving things.

**physical science**: (FIZ-i-kul SIY-uns) *n.* Any of the sciences that have to do with the nature and property of energy and nonliving things; physics, chemistry, astronomy, and geology are all physical sciences.

**plait**: (playt) *v.* To weave into.

**playwright**: (PLAY-riyt) *n.* A person who writes plays.

**plot**: (plaht) 1. *n.* A plan. 2. *v.* To plan.

**political science**: (pu-LIT-i-kul SIY-uns) *n.* The study of government and government organizations.

**pomegranate**: (PAHM-uh-gran-it) *n.* A hard, red fruit with many seeds.

**pore**: (pohr) *v.* To read or study carefully.

**practical**: (PRAK-ti-kul) *adj.* Able to be used or put into effect.

**presumptuous**: (pri-ZUHMP-choo-us) *adj.* Conceited.

**privation**: (priy-VAY-shun) *n.* The lack of basic needs.

**property**: (PRAHP-ur-tee) *n.* All things a person owns.

**Protestant Reformation**: (PRAHT-uh-stunt ref-ur-MAY-shun) *n.* A movement to reform the Roman Catholic Church.

# Q

**qualm**: (kwahm) *n.* Doubt; uncertainty.

# R

**rack**: (rak) *v.* To hurt or inflict pain.

**raid**: (rayd) *n.* A sudden or surprise attack.

**rase**: (rayz) *v.* To tear down.

**rash**: (rash) *adj.* Acting without thinking.

**realm**: (relm) *n.* A kingdom.

**rebellious**: (ri-BEL-yus) *adj.* Refusing to obey; revolting against someone in authority or power.

**recant**: (ri-KANT) *v.* To take back something that was said earlier.

**recognition**: (rek-uhg-NISH-un) *n.* Favorable attention or notice.

**refuge**: (REF-yooj) *n.* Shelter from danger.

**reign**: (rayn) *n.* The time during which a ruler is in power.

**remedy**: (REM-uh-dee) *n.* Something to correct a wrong.

**remission**: (ri-MISH-un) *n.* Forgiveness.

**remit**: (ri-MIT) *v.* To send.

**render**: (REN-dur) *v.* To give.

**represent**: (rep-ri-ZENT) *v.* To stand for; to serve as the spokesperson or agent for.

**rhyme**: (riym) *n.* A poem in which the ending lines have the same sound.

**righteousness**: (RIY-chus-nes) *n.* Acting in a just and moral way.

**rigor**: (RIG-ur) *n.* Strictness; harshness.

**robust constitution**: (roh-BUST kahn-sti-TOO-shun) *n.* Healthy body.

**royalty**: (ROI-ul-tee) *n.* A king, queen, or other person in a ruling family.

# S

**sagacity**: (suh-GAS-i-tee) *n.* Wisdom.

**salvation**: (sal-VAY-shun) *n.* Saving of the soul from sin and its consequences; the state of being saved.

**scabbard**: (SKAB-urd) *n.* Container for a sword.

**scandal**: (SKAN-dul) *n.* A situation that brings disgrace or is considered shameful by the community.

**schism**: (SIZ-um) *n.* A separation, division, or split, especially within a Christian church.

**scold**: (skohld) *v.* To find fault with; to be angry with.

**seemly**: (SEEM-lee) *adj.* Proper; socially acceptable.

**siege**: (seej) *n.* A persistent attempt to gain control.

**solitary**: (SAHL-i-ter-ee) *adj.* Lonely.

**spawn**: (spawn) *v.* To produce or bring forth.

**spoils**: (spoils) *n.* Goods or property taken after a conflict, especially a war.

**spur**: (spur) *v.* To urge.

**squadron**: (SKWAHD-run) *n.* A unit of soldiers.

**steed**: (steed) *n.* Horse.

**stupefy**: (STOO-puh-fiy) *v.* To stun or astonish.

**subordinate**: (suh-BOHR-di-nit) *adj.* Below another person in rank and importance.

**sufficient**: (suh-FISH-unt) *adj.* As much as is needed; enough.

**suited**: (SOOT-id) *adj.* Acceptable; appropriate.

**superstitious**: (soo-pur-STISH-us) *adj.* Believing in magic or having an irrational fear of something.

# T

**tablet**: (TAB-lit) *n.* A thin sheet used as a writing surface.

**temperate**: (TEM-puh-rit) *adj.* Moderate.

**textile**: (TEKS-til) *n.* A woven fabric; cloth.

**theology**: (thi-AHL-uh-jee) *n.* The study of religious ideas and questions.

**torment**: (TOHR-ment) *n.* Great physical or mental pain.

**traitor**: (TRAY-tur) *n.* One who betrays his or her country.

**tranquility**: (trang-KWIL-i-tee) *n.* Peace.

**transfixed**: (trans-FIKST) *v.* Motionless.

**trice**: (triys) *n.* A very short time; an instant.

**trinket**: (TRING-kit) *n.* Any small ornament, such as a small piece of jewelry.

**trow**: (trow) *v.* To think.

**try**: (triy) *v.* To test.

**tutor**: (TOO-tur) *n.* A person who teaches only one or two students at a time.

**typhus**: (TIY-fus) *n.* A disease that causes fever and skin rash.

# U

**unfurnish**: (un-FUR-nish) *v.* To strip.

**universal**: (yoo-nuh-VUR-sul) *adj.* Pertaining to all people.

# V

**valor**: (VAL-ur) *n.* Courage; bravery.

**vanquished**: (VANG-kwishd) *n.* Conquered or defeated.

**vantage**: (VAN-tij) *n.* Advantage; better position.

**vaunt**: (vawnt) *v.* To brag.

**vellum**: (VEL-um) *n.* The skin of a calf or lamb prepared for writing or painting upon.

**venom**: (VEN-um) *n.* Poison that some snakes and other animals inject with their bites.

**vessel**: (VES-ul) *n.* A container.

**vie**: (viy) *v.* To compete.

**villein**: (VIL-un) *n.* Serf.

**virtue**: (VUR-choo) *n.* Goodness; honesty; worth.

**vision**: (VIZH-un) *n.* An experience in which someone sees something that is out of the ordinary; a mystical or supernatural experience.

# W

**weary fancy**: (WEER-ee FAN-see) *n.* Tired imagination.

**widow**: (WID-oh) *n.* A woman whose husband has died.

**will**: (wil) *v.* To control one's own action.

**wounded**: (WOOND-uhd) *adj.* Hurt; injured.

**wretched**: (RECH-id) *adj.* Terrible.

## Vowel Pronunciation Key

| Symbol | Key Words |
| --- | --- |
| a | ant, man |
| ay | cake, May |
| ah | clock, arm |
| aw | salt, ball |
| e | neck, hair |
| ee | ear, key |
| i | chick, skin |
| iy | five, tiger |
| oh | coat, soda |
| oi | boy, coin |
| ohr | board, door |
| oo | blue, boot |
| ow | cow, owl |
| u | foot, wolf, bird, and the schwa sound used in final syllables followed by 'l,' 'r,' 's,' 'm,' 't,' or 'n,' for example, children (CHIL-drun) |
| uh | bug, uncle, and other schwa sounds, such as kangaroo (kang-guh-ROO) |

*Source: The vowel pronunciation key is derived from the* American Heritage Dictionary of the English Language, *1981;* Oxford American Dictionary: Heald Colleges Edition, *1982; and* Webster's New World College Dictionary, Third Edition, *1990. Please note that the surrounding letters may affect the vowel sound slightly.*

# INDEX

*Some entries include the Latin word* passim, *which means "here and there and everywhere." This word indicates that the entry occurs frequently in the text.*

# Photography and Illustration Credits

(t=top, b=bottom, c=center, l=left, r=right)

**Dover Publications:** *African Designs from Traditional Sources*—109 (l), 112 (b), 113 (t), 114, 119, 125; *Costumes of the Greeks and Romans*—45 (b), 46 (r), 47 (r), 49; *Dictionary of American Portraits*—150 (r), 153 (bl), 155, 159, 364, 365 (r), 413; *Portraits of Famous People*—28, 303 (r), 307, 308 (r), 315, 333 (t), 334, 351, 355, 428, 431; *Historic Costumes in Pictures*—55, 89, 309, 405 (b), 441; *Racinet's Full-Color Pictorial History of Western Costume*—308 (l), 407

**Library of Congress:** 3 (b, bc), 4 (tl, bl, br), 16, 31, 41, 56, 59, 62, 69, 71, 73, 74, 93 (l), 98, 101, 138, 141 (l), 150 (l), 179, 247, 249 (l), 250, 257, 266, 269, 271, 273, 277, 278, 282, 293, 301, 303 (l), 310, 313, 316 (l), 317, 320, 321, 322, 323, 324, 329, 333 (c, b), 335, 339, 340-341 (b), 344, 345, 348, 349, 360, 366, 371, 373, 375, 377, 378, 379, 381, 382, 383, 386, 393, 395, 398 (t), 401, 404, 405 (t), 409, 411, 414, 415, 416 (b), 419, 420, 421, 426, 432, 434, 435, 436, 437, 443 (t)

**North Wind Picture Archives:** 4 (lc), 121, 151, 153 (t), 156 (t, b), 157, 168, 173, 174-175, 177, 206, 208, 236, 237, 238, 240, 248, 256, 261, 263, 265, 272, 275, 280, 297, 319, 325, 337, 341 (t), 342, 343, 346, 353, 356, 361, 363, 385 (b), 387, 389, 392, 394, 396, 397, 408, 418, 423, 424, 427, 433, 442, 443 (t)

**Illustrators:** Gina Capaldi—4 (t, rc), 10 (tl, bl, br), 11, 14, 21 (t), 25, 26, 36, 37, 38, 39, 45 (t), 52, 60, 64, 65, 83, 85 (b), 87, 91, 93 (r), 94, 96 (r), 104 (b), 105, 107, 111 (r), 112 (t), 113 (b), 118, 122, 124, 129, 130 (t), 131, 134, 139, 141 (r), 145, 147, 148, 153 (blc, br), 158, 161, 167 (b), 171, 180, 181, 182, 194, 195, 196, 197, 199, 200, 204, 205, 211, 213, 216, 218, 219, 220, 224 (c), 227 (t), 234, 235, 241, 243, 244, 245 , 249 (r), 251, 253, 255, 259, 283, 287 (l), 327, 354, 398 (b), 422, 430, 438, 439, 443; Sabrina Lammé—21 (b), 224 (b), 285, 291, 292, 358, 367 (b), 368 (t), 369 (b); Fujiko Miller—188, 191, 198; Keith Neely—15, 29; Emmy Rhee—68 (r), 81, 146, 352; Ti Tong—33, 35 (t), 42, 43, 47 (l), 48 (tl), 70, 85 (t), 96 (l), 106; Leilani Trollinger—166, 221, 232, 359, 365 (l), 367 (t), 369 (t)

**Other Sources:** Bill Abbot/Wilderness Travel—184; American Numismatics Society—68 (l); Artville—10 (c), 12; Sarah Biondi—226; Michelle Chew—416 (t); Consulate General of Japan—215, 217, 222 (l, r), 223 (l), 224 (t), 230; Susan Douglass/Center on Islamic Education—58; Dale Frakes—100 (b); Getty Images—103, 104 (t), 306, 384; Patrice Gotsch—227 (b), 229 (t); Paul Helmle—3 (tc), 35 (b), 44; David Jemison, Life in Korea—202; Floyd Johnson—3 (t), 6, 7 (top), 9; Eric Jones Esq.—130, 132, 133; Hiroko Kawasaki—228, 229 (b); Jill Kinkade—170, 176, 183, 187 (t); Edith Leiby—385 (t); Alan Levy—169; Allison Mangrum—302, 305, 311, 312, 316 (r), 350; Larry Newton—110, 163 (r), 164; pdimages.com—336, 410; Pratt Wagon Works, Cove Fort, Utah—299; Roberta Stathis—8, 17 (t), 19; Tonantzin Dance Company ("Aztec Ceremonial Dancers")—142; West African Journey, L.C.—115; Kijana Wiseman, M.Ed. as 'The Griot,' Photo by Alvin McEwing—109 (r); www.anthroarcheart.org—126

*Every effort has been made to trace the copyright holders. We apologize in advance for any unintentional errors or omissions. We would be pleased to insert the appropriate acknowledgements in subsequent editions of this textbook.*

# Text Credits

*The authors and publisher gratefully acknowledge use of the material listed below:*

**23** The Law of the Twelve Tables: From *Roman Civilization*, Volume I, by Naphtali Lewis and Meyer Reinhold. Columbia University Press, 1951. **27** Polybius on Roman Government: From Polybius, *Rise of the Roman Empire*, translated by Ian Scot-Kilvert. **29** Julius Caesar: From John P. McKay, Bennett D. Hill, and John Buckler, *A History of Western Society*, Vol. 1, Houghton-Mifflin, 1995. **33** Cicero: From Cicero, *Selected Works*, translated by Michael Grant, Viking Press, 1960. **37** Rome's Greatest Poets: From Horace, *Odes*, translated by David West, Oxford University Press, 2000; Virgil, *The Aeneid*, translated by David West, Penguin Books, 1990; Ovid, *Metamorphoses*, translated by A.D. Melville, Oxford University Press, 1998. **4** Peter's "Good News": From Acts 3:17-26 in the Revised Standard Version of the Bible. Division of Christian Education of the National Council of Churches of Christ in the United States, 1971. **5** Marcus Aurelius: From Marcus Aurelius, *Meditations*, translated by Maxwell Staniforth, Penguin Books, 1964. **52** "Barbarians" in the Empire: From John McKay, Bennett D. Hill, and John Buckler, *A History of Western Society*, Vol. 1, Houghton Mifflin, 1995; From Procopius, *History of the Wars*, translated by H. B. Dewing, Harvard University Press & Wm. Heinemann, 1914, reprint ed. 1953-54; From James H. Robinson, ed., *Readings in European History*, Ginn and Co., 1904. **58** Muhammad: From Akram Zahoor, *Muslim History 570-1950*, ZMD, 2000. **6** Abu Bakr: Abdul Basit Ahmad, *Abu Bakr As-Siddi*

*The First Caliph of Islam,* Darussalam Publications, 2001. **63-64** Khadija: Anne Marie Schimmel, *Islam: An Introduction,* State University of New York Press, 1992. **65** Passages from the Qur'an: From *The Qur'an,* translated by M.H. Shakir, Kazi Publications, 1990. **80** Ibn-Sina: From Soheil Afnan, *Avicenna, His Life and Works,* G. Allen & Unwin, 1958; and Lenn Evan Goodman, *Avicenna,* Routledge, 1992. **81** Omar Khayyam: From Omar Khayyam, *The Rubaiyat,* translated by Edward Fitzgerald, St. Martin's Press, 1983. **90** Flowering of Jewish Civilization: From Martin A.S. Hume, *The Spanish People: Their Origin, Growth and Influence,* D. Appleton & Co., 1901. **94** Genoese Lady: From *The World's Story: A History of the World in Story, Song, and Art,* edited by E.M. Tappan, Houghton Mifflin, 1914. **98** Michael Kritovoulos: From Michael Kritovoulos, *History of Memed the Conqueror,* translated by Charles T. Riggs, Princeton University Press, 1954. **99** Life in the Islamic Empire: From Bernard Lewis, *The Muslim Discovery of Europe,* W.W. Norton, 1982; and Akram Zahoor, *Muslim History 570-1950,* ZMD, 2000. **108** King Tenkamenin: From Basil Davidson, *African Kingdoms,* Time Life, 1966. **112** Al-Bakri—Views of West Africa: From *Corpus of Early Arabic Sources for West Africa,* edited by N. Levtzion and J.F.P. Hopkins, and translated by J.F.P. Hopkins, Cambridge University Press, 1981; and Basil Davidson, *African Kingdoms,* Time Life, 1966. **113** Abu Hamid al Andalusi—Views of West Africa: From Basil Davidson, *African Kingdoms,* Time Life, 1966. **114** Sundiata: From D.T. Niane, *Sundiata: An Epic of Old Mali,* Longman Group Ltd., 1960. **116** Ibn Battuta—World Traveler: From Basil Davidson, *African Kingdoms,* Time Life, 1966. **118** Mansa Musa: From *Corpus of Early Arabic Sources for West Africa,* edited by N. Levtzion and J.F.P. Hopkins, and translated by J.F.P. Hopkins, Cambridge University Press, 1981. **120** The Salt Mines: From Basil Davidson, *African Kingdoms,* Time Life, 1966; and Jessica B. Harris, *The Africa Cookbook: Tastes of a Continent,* Simon & Schuster, 1998. **125** Leo Africanus—Views of West Africa: From Basil Davidson, *African Kingdoms,* Time Life, 1966. **126** How Do We Know ... the Maya?: See *Popul Vuh,* translated by Ralph Nelson. Houghton Mifflin, 1976; *Popul Vuh: The Mayan Book of the Dawn of Life* (revised edition), translated by Dennis Tedlock, Simon & Schuster, 1996; and *The Destruction of the Jaguar: Poems from the Books of Chilam Balam* translated by Christopher Sawyer-Laucanno, City Lights Books, 1987. **130** Maya Social Classes: From *Diego de Landa's Account of the Affairs of Yucatan: The Maya,* edited and translated by A.R. Pagden, J. Philip O'Hara, Inc. 1975. **135** Diego de Landa's

Account: From *Diego de Landa's Account of the Affairs of Yucatan: The Maya,* edited and translated by A.R. Pagden, J. Philip O'Hara, Inc. 1975. **136** Stephens and Incidents: From John L. Stephens, *Incidents of Travel in Central America, Chiapas, & Yucatan.* Richard L. Predmore (ed.), Rutgers University Press, 1949. **137** The Popul Vuh: From *Popul Vuh,* translated by Ralph Nelson, Houghton Mifflin, 1976. **138** How Do We Know ... the Aztecs?: From Bernardino de Sahagún, *Florentine Codex: General History of the Things of New Spain,* translated and edited by Arthur J.O. Anderson and Charles E. Dibble, School of American Research and the University of Utah Press, 1950-82 (originally written in 1575-1577). **140-141** Bernardino de Sahagún and the Aztecs: From Bernardino de Sahagún, *Florentine Codex: General History of the Things of New Spain,* translated and edited by Arthur J.O. Anderson and Charles E. Dibble, School of American Research and the University of Utah Press, 1950-82 (originally written in 1575-1577). **142-143** Diego Durán on the Aztecs: From Diego Durán, *Historia de Las Indias de Nueva España,* edited by Angel M. Garibay K. Porrúa, Mexico City, 1967 (originally written in 1581). **144** The Spaniards Describe Women in Aztec Society: From Diego Durán, *Book of the Gods and Rites and the Ancient Calendar,* translated and edited by Fernando Horcasitas and Doris Heyden, University of Oklahoma Press, 1971; Bernardino de Sahagún, *Florentine Codex, General History of the Things of New Spain,* translated and edited by Arthur J.O. Anderson and Charles E. Dibble, School of American Research and the University of Utah Press, 1950-1982 (originally written in 1575-1577); Diego Durán, *Book of the Gods and Rites and the Ancient Calendar;* and Bernardino de Sahagún, *Florentine Codex: General History of the Things of New Spain.* **147** Ahuitzotl: From David Damrosch, "The Aesthetics of Conquest: Aztec Poetry Before and After Cortes," *Representations* 33 (Winter 1991). **149-151** Moctezuma II: From Bernardino de Sahagún, *Florentine Codex: General History of the Things of New Spain,* translated and edited by Arthur J.O. Anderson and Charles E. Dibble, School of American Research and the University of Utah Press, 1950-82 (originally written in 1575-1577); and Bernal Díaz [del Castillo], *The Conquest of New Spain,* translated by J.M. Cohen. Penguin Classics, 1976 (originally written in the 1560s). **153-154** Malinche: From Bernal Díaz [del Castillo], *The Conquest of New Spain,* translated by J.M. Cohen. Penguin Classics, 1976 (originally written in the 1560s); and Anne Smittle, "The Story of La Malinche: 'The Mexican Eve:' A Woman of Historical Contradictions," http://home.earthlink.net/~wsmittle/malinche.htm: Dec. 4, 2000. **156-157** Collision of Two Worlds: Bernardino de Sahagún, *Florentine Codex: General History of the Things of New Spain*, translated and edited by Arthur J.O. Anderson and Charles E. Dibble, School of American Research and the University of Utah Press, 1950-82 (originally written in 1575-1577); Diego Durán, *Historia de Las Indias de Nueva España*, edited by Angel M. Garibay K. Porrúa, Mexico City, 1967, (originally written in 1581); and Miguel León-Portilla, *The Broken Spears: The Aztec Account of the Conquest of Mexico*, Beacon Press, 1962. **158** Bernal Díaz del Castillo: From Bernal Díaz [del Castillo], *The Conquest of New Spain*, translated by J.M. Cohen. Penguin Classics, 1976 (originally written in the 1560s). **159** Hernando Cortés: From Hernando Cortés, *Five Letters of Cortés to the Emperor*, edited and translated by J. Bayard Morris, Norton, 1962 (originally written in 1519-1526). **160** Francisco Lopez de Gomara: From Francisco Lopez de Gomara. *Cortés: The Life of the Conqueror*, translated and edited by Lesley Byrd Simpson, University of California Press, 1964 (originally written in the 1560s). **161** Aztec Poetry: From *Cantares Mexicanos: Songs of the Aztecs*, edited and translated by John Bierhorst, Stanford University Press, 1985 (originally written in the 1500s); and Fernando Alvarado Tezozomoc, *Cronica Mexicayotl*, translated by Adrian Leon. Universidad Nacional Autónoma de Mexico (originally written in 1609). **162-165** Foods that Changed the World: From Bernardino de Sahagún, *Florentine Codex: General History of the Things of New Spain*, translated and edited by Arthur J.O. Anderson and Charles E. Dibble, School of American Research and the University of Utah Press, 1950-82 (originally written 1575-1577); and Bernal Díaz [del Castillo], *The Conquest of New Spain*, translated by J.M. Cohen. Penguin Classics, 1976 (originally written in the 1560s). **166-168** Pachacuti: From Father Bernabe Cobo, *History of the Inca Empire*, translated and edited by Roland Hamilton from the holograph manuscript in the Biblioteca Capitular y Colombina de Sevilla with a foreword by John Rowe, University of Texas Press, 1979; Catherine Julien, *Reading Inca History*, University of Iowa Press, 2000; and Albert Marrin, *Inca & Spaniard: Pizarro and the Conquest of Peru*. Atheneum, 1989. **169** Honoring the Gods: From Cristobal de Molina, *The Fables and Rites of the Incas*, translated by Clements R. Markham, Hakluyt Society, 1873. **170-171** "El Inca" Tells about Life: From Garcilaso de la Vega, El Inca, *Royal Commentaries of the Incas and General History of Peru*, translated with an introduction by Harold V. Livermore, University of Texas Press, 1966

(originally written in the late 1500s/early 1600s). **172, 175** Atahualpa & Huascar: From Father Bernabe Cobo, *History of the Inca Empire*, translated and edited by Roland Hamilton from the holograph manuscript in the Biblioteca Capitular y Colombina de Sevilla with a foreword by John Rowe, University of Texas Press, 1979; and Albert Marrin, *Inca & Spaniard: Pizarro and the Conquest of Peru* Atheneum, 1989. **176-179** Collision of Two Worlds: From Father Bernabe Cobo, *History of the Inca Empire*, translated and edited by Roland Hamilton from the holograph manuscript in the Biblioteca Capitular y Colombina de Sevilla with a foreword by John Rowe, University of Texas Press, 1979; Catherine Julien, *Reading Inca History*, University of Iowa Press, 2000; and Albert Marrin, *Inca & Spaniard: Pizarro and the Conquest of Peru* Atheneum, 1989. **180-181** A Peruvian Chief' "Letter": From Huamán Poma, *Letter to a King: A Peruvian Chief's Account of Life Under the Incas and Under Spanish Rule*, arranged and edited with an introduction by Christopher Dilke and translated from *Nueva Coronica y Buen Govierno*, E.P. Dutton 1978. **182** Setting the Story Straight: From Garcilaso de la Vega, El Inca, *Royal Commentaries of the Incas and General History of Peru*, translated with an introduction by Harold V. Livermore, University of Texas Press, 1966 (originally written in the late 1500s/early 1600s). **183** When Worlds Meet: From Pedro Cieza de León, *Chronicle of Peru*, translated by Clements R. Markham, Hakluyt Society, 186 (originally written in 1553). **186** Hiram Bingham: From Hiram Bingham, *Lost City of the Incas: The Story of Machu Picchu and Its Builders*, Greenwood Press, 1948. **188-193** Confucius, Buddha, and Laozi: Laozi, from *Dao De Jing: The Book of the Way* translated by Moss Roberts, University of California Press, 2001; Confucius, from *Analects*, translated by E. Bruce Brooks and A. Taeko Brooks, Columbia University Press, 1998; and Conrad Schirokauer, *A Brief History of Chinese and Japanese Civilization* Harcourt Brace Jovanovich, 1989. **194** Buddhist Poetry: From Burton Watson, *Chinese Lyricism: Shi Poetry from the Second to the Twelfth Century* Columbia University Press, 1971; *Travels of a Chinese Poet: Tu Fu, Guest of Rivers and Lakes*, translated and edited by Florence Ayscough, Houghton Mifflin 1934 (originally written between 712-770); and *The Works of Li Po, The Chinese Poet*, translated and edited by Shigeyoshi Obata, Paragon Book Reprint, Corp 1965. **208** Marco Polo on China: From Marco Polo, *The Travels of Marco Polo*, translated by Ronald Latham, Penguin Books, 1958. **214-215** Prince Shotoku: From *The Cambridge History of Japan*, Vol 1, Ancient Japan, Cambridge University Press, 199

**216, 218-219** Lady Murasaki: From *The Tale of Genji* by Lady Murasaki, translated with a foreword by Arthur Waley, The Modern Library, 1960. **220** The Pillow Book: From *The Pillow Book of Sei Shonagon*, translated by Arthur Waley, George Allen, and Unwin, 1957. **221** Tales of Heike: From *The Ten Foot Square Hut and Tales of the Heike*, translated by A.L. Sadler, Angus & Robertson, 1928. **229-230** European Impressions: From *They Came to Japan: An Anthology of European Reports on Japan, 1543-1640*, edited by Michael Cooper, S.J., University of California Press, 1965. **223** Bashō: From *Introduction to Haiku* by Harold G. Henderson, Doubleday, 1958. **234** The Rule of St. Benedict: From Norman F. Cantor, *The Medieval Reader*, HarperCollins, 1994. **240** Einhard: From Einhard, *The Life of Charlemagne*, with a foreword by Sidney Painter and translated by Samuel Epes Turner, University of Michigan Press, 1960. **241** Alcuin of York: From *Alcuin: The Bishops, Kings, and Saints of York*, edited by Peter Godman, Oxford University Press, 1982. **242** The Song of Roland: From *The Song of Roland*, translated by Frederick Goldin, W.W. Norton & Company, 1978. **246** Beowulf: From Randolph Swearer, Raymond Oliver, and Marijane Osborn, *Beowulf: A Likeness*, Yale University Press, 1990. **248** King Arthur: From *Caxton's Mallory: A New Edition of Sir Thomas Malory's Le Morte D'arthur* (Based on the Pierpont Morgan Copy of William Caxton's Edition of 1485), edited by James W. Spisak, University of California Press, 1983. **255** Domesday Book: From James H. Robinson, *Readings in European History*, Ginn and Co., 1904. **256** Pope Urban II's Call a Crusade: From Norman F. Cantor, *The Medieval Reader*, HarperCollins, 1994. **258** Views of the Crusades: From Norman F. Cantor, *The Medieval Reader*, HarperCollins, 1994. **260** Anna Comnena: From James H. Robinson, *Readings in European History*, Ginn and Co., 1904. **262** Pope Gregory VII: From Robert Louis Wilken, "Gregory VII and the Politics of the Spirit," *First Things 89*, January 1999. **268** Abbot Suger and the Invention of the Gothic Cathedral: From Abbot Suger of St. Denis, *Libellus de consecratione ecclesiae Sancti Dionysii* (The Little Book on the Consecration of the Church of St. Denis), translated and edited by E. Panofsky, *Abbot Suger on the Abbey Church of St. Denis and its Art Treasures*, Princeton, 1946. **273** Magna Carta: From James H. Robinson, *Readings in European History*, Ginn and Co., 1904. **274** Hildegard of Bingen: From Norman F. Cantor, *The Medieval Reader*, HarperCollins, 1994. **281** Thomas Aquinas: From Norman F. Cantor, *The Medieval Reader*, HarperCollins, 1994. **282** King Edward I's Invitation: From James H. Robinson, *Readings in European History*, Ginn and Co., 1904. **284** The Divine Comedy: From Dante Alighieri, *The Divine Comedy*, translated by Seth Zinnerman, *Willow Springs, Spoon River Poetry Review, Metamorphoses*, Proceedings of the American Translator's Association, 1993. **286** Piers Plowman: From *Everyman's Library*, Rachel Atwater (ed.), translated by Donald and Rachel Atwater, J.M. Dent, 1957. **287-289** Black Death & How ... : From Norman F. Cantor, *The Medieval Reader*, HarperCollins, 1994. **290** Persecution of Jews: From Norman F. Cantor, *The Medieval Reader*, HarperCollins, 1994. **292** Peasant Revolt: From Norman F. Cantor, *The Medieval Reader*, HarperCollins, 1994. **293** Trial of Joan of Arc: From Norman F. Cantor, *The Medieval Reader*, HarperCollins, 1994. **294-295** Medieval Meals: From Norman F. Cantor, *The Medieval Reader*, HarperCollins, 1994. **296** I Cannot Get Enough Books: From *Letters from Petrarch*, translated by Morris Bishop, Indiana University Press, 1966. **300-302** Lorenzo di Medici: From Christopher Hibbert, *The House of Medici: Its Rise and Fall*, Morrow Quill Paperbacks, 1980. **308** Isabella d'Este: From *The Bed and the Throne: The Life of Isabella d'Este*, by George R. Marek, HarperCollins, 1963. **309** "It Is Not Seemly ...": Baldassare Castiglione, *The Book of the Courtier*, translated by George Bull, Penguin, 1976. **311-312** Niccolo Machiavelli: Niccolo Machiavelli, *The Prince and the Discourses*, translated by Luigi Ricci, revised by E.R.P. Vincent, introduction by Max Lerner, Modern Library, 1950. **314** Laura Cereta: From *Laura Cereta, Collected Letters of a Renaissance Feminist*, transcribed, translated, and edited by Diana Robin as part of the series *The Other Voice in Early Modern Europe*, Margaret L. King and Albert Rabil, Jr. (eds.), University of Chicago Press, 1997. **315-316** Michelangelo: From *Michelangelo: A Self-Portrait*, translated and edited by Robert J. Clements, Prentice-Hall, 1963; and Giorgio Vasari, *Lives of the Artists*, translated by Julia Conaway Bondanella and Peter Bondanella, Oxford University Press, 1998. **321** Miguel Cervantes: Miguel de Cervantes, *Don Quixote*, translated by Samuel Putnam, Viking Press, 1949. **323-324** William Shakespeare: William Shakespeare, *Romeo and Juliet*, edited by J.A. Bryant, Jr., New American Library, 1964. **330-331** Margery Kempe: From Margery Kempe, *The Book of Margery Kempe*, translated by Barry Windeatt, Penguin Books, 1985. **333** Martin Luther, *Reformation Writings of Martin Luther*, (Definitive Weimar Edition) translated by Bertram Lee Woolf, The Philosophical Library, 1953. **334** Anna Bijns: From Anna Bijns' "Poems," translated by Kristiaan P.G. Aercke, as published in *Women Writers of the Renaissance and Reformation*, edited by Katharina M. Wilson,

University of Georgia Press, 1987. **336** Thomas More and Henry VIII: From J.D.M. Derrett, "The Trial of Sir Thomas More," *English Historical Review 79*, 1964. **337** John Calvin: From John Calvin, "On Suffering Persecution" in *The World's Greatest Speeches*, edited by Lewis Copeland and Lawrence W. Lamm, Dover Publications, 1973. **339** Desiderius Erasmus: Desiderius Erasmus, *The Praise of Folly*, translated by Hopewell Hudson, Princeton University Press, 1941. **343** William Tyndale: From David Daniell, *William Tyndale: A Biography*, Yale University Press, 1994. **347** Vesalius: Andreas Vesalius, *On the Human Brain*, translated and introduction by Charles Singer, Oxford University Press, 1952. **349** Francis Bacon: From Francis Bacon, *The Advancement of Learning*, edited by William Aldis Wright, Oxford University Press, 1873. **351** Galileo and Suor Maria Celeste: From Dava Sobel, *Galileo's Daughter*, Walker & Company, 1999. **352** Johannes Kepler: From *Kepler's Conversation with Galileo's Sidereal Messenger*, translated by Edward Rosen, Johnson Reprint Corp., 1965. **353** Rene Descartes—Mathematician and Philosopher: From *Discourse on the Method for Conducting One's Reason Well and for Seeking Truth in the Sciences* (1637), translated by Donald A. Cress, Hackett Publishing, Co., 1998. **357** Isaac Newton: From *Let Newton Be!* edited by John Fauvel, Raymond Flood, and Robin J. Wilson, Oxford University Press, 1988. **361-362** Gomes Eanes de Zurara: From Peter Russell, *Prince Henry 'the Navigator': A Life*, Yale University Press, 2000. **377, 380** Christopher Columbus: From *The Diario of Christopher Columbus' First Voyage to America, 1492-1493*, translated by Oliver Dunn and James E. Kelley, Jr., 1989. **388** Amerigo Vespucci: From *The Letters of Amerigo Vespucci*, translated and edited by Clements Markham, Burt Franklin Publisher, 1894. **392** Vasco da Gama: From Gaspar Correa, *Lendas da India*, translated by Henry E.J. Stanley, the Hakluyt Society, 1869 (under the title, *The Three Voyages of Vasco da Gama*). **397** Bartolomé de Las Casas: From Bartolomé de las Casas, *In Defense of the Indians*, translated and edited by Stafford Poole, C.M., Northern Illinois University Press, 1974. **403** John Harrison—The Search for Longitude: From Dava Sobel, *Longitude*, Penguin, 1995. **406** Cardinal Richelieu—The Power Behind the Throne: From James H. Robinson, ed., *Readings in European History*, Ginn and Co., 1904. **407** Louis XIV: From John B. Wolf, *Louis XIV*, W.W. Norton, 1968; and *Memoirs of the Duke of Saint Simon*, translated by Bayle St. John, Swan Sonnonschein &

Co., 1900; and J.H. Elliott, *Richelieu and Olivares*, Cambridge University Press, 1984. **408** Philippe Duplessis-Mornay: Philippe Duplessis-Mornay, *Vindiciae Contra Tyrannos* from *Readings in Western Civilization, Early Modern Europe: Crisis of Authority*, edited by Eric Cochrane, C.M. Gray, and Mark Kishlansky, University of Chicago Press, 1987. **411-412** Queen Elizabeth: From Christopher Hibbert, *The Virgin Queen*, Perseus Books, 1991. **413-414** Sir Walter Raleigh: From Kenneth J. Atchity, *The Renaissance Reader*, HarperCollins, 1996. **415** James I: From *The Political Works of James I*, reprinted from the edition of 1616 with an introduction by Charles Howard McIlwain, Harvard University Press, 1918. **417** Thomas Hobbes: From Thomas Hobbes, *Leviathan*, edited by C.B. Macpherson, Penguin Books, 1977. **425** John Locke: John Locke, *Second Treatise on Government* (1690), edited by C.B. Macpherson, Hackett Publishing, 1990. **426** Baron de Montesquieu: From Montesquieu, *Spirit of Laws: A Compendium of the First English Edition*, translated by David Carrithers, University of California, 1977. **427** Jean-Jacques Rousseau: From Jean-Jacques Rousseau, *The Social Contract*, translated by Rose M. Harrington, G.P. Putnam's Sons, 1906. **429** Voltaire: From Voltaire, *Candide*, translated by John Butt, Penguin Books, 1947. **430** Madame du Châtelet: From Samuel Edwards, *The Divine Mistress*, D. McKay Company, 1970. **432** Wolfgang Amadeus Mozart: From Eric Schenk, *Mozart and His Times*, Alfred A. Knopf, 1959. **437** Thomas Jefferson: From Thomas Jefferson, The Declaration of Independence. In *Documents Illustrative of American History 1606-1863*, edited by Howard W. Preston. G.P. Putnam's Sons, 1893. **440** Declaration of the Rights of Man: From Declaration of the Rights of Man and Citizen. In *Readings in European History, Vol. II: From the Opening of the Protestant Revolt to the Present Day*, edited by James Harvey Robinson, Ginn & Co., 1906. **441** Declaration of the Rights of Woman: From Olympe de Gouges, *Declaration of the Rights of Woman and the Female Citizen*. In *Women in Revolutionary Paris 1780-1795*, translated by Darline Gay Levy, Harriet Branson Applewhite, and Mary Durham Johnson, University of Illinois Press, 1979. **442** France—After the Revolution: From John Carey, *Eyewitness to History*, Avon Books, 1987. **443** Edmund Burke: From Edmund Burke, *1793 Speech*. In *The Cambridge History of English and American Literature* (Vol. II), A.W. Ward and W.P. Trent et al. (eds.). New York: G.P. Putnam's Sons, 1907-21.

# Acknowledgments

We began working on this book more than two years ago with enthusiasm, optimism, and a naivete unbecoming to people our age. Our hope was to create an enjoyable, highly readable, fun, and educational resource for students. Our vision for this book was realized in large part because of the talent, hard work, and creativity of Liliana Cartelli, graphic designer, and Heera Kang, editor. We owe them our deep gratitude. We also thank all the editorial staff at Ballard & Tighe for their help and support. We dedicate *People and Stories in World History* to Tommy Haldorsen and Alexis Stathis—two very special people in the world and in our lives.

*Gregory Blanch & Roberta Stathis*
*December 2002*